A PROMISE FULFILLED

A PROMISE FULFILLED

HIGHLIGHTS IN THE POLITICAL HISTORY
OF
CATHOLIC SEPARATE SCHOOLS IN ONTARIO

by

Michael Power

Ontario Catholic School Trustees' Association

2002

Dedication:

To John Power (1796-1885), John Power (1850-1926) and John O'Connor Power (1884-1960), three generations of separate school trustees in Anderdon Township, Essex County and the Town of Sandwich (Windsor).

To the thousands of men and women who have served as separate school trustees throughout the province of Ontario, beginning in 1841 and continuing to this day.

To all past and present members of the executive and board of directors of the Ontario Separate School Trustees' Association, and since 1997, the Ontario Catholic School Trustees' Association.

© Ontario Catholic School Trustees' Association, 2002

National Library of Canada Cataloguing in Publication

Power, Michael, 1953-
    A promise fulfilled : highlights in the political history of Catholic separate schools in Ontario / by Michael Power.

Includes bibliographical references and index.
ISBN 0-9730665-0-4

    1. Separate schools—Ontario—History. 2. Catholic schools—Ontario—History. 3. Politics and education—Ontario—History. I. Ontario Catholic School Trustees' Association. II. Title.

LC504.2.O5P69 2002   372.071'2713   C2002-901444-1

CONTENTS

Message from the Presidents vii

Introduction viii

Acknowledgments x

Glossary of Terms and Abbreviations xi

Chapter One: Prelates and School Politics
                 The Case of Four Nineteenth Century Bishops 1

Chapter Two: The Catholic Laity and Separate Schools in
                 Nineteenth Century Ontario 73

Chapter Three: A Living Endowment: Religious Teachers 163

Chapter Four: A Divisive Debacle: Regulation 17 203

Chapter Five: The Bishops Take Control
                 The 1920s Campaign: Corporation Taxes,
                 High Schools and the Tiny Township Case 247

Chapter Six: The Grand Experiment
                 The Campaign of the 1930s: Martin J. Quinn
                 and the Catholic Taxpayers' Association 289

Chapter Seven: Completing the Separate School System
                 The Trustees Find their Voice: The Ontario
                 Separate School Trustees' Association 347

Epilogue: 1984-1997 473

Presidents of OSSTA/OCSTA, 1961 to the Present 495

Executive Directors of OSSTA/OCSTA, 1961 to the Present 497

Chaplains, 1961 to the Present 497

Trustee Award of Merit, 1974 to 2002 497

Select Bibliography 503

Index 509

MESSAGE FROM THE PRESIDENTS

The idea for this book originated in the spring of 1998 when the board of directors resolved to publish a brief political history of Catholic education in Ontario with particular emphasis on the role of Catholic school trustees.

When we commissioned Michael Power to work on the project, little did we realize the magnitude of the task we had undertaken and that it would eventually span over the term of three presidents. However, it soon became evident that to do justice to at least some of the major players in the evolution of our system, we would have to expand the project and invest the time and effort required to produce this book.

Our archives offered a veritable treasure of historical information which testifies to the commitment of our forebears to establish and maintain a faith centered, autonomous, Catholic education system in Ontario. From 1841 through to 1984, one constant theme runs through our story – the unwavering determination of the Catholic clergy, religious communities and laity to build the Catholic education system with which we are blessed today.

Catholic school trustees played a pivotal role in the evolution of Catholic education in Ontario. From the early years when their role was limited to hiring the local teacher, stoking the fire in the wood stove and generally keeping the school in an habitable condition, to the latter years when the trustees assumed the leadership mantle, their contribution has been critical to the survival and growth of the system. This book is our attempt to honour each and every man and woman who has served in this very important ministry.

We want to thank Michael Power for his determination to see the project through despite its ever-widening scope. We are particularly grateful to him for the meticulous research which has resulted in this factual account of events and for the enlightening insights into the personalities of some of the major players in our history.

We are extremely grateful to the past-presidents who graciously consented to dig deep into their memory banks to inform us about some of the less heralded yet significant accomplishments of our Association. Finally, we wish to express our appreciation to current and former directors and staff members for their valuable contributions to this project.

Regis O'Connor   Donald Petrozzi   Louise Ervin
Past-President   Past-President   President

INTRODUCTION

Catholic separate schools have been in existence in Ontario since 1841. They were part of the political compromise known as the Act of Union, which created the Province of Canada out of Upper Canada and Lower Canada, and reaffirming their legitimacy was absolutely essential to the formation of the new Dominion. Treating the Scott Act of 1863 as a sine qua non, the Fathers of Confederation enshrined separate school rights in Section 93 of the British North America Act of 1867, where they remain to this day.

But many questions were left unanswered at the time of Confederation. What did the Scott Act of 1863, and by extension Section 93 of the BNA Act, intend for the future of Catholic separate schools? Was tax-supported Catholic education limited to the elementary grades? What about the secondary grades? Was tax revenue for separate schools limited to that raised on Catholic-owned homes and businesses? What about corporation and utility taxes, which were becoming increasingly lucrative as the province slowly shed its rural persona and became an industrialized society? Most importantly, was the Scott Act the final word on separate schools? Were Catholic separate schools forever frozen in time, unable to grow and develop according to the changing needs of their students? Were they doomed to remain a nineteenth century anachronism that produced second-rate citizens?

These questions were the stuff of 125 years of separate school politics, as generation after generation of Catholic leaders lobbied successive governments to interpret the Scott Act the way Catholic ratepayers interpreted it — as a living, breathing piece of legislation that was designed to allow separate schools to evolve into an organic whole. Catholics believed that the Scott Act intended to lay a particular legal groundwork so that the separate schools could provide as complete an education for Catholic children as that enjoyed by the children of public school supporters, according to current pedagogical trends. In reality, though, Catholic parents and students were obliged to live with a truncated and inadequately funded school system that for decades was the much poorer sister of its public counterpart.

But poverty and a host of setbacks, far from destroying separate schools, were the foundation on which they flourished, in number as well as in spirit, as the Catholic cause on behalf of separate schools gradually built itself up into a towering presence in Ontario society. Far from withering and dying out, as was predicted by none other than Egerton Ryerson, separate schools stubbornly and solemnly resisted the pull of a more worldly logic and instead grew into the most successful institution established by the Catholic Church in Ontario.

The story of the survival and triumph of Catholic separate schools is rich in raw emotion, political rhetoric and legal manoeuvres. Separate schools were a topic that produced a lot of high-pitched yelling, especially during the latter half of the nineteenth century, when Catholics feared the disappearance of their schools at the hands of a hostile host culture, and also well into the twentieth century, when the status of the French language was added to the volatile vortex of public opinion. Catholics yelled at Protestants, Protestants yelled at Catholics and Catholics yelled at each other, occasionally all at the same time. Catholics were hardly unanimous on the secret ballot for the election of trustees, teacher certification and Regulation 17. Separate school controversies of all kinds, from the 1850s to the late 1930s, always appeared in print and usually with a vigour and nastiness that can only astonish the modern reader.

Then there were the quieter times, beginning in the 1940s, when back door Queen's Park diplomacy was the operative rule. Premiers and bishops, along with trustees and ministers of education, forged close working ties that allowed both sides to test each other's mettle in various ways that brought forth positive incremental benefits to separate schools without stirring up any of the old time rancour and division. The 1984 announcement on full funding aroused the last great blast against the existence of publicly-funded Catholic schools.

The cast of characters in the story that follows is a long and colourful one. It includes bishops and priests, who until quite recently were the natural leaders in separate school agitation; Catholic journalists and publishers; school inspectors; premiers and politicians; ministers of education and bureaucrats; lawyers and judges; educators; the Catholic Taxpayers' Association; the English Catholic Education Association of Ontario; the Ontario English

Catholic Teachers' Association; the Federation of Catholic Parent-Teacher Associations; the Association of Catholic High School Boards of Ontario; the Catholic section of l'Association française des conseils scolaires de l'Ontario; student activists; individual trustees and school boards; and from 1963 onwards the Ontario Separate School Trustees' Association, which assumed the mantle of leadership in political lobbying on behalf of separate schools and rightly deserves the extensive attention it receives in Chapter Seven.

Lastly, we must not forget the religious teachers, those thousands of Sisters and Brothers who were the mainstay of separate schools for more than a century. Their presence in the classroom was of course more educational than political. However, without them, there would have been no separate schools to fight for at Massey Hall in 1922, the Judicial Committee of the Privy Council in 1928, the Hope Commission in 1950, the Maple Leaf Gardens rally in 1970, the Supreme Court of Canada in 1987 and all the other times, too numerous to mention, that Catholic supporters of separate schools defended their rights in the public square.

This is a story about personalities, strong opinions, the role of organized religion in society and the emergence of the Catholic laity in their trusteeship of separate schools. It is a story of many failed attempts to gain redress, some brilliant successes and ultimate vindication in the legislature and the courts.

ACKNOWLEDGMENTS

I am indebted to many people. Without their generosity during the last three years, this book could not have been written. I am deeply grateful to all those who assisted in any way with the production of the manuscript and the correction of the page proofs. My thanks to the following:

To the Ontario Catholic School Trustees' Association (OCSTA), for offering me a chance to write this history and for being so patient and understanding.

To the OCSTA committee overseeing my work — Monsignor Dennis Murphy, Patrick Slack, John Stunt, Don Petrozzi, Louise Ervin and

Regis O'Connor — for their unflagging enthusiasm and honest commentary. To Anne Cadieux, director of administrative services at OCSTA, for handling all the details of meetings and contracts and being an excellent go-between.

To the manuscript readers — Kathleen Power, Dr. Mark McGowan, Suzanne Lout, John Burtniak (Chapters Four to Seven), Peter Meehan (Chapter Six) and M. Earle McCabe, Father Frank Kavanagh, Jim Sherlock and Frank Clifford (Chapter Seven) — for volunteering to plough through my prose, for being frank in their criticism of my work and for making many helpful suggestions.

To Marc Lerman and Suzanne Lout of the Archives of the Roman Catholic Archdiocese of Toronto (ARCAT), for providing me with a small mountain of documents and illustrations. To Father Carl Matthews, SJ, for the Matthews Papers. To Greg Brown of the Ontario Archives, for supplying the definitions to many words in the educational field no longer in use. To Diane Baltaz of the Diocese of Hamilton, for biographical information on Monsignor Vincent Priester. To Sister Juliana Dusel, IBVM, for material and illustrations on the Sisters of Loretto. To Sister Veronica O'Reilly, CSJ, Sister Mary Zimmer, CSJ, Sister Jean Rooney, CSJ and Linda Wicks, archivist, for material, books and illustrations on the Sisters of St. Joseph.

GLOSSARY OF TERMS AND ABBREVIATIONS

Glossary of Terms

The Constitutional Act of 1791 divided the old Province of Quebec into two distinct administrative units: **Upper Canada**, the predecessor of Ontario, and **Lower Canada**, the predecessor of modern-day Quebec. This arrangement ended in 1841, when Upper Canada became **Canada West** and Lower Canada became **Canada East** and were united as the Province of Canada. This lasted until 1867, when Canada West became the province of Ontario and Canada East became the province of Quebec within Confederation.

Until recently, the **Premier** of Ontario was known as the **Prime Minister** of Ontario. This appellation was found on all official documents originating from the Premier's office. Sometimes, the two terms were interchangeable in less formal circumstances. However, since Premier is the common term today, it is applied to all the Premiers (Prime Ministers of Ontario) who are mentioned in this work.

There is some confusion about **Grades** (Grades 1, 2, 3, etc.) and **Forms**. The word "Grades" was not used until the 1937-38 new curriculum. Before then, the literature referred to Form I (Grades 1 and 2); Form II (Grades 3 and 4); Form III (Grades 5 and 6); Form IV (Grades 7 and 8); and Form V (Grades 9 and 10). Form V was also known as the **Fifth Form** or **Fifth Classes**, which were taught in elementary school. The students in Fifth Form did work similar to that of the first two grades of secondary school. Since Fifth Form belonged to the elementary panel, Catholic separate schools had a legal right to offer it to their students. The large majority of Fifth Form classes were established in rural areas that did not have a local high school.

Continuation Classes, which in 1908 became **Continuation Schools**, were similar to Fifth Form, because they were set up in those districts that lacked a high school, but they were intended to be more like Junior High School than an extension of elementary school. Students wishing to enter Continuation Classes had to pass the High School Entrance Examination, and the teachers had to qualify as High School Assistants. Separate schools also had a right to establish Continuation Classes but only for Grades 9 and 10.

Junior High School was Grades 9 and 10; **Middle School** was Grades 11 and 12; and **Upper School** was Grade 13.

In 1871, the government instituted **high school entrance examinations**, which were usually written after Grade 8. This practice lasted until 1949. At different times, there were other kinds of entrance examinations, for Senior High School, Normal School, Model School and University.

xii

Normal School was Teachers' College.

Abbreviations

ACEBO	l'Association des commissions des écoles bilingues d'Ontario
ACFEO	l'Association canadienne-française d'éducation d'Ontario
ACHSBO	Association of Catholic High School Boards of Ontario
AFCSO	l'Association française des conseils scolaires de l'Ontario
AO	Archives of Ontario
ARCAT	Archives of the Roman Catholic Archdiocese of Toronto
BNA	British North America
CSJ	Congregation of St. Joseph
CTA	Catholic Taxpayers' Association
CWL	Catholic Women's League
DCB	*Dictionary of Canadian Biography*
ECEAO	English Catholic Education Association of Ontario
FCPTAO	Federation of Catholic Parent-Teacher Associations of Ontario
IBVM	Institute of the Blessed Virgin Mary
ICE	Institute for Catholic Education
MSSB	Metropolitan Separate School Board
NCE	*New Catholic Encyclopedia*
NDP	New Democratic Party
OCCB	Ontario Conference of Catholic Bishops
OCSTA	Ontario Catholic School Trustees' Association
OEA	Ontario Educational Association
OECTA	Ontario English Catholic Teachers' Association
OMI	Oblates of Mary Immaculate
OPSTA	Ontario Public School Trustees' Association
OSSTA	Ontario Separate School Trustees' Association

CHAPTER ONE

PRELATES AND SCHOOL POLITICS
THE CASE OF FOUR
NINETEENTH CENTURY BISHOPS

Bishop Alexander Macdonell, 1762-1840

*"To promote the advancement of the Catholic religion and
Catholic education is my greatest interest and desire and
what tends to that will afford me not only the greatest but
the only satisfaction I can enjoy in this life."*

— Bishop Macdonell to François Baby, 10 March 1839[1]

$\mathcal{B}$ishop Alexander Macdonell, Scottish immigrant, veteran missionary priest and the first Catholic bishop in Upper Canada, wrote these words near the end of a long, useful and sometimes controversial life in the service of the Church. They are a concise summation of a traditional Catholic belief that the future of the Church, as a spiritual and social institution, was closely tied to the establishment and upkeep of a system of Catholic schools. In the bishop's mind, religion and education were inseparable for the successful transmission of the faith to each new generation of believers and for the well-being of the faithful as a whole as they sought their rightful place in colonial society. This belief was not peculiar to Macdonell. It was shared by most of his Christian contemporaries, including two lieutenant governors of Upper Canada, Sir Francis Gore[2] and Sir Peregrine Maitland,[3] and Dr. Charles Duncombe, the author of a 1836 report on education.[4] Schools which deliberately excluded the teaching of religion were unthinkable and an absurdity. The idea was so strange it was rejected out of hand.

Just as alien to Macdonell was the desire among some Protestant politicians and educators to teach a common Christian

1

religion based solely on the Bible in all public schools. This too was considered a threat to the integrity of the Catholic faith. Catholics must have their own schools.

To this end, Bishop Macdonell, in concert with many priests and early trustees, founded a noticeable number of Catholic schools, not only outside the orbit of the 1807 and 1816 legislation on education but also well in advance of the 1841 Common Schools Act, which explicitly mentioned separate schools for the first time. In other words, Catholic schools existed for many years before separate schools came into legal operation. This is important to remember.

As we shall see, the Herculean struggle to set up those schools involved the bishop, priests and lay people and was fraught with numerous and nagging difficulties. During the first half of the nineteenth century, Upper Canadian Catholics were small in number, relatively disorganized and impoverished to a disabling degree. Thus we are not surprised to learn that Bishop Macdonell spent a good deal of his time and energy dunning the colonial and provincial administrations for money. He constantly reminded various colonial officials and lieutenant governors that Catholic loyalty to British institutions was tenuous and its continuance depended on government generosity to Catholic institutions, in particular to the payment of priests and teachers and the building of school houses. Meanwhile, the priests and trustees regularly reported to the bishop about Catholic schools in their respective settlements. From their many letters we are able to paint a picture, however imperfect, of the humble and struggling condition of these schools during Macdonell's episcopacy.

It was a truly heroic effort on everyone's part. But the manner in which Catholic institutions of learning secured a foothold in the province was due largely to the personality, presence and endeavours of Bishop Macdonell. To him, Catholics in the province of Ontario owe the foundation of a school system that was sufficiently visible and viable to be recognized in the 1841 legislation. Details of the bishop's biography and examples of his efforts on behalf of Catholic education will illustrate the nature and results of his work.

Of course, no degree of hard work and good will on Macdonell's part would have achieved anything of lasting value if he did not have the constant co-operation of priests and trustees working towards the same general goals in the parishes and missions of Macdonell's vast diocese. Samples of their work will also be given.

****

Alexander Macdonell was born on 17 July 1762 in Glengarry, Scotland.[5] Since he was a member of a Highland Catholic family, he was subjected to the disabilities of the penal laws, but it was Clan Macdonell's open support for Prince Charles Stuart, the Young Pretender, during the rebellion of 1745, that forced Macdonell to pursue his studies on the continent. He was educated at the Scots College in Paris and the Royal Scots College at Valladolid, Spain, where he was ordained to the priesthood on 16 February 1787. Macdonell was very orthodox in his theology and conservative in his politics. Catholicism and Toryism were the two pillars of his public life.

Returning to his native land as a missionary priest, Macdonell served at Badenoch, Lochaber and Glasgow. He quickly realized that one way for his people to survive the harsh economic and political climate of late eighteenth century Scotland, was their enlistment in the British army when opportunities arose. This divided loyalty — on the one hand, to the Catholic faith and the Catholic Church, and on the other, to the British government, which was certainly no friend of either the faith or the Church — apparently was not a theological problem for Father Macdonell. Rather, it was a practical matter of survival, one which he was to employ to great effect on behalf of himself and his fellow Catholics in Upper Canada.

Unemployed Highlanders in Glasgow were the most desperate group to which Father Macdonell ministered. Leaving Scotland in large numbers was the only way they could possibly cope with the calamity of the Highland clearances. Macdonell's response was to convince Alexander Ranaldson Macdonell of Glengarry, the Protestant chief of the clan, to raise a regiment of fencibles for duty outside of Scotland and England. The government accepted his proposal, and the Glengarry Fencibles were formed, with the clan chief as their colonel and Father Macdonell as their chaplain. The latter's appointment was dated 14 August 1794, making him the first Catholic chaplain in the British Army since the Reformation. The regiment was stationed on Jersey and Guernsey until 1798, when it was transferred to Ireland, where it was engaged in the formal suppression of the Irish rebellion in Wexford County and the Wicklow mountains.[6] They stayed in Ireland until 1802, the year the Peace of Amiens brought about the regiment's required disbandment. Two years later, Father Macdonell was leading the discharged soldiers to a new life in Glengarry, Upper Canada.

Alexander Macdonell's career in Upper Canada was nothing short of brilliant. Macdonell was the bishop of Quebec's vicar general for the entire province, beginning in November 1804; he was chaplain for the Glengarry Light Infantry Fencibles during the War of 1812; he was consecrated titular bishop of Rhesaena and suffragan to the bishop of Quebec in 1820; Rome appointed him the first bishop of the new diocese of Kingston in 1826. Ecclesiastical honours were followed by political recognition. Macdonell was appointed a member of the Legislative Council, taking his seat in 1831, and a confidante of Sir John Colborne, lieutenant governor of Upper Canada from 1828 to 1836, and of Lord Bathurst, the colonial secretary in London, who, in the course of one of Macdonell's lobbying sessions at the Colonial Office, introduced him to the Prince Regent. During the Rebellion of 1837-38, Bishop Macdonell was the backbone of loyalty in the eastern part of the province.

Macdonell was a great survivor of church and provincial politics, and he knew how to cajole and manipulate the colonial authorities for the benefit of his far-flung flock of Catholic settlers. Using St. Raphael's in Glengarry County as his missionary headquarters, the bishop, often alone, crisscrossed Upper Canada on numerous pastoral visits and traveled overseas five times in the cause of religion. He was a relentless and indefatigable campaigner, whose already difficult life was made all the more burdensome by several difficult priests, who were disobedient and quarrelsome to an extraordinary degree, and the radical element in the Legislative Assembly, who objected to his having a seat on the Legislative Council.

When Macdonell arrived in the province in 1804, he found two priests, one of whom left shortly thereafter, one small mission church (Assumption in Sandwich), no schools and no schoolmasters. By 1833, he was able to report to Colonel William Rowan, Colborne's civil secretary, that there were eighteen diocesan priests and more than thirty churches either built or in the process of being built; that he had constructed a school house in Glengarry and prior to 1826 had spent £1,300 of his own money hiring teachers for Catholic children; and that between 1827 and 1832, depending on the year, there were from seven to nine Catholic teachers supported by government funds.[7] To the lieutenant governor himself, Macdonell carefully listed the Catholic churches and schools by settlement and then listed those which still needed to be built. Concerning the schools, he wrote that they had already been established in Amherstburg, St. Andrew's, St. Raphael's (one for boys and one for girls) and Alexandria. The last three schools were in Glengarry and were more or less under his personal patronage. (For some odd reason he failed to mention that he had founded St. Raphael's Seminary in 1825.[8]) But five schools in four settlements after almost three decades of intense effort scarcely answered the growing demand for Catholic schools. Macdonell went on to inform Colborne that Catholics needed the government's assistance to build a school for boys and one for girls in Sandwich (now a part of Windsor), and schools in Guelph, York (the capital), Penetanguishene, Peterborough, Kingston, Perth, Bytown (Ottawa), Prescott and Gore of Emily.[9]

On the subject of Catholic teachers, the historical record as gleaned from Macdonell's own letters is sufficiently informative for one to appreciate the tenuous state of affairs experienced by teachers during his episcopacy. There are early references to three Scotsmen, James MacPherson, John A. Murdock and Angus McDonald [Macdonell] and to one Englishman, Richard Hammond. MacPherson arrived in 1816 and settled among the Scottish in Glengarry County.[10] Hammond, Murdock and McDonald appeared the next year.[11] All four teachers emigrated to Upper Canada on Lord Bathurst's promise that they would be paid from the government purse, in both money and land. But it seems that not one of them received a farthing or an acre and had to quit their posts for lack of money. Their leaving was another in a long string of embarrassments for Macdonell.

However, the situation improved in the 1830s. This came about because the government allowed Macdonell to give the teachers under his supervision a portion of the grant to the clergy.[12] This helped the bishop to attract and keep a steady complement of teachers. According to Macdonell's 1836 statement of the distribution of government funds, there were school teachers active in at least eight settlements throughout the province: York, Sandwich, Amherstburg, St. Raphael's, Alexandria, Glengarry, Kingston and the River Trench (Thames River near Tilbury). Their names were John Butler, Joseph Sawyers, William Kennedy, Patrick Dollard, John McSweeney, Mr. Parent, Angus Macdonell, John McIntosh, John Carroll, John Macdonagh, James Chisholm, John Farrell, John Hay and Allan MacDonell. Some were laymen and others were ecclesiastics studying for the priesthood. Among the latter can be counted several pioneer priests of the archdiocese of Toronto.[13] In addition to the men, Sister Marie-Clotilde Raizenne and three postulants, who belonged to the recently founded Congrégation de l'Enfant-Jésus, conducted a school for girls at Assumption parish in Sandwich, beginning in 1828. They had about fifty students and were assisted by an American lady.[14] Unfortunately, Sister Raizenne died after only a year, but her small community continued to teach in Sandwich at least until 1832, when they were paid £35 for their work.[15] Salaries for the male teachers ranged from a high of £30 for John Butler of York in 1832 to a low of £7 for John Macdonagh in the first half of 1833. If one lumps together full year and partial year sums and disregards the one payment to the religious women in Sandwich, the average salary was a little more than £15.

That there was any money for Catholic teachers was due almost entirely to Bishop Macdonell's tireless campaign for government funds, for both clergy and teachers, which began in earnest in a letter of 19 January 1817 to Lord Bathurst and which continued for the rest of the bishop's life. Along the way Macdonell overcame numerous obstacles a weaker man in a mitre might have found too forbidding to

6

face. He had to endure bureaucratic bungling in both the provincial administration and the colonial office, Sir Peregrine Maitland's political obstinacy towards public funding of Catholic education, the surprise bankruptcy of his London-based bank, the disputatious personalities of several of his senior priests, the rebellious petitions of a majority of York's Catholics in 1833 and endless delays trying to conduct business across the Atlantic ocean. Macdonell must have been a patient man, blessed with an abundance of hope for the future of Catholicism in Upper Canada, a hope, moreover, that could not be diminished by the drudgery of day-to-day details of running a diocese that covered the whole province.

Macdonell was a prolific letter writer, leaving a rich and varied archive of administrative detail. Surviving are pivotal letters to Lord Bathurst, Maitland, Thomas Cardinal Weld and Lord Goderich, in which Macdonell expresses his opinions on Catholic loyalty to the British government and the government's need to fund Catholic clergy and teachers who would be able to secure and enhance that same Catholic loyalty among the thousands of new immigrants arriving every year in the province.[16] We will look at a brief extract from one of these letters.

In reminding Bathurst in 1817 of the Prince Regent's promise of salaries to public school teachers, regardless of their religious persuasion, Macdonell reiterated what he thought would be necessary to sustain them in their work:

> £100 sterling per annum, and 200 acres of Land to Clergymen, and £50 sterling and 100 acres of Land to School Masters, could be all that could be required, or expected, by the Roman Catholics of that Province, for the people themselves would easily contribute whatever more might be necessary for the support of these public functionaries; and this bounty of the Government could not fail to operate as an additional tie on the loyalty and gratitude of the former, and a powerful stimulus on the latter to make them exert themselves in the assiduous discharge of their important duty.[17]

Bathurst readily agreed with Macdonell's logic. But as the next letter from Macdonell to William Morris, member of parliament for Perth, makes abundantly clear, political promises made in London were difficult to fulfill in York. The letter was dated 21 April 1827, ten full years after Macdonell's initial correspondence with Lord Bathurst!

This [letter] will probably be handed to you, by Mr. A.J. Murdock, one of the schoolmasters that followed me from Britain in 1817 on the promise of Earl Bathurst that they should receive salaries in this province as Catholic teachers. His Lordship indeed sent me positive orders to the Executive here to pay them their salaries and Col. [David William] Smith who was president at the time was disposed to comply with His Lordship's orders, but Dr. [John] Strachan and Justice [William Dummer] Powell who in fact administered the government of the Province thought themselves bound in honour and in conscience, as sound constitutional politicians, to check the growth of popery by all the means which Providence had then placed in their power and they shrewdly discovered that this might be done as effectually by starving to death as by burning to death. They accordingly refused in the most peremptory manner to comply with Earl Bathurst's orders respecting those teachers. I spent several years in fruitless exertions, in supplications, prayers and petitions, sometimes to the executive government of this province, sometimes to the Governor in Chief, taking half a dozen journeys between this [Glengarry] and York and Quebec upon the business of the forwarded petitions and memorials without number to the Colonial Department at home. At length in 1822 I was informed by Sir Peregrine Maitland that he observed in the Provincial estimate of that year an item of Three hundred pounds for Catholic teachers employed at that time in Upper Canada. Mr. Murdock having been under the necessity of quitting his post for want of support a considerable time before this period, and another having left his also although not from the same cause, I wished both these to come in for a share of the £300 per annum until their arrears should be paid up but to this Sir Peregrine Maitland would not consent without an express order from Earl Bathurst to that effect. He however promised if I would write a letter on the subject to Earl Bathurst, he would forward it, which I accordingly did. Next year, in 1823, by the kind advice of the Governor in chief the Earl Dalhousie, I went home myself to try to get matters to a satisfactory settlement and I was seven months in Britain before I found out whether the salaries of the teachers had been issued out from the Treasury or to whom they had been paid. At length I discovered that Six hundred pounds, the salary of the teachers for two years, were received by a Mr. Adam and lodged in a banking house in the Strand but for a long time after this Lord Bathurst declared in presence of Mr. Wilmot Horton that the teachers who deserted their posts were not entitled to anything, and it was by dint of teasing him that I almost extorted from him an order on the Treasury for Four hundred pounds to Mr. Murdock and a proportionate sum for each of the others. This order, however, remained unpaid for several months and might have remained unpaid to this date had not my relative and friend the Honourable Chas Grant, the Vice-President of the Board of Trade, interested himself on my behalf and procured an Order from the Chancellor of the Exchequer for the payment of the same.[18]

But that was not the end of the story. The money was deposited in the House of Maitland, Garden and Aldjo, who had been merchant bankers for Macdonell for over twenty years. The firm went bankrupt, leaving Macdonell without a penny. To make matters even worse, Mr. Murdock turned against the bishop.

Bishop Macdonell was also busy on the diocesan front when it came to protecting and nurturing Catholic education. Here are a few examples of his direct involvement on the subject of Catholic schools for Catholic children. He gave his permission to the Reverend Peter

Sweeney in Perth to conduct a school, but warned him not to let the management of the school interfere with his pastoral work. "If you could discharge the duties of both," wrote the bishop, "without the one injuring the other, I would be happy."[19] In a lengthy letter to John McDonald of Grey's Creek, who had a son in Macdonell's Glengarry school, the bishop wrote that "the terms of the school kept here under my supervision are, for board and tuition, thirty pounds currency per annum, to boys who continue in the school for twelve months, and at the rate of eight pounds per quarter to such as remain for a shorter period."[20] The father, who was a Protestant, objected to his son's having to attend Catholic prayers. Macdonell replied that it was not the intention of the school "to divert from their own persuasion those differing from the Catholic religion, for that is repugnant to the genuine spirit of the Catholic faith, whatever bigotry and malice may allege to the contrary."[21] No student would be prevented from leaving the school on Saturday or Sunday, according to his parents' wishes, but all students "must observe the same hours of study and the same practice of devotion."[22] No exceptions would be made.

On a more personal level, on 16 July 1827, Macdonell met with the church wardens of Assumption parish, in the presence of the assembled congregation, to ascertain from them when they intended to build schools. Answering a series of questions put to them by the bishop, they promised to construct two schools: a 50-by-35-foot convent school for the girls and a 45-by-35-foot school for boys.[23] Neither school was erected. Three years later, Macdonell addressed a stern letter to Father Joseph Crevier, the parish priest, and to the elders and church wardens, bluntly accusing them of shamefully neglecting the education of the parish children and warning them that "Catholics for want of education are not only kept in the background and neglected, but are made the hewers of wood and the drawers of water to those who came into the country adventurers and beggars."[24] These were harsh but prophetic words. They would be repeated almost verbatim nearly a century later by Bishop Michael Francis Fallon in his fight against bilingual education.

On 20 May 1832, Macdonell chaired a similar meeting at St. Paul's church in York. He told the people that it was urgent that they construct a schoolhouse on a lot that had been recently donated to the parish by the government. The property, which had been earmarked for school purposes, was probably at the corner of Jarvis and Richmond streets. Acting on the instructions of the bishop, a fundraising committee of prominent Catholics was formed. It included the Hon. James Baby, the Hon. Alexander Macdonell, Francis Collins, publisher of the *Canadian Freeman*, William Bergin, Michael Macnamara and Edward Barnett. The first donations came from three well known Protestants: H.J. Boulton, the attorney general, Peter Robinson, and William Dummer Powell, the chief justice.[25] But it took more than eight years for a school to open its doors. It seems that York's Catholics did not have the financial means to build one. In February 1835, William Bergin petitioned the House of Assembly to grant £500 to the Catholics of Toronto towards the construction of a school. Peter Robinson presented the petition, but nothing was done.[26] A more serious obstacle, though, was Father William O'Grady. A former parish priest in York and one of the trustees of the property, he had been banished by Macdonell as part of a very public quarrel and would not relinquish his hold on the property. Only after he died in August 1840, eight months after Bishop Macdonell had died, was the parish able to claim its school house.[27]

****

Of course, Bishop Macdonell did not labour alone in establishing a system of Catholic schools in Upper Canada. It was a two-way process. There were many Catholics, priests as well as lay people, who worked at the local level, employing teachers, making plans for schools and petitioning for land and financial relief. In Macdonell's papers, there is a wide range of letters on educational matters from Catholics-in-the-field. They reported from Catholic missions in York, Sandwich, Amherstburg, Belle River, St. Raphael's, Perth, Niagara, Penetanguishene, New Germany and Wilmot and Puslinch, near Guelph. In fact, Catholic school trustees were functioning as early as the 1820s. Since they would have been actively familiar with lay trusteeship of church temporalities, lay involvement in the management of Catholic schools would have appeared a natural duty to them. The following are two representative selections from this particular body of correspondence.

In a letter of 24 June 1828, Chief Waron, Chief Isidore and War Chief Thomas Split Log of the Huron tribe at Belle River wrote Bishop Macdonell:

> . . . Father we understood you well last summer when you advised us to send our children to school and it is but a few days since we had a council between us in which we all determined they should go to school. Father Bishop you tell us likewise that you should be glad if we should have a School House in our Village; we now agree it shall be so; Father listen to your children of the Huron chiefs, you ask us for a piece of Land for the use of a Roman catholic clergyman and school master. We shall obey your order, we have lots of the land and we shall give a piece for that purpose.[28]

Writing on the 18 August 1833, James Farling, Louis Corbiene and George Gordon, Catholic trustees in Penetanguishene, wrote a letter to the authorities supporting the Catholic teachers' petition for an allowance from the government:

> We The Undersigned Trustees Named by an assembly held in the Town of Penetanguishene on the Eighteenth Inst. for the Erection of a Catholic School in this Town do hereby certify that Mr. Anthony Lacourse has opened a School in the Town, has at present Twenty Six Scholars. We after having made the Necessary Inquiry of his Conduct and qualification as a Teacher found him worthy and suitable to the Patronage of a Catholic School for which he Solicits the Township Allowance Granted by Government.[29]

In York, although the congregation was stymied for many years in its desire to build a school, there was no shortage of teachers. John Harvey taught in a frame building at the head of Nelson (now Jarvis)

Street, near the farm of Samuel Peters Jarvis, in approximately 1830. Joseph Sawyers (Seyers or Siers) had a school on York Street between King and Richmond streets. John Butler, who later became a priest, taught at a school located on the corner of Jordan and Melinda streets. The names of both Sawyers and Butler appear on the list of teachers who received a portion of the government grant to Bishop Macdonell. James Murnane taught upwards of ninety pupils at Macdonell's house and chapel at the corner of Duchess and Jarvis streets. P.B. McLoughlin was the first teacher in the parish school. He was succeeded by Denis Heffernan. Also mentioned are the names of a Mr. McManus, who left Toronto because he had not been paid, a Mr. Gallagher and a Miss Roberts.[30]

However, not all was well between Bishop Macdonell and the more radical or democratic elements in the York congregation. Joseph McDougal and 167 others signed and delivered a petition to the House of Assembly. It was introduced into the House on 3 December 1833. The petitioners asked for legislation in the following areas of concern to the Catholic laity: repeal of all laws that gave the Crown "the power to reject or appoint to the vacant sees and parishes in this country Roman Catholic Bishops and priests"; prohibition of tithes payable to the Roman Catholic clergy; abolition of all pensions and sinecures given by the state to the Catholic clergy; revocation of the £1,000 currently granted to the Catholic bishop for the support of himself and the clergy; the reintroduction of the £1,000 grant to the Catholics of the province, £100 of which would be used for a school house in York and the rest for the general purposes of education.[31]

This was a bold and direct attack on Macdonell's administration of the diocese. It damned his close association with the government and blamed him for the lack of Catholic schools. Since the lion's share of the government grant went to the clergy, only a pittance was left for the teachers. Justice dictated that the entire grant go to education.

Peter Parry moved and Peter Shaver seconded a motion to have the petition sent to a four-person Select Committee, which would have the power to subpoena individuals and documents and report back to the House with a Bill. After several eviscerating amendments, the petition was abandoned.[32]

But that was not the end of the matter. A second petition was drawn up and delivered to the House of Assembly. It was signed by Peter McDougal and between 800 and 900 York Catholics and was a stinging assault on Macdonell's treatment of the Reverend William O'Grady. Except for a passing reference to the alleged "misapplication of the Government appropriation for the support of clergymen and schoolmasters," a charge which had never been substantiated, this petition had nothing significant to say about education.[33] Its real value, at least from the historian's point of view, is that it signaled the beginning of the passing of Macdonell's world. Time would satisfy the reformer's demands as spelled out in the first petition. Government stipends, pensions and sinecures for the Catholic clergy would end, and the funding of public education would become public policy.

****

Bishop Alexander Macdonell died of the lingering effects of pneumonia, on 14 January 1840, in Dumfries, Scotland, while on a tour to raise funds for Regiopolis College. His death was not unexpected. The bishop's eighteenth-century brand of ecclesiastical Toryism, steadfast Catholic loyalty and Church dependence on the munificence of the government went with him to the grave. It is difficult to assess the state of Catholic education in Upper Canada in 1840. Macdonell, his priests and many of the laity certainly busied themselves in the task of setting up schools, hiring teachers and building school houses. However, a constant lack of money, the absence of an efficient organization and nasty political disagreements of the kind occasioned by the 1833 petitions hobbled their work and stalled any real material progress. In the end, though, Macdonell and his contemporaries had accomplished enough in the name of Catholic education to prepare the coming generation of Catholics for the new and quite different era of separate schools.

Bishop Michael Power, 1804-1847

"I cannot reflect upon the full and frequent conversations which I have had with him [Bishop Power], on subjects of public instructions, and on the scrupulous regard which he ever manifested, for the views and rights and wishes of Protestants, without feelings of the deepest respect for his character and memory."
— Egerton Ryerson on the death of Bishop Michael Power,
October 1847 [34]

The death of Bishop Macdonell ended the "colonial" era of the Church in Upper Canada and interestingly coincided with the beginning of a new political experiment, the union of Upper Canada and Lower Canada to form the Province of Canada. Macdonell's passing had the additional effect of hastening the ecclesiastical process whereby the Diocese of Kingston was divided into two, giving birth to the Diocese (and later the Archdiocese) of Toronto. The new diocese, formally erected by Rome on 17 December 1841, extended over the western half of the province, in itself still a vast territory for any single bishop to govern.

The creation of this diocese would affect the tone and direction of the political debate on education in Canada West (Ontario) for many decades. It would also guarantee a place of prominence and controversy for many of the bishops and archbishops of Toronto in the prolonged and sometimes bitter debate over separate schools. Michael Power, the first bishop of Toronto, did not have to endure much of this bitterness. Since his episcopacy was short lived, and he cultivated cordial working relations with Toronto's Protestant élite, he was able to avoid direct conflict over separate schools. The same, though, was not true of his two immediate successors, Bishop Armand de Charbonnel and Archbishop John Joseph Lynch.

Michael Power was born in Halifax, on 17 October 1804, to William Power and Mary Roach, recent arrivals from Ireland.[35] On the advice of Father Edmund Burke, the vicar general, they sent their son when he was only twelve years of age to the Archdiocese of Quebec to prepare for Holy Orders. As soon as he had completed his theological studies in Quebec and Montreal, Power was ordained to the priesthood, on 17 August 1827, by Bishop John Dubois of New York.

Prior to his elevation to the episcopacy, Michael Power was a priest in an entirely French Canadian milieu. This was rather odd for someone who was the son of Irish immigrants and a native of Nova Scotia, but it demonstrated the ease with which this young but capable cleric could not only move but also thrive in a religious culture quite different from that of Halifax or from that which he was to face in his own diocese. Father Power was a missionary at Drummondville and then a parish priest at Montebello in the Ottawa Valley, at Sainte-Martine, near Salaberry-de-Valleyfield, and lastly at La Prairie, where he built an impressive stone church that remains in use today. Also, as vicar general of the Diocese of Montreal he accompanied Bishop Ignace Bourget on the latter's trip to Europe where he succeeded in convincing the Roman authorities to erect a new see in the western part of Canada.

Michael Power chose Toronto as his episcopal see, drew the boundaries separating Toronto from Kingston and was consecrated bishop on 8 May 1842. Entrusted to his pastoral care were approximately 50,000 Catholics, of whom 3,000 lived in Toronto. Sadly, his reign was all too brief, lasting less than five and a half years. During that time, he spent most of his energy organizing his administration, establishing regulations for the spiritual discipline of both clergy and laity and gathering funds to build a cathedral. He laid firm foundations for the future greatness of his nascent diocese, but he did not live to see the fruits of his labours. Those labours also included some work in the field of Catholic education.

However, before we outline Bishop Power's contributions to Catholic education in Ontario, we must do two things. First, we must make clear the fundamental importance of the following piece of legislation in the history of separate schools: "An Act to make further provision for the establishment and maintenance of Common Schools throughout the Province." Secondly, we must point out the several rather rich ironies which gave birth to this piece of legislation passed in 1841 (4 & 5 Victoria, c. 18).

Section IX of the 1841 statute incorporated the principle of separate (though not necessarily Catholic) schools. This was a first in school legislation for the province and set a precedent that has stood the test of time and political and legal hostility to this day. The section specifically recognized the right of any number of inhabitants living in any common school district to dissent from the religious instruction as provided in the Act and to elect their own trustee or trustees, who would hold the same powers and perform the same duties as the trustees of common schools. Separate schools would be subject to the same regulations and obligations as the common schools and would be entitled to their proportion of the school funds raised by assessment, according to the number of dissenting inhabitants. Furthermore, Section XVI stipulated that half of the members of the Board of Examiners in any incorporated town or city had to be Catholic and that the Catholic members of such board would be assigned to those common schools attended by only Catholic children.[36]

Ironically, if the Province of Canada, which had equal representation from Canada West (Upper Canada) and Canada East (Lower Canada), had not come into existence in February 1841, there would have been no provision for separate schools in the 1841 legislation. Even more ironic, though, was that the passionate call for separate schools was not so much Catholic, at least at this stage, as it was Anglican and Presbyterian, two of the more outspoken Protestant denominations to demand that the Bible be used as a textbook in the common schools. Bishop John Strachan[37] and Peter B. De Blacquière[38] led the Anglicans, who went one step further and asked for their own schools, and John Hamilton, a member of the Legislative Council, presented the petitions of the ministers and elders of the Presbyterian church.[39] Of the forty-two petitions submitted to the legislature during the prolonged debate on the school bill, thirty-nine dealt with the Bible.[40]

There were two Catholic petitions. The first was submitted by Bishop Rémi Gaulin of the Diocese of Kingston and the Reverend A. Mauseau and Reverend H. Hudon, administrators of the Diocese of Montreal. They asked that the bill not become law until the opinion of Catholics and other religious denominations were known. The second was signed by Archbishop Joseph Signay of Quebec and his coadjutor, Bishop Pierre-Flavien Turgeon. Their petition asked that no law be passed that would prejudice Catholic interests or ignore the principles of justice.[41]

Protestants as well as Catholics agreed that teaching the Christian faith was central to the common school curriculum. This was a core concept of the religious culture of the day and was shared by virtually everyone. What divided Protestant from Catholic was the proposed use of the Protestant version of the Bible in the schools and its interpretation at the hands of Protestant teachers.[42] For Catholics, this was anathema, a point on which no compromise could be made. William Morris, a Scottish Presbyterian and member of the Legislative Council, summed up the situation this way:

> With respect to the difficulty which is presented to our view by the Petitions which daily come before the House, from Roman Catholic and Protestant Bodies, I would just observe, that if the use, by Protestants, of the Holy Scriptures in their Schools, is so objectionable to our fellow-subjects of that other faith, the children of both religious persuasions must be educated apart; for Protestants never can yield to that point, and, therefore, if it is insisted upon that the Scriptures shall not be a class-book in Schools, we must part in peace, and conduct the education of the respective Bodies according to our sense of what is right.[43]

The newly minted legislature was at an impasse over one of its first bills and decided to create separate schools as the most practical solution to what could have become a political bombshell for all members. We must remember that separate schools were not controversial at the time. However, the battle over the Bible in schools, between the Anglicans (Church of England) and certain secularists in the press, who did not want the Bible in any school, continued to simmer and occasionally boil over. Besides the unintended irony of all this, the point here is that the law allowing publicly funded separate schools was in place before Michael Power became bishop of Toronto and that he accepted such schools as a right, not a privilege, for Catholics and as an integral part of the overall educational system.[44] He never wavered on these two points, even when the 1841 Act was superseded by new school legislation in 1843 (7 Victoria, c. 29), which pertained solely to Canada West.[45]

"An Act for the establishment and maintenance of Common Schools in Upper Canada" changed only the method whereby ratepayers in school districts could set up separate schools. Section 55 permitted dissent on the basis of the religion of the teacher:

> In all cases, wherein the Teacher of any such school shall happen to be a Roman Catholic, the Protestant Inhabitants shall be entitled to have a School with a Teacher of their own religious persuasion, upon the application of ten or more resident Freeholders or Householders of any School District, or within the limits assigned to any Town or City School; and in like manner, when the Teacher of any such school shall happen to be a Protestant, the Roman Catholic Inhabitants shall have a separate School, with a Teacher of their own religious persuasion, upon a like application.[46]

Section 56 stated that separate schools were to receive their rightful portion of the tax levy for schools "according to the number of Children of religious persuasion who shall attend such separate School, which share shall be settled and adjudged by the Township, Town or City Superintendent, subject to an appeal to the County Superintendent."[47] The separate school funding was to continue.

These two sections of the 1843 legislation affirmed the legal standing of separate schools. Bishop Power referred to them in a letter to Father Simon P. Saenderl, a Redemptorist priest in Wilmot Township. By these two clauses, the bishop wrote, "Catholics have a right to a school of their own and this ought to be the case in every school district when practicable. The Trustees must be in every case Catholics chosen according to Law and the School Master a member of the Catholic Church."[48] The bishop could not have been more emphatic in stating what would become the classic Catholic case for separate schools. He repeated his position to the Catholics of the mission in Belle River, Essex County:

> We avail ourselves of this opportunity to exhort you most earnestly to send your children to schools conducted by good, moral and Catholic masters from whom they may receive not only that elementary education which you are bound to bestow upon your children if it be in your power but likewise that they may receive at the same time under the guidance of your Pastor those principles of religion and morality which will enable them to become not only faithful adherents of the true church but useful members of society.[49]

Concerning Catholic children and the Protestant Bible, Bishop Power was just as adamant and unequivocal. To Father Michael R. Mills, the priest in St. Thomas, he gave this directive:

> You ought to know that the Bible cannot be made use of as a mere class book and that no Catholic child can attend the reading from the Protestant version of the Holy Scriptures. The Catholic children should be allowed to remain in a separate room until the usual lesson from the Holy Scriptures shall have been read; they can there read themselves a chapter from the authorized version of the New Testament. It would be preferable in every way if the parents of Catholic children could have a separate school of their own, but this must depend in a great measure on the number of Catholics in each locality.[50]

These three instructions from Bishop Power would set the tone for future debates about Catholic separate schools. They amply demonstrate that the bishop supported and defended separate schools for Catholic children, not only as a right but also as a spiritual necessity, everywhere in the province and that his opinions on this matter did not differ substantially from those of his episcopal successors in Toronto. They were of one mind when it came to separate schools. As Franklin Walker put it, "They supported legislative plans to further general education, but assumed that a progress common to all would mean like benefits for Catholic schools."[51]

On another front, Bishop Power gave practical effect to his beliefs on Catholic education. He supported John Elmsley, Samuel G. Lynn and Charles Robinson, three leading Catholic laymen, in their highly publicized fight to secure a larger portion of the school fund for Toronto's Catholic children.[52] He succeeded in persuading the Institute of the Blessed Virgin Mary (the Loretto Sisters) to send some of their members to his diocese. They arrived in the city on 16 September 1847 and opened Loretto Abbey on 29 September, making them the first teaching community in Toronto.[53] He invited the Society of Jesus (the Jesuits) to his diocese, and he particularly asked them to take an active role in teaching young Catholics.[54] This invitation finally bore fruit when the Jesuits opened Assumption College in Sandwich in 1857.[55] Bishop Power also invited the Christian Brothers, in 1847. They arrived four years later, in 1851, teaching classes at two places, St Michael's school on Richmond Street and at St. Paul's parish.[56]

On 21 July 1846, Bishop Power joined the Board of Education for Upper Canada, which later became the Council of Public Instruction. Under either name it would have been roughly equivalent to a modern-day provincial department of education.[57] Bishop Power was the board's first chairman, but his attendance at meetings came second to the fulfillment of episcopal duties in his vast diocese. It was regrettable that he was often absent and thus unable to check the ambitions of others, such as Egerton Ryerson, the province's chief superintendent of education since 1846 who had actually nominated Bishop Power. The board's principal functions were to establish a provincial Normal School (Teachers College), to set down rules for "Text books, Plans, Forms and Regulations" and to give advice and counsel to the superintendent.[58] In all these endeavours, the bishop worked harmoniously with Ryerson and his fellow board members. Indeed, Ryerson grew very fond of Power and was genuinely upset at the news of the bishop's death in 1847.

However, Bishop Power's decision to accept membership on the

Board of Education unintentionally gave Ryerson and his chief apologist, J. George Hodgins, many opportunities during the 1850s to use the example of Bishop Power's co-operation as a weapon against his immediate successor, Bishop Charbonnel, and to obscure, and actually bury, Bishop Power's true opinions on Catholic separate schools. For example, it was Power's absence in Europe, from January to June 1847, that allowed Ryerson, with the active support of John Strachan, to amend the Act of 1846, so that the establishment of separate schools would be in the hands of Protestant-dominated municipalities. This was anathema to Bishop Power. If he had been in the chair, it is higly unlikely that he would have tolerated the Ryerson-Strachan amendment or that it would have been proposed at all. Ryerson went so far as to claim that Bishop Power had agreed that the Catholic need for separate schools was limited to providing "protection from insult" in rural communities.[59] But this apparently private conversation hardly squares with the bishop's own letters and directives to Father Saenderl and Father Mills and to the Catholics of Belle River, which have already been quoted.[60]

Bishop Michael Power died of typhus on 1 October 1847, while bringing the sacraments and spiritual comfort to Irish famine victims. He is buried beneath the main altar of St. Michael's cathedral.

Bishop Armand-François-Marie de Charbonnel, 1802-1891

"Since we are under the blessed principles of religious liberty and equal civil rights, we must have, and we will have the full management of our Schools . . ."
– Bishop Charbonnel to Egerton Ryerson, 24 March 1852[61]

'I think our next step must be, if further legislation be called for, to take the sound American ground of not providing or recognizing separate schools at all."
– Egerton Ryerson to Francis Hincks, 6 September 1854[62]

Bishop Charbonnel and Egerton Ryerson were contemporaries. Although they were born within four months of each other, their place of birth, religion and culture set them worlds apart. Charbonnel was a member of an aristocratic French family and a Catholic prelate who looked upon Europe as his cultural home. Ryerson was born into a Loyalist family in Upper Canada and was a Methodist minister, who understood the British connection to be absolutely vital. The two men may have shared some of the same values, such as religious liberty in a democratic society, but they were the products of two strikingly different religious and political cultures. Thrown together during the 1850s, they collided over the future of Catholic education.

Any discussion of Bishop Charbonnel's combative role in the history of Catholic separate school agitation[63] must include an examination of the beliefs and attitudes of Egerton Ryerson. It would be negligent to talk about one without drawing in the other. As chief superintendent of schools in Upper Canada, from 1846 to 1876, Ryerson was the principal architect and defender of a unified common school system that was designed to be Christian but non-denominational, inclusive but tolerant of those who wished to separate from the mainstream for religious reasons.

There is no denying that Charbonnel's school politics, after 1852, could be very emotional and reactionary. The bishop's tactics were largely defined by Ryerson's unblinking opposition to his demands that Catholics had a right to open, staff and manage their own schools, wherever practicable, and that the government had a corresponding *obligation* to fund Catholic schools in a manner consistent with the funding of Protestant schools in Lower Canada. Ryerson's answer on both counts was consistently negative.

During the incendiary school struggles of the 1850s, the French-born Charbonnel was Ryerson's most dangerous antagonist. However unlikely it might appear to us, Charbonnel was more of a perceived threat to Ryerson's common schools than either John Strachan, the Church of England bishop, or George Brown, the Presbyterian and pugilistic proprietor of the *Globe*. Whereas Strachan's political influence, in steady decline since the 1841 Union, could be easily deflected, and Brown's hectoring in favour of completely secular schools could be dismissed as too radical for most Protestants, Charbonnel was the spiritual leader of a flock whose numbers steadily increased during the ten years he was bishop and whose priests and leading laity stubbornly clung to their ideal of Catholic schools for Catholic children, despite a chronic shortage of money, political trickery and endless roadblocks. As for Charbonnel himself, he never gave up. He doggedly pressed his double-barreled claim that separate schools for Catholic children were a spiritual necessity and a legal right not to be denied by anyone.

For his part in the great drama, Ryerson was Charbonnel's arch nemesis. Loyalist and pro-British to the core, Ryerson struck at the bishop, the foreign ecclesiastic, on numerous occasions, "smiting him hip and thigh" every time they clashed. Charbonnel could be his own worst enemy and thus the perfect foil to Ryerson. The bishop's passion, although genuine, often got the better of him and interfered with the facts at hand, leading to a series of humiliations and defeats. Ryerson, on the other hand, never allowed his emotions to rule his intellect. Politically adept and blessed with a keen eye for detail, he was in control of every fact in every dispute about provincial education and the current law governing its administration. No opponent — no politician for that matter — could match him in this regard. But it is the calculated measure of Ryerson's numerous counterblasts against Charbonnel that convinces one that the chief superintendent reserved his best salvos for the leader of the Catholic camp. Ryerson's rebuttals and explanations were often long-winded, tedious and repetitious. Nevertheless, they were an effective means of dulling most of his enemies into silence and submission.

However, it was one thing for Ryerson to pummel Charbonnel in debate, which he did so well to loud applause, but it was foolish of him to predict that Catholic separate schools would wither away. Their hoped-for disappearance was a pious prayer of Ryerson's that was often invoked in his published reports but mercifully remained unanswered. Time, that great leveler of opinion and political power, proved him wrong. That Catholic separate schools survived Ryerson's thirty years of active hostility is a judgment in favour of the kind of tenacity displayed by Charbonnel on behalf of these schools. It was the same kind of tenacity, albeit shorn of Charbonnel's emotionalism, that was shared by contemporary Catholic newspaper owners and countless school trustees and subsequently adopted by many of his episcopal successors in later showdowns over separate schools. The Catholic bishop and the Methodist bureaucrat waged a fierce and bitter battle over the status and fate of Catholic separate schools that did not end until Charbonnel resigned from the See of Toronto and returned permanently to Europe in 1860. The intensity of the war of words they waged against each other might surprise and perhaps shock some modern readers, unaccustomed as they are to the bombast and bullying of nineteenth century rhetoric, but politics in Upper Canada was often a rough-and-tumble affair and was tailor-made for divisive social and religious issues such as separate schools. Political adversaries penned their opinions bluntly, sometimes harshly, giving no quarter to their opponents and expecting none from them. Bishop Charbonnel and Chief Superintendent Ryerson were no exception.

Since so much ink was spilled over Catholic schools, in Charbonnel versus Ryerson, one is obliged to limit the reproduction of their opinions to representative samples, within the context of their respective biographies and the various pieces of legislation concerning separate schools.

****

Armand-François-Marie de Charbonnel was born on 1 December 1802, at Château du Flachat, near Monistrol-sur-Loire, France. He was the son of Jean-Baptiste de Charbonnel, Comte de Charbonnel, and Marie-Claudine de Pradier. His father had remained a Royalist during the French Revolution, and his older brother, Félix-Louis, had been killed in Paris at the time of the 1848 revolution.[64] He was a brilliant student at Montbrisson, Annonay (the home of the Basilian Fathers) and the Séminaire de Saint-Sulpice. After he turned down the offer of a philosophy professorship, when he was only twenty years of age, Charbonnel continued his theological studies and was ordained a priest on 17 December 1825. His first appointment was chaplain to the Duchesse de Berry. This was too retiring a position for a person of his gifts. The following year he joined the Society of Saint-Sulpice and began to teach.

Charbonnel enjoyed the classroom. At one time or another he taught at the Sulpician Seminary in Lyons and at seminaries in Versailles, Bordeaux and Aix-en-Provence. His specialties were dogmatic theology and sacred scripture. He was also a skilled preacher and retreat master, who declined civic honours and avoided advancement in the church. He refused to accept the cross of the Legion of Honour for saving the Lyons seminary from destruction at the hands of rioters in 1833, and he resisted pressure to take his slain brother's seat in the assembly. When it appeared that he would be promoted to the hierarchy in France or at the very least appointed a seminary rector, he decided to leave France and become a missionary in North America.

Charbonnel arrived at the Sulpician seminary in Montreal in 1839. Soon he was in constant demand to preach and give retreats. One of those retreats took place in Toronto, in 1845, at the request of Bishop Michael Power. It was a memorable event and five years later proved to be one of the decisive factors towards the selection of Charbonnel as Toronto's second bishop.

In 1841, Charbonnel moved to Baltimore, Maryland to learn English, a language he never mastered to the point where he felt comfortable speaking or writing it. In 1844, several years following his return to Montreal, Charbonnel vetoed the efforts of Bishop Antoine Blanc of New Orleans to have the pope name him his successor. Charbonnel preferred to carry on as a simple priest in Montreal. That decision almost inadvertently killed him. He nearly died during the 1847 typhus epidemic, the same scourge that swept away Bishop Power. Charbonnel's brush with death convinced him to complete his convalescence in France.

In the meantime, the young Diocese of Toronto struggled without a bishop for three years. Charbonnel's flight from promotion in the Church ended when the Canadian hierarchy promoted his name as its preferred candidate to the Holy See. He was ordained bishop by Pius IX in the Sistine Chapel on 26 May 1850 and assumed his episcopal duties in Toronto by 21 September.

Bishop Charbonnel inherited a vast diocese which was experiencing an evident growth in population, mainly from Irish immigration, but which was also in deep administrative and financial disarray. The number of Catholics had increased from approximately 50,000 in 1842, the year Power assumed control, to around 80,000 in 1850, the year Charbonnel came.[65] (Compare this to the entire province: from 1842 to 1851, there was a 157 percent increase, from 65,203 to 167,695.[66]) In Toronto itself, the Catholic population went from 2,500 in 1838 to 7,940 in 1850 and would grow to 12,000 by 1860.[67] These numbers are truly impressive by any standard, but the Catholic community in 1850 and for decades thereafter was pitifully short on collective wealth and the kind of political clout that came with it.

To compound matters, there was only one parish church for the entire city of Toronto — St. Paul's — and an unfinished cathedral saddled with a huge debt. According to the accounts, the diocese was insolvent; further, there were a mere twenty-eight secular priests to serve a diocese that stretched from Windsor on the Detroit River to Oshawa east of Toronto.

Bishop Charbonnel confronted each problem with enthusiasm and imagination. He set up the Cathedral Loan Fund and completed the cathedral decorations; he instituted the *cathedraticum*, an annual payment to the diocese amounting to ten percent of each parish's income; he recruited dozens of priests and encouraged many more to study for the priesthood; he built twenty-three churches; he successfully invited the Christian Brothers, the Basilian Fathers and the Sisters of St. Joseph to teach in Catholic schools; he guided the formation of the Toronto conference of the St. Vincent de Paul Society and founded the Toronto Savings Bank and the House of Providence; and he reformed the spiritual life and discipline of both priests and people. He was really the second founder of the diocese of Toronto and was responsible for the creation of the dioceses of London and Hamilton.

Central to Charbonnel's campaign to reinvigorate and regulate the Catholic faith among his people was the establishment of a well funded and properly managed system of Catholic schools where Catholic children could learn the faith free from the cultural and religious hegemony of the province's Protestant majority. His attempt to achieve this lofty but politically dangerous goal is the story of his struggle with Egerton Ryerson.

****

Egerton Ryerson was born in Charlotteville Township, Norfolk County, on 24 March 1803.[68] His parents were Joseph Ryerson and Mehetable Stickney. Ryerson's family were loyalists during the American Revolution and the War of 1812. Five sons, including Egerton, became Methodist ministers. Loyalism and Methodism, then, were the hallmarks of his formative years. They would shape and sustain many of his religious and political beliefs, and they would have a great effect upon the philosophical underpinnings of the province's common school system. Ryerson wanted schools that would be both broadly Christian and unmistakably British in their core values, traditions and outlook.

Ryerson was a man of many talents and achievements. As well as serving as a seasoned circuit rider and ordained Methodist clergyman, he was the first editor of the *Christian Guardian*, the Methodist newspaper, the first president of the Methodist Church in Canada and the first principal of Victoria College of the University of Toronto. He was a pamphleteer and polemicist of uncommon ability, demolishing not only Charbonnel but also Strachan and Brown and many other political and religious enemies. All his life, he was fearless in the face of considerable public malignity, a good deal of which came from Charles Donlevy's *Toronto Mirror*. But it is Ryerson's three decades at the helm of the Council of Public Instruction that demands our attention.

Appointed assistant superintendent in 1844 and then chief in 1846, Ryerson was an absolute marvel at administration. The reason for this was deceptively simple: he had a natural genius for running a department and imposing his will. To this genius he added "singleness of purpose, vigour in action, and an unusual facility for propaganda. Like Bentham and Voltaire who lived long and wrote much, Ryerson won acceptance of his ideas not only because they were so convincingly presented, but because they were so often repeated."[69]

Egerton Ryerson was a veritable workhorse, the ideal civil servant, and nothing if not consistent and clear in his ideas, opinions and prejudices. To the dismay of his Catholic critics, including Bishop Charbonnel, he was even more emphatic on all three counts whenever he pronounced on separate schools.

****

Ryerson believed that his mission was to remake an already existing common school system of nearly 2,500 elementary schools[70] into a province-wide system of education that would be universal (open to the children of all classes); free (no tuition or fees); practical; compulsory up to a certain age; Christian but non-denominational; thoroughly British and Canadian, with an emphasis on the Imperial tie; and financed by a combination of government grants from the School Fund and general property taxes. This system would be managed by a strong central authority whose policies and decisions would be implemented at the local level by trustees elected by the ratepayers in each school district or city ward. The system would include both common and grammar schools and would be an active concern of the government.[71]

Many of these components can be found in Ryerson's 1846 "Report on a System of Public Elementary Instruction for Upper Canada," a seminal document in the history of education in Ontario. Other items, such as the inclusion of grammar schools and the concept of compulsory education were to come later but were no less essential to his overall philosophy of education.

The great paradox of Ryerson's non-denominational (or non-sectarian) Christianity was that no such entity had ever existed in Upper Canada and was nowhere in evidence at the time he submitted his "Report." Christianity was not an homogenous religious expression — it had many different faces — and it could not be made homogenous by its well-intentioned inclusion in the curriculum of the common schools. Although Ryerson himself realized that Christianity had many "sects," he failed to deal with the paradox inherent in his non-sectarian Christianity. He thought doctrinal differences among Christians, at least in the common schools, could be easily papered over by offering a Bible-based moral instruction to everyone who wanted it, and allotting highly circumscribed and financially starved separate schools to those who did not. Those who did not, he called dissidents.

Ryerson's common school Christianity was really Protestantism in a different guise. It was a clever deception, but it did not fool the leaders of the Church in Ontario. Moreover, it was Christianity wholly subject to the interests of the state, which he called "the collective parent" in matters of educating the young.[72] It is little wonder then that he went to such great lengths to denounce those Catholics who, he charged, had handed over their parental authority to the priests as part of a bishop- and priest-directed plan of campaign to make Catholic separate schools a right.

On Christianity's pre-eminent place in the province's common schools and the existence of separate schools, as permitted by the Act of 1843, Ryerson had this to say:

> The inhabitants of the Province at large, professing Christianity, and being fully represented in the Government by Members of a Responsible Council — Christianity, therefore, upon the most popular principles of Government, should be the basis of a Provincial System of Education. But that general principle admits of considerable variety in its application . . .
>
> The foregoing observations and illustrations apply, for the most part, to a population consisting of both Protestants and Roman Catholics. The law provides against interfering with the religious scruples of each class, in respect both to religious books and the means of establishing Separate Schools.
>
> In School Districts where the whole population is either Protestant, or Roman Catholic, and where, consequently, the Schools come under the character of "Separate," there the principle of Religious instruction can be carried out into as minute detail as may accord with the views and wishes of either class of the population; though I am persuaded all that

is essential to the moral interests of youth may be taught in what are termed Mixed Schools.[73]

Most important in the above is Ryerson's opinion on the ability of Mixed Schools to deal with the moral interests of the students. It reveals his negative attitude towards separate schools, an attitude that hardened over the years on the receipt of each new demand from Catholic leaders for changes in school legislation. Mixed Schools were for all children and were sufficient to transmit the basic moral truths of the Bible. Separate schools were an entirely different matter. They were a temporary answer to peculiar local conditions as might be experienced in some rural communities and consequently were a privilege never to be extended or improved. (Ryerson once claimed that these conditions were nothing more than a conflict between Irish Catholics and Irish Protestants.[74]) Separate schools were part of the common school system, but they were well outside the pale of full legal recognition and had no hope of ever achieving an equal status with the Mixed Schools.

Ryerson tolerated separate schools because they had been the will of the legislature in 1841 and 1843, but he treated them as an unwanted inheritance, a lingering annoyance and nuisance. He believed that it was only a matter of time before the conditions that had given rise to them would cease to exist. Separate schools, then, were doomed to disappear on their own. That is why he never sought their outright abolition. To him the status quo, however unpalatable and irritating, made perfect political sense.

Ryerson's attitude towards separate schools never substantially changed at any time during his long tenure as chief superintendent. His own words easily prove this. They also demonstrate the extent to which he was determined to keep separate schools in a permanently crippled condition, and they reveal the deep-seated contempt he had for Catholic bishops, priests and laity. Here are seven representative samples from 1847 to 1858:

1847 Annual Report

It appears . . . there are only forty-one [Protestant and Catholic] Separate Schools in Upper Canada. These, I believe are generally of an inferior class. The number of them have been diminishing from year to year. The very small number of them shows that the provision of the School Law permitting their establishment is of very little importance, either for good or evil. I believe the fewer of these Separate Schools the better for the interests of youth, and the diffusion of General Education; but it is perhaps better to leave the Law as it is, in respect to Separate Schools, than to have an agitation arising from the repeal of it.[75]

Ryerson to Reverend William Fraser
31 March 1849

It was not intended to place *separate* Schools upon the same footing with mixed or public Schools. By the 31st section of the [1846] Act, equal advantages and protection are secured to all religious persuasions in the public Schools. And if, after that, the members of any religious persuasion in a School Section wish for a sectarian School or a School subservient to the peculiar interests of their own Church, they cannot expect the public money to be given in a same ratio to build up a sectarian interest as to support a School free from sectarian influence and equally open to all religious persuasions. Such is the principle of the law; and such is the principle on which it has been administered in all my decisions in respect to both Protestant and Roman Catholic separate Schools.[76]

Ryerson to the Globe, 22 July 1851

Though Separate Schools are permitted, they are not placed in the same position as "Mixed Schools," and can only be sustained by special exertions and sacrifices on the part of their supporters, who are equally taxed, with all other classes of their neighbours for the erection, furnishing and all expenses of the Mixed School, or Schools, and who, in addition, have to provide their own School-house and all incidental expenses of their School, as well as the balance of the Teacher's salary, by voluntary subscriptions among themselves. These Schools only receive a portion of the School fund, according to the average attendance of pupils, towards the making up, in part, of their Teacher's salary.[77]

1855 Annual Report

But if the parties for whom separate schools are allowed, and aided out of the Legislative School Grants, according to the average attendance of pupils . . . shall renew agitation upon the subject, and assail and seek to subvert the public school system, as they have done and endeavor to force legislation upon that subject against the voice and rights of the people of Upper Canada, by votes from Lower Canada, and the highest terrors of ecclesiastical authority, then I submit that the true and only alternative will be to abolish the separate school law altogether, and substitute the provisions of the national system in Ireland in relation to united secular and separate religious instruction, and extend it to Lower as well as Upper Canada.[78]

1857 Annual Report

I think it was a grave mistake, though dictated by the best motives, to introduce the principle of Separate Schools at all into the School Law of Upper Canada and Lower Canada in 1841. The equal protection of all parties and classes in the Public Schools was provided for, and no party had any right to claim more.[79]

If, therefore, the Roman Catholic Separate Schools are of little account, and feebly supported in comparison with the public schools, it is because the supporters of separate schools are less concerned and energetic in the education of their children than are the supporters of public schools, and isolate themselves from the latter . . . in spite of all appeals and influences to the contrary, the progressive portion of the Roman Catholic as well as of the Protestant population prefers the public schools to separate schools, combined action to isolated action, the principle which is the *magna charta* as well as characteristic of a free people, to the principle that has been the prop of every despotism which has oppressed mankind; the principle which makes a good education the right of every child in the land, to the principle, which, in every land where it has prevailed, has left the great majority of the most needy classes of children in ignorance.[80]

Ryerson to the Governor General
20 April 1858

The supporters of Dissentient [Protestant] Schools in Lower Canada are, as a whole, more intelligent and more wealthy, and know better how to proceed and manage their affairs, than the Supporters of Separate Schools in the rural parts of Upper Canada. This poverty and ignorance on the part of a great portion of the Supporters of Separate Schools in Upper Canada is not so apparent, or so much felt, when they are associated with other classes of the inhabitants in the management of local affairs; but when they stand out isolated from other classes, as they do in Separate school matters, from the intelligent counsel of local School Superintendents, and the co-operation of Municipal Councils, their inexperience and incapacity become painfully obvious, and the Priests, who frequently assume the whole

Correspondence and management in Separate School matters seem to possess little more practical talent and knowledge of legal modes of proceeding than those whom they influence to establish Separate Schools.[81]

Since this last document was written in 1858, Ryerson is speaking about Catholic separate schools and Catholic priests. He practically accused the entire Catholic community, and their priests especially, of ignorance and stupidity in their management of separate schools. Ryerson's judgment of the Catholic community, after twelve years as chief superintendent, came dangerously close to a vicious stereotype. One suspects that it was a sign of his frustration with the continuing viability of Catholic separate schools.[82] As we shall see, they did not disappear.

It was a frustration made all the more worse by Ryerson himself. Time and again, he claimed that Catholics had originally asked for separate schools as a "protection from insult" and for no other reason,[83] that "until 1852, Separate Schools were never advocated as a theory, much less as a doctrine, and less still as an article of faith"[84] and that it was Bishop Charbonnel who was primarily responsible for this radical change in the Catholic approach to separate schools. Since Charbonnel had served on the Council of Public Instruction, Ryerson felt betrayed by the bishop and took every opportunity to convey his hurt feelings.[85]

However, if Ryerson wanted to learn the reason for alleged Catholic mismanagement of Catholic schools and Charbonnel's supposed *volte face*, he had to look no further than the separate school provisions in the legislation he either engineered or was only too happy to enforce. This legislation can be divided into two groups: one, those acts passed from 1846 to 1850, prior to the arrival of Bishop Charbonnel, and two, those acts passed from 1851 to 1855, which were the government's response to Catholic agitation. Let us look at the first group.

Ryerson's first piece of school legislation was the result of his "Report on a System of Public Elementary Instruction for Upper Canada" and was passed on 23 May 1846. "An Act for the better establishment and maintenance of Common Schools in Upper Canada" (9 Victoria, c. 20) outlined the functions of the chief superintendent, set up a Board of Education for the whole province, and enunciated policies concerning district superintendents, textbooks, property taxes to support schools, government grants, school sections and the school-related duties of municipal councils. Although the "Report" never mentioned separate schools, Section 32 of the Act recognized their legal existence. Except for a few changes in wording, Section 32 was identical to Section 55 of the 1843 Act: the right to establish a separate school, either Protestant or Catholic, depended on the religion of the teacher in the common school of any given school section. If the teacher were Protestant, the right belonged to Catholics, on the application of ten or more freeholders or householders in the school section. Protestants had the identical right if the teacher were Catholic. From the Catholic point of view, the fatal flaw in both the 1843 and 1846 Acts was that hiring Catholic teachers for the common schools effectively blocked Catholics from setting up their own schools in the same districts.

In 1847, the legislature passed a crippling amendment to the 1846 Act. "An Act for amending the Common Schools Act of Upper Canada" (10 & 11 Victoria, c. 19) took away the right of freeholders and householders in cities and towns to petition for a separate school and gave that right to municipal councils. From now on, they would have the power "to determine the number, sites and descriptions of schools, and whether such school or schools shall be denominational or mixed." This amendment made it virtually impossible for Catholics to open new schools and receive their share of the school fund for schools already existing.

Two years later, Malcolm Cameron, a member of parliament, submitted to the legislature "An Act for the better Establishment and Maintenance of Public Schools in Upper Canada, and for repealing the recent School Act." Cameron's bill would have abolished separate schools, forbidden clergy visitors to the common schools and circumscribed the duties (and thus power) of the chief superintendent. Ryerson welcomed the abolition of separate schools but thought that the bill would destroy the common school system. Such was his hold over the government that even though the bill became law, he was given permission to run the schools as if it had not and to offer alternative legislation the following year.

Ryerson wasted little time. "An Act for the better establishment and maintenance of Common Schools in Upper Canada" (13 & 14 Victoria, c. 48) was passed on 24 July 1850. Section 19 restored the process whereby separate schools could be established, but it did nothing to make it easier to open those schools. The Act said that it was the "duty of Municipal Councils of any Township, and of the Board of School Trustees of any City, Town and incorporated Village, on the application in writing of twelve or more resident heads of families, to authorize the establishment of one or more separate schools." The word "duty" was an advance, but any good that might have come from it was negated by the Act's fourth proviso: "that no Protestant separate school shall be allowed in any school division except when the Teacher of a Common School is a Roman Catholic, nor shall any Roman Catholic separate school be allowed except when the Teacher of the Common School is a Protestant." This was the 1843 Act all over again.

Even if separate school supporters succeeded in opening a school in their school section, they usually found it impossible to keep it open. Their school taxes went to the common schools; their portion of the government grant for the teacher's salary was often inadequate; and they were denied public money to buy and furnish a school house.

****

Two months after the passage of the 1850 Act, Bishop Charbonnel entered the picture. There were two Catholic separate schools in Toronto in 1850. Six years of lobbying by Catholic trustees had failed to add to that pitiful number. On 14 October, having been in his diocese only three weeks, the bishop asked the city superintendent of common schools for one more school for the eastern part of the city. In his letter, the bishop stated the classic

Catholic case for separate schools:

> By the 19th Section of the new school act, separate schools
> can be demanded by parties therein mentioned, under certain
> salutary conditions and restrictions. Those portions of the
> Upper Canadian population which are in communion with
> the See of Rome have ever been most desirous of having the
> education of their youth conducted upon such principles as
> will ensure to them the intimate blending of religious
> teaching with secular learning: in mixed schools this is
> obviously impossible. Although by no means agreeing with
> us in the necessity, utility, or even good policy of such a
> concession, nevertheless our separated brethren of all
> denominations have, with few exceptions, consented to
> concede this point to us, and the Legislature has stamped the
> boon with the authority of an Act of Parliament, and has
> placed us in Upper Canada in the same favourable position in
> which the Protestant portion of the community in Lower
> Canada stand where they are not, as is well known, in many
> parts of that province, of the prevailing creed.
> Notwithstanding this advantage, the Catholic community of
> Upper Canada do not desire to stand up stiffly for their strict
> legal rights, when a harmonious understanding can be
> attained; they have every disposition to meet their separated
> Brethren upon equitable terms, and thereby avert the clashing
> and jarring which might ensure to their mutual interest great
> inconvenience, were the law to be rigidly followed out in all
> its details.[86]

Charbonnel was misinformed about the equal standing of
Catholics in Upper Canada and Protestants in Lower Canada in school
rights under the law. No such equality existed and would never exist as
long as Ryerson remained chief superintendent. And clashing and jarring
are all that the bishop received from the Toronto common school trustees.
They quickly dismissed his request by treating the entire city of Toronto
as one ward. At that, two separate schools were one too many!

Charbonnel immediately fired back, demanding seven new schools, one for each district that had a Protestant teacher in the common school. The board continued to resist, however, referring the matter to the attorney general. At this juncture, Ryerson intervened and offered remedial legislation. Passed on 30 August 1851, "An Act to define and restore certain rights to parties therein mentioned" (14 & 15 Victoria, c. 111) entitled applicants under Section 19 "to have a separate school in each ward, or in two or more wards united, in each city or town in Upper Canada." This was a simple and easy solution to what was really the obduracy of the Toronto Board, which refused to follow the plain meaning of the law.

Why, one might ask, did Ryerson intervene if he were such a staunch enemy of separate schools? Ryerson promoted this remedy because he was sufficiently astute to realize that the board's interpretation of the 1850 Act was not intended by the Act and also because, as he reminded Francis Hincks and John Rolph, separate schools were declining in number and were bound to extinction. Any remedy of the type offered in the 1851 Act would do nothing to slow or stop this decline.[87] Ryerson had the statistics. There were only forty-six separate schools in all of 3,000 school sections in Upper Canada in 1851. Of these, twenty-one were Catholic.[88] For the following year, the numbers were even lower: there were four Protestant separate schools and sixteen Catholic ones.[89] Ryerson annihilated Protestant separate schools[90] and put to rest forever Bishop Strachan's wish to open Anglican separate schools. Ryerson would have done the same to the Catholic separate schools if Charbonnel had not persisted in his agitation on their behalf. It bears repeating that Ryerson's big mistake was to wish away Catholic schools, by confidently predicting their demise, year after year, and to boast to his political masters that any concession to the Catholics was too insignificant to alter the course of his oft-repeated predictions.

Round one went to Charbonnel. He managed to wring a substantial amendment to the 1850 Act that led to the founding of more separate schools in Toronto. Round two quickly followed and proved more difficult. It offered a stage for Charbonnel to vent his

Gallic fury against Ryerson and for Ryerson to humiliate Charbonnel. In the end, other concessions flowed from the government, which over time helped to stop and then reverse the decline in the number of separate schools. The process was slow and painful but ultimately victorious.

The battle began with a letter of 15 January 1852, from J.B. Williams, a separate school trustee in Chatham, to the Hon. S.B. Harrison, chairman of the Council of Public Instruction. At the root of the complaint was the total legal subservience of separate school supporters to the whims and prejudices of the trustees of the common school. The latter decided the merits of separate school applications, collected all school taxes and controlled the apportioning of the School Fund. The immediate problem was the pathetic sum of money the separate board received from that fund.

> In the month of March last, the Roman Catholics of this place applied to the Board of Trustees for the establishment of a Separate Roman Catholic School, which was granted, and the School was organized and has been in successful operation since the 12th May.
>
> The inhabitants of the Town, or rather the Trustees having decided upon having Free Schools during the last year, and also upon the erection of a Public School House, at an expense of £1200, a heavy tax has consequently been levied from us, of course, amongst the other citizens; to this we submitted cheerfully, under the impression, however, that we would be allowed a proportion thereof, for the payment of our teacher, and have the use of a reasonable part of the School House or an equivalent, but so far, the Board of Trustees refuse us both, and we have received no support whatever, excepting the small sum of £4 10s. out of the Provincial Grant.[91]

During an episcopal visitation of the southwestern part of his diocese, Charbonnel heard complaints about Chatham that prompted a letter to Ryerson, postmarked 7 March 1852:

40

I hear from Chatham, subsequently to my appeal to your equity and to your answer, that there the negroes are incomparably better treated than the Catholics; that the latter have received for their Separate School, attended on average by 46 pupils, only £4 10s, Government money, and are offered as little out of about £300 taxes raised for the payment of Teachers, to which the Catholics have much contributed as well as to the high sum levied for the building of a new School-house; that in another Mixed School the anti-Catholic history of England, by Goldsmith, is perused as

Again, Rev. and dear Doctor, where is the equity of such a management? Where that liberal spirit professed in pamphlets, public speeches, reports, etc.? And am I not right to call our most deplorable system of education a regular disguised persecution? And still I have at hand facts of a worse character.[92]

Ryerson revealed his liberality in a response to a similar demand from the separate school trustees in Belleville, dated 12 February 1852. If Catholics wanted their own separate schools, they would have to pay a steep price:

The School law provides for the equal protection of the peculiar religious rights and scruples of all religious persuasions; but if the members of any religious denomination in a municipality are not satisfied with the enjoyment of equal privileges with the members of other religious persuasions of their fellow-citizens, but insist upon a School exclusively devoted to their own denominational interest, they cannot ask, upon any ground of constitutional right or justice between man and man, that public money, Municipal authority and property, shall be employed to the same extent to build up denominational interest as to promote interests which are common to all classes of citizens without regard to sect or party.[93]

In other words, Catholic separate school supporters were on their own. A copy of this letter was forwarded to Bishop Charbonnel. Also sent was a letter of 13 March 1852, replying directly to his concerns about Chatham. In it, Ryerson brushed off Charbonnel's concerns about Goldsmith's history by claiming that no child was required to read it. He then continued:

> I have observed, with regret, that demands for exemptions and advantages have recently been made on the part of some advocates of Separate Schools, which had not been previously heard of during the whole ten years of the existence and operation of the provisions of the law for Separate as well as Mixed Schools. I cannot but regard such occurrences as ominous of evil. It is possible that the Legislature may accede to the demands of individuals praying, on grounds of conscience, for unrestricted liberty of teaching; exempting them from all School taxes, with a corresponding exclusion of their children from all Public Schools, leaving them perfectly free to establish their own Schools at their own expense; but I am persuaded the people of Upper Canada will never suffer themselves to be taxed, or the machinery of their Government to be employed for the building and support of denominational School houses, any more than for denominational places of worship and clergy.[94]

Ryerson finished by pointing out that the Catholic claim to a share of the School Fund for the erection of schoolhouses was especially weak given the fact a separate school ceased to exist as soon as the common school in the district hired a Catholic teacher.

Charbonnel was furious. He bellowed back on 24 March in a torrent of raw emotion:

> O beautiful protection! beautiful harmony! O admirable means of teaching God and his ordinances! admirable way of making children improve in religion, faith, piety, unity, charity, and in reading into the bargain!

And you are astonished, Rev. Doctor, at our demand, of having nothing to do with such a chimera, such a mixture, such a regular school of pyrrhonism, of indifferentism, of infidelity, and consequently of all vices and crimes.

    ... since your School system is the ruin of religion, and a persecution for our Church, since we know, at least, as well as any body else, how to encourage, diffuse, promote education . . . and better than you . . . how to teach respect toward authority, God and his Church, parent and government — since we are under the blessed principles of religious liberty and equal civil rights, we must have, and we will have the full management of our Schools, as well as Protestants in Lower Canada; or the world of the 19th century will know that here, as elsewhere, Catholics, against the constitution of the Country, against the best and most sacred interests, are persecuted by the most cruel and hypocritical persecution.[95]

Ryerson replied in a letter of 24 April, which ran for many tightly-packed and densely argued pages. He countered by repeating the standard catalogue of assertions: that Bishop Power did not advocate separate schools for Catholics; that Charbonnel brought into Upper Canada foreign ideas on education; that separate schools existed only as a temporary protection; that their introduction was regrettable; and that separate schools would die out.[96]

The jousting continued until Charbonnel ended it in a brief note of 22 May, promising Ryerson that by "making use of all constitutional means, in order to obtain our right, I will not upset the Government of Canada nor its institutions."[97] Charbonnel did not upset the government so much as he was to anger Ryerson during the next five years.

Round two ended in another legislative concession. On 13 June 1853, the legislature passed "An Act supplementary to the Common School Act for Upper Canada" (16 Victoria, c. 185). It exempted separate school supporters from paying common school taxes and incorporated separate school trustees, who were given the right to collect their own taxes as well as the responsibility to give annual notification to the municipal authorities of those who supported the separate schools. Although the Act removed a serious tax burden and gave separate school trustees independence of action in terms of collecting taxes, it did not change the process whereby separate schools were established, the importance of the religion of the teacher or the way in which the School Fund (legislative grant) was divided.[98]

Charbonnel was happy with the changes[99] but livid over the fact that common school trustees could easily demolish already existing separate schools in their respective districts by the simple expedient of hiring Catholic teachers. The Toronto common school trustees were quick to exploit this loophole in the law. Charbonnel took his case to Francis Hincks, the inspector general, in letters of 2 August and 7 October 1853, bitterly complaining of the supervisory power of local boards over separate schools.[100] Eight bishops then weighed in with a petition of 4 June 1854, asking the legislature to designate a portion of the sale of the Clergy Reserves for separate schools. The bishops wrote of "witnessing with the deepest sorrow the evil which commonly results from Mixed Schools."[101] They claimed that they desired "no exclusive privileges, their sole prayer being that the law which governs the Separate Schools in favour of the Protestants of Lower Canada, may be put in force in favour of the Catholics of Upper Canada."[102] For the bishops, equity in educational matters was a right, not a privilege granted by the majority. Besides episcopal pressure, there were at least thirty separate schools disputes in 1854 that landed on Ryerson's desk.[103]

The government responded with another piece of legislation known as the Taché Act, named after Étienne-Paschal Taché. Passed on 30 May 1855, after hurried and acrimonious debate, "An Act to amend the laws relating to Separate Schools in Upper Canada" (18 Victoria, c. 131) was restricted to Catholics in Upper Canada and became known as the first Separate School Act. Catholics now controlled the process by which they applied to set up Catholic schools. All that was needed was for five Catholic heads of families to inform the common school and municipal authorities of their intention. This eliminated a great deal of needless interference and acrimony at the local level. Also, no longer was the religion of the teacher of crucial importance. Common schools could not hire Catholic teachers as a means to close down existing Catholics schools or block applications for new ones in their respective districts. The Act continued to exempt separate school supporters from paying common school taxes and to allow separate schools to receive a share of the school fund based on average attendance.

Charbonnel thought that he had successfully bargained for substantially more, but he had been easily and brilliantly duped. During third reading of the bill, which took place after he had left Quebec City, where the legislature was sitting, the government under the guidance of John A. Macdonald tacked on several amendments so crippling in their effect that they devalued whatever progress the Act in its final form had accomplished. In a letter of 17 November 1855, Charbonnel listed six "contaminations which have most shamefully polluted the 3rd reading of the last Act on Separate Schools." They were:

1. The annual declaration of the supporters of sep. Schools to the clerk of the municipality; 2. The exclusion of school supporters from the benefit of public assessment and collection for school purposes; 3. The obligation of Roman Catholics to contribute to Protestant schools, school-houses & libraries; 4. Our exclusion from all school-funds, but the Government grant; 5. The nullity of the election of trustees, when within two months the separate school is not established; 6. The multiplicity of school trustees and wards in cities and town. None of these fetters shackle protestants in Lower Canada.[104]

Number 2 reflected Ryerson's absolute opposition to municipalities collecting separate school taxes. Number 3 concerned the liability of Catholics to honor long-term common school tax assessments, even after they had established a separate school in the same district. Number 4 was another Ryerson fixation: he blocked all efforts to have the government share public funds with separate schools beyond the miserly sum due to them from the School Fund for teachers' salaries. Number 6 referred to the prohibition of two or more Catholic school sections uniting to establish a separate school. This was a vexatious problem for Catholics in rural areas.

Having been made to look foolish, Charbonnel made matters worse by declaring in his 1856 Lenten Pastoral that Catholic electors and politicians who did not use their power to support separate schools were guilty of mortal sin; that parents who did not support separate schools or send their children to them were guilty of mortal sin; and that any confessor who gave absolution to such people was also guilty of mortal sin.[105]

This was a gigantic political blunder, for it played right into the hands of Ryerson. In his 1856 *Annual Report*, Ryerson charged the critics of the common schools with "sectarian bigotry" and "ecclesiastical despotism."[106] In January 1857, he went one step further in a wide-ranging attack upon the Catholic hierarchy by labeling them "enemies of God and man."[107]

There the matter stood until the passage of the so-called Scott Act in 1863. The Bowes Bill of 1856 failed to reach third reading. It would have allowed separate school supporters to prove their exemption from common school taxes by simply producing a tax receipt. The Felton amendment that would have placed Catholic separate schools in Upper Canada on a par with the Protestant separate schools in Lower Canada also went down to defeat. Happily, George Brown's motion to repeal all separate school legislation endured a similar fate.[108]

A truce in the war of words between Charbonnel and Ryerson took place when both men, for different reasons, departed for Europe almost at the same time during the summer of 1856. Charbonnel stayed until June 1858. The war, though, was resumed by Reverend J.M Bruyère, the rector of St. Michael's cathedral, when he openly contested Ryerson's circular of 15 November 1856, which suggested that the funds from the secularized Clergy Reserves be used exclusively to buy teaching aids for common schools and books for public libraries. Bruyère correctly demanded that separate schools also enjoy a portion of this bounty. It was a nasty confrontation. In the heat of the debate, Bruyère referred to Ryerson as Julian the Apostate and the "hypocrite son of John Wesley." Ryerson replied the way he always replied — by repeating his favourite themes. He claimed that Catholics did not have any real grievances against the current school law; that Bishop Power and Bishop Macdonell did not want separate schools; that only foreign ecclesiastics wanted them because they hated British institutions; and that Catholic parents were sending their children to them because they feared excommunication. It was all the fault of the priests.[109] The *Globe* joined the fray by spouting its standard anti-Catholic and anti-clerical invective:

> Priestly superstition, that dark dungeon in which Rome has always sought to imprison the human mind, was illuminated in spite of its bolts and bars by the glorious light of the Common School. Thousands who would otherwise have submitted themselves willingly to the keepers of the prison house, fled from the loathsome presence, as soon as they obtained, by the aid of mere secular light and truth, a dim view of its hideousness.[110]

Brown, like Ryerson, was guilty of wishful thinking. Neither man was able to will the extinction of Catholic separate schools. Because of their own prejudices, they overlooked the genuine desire of many Catholic people to have their own schools, despite all the impediments placed in their way and all the malevolence hurled against the Church. Proof of this desire is the fact that by 1860, the last year Charbonnel was bishop of Toronto, there were 115 Catholic separate schools attended by 14,780 Catholic students.[111]

****

Bishop Charbonnel left for Europe in February 1860 and resigned from his diocese on 26 April. He was succeeded by Bishop John Joseph Lynch. As titular bishop of Sozopolis, Charbonnel joined the Capuchins and became an auxiliary of the archdiocese of Lyons. In 1880, he was raised to the status of an archbishop. For two decades he traveled widely in his native France, preaching, giving retreats, ordaining priests and conducting administrative work. In 1883, he retired to the Capuchin monastery at Crest where he died on 29 March 1891.

Egerton Ryerson, meanwhile, continued as chief superintendent until he retired in February 1876. (He will appear in the final part of this chapter.) Only near the end of his lengthy tenure did the government dare to set up a ministry of education. Ryerson's final contribution to the legislative history of education in the province was the 1871 School Act. He died in Toronto on 19 February 1882 and was buried in Mount Pleasant Cemetery.

Archbishop John Joseph Lynch, 1816-1888

"We ask simply to educate our children as Catholics; to be allowed the privilege of spending our own money to the best advantage for that object; we claim our just share of State appropriation for educational purposes; – in a word, to have extended to us the rights and privileges which the Protestant minority of Lower Canada enjoy, and which we are willing they should continue to enjoy." – Canadian Freeman, 23 May 1861

John Joseph Lynch was bishop and then archbishop of Toronto for twenty-eight years, from 1860 to his death in 1888. He was the most powerful and influential Catholic prelate of his generation, outside of Quebec, and the next-to-last of the Irish-born bishops to rule Toronto's Catholic community. His involvement in the separate school wars took place against the backdrop of major political, cultural, economic and demographic change, which would alter the tone and the direction of the Catholic school campaign for the rest of the nineteenth century. It would also recast the respective roles of the clergy and laity in that struggle.

The most radical alteration to the political landscape was Confederation. As part of the negotiated dissolution of the Union of Canada West and Canada East, the new constitutional arrangement gave the provinces sole jurisdiction over education. As a barely disguised sop to the Catholics in Ontario and the Protestants in Quebec, the politicians enshrined educational rights existing at the time of Confederation in Section 93 of the British North America Act. This was a comfort to those Catholics who supported Confederation at the urging of politicians such as Thomas D'Arcy McGee, but the BNA Act was a severe blow to the political mechanics that had saved separate schools from extinction in the years leading up to Confederation. No longer would Catholics in Canada West be able to count on the legislative votes of their co-religionists in Canada East. As of 1 July 1867, Catholics in Ontario would virtually stand alone in their school battles, a religious minority left to the mercy of their Protestant critics. Freed from the "political interference" of Quebec-based Catholic politicians, Protestant Ontario as a distinct political entity emboldened Egerton Ryerson, George Brown and the Conservative Party in their opposition to extending any rights or privileges to Catholic separate schools. To them the 1863 Scott Act was final but its inclusion in the constitution was not.[112] Gone too were the political alliance between Catholics in Canada West and Protestants in Canada East, at least in matters pertaining to their education rights, and the uncanny ability of separate school agitation to divide the Orange Order and the Reform Party (the forerunner of the Liberal Party). Ironically, Confederation reunited and intensified Orange opposition to separate schools and transferred formal political opposition to them on the provincial level from the Liberals to the Conservatives.

Archbishop Lynch's answer to the new political reality in Ontario was twofold. He carefully avoided alienating Ryerson, before as well as after 1867. There was no use publicly confronting the chief superintendent as Charbonnel had done. Ryerson irritated Lynch to no small degree, but Lynch thought it was wiser to wait for Ryerson to retire from public office and to refrain from the kind of emotional outbursts that characterized Charbonnel's fateful dealings with the Methodist minister turned education bureaucrat. Meanwhile, Lynch was savvy enough to form a close working relationship with Sir Oliver Mowat's Liberal government, thereby ensuring that he would always have a hand in at least the administration of school policy as it directly affected the teaching of Catholic children.

This relationship worked well but only to a limited degree. Its end result was often political controversy of a type that brought nothing but scorn and contempt on Lynch's head and acute embarrassment to the Mowat Liberals. This was particularly true during the 1883 and 1886 provincial elections, which were even nastier than usual by contemporary standards. Moreover, any lasting good that the "Lynch-Mowat Concordat" achieved for separate schools was ultimately overshadowed by a fierce struggle between Lynch and leaders of the lay Catholic elite over control of the Toronto Separate School Board and the introduction of the secret ballot in trustee elections. (See Chapter Two for a treatment of these two issues.) The traditional Irish concept of automatic obedience, on the part of the Catholic faithful, to the demands of properly constituted spiritual authority in temporal affairs was coming to an end and more quickly than in the contest between the clergy and laity over the daily administration of separate schools.

The problems accruing from this cultural shift concerning ecclesiastical authority and the rise of the laity were compounded by the often baleful effects of industrialization and urbanization on the Catholic faithful and the fact that although there was an increase in the overall number of Catholics in Toronto, by 1890 they formed a smaller percentage of the city's population due to massive Protestant immigration. In effect, the minority status of Catholics was not only confirmed but also entrenched in the province's largest city, which also happened to be the provincial capital. This ensured tough times for separate school supporters, both in Toronto and its outlying areas and also throughout the rest of the province.

****

The son of James Lynch and Ann Connolly, John Joseph Lynch was born on 6 February 1816 in County Fermanagh, Ireland.[113] Since his parents were fairly prosperous, Lynch was given a respectable education. He attended school in Lucan, County Dublin, at the Academy of St. Joseph in Clondalkin and at St. Vincent's College in Castleknock. St. Vincent's was managed by the Congregation of the Mission. Their members were commonly known as either Lazarists or

Vincentians, and they specialized in missionary work. Lynch joined the community in 1837 and received his theological training at the Seminary of Saint-Lazarre in Paris.

After ordination at Maynooth in June 1843, he spent three years at St. Vincent's and in different parts of Ireland. In 1846, his dreams were fulfilled when he was transferred overseas. His first assignment was Texas where he was a horseback preacher during the Mexican-American war. Felled by typhoid fever, he was made superior of St. Mary of the Barrens in Perryville, Missouri. He stayed there from 1848 to 1856. Then, at the invitation of Bishop John Timon of Buffalo, he founded Our Lady of the Angels Seminary in Lewiston, New York (now Niagara University).

Lynch was a brilliant administrator, an excellent preacher and a powerful lecturer, three qualities which brought him to the notice of Bishop Charbonnel and convinced him that Lynch was the perfect candidate to oversee his largely Irish diocese. Lynch was consecrated coadjutor bishop on 20 November 1859 and succeeded to the See of Toronto on 26 April 1860. For his support of the doctrine of papal infallibility at the First Vatican Council, he was elevated to the status of an archbishop on 15 March 1870.

****

A month before Lynch officially became the third bishop of Toronto, Richard William Scott, the member for the city of Ottawa, introduced a private member's bill to correct deficiencies in the 1855 Taché Act. It was the first of four attempts to bring a measure of relief to separate school supporters and would culminate in the 1863 Act. This was the same Act that was protected by Section 93 of the BNA Act, the 1867 version of the Canadian constitution.

Scott belonged to one of the province's few Irish Catholic families to have achieved prominence in Upper Canada.[114] An old-fashioned war-horse for whom politics was a way of life, Scott promoted Ottawa as the capital of the new Dominion, served in Edward Blake's provincial cabinet and Alexander Mackenzie's federal cabinet, was a very active Senator from 1874 to 1913 and was made a knight bachelor in 1909. During his lifetime, he was known more for his authorship of the Canada Temperance Act of 1878 than he was for his school legislation.

Scott's Bill on separate schools was initially introduced on 16 March 1860.[115] Approved by Bishop Edward John Horan of Kingston and Bishop John Farrell of Hamilton, it gave Catholics the right to set up separate schools in incorporated towns and villages and relieved them of the duty to give annual notice of their support of separate schools. However, the government obliged Scott to withdraw his Bill because of a lack of time to consider it. Undaunted, Scott introduced another school Bill in April 1861. This proposed legislation contained three additional clauses; the most daring one would have allowed separate schools a share in all educational monies. Involved in the private negotiations prior to the Bill's introduction were Scott, Ryerson, John A. Macdonald, Bishop Lynch and the Reverend Angus Macdonell, vicar general of the diocese of Kingston.[116] This seems to be Lynch's first venture into the political minefield of school legislation. He escaped unscathed — this time.

What remains unclear is the extent, if any, to which these negotiations determined the actual wording of Scott's second Bill. Typical of the separate school controversy, as it was to unfold in the coming years, was an astonishing lack of consensus among backroom negotiators as to what amendments were accepted or rejected and if the proposed legislation was a final settlement of what had become for all parties a paralyzing process. In any event, Scott's 1861 Bill also died on the order paper.

The attempt to give separate schools a share in all educational funding was anathema to Egerton Ryerson. He responded with a Bill of his own in March 1862, which was limited to three important but relatively minor issues: annual notices of tax exemptions, separate schools in incorporated villages and separate school union sections.[117] This time Lynch was a key player in the drafting of legislation. In a letter to John A. Macdonald, Ryerson had this to say of the Catholic bishop of Toronto:

I found him a very moderate & practical man. He showed me

the notes which he had prepared on the subject, and I showed him mine; and we found that we were agreed. He asked for nothing more than what was enjoyed by Roman Catholics under the Separate School provisions of the Supplementary Act of 1853; and that was just what I propose to restore to them.[118]

Ryerson's version of his conversation with Lynch may be correct. But we must keep in mind that Lynch, like his brother bishops, tended to ask only for the absolute minimum at any given time because they believed (quite correctly) that since Ryerson was the final arbiter on all separate school matters, only the minimum would be granted. His opinion was the law of the land. Ryerson was so pleased with Lynch that he proposed to make him a member of the Council of Public Instruction. Lynch wisely accepted.[119]

If Ryerson thought that his Bill would obviate a third try on Scott's part, he was wrong. Scott had his own ideas. Twice thwarted, he introduced a third Bill, in early April 1862. It produced quite a shock in Ryerson. Instead of addressing issues arising from the 1855 Taché Act, it took as its model the Hon. John Elmsley's 1857 draft legislation, in which the following would be granted: separate schools in incorporated villages; unlimited union of school section trustees; exemption of all Catholic-owned property, regardless of its location, from education taxes; appointment of priests as *ex officio* trustees; Church control of rules and curriculum; exemption from all common school holidays and vacations and the freedom for separate schools to set their own.[120]

Ryerson would have none of it. When Scott moved second reading of his Bill, on 28 April, he agreed to submit both his Bill and Ryerson's Bill to committee. He had little choice. His was a private member's bill, which had yet to garner even lukewarm support from the government, and Ryerson was one civil servant whom politicians on both sides of the legislature were loathe to alienate.

It was at the committee stage that Ryerson demonstrated his power and persuasiveness. He was able to gut Scott's Bill so that essentially it resembled his own. At a meeting on 1 June, Scott, the

Reverend C.F. Cazeau, vicar general of Quebec, and Angus Macdonell of Kingston agreed to Ryerson's amended version of the Bill. In Ryerson's estimation, the amended Bill was not only a final settlement of the separate school question — absolutely irrevocable — but it was also accepted as final by Scott and the two vicars-general. Furthermore, it was Ryerson's understanding that when Cazeau and Macdonell put their stamp to the Bill, they had acted in the name of the Catholic bishops of the Province of Canada. Ryerson's insistence that the Catholic hierarchy had agreed to the finality of this legislation would plague the Catholic camp for many years to come.[121] Within several years, Ryerson's claim to finality, which he argued in print on many occasions, would be his most effective weapon in the battle to stop the agitation to expand and equalize separate school rights in both Canada West and Canada East before Confederation became a constitutional reality.

By June 1862, Scott's heavily amended legislation was ready for third reading. It was the best agreement Catholics could hope for given the adamant and skillful opposition of Ryerson to anything remotely resembling the Elmsley legislation. But that was not the end of the matter. Even though an agreement had been brokered, Scott had to wait until the following year to shepherd the Bill through the legislature.

Third and final reading finally took place on 12 March 1863. The voting was 76 yeas to 31 nays, a resounding majority. Among the members from Canada East, the vote was a clean sweep of 54 yeas. French Canadian Catholics had come to the rescue once again. In Canada West, the vote was 22 yeas to 31 nays. Given that the then premier of the province, John Sandfield Macdonald, a Catholic, was an avowed enemy of separate schools, the negative vote was not surprising.[122] "An Act to restore to Roman Catholics in Upper Canada certain rights in respect to Separate Schools" (26 Victoria, c. 5) received Royal Assent on 5 May 1863.

Lynch congratulated Scott in a letter of 18 March:

> I most heartily thank you for your noble efforts to settle finally our school difficulty.

I do hope that your bill will become law, and exonerate us from the very disagreeable and difficult duty of fighting a religious battle on the political arena of the hustings.

Please accept my dear Sir, the expression of my high esteem and regard.[123]

The day after the Act became law, Lynch telegraphed Scott: "Please accept assurance of perpetual gratitude of Catholics of Canada."[124]

What, then, did the Scott Act of 1863 achieve for separate schools in Canada West, the same legislation that was subsequently safeguarded by Section 93 of the B.N.A. Act of 1867? Scott himself answered that question in an article published in *Canada: An Encyclopedia of the Country:*

1. The right to establish Separate Schools in incorporated villages.

2. Trustees might be chosen from residents of an adjoining section.

3. The establishment of the schools was made independent of the good-will of the Reeve of the Municipality or of the Chairman of the Board of Common School Trustees.

4. School sections, though in adjoining municipalities, might be formed into a union section.

5. Trustees were given the power not before possessed of obtaining a copy of the assessors' or collectors' roll.

6. Catholic children outside the school section had the right to attend the school.

7. Supporters of Separate Schools were relieved from the necessity of giving notice to the Clerk of the Municipality before the 1st of February in every year. Under the Act the notice if given before the 1st of March in any year did not require to be renewed in the subsequent year.

8. Catholics resident within three miles of the school-house might become supporters of the school though living in an adjoining municipality.

9. The Christian Brothers and Nuns of the teaching orders, being qualified by law in Lower Canada, were to be considered as qualified teachers without examination.

10. Catholic clergymen became *ex-officio* visitors of Separate Schools.

11 As disputes had frequently arisen between the Trustees and the Chief Superintendent of Education an appeal from his decision was given to the Governor-in-Council.[125]

In return for these administrative concessions (they were hardly rights or privileges), Catholic separate schools had "to accept inspection by provincial inspectors, centralized control of curriculum and textbooks, and government control of all teacher training."[126] As a result, authority over separate schools still remained in the hands of Ryerson and his education bureaucrats. Catholic schools were doomed to remain the hobbled poorer cousins of the common schools. The issues of the religion of school inspectors and the right to remove offensive textbooks from the curriculum would become major flashpoints for Lynch during the second half of his episcopacy. Wrangling over teaching certificates would continue into the twentieth century.

****

For Catholics in Canada West, the advent of Confederation changed the parameters of separate school politics. The Scott Act was no longer sufficient, if their ultimate goal was to enjoy the same educational rights and privileges as the Protestant minority of Lower Canada. In 1865, when a new Dominion was on the horizon, Catholics in Canada West initiated a province-wide agitation for a radical restructuring of separate school legislation. They had full support of their Protestant allies in Canada East. Catholics pressed their demands in newspaper editorials, petitions and resolutions, in the legislature, at a monster meeting of Kingston's Catholics led by James O'Reilly and at rallies in Toronto, Ottawa, Belleville and Chatham. Never before had the province's Catholics, the clergy and the laity working closely together, been so united and so vocal in their defense of separate schools.

Ryerson cried foul. He accused the Catholic hierarchy of breaking their word on the finality of the 1863 Scott Act, and he lashed out at every Catholic editorialist and agitator in the province.[127] Lynch had to defend himself and his fellow bishops in the press:

> You will confer a favour on me by giving space to the following remarks, which I write with a view of correcting a mistake concerning my acceptation of the Separate School Bill of 1863. When earnestly pressed to accept that Bill as a finality, I studiously avoided the term, and was taken to task by a city journal *[Globe]* for doing so, the expression savoured too much of the perfection of human progress, and seemed to place a bar to the claims and exigencies of the future. I said I was content with the Bill, as were also my brothers in the Episcopacy, as far as I know their sentiments. But, since the BNA provinces wish to take a consolidated form, (and we hope a form that will last for a long time) and as the important question of education is to be placed on a permanent basis, I consider we should be yielding greatly in zeal for the good of posterity, were we to content ourselves with anything less than the Protestant minority of Lower Canada claim. I therefore rejoice that I did not use the word *finality*, which even had I used, could certainly not be interpreted to mean "final" under any and all circumstances, but final, so long as the position of the two provinces remained unchanged.[128]

Of course, Lynch had written the word "finally" in his letter of 18 March 1863 to Scott. (Other Catholic bishops and priests and even D'Arcy McGee had also used the word in one form or another.) But Lynch claimed to have avoided its use where it mattered the most — in the public forum. Hence the *Globe's* criticism towards him. However, the word, even if it had been used by every Catholic in the province at the time of the passage of the Scott Act, was no longer operative. The prospect of Confederation had changed the political playing field. Underlying Lynch's objections, though never stated explicitly by him, is the recognition that the British tradition of making and amending laws hardly allows for the concept of immutability. Laws, even constitutions themselves, change with time and circumstance. Lynch was right to point out that to have ascribed to finality, in the way Ryerson expected him and the rest of the hierarchy to, the bishops would have bound all future generations of his fellow Catholics to a law passed in 1863.

However, it was Ryerson, the chief superintendent of education, who believed that the Scott Act was frozen for all time. Since his influence over politicians during the twilight of the legislature of the United Canadas was far more pervasive and masterly than any strength the Catholics of Canada West could muster, it was his opinion that was bound to win the day. And it did.

Louis Langevin introduced a school Bill for Lower Canada on 31 July 1866. He was followed by Robert Bell, a Protestant member for Russell, who introduced a school Bill for Upper Canada. The title of Bell's Bill sums up the principal aim of the 1860s Catholic campaign in Canada West, and it mirrors the intentions of the Langevin Bill: "An Act to restore to Roman Catholics in Upper Canada certain rights in respect to separate schools, and to extend to the Roman Catholic minority in Upper Canada, similar and equal privileges with those granted by the legislature to the Protestant minority in Lower Canada."[129] Bell's legislation would have established a completely Catholic separate school system, according to John Moir, with its own Catholic Deputy Superintendent of Education, normal school and Council of Public Instruction. Separate schools would be entitled to a proportional share of corporation taxes, and they would be eligible for legislative grants for all levels of education (high school and college). Municipalities would collect separate school taxes, and the property of non-resident Catholics in any school section could be assessed to support separate schools.[130]

No wonder Ryerson called the Bill outrageous. He argued that since the new constitution gave the provinces exclusive jurisdiction over education, any changes to the school law should be left to the discretion of the individual provinces. On 7 August, the government dropped both Bills when it became apparent that the Catholic legislators from Canada East would not support the Langevin Bill if the Protestant legislators from Canada West would not support the Bell Bill. A golden opportunity to end Catholic grievances over education was passed over in the name of political expediency. Egerton Ryerson and his Protestant allies won the day. It would take Ontario's Catholics nearly 120 years to secure what could have been theirs in the summer of 1866. In the meantime, they continued the separate school struggle within the confines of the 1863 Scott Act as guaranteed to them in Section 93 of the BNA Act. (For the full text of Section 93, see pages 484-485.)

****

The constitutional arrangement of 1867 severely restricted the area in which Lynch and the Catholic camp could improve the fortunes of separate schools in Ontario. As bishop (and after 1870 archbishop of Toronto), Lynch became the de facto chief defender of the province's separate schools. He took his role seriously and used his powers of persuasion wisely and effectively. As a diplomat and negotiator, he knew the limits of his own political influence and followed to the letter his own conservative instincts.

That Lynch was able to accomplish anything of lasting significance was due mainly to his support of Sir Oliver Mowat's provincial Liberals. It was an adroit political move. Mowat was in office from 1872 to 1896. The door to the premier's office was always open, and Lynch was often seen going through it. Their relationship was so close, their political enemies dubbed it "The Lynch-Mowat Concordat."[131] The Liberals even tried to corral Ryerson (although not very successfully). On the latter's retirement in 1876, they set up a department of education with Adam Crooks as the first minister of education.

Archbishop Lynch's two most important contributions to the welfare of the province's separate schools were the 1879 "Crooks amendments" and the 1882 appointment of the first Catholic school inspector for separate schools. The "Crooks amendments" were five in number and can be found in "An Act Respecting Public, Separate and High Schools" (*Statutes of Ontario*, 42 Victoria, c. 34). C.B. Sissons, an historian unsympathetic to separate schools, described them this way:

> (1) Permission was granted for setting up Roman Catholic Model Schools for the training of third-class teachers, and for the appointment from each such school of a representative on the County Board of Examiners.
>
> (2) The law was clarified in the matter of accepting Quebec certificates in Ontario . . .
>
> (3) Permission to vote at separate school elections was granted to any Roman Catholic who might live outside the municipality in which the separate school was situated, but within three miles of the school in a direct line.
>
> (4) Permission was granted to a Roman Catholic owner of unoccupied land in any municipality to have the land assessed for the support of separate schools, without regard to his place of residence.
>
> (5) The assessor of a municipality was permitted to assess a person as a separate school supporter merely if he knew personally that the ratepayer was a Roman Catholic.[132]

Additional concessions of a comparatively more minor nature were included in legislation passed in 1886, "An Act respecting Separate Schools" (*Statutes of Ontario*, 49 Victoria, c. 46). The government's amendments allowed tenants to direct their portion of the landlord's taxes to separate schools, made it possible for corporations to pay separate school taxes according to the property of their Catholic shareholders and allowed the use of municipal tax-gathering machinery to collect taxes on behalf of separate school supporters. However seemingly innocuous these changes to the legislation were, as least from the point of view of the Liberal government, they nevertheless became the ammunition for the last great no-popery campaign in the province of Ontario.[133]

More significant was the 1882 government regulation that appointed a Catholic as inspector of Catholic separate schools. This simple administrative change brought an end to decades of unproductive confrontations between Protestant inspectors and Catholic clergy and teachers and ushered in an era of necessary self-criticism. Since Catholic ratepayers were generally less well off than their Protestant counterparts and had no access to public money other than their own property taxes and the legislative grant, Catholic schoolhouses were often substandard and the quality of teaching left much to be desired. The early inspection reports of the legendary James F. White, the first Catholic school inspector, and Cornelius Donovan, who worked with White beginning in 1884, forced Catholics to improve the schools they already had and to seek out better qualified teachers. The careers of both White and Donovan will be examined in Chapter Two.

Less beneficial to the well-being of the province's separate schools, and certainly injurious to Lynch's public reputation, was his participation in the vetting of school textbooks. The Mowat government let Lynch know that his objections would be taken seriously, and Lynch dutifully let Mowat and his ministers know where he stood on works he found anti-Catholic and thus unsuitable for Catholic children. These included sections from *Collier's British History*, Sir Walter Scott's *Marmion* and Coleridge's "Christabel." Even more questionable was the government's invitation to Lynch to help select Scripture readings for common school students. (Lynch was asked because the majority of Catholic students attended common schools.) The final selection of readings was sarcastically dubbed the Ross Bible, after George Ross, the second minister of education, and the compilation was rejected by the Toronto Public School Board. News that the ministry had withdrawn *Marmion* in 1882 at the behest of Lynch led to bitter denunciations of the archbishop and the entire separate school system in the 1883 election. The Ross Bible fiasco of 1884 brought forth more anti-Catholic invective against Lynch. Two years later, *The Mail*, a Conservative newspaper in Toronto, conducted a vicious campaign to abolish separate schools.[134] Lynch's biggest humiliation, though, came at the hands of Egerton Ryerson. When Ryerson drew up plans for a publicly-funded high school system, in 1871, he ignored Lynch and made no provisions in the legislation for Catholic schools. Lynch's overly cautious attitude towards universal secondary education — that it might not be a good thing for the urban working class or the children of farmers — played right into Ryerson's hands and would cost Catholics dearly for the next century.

****

Archbishop John Joseph Lynch was deeply devoted to Catholic separate schools and never let the pummeling he took at the hands of the press lessen his devotion to Catholic school children. Lynch addressed trustees, gave advice on the management of schools and distributed prizes at graduation exercises; he paid $100 bonuses to Catholic teachers with a first-class certificate; he took an avid interest in the accounts and attendance records of different school boards and complained about Ryerson's dominance on the Council of Public Instruction; he recommended many teachers; and in 1877 he published a catechism, *Questions and Answers*. His episcopacy witnessed a dramatic increase in the number of students and schools throughout the province, from 14,708 students in 115 schools, in 1860, to 34,571 children in 259 schools, in 1890.[135] Although Lynch cannot be given full credit for the continuing success of separate schools — that is due to the whole Catholic community — one must acknowledge him for providing aggressive yet intelligent leadership during a time when Catholic separate school supporters laboured tirelessly under the yoke of restrictive legislation, anti-Catholic bigotry in the press and a poverty from which it would take another generation to escape. Lynch's undoing was his inability to accept the rise of the laity in separate school politics.

Archbishop John Joseph Lynch died in Toronto on 12 May 1888 and was buried outside St. Michael's cathedral, next to the wall near the north transept.

[1] Archives of Ontario [hereafter AO], MU 1770, *Macdonell Letters*, 4: 558. Macdonell to François Baby, 10 March 1839.

[2] J. George Hodgins, *Documentary History of Education in Upper Canada*, 28 vols. (Toronto: Warwick Bros. & Rutter, 1894-1910), 1: 62. To the House of Assembly in 1808, Gore said that public schools were "institutions which, I trust, will be the means not only of communicating useful knowledge to the youth of this Province, but also of instilling into their minds principles of Religion and Loyalty."

[3] Ibid., 1: 169. To the House of Assembly in 1820, Maitland said: "Provision for religious instruction and the diffusion of Education are becoming daily more important in this Province."

[4] Ibid., 2: 303.

[5] "McDonell, Alexander," *Dictionary of Canadian Biography* [hereafter *DCB*], 14 vols. (Toronto: University of Toronto Press, 1967-1998), 8: 544-51. J.E. Rea notes that the bishop only began signing his sign "Macdonell" after 1838. However, since the form "Macdonell" is used in most of the historical literature, including Rae's one work on the bishop, I will use "Macdonell." For additional biographical details see the two following works: Kathleen M. Toomey, *Alexander Macdonell: The Scottish Years 1762-1804* (Toronto: The Canadian Catholic Historical Association, 1985); J.E. Rea, Bishop Alexander *Macdonell and the Politics of Upper Canada* (Toronto: Ontario Historical Society, 1974).

[6] Hugh Joseph Somers, *The Life and Times of the Hon. and Rt. Rev. Alexander Macdonell, D.D. First Bishop of Upper Canada 1762-1840* (Washington, D.C.: The Catholic University of America, 1931), 170. Letter of Macdonell to Sir George Drummond, 1 March 1815.

[7] Ibid., 206-8. Macdonell to Col. William Rowan, 16 February 1833.

[8] Hodgins, *Documentary History of Education in Upper Canada*, 2: 193. The College of Regiopolis was incorporated in 1837 (7 William IV, c. 56). In a petition, submitted to the House of Assembly on 12 March 1839, Bishop Macdonell asked that Regiopolis College receive the same financial aid (£4,100) as was given to Upper Canada Academy and the Methodist Seminary at Coburg. See Hodgins, *Documentary History of Education in Upper Canada*, 3: 146.

[9] Somers, *The Life and Times*, 210-11. Macdonell to Colborne, 1832.

[10] Ibid., 173-74. Macdonell to Lord Bathurst, 10 April 1824.

[11] Hodgins, *Documentary History of Education in Upper Canada*, 5: 307-8.

[12] AO, MU 1770, *Macdonell Letters*, 3: 344. Major George Hillier to Macdonell, 19 November 1827

[13] Hodgins, *Documentary History of Education in Upper Canada*, 2: 285-86. See also AO, MU 1771, *Macdonell Letters*, 9: 1290. "Statement of the sums of money received, out of the revenue of the Province of Upper Canada by Rectors and other religious teachers of the Catholic Church in the year 1832."

[14] E.J. Lajeunesse, *Outline History of Assumption Parish, 1767-1967* ([Windsor: [Assumption Church]:1967), 32-33. See also Archives of the Roman Catholic Archdiocese of Toronto [hereafter ARCAT], M AC21.04. Sr. Raizenne to Sir John Colborne, 17 December 1828.

[15] Hodgins, *Documentary History of Education in Upper Canada*, 2: 285.

[16] Ibid., 5: 307-8. Macdonell to Bathurst, 10 January 1817; Somers, *Life and Times*, 173-74. Macdonell to Bathurst, 10 April 1824; Ibid., 180-83. Macdonell to Maitland, 9 March 1826; Ibid., 189-90. Macdonell to Thomas Weld, 6 May 1827; Ibid., 193-94. Macdonell to Thomas Weld, 26 November 1828; Ibid., 208-210. Macdonell to Lord Goderich, 22 March 1833.

[17] Hodgins, *Documentary History of Education in Upper Canada*, 5: 307. Macdonell to Bathurst, 10 January 1817.

[18] AO, MU 1770, *Macdonell Letters*, 2: 236-38. Macdonell to William Morris, 21 April 1827.

[19] Ibid., 1: 21. Macdonell to Rev. Peter Sweeney, 19 June 1820.

[20] Ibid., 1: 26. Macdonell to John McDonald, 3 July 1820.

[21] Ibid.

[22] Ibid.

[23] Ibid., 4: 556-57. Meeting of the Church Wardens of Assumption Parish, Sandwich, 16 July 1827.

[24] Lajeunesse, *Outline History*, 33. Letter of Macdonell, 20 November 1830.

[25] Edward Kelly, *The Story of St. Paul's Parish Toronto* (Toronto: St. Paul's Parish, 1922), 79-82.

[26] Hodgins, *Documentary History of Education in Upper Canada*, 2: 163.

[27] For more on this controversy, see "O'Grady, William John," *DCB*, 7: 661-65.

[28] ARCAT, M AC0601. Letter of Waron, Chief at River Canard, et al. to Bishop Macdonell, 28 June 1828.

[29] Ibid., M AC1602. Petition for the Erection of a Catholic School in Penetanguishene, 18 August 1833.

[30] Kelly, *The Story of St. Paul's Parish Toronto*, 79-82; John R. Teefy, ed., *Jubilee Volume of the Archdiocese of Toronto and Archbishop Walsh* (Toronto: Geo Dixon, 1892), 268-69. For Gallagher and Roberts, see ARCAT, M AB30.01. Reverend William Patrick McDonagh to Macdonell, 25 January 1835; M AB31.12. Letter of Reverend William Patrick McDonagh to Macdonell, 6 August 1838.

[31] ARCAT, M CB1005. "To the Honorable the Commons House of Assembly of the Province of Upper Canada, in Provincial Parliament Assembly." For a typed version of this petition, see AO, MU 1771, 9: 1312-14. This version lists eight other names: James King, Paddy Handy, Patrick Atkinson, Thomas Ryan, Peter McDougall, Cornelius Keller, Charles Donne and Maurice Malone.

[32] Hodgins, *Documentary History of Education in Upper Canada*, 2: 140-41.

[33] AO, MU 1771, 9: 1315-20. Petition, no date, but it must have come right after the first petition because Macdonell replied to this one in a letter dated 10 December 1833. Ibid., 9: 1322-32.

[34] Hodgins, *Documentary History of Education in Upper Canada*, 7: 100.

[35] "Power, Michael," *DCB*, 7: 705-6; Murray W. Nicolson, "Michael Power, First Bishop of Toronto, 1842-1847," Canadian Catholic Historical Association [hereafter CCHA], *Historical Studies*, 54 (1987): 27-38.

[36] These two sections of the 1841 Act are reproduced in full in J. George Hodgins, *The Legislation and History of Separate Schools in Upper Canada* (Toronto: William Briggs, 1897), 23-24. An interpretation of Section IX is presented in Franklin A. Walker, *Catholic Education and Politics in Upper Canada* (Toronto: The English Catholic Education Association of Ontario, 1955; reprint, Toronto: The Federation of Catholic Education Associations of Ontario, 1976; reprint, Toronto: Catholic Education Foundation, 1985), 45.

[37] Hodgins, *Documentary History of Education in Upper Canada*, 4: 20.

[38] Ibid., 4: 33-35.

[39] Ibid., 4: 29.

[40] Hodgins, *Legislation and History of Separate Schools*, 22.

[41] Hodgins, *Documentary History of Education in Upper Canada*, 1: 22.

[42] Protestants used the Authorized (King James) Version of the Bible and Catholics used the Douay Version. The AV version of the Old Testament did not consider as inspired text those books which did not appear in the Hebrew Scriptures and consequently relegated to the Apocrypha eleven books, either in whole or in part, which appear in the Douay Version.

[43] Hodgins, *Legislation and History of Separate Schools*, 19.

[44] E.F. Henderson et al., *Historical Sketch of the Separate Schools of Ontario and Minority Report, 1950* [hereafter *Historical Sketch*] (Toronto: The English Catholic Education Association of Ontario, [1950]), 19.

[45] We know that Bishop Power submitted several remarks on this bill to Dominick Daly, the provincial secretary, but we have no idea what he wrote or if his lobbying had any effect on the final wording. See Walker, *Catholic Education and Politics in Upper Canada*, 47.

[46] As quoted in Walker, *Catholic Education and Politics in Upper Canada*, 48.

[47] Ibid.

[48] ARCAT, LB02.176. Bishop Michael Power to the Reverend S. Saenderl, 28 June 1844. Bishop Power mistakenly numbered these two clauses 50 and 51.

[49] Ibid., LB01.139. Episcopal Mandate, September 1845.

[50] Ibid., LB02.247. Bishop Michael Power to Reverend Michael R. Mills, 8 July 1845.

[51] Walker, *Catholic Education and Politics in Upper Canada*, 55.

[52] ARCAT., P AA10.06. Bishop Michael Power to Reverend Angus Macdonell, 11 December 1844. This Macdonell was a nephew of Bishop Macdonell. For more details about this quarrel, see Chapter Two.

[53] Walker, *Catholic Education and Politics in Upper Canada*, 53. See also *Walking the Less Travelled Road: A History of the Religious Communities within the Archdiocese of Toronto 1841-1991* (Toronto: Archdiocese of Toronto, 1993), 78-79.

[54] ARCAT, PRC24.10. Bishop Power to Reverend T. Roothaan, superior general of the Jesuits, 12 November 1842.

[55] Of course, Bishop Power's invitation to the Jesuits cannot be construed as support for separate schools. I have included the invitation to show that the bishop was busy working on more than one front on behalf of Catholic education. The situation of the

Loretto Sisters is a little more complex. Although it is true that they too charged a fee for school services, it is also true that they would play an integral role in staffing separate schools in the archdiocese of Toronto. Bishop Power could not have predicted that outcome, but his invitation to them made such an outcome possible.

[56] ARCAT, PAA10.13. Bishop Power to Msgr. Reisache, Archbishop of Munich, 8 May 1847. *Walking the Less Travelled Road*, 21.

[57] Hodgins, *Documentary History of Education in Upper Canada*, 6: 232.

[58] Ibid., 6: 231.

[59] Hodgins, *Legislation and History of Separate Schools*, 30. Ryerson expressed this version of events in an open letter to *The Leader*, 27 February 1857.

[60] See also Mark McGowan, "What did Michael Power Really Want? Questions Regarding the Origins of Catholic Separate Schools in Canada West, CCHA, *Historical Studies*, 68 (2002): 85-104.

[61] *Copies of Correspondence Between the Roman Catholic Bishop of Toronto and the Chief Superintendent of Schools on the Subject of Separate Common Schools in Upper Canada with an Appendix, Containing Documents Referred to in the Correspondence* [hereafter *Copies of Correspondence* (1852)] (Quebec: John Lovell, 1852), 10.

[62] *Copies of Correspondence Between the Chief Superintendent of Schools for Upper Canada and Other Persons on the Subject of Separate Schools* [hereafter *Copies of Correspondence* (1855)] (Toronto: Lovell & Gibson, 1855), 24.

[63] At this point in the narrative, we must clarify the phrase "separate schools." During Ryerson's tenure as chief superintendent of schools, there were three classes of separate schools: one based on different languages, such as French, German, Scots Gaelic and Algonkian; one based on racial groups, such as blacks and Natives; and one based on religious denominations, such as Protestant and Catholic. Consequently, "separate" did not automatically denote "denominational." However, the two words almost became synonymous when Ryerson engineered separate school legislation exclusively for Catholic separate schools and their supporters. See: J. Donald Wilson, "The Ryerson Years in Canada West," in *Canadian Education: A History*, ed. J. Donald Wilson, Robert M. Stamp and Louis-Philippe Audet (Scarborough: Prentice-Hall, 1970), 231-32.

[64] "Charbonnel, Armand-François-Marie de," *DCB*, 12: 182-85.

[65] Ibid., 183.

[66] John S. Moir, *Church and State in Canada West* (Toronto: University of Toronto

Press, 1959), 148.

[67] "Charbonnel," *DCB*, 12: 184.

[68] "Ryerson, Egerton," *DCB*, 11: 783-95.

[69] *Historical Sketch*, 25.

[70] Common schools were elementary schools; grammar schools became high schools; the Normal School was Teachers College; and models schools were for teachers-in-training.

[71] Hodgins, *Documentary History of Education in Upper Canada*, 6: 142. See also "Ryerson," *DCB*, 11: 789 for a concise rendering of Ryerson's philosophy of education for the province's schools.

[72] *Dr. Ryerson's Letters in Reply to the Attacks of Foreign Ecclesiastics Against the Schools and Municipalities of Upper Canada* (Toronto: Lovell and Gibson, 1857), 70.

[73] Hodgins, *Documentary History of Education in Upper Canada*, 6: 158.

[74] J. George Hodgins, *Historical and Other Papers and Documents Illustrative of the Educational System of Ontario, 1856-1872,* 6 vols. [hereafter, *Historical and Other Papers and Documents*] (Toronto: L.K. Cameron, 1911), 2: 125.

[75] Ibid., 2: 167.

[76] Walker, *Catholic Education and Politics in Upper Canada*, 74, fn. 39.

[77] Hodgins, *Documentary History of Education in Upper Canada*, 10: 89.

[78] Egerton Ryerson, *Annual Report of the Normal, Model, Grammar and Common Schools, in Upper Canada, for the Year 1855* (Toronto: John Lovell, 1856), 11.

[79] Hodgins, *Documentary History of Education in Upper Canada*, 13: 214.

[80] Egerton Ryerson, *Annual Report of the Normal, Model, Grammar, and Common Schools, in Upper Canada, for the Year 1858* (Toronto: John Lovell, 1859), viii-ix.

[81] Hodgins, *Historical and Other Papers and Documents*, 2: 109-10.

[82] Moir, *Church and State in Canada West*, 155.

[83] We have already dealt with this in the section on Bishop Power. While it is true, as Sissons claims, that the phrase was initially used by Catholics, it is just as true to say

that Ryerson turned it to his own advantage and repeated it *ad infinitum, ad nauseum*, as if the Catholic position on separate schools was a static thing, never to change and always to be limited to unchanging rural communities. Of additional interest to the modern reader is the power this phrase assumed in the hands of Ryerson's many apologists. See C.B. Sissons, *Church & State in Canadian Education: An Historical Study* (Toronto: Ryerson Press, 1959), 25-26; and Moir, *Church and State in Canada West*, 151. For a rebuttal of Ryerson's claim, see *Historical Sketch*, 43-44.

[84] Hodgins, *Historical and Other Papers and Documents*, 2: 125.

[85] Hodgins, *Legislation and History of Separate Schools*, 120, 144; ibid., *Documentary History of Education in Upper Canada*, 13: 10; ibid., *Historical and Other Papers and Documents*, 2: 125.

[86] ARCAT, LB03.018. Charbonnel to the City Superintendent of Common Schools, 14 October 1850.

[87] Hodgins, *Documentary History of Education in Upper Canada*, 10: 90-91.

[88] Egerton Ryerson, *Annual Report of the Normal, Model and Common Schools, in Upper Canada for the Year 1850* (Toronto: John Lovell, 1851), 14-15. This information can also be located in Hodgins, *Legislation and History of Separate Schools*, 57.

[89] *Copies of Correspondence* (1852), 62-63.

[90] Wilson, "The Ryerson Years in Canada West," 237. In 1896, there were ten Protestant separate schools; in 1938, four; and in 1967 just two. In stark contrast, there were 1,380 Catholic separate schools in 1967.

[91] *Copies of Correspondence* (1852), 31.

[92] Ibid., 7.

[93] Ibid., 39. For the Belleville controversy, see Ibid., 34-41. There were additional Catholic protests in 1852 from Georgetown and Wilmot. See Ibid., 42-55.

[94] Ibid., 8.

[95] Ibid., 10-11.

[96] Ibid., 11-17.

[97] Ibid., 27.

[98] Moir, *Church and State in Canada West*, 155.

[99] ARCAT, AA04.12. Pastoral Letter of 18 July 1853.

[100] Ibid., LB02.358. Bishop Charbonnel to Inspector General Francis Hincks, 2 August 1853; and LB02.362. Bishop Charbonnel to Inspector General Francis Hincks, 7 October 1853. There was also a third letter: LB02.365. Bishop Charbonnel to Inspector General Hincks, 19 October 1853.

[101] Hodgins, *Documentary History of Education in Upper Canada*, 11: 109.

[102] Ibid.

[103] *Copies of Correspondence* (1855), 55-77.

[104] ARCAT, LB03.078. Bishop Charbonnel to Fathers Lynch and Birne of Renfrew, 17 November 1855.

[105] Ibid. C AA04.25. Lenten Pastoral, March 1856.

[106] Hodgins, *Documentary History of Education in Upper Canada*, 13: 61.

[107] *Dr. Ryerson's Letters in Reply to the Attacks of Foreign Ecclesiastics*, 69.

[108] Moir, *Church and State in Canada West*, 162-63. W.L. Felton was an Anglican.

[109] Ibid., 165. See also Walker, *Catholic Education and Politics in Upper Canada*, 208-13.

[110] *Globe*, 21 February 1857, 2.

[111] Egerton Ryerson, *Annual Report of the Normal, Model, Grammar, and Common Schools in Upper Canada for the Year 1860* (Quebec: Hunter, Rose & Co., 1861), Table F.

[112] "In a free country no constitutional system ought ever to be put forward as a finality." *Globe*, 28 November 1864, 2.

[113] "Lynch, John Joseph," *DCB*, 11: 535-38; Gerald J. Stortz, "Archbishop John Joseph Lynch of Toronto: Twenty-eight Years of Commitment," CCHA, *Study Sessions*, 49 (1982): 5-23.

[114] "Scott, Sir Richard William," *DCB*, 14: 913-16; W.L. Scott, "Sir Richard Scott, K.C. (1825-1913)," CCHA, *Report* (1936-1937): 46-71.

[115] Hodgins, *Documentary History of Education in Upper Canada*, 15: 24-26.

[116] Scott, "Sir Richard Scott," 65, Angus Macdonnell to Richard Scott, 24 April 1861.

[117] Hodgins, *Documentary History of Education in Upper Canada*, 17: 192-94.

[118] Walker, *Catholic Education and Politics in Upper Canada*, 264, fn. 61.

[119] Hodgins, *Documentary History of Education in Upper Canada*, 17: 194-95.

[120] For a copy of Elmsley's proposed legislation, see Hodgins, *Documentary History of Education in Upper Canada*, 13: 164-76. For a copy of Scott's third separate school Bill, April 1862, see Ibid., 17: 198-220; see also Moir, *Church and State in Canada West*, 168-75.

[121] Ryerson would pound away on this point, *ad infinitum, ad nauseum*. See Hodgins, *Legislation and History of Separate Schools*, 152-83.

[122] John Sandfield Macdonald, who would become the first premier of Ontario, was a nominal Catholic who "opposed the religious segregation of children but accepted the bill to achieve educational tranquillity." See "Macdonald, John Sandfield," *DCB*, 10: 462-69.

[123] Scott, "Sir Richard Scott," 68, letter of John Joseph Lynch to Richard Scott, 18 March 1863.

[124] Ibid., 69, telegram from Bishop Lynch to R.W. Scott, 6 May 1863.

[125] Richard W. Scott, "Establishment and Growth of the Separate School System in Ontario," in *Canada: An Encyclopedia of the Country*, 5 vols. (Toronto: Linscott Publishing, 1898-1900), 3: 185.

[126] Wilson, "The Ryerson Years in Canada West," 237.

[127] Hodgins, *Documentary History of Education in Upper Canada*, 18: 304-16 and also additional material in volume 19, especially his letter to *The Leader* (Toronto) of 18 March 1865.

[128] *Globe*, 6 March 1865, 2.

[129] Hodgins, *Documentary History of Education in Upper Canada*, 19: 211-12.

[130] Moir, *Church and State in Canada West*, 178.

[131] Gerald J. Stortz, "John Joseph Lynch, Archbishop of Toronto: A Biographical Study of Religious, Political and Social Commitment" (Ph.D. diss., University of Guelph, 1980), Chapter V, "The Lynch-Mowat Concordat."

[132] Sissons, *Church & State in Canadian Education*, 61.

[133] See Franklin A. Walker, *Catholic Education and Politics in Ontario*, vol. 2 (Toronto: Federation of Catholic Education Associations, 1976), Chapter 5. The amendments are explained and defended in C.R.W. Biggar, *Sir Oliver Mowat: A Biographical Sketch*, 2 vols. (Toronto: Warwick Bro's & Rutter, 1905), 1: 465-73.

[134] Walker, *Catholic Education and Politics in Ontario*, 2: Chapter 4.

[135] Stortz, "John Joseph Lynch, Archbishop of Toronto," 8.

THE CATHOLIC LAITY AND SEPARATE SCHOOLS
IN NINETEENTH CENTURY ONTARIO

Introduction

> *"Education without religion we believe to be a curse;*
> *and therefore not worth paying for."*
>
> — *True Witness and Catholic Chronicle*, 9 March 1855, 4.

> *"We are frequently told by the opponents of Separate Schools*
> *that the Hierarchy and priesthood of the Catholic Church*
> *desire to enslave the minds of their people to keep them in*
> *darkness and ignorance, and hence their objection to allow*
> *the effulgent light of the Common School system to shine upon*
> *their benighted flocks."*
>
> — Editorial, *Canadian Freeman*, 9 April 1863, 2.

*T*he above two quotations remind us of two constants that defined the often overlooked role of the Catholic laity in the separate school struggle in nineteenth century Ontario. The first constant was the genuine desire of many Catholic parents to have their children educated in Catholic-supported schools in which the Catholic faith would be taught, untainted by Protestantism, along with the usual array of secular subjects. For these Catholic parents, education without religion — and by religion they meant the Catholic religion — was indeed a curse not worth the cost of the common schools. If there had not been Catholics in sufficient numbers across the province who fervently and openly believed this to be true, and acted upon it at election time, separate schools would certainly have died out according to the wishes of Egerton Ryerson. The mere survival of

Catholic separate schools, during decades of legal wrangling and intense anti-Catholic feeling, is proof that there existed a large pool of Catholic ratepayers, led by their elected trustees, willing to make numerous sacrifices to ensure the system's long-term viability. By the close of the 1880s, their efforts began to bear considerable fruit. Catholic schools and school boards became a *system*, gradually expanding and improving to the point where friend and foe alike agreed that Catholic schools were destined to survive and in time would likely continue to grow ever larger and stronger.

Of course, Catholic opinion on the subject of religion and education was hardly uniform in the nineteenth century. Some overly zealous Protestants, such as the leadership of the Loyal Orange Lodge, may have believed that the Catholic laity jumped at every command from bishop and priest, but their view of the Catholic world was skewered by ignorance and bigotry. In the midst of considerable separate school militancy, described in some detail in the opening chapter, there were plenty of Catholic parents who were simply ambivalent towards Catholic education and consequently made the work of securing Catholic educational rights all that more difficult. Reasons for this ambivalence range from the independent thinking typical of country folk to a latent anti-clericalism to an underdeveloped relationship between priest and people at the parish level. But this is only historical speculation. People were ambivalent for reasons best known only to themselves.

But an even thornier complication was that the overwhelming majority of people in Ontario lived in the countryside, mostly on small family farms and in hamlets, villages and towns. This settlement pattern prevailed well into the twentieth century. Rural society was defined by scattered populations. Being a minority, rural Catholics were often more isolated than was the case with their Protestant neighbours. For these Catholics, then, any desire to have a separate school for their children was usually impractical and thus impossible. This was one of the major reasons why so many Catholic children attended the common schools for so many years. Egerton Ryerson was fond of telling the public that despite the existence of publicly funded Catholic separate schools for several decades, up to three-fourths of Catholic children on the school rolls continued to attend common schools. However, he never bothered to acknowledge the obvious reason for that lopsided figure — Ontario as a rural society — or the fact that he did everything in his power to prevent Catholics from establishing their own schools.

Father John Walsh, parish priest at St. Mary's in Toronto and the future bishop of London and archbishop of Toronto, offered his own explanation in 1866, using the most recent census as his evidence.[1] He wrote in the *Canadian Freeman* that Catholics who lived in cities, towns and even incorporated villages generally availed themselves of separate schools, their number and proximity to each other allowing them to do so, but that Catholics who lived outside any type of urban area, in smaller groupings, or were distant from each other had an almost impossible task organizing their own schools and could hardly be faulted for attending the common schools. Their best hope, then, was to have Catholic teachers.

James G. Moylan also took Ryerson to task for avoiding the obvious, four years before Father Walsh did, but he argued that the Ryerson-engineered inequities in the law concerning the union of school sections were designed to keep Catholic parents in rural areas from setting up Catholic schools (see below).

Be that as it may, the separate school system flourished, beginning with the 1863 Scott Act and most definitely after the introduction of Catholic school inspectors in 1882, despite formidable legal, financial and practical hurdles. This happened because there were enough Catholic laity, with school trustees in the forefront, aggressively committed to their existence. No lay support meant no separate schools.

This brings us to our second constant — the infamous and oft-repeated canard that it was only the bishops and priests who wanted separate schools, as yet another means to control their flocks, and that the Catholic rank and file would have gladly accepted Ryerson's common schools, if they had not been bullied by their religious leaders into endless agitation. Nothing could have been further from the truth. As we have already seen in Chapter One, the bishops were forefront in every separate school battle, but they were hardly generals without an army. That army was the Catholic laity. It was for them and *with them* that all the great battles were waged. Also important is the fact that from the laity there sprang many defenders of separate schools whose work proved crucial to their survival. Where the clergy could not tread, these lay defenders did so gladly, taking the fight to the public square of political opinion, always fearlessly and on occasion ferociously.

This chapter is devoted to an examination of the pioneering work of a selection of these lay leaders. They are John Elmsley, convert to Catholicism and philanthropist; Charles Donlevy and James G. Moylan, two newspaper proprietors (other proprietors will be mentioned in a postscript); local trustees; Catholic Institute members; James F. White, the first government-appointed Catholic school inspector; and some of the notable personalities who were involved in the bitter fight for lay control of the Toronto Separate School Board and the introduction of the secret ballot in trustee elections. Catholic culture in Ontario was very robust during the last half of the nineteenth century and never more so when it came to the topic of Catholic separate schools.

John Elmsley, 1801-1863

John Elmsley was the greatest benefactor of the Catholic Church in pre-Confederation Toronto. From his conversion in 1833 to his death thirty years later, he participated in nearly every good work, including the advancement of Catholic education, undertaken and promoted by his fellow Catholics. Bishop Alexander Macdonell considered his embrace of the Catholic faith a miracle. It would be no exaggeration to claim that the Diocese of Toronto under Bishop Power and Bishop Charbonnel would have been a much poorer and backward institution, one whose growth would have been held in check for a decade or two, had it not been for Elmsley's incredible and timely generosity.

Born in the provincial capital of York, on 19 May 1801, John Elmsley was the son of Chief Justice John Elmsley and Mary Hallowell, a Loyalist from Boston of Protestant convictions just as fervent as her husband's.[2] After the premature death of his father in

1805, his mother moved the family to England where he was educated and enlisted in the Royal Navy on the suggestion of one of his maternal uncles who was an admiral. He served in the navy from 1815 to 1824, rising from 1st class volunteer to lieutenant, seeing service on the Irish, North American and Nore stations. Elmsley retired on half pay and returned to his native York in 1825 to manage his late father's considerable landholdings.

An Anglican and a Tory, Elmsley lived and prospered as a member of the so-called Family Compact. In 1831, he married Charlotte Sherwood, the Catholic daughter of Levius Peters Sherwood, who was a judge on the Court of King's Bench in Upper Canada. They were actually married twice, first in St. Paul's and then in St. James, a local custom in the case of mixed marriages that was frowned upon but tolerated by the Catholic authorities.

Elmsley was not an idle man. He supplemented the income from his inheritance by investing his time and money in a wide range of commercial activities and business arrangements. He was a shareholder and director of the Bank of Upper Canada; the founder, president and secretary of the Home District Agricultural Society; an incorporator of the British American Assurance Company; a major shareholder in the Welland Canal Company; a promoter and director of the City of Toronto and Lake Huron Rail Road Company; the co-founder of the Farmers' Bank; and a director of the Home District Mutual Fire Company.

Always a sailor at heart, Elmsley sided with the government during the Rebellion of 1837-38. Under Captain Andrew Drew, he partook in the *Caroline* incident on the Niagara River and was later in command of the steamer *Thames* and the *Chief Justice Robinson*. In the 1840s, Elmsley was captain of the steamer *Cobourg*, on the Kingston-Toronto route, and captain and part-owner of the *Niagara* (later the *Sovereign*), also on the Kingston-Toronto route, as part of the Royal Mail line. (For the rest of his life he was referred to as Captain Elmsley.)

Then there was the world of provincial politics. Sir John Colborne, the lieutenant governor, appointed Elmsley to the Executive Council, in September 1830, and then to the Legislative

Council, in January 1831. Such appointments were Elmsley's due because of his social standing and Tory leanings. However, his time on the Executive Council ended in a nasty dispute with Colborne over the practice of speculating in United Empire Loyalist location rights to land in the province. Elmsley defended the practice so vigorously that he was obliged to resign his seat in 1833. Re-appointed three years later by Sir Francis Bond Head, Elmsley was once more forced to leave, this time in 1839, because he had refused to obey a lawful order to move his men to Lake Erie to support Captain Drew in the final stages of the Rebellion. Elmsley would not budge until he had received a higher rank than Drew's. He could be a stubborn and proud man. Once he had made up his mind on a course of action, he never backed down, regardless of the criticism leveled against him, choosing instead to ignore the opinions of others. By the end of the 1830s, he began to look more like a Reformer than a Tory.

Notwithstanding his disastrous entanglements with various lieutenant governors, Elmsley continued to sit on the Legislative Council until the Union of the Canadas in 1841. His support of the Union earned him the scorn of Charles Donlevy of the *Toronto Mirror*.[3] The Irish Catholic Donlevy wondered what kind of Catholic Elmsley was to have seconded a motion by the Anglican Bishop John Strachan, which, according to the *Mirror*, would have abolished the French language and disfranchised French Canadians, most of whom were Elmsley's fellow Catholics. The motion died, but the sting of the *Mirror's* attack did not.

This brings us to the pivotal matter of John Elmsley's conversion to the Catholic faith, his place in the history of the Church in Toronto and naturally his work on behalf of Catholic education. Elmsley entered the Church in 1833, the same year he left the Executive Council for the first time. He was led to abandon the Anglican fold by the Bishop of Strasbourg's spirited defense of the Real Presence of Our Lord in the Eucharist. Elmsley was so convinced by the bishop's work that he paid for the printing and distribution of 5,000 copies of a translation of the bishop's commentary on the sixth chapter of St. John's Gospel. His conversion was the talk of the town and provoked John Strachan, the Anglican rector of St. James at the time, to preach from the pulpit against the errors of "Romanism" and to write two pamphlets denouncing the doctrine of transubstantiation and warning his congregation of the dangers of popery. Not to be outdone, Father W.P. MacDonald, vicar general in Kingston, replied for the Catholic side with his own publication, defending the doctrine and Elmsley's conversion.

As the pamphlet war raged around him, Elmsley quietly joined St. Paul's parish. If he was hoping for an oasis of calm, however, it was not forthcoming. The only Catholic parish in the city, St. Paul's was still recovering from a self-destructive schism between its former priest, Father William J. O'Grady, and his Reform allies, and Bishop Macdonell and his Tory supporters in the parish. Relations between Elmsley, the wealthiest member of the parish, and the new priest, Father William Patrick McDonagh, deteriorated within several years and almost precipitated another faction fight among Toronto's small but volatile Catholic community.

Since he was St. Paul's richest and best connected Catholic, a plum of a convert and a born leader, Elmsley quickly became the parish treasurer and one of its three wardens (a lay trustee responsible for parish temporalities). As well, Bishop Macdonell made him his lay vicar general, an unusual appointment for the day. Unhappily for everyone, Elmsley's strong belief in voluntarism — that Catholics should support their clergy and pay for their churches with their own money and not the government's — ran into a wall of silent resistance from rich and poor alike. Aside from pew rents, there were few means to raise money to pay down the debt, and no one could be forced to pay rent for a pew. As a result, the pews at Sunday Mass were mostly empty and the aisles were jammed with people.

Elmsley's solution to Catholic miserliness was to initiate a lay takeover of the parish administration, which restricted the number of voters in the elections for warden to those who could annually contribute £ 5 to the building fund and 10 shillings in taxes, an entrance admission of 2 pence for Sunday Mass, precise rules for the celebration of the liturgy, strict controls on the parish priest and a demand that the bishop close the church for several months as a means to force the people to pay up. This was an ironic way to promote voluntarism![4]

Although Elmsley had the blessing of the Bishop Macdonell and his co-adjutor, Bishop Rémi Gaulin, and other leading members of the parish, such as his brother-in-law, Dr. John King, his elitist meddling in parish affairs offended Father McDonagh and his mainly Irish congregation. Things came to a head when Elmsley failed to have McDonagh removed from the parish. Elmsley resigned as church warden in 1836 and turned his attention towards his many business pursuits. In one final confrontation with McDonagh, in 1840, Elmsley refused to sanction the parish's request to build a school on the lot provided for it.[5] When one considers Elmsley's later support for separate schools, this too was highly ironic.

The creation of the Diocese of Toronto, in December 1841, was a Godsend in John Elmsley's life. The new diocese freed him from the hothouse of petty parish politics and gave him a much wider outlet for his energies and ambitions on behalf of the local church. It provided the right backdrop for him to become a progressive philanthropist. He served under three bishops — Power, Charbonnel and Lynch — and kept the diocese afloat between the death of Bishop Power in 1847 and the arrival of Bishop Charbonnel in 1850. Another fortuitous event was the recognition of separate schools in the 1841 Common Schools Act. His days as an appointed member of the government having ended with the Act of Union, Elmsley channelled his political acumen into separate school politics, in the process becoming an ardent defender of Catholic schools and a skilled negotiator on their behalf.

But Elmsley's Catholic career could not have unfolded as it did if he had remained aloof from the great unwashed of his adoptive Church. They were the Irish. He had alienated them at St. Paul's but won their admiration during the summer of 1847 when thousands fleeing the Famine in Ireland crowded the wharves and streets of Toronto looking for food and shelter. Their tragic appearance set the stage for what historian Murray Nicolson called Elmsley's second conversion. Of his heroic work among the Famine Irish, the *Canadian Freeman* wrote:

He flung himself with ardor into all works of charity. Amidst the ridicule of his former friends, some of whom abandoned him, he went about doing good. His care of the poor, of the widows and orphans of those who were swept away by fever, was incessant. With the tenderness and devotion of a Sister of Charity, he visited the fever sheds, regardless of contagion. He nursed and tended the sick; he consoled the dying; he buried the victims of the terrible scourge; he washed with his own hands the poor bereaved orphans whose condition would have excited disgust in the minds of those who lay claim to no ordinary share of humanity and benevolence.[6]

Elmsley made many contributions to the material welfare of the Diocese of Toronto. They deserve to be listed and should be treated as the context in which he worked so diligently on behalf of Toronto's beleaguered separate schools. Elmsley organized the Christian Doctrine Society, a catechism class for adults, in 1840; he organized volunteers to dig the foundations of St. Michael's Cathedral; he set up and managed the Cathedral Loan Fund; along with Samuel Goodenough Lynn, a prosperous merchant and another convert from Anglicanism, he guaranteed the cathedral's massive $57,600 mortgage, which allowed the consecration of St. Michael's to proceed in September 1848; he donated the land from his Clover Hill estate for the Basilian-run St. Michael's College and St. Basil's Church and St Joseph's convent and academy (he tried but failed to convince the Jesuits to build a college on his property[7]); with the advice and help of his wife, he established the Catholic Ladies of Toronto, in 1849, as a conduit for women's social work in the city; he was an early and faithful member of the St. Vincent de Paul Society; he had a hand in founding the Catholic orphanage on Nelson (Jarvis) Street, the House of Providence and the Boys Industrial School; he captained the *James Coleman* for an 1851 cathedral fund-raising tour to Halifax[8]; he was the bishop's secretary in 1852; he was a member of the Catholic deputation to the Duke of Newcastle, in 1860, protesting the erection of an Orange arch in anticipation of the visit of the Prince of Wales[9]; and for a number of years he conducted catechism classes for the boys of St. Paul's parish, distributing prizes, prayer books and rosaries. Roderick A. O'Connor, who became the third bishop of Peterborough, was one of his catechism students and fondly remembered how Captain Elmsley used to march his students, military style, to the church after lessons.[10] Elmsley had spent so much of his money on Catholic projects that his vast fortune was effectively depleted within ten years of his death in 1863. When Archbishop Lynch asked Mrs. Elmsley in 1871 to purchase a site for a Catholic hospital all she could promise was to furnish a room.[11]

Besides his extensive charity work, John Elmsley was an apologist for the Catholic Church. One example of his rising to the Church's defense can be found in a letter to the *Colonist*, dated 29 March 1856. It was not only a follow-up to a previous letter concerning Bishop Power (see below) but also a critique of the then current Protestant translation of the Bible into English and a blast against the old chestnut that Catholics were not allowed by their priests to read Sacred Scripture. Elmsley directed his remarks on this last point to a John Fletcher:

> In conclusion permit me to remark that it is most extraordinary, that Mr. Fletcher should renew the thousand times refuted slanders, that "in this Colony or anywhere else, efforts are being made to keep the Book of God out of the hands of the common people." We have two Catholic Booksellers in this city, either of whom will inform Mr. Fletcher, if he will favor them with a call, that they have always on hand, for sale, a large number of very cheap Catholic translations of the Holy Scriptures; and that they actually do sell, annually, large quantities thereof, to any party or parties whatsoever, without let, hindrance, molestation, or denial, of any authority, ecclesiastical or secular; and they will freely challenge either Mr. Fletcher or any body else to prove that Catholics have not "free permission, to have their Bibles read in their dwellings and school houses." The efforts of the ecclesiastical authorities are directed to the grateful task of spreading the Book of God

amongst their flocks, but to keep translations with many errors out of their hands.[12]

There is a reference in this letter to reading the Bible in school-houses. This was John Elmsley, separate school trustee, talking. By the time he wrote this letter, in 1856, he was a veteran of many a school battle. He was a trustee, beginning in 1841, and oftentimes acted as the board's secretary, treasurer and main spokesman in their dealings with Egerton Ryerson.[13] (For a time, he was also treasurer of the Toronto Catholic Institute, a separate group that included many trustees.[14]) Also in 1841, he built Toronto's first Catholic separate school, a frame structure on Richmond Street at the rear of the Lombard Street fire hall. For many tireless years, Elmsley was one of several board-appointed school inspectors. Their task was to supervise "the intellectual, moral and religious education of the Catholic youth" of Toronto.[16] He was an agent for the distribution of the legislative grants to separate schools and the best known member of a committee of collectors who went to every Catholic home and business in Toronto, in 1854, asking for extra subscriptions.[17] Franklin Walker claims that Elmsley's own taxes and donations helped to keep Catholic schools functioning until the 1855 Act provided more revenue.[18] And Nicolson goes one step further: "Without the generosity of Charbonnel and Elmsley the whole separate school system [in Toronto] would have failed."[19] The bishop was certainly the system's biggest financial patron, but not even his money would have been enough without that of Elmsley's.[20]

John Elmsley was involved in practically every stage of the drawn-out war of words leading up to the 1863 Scott Act. On no fewer than five different occasions, he made public his opinions, and in 1857 he submitted to Egerton Ryerson draft legislation for separate schools.

Six months following the passage of the 1843 school act, Elmsley, S. G. Lynn and Charles Robinson sent a letter to G.A. Barber, superintendent of education for the city of Toronto, asking him to petition the Toronto City Council for several separate schools. At that time, municipalities had the power to accept or reject the petitions of separate school supporters for new schools. Dated 8 August 1844, the letter says:

> With reference to the conversation which passed between you, and the Committee of a public meeting of the Roman Catholics of the city of Toronto, at an interview with you this morning, they have now the honour to state that the main object of the Roman Catholic body is to have two or three separate schools within the limits of the city and (if it can be accomplished) to have allotted to those separate schools an apportionment of the Committee School Fund in proportion, either to the number of children attending such separate schools, or to the aggregate Roman Catholic population of the city.
>
> They would respectfully submit that the spirit of the Act for the establishment and maintenance of Common Schools in Upper Canada, passed 9 December 1843, favors the wishes and views of the Roman Catholics in this respect, and they sincerely trust that you, with the concurrence of the Common Council of the city, will be enabled to comply with these views.
>
> They would also beg permission to suggest that if separate schools can only be established in strict conformity with the letter of the law, the apportionment of any one School District, when divided between Protestant and Roman Catholic schools, will necessarily be so small as to render a separate maintenance for both impracticable; but, in taking the spirit of the Act, the intention of the Legislature, the Committee feels assured, will be carried out . . .[21]

Barber readily agreed with the Catholic position. "Taking the *spirit* of the School Act as my guide and comparing its provisions with the former statute," he wrote to the city council, "I am of the opinion that the Legislature intended to secure to the Roman Catholic population of each township, town, or city, a separate school or schools; with a teacher or teachers of their own religious

84

persuasion."[22] But council ignored Barber's support of a Catholic interpretation of the spirit of the 1843 Act. Instead, they rigorously applied the letter of the law and denied Catholics any new schools.[23] This prompted M.T. O'Brien and other Toronto Catholics to bring a petition to the legislature, "praying that the Common School act may be amended so that they be allowed a just portion of the Common School moneys."[24] This grievance would not be rectified in full until the passage of the 1851 Act.[25]

One defeat did not deter Elmsley. In a debate on common schools on 6 December 1847, at which Ryerson explained the new legislation and others disapproved of sectarian schools, Elmsley rose to object to Protestants teaching Catholics and to Catholic children reading the common school version of the Bible unsupervised by their priests. Brave man, Elmsley was the only Catholic at the debate. A report on his speech appeared in the *Banner*:

> Many things were taught in these [common] schools which reflected on Roman Catholics — such as in the history of Henry VIII, which was given so differently in Protestant from Roman Catholic authors. Above all things there was the Bible, which Protestants made a school book of, but which Roman Catholics, not from disrespect, but from greater reverence did not give their children to read, without being accompanied by explanations approved by the priests. He believed that if children read the Bible without that safeguard they would become *not* Protestants but infidels. As he was the only Roman Catholic present, he felt called on to represent their feelings. There were many Roman Catholic children running about the streets idle, who would be at school if it were not for the Protestant teachers to whom they must be sent; but this the parents would never do; they would rather they were not educated at all.[26]

Interestingly, George Brown of the *Globe* agreed with Elmsley: that if Catholics were so adamant about having their children educated apart from Protestant children, the only remedy was separate schools for Catholics — at least for now, if they were so foolish to insist on having them. When Catholics (and Anglicans) applied to the Toronto Board of Trustees for separate schools, in June 1848, they were flatly refused. The *Globe* applauded the decision.[27]

The problem of uneducated Catholic urchins on the streets of Toronto was a serious one in the Famine year 1847. It would only worsen during the three-year wait for a new bishop and legislation that would give Catholics the right to establish their own schools without the interference of common school trustees, who hardly had an interest in promoting Catholic education. As already noted above, a legislative remedy did not happen until the remedial Act of 1851.

At the urging of Father John Carroll, John Elmsley and S.G. Lynn wrote a letter to Bishop Charbonnel, in advance of his arrival in 1850, about the need to educate the children of his diocese, many of whom were the products of the worst poverty and ignorance. The two men did not mince their words:

> The elevation of these degraded people should be we venture to submit the earnest and unceasing object of Your Lordship's untiring efforts; and we conceive that in no way can Your Lordship better endeavour to attain this most desirable end than in extending to them the blessings of a sound religious Education. The parents of the children inhabiting these places are in some cases altogether too poor to be able to pay for the schooling of their little ones, but in most cases they infinitely prefer the indulgence of their own sensual propensities to the instruction of their youth, and their large numbers of young persons are annually thrown upon society steeped in all the mischievous consequences of idle and dissolute training.[28]

Little wonder, then, that having read these words penned by the diocese's two leading laymen, Charbonnel plunged right into the separate school controversy (see Chapter One).

The struggle continued. In 1853 and 1854, Elmsley acted on behalf of the Catholic ratepayers of St. David's Ward and St. James'

Ward and also on behalf of all the separate school trustees in Toronto. He was deputed to write directly to Egerton Ryerson concerning a series of critical issues arising from the application of the school acts of 1850 and 1851. Those issues included the still tortuous difficulty in setting up new Catholic schools in the face of stiff opposition from the common school trustees and their many allies on the city council; insuring that the names of separate school supporters were excluded from paying their taxes to the common schools; and the recording of correct information on the attendance returns of children in separate schools.

On 29 August 1853, Elmsley, representing twelve heads of families in St. David's Ward whose petition for a separate school had been denied, argued the following case:

> The applicants were refused a separate school in January last, upon the ground that there was a Catholic teacher employed in their ward, but they had hoped and expected that the supplementary act of last session of Parliament, would have smoothed all difficulties, and healed all wounds; and that upon their renewed application, subsequent to the passing of that act, they would have been at once permitted to enjoy the advantage of a separate school within their limits.
>
> The reply of the city board of school trustees, however, destroys all hope; unless by a re-consideration of the decision they have made, they see fit to revise it. In this view I have been instructed to address a communication to you as Chief Superintendent of common schools in order to ascertain whether in your judgment the city board takes a correct view of the law. The applicants now see that they are placed in a worse position than they were when the city was under the school section system; because then, although there were three school sections in the ward yet in only one of them was there a Catholic teacher, and therefore of course the only portion of the ward deprived of the privilege of having a separate school. Now the whole ward is, if the city board be

right in their decision, to be subjected to the same disability as a portion of it formerly was, although the teachers in all other portions of the ward were then, have continued to be, and still are, Protestant.

The short act of 1851, was, as its title and preambles signify, destined to restore rights, to remove doubts; it declares that it is inexpedient to deprive parties of rights which they enjoyed under preceding school acts. The applicants of St. David's ward therefore think that it could not possibly have been the intention of the legislature by that act, or by any other measure, to deprive them of the right of having a separate school, at least for such portions of it as possessed the right under the school section system; and that therefore the concluding proviso of the act of 1851 does not subject the whole ward to the obligation to which only one section of it had been formerly subjected under preceding school acts.

There are now nearly three hundred children of Catholic parentage, who attend the Catholic school in St. David's ward. There are six teachers in the ward employed by the board, only one of whom is a Catholic. Can it be possible that the legislature contemplated that so many pupils should be deprived of the benefit of a separate school upon such a ground. The applicants respectfully suggest that the intentions of the legislature were not such, and to you, Sir, they appeal for redress.[29]

Ryerson came down on Elmsley's side. Even though Ryerson agreed with the city board of school trustees that "where the teacher of the public school is a Roman Catholic, a separate school Roman Catholic school cannot be allowed in the ward," he claimed that the 1850 Act "assumed the existence of but one teacher."[30] Therefore, since there were six teachers in the common school, of whom only one was a Catholic, the Catholics in St. David's Ward were allowed to have a separate school. It was a very technical but sufficient interpretation of the law.

The next matter concerned the Catholics of St. James' Ward. As the secretary-treasurer of that ward's separate school trustees, Elmsley wrote to Ryerson, on 27 October 1853, that the names of many Catholics who indicated their willingness to subscribe to separate schools had not been left off the collector's roll for the city school rate. In other words, they had been counted as common school supporters and taxed accordingly. The mix-up was more than just unfortunate. It was a potential disaster and another case in point of the Byzantine-like regulations that made life for separate school supporters rather bewildering.

In order to be exempted from common school rates, separate school supporters had to give their names as well as the amount they would subscribe. This amount had to be "equal to the assessment for school purposes" and also equal to the amount "such persons would have to pay if no such separate schools were in existence."[31] However, the trustees of St. James's Ward could not insert the amount to be subscribed for many Catholic ratepayers until they had been informed of the common school rate. But the city council had not determined the rate until September, two full months after the 30 June deadline for filing the names of separate school supporters to be exempted from the collector's rolls. Elmsley continued:

> Neither did there exist any reliable data upon which the Roman Catholic trustees could have an approximation to the amount. In the first place, they could not undertake to fix the school rate for 1853 at the same figure as that of 1852; had they done so they would have been 1d. in the £ short of the amount, and then the clerk of the council would indeed have had just grounds for declining to exempt them from paying the tax. In the next place, the Roman Catholic trustees could not fix the value of the assessable property of the citizens for 1853, because a very great increase in the value of all kinds of property had taken place in the course of the past twelvemonth. In my own case, land has been valued at more than double the valuation of 1852, by the assessors, and whereas my taxes for last year amounted to £45, they reach

this year £97 — and thus had my subscription been based upon an assessment of £45, or even twice £45, I should have been shut out of the privilege of subscribing to the separate schools, upon the ground of having subscribed an insufficient amount. Several of my co-religionists would have been in the same condition.[32]

Elmsley had the support of Charles Daly, clerk of the city council. In his response, Ryerson rejected Elmsley's argument. The names of separate school supporters had to be accompanied by a statement of their subscription. But in view of Daly's explanation that the subscriptions were missing due to no fault of the Catholics, Ryerson allowed Elmsley to circulate a subscription paper to each separate school supporter whose name had not been excluded from the collector's rolls. On this paper each supporter would be obliged to insert the amount of his subscription, which was now possible since Ryerson's decision was handed down in October.[33]

The question of attendance returns affected every separate school in the city of Toronto. The law required separate school trustees to submit half yearly attendance returns, on or before 30 June and 31 December. These returns had to show the names and subscriptions of separate school supporters, the names of the school children and their daily and average attendance. The local superintendent, who would receive these returns, would determine from the information on them what names to exclude from the collector's rolls for the general school rate and the amount of the half-yearly legislative grant. The latter was calculated solely on the average attendance of the pupils.

Elmsley had to contend with two problems. One, the municipal clerk demanded to use the actual as well as the average attendance of the pupils to determine the amount of the exemption. Elmsley objected to this and Ryerson agreed, but Ryerson added that the actual attendance must appear on the forms for the benefit of the superintendent. Two, Elmsley wondered why there had to be half yearly attendance returns when the collector's rolls were finalized but once a year, in either August or September, and thus no change in the list could take place until the following year. Ryerson answered this by saying that since an equitable apportionment of the money from the legislative grant was based on the attendance returns, and that the grant was given half yearly, the returns also had to be half yearly.[34]

This exchange continued with several more extraordinarily lengthy letters from both Elmsley and Ryerson. It is apparent from this and other exchanges between Ryerson and Catholic trustees that only Ryerson really understood the school legislation and that without lawyers to advise them, Catholic trustees, including the indefatigable Elmsley, were always at a disadvantage when they had to bow to Ryerson's judgments on the meaning and application of the law in regards to separate schools.

Elmsley was part of the counterattack against Ryerson and his allies in the press when the chief superintendent insisted that Bishop Power's support of separate schools was strictly limited. Elmsley's contribution was in the form of an open letter to the *Colonist* in 1856:

> The affectionate regard that I entertain for the revered memory of our late beloved friend and Pastor, Bishop Power, impels me to put forth my humble endeavors, to rescue his sacred character from the obloquy that you have attempted to cast upon it, in your newspaper of the 14th inst.
>
> Following the unhappy example of Dr. Ryerson, and indeed almost using his words, you have thought proper to allege that Bishop Power, *"understood the working of the Public School system, and died contented."*
>
> As to the first portion of this allegation, I am in a position to state, that Bishop Power was certainly not long in coming to a perfect understanding of the workings of that infidel system; to the latter portion, that he died contented therewith, I am equally competent to state, and do hereby declare, that is totally void of truth.
>
> His Lordship did me the honor to confide to my charge a large share in the working of the Catholic Separate School system, from the moment that he understood the workings of the other, or mixed system, until it pleased Almighty God to

call him to the enjoyment of his reward in Heaven.

In favor of Catholic Schools he devoted his best energies; and were he now living, he would set himself vigorously to the work of counteracting the effects of those Educational establishments which practically ignore the Dogmas of the Christian Religion, and are rapidly subsiding into pure Deism.

May I beg the favor of you to give this communication a place in your paper, in order that the contradiction may be co-extensive with the allegation — that Bishop Power died contented with the working of the Public School system; and also that the real friends of that truly Catholic and Apostolic Prelate may feel assured, that the injurious imputation you have tried to fasten upon his character is totally without foundation.

Your encomiums, in so far as they relate to the line of conduct you have attributed to him, are severe reproaches; and I am most happy in having it in my power to state, for the benefit of all whom it may concern, that our late Bishop was a most energetic advocate and supporter of Catholic Separate Schools, and most resolutely opposed to mixed [schools].[35]

Elmsley could not have been clearer in his denunciation of the claim that Bishop Power was content with the common schools. As if to make sure that everyone understood this, the Reverend J.M. Bruyère quoted Elmsley's letter in his own quarrel with Ryerson.[36] However, Elmsley's words, as forthright as they were, did not stop Ryerson from repeating his claim.

Protecting the reputation of Bishop Power was not the only controversy in 1856 that commanded Elmsley's attention. There was the "Bowes Bill" that would have amended the Taché Act in favour of separate school supporters. The bill had reached second reading by March 1856 but was stalled by a loud and menacing no-popery campaign that claimed that Protestant money would be used to finance Catholic separate schools. The claim was preposterous, of course, but repeated *ad nauseum, ad infinitum*, it made for compelling politics in a Protestant province.

To counter this claim, the Toronto Separate School Board issued a handbill, dated 1 April 1856 and signed by Charles Robinson, chairman, and John Elmsley, secretary. The handbill repeated the standard Catholic claims: the right of Catholics in Upper Canada to their own separate schools, being based on the liberty of conscience, was the same as that of Protestants in Lower Canada having their own schools; the method whereby government grants to schools were apportioned should be the same in both provinces; and Catholics had absolutely no interest in spending Protestant money on Catholic schools but only in being exempted from supporting the common schools.[37]

Elmsley's last major contribution to the struggle was his draft legislation. Actually, he proposed two bills, one for Catholic separate schools and one for separate schools for other denominations. He submitted his bills to Ryerson on 4 March 1857. The denominational bill went nowhere. The separate school bill, even though Ryerson rejected it too, inspired Richard Scott's third attempt to legislate on behalf of separate schools (see Chapter One).

John Elmsley died at his St. Joseph Street home on 8 May 1863. He was buried in the crypt of St. Michael's Cathedral but his heart was deposited in the west wall of St. Basil's Church. His wife, Charlotte, died on 2 October 1883, at the age of 71, and was buried next to her husband at the cathedral. Of John and Charlotte's ten children, only two outlived their father. Sophia Stuart, his second daughter, became a Benedictine nun and lived at St. Mary's Priory at Princethorpe, near Rugby, England. She died on 31 March 1873. Remigius, his fifth son, died at his Toronto home many years later, on 15 September 1910, and is buried in Mount Hope Cemetery. He figures in our story near the end of this chapter.

Two Newspaper Proprietors

The journalism and editorial writing of Charles Donlevy of the *Toronto Mirror* and James G. Moylan of the *Canadian Freeman*, another Toronto-based newspaper, in defending and promoting Catholic separate schools in Ontario, was integral to the very survival of publicly-funded Catholic education in the province. Any concession, large or small, that Catholics had won on school matters could not have been extracted from politicians without the spirited and relentless agitation of these Catholic newspapers. They beat a loud drum. This was especially true during the tumultuous 1850s and 1860s, when the political rhetoric on schools, wrapped in layers of mutual suspicion and the blinding fog of religious history, was usually nasty, personal and socially divisive.

The *Toronto Mirror* and *Canadian Freeman* were veritable bulwarks against those individuals and factions within the Protestant community that feared and despised Catholicism in almost equal measure and barely tolerated the existence of Catholic separate schools.[38] These two newspapers served many purposes. They were sources of current news about Ireland and the Irish in North America; advertised Catholic businesses; served as barometers of pride in the progress of their community; and occasionally acted as forums for Catholic self-criticism. Concerning separate school politics, they were an invaluable source of information on the province-wide state of Catholic agitation for improved legislation as well as platforms for local Catholics to air their grievances on school matters. Their editorials shaped and led Catholic opinion on separate schools to a degree unimaginable today.

The strength of the *Toronto Mirror* and *Canadian Freeman* — which made them such potent weapons in the Catholic arsenal — was their financial and political independence from the Catholic hierarchy. This was a paradox that worked to their advantage. Neither paper was an official diocesan mouthpiece, despite considerable braying to the contrary from the Protestant press, and although genuinely loyal to Church authority, neither paper was subservient to episcopal direction. Truth to tell, it was the Catholic hierarchy who needed the newspapers to be the voice of separate school supporters in the public square, where their own course of action was circumscribed. They and the Catholic community at whose head they stood and acted in religious matters (and for Catholics, schools *were* a religious matter) were fortunate to have such able and selfless advocates of separate schools in the persons of Charles Donlevy and

James G. Moylan.

These two men enjoyed a freedom of words and action not available to the Catholic clergy or to the vast majority of the Catholic laity, including the average school trustee in the 1850s and 1860s. No wonder then that they stood at the pinnacle of Catholic lay power, for the most part immune from criticism within their own religious community. When it came to separate schools, a subject dear to their hearts, they pumped the ink wells dry in their defense of the right of Catholic parents to have their taxes support a system of schools in which the teaching of the Catholic religion was central to the curriculum and safe from the assaults of Protestant teachers.

The *Toronto Mirror* and the *Canadian Freeman* published a steady stream of material on separate schools: numerous editorials, which sometimes went into excruciating detail; the results of trustee elections; the proceedings of school board meetings; reports of the annual examinations of Catholic pupils; in-depth discussions of proposed changes to separate school legislation; letters (usually complaints) from trustees, parents and teachers from all parts of the province; denunciations by name of the alleged enemies of separate schools, including any politician, either Protestant or Catholic, who voted against legislation perceived to be beneficial to separate schools; lengthy and often emotional replies to the separate school editorials of such newspapers as the *Patriot*, the *Banner*, the *Examiner*, the *Globe*, the *Christian Guardian*, *Le Journal de Québec*, and the *Canadian Free Press*; and lastly commentaries on Ryerson's annual education reports.

****

Charles Donlevy was born in either 1812 or 1813 in Ballymote, Ireland and settled in Toronto in the mid-1830s.[39] He quickly rose to prominence in the city's Irish Catholic community and remained one of its most dynamic leaders for the remainder of his short life. He was a member of the St. Patrick's Benevolent Society, the Total Abstinence Society, the Catholic Colonization Society, the Reform Association of Canada, the Loyal Irish Repeal Association of Toronto and the

Catholic Institute. In 1853, he was elected a separate school trustee for St. James's Ward and was chairman of the Toronto Separate School Board. Donlevy's causes were many and varied; Irish Catholics throughout the province were his natural constituency; and his newspaper enjoyed a healthy circulation.

After serving a printing apprenticeship with John and Michael Reynolds, Donlevy along with Patrick McTavey founded the *Toronto Mirror* in 1837. Six years later, Donlevy was the sole proprietor. Under his tireless direction, the *Mirror* became "one of the most important voices of Irish Catholic reformers in Upper Canada."[40] By extension, it was also one of the more effective bully pulpits from which the "gospel" of separate schools was preached with great and lasting effect.

A survey of seventy-five news items, editorials and letters to the editor, published in the *Mirror* between 1837 and 1858, reveals Donlevy's shift away from a general and uncritical embrace of common schools to a radical stance on separate school rights. His radicalism took full flight in 1850 and probably mirrored the growing school rights radicalism of city and town Catholics, who, having already established separate schools, bore the brunt of anti-Catholic hostility. If competing personalities were factors in bringing about this change in Donlevy, the names of two familiar protagonists come to mind. They were the Methodist Egerton Ryerson, the chief superintendent, and the Presbyterian George Brown, publisher of the *Globe* and the major instigator of the 1850s no-popery crusade. Donlevy developed a malignant hatred for both men, seeing them as persecutors of the Catholic minority. On a more positive note, it must be said that Donlevy's radicalism was more than mere animus. It was rooted in a liberal belief, actively shared by many Catholics, that state aid to Catholic schools affirmed the rights of parents to educate their children as they saw fit.[41]

For the first ten years of the *Mirror's* existence, Donlevy supported the concept of a province-wide system of common schools, financed by everyone's taxes and managed by locally elected trustees.[42] He made no direct mention of Catholic separate schools but played up the link between the lack of education and the prevalence of crime among the young, a common theme in nineteenth-century social thinking.[43] The paper applauded the legislation of 1843 in two editorials. In an uncharacteristic move, however, it also attacked G.A. Barber, the city of Toronto superintendent of common schools, for refusing to grant a certificate to a teacher in a Catholic school.[44] In 1845, the *Mirror* reasserted its support for common schools.[45]

There matters stood, dormant, until 1848. That was the year Donlevy strongly objected to the 1847 Act which replaced locally elected school trustees with municipally-appointed ones. (He also opposed an increase in school taxes from one pence to four pence in the pound.)[46] Appointing trustees, Donlevy argued, was undemocratic and gave too much discretionary power to the chief superintendent and his numerous cronies at the local level. Perhaps Donlevy correctly intuited Ryerson's rise to predominance in education, even at this early stage, and feared that the worst was yet to come. Be that as it may, Donlevy's initial reaction was to christen him "Leonidas," a reference to the 5th Century B.C. Spartan king who died at the battle of Thermopylae, and in a later editorial to scornfully call him "the Prussian saddlebag centralizer."[47] When there was mention that the grammar schools would fall under Ryerson's jurisdiction (which eventually happened), Donlevy was horrified at the news but mollified himself by musing that a change in government would surely mean Ryerson's fall from grace. It was a terrible misjudgment.[48] Ryerson would stay at his post until retirement in 1876 and would remain a pesky thorn in Donlevy's side. As time went on, that thorn only grew bigger, causing more pain to Donlevy and his allies as separate schools became *the* political issue of the 1850s. It proved nearly fatal to Donlevy's politics following the Ryerson-engineered collapse of the Bowes Bill and the defeat of the Felton amendment, in 1856.

Bitter were the words, then, that Donlevy heaped on Ryerson in an 1857 editorial:

> From the North route we hear of the most strenuous and successful efforts being made to establish Catholic schools, and provide for them efficient teachers. In the space

of one month, no less than five or six have been established in one large mission alone, and the people are being prepared for still further progress in the same direction. On all sides, too, we find that the privileges granted by the present Separate School law are regarded with the utmost contempt. Many look with absolute disgust upon the pittance doled out to their schools by the Education Department; and in several instances, we understand, they have not considered it of sufficient moment to take the trouble of making the necessary returns. Considering that these documents are a species of feudal tribute, whereby, for a consideration, the Rev. Egerton Ryerson is acknowledged as their lord and master, the Trustees of these schools have determined to have nothing to do with him or his department . . . The Chief Superintendent delights in honoring the "glorious School system of Upper Canada." Transcendental must its good qualities indeed be, when schools that have been recently established, scorn to be affiliated to or to reap any pecuniary advantages from it. From every part of the country there is but one cry, which finds its re-echo in the ablest organs of public sentiment, and the meaning and essence of which is, a contempt for the present educational laws, and a dislike (to speak as mildly as possible) to the hand which guides the machinery of the Department of Public Instruction.[49]

The other thorn in Donlevy's flesh was George Brown of the *Globe*. The two newspaper proprietors carried on a spirited war of words in 1851. Brown used separate schools as a rallying cry against all things Catholic and demanded their abolition in Upper Canada (without thinking through the consequences of such an act on the Protestant minority of Lower Canada). Brown employed inflammatory and disparaging language whenever he wrote about Catholics. In his mind, they were Romanists and papists; their faith was nothing more than a sectarian prejudice; their schools were sectarian schools and as such anathema to Reform principles; and their priests practiced popish priestcraft over their people, keeping them in perpetual ignorance and slavery.

Donlevy took strong exception to such pejorative insults from a fellow journalist. He replied by calling Brown in print "ignorant as he is bigoted" and "a nuisance to society and a traitor to his party." That party was the Reform Party. As Brown's Clear Grit, no-popery faction gained ascendancy within it, Irish Catholic reformers were left with nowhere to turn, a development the lifelong Reformer Donlevy deeply resented.[50]

For each blast Brown hurled against separate schools, Donlevy replied with a counterblast of equal or greater intensity. For example, in the lead up to the passing of the 1851 Act, Donlevy published the classic Catholic argument for separate schools.[51] For good measure, he followed this editorial a week later, on 15 August 1851, with a direct and uncompromising response to the anti-Catholic tirades of a man who is now acknowledged a Father of Confederation:

> Our *terrestrial* cotemporary is quite furious against the granting of Separate Schools to Roman Catholics. He contends that it will be the destruction of our National School system, and that "national education in all its integrity" must be a foremost test at the approaching election. This is all bombast — quite in keeping with the tone and temper of the *Globe* on all subjects affecting Roman Catholics. We have not the slightest objection that national education should be made a prominent test at the election, but we protest against the tyranny of compelling parties to send their children to schools which they regard as dangerous to faith and morals.
>
> The position of Roman Catholics as distinguished from the Protestant community, differs widely from the position which any one denomination of that community occupies as compared to the rest. All Protestant sects unite most cordially in their denunciations of Popery, and agree among themselves upon all points of vital importance, so far as salvation in a future world would be concerned. The great principle of Protestantism consists in the right of private judgment on all questions touching religion, and this principle is regarded not only as a right but an obligation.

Such being the case, we cannot understand what danger could attend the education of children of various Protestant denominations in the same school.

With Roman Catholics the question is very different indeed. Theirs is not a difference of opinion from the Protestant population, but a difference of *Faith* — a difference in the belief of certain dogmas which they are taught to regard as of the greatest importance, while any deviation from this belief would be attended with future punishment.

We could easily dwell on this subject to a much greater length, but we are confident that the liberal and intelligent require no proofs to convince them of the *justice* of the Roman Catholic demands, while no amount of proof or argument could induce the *Globe* to stay his onslaught. We are confident he will yet have still greater cause to regret his course than he has hitherto had.[52]

This editorial, and many others like it, assumed a view of the world in which religious faith in the here and now was absolutely central to the future well being of every individual. It was an assumption shared by all Christians but not in the same manner. Since Catholics *were* so different from their Protestant neighbours, in this most fundamental aspect of Christian life in the nineteenth century, the hierarchy and lay leaders like Donlevy felt that a separate system of education for Catholic children was necessary to preserve the manner in which Catholics as a *community of believers* lived their religious faith and insured its long-term survival.

Although Ryerson and Brown were formidable opponents of separate schools and occasionally succeeded in driving Donlevy to excitement and exhaustion, they were hardly the only fronts on which he wielded his pen in defense of the Catholic Church and her schools. The pages of the *Toronto Mirror* reveal just how busy and determined he was. Donlevy championed Bishop Charbonnel, Father J.M. Bruyère and Maurice Carroll of Georgetown in their respective quarrels with Egerton Ryerson;[53] he published lengthy letters from trustees in Brantford, Picton, the townships of Nichol, Adjala, Tecumseth and Mountain (to name but a few examples);[55] he wrote numerous times on the vexatious problems concerning the proper collection and allocation of school taxes, a sore point endured by trustees for many years; he organized and advertised petition drives in connection with forthcoming legislation;[56] he complained about the unequal distribution of the legislative grant and political attempts to secularize the clergy reserves for the sole benefit of common schools;[57] he belonged to the Catholic Institute; in addition to the *Globe*, his main journalistic opponent, he fought skirmishes with a half dozen other newspapers; he scrutinized the operations of the Toronto Separate School Board; and he even criticized the lethargy of separate school supporters on election day (trustee elections took place early each year).[58]

Charles Donlevy died on 22 July 1858, penniless, and was buried in the crypt of St. Michael's Cathedral. His remains lie not too far from that other Catholic stalwart, John Elmsley. Since Donlevy was only in his mid forties, his sudden passing was a shock to Catholics everywhere and a blow to the separate school cause. Patrick A. O'Neill continued to publish the *Mirror* until 1866, but it was superseded as the pre-eminent voice of Irish Catholics in Upper Canada by James G. Moylan's *Canadian Freeman*.

****

James George Moylan was born on 11 January 1826 in Maynooth, Ireland.[59] Educated at St. Jarlath's College in Tuam, County Clare and at the Royal College of St. Patrick in Maynooth, he worked for British customs in London for three years before he emigrated to the United States and found employment at the Chilean Embassy. From 1852 to 1856, he wrote for *The New York Daily Times*, first as its Washington correspondent and later as a member of its New York staff. In 1856, he moved to Guelph, Upper Canada to teach classics at the Jesuit college there. Two years later, Moylan and James J. Mallon bought the four-year-old *Catholic Citizen* in Toronto and rechristened it the *Canadian Freeman*. By 1859, Moylan was the paper's sole proprietor and a major contributor to its pages. Moylan's writing was exceptionally clear and logical, and he generously sprinkled it with Latin words and phrases. Absent was the bitterness and emotion that marred so much Catholic journalism during this period, but clarity and logic aside, Moylan could also be viciously witty at the expense of his opponents. He saved some of his most savage barbs for George Brown and Egerton Ryerson.

Moylan's main constituency was his fellow Irish Catholics, who made up the majority of Catholics then living in the province. He was close to Thomas D'Arcy McGee and to Bishop/Archbishop John Joseph Lynch of Toronto. He favoured the union of the two Canadas as the best political arrangement for protecting minority rights in both provinces, and for a long time he was cool to the idea of confederation. In time, however, he changed his political stripes and embraced John A. Macdonald and his Conservative party. Like Donlevy of the *Mirror*, Moylan had been a Reformer but felt compelled to leave the party over Brown's hostile ranting against the Catholic Church. In any event, Moylan was essentially a social and political conservative. He was passionate about Ireland but felt that Canada was no place to fight the homeland's struggle against British misrule. He also believed that there existed plenty of room for both Irish and Catholic values in Canadian society. In that particular vein, he was a consistent backer of the extension of separate school rights.

The *Canadian Freeman* provided extensive coverage of two distinct but related avenues of separate school agitation: the political debate prior to the passage of the Scott Act of 1863, and the campaign to legislate the same school rights for both provinces before confederation took effect. Concerning the Scott Act, Moylan never understood it to be final. He believed that it had too many shortcomings to be considered the last word. Besides advocating the necessity of petition drives and denouncing Catholic traitors in the strongest language, he wrote an entire series of editorials replying to those two critics of Catholic education, George Brown and Egerton Ryerson. They were masterful pieces. The 1865-66 agitation, on the other hand, was an embarrassing flop and prompted Moylan's bitterest words on the school question, following the rejection of Robert Bell's

Bill in 1866.

In early 1862, Moylan consulted clergymen, teachers and trustees as he prepared to comment on Scott's Bill. He argued that Catholic separate schools needed to be free from the chief superintendent's interference. They must have their own superintendent, who would be appointed by the bishops and would work in conjunction with the chief superintendent, as well as their own local superintendents. Their educational rights should be the same as those enjoyed by the Protestant minority in Lower Canada. This meant that they should have not only elementary schools but also their own academies (grammar schools), model schools, normal school and even university. Lastly, Catholic trustees should not have to take an oath to the accuracy of their attendance returns to the chief superintendent. Their word should be no less trustworthy than the word of common school trustees on *their* returns.[60]

Two *Globe* editorials of 3 and 9 May 1862 repeated the now standard and rather stale untruths levelled against separate schools. Moylan calmly replied that the Scott Bill would not harm common schools nor would it introduce clerical domination. Catholics, Moylan continued, rejected secular education controlled by denominationalism as much as they did the godless variety, which forbade any mention of "God's providence, and even of His existence, or the existence of revelation."[61] The careful teaching of the faith to each succeeding generation of Catholic youth was so central to the concept of what constituted a Catholic education that compromise was unthinkable. Moylan denied that separate education produced estrangement and intolerance among the different classes of citizens and that Catholics wanted Protestant money for Catholic schools. He asked why Catholics should be forced to pay for schools they would not use.[62]

Moylan ended one editorial with these words of warning and hope. They read like a manifesto:

> The *Globe* and its fanatical phalanx may tell us that they "cannot hold out the slightest hope that there will be any change of views on the subject" [of separate schools]; but we

tell them in reply that the day of religious equality may be postponed for a time, it cannot be averted long. The hour for exclusive privileges and monopolies are gone – there is a power in strong religious convictions which it is impossible to cope with; they burst the bonds that seek to confine them. We look around and see everywhere evidences amongst us of increasing religious earnestness. We see new churches springing up and filled in all directions – religious orders increasing and developing – troops of holy men and women educating the poor and ministering to every want of suffering humanity. We believe that such faith as this will have its reward. There is a latent power in earnest faith which bears all before it, like one of those huge billows of ocean which seems to move sluggishly, but still carries all that opposes it with resistless force. The day of religious equality, we reiterate, is nigh, when we shall all live in peace, because no class will have to reproach the other with injustice.[63]

However convinced Moylan may have been about the power of religious conviction to bring about equality for separate schools, from his clash with Ryerson in July 1862, he must have known that the peace and justice he sought would be a long time coming. The occasion that burst his Utopian bubble was the publication of two letters by Ryerson in the *Leader*, on 18 July, in response to the demands of the Anglican Synod for their own schools. In the one letter that referred to Catholic separate schools, Ryerson wrote:

There is not a vestige of desire for Separate Schools throughout the Townships of Upper Canada in any section of the Protestant population; and the desire for them exists among only a small minority of the Roman Catholic population itself; for, according to the best data within my reach, the School population connected with the Roman Catholic Church in Upper Canada is 68,675; of whom 53,760 attended the schools; but of this 53,760 children attending the schools, only 13,631, or one fourth of them attend *Separate*

Schools, while 43,760 or three fourths of them attend the mixed or public schools. Notwithstanding the efforts employed to induce Roman Catholics to send their children to the separate schools, and the facilities afforded to such schools, the fact that three-fourths of the Roman Catholics in Upper Canada send their children to the public schools, instead of the separate schools, shows how averse the great body of the Roman Catholics are to separate their children in their day-school education from those of their protestant neighbours, and how strong is the principle of co-operation and union against that of isolation and separation among all classes of the population in the home education of their children, and especially when the law as effectually protects the religious rights and feelings of Roman Catholics in the public schools as it does those of any class of Protestants, and as there is not known a single instance of proselytism of a Roman Catholic child during twenty years in all the public schools of Upper Canada.[64]

Ryerson was probably correct about the sentiment concerning Protestant separate schools. However, he must have conveniently forgotten the Maurice Carroll proselytism case in Georgetown, in 1852, and he was certainly being disingenuous when he tried to prove with incorrect figures that Catholics as a body did not support separate schools, as if he himself had not had a large say in the matter. Moylan was furious. Here is the main body of his answer:

Now, let us review Dr. Ryerson's figures and facts. He tells us that out of the entire Catholic school population of 53,760 attending the schools, only 13,631 attend the separate schools, and 43,760 children go to the common schools. We cannot understand how or where the Doctor procured the last set of figures. According to our notion of subtraction 40,129 is the proper remainder, after deducting 13,631 from 53,760. This would show that more than one-third, and not one-fourth, of the Catholic children – as erroneously stated by Dr.

Ryerson – avail themselves of the separate schools in operation. Assuming, then, as correct the number of children set down as attending separate schools, we contend, that the Chief Superintendent, so far from showing any disinclination on the part of Catholic parents "to separate their children in their day school education from those of their Protestant neighbors," proves quite the *reverse*, as we shall immediately *demonstrate*. There are in Western Canada [Upper Canada] about 120 separate schools established. The total number of children attending those schools, according to the Doctor's data, is 13,631. This would give an average attendance of 113¹/₂ pupils to each school. We challenge the Chief Superintendent to indicate a corresponding average in the same number of common schools selected from the localities in which separate schools are in operation. This he cannot do. Neither can he produce a half dozen authenticated instances, throughout the whole of Upper Canada, where Catholic parents send their children to a common school when there is a separate school available. If Dr. Ryerson, therefore, cannot show for 120 common schools, established in the immediate vicinity of separate schools, an attendance of 13,631 pupils, and if, further, he be unable to prove that Catholics give a preference to common schools, when they have a school of their own within reach, all he has said on the score of separate schools is not worth a straw.

It is to the iniquitous and unfair law that prevents Catholics in various sections from uniting to establish separate schools, and not to the cause assigned, that the common schools are indebted for so large a proportion of Catholic pupils. The figures quoted from Dr. Ryerson's letter incontestably prove, that wherever separate schools are established they are well attended.

Let the law be amended in such a way as to afford Catholics those "facilities" to which Dr. Ryerson – jocosely, no doubt – alludes, and we venture to say, that the entire Catholic school population, or at least all in the enjoyment of the "facilities," will be found attending separate schools.[65]

Moylan confronted Ryerson in print again, in March 1865. Ryerson had published a pamphlet in which he set down three major objections to separate schools. One, they suffered from "a chronic and inherent weakness" that made them sickly and stunted their growth. Two, the isolation of Catholic children from the rest of society produced an inferior education that would leave them in later life at the bottom of the economic ladder. Three, Catholics only had themselves to blame for their social and economic inferiority, which inevitably led to envy on their part of the more successful in society and a tendency to resort to Fenian-like violence and anarchy as a way of securing wealth and power for themselves.

To the first objection, Moylan replied that if separate schools suffered any kind of "chronic and inherent weakness" it was the fault of the "stunted" separate school law, for which Ryerson himself was chiefly responsible. "Give to Separate Schools the same advantages and facilities that Common Schools enjoy and the 'chronic and inherent weakness' — if any such really exist — will soon disappear."[66] To the second, Moylan wrote that Catholics, regardless of their education or abilities, were treated as second-class citizens in the province:

> If Catholic young men are found in the humbler avocations and walks of life in Canada, it is not by reason of their incompetency to fill more lucrative and respectful positions. The cause lies deeper, and may be fairly traced to that spirit of exclusiveness and prejudice which unhappily, as Dr. Ryerson admits, pervades the whole Protestant community of Upper Canada. This rule of proscription is carried into force in every branch of business throughout the country. Catholics, no matter how high their attainments or irreproachable their character, are excluded from places of trust and emolument, simply and solely through hatred of their religion . . .
>
> We would remind Dr. Ryerson that, in Canada, every

impediment is thrown in the way of our Catholic youth. They live among a hostile majority, who, with a few noble exceptions, are ever ready to close every door against them that would lead to wealth or position.[67]

To the third, Moylan charged that Ryerson had published a libel against the entire Catholic community without furnishing a shred of proof. Moylan continued:

[Catholics] are not office-seekers nor place-beggars. They are not dissatisfied with the Government of the country in any respect, save as regards the anomalous and degrading distinction which the law has established in reference to the education of the minorities in Upper and Lower Canada. This they resent and protest against, and they will continue to resent and protest against the grievance until a remedy be applied.[68]

Moylan was front and centre of that resentment and protest. He never criticized Richard Scott for the contents of his 1863 legislation. Like every other informed Catholic in Upper Canada, Moylan readily knew that Scott's three-year legislative initiative had been effectively eviscerated by Ryerson, with the complete connivance of the government of the day. In February 1865, Moylan denounced the 1863 Act in language uncharacteristically emotional for him: "A more cruel hoax, — a more transparent deception, under the show of granting a measure of justice, of conferring benefits, never has been practiced by a Government on a whole community."[69] To prove his point, he referred his readers to the situation of the separate school in Oakville. For the teaching of 120 children, the school received a government grant of $48 in 1862 and 1863. For the teaching of approximately three times that number of children, the united grammar and common school received $765 in 1862 and $795 in 1863. It is unclear from the account in the *Canadian Freeman* how the education authorities arrived at such an obvious inequity in funding. However, such inequity was not even the major bone of contention. What galled Oakville's Catholic ratepayers was the fact that every penny of interest from the Clergy Reserve Fund went to the united grammar and common school. In 1862, the interest amounted to $227. When Father J. Ryan, parish priest and chairman of the Catholic school board in Oakville, asked for the Catholic share of the Clergy Reserve Fund, citing section 20 of the 1863 Act, he was refused. The municipality justified its answer on the grounds that starting in 1857 the interest from the fund could only be applied to schools in town, and since there was no Catholic separate school in Oakville in 1857, section 20 of the 1863 Act did not apply to the town.

It was this kind of petty interference and convoluted thinking that drove Catholic trustees and their public defenders, like James G. Moylan, to despair. That despair deepened in 1865 when John A. Macdonald, speaking on behalf of the government, declared that although changes to the law on education would be made for the Protestant minority in Lower Canada, none would be made for the Catholic minority in Upper Canada because they were satisfied with the law as it was![70] The withdrawal of Robert Bell's bill in August 1866 was the final blow to Moylan's valiant drive to achieve educational equality for Catholics in Ontario. Describing the scene on the floor of the legislature when Bell introduced his legislation, Moylan acidly wrote: "In the course of our lives, we have not seen an exhibition of such gross and disgusting bigotry, as that displayed by Protestant M.P.P.'s."[71]

In 1869, Moylan accepted a patronage position as emigration agent for the Canadian government in Ireland. He continued to publish the *Canadian Freeman* until 1873. A year before the paper's demise, he commenced an entirely new career as an inspector of federal penitentiaries. This was to last until 1895. James George Moylan died in Ottawa on 18 January 1902, one of the last of the old Irish guard who had battled so hard and so brilliantly on behalf of separate schools.

****

By way of a postscript to this section on newspaper editors, the names of other Catholic newspapers and their owners from this period should be mentioned. They were the *Catholic Citizen* (1854-1858), Thomas and Michael Hayes; the *Tribune* (1874-1887), owned by Thomas McCrosson[72] from 1877 to 1879; the *Irish Canadian* (1863-1892), Patrick Boyle; *Catholic Weekly Review* (1887-1892), Gerald Fitzgerald and Philip de Grouchy; and the *Catholic Register*, which began publishing in January 1893 as a result of the amalgamation of the *Irish Canadian* and the *Catholic Weekly Review*. These papers were based in Toronto. Another newspaper worth mentioning is George Edward Clerk's *True Witness and Catholic Chronicle*. Published in Montreal, it paid close and critical attention to separate school affairs in Upper Canada and was probably the most militant Catholic newspaper of its day.[73] McCrosson's *Tribune* and Boyle's *Irish Canadian* publicized Remigius Elmsley's celebrated confrontation with Archbishop Lynch over control of the Toronto Separate School Board. Boyle was also a major player in the secret ballot controversy.[74]

School Trustees

Local school trustees were the administrative backbone of Ontario's fledgling separate schools. They did everything within their limited power and resources to make and keep Catholic education a practical and living reality in their respective communities. It was never an easy task. This was particularly true for those trustees in the 1850s and 1860s, when Catholic schools began to sink permanent roots in the Ontario landscape. The fact that the trustees were financially hobbled and had few legal resources was a source of frustration and anxiety. Many of them were simple country folk, who were not educated themselves, and among their number were those who could not sign their own names to education department documents. They worked in isolation from their fellow trustees because the distances between rural communities, where the majority of them lived, made communication so difficult. A province-wide association for the coordination of their political activities was a long way off in the future. For many trustees in the hinterland, writing to one of the Catholic newspapers was the only way to make contact with the outside Catholic world on whom they relied for advice and support.

Odd as it may seem to us, rarely, if ever, were the trustees consulted by either the bishops or Catholic politicians about the course Catholic ratepayers should take in pressing their demands for better legislation. Leaders in their own communities, trustees were expected to follow the commands of the Church's clerical and lay élite. That they did so, willingly and consistently over a long period of time, ensured a future for separate schools that Egerton Ryerson was convinced would never happen.

Perseverance, diligence and a commitment to the Catholic faith and a homegrown Catholic culture — these were the things that sustained Catholic trustees in their struggle to maintain separate schools. With little guidance and no experience, they set up school boards, founded schools, hired teachers and built schoolhouses. They visited their schools, submitted their annual reports and semi-annual attendance records, assembled the tax rolls, collected property taxes and subscriptions, petitioned for amendments to the school legislation, dealt with hostile common school trustees and their allies on the municipal councils, and struggled to understand and interpret the law to the benefit of separate school supporters and their children.

****

The most difficult years for Catholic trustees stretched from 1850 to 1867. It was a time when Ryerson consolidated his power over all aspects of provincial education and when the Catholic trustees in nearly every region of the province defied the odds and Ryerson himself by continuing to establish separate schools. The rate of increase was never spectacular in any given year. Rather, it was gradual but the rate of retention was excellent. The number of schools which ceased to exist for whatever reason was small. It was also a time of confusion for both common school and separate school trustees concerning the interpretation and application of the law.

Confusion seems to have been the order of the day when it came to the 1850 Act and the 1853 Supplementary Act. Ryerson was the sole person in the province able to interpret the legislation. This is not surprising, since he was the architect of every education act until his retirement. According to his own 1855 publication, *Copies of Correspondence Between the Chief Superintendent of Schools for Upper Canada and Other Persons on the Subject of Separate Schools*, Ryerson answered queries concerning the law and pronounced judgment on problems submitted by trustees on both sides of the school divide. Some letters reeked of anger and bitterness directed towards the other side, but most correspondence was written out of a sincere concern to adhere to the law, if the letter writers only knew what the law required of them.

Ryerson published letters from trustees who lived in the following cities, towns, villages and school sections of Ontario: Toronto (see John Elmsley), Kingston, Bytown (Ottawa), Belleville, Brantford, Goderich, Perth, Prescott, Peterborough, Picton, Amherstburg, Chatham, Guelph, Thorold, Kitley, Hallowell, Seymour West, Brock, Wellesley, Wilmot, Nichol, Pilkington, the Township of Williams, Metcalfe and Sandwich. It was Ryerson who defined the meaning of such crucial phrases as "common school fund," "school moneys," "amount subscribed" and "amount paid." And it was Ryerson who answered questions on the election of separate school trustees, voter eligibility, the hiring and payment of teachers, the separate school share of the legislative grant for teachers' salaries, local superintendents, exemptions from municipal taxation, separate school rates for non-residents, the corporate status of school boards, the formation of separate school sections from parts of two townships, the proper method for filling out forms, the union of school sections and the distribution of the *Journal of Education*.

One of the most contentious issues facing Catholic trustees was the proper process whereby Catholic ratepayers were allowed to have their own separate school. The 19th section of the 1850 Act spelled out that process, which took place in four orderly steps:

1) twelve heads of families have to apply to the board of school trustees for a separate school
2) the boundaries of the separate school section have to be determined
3) the school board calls the first meeting for the

election of separate school trustees

4) application for a school must be made before the 25 December

Ryerson did not allow for any deviation from this sequential process. He was rigid and unbending in his interpretation and application of the 19th section, notwithstanding the hardships of rural life and the fact that the typical trustee was in no position to be as familiar with the intricacies of the legislation as he was. Consequently, there were instances of Catholic trustees not knowing if their school was legal and eligible to receive its just portion of the legislative grant. This happened in Brantford.

Writing on 13 September 1853, Thomas Daly, chairman, and Joseph Quinlan, secretary, of the trustees of Brantford's Roman Catholic Separate School, petitioned Ryerson:

> That a school was established by Roman Catholics, in the town of Brantford, in the month of November last, for the education of the children of Roman Catholics.
>
> That it was considered advisable at that time to postpone taking the necessary steps to have the limits of the said school defined, as well as to defer the election of trustees till the looked for action in the matter of common schools was taken by the legislature [a reference to the 1853 Supplementary Act].
>
> That from the time of establishing the same, (hitherto) the said school has been in operation, having been supported wholly, or chiefly by the voluntary contributions of Roman Catholics.
>
> That in pursuance of the common school act passed in 1852 [?], in the months of December and June last, returns of the names of the contributors to such school, the number of pupils who had attended the same, and of all other particulars required by the said act, were made; an election of school trustees was held in the month of June aforesaid, and the limits of the said school were set out as required by the said act.

That in the apportionment of school moneys for the present year, no moneys were allotted to the said school.

Your petitioners would therefore pray that you would be pleased, under the authority vested in you as Chief Superintendent, to apportion to the said school such a sum of money as in your discretion you may deem just.[75]

The Brantford trustees were well intentioned and had obviously followed the law as best as circumstances allowed them, but their understanding of the process for establishing a separate school was woefully inadequate. Ryerson's reply of 15 September 1853 was a straightforward rendition of the requirements of the law:

. . . with the information which you furnish, I cannot express any opinion as to the claims which you make to share in the common school fund for the current year.

You state that an election of trustees for the separate school was held in June, yet that the separate school was established in November last. By referring to the 19th section of the common school act, you will perceive that the formation of a school section and the election of trustees must precede the establishment of a separate school. According to law, no school, either as a common or separate school, can have legal existence or share in the common school fund until after the formation of the school section and the election of trustees after public notice as required by law. Any school, otherwise established, whether by a religious persuasion, or by private enterprise, must be regarded as a private school, and cannot share in the common school fund.

If your school therefore was organized according to law, before the commencement of the current year, it has a right to share in the current year's common school fund; not otherwise.

The 4th section of the supplementary school act makes no change in the mode of establishing separate schools; it changes only the mode of supporting them, and grants certain exemptions to parties supporting them when established according to law.[76]

Next in importance for Catholic trustees was the legislative grant, which was money given directly by the government to the school board for teacher's salaries. The sum was based on average attendance compared with that of the public schools in the same municipalities. The grant never amounted to very much money, but since it represented government funding of separate schools, it was an important symbol. (In 1854, the separate school in Brockville had 140 students and an average attendance of 84, for which it received the princely sum of £ 22.[77])

Typical of the confusion surrounding this issue was a letter, dated 27 August 1853, from Dr. P.A. McDougall, secretary of the separate school in Goderich, to Ryerson. The blank reports he mentions are the official forms for the semi-annual attendance returns:

> I have the honor to acknowledge the receipt of your letter of the 5th instant, and in reply, to state that we applied in due time to the local superintendent for a blank report, but could not obtain any; and in the absence of such blank report, we drew up a report and forwarded it to the local superintendent, who, it appears, although he visited the separate school as superintendent, forwarded the report to the trustees of the common schools, of the town of Goderich, since which time we have heard nothing of the report, nor of any money being apportioned to our school.
>
> It is evident that efforts are being made to defraud the Roman Catholic separate school of the town of Goderich, of what is justly and legally their right, the government grant. And, if possible, the trustees would like to know upon what grounds and by what means it is done.
>
> Therefore, we beg to be informed upon the following points, viz:
> 1st. To whom should the trustees of separate schools

apply for blank reports, and when filled up, to whom should they be sent? (Our local superintendent says not to him.)

2nd. Whose duty, if any, is it to furnish the trustees blank reports?

3rd. Is it part of the local superintendent's duty to send the report of separate schools to the board of common schools?

4th. Are not the trustees of separate schools a body corporate, and entitled to some privileges, as the trustees of common schools?

5th. What ought we to do, or what can we do, under the circumstances, to obtain our portion of the government grant?[78]

The question about trustees being a body corporate was probably the most important of the five questions that Dr. McDougall asked. The annoying business of the blank reports demonstrates ignorance of duty on the part of the superintendent and a lack of communication between a board and education headquarters in Toronto.

Ryerson's reply of 31 August 1853, was conciliatory:

. . . the school grant apportioned to the town of Goderich, has not yet been paid, on account of the returns required by law not having been made by the clerk of the town council. When paid, the report which you have made will, of course, be taken into consideration by the town board of school trustees.

I intended to have supplied each set of trustees with a blank report directly from this department. But as I had no return of your school, when the lists were made out, I did not send to your trustees either a blank report, or a copy of the *Journal of Education*, which I have now the pleasure of forwarding.

The trustees of a separate school are a corporation, and are entitled to all the reports, &., through the local

116

superintendent, provided to any other school corporation.[79]

Then there was the intransigence of some common school boards which refused to grant separate schools to Catholics who had correctly followed the law in petitioning for one. Father John Holzer, S.J., the pastor at Guelph, wrote to Ryerson on 19 December 1853:

> The Roman Catholics of Guelph, having erected a school house sufficiently large to contain 300 pupils, beg leave to inform you, that they desire to establish a separate school according to the provisions made by the Legislature in their favour.
>
> I regret to be under the necessity of informing you, that the petition got up by them for that purpose, has been rejected by Doctor Henry Orton, the chairman of the board of trustees of the common schools of Guelph.
>
> *Per parenthesis* – (He very insultingly told us, he would not have anything to do with it, and consequently would not bring it forward.)
>
> Now, sir, we appeal to you for redress, and hope to meet with a favorable and positive answer, in regard to procuring the privileges extended to Roman Catholics by the School Acts of 1850 and 1853.
>
> In the meantime, it is our intention to open our school about the beginning of the ensuing year.[80]

Ryerson's answer to Father Holzer, dated 21 December 1853, made it abundantly clear that the application of twelve heads of families for a separate school left no room for a negative reply from the common school board of trustees.[81] They had to obey the law.

The 1855 *Copies of Correspondence* printed only that correspondence which made Ryerson's administration of the school system shine in the eyes of his political masters. It was very self-serving and highly effective. But that is not the point. The six letters we have used in this section illustrate in a representative way the types of obstacles faced by Catholic trustees during the first bloom of their corporate existence in the 1850s. Of course, six letters do not make the whole story, but they give us a fair enough idea of the onerous duties Catholic trustees took upon themselves in order for their fellow Catholics to have separate schools.

****

Conflicts persisted and some trustees chose, from time to time, to air their grievances and opinions in the Catholic press, a friendly and receptive arena in which there was no fear of Ryerson's retorts. Charles Donlevy of the *Toronto Mirror* made this a regular feature of his paper. James G. Moylan of the *Canadian Freeman* followed suit. Two selections, one from each newspaper, will suffice to make our point that Catholic trustees were none too shy in attacking their political enemies. Trusteeship was one of the few platforms for aspiring Catholic politicians in nineteenth century Ontario. The more educated among the Catholic trustees tended to make the most of their special status in the Catholic community.

The first excerpt is taken from a letter signed "A Trustee" of the R.C. Separate School, Brantford, and is dated 8 February 1856. After spending the opening two paragraphs poking fun at the *Leader, Guardian, Herald* and *Globe* newspapers, he lodges his complaint:

A Catholic residing about two miles from this town (Brantford) gave notice to the Local Superintendent, according to law, before the 30th June last, that he was a supporter of the Roman Catholic Separate School, and would pay his taxes to it; but behold you! the Trustees of the Common School of the section in which he lives sued him a few days ago for taxes; and although the Trustees of the Separate School knew that the *spirit* and *letter* of the law were in their favor, and also the first proviso of the 12th section of the supplementary School Act, still it was considered useless to defend the case, inasmuch as the abettors of "godless schools" have power, by quibbling, to baffle the intention of the legislature, and to cheat Catholics of their rights. Moreover, the same man and another Catholic neighbor went, in January last, to give notice and get their certificates, in accordance with the amended School Act, from the Township Clerk, who is an able lawyer residing in Brantford, but were refused on the quibbles on which the abettors of Common Schools give to the words *"neighboring school section"* mentioned in the Separate School Act; also that a letter was received from Rev. Dr. Ryerson prohibiting the giving of such certificates. This man's taxes amounted to $16, of which, together with costs, the common school abettors have defrauded the separate school in which children are taught that if by counsel, by command, or even by silence, they become accessory to the neighbor's loss, they are bound to restitution. Then how can the *First Pastor* [the bishop] of this diocese, knowing such injustice towards Catholics, remain silent, and not forewarn electors to return members to the Provincial Parliament who will mete equal justice to Catholics. Now will the *Leader* consult the *Guardian*, and authorize the *Herald* to report to the *Globe* in what catalogue of mortal sins will the fraud of $16 be placed?[82]

Peter Murtagh, a trustee in St. Thomas, wrote a lengthy letter to the *Canadian Freeman*, dated 5 May 1862. We quote the part devoted to Egerton Ryerson's decisive intervention during Richard Scott's second attempt to carry a school bill through the legislature. Murtagh's frustration at Ryerson's power over the politicians is plainly evident. Catholic trustees from across the province were just as frustrated as Murtagh, during the 1860s, and their hatred of the chief superintendent was no less vitriolic. Murtagh wrote:

> Speaking of the Education Department, it will be impossible to disconnect the name of its Chief from that institution. In his annual ponderous Blue Book, which he is pleased to style a Report, arguments are set forth, and insinuations made against the principal advocates of Separate Schools. Not content with this mode of ventilating his

antipathy, at the public expense, he avails himself of the broad columns of the daily press and of his own official journal, to hurl forth his thundering mandates. No sooner had Mr. Scott introduced the Bill for the amendment of the law, than out comes the great Mogul himself, and pretending to vent his wrath at Mr. Brown, of the *Globe*, unmasks himself as an assailant of Mr. Scott and his Bill through the columns of the *Leader*.

The amendment before the House is not by any means liberal enough, yet the Chief Superintendent rises, as he says, from a sick bed, to oppose it and substitute one of his own, for confusion's sake. Nothing, in his opinion, can be sound, except he has a hand in the working of it. Think of the position this man assumes. He is at the head of a Department, without being responsible to the people — an anomaly in representative government. He dictates laws to parliament; and although not having formally a seat in Cabinet, is virtually a member of every administration in power, or, at least, dictator to them. If he were liberally and honestly inclined in the great work of Education, his own head-quarters at Toronto should be remodelled accordingly. In the staff of professors, teachers, secretaries and clerks, it is said he has not one Catholic employed. Is this the policy to exhibit fair play to those who are of right dissatisfied with his sectarian exclusiveness. He is the head and foot of every educational institution that affects the common classes of society. He stands on the might of his versatile goose quill, and the well-known redundancy of ephemeral logic he is so flatulently capable of exercising, to guff and intimidate people, and always pretends to be impartial. He will assert that there is no sectarianism in his system of mixed schools, but everyone knows this to be fallacious . . .[83]

Murtagh's trenchant criticism of Ryerson's unenthusiastic commentaries on separate schools was definitely valid. Samples of Ryerson's windy opinions can be found in his 1855 and 1858 annual reports and in his 1858 *Confidential Report to the Governor General*. Murtagh also had a point about Ryerson's seeming political invincibility. He served every government and was master of them all in educational matters. His will was law, and he felt no compunction in exerting his will. Murtagh, or any other trustee who vented his spleen in the press, was powerless to stop him. Not even the will of the Catholic people, as expressed in numerous petitions to parliament, could change the chief superintendent's attitude towards separate schools.

****

Between 1844 and 1866, Catholics submitted a host of petitions to the legislature on separate school matters. These petitions are strong evidence that the rank and file of the Church, regardless of their station in life, were just as interested in having their own schools as were their ecclesiastical leaders. In the vanguard of the various petition drives stood the trustees. Although the first names on petitions were not always identified as trustees, one would not be overreaching to assume that in many cases these names belonged to trustees, the leaders of the Catholic community on education. These names were mainly Irish in origin, with some Scottish, French, German and English, reflecting the nineteenth century Catholic settlement patterns in the provinces.[84]

Encouraged by their bishops and parish priests and urged on by Catholic newspaper editors, ordinary Catholics used petitions as the best means at their disposal to voice their grievances and demands. Depending on the year and the major grievance at hand, Catholics petitioned for a more equitable share of the legislative grant; amendments to the 19th section of the 1850 Act; amendments to the Supplementary Act of 1853; an equitable distribution of the funds arising from the sale of the Clergy Reserves; and, naturally, a law that would extend to the Catholic minority of Upper Canada the exact same educational rights and privileges lawfully enjoyed by the Protestant minority in Lower Canada. This last demand was a mainstay of Catholic thinking and a favourite of the bishops, who delivered their own petitions in 1854 and 1866.[85]

In 1859, more than 100,000 Catholics signed petitions in favour of far-reaching reforms that would have removed Catholic schools from Ryerson's supervision, facilitated the union of county school sections and provided for secondary schools and a normal school.[86] In 1865, Moylan's *Canadian Freeman* published a "Memorial of the Catholics of Upper Canada to the Executive and the two Branches of the Legislature in Parliament, assembled, respecting the Education of the Catholic minority."[87] Not to be outdone, the Catholics of Kingston held a giant meeting at the beginning of February 1865 and drew up their own petition and sent it to the House of Assembly. Since it encapsulates the grievances and demands of several decades of Catholic petition drives, it stands on its own merits:

> The Petition of the Roman Catholics of the City of Kingston Respectfully Sheweth –
>
> That the existing Separate School Law in Upper Canada is inadequate to the wants and purposes of Roman Catholics, and requires amendment.
>
> That your petitioners are desirous of having the law so amended as to secure to the Catholics of this section of the Province [Upper Canada] efficient schools and educational institutions.
>
> That in view of the Confederation of the British American Provinces, we believe it is the intention of the Government to protect the rights and privileges of the minorities both in Upper and Lower Canada in the maintenance of dissient schools by a constitutional enactment; we are therefore anxious that the Roman Catholics of Upper Canada should, like their Protestant fellow-subjects of Lower Canada, seek to obtain the sanction of the authorities to such a School Law as will secure the educational institutions of both minorities upon an equal footing.
>
> That the property of the Roman Catholics should not be

taxed for the support of Schools which they are not, from conscientious convictions, at liberty to send their children to.

That the Catholic Ratepayers should pay their School Tax to such schools as they may designate, whether they are residents of the Municipality or not; and that the school rate imposed on incorporated companies and public bodies composed of Catholic and Protestant shareholders should be divided in the same proportion as the governmental grant to schools.

That a Normal School should be established and endowed by the Government, distinct from the present Normal School at Toronto, for the training and instruction of Roman Catholic School Teachers; and that to secure the efficient working of the Separate Schools, a Catholic Council of Public Instruction should be established, and a Catholic Superintendent appointed to be in direct communication with the Government.

That the Nineteenth Section of the Separate School act of Upper Canada, 26 Victoria, Chapter 5, should be repealed, and the law amended so as to confer upon a Catholic Superintendent of Education, the power of defining the boundaries of Separate School Sections, as now possessed by Township Municipalities for defining and establishing the boundaries of Common School Sections in Upper Canada.

That the Catholic Colleges [secondary schools] in Upper Canada should be adequately endowed as Provincial Institutions, separate from any provision that may be made for Common Schools and that a Catholic University should be established and endowed in this section of the Province with like privileges, powers and advantages as the University of McGill in Lower Canada.

May it therefore please your Honorable House to grant adequate relief in the premises to your petitioners, and thereby secure to them under the new Constitution their civil and religious rights and privileges in the education of their children and the maintenance of their schools and seats of learning.[88]

The petition of Kingston's Catholics was fruitless. The only tangible benefit the province's Catholics did receive on the eve of Confederation was the entrenchment of the 1863 Scott Act as Section 93 of the British North America Act. However, as we have already recognized at the end of Chapter One, this single concession had large practical consequences. It meant no equality on educational rights with the Protestants of Lower Canada. Among other things, this translated into no government-funded Catholic high schools and no share for Catholic school boards in corporate or public utility taxes. Attempts to resolve these two issues would dominate separate school politics in the twentieth century.

****

In light of all this, an obvious question arises. What, then, did Catholic school trustees in Ontario accomplish between 1855, the year of the Taché Act, and 1899, at the close of the nineteenth century? The answer can be found in the official government statistics on separate schools. Catholic trustees may have had no influence on the content of legislation governing the existence and administration of the schools entrusted to them, but they had the power in law to build a system of Catholic education, one school at a time. This they did, with the generous financial support of the clergy, religious and laity.

There were three main sources of financial support for separate schools: the legislative grant for teachers' salaries; local tax on supporters (property tax); and subscriptions from supporters (voluntary donations from clergy and laity). For a brief period, there was also something called a rate bill, but that seems to have been folded into the local tax. Starting in the early 1860s, the government distributed additional money, taken from the Clergy Reserves Fund, for maps, apparatus, prizes and libraries. These grants were quite small, almost negligible, but were valued as a symbolic Catholic victory in the war over the disbursement of the proceeds from the Clergy Reserves.

Of the three main sources of revenue at the disposal of separate schools, property taxes generated the largest source of money. Voluntary subscriptions came second and the legislative grant was always a distant third. As time wore on, voluntary subscriptions were two to more than three times as much as the legislative grant. In other words, Catholics paid from their own pockets more than 80 percent of the cost of having their own schools, if one combines property taxes and voluntary subscriptions. Catholics proved false the old time-worn chestnut that Protestant money would have to pay for Catholic schools. Also, their generosity far outweighed the sum that any nineteenth century government was willing to give for Catholic schools. Having a right in law was one thing, but having the money to enjoy that right was another story.

Given that the separate schools were consistently cash-starved, what the trustees and Catholic ratepayers accomplished, between 1855 and 1899, was truly remarkable. Let us look at the following years — 1855, 1860, 1865, 1871, 1875, 1880, 1884, 1890 and 1899 — in these terms: the number of schools, teachers and students; the number of cities, towns, villages and school sections (townships) in which separate schools were located (in 1875, the tabulation changes from school sections to counties and incorporated villages); and the total revenue out of which the trustees had to pay teachers' salaries, purchase property and equipment and build and maintain school houses.

1855 — 41 schools, 57 teachers, 4,885 students; in 2 cities, 11 towns (including 2 town municipalities), 1 village and 23 school sections; total revenue £3, 445

1860 — 115 schools, 162 teachers, 14,708 students; in 5 cities (Toronto, Hamilton, Kingston, London and Ottawa), 22 towns, 8 villages and 52 school sections; total revenue $31,360

1865 — 152 schools, 209 teachers, 18,101 students; in 5 cities, 24 towns, 11 villages and 69 school sections; total revenue $46,219

1871 — 160 schools, 249 teachers, 21,206 students; [no location statistics for this year]; total revenue $69,818

1875 — 156 schools, 210 teachers, 22,673 students; [no location statistics for this year]; total revenue $90,626

1880 — 196 schools, 344 teachers, 25,311 students; in 9 cities, 31 towns and 31 counties and incorporated villages; total revenue $136,873

1884 — 207 schools, 427 teachers, 27,463 students; in 10 cities, 33 towns, 28 counties and incorporated villages and several districts; total revenue $190,045

1890 — 259 schools, 569 teachers, 34,571 students; in 11 cities; 33 towns, 30 counties and incorporated villages and several districts; total revenue $313,325

1899 — 352 schools, 764 teachers, 41,796 students; in 12 cities, 44 towns, 29 counties and incorporated villages and 2 districts; total revenue $401,154[89]

The Catholic Institutes

The Catholic Institute of Toronto and its branch institutes throughout the province flourished during the first half of the 1850s. Loosely modelled on the Catholic Institutes of England and on the province's Mechanics' Institutes, they acted as an excellent conduit of public political expression that was unabashedly Catholic in its membership, outlook and desires. They were the brainchild of the laity, the clergy being invited to participate only after the formation of the first Institute, and many members of these Institutes were also Catholic school trustees. Among the trustees were three people whom we have already encountered in this chapter: John Elmsley, Catholic convert; Charles Donlevy, newspaper editor; and Peter Murtagh, St. Thomas school trustee. Murtagh was secretary of the Catholic Institute of London and a frequent lecturer to its members.[90]

The first Catholic Institute was founded in Toronto on 20 August 1851. Between three and four hundred Catholics packed the schoolhouse on Stanley Street. They passed three resolutions and elected their first executive: Charles Robertson, president; C. Donlevy, vice-president; M.S. McCoy, secretary; and M.P. Hayes, treasurer. They also chose a committee of management. They were

Denis Hefferman, Francis O'Connell, Angus McDonnell, Peter J. O'Neil, P.F. Kavanagh, Francis Sullivan, Bernard Cosgrove, William Halley, Robert O'Brien, J. Hallinan, John Shea, D.K. Feehan, W.J. McDonnell, Clement Kane and Patrick Doyle.[91] In the preamble to their "Rules and Regulations," we find the stated objectives of the Institute:

> The object of the Catholic Institute is UNITY AMONG CATHOLICS – for the establishment and protection of their civil and religious rights and privileges – sound religious and secular instruction of their youth – the encouragement of Public Lectures – the formation of Libraries and Reading Rooms – the extension of useful knowledge, and the attainment of that position in the community to which their number and influence entitle them.[92]

In addition to educating their fellow Catholics by sponsoring public lectures, libraries and reading rooms, the Institute wanted to stake out political territory for Catholics as a community so that they could act as a unified body of political opinion on those issues directly affecting them. In the minds of the Institute's founders, it was a political necessity that Catholic electors speak with one voice at election time and reject those politicians who were anti-Catholic or worse, played up to Catholic electors only to abandon them once the election was over. In their quest for unity, the Toronto Institute published an address to their co-religionists of Canada West, in September 1851, explaining the goals and organization of the Institute and urging Catholics to form their own local branches.[93] The address achieved impressive results in a short period of time. By 21 March 1852, Catholics had organized Institutes in Kingston, London, Hamilton, Guelph, Pembroke, Niagara, Lindsay, Peterborough, St. Thomas, Sandwich, Bytown and Perth.[94]

Predominant among the political concerns of the Institute was the status of separate schools. To pressure politicians to amend legislation concerning Catholic educational rights, the different Institutes, with Toronto usually taking the lead, sponsored large public meetings, at which Catholic electors were urged to vote only for those candidates favourably disposed towards separate schools, even if that meant abandoning the Reform Party; spearheaded petition drives; and drew up resolutions that were later published in Catholic newspapers for the political edification of their fellow Catholics.

As the election of November-December 1851 neared, many Institutes addressed the Catholic electors of their respective ridings. The address of the Guelph Institute to the Catholic Electors of the County of Waterloo, dated 17 November 1851, was typical. It spoke of the religious liberties in education which Catholics as British subjects enjoyed, of the imminent threat to the entire system of separate schools, posed by politicians determined to secularize public education, and of the respective positions of the two candidates on the subject of separate schools. The Institute was careful not to tell Catholic electors how to vote. Such advice would have brought criticism upon the local Catholic community. The address reads:

It is not unknown to you that the most active and untiring exertions are now making throughout the Province, by parties inimical to the faith we inherited from our forefathers, to deprive us of privileges we have for many years enjoyed, and of which we cannot now be deprived without a virtual breach of that religious liberty possessed by us as British subjects. As the School Law has for many years existed, Catholics, and Members of other Religious denominations, are permitted, when they have conscientious objections to the Teachers, or to the mode of tuition adopted in the Common Schools of their respective localities, under certain restrictions to retain their School Rates to establish and maintain Separate Schools. A cry has been got up in certain quarters against this system, and a determination exhibited to put down these so-called Sectarian Schools, and to compel Catholics to pay their proportion of School Rates and Taxes, whether they send their children to the Common Schools or not — thus compelling them, under such circumstances, to pay for the education of the children of

Protestants in the Common Schools, while their own children must either be educated at their own charges, or remain entirely destitute of education. Catholics desire no privileges as members of the State, but such as they are heartily willing to grant to all their fellow subjects; but they will not succumb to a system which would rob them of their money, or cause them to violate their conscience. Two candidates are now in the field solicitating your Suffrages as Representatives for the County of Waterloo. Mr. Fergusson, the late Member, is pledged to put down Sectarian Schools, and so to strike at our religious liberties; Mr. Wright pledges himself to maintain the law as it now is, and to secure to us the right we have hitherto enjoyed. Fellow Catholics, it now rests with you to exercise your elective franchise according to the best of your judgment, without any dictation from this Society.[95]

Despite the Guelph Institute's efforts to influence the outcome of the Waterloo election, Adam Johnston Fergusson won the seat.

In May 1852, the Toronto Institute passed a resolution demanding that Catholics have a right to elect their own school trustees.[96] In August, it directed a province-wide petition that asked the legislature to pass an explanatory statute that would clear up the many ambiguities in the 1850 Act. These ambiguities, it was alleged, allowed hostile common school trustees and municipal authorities to make decisions harmful to the welfare of separate schools. The Toronto Institute cited the fact that although Catholics were one-fourth the population of the city, in 1852, they received from the Board of School Trustees only one-twelfth of the money applicable for school purposes.[97] This was manifestly unfair. In 1854, the problem was the Supplementary Act of 1853. That too was found woefully inadequate. Its language was open to all sorts of distortion and misdirection by parties prejudiced against an application of the school law that would benefit separate school supporters.[98] Another pressing issue was the equitable distribution of the funds arising from the Clergy Reserves. Toronto and Perth submitted petitions on the matter to the legislature.[99]

After the passing of the 1855 Taché Act, the public work of the Catholic Institutes on behalf of separate schools seems to have slowly declined. Perhaps many Catholics felt that the 1855 legislation answered their prayers or were too worn out from the agitation of previous years to sustain the fight. There are newspaper references to the activities of the Institutes in Perth, London, St. Thomas and St. Catharines but not to the same degree as witnessed from 1851 to 1854. The Toronto Institute is mentioned in an 1857 editorial in the *True Witness*, which called for the abolition of the whole common school system.[100] It appears, though, that the Toronto Institute collapsed near the end of the 1850s. The sudden death of Charles Donlevy may have been a decisive factor in its demise. The Toronto Institute was reconstituted in 1860 under Bishop John Lynch and Father John Walsh. But the membership was small, and Bishop Lynch's insistence that it be strictly non-political made sure that it never recaptured the spirit the Institute enjoyed in its early years. Another distinctly Catholic organization like the Institute would not come on the scene until the formation of the Ontario Catholic League in December 1870.[101]

Catholic School Inspectors

Until 1882, Protestant school inspectors were in charge of inspecting Roman Catholic separate schools. High school inspectors were given the task in cities and towns, and if needed, county inspectors assisted them; in the townships and incorporated villages, where the majority of separate schools were located, county inspectors were responsible for the inspections. In many instances, these inspectors were Protestant clergymen. This was an annoyance and sometimes an humiliation for Catholics. On occasion, confrontations arose.

In 1865, the Christian Brothers in Kingston refused to allow Reverend George Paxton Young, the high school inspector, into their classrooms without first obtaining the permission of Bishop Edward John Horan. This earned the bishop and the brothers a strong rebuke from Egerton Ryerson, who was quite correct to point out to them that

130

according to the law the right to appoint school inspectors lay with the chief superintendent and not with the teachers, trustees or bishops.[102]

Another incident occurred in 1871. "To our great amazement," wrote Archbishop Lynch of Toronto, "we find that our separate schools are visited by the Inspectors of the Common Schools." He continued: "We take this occasion to protest against this intrusion, as it is contrary to the spirit of the Law establishing Separate Schools; and we will be obliged to give notice to the Trustees not to receive those visits; not that we are afraid of them, but we do not want their interference."[103]

As a member of the Council of Public Instruction and as the Catholic school superintendent in Toronto, Lynch should not have been so astonished to learn that there were no Catholic inspectors for Catholic schools. For his part, Ryerson answered Lynch much the same way as he had answered Horan — that the law governing school inspectors must be obeyed and that it was his responsibility to enforce the law. That said, one wonders if Ryerson had ever appointed Catholics to the position of school inspector or encouraged county councils to do so. One can only conclude that if he had made such a move, he would have trumped his Catholic critics with it. It appears that he did not trust Catholics to inspect their own school and that this lack of trust had become so well-entrenched as policy that it survived his own administration for six years.

This was unfortunate because if Catholic separate schools were ever to improve themselves, any criticisms of their many shortcomings would have to come from Catholics in positions of authority within the educational system. In other words, it would have to be Catholic self-criticism. Time would prove the truth of this assertion. Self-criticism was the only avenue by which Catholics would put aside their suspicion of legitimate criticism, simply because it came from Protestants, and overcome the self-destructive inertia that such suspicion bred in the management of their schools.

A rare example of Catholic criticism of separate schools appeared in the *Globe*, in a letter of 21 August 1877. Of course, the *Globe* had its own agenda for publishing it, and, moreover, the letter was signed Don Pedro McPatrick, an obvious pseudonym. But the letter is interesting, despite its trenchant tone and generalizations, because the many deficiencies it highlights would later surface in the early Catholic inspection reports and even play a role in the secret ballot uproar of 1888.

The writer of the letter, who must have been a Catholic, made a number of powerful claims: that separate schools produced few scholars worthy of the name, that many Catholic parents sent their children to separate schools only for first holy communion and confirmation, after which the parents removed them to the public schools, and that few religious or even lay teachers held teaching certificates issued after 1871. "Furthermore," he writes, "not being subject to inspection, the [teachers] have no incentive to self-improvement or the advancement of their pupils. All the Superintendent looks for is a good religious instruction, and if satisfactory the teacher and pupils get any amount of praise for their learning. Those who deny these statements will please inform the public how many qualified teachers are employed at present in the cities of Ottawa, Kingston, Belleville, Toronto, Hamilton, St. Catharines, Brantford, and London."[104]

McPatrick devoted the second half of his letter to an attack on Brother Arnold and the Christian Brothers in Toronto. He asked them a rhetorical question: how many qualified teachers, lawyers, doctors, civil engineers and provincial land surveyors had the Brothers produced after twenty-seven years running the city's separate schools. Their alleged failure in this regard proved, as far as McPatrick was concerned, that the system had failed Catholic children and had lost its significance.

The separate schools carried on, as we have seen, but something quite daring had to be done to save them from becoming hopelessly mediocre. That happened in 1882, when the provincial government created a new position in the ministry of education: Catholic inspector of Catholic separate schools. This radical departure from past practice rested on the rather bold assumption that only Catholics should act as inspectors of Catholic schools. It was unheard of in Ryerson's day but was long overdue and found its fulfillment in the brilliant career of the man who assumed the enormous burden of breathing new life into Catholic education as the nineteenth century came to a close.

No better qualified person than James Francis White could have been chosen as Ontario's first Catholic inspector of Catholic separate schools. Born in Trenton, Ontario, on 18 November 1857, White was the son of James White and Ellen Maloney. He was a rarity among his generation of Catholic students for having attended high school. Even rarer was his winning the coveted Dufferin Gold Medal when he graduated from the Toronto Normal School, at seventeen years of age, and his earning a 1st Class Provincial Certificate. Talented and ambitious, White quickly climbed the teaching ladder and became the principal of the separate school in Brockville and then in Lindsay. He was a school inspector from 1882 to 1903, the year he was appointed principal of the Ottawa Normal School. He helped to prepare various textbooks for use in the separate schools and was the author of "Separate School Law and the Separate Schools of the Archdiocese," which appeared in *Jubilee Volume of the Archdiocese of Toronto*. In 1905, the University of Ottawa conferred on him an honourary LLD.[105]

For his inaugural report on separate schools, dated December 1882, White travelled 500 miles by horse-drawn carriage and 4,500 miles by rail or water, from Windsor in the south to Mattawa in the north and to the eastern boundary of the province, with the exception of Haldimand, Durham, Dundas and Russell, which did not have separate schools. Alone, he inspected 135 schools, 266 teachers and 19,783 children and planned to visit the remaining 58 schools and 115 teachers over a two-month period beginning in April 1883. No wonder he asked for an assistant!

White did not mince words. His 1882 report is frank and forceful in its revelations, judgments and suggestions. He commented on financial conditions, the lighting, heating and ventilation of school houses, the urgent need to use only authorized textbooks, the enforcement of the 1879 regulations governing Quebec teaching certificates, the different methods whereby reading, grammar and history were taught, the general work of separate schools and widespread parental indifference to their children's regular school attendance. He ended by providing a comparative table showing the significant difference in the cost of education between separate schools and common schools.

On the precarious financial condition of separate schools in rural areas, White wrote that "From year to year they lead a struggling existence, but there is no guarantee of their permanency. Many seem in danger of extinction at the end of each year, for their supporters of one year may next year pay their taxes to a Public School. Often where a few persons have made a brave struggle to establish a school, and have taxed themselves heavily to maintain it, the withdrawal of a few supporters has caused it to die out."[106] It would take several more decades for this unfortunate tendency to run its baleful course. Until then, the lack of consistent financial support would plague the smaller schools in the countryside.

White was firm in his demand that the government enforce the 1879 school law amendments on Quebec teaching certificates. Only those obtained before the passing of the BNA Act in 1867 were valid:

> Of the thirty-four teachers in our schools having Quebec certificates, but very few obtained them previous to 1867. There are two principal reasons why these certificates should not be recognized here. So low is the standard for examinations, that a First Class Certificate from that Province ranks scarcely equal to a Third from our own. Attendance at a training school and the passing of a professional examination, are not requisite before obtaining a certificate. Thus it results that most of these teachers have no system of teaching except that which each one evolves for himself. The inspection of their schools proved that many of them are totally unqualified for their positions. Their examinations were passed in Quebec, solely because it is a matter of no difficulty to obtain a certificate there. In favour of schools requiring French teachers, provision may be made that persons holding Quebec certificates be legally qualified for such positions. But in schools engaging English-speaking teachers, none but those having certificates obtained in this

Province should be considered qualified.[107]

This was harsh and uncompromising criticism of the poor training of teachers in Quebec as much it was of those separate schools in Ontario who hired them. At the same time, though, White was careful to point out to the minister of education that "where conditions have been at all equal for the two systems, Separate Schools show results in no way inferior to those of the Public Schools."[108] But achieving equality was elusive. Separate schools had far less money than the public schools to spend on their students. In three categories — Counties, Cities and Towns — the public schools were able to spend $5.70, $9.30 and $6.20, respectively, for an average expenditure of $6.02 per student. Meanwhile, their poorer cousins, the separate schools, were able to spend only $4.70, $4.78 and $5.66, respectively, for an average expenditure of $4.99 per student. The largest gap in spending between the two systems occurred in cities. There the public schools were able to spend $4.52 more per student than the separate schools.[109]

In his 1883 report, besides the standard array of concerns, White wrote of the absolute necessity for a Manual of School Law as the best means to deal with any lingering doubts about the status and operations of Catholic separate schools, which had plagued Catholic trustees for the better part of forty years.

There is wide-spread ignorance of Separate School law, and frequently its provisions are not observed . . . because of the difficulty of determining what *are* its requirements. In the compendiums now used, the Separate School law is given in some half-dozen pages, and for fuller information and guidance on many points, reference is made to certain provisions of the Public Schools Act which apply. This of itself is confusing enough; but the greatest difficulty is experienced when matters are to be settled of which no special mention has been made in either of these places. Such cases are not easily settled without the trouble and expense attendant on a decision of one of the courts. The Hon. the

Minister would confer a great boon on trustees and other officers of Separate Schools by issuing a special manual containing full provisions for their guidance, together with decisions thus far rendered on disputed points.[110]

White concluded his second report with an urgent plea for the better training of teachers. More of them had to take advantage of the lectures and training provided by the Normal Schools. "At the expense of a few extra dollars," White wrote by way of admonition, "trustees, supported by parents, should *insist* that they whose delicate and difficult task is to develop the intelligence and mould the character of children, shall have the special training *absolutely indispensable* for its proper performance."[111] The fact that there had been improvements of late in teaching methods in separate schools did not mitigate the need for "harsh and severe criticisms" if further improvements were to be realized.

In 1884, White received an assistant inspector, Cornelius Donovan, MA, from the University of Toronto.[112] The two men divided the province between them, with Donovan visiting the schools north and west of Toronto and White taking the schools in the rest of the province. Donovan was also unsparing in his pointed criticism of the many shortfalls in the schools he inspected, but he concluded his first report with words that should have alarmed White, his superior:

> On a general view of the situation, the friends and supporters of the Roman Catholic Separate Schools have reason to feel proud of their system: it was founded under difficulties that would have prevented the existence of many others and it has been maintained amid trials that would have caused others to perish. When we consider the struggles sustained, in years gone by, for rights and privileges; and how very few of the schools are to-day in positions of abundant wealth; the wonder is — not that the system now rests on a solid foundation, not that the Separate Schools of Ontario are, generally speaking, in a flourishing condition — but that they have *any* existence at all. All honour to the clergy who have

bestowed their time, their labour and the contents of their slender purses unsparingly, towards establishing, maintaining and forwarding their respective schools; all honour to the religious teachers who have been devoting their lives and talents, without any personal remuneration, to the noble purpose of a plan of education founded and conducted on Christian principles.[113]

Besides forgetting to mention the trustees and parents, without whom separate schools could not have existed, Donovan's congratulatory flourish was full of unintended irony. James F. White for one did not want separate schools to rest on their laurels. It was not enough to have survived. Having Catholic inspectors for Catholic schools was the catalyst for much needed reform. If school trustees and Catholic ratepayers failed to reform their schools in all aspects of their administration, from teacher training to uniform textbooks to properly built schoolhouses, separate schools would crumble from within and Catholics would only have themselves to blame. Although Donovan was to prove himself a very able school inspector, a real boon to improving separate schools, he seemed to be blissfully unaware, at least in 1884, that separate school supporters wanted more than idle boasting about having survived Ryerson and company. They wanted more lay control of the school system and were willing to play hardball politics to get it.

The struggle over control of the Toronto Separate School Board had taken place in 1878, six years before Donovan's report, and the battle over the secret ballot for separate school board elections reached a crescendo in 1888, four years afterwards. In both confrontations, Catholic trustees, regardless of where they stood on either issue, displayed a vigor and independence which in the long run would help to ensure the continued growth and betterment of the province's Catholic separate schools.

The Toronto Separate School Board, 1876-1879
The years 1876 to 1879 were a watershed in the history of the

Toronto Separate School Board and by extension in the collective history of separate school boards throughout the province. After more than a decade of relative calm and prosperity for separate school supporters, these years witnessed the first sustained threat to the intrinsically paradoxical nature of Catholic school management. "The Separate School Board," writes historian Brian Clarke, "was a public institution in which the laity had a role on the local level as parents, taxpayers, and school trustees, and at the same time a religious institution that was tied to the Catholic Church's structures of authority."[114] In whose hands, then, did authority over Catholic separate schools reside? It was a question that begged for an answer, but when it was finally asked, it provoked a nasty and very public quarrel among Catholics never before seen in Toronto.

According to Archbishop Lynch, since Catholic education was primarily a religious affair, the direction of separate schools fell within the magisterium of the Church. The primary duty of the lay trustees was to assist the clergy and to obey their directives. It was the clergy who had real authority over the religious *and* intellectual formation of Catholic children. This point of view was shared not only by the clergy, as one would suspect, but also by many lay Catholics, who were in the habit of following their pastors. It had worked well during the period that that produced the Scott Act of 1863, but it was bound to lose its moral legitimacy as soon as separate schools were left on their own to survive within a specific legal framework guaranteed by the constitution. It also had practical consequences peculiar to separate schools that were fated to look old-fashioned as the century wore on. It was not unusual for priests to step out of the pulpit and perform duties unconnected to their sacerdotal calling. They collected property taxes, stood for election as trustees and were present in force at the polling stations on voting day, making sure that candidates who stood by the archbishop were elected. Of course, they did not always succeed, but the sight of three or four priests at a polling station was often enough to convince the electors, who voted by a public show of hands, to side with the "clerical party." Defying the clergy took courage and was done only when the stakes were high; voting in a member of "lay party" was almost an act of rebellion.

The dissident trustees never questioned the rightful place of the clergy in the religious formation of Catholic children. Nor did they question the right of priests to be trustees. Even the most radical of the dissidents could not imagine separate school boards without priest trustees. However, they also believed that the priest as trustee had no more authority than any other trustee and that lay members were more than mere "yes-men" to the clergy. In the minds of the dissidents, differences of opinion on school matters, between clerical and lay members of the board, did not involve faith or morals, and consequently their resolution was not subject to Church authority but to debate and voting at school board meetings. In the final analysis, they wanted to implement sound financial practices for the schools and believed that this could be accomplished only if the laity took charge of the school board. Catholic schools, as poor as they were, belonged to all Catholic ratepayers and needed their own school-oriented bureaucracy, independent of church government, in order to manage their increasingly complex affairs. The dissidents challenged assumptions and past practices and in the process incurred the wrath of the archbishop himself, who was no slouch when it came to political brinkmanship. Lynch would win the battle, but victory would elude him because his flock was changing. Middle-class Catholics had few avenues of political activity in the 1870s and 1880s. A number of them openly embraced separate school politics as a rare opportunity to exercise leadership within the Catholic community. Their desire to take a lead in the governance of separate schools, an institution funded by their taxes, reflected a maturity and self-confidence that the clergy and their conservative lay supporters found unsettling, to say the least.

In the first flush of the post-Ryerson period in education, a group of Catholic trustees in Toronto fell afoul of Archbishop Lynch when they sought to clarify and limit the role of the archbishop and his priests in the management of the city's separate schools. So many and so complex were the issues raised by the dissidents, especially during the tumultuous year of 1878, that it would be best to list them:

1) the renewal of leases on land owned by the Episcopal Corporation but used for school purposes
2) the ownership of school buildings
3) the archbishop in his role as superintendent of schools
4) the manner in which school board elections were conducted
5) full disclosure of separate school receipts and expenditures from 1863 to 1878
6) charges that the Episcopal Corporation misspent school funds
7) the call for the secret ballot in trustee elections
8) the lack of school inspectors
9) the qualifications and salaries of teachers
10) the absence of a standard set of text books for classroom use
11) scholarships for students

The Toronto Separate School Board was in danger of imploding. There were too many contentious issues confronting it. Self-destruction was always at hand. Large crowds of curious Catholics attended the biweekly board meetings at St. John's Hall and took sides, some cheering on the clerical party and others the lay or dissident party, to the unfeigned delight of the newspaper reporters. Proceedings were often marred by shouts, laughter, angry words, charges and counter-charges, hot denials, hisses and boos and personal attacks. Partisanship was evident in nearly every utterance. Motives were questioned. The clergy were on the defensive and looked weak. Many meetings began in disorder and ended in total confusion.

The conflict began quietly. In a letter dated 16 March 1876, Remigius Elmsley, the chairman of the separate school board, asked Archbishop Lynch for a complete record of the Episcopal Corporation's administration of school property.[115] All but one separate school in the city was situated on land leased from the archdiocese, a situation that left the school board vulnerable. It hoped to embark upon an ambitious building program but was unsure if

Lynch would give them long-term leases. Particularly irritating to Elmsley was the use of a good deal of the Richmond Street property for purposes other than education. Situated on the property when Lynch arrived in Toronto in 1859 were a school, an orphanage, a home for respectable women called Notre Dame and run by the Sisters of St. Joseph and a rent-paying tavern. Lynch moved the orphanage to the House of Providence but had turned it into a residence for the Christian Brothers and defended the existence of Notre Dame. By 1876, the school was in disrepair and far too small to accommodate all the Catholic children who should have been attending it.

Remigius "Remy" Elmsley was the son of John Elmsley, who had built the city's first Catholic school on the Richmond Street property, in 1841, and who also had assisted in the erection of the orphanage there.[116] No one, least of all Lynch, missed the irony of Remy being the one to fire the first salvo in what became a war of words that started over a piece of property that had been overseen for many years by Remy's father.

Lynch replied to Elmsley in a letter of 1 April 1876. He insisted that the school board had no legal claim to the Richmond Street property. It had been acquired by Bishop Macdonell in 1829 and re-deeded to Bishop Power in 1846 for the Episcopal Corporation. That might have ended the matter except that the query about Richmond Street led to one about the archbishop's handling of school funds up to 1876, when they were finally handed over to the board, and his refusal to give a detailed financial statement. Father Francis Patrick Rooney, the vicar general, vetoed any further discussion, forcing Elmsley into a minority position and a temporary retreat.

The retreat lasted until November 1877. Having been silenced at the board, Elmsley and his allies petitioned Bishop George Conroy, the Apostolic Delegate. It was a remarkable document, detailing the miserable state of four of the city's separate schools and the paltry pay of the teachers and accusing the archbishop of misappropriating the equivalent of $1,200 in school funds and demoting the trustees to nominal status.[117] The petition had no effect. It died on Conroy's desk.

In addition to Elmsley, signatories to the petition were Thomas

Devine, chairman of the board in 1877, George Evans, Joseph Power, John Marvyn, James E. Robertson and W.J. Smith. These were the dissident trustees. Evans, Power and Robertson continued as members of the 1878 board. Three became four when Joseph J. Walsh joined their ranks. In the May 1878 by-elections, only Power and Walsh were returned. Elmsley was centre stage in the August 1878 meeting of Toronto's Catholic élite with Archbishop Lynch concerning the separate school financial statement, and he would run for re-election to the board in 1879. However diminished in number the dissidents may have been during the ensuing controversy, they still managed to convince the archbishop's supporters on the board to strike committees on the Richmond Street property and the school board finances for the past fifteen years and to force Lynch to submit a superintendent's report and to treat their opposition seriously. Little did the dissidents know just how determined the archbishop would be to crush them.

The first clash between Archbishop Lynch and the lay faction took place immediately after the January 1878 elections. In five wards, two sets of trustees had been chosen. The dissident trustees had organized polling stations at fire halls, where a municipal official recorded the outcomes. In his capacity as local superintendent, Lynch voided the results of those elections and only accepted those candidates chosen at schoolhouse polling stations, where the clergy were present. In retaliation, J.E. Robertson moved that the board hire Francis J. Taylor, an education department official, as superintendent. This was an open insult to Lynch. Taylor had no idea that he had been nominated, the motion failed, and round one went to Lynch.[118]

The next round also went to the archbishop. At a meeting of 3 April 1878, Robertson, Evans, Power and Walsh resigned from the board. Evans said that "there were influences at work in the Board detrimental to the interests of Catholic education. The fact was that lay members had no power of control in the Board."[119] The by-election took place on 16 May. Roberston and Evans lost in St. Patrick's Ward and St. Stephen's Ward, respectively, but Power and Walsh were returned as the two trustees for St. George's Ward.

Heard loud and clear during the electioneering was the editorial

142

voice of Patrick Boyle of the *Irish Canadian*. Boyle was no friend of Archbishop Lynch. He had earned Lynch's enmity in 1876 when he attacked Christopher Findlay Fraser, the most important Catholic politician in Premier Oliver Mowat's Liberal government.[120] Lynch responded by denouncing Boyle and pressuring his parish priests to cancel their subscriptions to his newspaper.[121] Two years later, an unrepentant Boyle threw his support behind the candidacies of the dissenting trustees. For the benefit of his Catholic readership, he drew a line separating the role of archbishop from that of superintendent and the role of priest from that of trustee:

> Between the Priest and the Trustee, between the Archbishop and the Superintendent, we certainly draw very broad distinctions; and in doing so in the case of the Separate Schools, public institutions sustained by special taxes levied according to law on ourself and our co-religionists, we but stand in a respectful though determined assertion of our right as a Catholic ratepayer and Catholic parent . . . once chosen for office under the Law, they [the trustees] stand in reference to that office outside their sacred character, subject as officers to praise or blame according to their acts, like other citizens elected by popular suffrage to a public trust.[122]

This plea to the levelling nature of the democratic process was akin to heresy in Catholic circles and was a direct challenge to the manner in which the clergy exercised their authority in the administrative affairs of the school board. Boyle continued by spelling out the reform agenda:

> An improvement in the quality of the schooling, a more business like, earnest and vigorous administration of the business, a full and properly vouched system of accounting for the funds, a recovery of the Richmond Street property for the benefit of the children, are all at stake in the pending election. These facts pointing plainly to a duty which it is sheer nonsense, if not downright wickedness, to say involves

any violation of proper respect for his Grace the Archbishop, we avoid any aggravation of the unnecessary, and indeed improper, passions which exist on the subject, by discharging our duty in the premises with the simple declaration that the existence of the Separate Schools and the suppression of religious scandal, unite in a call on every Catholic ratepayer of St. Patrick's, St. George's and St. Stephen's Wards, to go to the polls next Thursday; and as an act of solemn duty to cast his vote for those gentlemen who have been so faithful to the cause of the Catholic children of the City — Messrs. Robertson, Evan, Power and Walsh.[123]

The results were not to Boyle's liking. Disgusted, he published lengthy reports on the polling in each ward and found Frank C. Flannery's defeat of James E. Robertson in St. Patrick's Ward particularly galling. Martin Murphy had proposed Robertson and Alex Macdonell had seconded the nomination:

Mr. Murphy said he had proposed Mr. Robertson on the occasion of his election [in January 1878]; and having since then watched his conduct in the School Board, he saw no reason to regret the course he had adopted. He entirely approved of everything his nominee had done as Trustee for St. Patrick's Ward. The influences at work against his re-election were terribly strong. The most popular Priest in the city had canvassed one end of the Ward, while another Priest had done his best in the other, to defeat Mr. Robertson. Not satisfied with using every fair means to accomplish their object, his opponents had consented to slander his fair name. They had reported that he desired to get rid of the Brothers and Sisters as teachers, to make way for lay teachers. They gave him credit for having made an attempt to entirely sweep away the Schools. They even went so far as to make him responsible for the writing of certain letters to Mr. Flannery's employer, Alderman Hughes, requiring him to compel Mr. Flannery to withdraw his candidature, and threatening, in the event of his neglect or refusal, to oppose Mr. Hughes whenever he presented himself for the suffrages of his fellow citizens . . .

Mr. Flannery denied that he had charged his opponent with the writing of the letters, all he had stated being that they were written by Mr. Robertson's friends. It was not true the popular priest referred to by Mr. Murphy had used influence on his (Mr. Flannery's) behalf. He merely introduced him to the electors, never asking anyone to vote for him in preference to his opponent.

The Rev. Father [Patrick] Conway desired to say he was present in behalf of Father [Joseph M.] Laurent, who was unavoidably absent. He was authorized by that gentleman to state that he had never asked any one to vote for Mr. Flannery in preference to Mr. Robertson, and that he had never said a single word detrimental to Mr. Robertson's character.

A poll was then demanded by two electors, and was opened. The excitement during the day was at times quite lively, especially about one 'o'clock, when it was announced the vote was a tie. Cab-loads of women were brought in during the day, Mr. Flannery polling about 85 of them to Mr. Robertson's 4. A very large proportion of the votes cast were objected to on various grounds. At the close of the poll the vote stood: Flannery, 105; Robertson, 89. Mr. Flannery was zealously assisted by Fathers Conway, Laurent and Rooney, while his opponent had the services of several energetic laymen. If it be true that the 194 who voted, with over 60 who failed to show up, are all supporters of the Separate Schools, the taxes collected would appear very much less than they should be.[124]

Boyle continued his campaign. In a three-column editorial of 5 June 1878, he demanded that the Richmond Street property be conveyed unconditionally to the school board; he chided electioneering priests; and he claimed that the board had paid $758 to repair the old convent at St. Mary's and then another $525 to remove the sisters. These were but two examples, Boyle wrote, of the school board's misuse of funds earmarked specifically for the education of Catholic children.[125]

It was Archbishop Lynch's turn to reply. In fact, he had already begun his countermoves. He had submitted his superintendent's report, as requested, on 3 April 1878, which included conciliatory noises on the Richmond Street property.[126] In anticipation of the May by-election, he had conducted a well organized tour of Toronto's separate schools, on 10 May, in the presence of Adam Crooks, the minister of education, loyal trustees and several prominent clergymen. It was brilliant public relations.[127] Next, Lynch wrote a long-winded explanatory letter to the Apostolic Delegate, dated 24 May 1878, in which he denounced trustees Robertson, Smith, Evans, Power and Walsh.[128] Now, in response to Boyle's allegations of 5 June 1878, Lynch sent the following letter to the *Globe*:

> Finding that for some time past grave charges have been made and published against the management of the funds of the separate schools of Toronto, we hereby declare that there has been no misappropriation so far as we can learn; but on the contrary, the Episcopal Corporation and the clergy of the city, since the establishment of the Catholic schools in 1851, have contributed thousands of dollars towards the building and maintenance of said schools.[129]

Boyle was unimpressed. He thought that the archbishop's words were too qualified to amount to anything substantially true. The remaining dissidents on the school board, meanwhile, continued to press for long-term leases to church property used by the board and for a legal opinion on the title to the Richmond Street property. The board meetings of 23 and 30 July 1878 failed to resolve anything on either issue.[130]

The initiative returned to Archbishop Lynch. On Sunday, 28 July 1878, he ascended the pulpit of St. Michael's cathedral and blasted his critics on the board and in the press. Controversial though it was, this move paid handsome dividends for the archbishop. "A certain number of men got on the School Board," Lynch declared to the assembled, "and they commenced a sort of Government Opposition tactics to run down and declare all was wrong in the past, and called for all the accounts for fifteen years, indirectly accusing the Bishop, Priests, and Catholic Trustees of managing the Separate School dishonestly. This was resisted and justly so."[131] He called these men people of "very little religion" and "wolves in sheep's clothing" whose behaviour was so shameful it was scandalizing honest Protestants! He spoke at length about the ten thousand dollars the Episcopal Corporation and clergy had donated to the schools since 1851 and about the leases and the Richmond Street property. He also denied that he had withheld any relevant documents from the special committee struck in April 1878 to examine the last fifteen years of the board's financial transactions.[132]

When Lynch directed his remarks to the editor of "a certain paper in this city" he was obviously referring to Patrick Boyle:

> A certain paper in this city is repeating day after day, for the last two months, that we are keeping back the accounts, because if we gave them the character of the Episcopal Corporation would be ruined. It has been written to the editor officially that the Investigating Committee have all the vouchers, receipts, etc., in their hands. But when you find a Protestant paper taking such an active part in vilifying the Bishop and Priests, it is hardly necessary to put you on your guard against those persistent wholesale lies. A bad feature in this nefarious proceeding is that a few bad Catholics are supplying these untruths. These men have a fair face to me, but their names have been given to me. They are doing their utmost for sinister purposes of their own to damage my character and that of the priests, but they have overshot their mark, and they will not succeed.[133]

How far the archbishop's critics had overshot their mark was shown at a special meeting Lynch called for Monday evening, 7 August 1878. Gathered at St. Michael's Palace were approximately sixty of Toronto's foremost Catholics, including the Hon. Frank Smith, Eugene O'Keefe, John O'Donohoe and Thomas McCrosson, publisher of the *Tribune*. Absent was Patrick Boyle, the *bête noir* of the entire affair. Not in attendance as well were any former or current dissident trustees, save one. Remy Elmsley accepted the archbishop's invitation.

The primary purpose of the meeting was to have Bishop Jean-François Jamot, Lynch's former vicar general, read and explain an official statement of receipts and expenditures for the city's separate schools, from August 1863 to December 1873. The statement's bottom line showed that the trustees owed the Episcopal Corporation in excess of $3,000! This was Lynch's trump card in the response to the much ballyhooed charge of malfeasance.

There was only one dissenting voice at the palace that night. It belonged to Remy Elmsley. He objected not so much to the statement's conclusion as he did to its having been made public well in advance of the school board's own investigations. To John O'Donohoe's motion, seconded by Eugene O'Keefe, that the meeting accept Bishop Jamot's financial statement, Elmsley proposed an amendment, seconded by W.J. Smith, that the meeting adjourn for two weeks so that the school board committee could table its own findings. Elmsley did not want the archbishop to upstage the school board in an investigative process that properly belonged in the hands of a board-appointed committee. This tense exchange followed:

> Mr. O'Donohoe said this meeting had nothing to do with the report that was to come. The meeting was one to consider a question affecting the entire Catholic body and the integrity of their clergy.
>
> Mr. Elmsley said his Grace had consented to an investigation on the receipts and expenditures of the School Board for past years. He had allowed the Committee access to the books in order to get the particulars. He was therefore a party to the Committee, and the speaker thought, in justice to the gentlemen who composed that Committee, and in justice to the Archbishop himself, that the report which these

gentlemen were about to submit ought to be brought down and submitted to the Catholic body of Toronto before they passed any opinion on the matter. They (the people) had heard one side; let them hear the other. Let them in justice to the gentlemen he had named hear the report, and then, if they were of the same opinion as the present meeting, let them adopt Mr. O'Donohoe's resolution. Then the matter would be hushed forever; but first let them get a full return. The real question was, had all the money been paid out for the benefit of their schools? An instance he thought was to the contrary was the payment of $700 to the sisters of St. Mary's for repairs to their home. The reason given for this outlay was that the nuns had been asked to take little children while their mothers were at work; they had complied with this, and the little ones were kept in a room of the sister's building till the mothers came for them. This had been put down as a Separate School work, and the $700 so expended was charged to the St. Mary's school account. This was one of the instances which the Committee would report.

Bishop Jamot said that the sisters who had thus got their house repaired only received $200 a year for teaching, and the Episcopal corporation could not do otherwise than furnish them with shelter and keep their houses in repair . . .

Archbishop Lynch said that Mr. Elmsley in stating that he (the Archbishop) had consented to the appointment of the Committee, had hardly put the matter correctly. He did not think he had been consulted about it. He did not think it was fair to go behind the public record of 1874. It was not business-like; such a course was never followed out in any commercial corporation. He had intended at first not to invite any of the trustees to the meeting, as it might embarrass them in their subsequent proceedings. Representations to the contrary, however, having been made to him, he had changed his mind, and had invited them to attend merely as Catholics. He was acting on the principle now that when one's house was on fire one should put it out as soon as possible. The trustees could act as they saw fit.[134]

Elmsley was obliged to withdraw his amendment and the motion passed.

If Remy Elmsley was trying to buy time for the school board committee to produce a statement contrary to Bishop Jamot's, he would have been sorely disappointed when the committee submitted its report on 15 October 1878. It found in favour of the Episcopal Corporation, agreeing that the board owed money to the corporation.[135] There the matter died. The school board turned its attention to the Richmond Street property. Only Patrick Boyle found fault with the report, but his sound and fury signified nothing but irritation.[136] The archbishop had the last word in a circular of 9 December 1878, which was read from every pulpit in Ontario.[137]

Archbishop Lynch and Remy Elmsley had one more confrontation. It took place after the 8 January 1879 school elections. Elmsley was one of four candidates returned as trustees by the municipal returning officer. Elmsley was declared the winner in St. John's Ward. The three other reformers were Albert J. Furniss, St. James's Ward, J.E. Costello, St. Thomas's Ward and Michael Walsh, St. Andrew's Ward.[138] Lynch, in his capacity as local superintendent, voided their election. This time, though, the archbishop went one step further. Afraid that Elmsley might take the case to court, Lynch ordered Father Charles Vincent, the parish priest at St. Basil's, to deny Elmsley absolution. This forced Elmsley to choose between what he called his rights as a citizen and his faith. He chose his Catholicism but under strong protest. Having humbled Elmsley, the archbishop then took to the pulpit on Sunday, 12 January and denounced "bad men" who were harming Catholic schools and attacking the Church.[139]

Archbishop Lynch had vanquished his enemies and was now ready to deal with the Richmond Street fiasco. The matter was settled in June 1879, to the satisfaction of the trustees and brought a measure of peace. Oddly enough, this was predicted by Patrick Boyle as early as June 1878, when he wrote that the proper conveyance of the property to the school trustees would remove "that bone of contention by which the clergy are separated in this School business from the rate-payers and parents."[140]

Despite the utter defeat of the dissidents, who could not elect even one member for the 1879 board, the Richmond Street resolution was really a victory in the struggle for lay control of the Toronto Separate School Board. The old haphazard ways of doing board business were passing. Clerical domination of the board would also end. Bishop John Walsh of London sensed a solution to the scandal of clerical/lay divisions on the Toronto board when he suggested to Archbishop Lynch, in a letter of 2 December 1878, that he should foster the election of loyal laymen rather than his priests.[141] Lynch ignored the advice, but the passage of time would prove the wisdom of Walsh's suggestion.

The Secret Ballot, 1888

The battle over the introduction of the secret ballot in separate school elections was another defining moment in the history of the gradual laicization of the Toronto Separate School Board. Since its political complexity mirrors in many respects that of the 1878 battle between Archbishop Lynch and dissident trustees, we are precluded from discussing 1888 in any detail. Franklin Walker devotes a full and entertaining chapter to the controversy, in *Catholic Education and Politics in Ontario*, and Brian Clarke gives a masterful interpretation of the secret ballot agitation within the context of Irish Catholic nationalism, in *Piety and Nationalism*.

For our purposes, we note that the secret ballot was not introduced for provincial and municipal elections until 1874 and that Premier Oliver Mowat did not do the same for separate school trustee elections out of deference to his good friend, Archbishop Lynch. The secret ballot was still very much a novelty when trustees W.J. Smith and J.E. Robertson called for its implementation in early 1878.[143] In February 1879, 140 Catholics signed a petition asking for the ballot. This ignited a series of petitions and counter-petitions to the legislature that carried on into January 1883.

On one side stood Archbishop Lynch, the major ecclesiastical player. He opposed the ballot for several reasons: one, he thought that honest people had no reason to hide their votes, and two, he said that "Catholic education is essentially a religious affair to be managed with judgment and economy by the clergy, assisted by good

Catholics."[144] It was the same line of reasoning he had used ten years earlier — the laity were subordinate to the clergy in the ongoing administration of the separate schools. The archbishop feared that the secret ballot would destroy clerical control and eventually the school system itself. He was correct about the loss of clerical control but groundless about the viability of separate schools managed by trustees elected by secret ballot. Similar to Egerton Ryerson's mistrust of Catholics inspecting Catholic schools, Lynch simply did not have enough faith in the Catholic laity to entrust them with the management of separate schools. Moreover, he was inclined to believe that politically ambitious laymen looked at membership on the school board as a means to line their own pockets or to advance the cause of Irish nationalism.

On the other side was Daniel P. Cahill, a Toronto manufacturer and secretary of the Irish National League. Cahill treated separate school elections as civic affairs, not as religious events, and he thought that the secret ballot, already in use for more than a dozen years, would be a more just and efficient way to conduct elections. Cahill himself was elected to the school board in January 1888. He was joined by five other Irish nationalists.

As soon as one of them, D. Kelly, proposed that the board petition the legislature for the secret ballot, Archbishop Lynch responded in full force, with a series of circular and pastoral letters, a campaign of private letters soliciting support, the suspension of two priests for taking a pro-ballot stance — Father Denis Morris and Father John Laurence Hand — and direct intervention in an April 1888 by-election in St. Andrew's Ward. Determined to win at all costs, Lynch chose the Hon. Timothy Warren Anglin to be his candidate. Anglin was a well known Irish Catholic heavyweight and a former speaker of the House of Commons. His opponent was Samuel Dunbar, secretary of the Toronto Plasterers' Union. Lynch and his vicar general, Father Rooney, publicly attacked Dunbar to great effect and called out their supporters in the St. Vincent de Paul Society and among the Catholic women voters, also to great effect. Anglin won a landslide victory, 175 to 90.

It was to be Archbishop Lynch's final battle. He died on 12 May

1888. His supporters on the separate school board made sure that the pro-ballot trustees, including Cahill, were defeated in the 1890 election. However, it was another Pyrrhic victory for the old politics. Four years later, The Separate Schools Act was amended to allow boards the option of a secret ballot.[145] Responsible for the legislation was James Conmee, the Liberal member from Algoma West and one of the few Catholics in the legislature.[146]

---

[1] *Canadian Freeman*, 20 December 1866, 2.

[2] Biographical material on John Elmsley is taken from the following sources: "Elmsley, John," *DCB*, 9: 239-42; "Elmsley, John," *New Catholic Encyclopedia* [hereafter *NCE*] (Washington, D.C.: Catholic University of America, 1967), 5: 286-87; Brother Alfred [A.J. Dooner], "The Honourable John Elmsley: Legislative and Executive Councillor of Upper Canada (1801-1863)," CCHA *Report* (1936-37): 23-40; Murray W. Nicolson, "John Elmsley and the Rise of Irish Catholic Social Action in Victorian Toronto," CCHA, *Historical Studies* (1984): 47-66.

[3] *Toronto Mirror* [hereafter *Mirror*], 27 December 1839, 3.

[4] An excellent re-telling of this whole complicated episode can be found in Nicolson, "John Elmsley and the Rise of Irish Catholic Social Action in Victorian Toronto," 49-57.

[5] Murray W. Nicolson, "The Catholic Church and the Irish in Victorian Toronto" (Ph.D. diss., University of Guelph, 1980), 382.

[6] *Canadian Freeman*, 14 May 1863, 2: "Death of the Honorable Captain Elmsley."

[7] "Tellier, Remi-Joseph," *Dictionary of Jesuit Biography: Ministry to English Canada*, 1842-1987 (Toronto: Canadian Institute of Jesuit Studies, 1991), 333.

[8] "Elmsley, John," *DCB*, 9: 241; *Jubilee Volume of the Archdiocese of Toronto*, 153.

[9] *Jubilee Volume of the Archdiocese of Toronto*, ix.

[10] Kelly, *The Story of St. Paul's Parish, Toronto*, 82-83.

[11] Nicolson, "John Elmsley and the Rise of Irish Catholic Social Action in Victorian Toronto," 66.

[12] Reprinted in the *Mirror*, 4 April 1856, 3.

[13] *Mirror*, 27 January 1854, 3.

[14] Ibid., 23 September 3.

[15] According to J. Ross Robertson, the Catholic Church owned a large tract of land at the corner of Nelson (Jarvis) and New (Richmond) streets, which extended westward along the south side of Richmond Street. The school was located on a portion of this property. The front was on Richmond Street and the gables were facing east and west. See *Robertson's Landmarks of Toronto: A Collection of Historical Sketches of the Old Town of York from 1792 until 1833, and of Toronto from 1834 to 1893* [Vol. 1] (Toronto: J. Ross Robertson, 1894), 124-26. See also Brother Alfred, "The Honourable John Elmsley," 33.

[16] *Mirror*, 29 January 1858, 3.

[17] Ibid., 12 May 1854, 2

[18] Walker, *Catholic Education and Politics in Ontario*, 2: 42.

[19] Nicolson, "The Catholic Church and the Irish in Victorian Toronto," 384.

[20] ARCAT, LB03.030. Bishop Charbonnel to John Elmsley, thanking him for his support of Toronto's Catholic schools, 9 February 1851.

[21] *Globe*, 3 September 1844, 2.

[22] Ibid.

[23] Ibid.

[24] Hodgins, *Documentary History of Education in Upper Canada*, 5: 156.

[25] Walker, *Catholic Education and Politics in Upper Canada*, 99.

[26] Ibid., 72-73; originally appeared in the *Banner*, 10 December 1847.

[27] *Globe*, 14 June 1848.

[28] ARCAT, C AE01.03. Letter of John Elmsley and S.G. Lynn to Bishop Charbonnel, 10 October 1850.

[29] *Copies of Correspondence* (1855), 59-60.

[30] Ibid., 60.

[31] Ibid., 62.

[32] Ibid.

[33] Ibid., 64.

[34] Ibid., 66-77.

[35] *True Witness and Catholic Chronicle* [hereafter *True Witness*], 28 March 1856, 5. The letter was also reproduced in the *Mirror*, 21 March 1856.

[36] Ibid., 16 January 1857, 4-5.

[37] Walker, *Catholic Education and Politics in Upper Canada*, 186-87.

[38] See Neil Gregor Smith, "Religious Tensions in Pre-Confederation Politics," *Canadian Journal of Theology* 9 (October, 1963): 248-62.

[39] "Donlevy, Charles," *DCB,* 8: 228-31.

[40] Ibid., 228-29.

[41] Franklin A. Walker, "The Political Opinion of Upper Canadian Catholics," CCHA *Report*, 22 (1955), 83.

[42] *Mirror*, 13 February 1839, 3; 8 September 1843, 3.

[43] Ibid., 5 June 1846, 3.

[44] Ibid., 14 March 1845, 3; 8 August 1845, 3.

[45] Ibid., 3 October 1845, 2.

[46] Ibid., 21 January 1848, 2; 24 March 1848, 3.

[47] Ibid., 12 May 1848, 2.

[48] Ibid., 26 July 1850, 2-3.

[49] Ibid., 3 April 1857, 2.

[50] Ibid., 24 January 1851, 3; 30 May 1851, 3; 15 August 1851, 3.

[51] Ibid., 8 August, 1851, 3.

[52] Ibid., 15 August 1851, 3.

[53] For Charbonnel, see *Mirror*, 31 December 1852, 2; 7 January 1853, 3; 15 July 1853, 3; 11 November 1853, 3; 21 July 1854, 3; for Bruyère, see *Mirror*, 4 April 1856, 3; for Carroll, see *Mirror*, 2 April 1852, 3; 9 April 1852, 2; 23 April 1852, 2.

[54] *Mirror*, 15 February 1856, 2; 7 March 1856, 1; 4 April 1856, 2; 31 October 1856, 2.

[55] Ibid., 12 May 1854, 2.

[56] Ibid., 21 May 1852, 3; 20 August 1852, 2; 10 September 1852, 3.

[57] Ibid., 4 September 1857, 3; 1 October 1852, 2.

[58] Ibid., 30 January 1857, 2.

[59] "Moylan, James George," *DCB,* 13: 742-45.

[60] *Canadian Freeman*, 1 May 1862, 2.

[61] Ibid., 22 May 1862, 2.

[62] Ibid., 8 May 1862, 2; 22 May 1862, 2.

[63] Ibid., 8 May 1862, 2.

[64] As quoted in the *Canadian Freeman*, 31 July 1862, 2.

[65] *Canadian Freeman*, 31 July 1862, 2.

[66] Ibid., 30 March 1865, 2.

[67] Ibid.

[68] Ibid.

[69] Ibid., 9 February 1865, 2.

[70] Ibid.

[71] Ibid., 9 August 1866, 2.

[72] "McCrosson, Thomas," *DCB*, 13: 620-21.

[73] "Clerk, George Edward," *DCB,* 10: 174-76; Agnes Coffey, "George Edward Clerk, Founder of the 'True Witness': A Pioneer of Catholic Action," CCHA, *Report* (1934-35): 46-59.

[74] Gerald J. Stortz, "The Irish Catholic Press in Toronto, 1874-1887," CCHA *Study Sessions*, 47 (1980): 41-56; Mark G. McGowan, *The Waning of the Green: Catholics, the Irish and Identity in Toronto*, 1887-1922 (Montreal & Kingston: McGill-Queen's University Press, 1999), Chapter Six.

[75] *Copies of Correspondence* (1855), 126.

[76] Ibid., 127.

[77] AO, RG 2-19, Box 1. "Roman Catholic Separate School Trustees Annual Reports and Semi-Annual Attendance Returns 1852-71," Brockville, 1854.

[78] *Copies of Correspondence* (1855), 135.

[79] Ibid., 136.

[80] Ibid., 153.

[81] Ibid., 153-54.

[82] *Mirror*, 15 February 1856, 3.

[83] *Canadian Freeman*, 22 May 1862, 2.

[84] Petitions and names of petitioners can be located in the following sources: prior to 1852, see Hodgins, *Documentary History of Education in Upper Canada*, 5: 156, 8: 110, and 9: 1; and *Journals of the Legislative Assembly of the Province of Canada*, 26 vols. (Ottawa: Hunter, Rose & Co., 1842-1866), 9: 28, 69, 127; 10: 102; for 1852 and following, see *Journals of the Legislative Assembly of the Province of Canada, 1852-1866: General Index* (Ottawa: Hunter, Rose & Co., 1867), 15, 16, 210, 227, 344.

[85] *Journals of the Legislative Assembly of the Province of Canada, Session 1854-5*, 13: 236-37; Ibid., *Session 1866*, 24: 293-94.

[86] Walker, *Catholic Education and Politics in Upper Canada*, 246-49; *Canadian Freeman*, 11 February 1859, 2; 1 April 1858, 2; 31 July 1862, 2.

[87] *Canadian Freeman*, 26 January 1865, 2.

[88] Ibid., 16 February 1865, 1-2.

[89] Egerton Ryerson, *Annual Report of the Normal, Model, Grammar, and Common Schools in Upper Canada for the Year 1855* (Toronto: John Lovell, 1856), Table G; Ibid., *Annual Report of the Normal, Model, Grammar, and Common Schools in Upper Canada for the Year 1860* (Quebec: Hunter, Rose & Co., 1861), Table F; Ibid.,

Annual Report of the Normal, Model, Grammar and Common Schools in Upper Canada for the Year 1865 (Ottawa: Hunter, Rose & Co., 1866), Table F; Ibid., *Annual Report of the Normal, Model, High and Public Schools of Ontario for the Year 1871* (Toronto: Hunter, Rose & Co., 1873), Table F; Minister of Education, *Annual Report of the Normal, Model, High and Public Schools of Ontario for the Year 1875* (Toronto: Hunter, Rose & Co. 1877), Table F; *Report of the Minister of Education (Ontario), for the Years 1880 and 1881* (Toronto: C. Blackett Robinson, 1882), Table F; *Report of the Minister of Education (Ontario) for the Year 1885* (Toronto: Warwick & Sons, 1886), Table F; *Report of the Minister of Education (Ontario) for the Year 1891* (Toronto: Warwick & Sons, 1891), xx, Table F; *Report of the Minister of Education (Ontario) for the Year 1900* (Toronto: L.K. Cameron, 1901), vii, Table F.

[90] Elmsley was treasurer of the Toronto Catholic Institute in 1853, see *Mirror*, 23 September 1853, 2; Donlevy was vice-president of the Institute and a mover of a resolution at the October meeting, see *Mirror*, 22 August 1851, 3 and 10 October 1851, 2; Murtagh's name appears at least four times in the *Mirror*, 21 November 1851, 3; 3 January 1852, 3; 23 January 1852, 3 (full text of lecture); 9 April 1852, 3.

[91] *Mirror*, 8 August 1851, 3; 22 August 1851, 2.

[92] ARCAT, C AC0202, "Rules and Regulations of the Catholic Institute, Toronto, C.W."

[93] *Mirror*, 26 September 1851, 3.

[94] Ibid., 15 October 1852, 3.

[95] Ibid., 28 November 1851, 3.

[96] Ibid., 21 May 1852, 3.

[97] Ibid., 13 August 1852, 2.

[98] Ibid., 5 May 1854, 3.

[99] *Journals of the Legislative Assembly of the Province of Canada Session 1854-5*, 13: 84, 212.

[100] *True Witness*, 4 December 1857, 4.

[101] *Canadian Freeman*, 2 August 1871, 2.

[102] Hodgins, *Documentary History of Education in Upper Canada*, 19: 9-11.

[103] Ibid., 23: 158.

[104] *Globe*, 24 August 1877, 2.

[105] Henry James Morgan, *The Canadian Men and Women of the Time*, 2nd ed. (Toronto: William Briggs, 1912), 1159; *Globe*, 22 May 1922, 14, 15; *Catholic Register*, 1 June 1922, 8 and 8 June 1922, 2; J. Castell Hopkins, *The Canadian Annual Review of Public Affairs 1922* (Toronto: Canadian Review Company, 1923), 902; burial records from Mount Hope Cemetery, Toronto.

[106] *Report of the Minister of Education (Ontario) 1882* (Toronto: C. Blackett Robinson, 1883), 131.

[107] Ibid., 133.

[108] Ibid., 135.

[109] Ibid.

[110] *Report of the Minister of Education (Ontario) for the Year 1883* (Toronto: C. Blackett Robinson, 1884), 135.

[111] Ibid., 137.

[112] "Donovan, Cornelius," *Dictionary of Hamilton Biography* (Hamilton: Dictionary of Hamilton Biography, 1981), 1: 63.

[113] *Report of the Minister of Education (Ontario) for the Year 1884* (Toronto: "Grip" Printing, 1885), 160.

[114] Brian P. Clarke, *Piety and Nationalism: Lay Voluntary Associations and the Creation of an Irish-Catholic Community in Toronto, 1850-1895* (Montreal & Kingston: McGill-Queen's University Press, 1993), 219.

[115] Franklin Walker gives an excellent account of the controversy. See *Walker, Catholic Education and Politics in Ontario*, 2: Chapter Two. The newspapers covered separate school board meetings in great detail. See the *Globe, The Evening Telegram, Canadian Freeman* and *The Tribune*.

[116] "Mr. Remy Elmsley Dead," an obituary in the *Globe*, 16 September 1910, 8.

[117] Walker, *Catholic Education and Politics in Ontario*, 2: 32-33.

[118] *Globe*, 16 January 1878, 4.

[119] Ibid., 4 April 1878, 4.

[120] "Boyle, Patrick," *DCB*, 13: 106-8.

[121] ARCAT, L TA01.28. Letter from Archbishop John Joseph Lynch to P. Boyle, 7 December 1876; LAH2119. Circular Letter of Archbishop John Joseph Lynch to Whom it may concern, 6 December 1876.

[122] *Irish Canadian*, 15 May 1878, 4.

[123] Ibid.

[124] Ibid., 22 May 1878, 4.

[125] Ibid., 5 June 1878, 4.

[126] *Globe*, 4 April 1878, 4

[127] Ibid., 11 May 1878, 3; *Irish Canadian*, 15 May 1878, 2.

[128] Walker, *Catholic Education and Politics in Ontario*, 2: 44-45.

[129] *Globe*, 8 June 1878, 4; *Irish Canadian*, 12 June 1878, 4; *The Tribune*, 14 June 1878, 4.

[130] *Irish Canadian*, 31 July 1878, 7.

[131] *The Tribune*, 2 August 1878, 4.

[132] *Globe*, 4 April 1878, 4. The committee was composed of Father Thomas J. Morris, Father Patrick Conway, C.B. Doherty and W.J. Smith.

[133] *The Tribune*, 2 August 1878, 4.

[134] *Globe*, 8 August 1878, 4; *Irish Canadian*, 14 August 1878, 3; *The Tribune*, 16 August 1878, 2.

[135] *Globe*, 16 October 1878, 4.

[136] *Irish Canadian*, 23 October 1878, 4.

[137] Walker, *Catholic Education and Politics in Ontario*, 2: 52-54.

[138] *Globe*, 9 January 1879, 4.

[139] Walker, *Catholic Education and Politics in Ontario*, 2: 55-56.

[140] *Irish Canadian*, 5 June 1878, 4.

[141] ARCAT, L A021.11. Bishop John Walsh to Archbishop John Joseph Lynch, 2 December 1878.

[142] Walker, *Catholic Education and Politics in Ontario*, 2: Chapter Three; Clarke, *Piety and Nationalism*, 245-49.

[143] *Globe*, 20 February 1878, 4 and 7 March 1878, 4.

[144] As quoted in Clarke, *Piety and Nationalism*, 246.

[145] "An Act to Amend the Separate Schools Act" (1894, *Statutes of Ontario*, c. 59).

[146] "Conmee, James," *DCB,* 14: 229-31.

**Bishop Alexander Macdonell
(1762-1840)**
*Courtesy Archives of the R.C.
Archdiocese of Toronto (ARCAT)*

**Bishop Michael Power
(1804-1847)**
*Courtesy Archives of the R.C.
Archdiocese of Toronto (ARCAT)*

**Bishop Armand-François-Marie
de Charbonnel
(1802-1891)**
*Courtesy Archives of the R.C.
Archdiocese of Toronto (ARCAT)*

**Archbishop John Joseph Lynch
(1816-1888)**
*Courtesy Archives of the R.C.
Archdiocese of Toronto (ARCAT)*

**Egerton Ryerson
(1803-1882)**
*Credit: J. George Hodgins,
Schools and Colleges in Ontario,
1792-1910, v. 3, p. 76*

**George Brown
(1818-1880)**
*Credit: Canada: An Encyclopedia of
the Country, v. 5, p. 197*

**John Elmsley
(1801-1863)**
*Courtesy Archives of the R.C.
Archdiocese of Toronto (ARCAT)*

**Sir Richard William Scott
(1825-1913)**
*Courtesy Archives of Ontario
(S 218)*

**Sir Oliver Mowat (1820-1903)
Premier of Ontario,
1872 to 1896**

**Adam Crooks (1827-1885)
First Minister of Education,
1877-1883**

To the Catholic Electors of St. David's Ward
Toronto Mirror, 7 July 1854, p. 3

CATHOLIC SCHOOL NOTICE.

Meetings of the Catholic Ratepayers of the several Wards of this City, will be held at the undermentioned places, on Wednesday next, the 13th instant, at ten o'clock in the forenoon, for the purpose of electing trustees of the Roman Catholic Separate Schools for the year 1858:

In the Ward of St. David, St. Paul's School House.

Ward of St. Lawrence—Richmond-Street-East School House.

Ward of St. James—Stanley-Street School House.

Ward of St. John—Richmond-Street-West School House.

Ward of St. Andrew—Do. do.

Ward of St. Patrick—St. Mary's School House.

Ward of St. George—Do. do.

By order of the Board of Trustees,

J. ELMSLEY, Secretary.

Toronto, 7th January, 1857.

A TEACHER WANTED

FOR NICHOL ROMAN CATHOLIC SE-PARATE SCHOOL No. 1. Salary in accordance with the times. None need apply but those of good testimonials as regards character and ability; if by letter post-paid, addressed to the Rev. F. Dumortier.

CORNELIUS O'CALLAGHAN,
JOHN GREENE,
Trustees.

Direct Thorpville P. O., C. W.

TEACHER WANTED.

WANTED FOR THE FEMALE department of the Perth Separate School, a Female Teacher, holding a first class certificate ann good testimonials, to take charge 1st January, 1868.

W. WALSH,

-543tf   Secretary.

SCHOOL WANTED.

IMMEDIATELY by a young man, who holds a Second-Class certificate, having seven years' experience in teaching in Canada; can produce the highest testimonials, from clergymen and trustees. Address, post-paid, " J., Teacher, Hamilton, P. O."

Teacher Wanted,
Perth, Ontario
Canadian Freeman
17 December 1868, p. 3

REPORT—*Continued.*

THE *UNDERSIGNED* hereby declare that the above Report has been compiled in accordance with the *General Instructions* on the back, and that it contains a true and full account of ALL MONEYS RECEIVED for the use of their Separate School during the year ending 31st December, 186 , and of the EXPENDITURE thereof, and of ALL OTHER MATTERS stated in said Report, to the best of their knowledge and belief.

Dated this ___ day of *January* ___ 186 7

William Kelly

Joseph X Mignaud
    mark

John X Rivers
    his mark

Peter Doran *Teacher.* *Second* class Certificate or Religious order.

Trustees of the Roman Catholic Separate School in Common School Section

No. 3 & 4

Township of *Anderdon*

Anderdon

given by the Essex County Board

If the Trustees have a proper Corporate Seal, which is now by law indispensable, one may be obtained through the Education Office, Toronto, for $5.

Assistant Teacher. ___ class Certificate or Religious Order.

ilar manner. This Report to be sent to the Local Superintendent not later than the 15th January, 186 .

**Annual Return of the Separate School in School Sections 3 and 4
Anderdon Township, Essex County, 11 January 1867.
Two out of the three trustees could not sign their names.**
Courtesy Archives of Ontario RG 2-19, Box 1

Roman Catholic
Separate School,
Preston, 1889

Separate School, Paris, 1910

St. Mary's Roman Catholic School, Bathurst Street, Toronto, c. 1890s
Credit: John R. Teefy, ed., Jubilee Volume: The Archdiocese of Toronto, 1842-1892

Separate School, Glenbournie, Frontenac County, 1878-1946
Credit: L.J. Flynn, At School in Kingston 1859-1973, p. 49

St. Peter's School, London, 1902, Sister Carmel Moylan, CSJ
Courtesy Archives Mount St. Joseph London

St. Martin's School, London, Grades 7 and 8, Sister Assumption Healy, CSJ, (c. 1948-1952)
Courtesy Archives Mount St. Joseph London

Teaching New Canadians to Read, St. Peter's School, London, Sister Cajetan Dorresteyn, CSJ (c. 1948-1956)
Courtesy Archives Mount St. Joseph London

Art Class, Windsor, Sister Mary Perpetual Help Dufour, CSJ (c. 1965-1973)
Courtesy Archives Mount St. Joseph London

St. Paul's School, Girls' Class, Toronto, c. 1900
Courtesy Archives of the R.C. Archdiocese of Toronto (ARCAT)

St. Gertrude's School, Oshawa, Grade 8 Graduating Class, June 1964
Courtesy Sisters of St. Joseph Toronto Archives

Oshawa Catholic High School, First Graduating Class, September 1966
Courtesy Sisters of St. Joseph Toronto Archives

St. James' School, Colgan, Staff, 1967
Courtesy Sisters of St. Joseph Toronto Archives

Sister Stephanie Sinkewicz, CSJ,
Courtesy Sisters of St. Joseph Toronto Archives, Catholic Register, 9 November 1968

**Mother Ignatia Lynn, IBVM
(1836-1912)**
*Courtesy Institute of the Blessed
Virgin Mary Archives North America*

**Eucharistic Crusade,
St. Cecelia's School,
Toronto, c. 1960
Sister Victor Dudgeon,
IBVM, Principal,
1956-1964**
*Courtesy Institute of the
Blessed Virgin Mary
Archives North America*

**St. Joseph School,
Stratford, Sister
Rosemary Smith,
Principal, c. 1965**
*Courtesy Institute of the
Blessed Virgin Mary
Archives North America*

Archbishop Neil McNeil
(1851-1934)
Courtesy Archives of the R.C.
Archdiocese of Toronto (ARCAT)

Bishop Michael Francis Fallon
(1867-1931)

Cardinal James Charles McGuigan
(1894-1974)
Courtesy Archives of the R.C.
Archdiocese of Toronto (ARCAT)

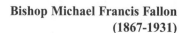

Mitch Hepburn (Right),
Premier of Ontario, 1934-1942
Courtesy: John T. Saywell

Martin J. Quinn,
Catholic Taxpayers' Association

John P. Robarts,
Minister of Education, 1959

**William G. Davis,
Minister of Education, 1963**

**Bishop Joseph F. Ryan
(1897-1973)**
*Courtesy Diocese of Hamilton
Archives*

**Monsignor Vincent Priester,
First Executive Director,
English Catholic Education
Association of Ontario (ECEAO)**

Elect
FR. FOGARTY
Metro Toronto Separate School Board
TO
OSSTA

Father Patrick H. Fogarty, CSC, Second Executive Director,
English Catholic Education Association (ECEAO)

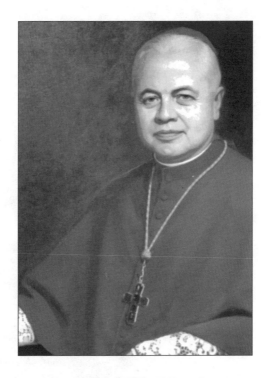

Archbishop Philip F. Pocock
(1906-1984)
Courtesy Archives of the R.C. Archdiocese of Toronto (ARCAT)

**Cardinal G. Emmett Carter
(b. 1912)**
*Photo Credit: Peter Caton/
Gerald Campbell Studios*

**Sean Conway
Minister of Education, 1985**

A LIVING ENDOWMENT:
RELIGIOUS TEACHERS

Introduction

$\mathcal{O}$n the first two chapters, we dealt with a selection of nineteenth-century bishops, laymen and school trustees in their decades-long struggle to establish Catholic separate schools. They did so by means of lobbying, legislation and amendments to the law and then by making sure that their educational rights were entrenched in the British North America Act. As soon as the bishops and their lay allies had secured the constitutional status of Catholic separate schools, they sought to place them on a more solid and long-term financial footing, one that would guarantee their schools' ability to flourish in step with the Catholic community as it grew and prospered. Politics, personalities, confrontations and the legislative history of separate schools were the main ingredients of these chapters. Also examined was the quiet and steady work of local trustees. Rarely recognized outside their own communities, these ordinary folk were the leaven of a slowly emerging province-wide separate school system.

However, school trustees, even those in Toronto, were sorely limited in their ability to foster separate schools by the political and practical realities of the day. The reason for this was as simple as it was unappetizing. The Catholic hierarchy and its lay allies in the secular world, no matter how politically adept they might have been, were far more successful in entrenching Catholic schools in law than they ever were in convincing the province's politicians to fund these schools according to the legitimate needs of the Catholic children who attended them. The prevailing political and cultural mentality agreed, albeit grudgingly, that Catholics had a right in law to separate schools but also that this right was a very limited one and that Catholic separate schools would have to function on a starvation diet of local property taxes and puny legislative grants.

How, then, did Catholics in Ontario manage to have 352 schools, 764 teachers and almost 42,000 pupils, by 1899?[1] This was no mean feat. By the close of the nineteenth century — thirty-seven years after the passage of the Scott Act — it was evident to both friend and foe of Catholic education that the existence of Catholic separate schools would not end as Egerton Ryerson had often predicted in his annual reports. But Ryerson was hardly a fool. He understood that no combination of bishops, priests, politicians, school trustees, lay teachers and parents could keep separate schools alive as a system for more than a generation, given the paltry amount of public money at their disposal. The relative poverty of Catholic taxpayers and legislative requirements, it was commonly believed, would wear down the patience of Catholic ratepayers. Ryerson's prediction, then, should have come true well in advance of his own retirement. But it obviously did not. Why?

The answer lies in the Counter Reformation invention of active Religious communities of men and women who lived according to vows and worked in the world outside the cloister, and this invention's profound manifestation in Ontario at the same time that universal publicly-funded elementary education was becoming the norm in North America. The Methodist Egerton Ryerson, for all his worldly experience and political power, could hardly have foreseen the flowering of this kind of Catholic Religious life in the province that took root in the mid nineteenth century and that would come into full bloom in the middle of the next century. Nor could Ryerson, even as czar of education, have predicted the extraordinary degree to which so many Religious communities would devote themselves to teaching separate school children.

The participation of Religious in Catholic education took on a dynamic of its own. The steadying and unifying presence of so many Religious teachers in separate schools, over such a long period of time, working for salaries well below the prevailing rates of pay, saved

Catholic elementary education from extinction. Without the selfless devotion of thousands of Sisters and hundreds of Brothers, whose vocation was to teach, there would be no Catholic separate schools today in Ontario.[2] Some might reply that there still would have been Catholic schools, most likely along the American parochial model, but they would have been far fewer in number. As a result, popular Catholic culture would have been quite different from that which was experienced by no fewer than five generations of the province's Catholics. This statement is far more than just a bromide nostalgically repeated by the last generation of Catholics to be taught by nuns. Every Catholic should treat it as a significant historical fact, one worth celebrating and examining in some detail.

This chapter is divided into five sections: A Portrait of Service; Sisters of St. Joseph; Ladies of Loretto; the Grey Sisters of the Cross; and the Teacher Certification Crisis.

A Portrait of Service

In this section, we will make some overall statements on the presence of Religious communities in Catholic separate schools. Included in our discussion will be lists of all those communities that supplied teachers. Our time frame is one hundred and twenty-five years, from 1850 to 1975. Following this, we will present some statistics concerning Religious teachers in the separate schools of the archdioceses of Toronto and Ottawa and of the dioceses of Hamilton and London, for the years 1915, 1935, 1946, 1960, 1970 and 1975.

It is our hope that this chapter, as brief and impressionistic as it is, will serve as a timely introduction to a field of study largely ignored by historians and unknown by the average Catholic, and that it will also be a springboard for others to pursue a more in-depth exploration of the topic of Religious teachers in separate schools.

****

Of the utmost importance for Catholics to realize and appreciate is that Religious teachers came from many different Religious communities, and that they left their mark in practically every major Catholic corner of the province. The number of Religious communities who provided teachers may come as a surprise to many people. There were no fewer than forty-seven of them.[3] They taught in separate schools in every diocese, archdiocese and vicar apostolic in Ontario, at one time or another, to varying degrees of commitment in terms of personnel, years of service and the number of schools and dioceses in which they served. The Religious commitment to Catholic elementary education was profound. It began in earnest at a juncture in the history of separate schools when trustees could not have managed to run their schools without the Sisters and Brothers. As well, that commitment was a very visible sign of the strength and vitality of a distinctly Catholic culture that produced so many Religious in the first place, and of the willingness of these Religious to assume the generally thankless task of helping to keep an impoverished school system afloat until the better days of the 1960s.

Of the forty-seven Religious communities who supplied teachers to the separate schools, only five were male Religious:

Christian Brothers (Brothers of the Christian Schools)
Brothers of the Sacred Heart
Brothers of the Presentation
Holy Cross Brothers
Brothers of St. Louis

The Christian Brothers were the most prominent. Their members taught generations of students in Ottawa, Toronto and St. Catharines and for periods in Sault Ste. Marie, Kingston, London and Windsor. Unfortunately, they were the unwitting lightning rods of a bitter tug of war in the teacher certification controversy which plagued separate schools for many years and which was not resolved until 1907 (see the final section of this chapter). The remaining communities of Brothers, as important as they were to the schools where they taught, provided only a small number of teachers for a few schools and were usually located in no more than one diocese and served for relatively brief periods of time.

The story was markedly different for the female Religious

communities. There were forty-two of these, acting as the backbone of the system from one end of the province to the other:

Congregation of the Sisters of St. Joseph (Sisters of St. Joseph)
Institute of the Blessed Virgin Mary (Ladies of Loretto)
Sisters of the Holy Names of Jesus and Mary
Sisters of the Holy Cross and Seven Sorrows
Sisters of Providence
Sisters of the Holy Cross
Ladies of the Sacred Heart
Benedictine Nuns
Congregation of Notre Dame
Sisters of Charity of Providence
Ursuline Sisters (Order of St. Ursula)
Grey Sisters of the Cross
Sisters of the Presentation of Mary
Sisters of St. Mary of Namur
Sisters of the Assumption
School Sisters of Notre Dame
Notre Dame des Missions
Sisters of the Sacred Heart
Sisters of St. Ann
Grey Sisters of the Immaculate Conception
Daughters of the Heart of Mary
Sisters of Our Lady of Perpetual Help
Sisters of Service
Missionary Sisters of Our Lady of Africa
Daughters of Divine Charity
Sister Servants of Mary Immaculate
Sisters of St. Martha
Sisters of Jesus and Mary
Religious Hospitalers of St. Joseph
Sisters of the Faithful Companions of Jesus
Felician Sisters
Missionary Sisters of the Precious Blood
Sisters of St. Joseph of Cluny

Sisters of Sion
Franciscan Missionaries of Mary
Carmelite Sisters of the Divine Heart of Jesus
Servants of Mary
Sisters of the Little Jesus
Irish Ursulines
Vincentian Sisters of Charity
Our Lady's Missionaries
Sisters of St. Joan of Arc

(Note: The Benedictine Nuns were from Duluth, Minnesota and taught in Fort Frances from 1905 to 1908.)

Of these forty-two communities, the Sisters of St. Joseph were by far the most numerous and active. By 1896, they already placed 146 teachers! Next in number were the Ladies of Loretto with thirty-six teachers and the School Sisters of Notre Dame with thirty teachers.[4] With time, the Sisters of St. Joseph provided principals and teachers for more than 400 separate schools all over Ontario.[5] Theirs was a singular accomplishment and more will be written about them in the next section. More too will be written about the Ladies of Loretto, who arrived in Toronto in 1847, on the invitation of Bishop Michael Power, and were to staff numerous schools in the archdiocese of Toronto and elsewhere. Lastly, we will examine the work of the Grey Sisters of the Cross, as an example of a French-speaking community who provided many teachers for the separate schools of the Archdiocese of Ottawa.

****

What else can we say with certainty about these Religious teachers? Four recognitions come to mind. One, Religious taught in cities and towns, where they could establish a house of residence, and they lived in community, not as individuals. Only on rare occasions did a Religious instruct students in a one-teacher rural school. Also, Religious were none too numerous in the more isolated parts of the province's far north. Their resources were finite, and urban areas, where Catholics were settling in ever greater numbers, especially after 1900, offered the best opportunities for them to live their vocations as teachers.

Two, from the late 1870s to the early 1900s, Religious teachers were so numerous that the need to keep lay male teachers, except in rural schools, had greatly diminished, and it was not uncommon for small to mid-size separate schools in many urban areas to be staffed entirely by Religious. A large number of separate school teachers in the 1850s and 1860s had been Catholic men, but, by 1896, they counted for only one out of every eight teachers. In the words of James F. White, school inspector, they were in danger of disappearing.[6] That never happened, but lay male teachers composed a scant minority for the next sixty years. Their absence from the classroom and the fact that there were far more female than male Religious teachers turned separate schools into highly feminized places of learning. (This preponderance of females in the ranks of separate school teachers was only reinforced and even expanded with the re-introduction of lay teachers in the second decade of the twentieth century. In the majority of instances, the new teachers were female. This state of affairs extended into the 1950s and can be easily traced in the various volumes of a government publication called *Schools and Teachers in the Province of Ontario.*)

Three, although we have already alluded to low salaries for Religious (and will do so later on in reference to the Sisters of St. Joseph), a few figures from the mid-1940s should suffice to illustrate our point just how low Religious salaries were. Compared to their public school counterparts, separate school teachers were poorly paid, and compared to their lay Catholic counterparts, Religious teachers were the poorest of the poorly paid, a state of affairs that lasted well into the 1960s. For example, as late as November 1945, there were 276 lay teachers (out of a total of 852) who earned less than $1,200 a year, and 781 Religious (out of a total of 1,029) who earned less than $800 per year.[7] On the other hand, public school teachers in Toronto for the same period, earned $2,400 per year.[8] When the Ontario English Catholic Teachers' Association pressed for minimum salaries for both lay and Religious teachers, beginning in 1945, Religious were very reluctant to ask for a minimum salary for themselves. They feared that such a demand would violate their vow of poverty, arouse an angry response from the government and the public and force separate school boards to raise taxes.[9] In 1947, the teachers' association agreed to press for a $1,500 minimum for lay teachers and an $800 to $1,000 minimum for Religious teachers. It took until 1950 for everyone to agree that a Religious would be paid two-thirds of a lay teacher's salary. This arrangement lasted for fifteen years and was finally superseded by the full implementation of the Ontario Foundation Tax Plan, which gave separate school boards for the first time in their history the financial wherewithal to pay decent salaries to all its teachers.[10]

Four, as the twentieth century unfolded, especially after the First World War, the need for qualified lay teachers became paramount. School populations and the number of schools increased to the point where the ability of Religious communities to provide teachers was outstripped by demand. The pioneer days of three or four Religious solely in charge of several hundred children in a four-room school were over. This trend towards the laicization of the teaching ranks did not stop until Religious teachers were the exception rather than the rule.

****

Now let us look at some numbers for Religious teachers and lay teachers and Religious teachers as a percentage of the whole body of teachers.[11]

Archdiocese of Toronto
(Note: after 1958, the figures exclude what became the Diocese of St. Catharines.)

1915	Religious: 148	Lay: 70	Total: 218	% of Religious:	68%
1935	Religious: 169	Lay: 278	Total: 447	% of Religious:	38%
1946	Religious: 201	Lay: 256	Total: 457	% of Religious:	44%
1960	Religious: 254	Lay: 1,068	Total: 1,322	% of Religious:	19%

1970 Religious: 184 Lay: 3,097 Total: 3,281 % of Religious: 5%
1975 Religious: 123 Lay: 3,823 Total: 3,946 % of Religious: 3%

Archdiocese of Ottawa
(Note: includes figures for those schools in Ontario)

1915 Religious: 225 Lay: 69 Total: 294 % of Religious: 76%
1935 Religious: 169 Lay: 156 Total: 325 % of Religious: 52%
1946 Religious: 256 Lay: 343 Total: 599 % of Religious: 42%
1960 Religious: 280 Lay: 769 Total: 1,049 % of Religious: 26%
1970 Religious: 186 Lay: 1,563 Total: 1,749 % of Religious: 10.5%
1975 Religious: 115 Lay: 1,978 Total: 2,093 % of Religious: 5%

Diocese of Hamilton

1915 Religious: 127 Lay: 45 Total: 172 % of Religious: 73%
1935 Religious: 186 Lay: 83 Total: 269 % of Religious: 69%
1946 Religious: 190 Lay: 97 Total: 287 % of Religious: 66%
1960 Religious: 216 Lay: 556 Total: 772 % of Religious: 27%
1970 Religious: 170 Lay: 1,775 Total: 1,945 % of Religious: 8%
1975 Religious: 92 Lay: 2,102 Total: 2,194 % of Religious: 4%

Diocese of London

1915 Religious: 149 Lay: 57 Total: 206 % of Religious: 72%
1935 Religious: 308 Lay: 80 Total: 388 % of Religious: 79%
1946 Religious: 280 Lay 197 Total: 477 % of Religious: 58%
1960 Religious: 349 Lay 613 Total: 962 % of Religious: 36%
1970 Religious: 200 Lay: 1,818 Total: 2,018 % of Religious: 9%
1975 Religious: 126 Lay: 2,152 Total: 2,278 % of Religious: 5%

Diocese of Sault Ste. Marie

1915 Religious: 60 Lay: 92 Total: 152 % of Religious: 39%
1935 Religious: 115 Lay: 171 Total: 286 % of Religious: 40%
1946 Religious: 167 Lay: 262 Total: 429 % of Religious: 38%

1960 Religious: 177 Lay: 724 Total: 901 % of Religious: 20%
1970 Religious: 169 Lay: 1,622 Total: 1,791 % of Religious: 9%
1975 Religious: 106 Lay: 1,714 Total: 1,820 % of Religious: 6%

Despite some anomalies in the figures, such as the rise in the percentage of Religious teachers in the archdiocese of Toronto in 1946 and in the diocese of London in 1935, and the almost same percentage of Religious teachers in the diocese of Sault Ste. Marie for the years 1915, 1935 and 1946, we can detect a pattern of development. In 1915, Religious teachers dominated the separate school teaching staff in aggregate numbers as well as in the percentage of the total number of teachers employed in the system. (The diocese of Sault Ste. Marie is the exception in this regard.) But this is somewhat misleading because 1915 can also be looked at as the beginning of the end of such an intensive Religious presence in the classroom. Although the total number of Religious teachers steadily increases up to 1960 — except in the archdiocese of Ottawa in 1935, which produced a decrease, and in the diocese of London in 1946, which produced an increase that could not be maintained afterwards — their percentage of the total number of teachers declines until it reaches single digits in 1975, ranging from 3% to 6%. Religious teachers in our five ecclesiastical divisions achieved their largest aggregate total in 1960 — almost 1,300 teachers — but this too is misleading. Between 1960 and 1970, the number of Religious teachers in Catholic classrooms dropped at rates that reduced them to a shadow of their former presence in separate school classrooms.

The history of Religious teachers in separate schools has come full circle. There were few of them in the 1850s and there were few of them in 1975, the end year of our study. Ironically, few remain in this age of publicly-funded schools and looming teacher shortages. But that is not the point. If Religious teachers had not appeared on the separate school scene in such impressive numbers, starting in the 1870s, and had not maintained their involvement at such high levels for the following eighty years, there would have been no circle to complete, no story to tell of their heroic sacrifice. Let us now look at the teaching work of three Religious communities, the Sisters of St.

Joseph, the Ladies of Loretto and the Grey Sisters of the Cross.

Sisters of St. Joseph

Bishop Henri de Maupas and Father Jean Pierre Médaille, a Jesuit priest, founded the Sisters of St. Joseph in Le Puy, Velay, France in 1648. Following the French Revolution, Mother St. Jean Fontbonne restored the congregation in Lyons, France in 1807 and established the congregation's first American Motherhouse at Carondelet (St. Louis, Missouri) in 1836. Among the six Sisters dispatched to St. Louis were two Fontbonne sisters, who were also nieces of Mother St. Jean Fontbonne. They were Sister Fébronie [Antoinette] and Sister Delphine [Marie Antoinette]. They were joined by their brother, Father Jacques Fontbonne.[12]

In 1847, the Sisters of St. Joseph founded a second house. It was located in Philadelphia, Pennsylvania. Three years later, Sister Delphine was appointed superior of the novitiate and orphanage in that city. Most likely, she would have spent the remainder of her life in the United States had it not been for the 1851 visit of Bishop Armand de Charbonnel of Toronto. There was a connection between the Charbonnel and Fontbonne families: Bishop Charbonnel's father had been instrumental in helping Mother St. Jean restore the congregation in Lyons. When Charbonnel heard that there was a Fontbonne in Philadelphia, he came in person to recruit her for his own diocese, which was in desperate need of a second community of Sisters. Bishop Francis J. Kenrick of Philadelphia listened to Charbonnel's pleading and agreed to release Sister Delphine for the diocese of Toronto. Kenrick was probably reluctant to grant her departure, since the Sisters had only begun to establish themselves in his own diocese, but his decision to bid her good-bye must have been an inspired one. Little did he or Charbonnel realize at the time what an amazing source of spiritual and corporal good works the Sisters of St. Joseph would be throughout the province, and what a saving grace they would be as principals and teachers to the survival and success of separate schools. From Toronto, the Sisters launched new congregations in Hamilton (1852), London (1868) and Peterborough (1890), and from the last mentioned, they branched out into Pembroke

(1921) and then Sault Ste. Marie (1936-37).

Sister Delphine did not depart Philadelphia alone. Accompanying her to Toronto were Sister Alphonsus [Sarah] Margerum, Sister Mary Martha [Maria] Bunning and Sister Mary Bernard [Ellen] Dinan. After a week-long journey by carriage and boat, they arrived on 7 October 1851 and were greeted joyfully by John Elmsley, a future benefactor, and other members of the Catholic community.

The Sisters immediately took control of the orphanage on Nelson Street, rearranging and transforming it from top to bottom. In 1852, one Sister was teaching at St. Patrick's school on Queen Street. A year later, two Sisters were teaching at St. Paul's school on Power Street. This was the humble beginning of a grand teaching tradition. Sadly, Sister Delphine was a victim of Toronto's 1855 typhus epidemic. Under normal circumstances, her energy, enthusiasm and administrative brilliance would have guaranteed her a place in the pantheon of Catholic pioneers. That was not to be. She died on 7 February 1856, at age forty-two, and was buried in St. Michael's cemetery, leaving behind a Religious community of thirty-eight members.

Sister Alphonsus suffered the same fate. She too died of typhus, in 1855, but not before she left her imprint on Toronto's fledgling separate schools. She was the Sister teaching at St. Patrick's in 1852. To honour her work among Catholic school children, the Lombard Street school was named St. Alphonsus, her name in religion.[13]

The German-born Sister Mary Martha was the first superior of the Hamilton convent. She and two novices arrived in April 1852. They came at the invitation of Father Edward John Gordon, the vicar general, who asked them to manage the orphanage. In 1853, the Sisters assumed direction of the city's separate schools and continued to do so after the erection of the Diocese of Hamilton in 1856. By 1862, the year Bishop John Farrell forced Sister Mary Martha to resign and leave the diocese, the Hamilton congregation had twenty-eight members and the support of thousands of people in their annual fund-raising efforts.[14] Sister Mary Martha died in Toronto on 13 June 1868.

Of the four Sisters who came to Toronto in 1851, Sister Mary Bernard enjoyed the longest and most fruitful career. Born in Macroom, Ireland and raised and educated in Philadelphia, she was mistress of novices from 1852 to 1856; she worked in Amherstburg, Niagara Falls, Buffalo and Hamilton from 1856 to 1860; she was assistant to the superior general in Toronto from 1860 to 1864, superior in St. Catharines for several terms between 1864 and 1869 and superior general in Toronto from 1869 to 1874, the year she was deposed by Archbishop John Joseph Lynch; after an absence of thirteen years, she returned to Toronto in 1887 and commenced her greatest apostolic work, Sacred Heart Orphanage at Sunnyside.

Sister Mary Bernard was the first member of the Canadian congregation to celebrate her golden jubilee. By the time of her death on 20 September 1901, the community had grown from four members to more than two hundred.[15]

Let us briefly survey the work of the Sisters of St. Joseph in the separate schools of the archdiocese of Toronto and the dioceses of Hamilton, London and Peterborough. Once again, the figures presented below do not pretend to tell the whole story, but, as selective as they are, they still provide the reader with a good idea of the extent of the community's separate school teaching apostolate.

Archdiocese of Toronto

1872: Sisters are teaching in 5 schools in Toronto and in schools in Barrie and St. Catharines

1873: 29 Sisters are engaged in teaching

1878: Sisters are teaching in 8 schools, including Sacred Heart Orphanage, in the city of Toronto; 1,805 boys and girls

1889: Sisters are teaching in 8 schools, including House of Providence, in the city of Toronto; 2,280 boys and girls

1891: 45 Sisters (out of a total of 79 teachers) in the city of Toronto

1915: 94 Sisters in 21 schools in the archdiocese of Toronto

1921: 92 Sisters in 27 schools, archdiocese of Toronto; a Sister of St. Joseph is principal in each of these schools

1935: 81 Sisters in 26 schools, archdiocese of Toronto

1946: 84 Sisters in 26 schools, archdiocese of Toronto
1960: 76 Sisters in 30 schools, archdiocese of Toronto
1970: 44 Sisters in 30 schools, archdiocese of Toronto
1975: 25 Sisters in 20 schools, archdiocese of Toronto[16]

In 1873, there were 29 teaching Sisters; in 1975, there were 25 teaching Sisters. In 102 years, the community had ended where it began in terms of the number of its members who were in separate school classrooms.

Now for a few words on salaries. In 1908, there were fifty-four Sisters teaching in eleven schools, including the Sunnyside orphanage, in the city of Toronto. Each Sister earned the handsome sum of $50 every three months for a grand total of $200 per year. Teaching with them were four lay teachers. One earned $100 every three months, or $400 per year, and the other three earned $75 every three months, or $300 per year. For the three-month pay period of October to December 1908, the payroll for fifty-four Sisters was $2,700. When one adds the $325 paid to the four lay teachers for the same pay period, the separate school board was able to operate eleven schools for three months for $3,025!

Improvements in teachers' salaries were hardly dramatic. For the year ending 31 December 1919, there were forty-six single women teaching in the Toronto separate schools. The top annual salary was $775. This was earned by a Miss M. Heenan, who had a second class permanent teaching certificate and nineteen years experience. The lowest annual salary was $675. This was earned by a Miss C. Keven, who had a second class interim teaching certificate and no more than four months teaching experience. The range of salaries earned by the Sisters at the end of the same year would have been less than the $675 to $775 range. To put this in even greater perspective, twelve years later, in January 1932, the annual salary for a teaching Sister was $630.[17]

In terms of years of teaching experience, the Sisters of St. Joseph had no rivals in the separate schools. The figures below compare the experience of single female teachers to Sister teachers in the city of Toronto separate schools, for the year ending 31 December

1916. There were 37 single female teachers and 63 Sister teachers.

Among the 37 single female teachers were one teacher who had taught only 8 months and another one who was only an occasional teacher. If these two are eliminated from our calculations, there were 35 single female teachers who had a combined teaching experience of 190 years or on average 5.4 years in the classroom. There were 28 single female teachers who claimed between 1 and 9 years experience and 7 who claimed between 10 and 19 years experience. Only one single female teacher had 19 years of service.

Among the 63 Sister teachers were 13 who had taught for less than a year. If these thirteen are eliminated from our calculations, there were 50 Sister teachers who had a combined teaching experience of 910 years or on average 18.2 years in the classroom. There were 14 Sister teachers who claimed between 1 and 9 years experience; 10 Sisters between 10 and 19 years experience; 19 Sisters between 30 and 39 years of experience; and one brave Sister who had been teaching for 40 years![18]

Diocese of Hamilton

We have already alluded to the arrival of the Sisters of St. Joseph in Hamilton in 1852, under the very capable leadership of Sister Mary Martha Bunning, and their taking charge of the separate schools the following year. They survived the 1854 cholera outbreak, which killed more than five hundred people. When the Hamilton separate school board opened St. Patrick's school and St. Mary's school in the city's downtown, the trustees did not hesitate to entrust them to the Sisters of St. Joseph. Indeed, the Sisters were the only Religious community teaching in the city's separate schools until the arrival of the Ladies of Loretto in 1865.[19] One of their first students at St. Patrick's was Cornelius Donovan, destined to be appointed the second Catholic inspector of separate schools in the province.

By 1900, the Sisters were teaching 1,440 students in seven Hamilton schools and another 1,030 students, including orphans, in schools located in   Paris (1858), Brantford (1859), Arthur (1873), Dundas (1879) and Owen Sound (1886).[20]

1915: 58 Sisters in 13 schools	1960: 63 Sisters in 29 schools
1935: 57 Sisters in 16 schools	1970: 55 Sisters in 34 schools
1946: 57 Sisters in 20 schools	1975: 29 Sisters in 22 schools[21]

Diocese of London

The Sisters of St. Joseph arrived in London 11 December 1868. They were met at the train station by Bishop John Walsh, Monsignor Jean-Marie Bruyère, the vicar general, and Father P. Egan, the pastor of St. Peter's parish. They were five in number: Mother Teresa Brennan, the first superior, Sister Ignatia Campbell, Sister Ursula McGuire, Sister Frances O'Malley and Sister Appolonia. They were accompanied by Mother Antoinette Macdonell, the superior general of the Motherhouse in Toronto. The Sisters' first convent was a small two-storied, white brick house facing Kent Street near St. Peter's and within easy walking distance of the school. Built by the Dominicans, the Kent Street house was intended for the Christian Brothers and was now to be used by the Sisters of St. Joseph![22]

In January 1869, three Sisters began teaching at St. Peter's separate school. They were Sister Ignatia, Sister Ursula and Sister Bonaventure Farley.[23] They taught the girls. Samuel Brown, who had been headmaster since 1860, was in charge of the boys. The school board paid each Sister $100 per year. This was hardly enough to feed the school mice, but the board's parsimony can be explained. Ever since the opening of St. Peter's in January 1858, the trustees had to overcome nearly every imaginable obstacle to keep open just one school. From the board's first report, dated 31 December 1858, we read that friend and foe alike made their work well nigh impossible. Bishop Pinsoneault removed the Sisters of Charity of Providence, upon whom they were depending to teach the girls, and then removed the seat of his diocese from St. Peter's in London to Assumption Church in Sandwich (Windsor). Next the Christian Brothers declined the board's invitation to take charge of the boys. To pay salaries, the trustees had to sponsor a soiree and even take out a bank loan. To re-open the school in September 1858, they relied on a substantial donation from Thomas D'Arcy McGee, private subscriptions and a monthly collection at the church door. To complicate matters, the

178

trustees also spent $1,200 to build a brick school house at Mount Hope (on Richmond Street North) for the Ladies of the Sacred Heart, who ran a boarding school. The original school had been an old barn.[24] (The Sisters of St. Joseph moved to Mount Hope in October 1869, kept the name and turned it into a home for orphans and the aged.)

The trustees, with the help of the Dominicans at St. Peter's, managed to keep St. Peter's school afloat for the next ten years, but indifference on the part of many Catholics, plus a constant shortage of money, prevented any attempt to open more separate schools in the city. Three events were to transform the fortunes of Catholic education in the diocese: the appointment of John Walsh as second bishop of London; the return of the seat of the Diocese to London; and the 1870 decision to turn the Sisters of St. Joseph stationed in London into an independent Diocesan Congregation. Mother Ignatia Campbell was the first superior general, and Mount Hope became the Motherhouse.

Progress on the provision of teachers for separate schools was naturally slow, because it took time to attract new candidates to Religious life and afterwards to train capable teachers among the recruits. But, as the nineteenth century came to a close, the Sisters of St. Joseph were well on their way to becoming the most important source of Religious teachers for the Diocese of London. By 1900, they were teaching 500 students in five schools in London, and another 950 students in schools located in Goderich, St. Thomas, Ingersoll, Belle River and Walkerville (now a part of Windsor).[25]

1915:	87 Sisters in 15 schools	1960: 139 Sisters in 69 schools
1935:	116 Sisters in 29 schools	1970: 91 Sisters in 63 schools
1946:	138 Sisters in 41 schools	1975: 64 Sisters in 51 schools[26]

Longevity and generosity were hallmarks of the Sister teachers in the Diocese of London. Noteworthy are these facts: 117 Sisters of St. Joseph taught in the separate schools and the Catholic high school in St. Thomas, from 1879 to 1996; the Sisters taught in Belle River beginning in 1889 and in the separate schools there, from 1899 to

1984; 70 Sisters taught in the separate schools and the Catholic high school in Goderich, from 1873 to 1992; 163 sisters taught in the separate schools and the two Catholic high schools of Sarnia, from 1906 to 1998; they taught in separate schools in London from 1869 to 1997; and beginning in 1894, they taught for more than a century in Windsor schools.[27]

Diocese of Peterborough

The Diocese of Peterborough was founded on 11 July 1882 and originally stretched from Port Hope and Cobourg on Lake Ontario to the Manitoba and Ontario border and included Peterborough, Lindsay, Parry Sound, North Bay, Sudbury, Sault Ste. Marie, Fort William and Port Arthur (Thunder Bay), Fort Frances, Kenora and dozens of other communities. It was a huge diocese, and the Sisters of St. Joseph of Peterborough taught in separate schools in many of these communities.

Although the Sisters had been teaching in Cobourg since 1883, it would take until 1890 for them to sink a permanent foundation in the diocese. That was the year a diocesan congregation, independent of Toronto, was formed at the request of Bishop R.A. O'Connor, and three Sisters arrived in Lindsay to take over the academy that had been run by the Ladies of Loretto since 1874. The three Sisters were Sister St. Edward Gormley, Sister Dionysia O'Connor and Sister Theodosia O'Meara. Assisting them were Mother Austin Doran and four single women teachers: Susan Maloney, Essie Cummie, a Miss Sullivan and Margaret Whalen. On the advice of the bishop and Monsignor P.D. Laurent, the Sisters dispensed with the distinction between select and parish students and taught all the children on the main floor. As time passed, the Sisters sent teachers to St. Mary's and St. Dominic's, two historic separate schools. As late as 1980, they were able to send one of their members to the new John Paul II elementary school.

In 1894, the Sisters assumed the management of Sacred Heart School in Peterborough and were to remain there until 1986. The first three teachers were Sister St. Edward Gormley, Sister St. Charles Duffy and Sister Celestine Twomey. After Sacred Heart, the Sisters taught in St. Mary's (1903), which had been staffed by the Congregation of the Notre Dame since 1867, St. Peter's Junior School (1906) and Immaculate Conception (1913). To these schools were added a roster of later and more modern ones: St. John the Baptist, St. Anne, St. Alphonsus, St. Pius, St. Teresa and St. Paul. The Peterborough Sisters also taught in separate schools in Port Arthur, from 1890 to 1937; Fort William, from 1890 to 1940; Sault Ste. Marie, from 1902 to 1937; North Bay, from 1906 to 1937; Sudbury, from 1922 to 1937; and in the Diocese of Pembroke.[28] (When the Sisters of St. Joseph of the Diocese of Sault Ste. Marie were established in 1936-37, they taught in those areas of Northeastern and Northwestern Ontario formerly served by the Sisters of St. Joseph of Peterborough.)

The chart below pertains to the diocese of Peterborough as it is currently constituted.[29] Since the Sisters of St. Joseph were virtually the only Religious community supplying teachers to the diocese during the years 1915 to 1975, the chart can be used as a barometer of Religious involvement in the diocese's separate schools.

1915: 26 Sisters in 6 schools	1960: 45 Sisters in 17 schools
1935: 35 Sisters in 11 schools	1970: 34 Sisters in 20 schools
1946: 36 Sisters in 8 schools	1975: 28 Sisters in 17 schools[30]

Institute of the Blessed Virgin Mary (Ladies of Loretto)

Mary Ward and seven companions founded the Institute of the Blessed Virgin Mary at St. Omer, France, in 1609. Born on 23 January 1585, Mother Ward was the daughter of Marmaduke Ward and Ursula Wright, both of whom were loyal Catholics and outstanding recusants during the reign of Elizabeth I. The Institute was not cloistered; it adopted the Rule of the Society of Jesus; and it dedicated its labours to the instruction of the young. Mother Ward died in York, England on 20 January 1645. Frances Bedingfeld, a companion of hers, opened Micklegate Bar Convent in York, in 1686. This was the first Catholic convent in England since the Reformation.[31]

It was to this convent in York, more than 125 years later, that Dr.

Daniel Murray, coadjutor archbishop of Dublin, would send Frances Ball (1794-1860). She entered the novitiate on 11 June 1814 and made her religious profession on 9 September 1816.[32] As Mother Teresa Ball, she established the Irish branch of the Institute at Rathfarnham, outside Dublin, in 1821, and it was from here that five Loretto Sisters departed for Toronto on 11 August 1847. They arrived on 16 September, unheralded, in a city inundated with thousands of Famine Irish, many of whom would die from typhus before they could continue their journey to the countryside.

The five Sisters were Mother Ignatia Hutchinson, who was the first superior, her younger sister, Sister Berchmans Hutchinson, Sister Gertrude Fleming, Sister Bonaventure Phelan and Sister Teresa Dease. By March 1851, three of these sisters were dead: Sister Bonaventure on 11 April 1849; Sister Gertrude on 25 December 1850; and Sister Ignatia on 9 March 1851. Distraught at the death of her sister, Sister Berchmans returned to Ireland. On 19 March 1851, Sister Teresa Dease was appointed superior and is considered the founder of the Institute in North America.[33] Sister Teresa's term of office lasted more than thirty-eight years. During that time she managed the inaugural phase of the Loretto Sisters' remarkable engagement in Catholic education, including the provision of teachers for the separate schools of the archdiocese of Toronto and in other Ontario towns and cities.

Initial success, though, came at a terrible price. We have already alluded to the tragic passing of three of the founding Sisters. But their deaths had been foreboded, in a manner of speaking, by a disaster that struck just two weeks after the arrival of the five Sisters in Toronto. Nothing prepared them for the passing of their patron, Bishop Michael Power, who died on 1 October 1847. To compound matters even further, a fire in early April 1849 destroyed most of Toronto's business district on King Street East and forced the Sisters to move from their first convent at 45 Duke Street (Adelaide Street East) to a new home at the south-east corner of Simcoe and Wellington. Although superior in nearly every way to their Duke Street address, the new convent was a considerable distance from the east-side schools where the Sisters taught. But the Loretto Sisters thrived on a long tradition of adaptability to prevailing circumstances and did not hesitate to dispense with social conventions if they impeded the progress of their work. This explains their decision to reach out beyond their tuition-paying students and include in their mandate the city's separate schools; it also explains their willingness to walk alone to and from school, if necessary, to instruct not only girls but also boys, to accept a more Canadian curriculum and later on to send their teaching Sisters to the Toronto Normal School for professional training and certification.

To Sister Gertrude Fleming goes the honour of being the first Religious of any community to teach in Toronto's separate schools. In early 1848, she was teaching the girls of St. Paul's parish on Power Street.[34] Her next posting was St. Francis Xavier school on Church Street, close to the cathedral, where she was later joined by Sister Joachim Murray, who had arrived from Ireland in June 1849.[35] Institute records for the next fifty years indicate that the Loretto Sisters taught at a "day school" on Church Street and at "poor schools" near the Simcoe Street convent, in St. Patrick's Market on Queen Street West (the Christian Brothers taught the boys on the second floor), in St. Joseph's convent on Jarvis Street and at St. Mary's on Bathurst Street. It is unclear if the terms "day school" and "poor school" refer to separate schools, but one is inclined to believe that they did because of the 1850 legislation that restored the process whereby separate schools could be legally established. In any event, before the close of the nineteenth century, the Sisters went on to teach at the following schools: St. Michael's on Bond Street, St. Helen's in Brockton (West Toronto), St. John's (later St. Martin's) on Parliament Street, Our Lady of Lourdes, Holy Family in Parkdale, St. Vincent's and St. Cecilia's.[36]

None of this could have happened if the Institute had not replenished their initial losses with more recruits from Ireland and attracted new postulants among Canadian-born women. This is exactly what they did. We have already mentioned Sister Joachim Murray joining Sister Gertrude Fleming. Other Sister teachers from this era include Sister Joseph MacNamara, Sister Ignatia Lynn, Sister Teresa Corrigan, Sister Gonzaga Donovan, Sister Magdalen Shea,

Sister Stanislaus Hennigan, Sister Francis de Sales and a Sister Ambrose.[37] Sister Ignatia Lynn was the eldest daughter of Samuel Goodenough Lynn, who had welcomed the Sisters into his home in 1847. She entered the Institute twelve days shy of her fifteenth birthday and was a member for sixty-two years, succeeding Mother Dease as superior in 1889. She died in 1913.[38]

In addition to their work in Toronto, the Loretto Sisters taught for various periods of time during the nineteenth century in separate schools in Brantford, London, Guelph, Belleville, Stratford, Niagara Falls and Lindsay.[39] Since the greater portion of their work in the twentieth century took place in the archdiocese of Toronto, the figures below concern only that ecclesiastical jurisdiction.

1915: 19 Sisters in 6 schools	1960: 49 Sisters in 25 schools
1935: 49 Sisters in 17 schools	1970: 26 Sisters in 19 schools
1946: 50 Sisters in 19 schools	1975: 16 Sisters in 13 schools[40]

Grey Sisters of the Cross (Sisters of Charity of Ottawa)

The Grey Sisters of the Cross, now known as the Sisters of Charity of Ottawa, are the oldest community of female religious in the Archdiocese of Ottawa. They arrived in Ottawa on 20 February 1845, when it was still Bytown and still a part of the diocese of Kingston (Ottawa was incorporated in 1855, and the diocese of Ottawa was erected in 1847). The Grey Sisters of the Cross, a self-governing religious community, are an offshoot of the Sisters of Charity of l'Hôpital Général in Montréal, which was founded by Madame Marguerite d'Youville, a widow, and three companions, Louise Thaumur, Catherine Cusson and Catherine Demers. (Madame d'Youville was canonized in 1990 as the Church's first Canadian-born saint.) Originally a lay association in 1737, the Sisters of Charity of l'Hôpital Général was officially recognized as a religious community in 1755. Their habit was the colour of grey, in open defiance of the many years of public ridicule they quietly endured, including the oft-repeated insult of being called *les soeurs grises*. The French word *gris* means grey but also tipsy or drunk, and the name *les soeurs grises* meant only one thing — tipsy or drunken nuns.[41]

On the invitation of Father Adrien Telmon, the parish priest of Bytown, Bishop Patrick Phelan, co-adjutor to the bishop of Kingston, and Bishop Ignace Bourget of Montreal, the Montreal community sent six young women to what was then a bustling lumber town of many French-speaking Catholics but few Church-run institutions, such as elementary schools, hospitals or relief agencies, to support them in their daily lives. The Oblates of Mary Immaculate, a male religious community, had arrived in Bytown in 1844, but they alone could not meet all the spiritual and temporal needs of local Catholics. Thus the invitation to the daughters of Madame d'Youville. Chosen to found a new community in Bytown, under circumstances best described as primitive, were the following: Élizabeth Bruyère, Éléonore Thibodeau, Marie-Antoinette Howard, Marie-Ursule Charlebois, Elizabeth Devlin and Mary Jones, a domestic.[42]

Élizabeth Bruyère was appointed the first superior. She was only twenty-six years old at the time. Born on 19 March 1818 at L'Assomption, Quebec, she received an uncommonly excellent education in matters spiritual, intellectual and domestic, and she was a teacher before she entered the novitiate in 1839. She was a natural leader, able to motivate her small band of sisters and attract many new recruits as she led them in the difficult tasks of opening schools (the first on March 1845 and the second in 1848), orphanages and different types of hospitals. Mother Bruyère remained at the helm until her death in Ottawa, on 5 April 1876.[43]

The contribution of the Grey Sisters of the Cross to the separate schools of the Archdiocese of Ottawa began in 1856, when the Ottawa Separate School Board was formed — the first six teachers hired by the board were Grey Sisters — and it continued, uninterrupted, for more than one hundred and twenty-five years. According to one historian, "They were truly responsible for establishing Catholic education in the Ottawa Diocese."[44]

1915:	148 Sisters in 26 schools	1960:	129 Sisters in 54 schools
1935:	128 Sisters in 20 schools	1970:	71 Sisters in 34 schools
1946:	127 Sisters in 27 schools	1975:	62 teachers in 34 schools[45]

The Teacher Certification Crisis

In 1907, the Conservative government of James Whitney legislated a reasonable and balanced solution to the long standing and vexatious problem of the absence of professional certification of Religious teachers in Ontario's separate schools. The legislation was a response to a Privy Council decision that upheld lower court rulings in favour of forcing the Christian Brothers in the Ottawa separate schools to acquire proper state certification in order to teach in Ontario. The ability of Religious teachers to avoid certification as a requirement of employment was a problem peculiar to separate schools, and the solution for it eventually came not from the Church's critics, but from Catholic laymen, who outflanked the bishops by openly supporting reform and dealing directly with Premier Whitney. It was a problem that had for its origins an unrealistic interpretation of the first paragraph of Section 93 of the British North America Act. It was a problem that revealed the dangerous extent to which the existence of separate schools depended upon inordinately large numbers of poorly-paid Religious teachers to keep the system functioning, especially in the cities and towns, and conversely that highlighted the real need for more equitable funding for separate schools. It was a problem that pitted the bishops against laymen and caused friction between lay teachers, for whom provincial certification was a requirement, school trustees, who hired the teachers, and Religious teachers whose rates of pay were ridiculously low. And it was a problem that exposed dangerous fault lines within the Catholic community over French as a language of instruction in separate schools and the future, if any, of English-French (or bilingual) schools in those parts of Ontario where French-speaking Catholics were sufficient in number to warrant their existence and to attract the negative attention of those hostile to the existence of separate schools in any guise.

In the final analysis, the Catholic community, minus the bishops and many priests, demonstrated a healthy maturity and a refreshing self-confidence in demanding state certification for all its separate school teachers. The large Religious contingent of Catholic teachers needed proper teaching qualifications, and rank and file

Catholics were not afraid to initiate change and accept the consequences. The laity deeply appreciated the enormous sacrifices the Sisters and Brothers were making on behalf of separate schools, but they also realized that a more professional teaching corps was an absolute necessity if separate schools were ever to gain an equal footing with the public schools. Catholic ratepayers were largely satisfied with the 1907 legislation. It improved the quality of teaching in separate schools and enhanced the reputation of Catholic elementary education. However, since the controversy over the state certification of Religious teachers was played out in an English-versus-French context, separate schools were unfortunately headed for another controversy. Hardly had Catholics accepted the 1907 legislation on teacher certification than they found themselves embroiled in a nasty language war that threatened to destroy the entire separate school system.

****

Separate school politics, regardless of the prevailing crisis, always had many players from different camps. The resolution of the teacher certification crisis was no exception. The players were provincial politicians, bishops, school trustees, separate school inspectors, the courts and the newspapers. (Of course, the Christian Brothers were also players, but despite their position at the centre of the controversy, they chose to be passive participants, reacting to events instead of taking a hand to shape them to their own benefit.) But there was one decisive difference in the political process this time. The dialogue between bishop and politician, a distinctive feature of Sir Oliver Mowat's Liberal government, was overtaken by the courts at the instigation of a Catholic teacher, and then, during the final stages of the crisis, it was transformed into a dialogue between another Catholic layman and the premier.

Let us parse the history of the state certification of Religious teachers into its constituent parts. First, there was the political process at Queen's Park in Toronto. The issue had remained relatively dormant since Confederation, but it erupted in January 1890, when the opposition Conservatives led by W. R. Meredith launched a classic broadside against separate schools. In addition to calling separate schools a mistake, Meredith cautioned the government about French-language schools and their willingness to teach English, which had been compulsory since 1885, and denounced so-called clerical control of separate schools and Catholic representation on High School Boards. Along with the caution and the denunciations, Meredith demanded that Catholic ratepayers be given the secret ballot and be required by law to make a specific declaration of their tax support for separate schools and that Religious teachers in separate schools take the same provincial examinations for teaching certificates as that required of all other teachers.[46]

Debate on separate schools took place in March and attracted overflow crowds to the legislative assembly. George W. Ross, minister of education, and Christopher Finlay Fraser, the minister of public works and the government's pre-eminent Catholic, gave brilliant and lengthy speeches — Fraser spoke for three hours — defending the government's handling of separate school issues, including the certification controversy.[47] To that demand, Ross responded by saying that a regulation requiring professional certification of Religious teachers would infringe on minority rights guaranteed in the constitution. The Catholic bishops shared this opinion. When Meredith proposed the outright abolition of separate schools, which he claimed could be accomplished on application from the Ontario government to the Dominion government, Fraser responded that any attempt to abolish them would break a solemn pact and be an act of wholesale thievery.

The parliamentary performances of the two men were enough to put a stop to any further official attacks on separate schools — for the time being. As a token to the opposition, the government re-affirmed the principle that every ratepayer was automatically a public school supporter unless he notified the local clerk otherwise. Furthermore, the secret ballot became law in 1894. When Meredith re-opened the separate school debate in 1894, he did not get too far. However, Meredith need not have worried. By 1894, the centre of political gravity on separate schools had already shifted from Queen's

Park to the hothouse of separate school board politics in the divided city of Ottawa.

What began as a critical examination of the state of French schools, penned by a Catholic school inspector, evolved into a public attack on the Christian Brothers and from there into a demand for the state certification of all Religious teachers in the separate schools of Ontario. The Mowat Liberals were fond of commissions and special reports as a way to buy time on prickly political problems. They had set up a commission to report on public schools in which the French language was taught (1889) and another to report on the schools of Prescott and Russell counties (1893).[48] By the time of the latter commission, however, the scene had moved to the nation's capital.

The Ottawa separate school board was united by religion but divided by language. Beginning in 1886, it managed its schools by means of two distinct committees. There were ten French trustees to run the French schools and ten English trustees to run the English schools. Each committee would have one trustee from each of the city's ten wards, and both committees would share school taxes and government grants on a proportional basis. The committees were in effect two school boards disguised as one, but it was a workable fiction as long as the committees remained separate solitudes in their own spheres of influence and kept the local Church hierarchy and the government at arm's length.

The fiction did not last. Archbishop Joseph Thomas Duhamel of Ottawa was like every other Catholic bishop in Ontario on the subject of separate schools. He was very protective and believed that he had a right to interfere in school board politics at crucial moments. From Duhamel's point of view, that right to interfere was even greater in the matter of French schools.[49] As far as the government and the department of education were concerned, their man on the ground in separate school matters was the school inspector. In the person of James Francis White, they had not only an able ally but also a sterling Catholic who was thoroughly committed to the welfare of separate schools and had been fearless in advocating reform since his first report in 1882. No one could ever accuse White of being hostile to Catholic education or of being a stooge of Queen Park Protestants.

In 1892, White wrote a confidential report on the sorry state of Ottawa's French schools for the separate school board's French committee. It was a scathing seventeen-point indictment of nearly every aspect of the day-to-day management of these schools: teachers, textbooks, grading, examinations, the teaching of English, French writing skills, the length of the school day, pupil attendance, heating, ventilation and disinfection and the need for new schools. When the report was leaked, the government decided to publish it as part of White's annual report and also as a Sessional Paper.[50]

Perhaps it was White's report that prompted Flavien Moffet to run for a seat on the Ottawa separate school board in the January 1893 elections. Moffet was Ottawa's version of Remigius Elmsley, an example of a rebellious layman whose school politics, while hardly radical in tone or content, were sufficiently novel to threaten the status quo. Moffet wanted the secret ballot in trustee elections, a reduction in school taxes and uniformity in school textbooks. Archbishop Duhamel opposed his candidacy and allowed him to be denounced from parish pulpits. Moffet lost. The margin of defeat was only forty-six votes.

Undaunted, he continued his public campaign to expose the true state of the city's French-speaking separate schools. He targeted the Christian Brothers, accusing them of poor teaching methods, making their students buy too many textbooks and charging too much for their notebooks. Moffet also complained that the school board had no control over the Brothers. The campaign worked. Moffet won a seat in January 1894.[51]

Inspector White repeated and amplified many of Moffet's complaints in his 1895 report to the minister of education. White went so far as to threaten to recommend to the ministry that legislative grants be suspended if the Brothers refused to reform.[52]

When the government decided to act, it appointed another commission, this time to investigate Ottawa separate schools. The commissioners finished their report by August 1895. Their findings, given extensive coverage in the *Globe*, produced shock waves far beyond Ottawa.[53] While the commissioners praised the work of the Sisters who taught in the French schools, they were extremely harsh in their criticism of the Brothers. In their judgment, the pedagogical work of the Brothers in every subject they taught fell woefully short of expectations. Their extensive reliance on memory work and the mechanical recitation of answers, without too much effort to determine whether their students understood what they were repeating, earned special condemnation and a call for professional certification of the Brothers if they were going to continue to teach in Ontario schools.

The upshot of the 1895 report was the departure of the Brothers from both the English and French separate schools in the city of Ottawa. They left on 1 October, under protest. Five days later, Inspector White was busy working with the board to find replacement teachers. The Christian Brothers returned in 1902. Their presence ushered in the next round in the certification crisis.

Between 1895 and 1904, Inspector White, along with the other separate school inspectors, was at diplomatic loggerheads with the Catholic bishops on the need for certification. The inspectors urged the bishops — in particular Archbishop Duhamel of Ottawa, Archbishop Charles Hugues Gauthier of Kingston and Archbishop Denis O'Connor of Toronto — to accept Normal school training and examinations for Religious teachers. The bishops always demurred, citing the first paragraph of Section 93 of the British North America Act: "Nothing in any such law shall prejudicially affect any right or privilege with respect to denominational schools which any class of persons have by law in the Province at the Union." In the matter of certification, this meant only one thing: since the Confederation agreement of 1867 had granted the right to Religious to teach in Ontario without having provincial certificates, no law could take away that right.

In fairness to the bishops, the Mowat government agreed with their position. Moreover, as the bishops were anxious to point out to their critics, Religious teachers had experience in the classroom and a public record, and they were sufficiently qualified according to the teaching regulations of their own Religious communities and from attendance at lectures in their residences given by Normal school professors.[54]

There matters stood until 4 July 1904, when J.D. Grattan brought a lawsuit against the Ottawa separate school trustees over their decision to hire the Christian Brothers to teach in Notre Dame parish separate school and to build for them a residence on school property. Grattan was a Catholic teacher and tax supporter of separate schools. The case was heard in the Ontario High Court of Justice before Mr. Justice MacMahon, who was also a Catholic. How ironic that Catholics would decide the fate of a group of Catholic teachers!

Grattan's case was a straightforward one. He argued that the board's contract with the Brothers was void because the Brothers, who had come from Quebec, did not possess teaching certificates issued by the province of Ontario. The business of building a residence for them at the ratepayers' expense was a side issue. (It was eventually dropped.)

Referring to the Separate Schools Act and the Public Schools Act (*Revised Statutes of Ontario 1897*), N. A. Belcourt, on behalf of the trustees and the Brothers, argued that the BNA Act had guaranteed the qualifications of teachers from both Ontario and Quebec. In other words, a teacher certified in Quebec had a right to teach in Ontario and vice-versa.

In his ruling of 11 July, Justice MacMahon came down on the side of Grattan. He said that the Act only applied to those teachers certified at the time of Confederation, of whom very few, if any, were still teaching in the separate schools in 1904. After Confederation, certification was mandatory for all new Religious teachers in Ontario. The trustees were ordered to pay costs.

The defendants appealed the decision to the Ontario Court of Appeal. This court agreed with MacMahon in a ruling dated 14 November 1904.[55] The next step was a further appeal, either to the Supreme Court of Canada or to the Judicial Committee of the Privy Council in Britain. The bishops, who had re-entered the picture, chose the latter course of action. The following stated case was submitted by mutual agreement between the government and all parties to the matter:

Are members of the communities, including the Brothers of the Christian Schools and certain religious communities composed of persons of the female sex, including the Community General Hospital, Alms House and Seminary of Learning and the Sisters of Charity of Ottawa, commonly called the Grey Nuns, who became members since the passing of the British North America Act, 1867, to be considered qualified teachers for the purposes of the separate schools act, and, therefore, eligible for employment as teachers in the Roman Catholic Separate Schools within the Province of Ontario, where such members have not received certificates of qualification to teach in the public schools in the Province?[56]

The Judicial Committee of the Privy Council gave its answer to this question in a judgment dated 2 November 1906. The committee upheld the decisions of the two lower courts. The process now returned to the political arena.

The bishops were now forced to accept state certification of all teachers in separate schools. They had no further bargaining chips except one. They sought the unconditional qualification of Religious teachers. In other words, Religious would receive the necessary certification without having to attend Normal School and pass the requisite examinations. Such a demand, made out of fear that the Brothers would leave Ottawa, was unpalatable to the Whitney government, which had come to power in the 1905 election and was unwilling to lose face on this issue.

It was now James F. White's turn to intervene. Principal of the Ottawa Normal School since 1903, White strongly objected to the bishops' position. In a letter of 13 March 1907, he wrote Premier Whitney that since certification of teachers was not a matter of faith or morals, the Catholic bishops spoke only for themselves. They did not know the mind of the Catholic people of Ontario on this issue. However, after twenty years as an inspector of separate schools, travelling to all parts of the province and talking to all segments of the Catholic population, White was confident that he knew "the opinions of Catholics upon this subject, and I am sure that at least nine-tenths of the Catholics of the province wish to have only qualified and capable teachers placed in charge of their schools."[57] The bishops' desire to keep the Brothers, who taught only in Ottawa and Toronto, should not override the interests of the great majority of separate school supporters and their children. White continued, pointing out a huge inequity in the separate school system: "At present, the religious teachers are in charge of nearly all the urban schools — the largest and most important under the Separate School System. Then, if no qualification is to be demanded of them, no qualification should be asked either of the teachers of small rural schools."[58] The last option was legally impossible.

After meeting with separate school inspectors, White wrote a second letter to the premier. Dated 23 March 1907, it arrived on Whitney's desk when the government was drafting legislation in response to the Privy Council ruling. White and the inspectors recommended a moderate, non-punitive approach to certification that would award permanent certificates, valid only in separate schools, to experienced teachers, after they had successfully completed a short Normal school course.[59] Whitney was willing to be persuaded. The government had already agreed to pay the legal expenses of the Ottawa trustees and the Brothers in their two appeals. It was now willing to listen to a Catholic solution to a Catholic problem that had been a bugbear to successive governments and an embarrassment to Catholic educators for decades.[60]

"An Act respecting the Qualifications of Certain Teachers" (*Statutes of Ontario*, 7 Edw. VII, c. 52) received royal assent on 20 April 1907. Sometimes referred to as the Seath Act, after John Seath, the superintendent of education, its passage through the legislature caused hardly a ripple of rancor. Guided by White's opinions to Whitney, the act provided for three classes of certificates valid only in separate schools. In order to certify teachers, regardless of the class of certification, the Act counted applicants' years of teaching experience up to 1 July 1907 and expected applicants to have completed their professional training no later than 31 December 1908. Permanent professional certificates would be awarded to those teachers who had seven years' teaching experience, of which five had to have been spent in a separate or public school in Ontario, and who had completed one summer session of Normal School professional training lasting a minimum of four weeks; second class certificates would be given to those who had five years' teaching experience, completed a four-week summer course and passed the required examinations; third class certificates would be given to those who had three year's experience, took a four-week summer course and passed the required examinations.

As an act of courtesy, the Whitney government acceded to Archbishop Duhamel's request for a special bilingual teacher training school in Ottawa that would be divided into two sections, one for the male Religious and one for the female Religious. The school opened in September 1907, and the process of certifying Religious teachers began.[61]

As serious as the certification crisis was for separate schools, its happy resolution in 1907 prompted leading Catholics to remind the government that the real culprit behind the crisis was a lack of adequate funding. By depriving separate schools of their share of corporate and utility taxes, the government had hamstrung Catholics in their heroic efforts to provide their children with a first-class education. Catholics were fortunate to have Religious communities willing to teach at low wages, year after year, but it would take far more than poorly paid Sisters and Brothers to build a system equal in quality to the public schools. Although the lobbying for equitable funding would dominate separate school politics right into the 1990s, of more immediate concern, however, was the status of bilingual schools as part of the separate school system. Were they a necessary component or an Achilles' heel?

---

[1] ARCAT, MG S020.200(a), "Catholic Separate Schools on Ontario," a compilation of statistics from 1856 to 1936.

[2] Many Catholic priests were also teachers, such as the Basilians, the Jesuits and the Oblates and even some diocesan priests, but they taught in the private Catholic high schools. As a result, prior to the 1960s, when separate school boards began to absorb grades 9 and 10, very few, if any, priest teachers would have taught in the separate

(elementary) schools.

[3] *Le Canada Ecclésiastique Almanach-Annuaire du Clergé Canadien* 1891 [hereafter *Le Canada Ecclésiastique*] (Montreal: Cadieux & Derome, 1891). Other years include 1892, 1893, 1894, 1895, 1900, 1903 and 1911; *The Ontario Catholic Year Book and Directory* 1915 (Toronto: 1915). Other years include 1922, 1930, 1935, 1940, 1946, 1950, 1955, 1960, 1965, 1965, 1970 and 1975. Another source was J. George Hodgins, *The Establishment of Schools and Colleges in Ontario* 1792-1910, vol. 2 (Toronto: King's Printer, 1910), Part VII, "Roman Catholic Separate Schools of Ontario," 145-79.

[4] Province of Ontario, *Sessional Papers*, 1897 (No. 1), 226.

[5] Letter of Sister Veronica O'Reilly, csj to the author, 30 November 1999.

[6] Province of Ontario, *Sessional Papers*, 1897 (No. 1), 226.

[7] Assumption University Archives, RG I, Box 8, File 137, Papers of Father Vincent J. Guinan, CSB, OECTA Salary Statistics, November 1945. Father Guinan was a member of the Religious Committee of OECTA. See RG I, Box 8, files 142 and 143.

[8] Ibid., RG I, Box 8, File 149, John M. Bennett to Father Vincent J. Guinan, CSB, 15 March 1944.

[9] Ibid., RG I, Box 8, File 142, Minutes of the meeting of Committee of Religious held at St. Michael's College, November 19, 1944.

[10] Robert Thomas Dixon, *Be a Teacher: A History of the Ontario English Catholic Teachers' Association 1944-1994* (Toronto: Ontario English Catholic Teachers' Association, 1994), 61-62.

[11] Several comments are in order concerning the charts that follow. One, the ecclesiastical divisions of Toronto, Ottawa, Hamilton, London and Sault Ste. Marie are sufficiently large, in terms of both geographic size and total Catholic population, to give one a fairly accurate pattern of the rise and fall of Religious involvement in separate schools. That involvement was measured in two ways: the total number of Religious teachers from all communities and this total as a percentage of the entire teaching body, for the selected years under examination. Our choice of years is arbitrary but not without meaning. Each one is tied into a landmark: 1915, the First World War; 1935, the height of the Great Depression; 1946, post-Second World War; 1960, the high-water mark in the history of Religious teachers; 1970, the evident decline of Religious participation in teaching; 1975, the confirmation and continuation of that decline.

Two, our statistics were derived from information in *The Ontario Catholic Year Book and Directory*, the successor to *Le Canada Ecclésiastique Almanach-Annuaire du Clergé Canadien. The Year Book and Directory* is divided into dioceses and each diocese is divided into its constituent parishes and missions. Included in the parochial information are the number of schools attached to the parish as well as the number of Religious and lay teachers in each school. (The two exceptions to this are the 1915 reports from the dioceses of London and Hamilton. They counted only Religious teachers and failed to give information on rural schools and their lay teachers. However, we were able to overcome this deficiency by subtracting the number of reported schools from the total number given in the recapitulation at the end of the reports. For London, this subtraction gave us fifty-seven additional schools, to each of which we assigned one lay teacher. For Hamilton, the subtraction of reported schools from the total number given in the recapitulation produced seventeen additional schools, to each of which we assigned one lay teacher.)

Three, by the term separate school we mean not only the elementary grades, kindergarten to eight, but also in some instances the Fifth Form or Fifth Classes, grades nine and ten, which later became Continuation Classes and then Continuation Schools. Anyone who taught these classes would have been an employee of the separate school board and would have been paid the wages of an elementary school teacher. As it turns out, Religious teachers were often in charge of Continuation classes.

See Glossary of Terms for definitions of Fifth Form, Fifth Classes, Continuation Classes and Continuation Schools. For the politics of Continuation Schools, see Walker, *Catholic Education and Politics in Ontario*, 2: 329-33. Thanks to Father Carl Matthews, S.J. for clarifying certain aspects of Continuation Classes, in particular that their existence was an option left open to each individual separate school board, and that it was not until the 1960s that boards started to take over grades 9 and 10 in private Catholic High Schools. The students were counted as elementary students for purposes of the legislative grant, as long as the board did not increase its property taxes to finance the takeover and administration of these grades. Furthermore, during the 1970s and 1980s, the funding for grades 9 and 10 gradually improved by means of a "weighting factor." For students in these grades, the school board received 107% of the amount given for students in kindergarten to grade 8. The percentage increased to 115% to 122% to 130%, etc., etc. "Besides," Father Matthews writes, " the increased enrolment due to the addition of Grades 9 and 10 (and JK!) decreased the 'assessment per pupil' and thereby increased the grant per pupil, JK to 8! Part of that miraculous increase was then available for 9 and 10 expenses. Hence by 1984, JK to 10 were in good financial shape for most Catholic boards and enrolment boomed." Reverend Carl Matthews, S.J. to the author, 1 November 2000.

[12] "St. Joseph Sisters," NCE, 12: 899-901; Sister Mary Agnes [Agnes Murphy], *The Congregation of the Sisters of St. Joseph: Le Puy, Lyons, St. Louis, Toronto* (Toronto: 1951), Chapter Eight; "Fontbonne, Marie-Antoinette," *DCB*, 8: 298-99.

[13] Elizabeth M. Smyth, "The Lessons of Religion and Science: The Congregation of the Sisters of St. Joseph and St. Joseph's Academy, Toronto 1854-1911," (D.Ed. diss., University of Toronto, 1989), 45.

[14] "Bunning, Maria," *DCB,* 9: 103-4; Smyth, "The Lessons of Religion and Science," 44-45; Sister Mary Agnes, *The Congregation of the Sisters of St. Joseph*, 113-14.

[15] "Dinan, Ellen," *DCB,* 13: 275-76; Sister Mary Bernita Young, *Silent Growth: The Life and Times of Sister Bernard Dinan* (Toronto: 1986).

[16] Figures for 1872 and 1921 are from Congregation of the Sisters of St. Joseph, Toronto [hereafter CSJT] Archives, Education School Lists; figures for 1873, 1878 and 1889 are from Young, *Silent Growth*, 13, 22 and 23, respectively; figures for 1891 are from *Jubilee Volume of the Archdiocese of Toronto*, 269; figures for 1915, 1935, 1946, 1960, 1970 and 1975 are from *Ontario Catholic Year Book and Directory* for the corresponding years.

[17] These figures are from CSJT, Archives, Education School Lists.

[18] Ibid.

[19] Patrick J. Brennan, *Resilient Roots: A Short History of Catholic Education* [Hamilton: Hamilton-Wentworth Roman Catholic Separate School Board, 1994], 1-2.

[20] *Le Canada Ecclésiastique* 1900, 206.

[21] *Ontario Catholic Year Book and Directory* for the corresponding years.

[22] John K.A. Farrell [O'Farrell], "The History of the Roman Catholic Church in London, Ontario 1826-1931," (master's thesis, University of Western Ontario, 1949), 60-61.

[23] There is a discrepancy concerning the third Sister. Farrell says it was Sister Frances O'Malley. However, Sister Bonaventure Farley is the name given in Sister M. Julia Moore, "The Sisters of St. Joseph: Beginnings in London Diocese 1868-1878" [London: 1978], 9. There is also a photograph of Sister Bonaventure on the preceding page. This work does not list the names of the Sisters who arrived on 11 December 1868. It only gives the name of the superior general.

[24] Ibid., Appendix H, 191-93.

[25] *Le Canada Ecclésiastique* 1900, 213.

[26] *Ontario Catholic Year Book and Directory* for the corresponding years.

[27] Information supplied in a letter of Sister Mary Zimmer, CSJ to the author, 19 July 2000.

[28] This information was taken from various chapters of Sister Eileen Gahagan et al., *As the Tree Grows: Celebrating 100 Years of the Sisters of St. Joseph Peterborough 1890-1990* [Peterborough: 1993].

[29] The diocese of Peterborough, established in 1882, began as the Apostolic Vicariate of Northern Canada, in 1874. Bishop Jean-François Jamot was the bishop.

[30] *Ontario Catholic Year Book and Directory* for the corresponding years.

[31] "Loretto, Ladies of (Institute of the Blessed Virgin Mary)," NCE, 8: 994-95; Kathleen McGovern, *Something More than Ordinary: The Early History of Mary Ward's Institute in North America* (Richmond Hill, Ontario: 1989), 1. The Institute should not be confused with the Sisters of Loretto at the Foot of the Cross.

[32] McGovern, *Something More than Ordinary*, 65-66.

[33] "Dease, Ellen," *DCB*, 11: 240-41.

[34] Marion Norman, "Making a Path by Walking: Loretto Pioneers Facing the Challenges of Catholic Education on the North American Frontier," CCHA *Historical Studies*, 65 (1999): 96.

[35] Ibid., 99.

[36] Ibid., 106.

[37] Ibid., 99-100.

[38] McGovern, *Something More than Ordinary*, 101.

[39] Norman, "Making a Path by Walking," 106.

[40] *Ontario Catholic Year Book and Directory* for the corresponding years. Additional information supplied by Sister Juliana Dusel, IBVM, archivist, Loretto Abbey, Toronto.

[41] "Grey Nuns," NCE, 6: 802-3; "Grey Nuns," *Canadian Encyclopedia Year 2000 Edition* (Toronto: McClelland and Stewart, 1999), 1018.

[42] Robert Choquette, "An Historical Overview," in Pierre Hurtubise, Mark McGowan and Pierre Savard, *Planted by Flowing Water: The Diocese of Ottawa 1847-1997* (Ottawa: Novalis, 1998), 13.

[43] "Bruyère (Bruguier), Élizabeth," *DCB*, 10: 107-8.

[44] Lionel Desjarlais, "Catholic Education in the Diocese: An Overview," in *Planted by Flowing Water*, 206.

[45] *Ontario Catholic Year Book and Directory* for the corresponding years.

[46] Walker, *Catholic Education and Politics in Ontario*, 2: 157-58.

[47] *Globe*, 26 March 1890, 1, 4-6.

[48] *Report of Commissioners on Public Schools in Ontario in which the French Language is Taught* (Toronto: 1889); *Report of Commissioners on Schools in the Counties of Prescott and Russell* (Toronto: 1893).

[49] "Duhamel, Joseph-Thomas," *DCB*, 13: 296-301.

[50] *Report of the Minister of Education (Ontario) for the Year 1892* (Toronto: Warwick & Sons, 1893), 145-46; Province of Ontario, *Sessional Papers 1893*, No. 50.

[51] Robert Choquette, *Language and Religion: A History of English-French Conflict in Ontario* (Ottawa: University of Ottawa Press, 1975), 59-61. For one of the more complete and detailed versions of the certification crisis, see Walker, *Catholic Education and Politics in Ontario*, 2: Chapter 8.

[52] Choquette, *Language and Religion*, 61.

[53] *Globe*, 17 August 1895, 9; Province of Ontario, *Sessional Papers* 1896, No. 1; also *Report of the Commission Relation to Ottawa Separate Schools* (Toronto: 1895).

[54] Walker, *Catholic Education and Politics in Ontario*, 2: 200-201.

[55] For a text of the ruling of the Court of Appeal, see Francis G. Carter, *Judicial Decisions on Denominational Schools* (Toronto: Ontario Separate School Trustees' Association, 1962), 231-34: Grattan v. Ottawa Separate School Trustees, Court of Appeal, 1904, *Ontario Law Reports*, 433.

[56] *Globe*, 3 November 1906, 1.

[57] AO, F5 MU 3122, Sir James Pliny Whitney Papers, James F. White to Premier Whitney, 13 March 1907.

[58] Ibid.

[59] Ibid., James F. White to Premier Whitney, 23 March 1907. Both letters (13 March 1907, 25 March 1907) are quoted in Walker, *Catholic Education and Politics in Ontario*, 2: 218-20.

[60] *Globe*, 30 March 1907, 6.

[61] Choquette, *Language and Religion*, 68.

A DIVISIVE DEBACLE:
REGULATION 17

*R*egulation 17 was a circular issued by the Ontario Department of Education in July 1912. It addressed the school year September 1912 to June 1913 and was amended in August 1913. (Its correct name was actually Instructions 17.) Regulation 17 had two seemingly contradictory aims. On the one hand, it sought to diminish the use of French as a language of *instruction and communication* in the English-French schools of the province, and on the other hand, it attempted to regularize and entrench the French language as a *subject of study* in all the province's schools.

To accomplish both aims at the same time, it was politically necessary that Regulation 17 open by reiterating the government's long-held position that there existed only two classes of publicly-funded schools in Ontario — public schools and Roman Catholic Separate Schools — and that the constitutional guarantee of these two classes of schools was the result of religion. Neither race nor language nor a combination of the two had played a role in the creation of Roman Catholic Separate Schools. This was understood by all political parties in 1867, and nothing since Confederation had subverted that understanding. It was non-negotiable. However, in the practical world there also existed in both publicly-funded systems a third class of schools called English-French schools, in which French was the prevailing language of instruction and communication. These were the so-called bilingual schools variously found in Essex and Kent counties, Eastern Ontario, the city of Ottawa and the unorganized districts of Northern Ontario. (There were also schools in and around Berlin, later called Kitchener, in which German was the language of instruction. Few in number and relegated to one area of the province, these schools had already begun by 1910 to make English the language of instruction and German a subject of study. Consequently, they were not a political problem.)

By November 1910, Sir James P. Whitney's Conservative government was ready to address the anomalous nature of English-French schools, which had been operating virtually unchecked for nearly two decades but without any legal provision for their existence. Remaining steadfast to its understanding of the BNA Act, the Whitney government was determined not to let English-French schools acquire by default a kind of legal status akin to that enjoyed by the Roman Catholic separate schools. For the government, this was the crux of the problem.

English-French schools were curious creatures of geography, isolation, local history, the migration of French Canadians, benign policies on the part of previous Liberal governments and school trustees who had successfully ignored the centralizing tendencies of the education bureaucracy in Toronto. Regulation 17 did not make the first occasion that the government had visited the troublesome business of the status of English-French schools. But this particular set of Instructions, unlike all others before it, would open a Pandora's box of political nightmares that only the passing of time would dispel.

****

The nub of the Regulation 17 controversy can be summed up in two different but related questions:

1) To what extent, if any, should the French language continue to be used as a language of *instruction and communication*, as well as a *subject of study*, in both the public and Roman Catholic separate schools?
2) To what extent, if any, did the existence of English-French schools imperil the financial future of Roman Catholic separate schools?

The first question, which was of concern to everyone, was essentially a political problem that needed a political solution. A solution was finally found in 1927, fifteen years after Regulation 17 was first issued. In the meantime, the political wrangling at both the provincial and federal levels exposed deep and dangerous divisions within Canadian society that threatened national unity and the fragile framework of the constitution. The often fierce battle over bilingual schools pitted an increasingly vocal French Canadian nationalism, largely of Quebec origin, against the dominant British Imperial culture of early twentieth century Ontario. It also divided English-speaking or "Irish" Catholics, as their foes were fond of calling them, from French-speaking Catholics, and it exposed the double-minority status of the latter.[1] French-speaking Catholics were a small minority within Ontario's Catholic community, which itself was a minority within an overwhelmingly Protestant province. (The exception to this minority status was the city of Ottawa. There French-speaking Catholics were a majority, and the Ottawa separate school board was split along language lines, making the reaction to Regulation 17 in that city all that more bitter.) And we must not forget that a good deal of the ensuing uproar over Regulation 17 was played out against the backdrop of the First World War, which on its own was causing considerable friction between the "two Canadas." Our focus will be on the division that Regulation 17 caused within the Catholic fold.[2]

The second question was of the utmost importance to supporters of Catholic separate schools. Unable to share in the mother lode of property taxes paid by public utilities, corporations and a myriad of local industries in receipt of municipal bonuses — the so-called bonused industries — separate school trustees found themselves during the opening decade of the twentieth century increasingly handcuffed in their efforts to operate their schools in an efficient and modern manner. All the separate school gains of the nineteenth century, won at tremendous cost to Catholic parents, were in danger of being swallowed up by a simple but painful lack of money to move forward. Keeping open existing schools on a bare bones budget was a challenge at the best of times; setting up new schools or building additions was an exhausting and protracted business, fraught with endless complications; and having to end public-funded Catholic education at the high school entrance examinations in grade eight frustrated many parents and their children. Moreover, the teacher certification crisis that was resolved in 1907 revealed to Catholic ratepayers the embarrassing extent to which separate school standards were inferior to those of the public schools. The nasty clash over English-French schools amplified what had become a collective sense of inferiority.

As the controversy slowly played itself out, it seems that a majority of Ontario's Catholics, including all the English-speaking bishops, agreed that an official Catholic defense of bilingual schools would forever dash any chance of achieving favourable legislation on corporate taxes and high schools. In their minds, such legislation was crucial to the long-term future of the entire separate school system. Although French-speaking Catholic leaders argued against this type of thinking, and one conceivably could carry on the same argument today, the fact remains that in the Ontario of 1910 and for many years thereafter, the majority of Catholic ratepayers feared that the Loyal Orange Lodge, still a force to be reckoned with, and their fellow travellers in elected office would turn any controversy over bilingual schools into the ammunition they needed to destroy all separate schools.

Reasonable grounds existed for harbouring this fear. In 1910, it was Premier Whitney's understanding that there were 250 English-French schools out of a total of 6,344 elementary schools.[3] Expressed in terms of a percentage, English-French schools formed a minuscule 4% of all elementary schools in the province. The political problem for Whitney was not one of numbers but of perception. Why did there exist even one English-French school when there was no provision in law for them to exist? Whitney's further understanding was that of the 250 English-French schools, 195 were separate schools and 55 were public schools. For the premier, therefore, the central political truth was that the "problem" of English-French schools belonged to everyone.

However, Catholics who were aware of the same or similar figures came to a different conclusion. In 1910, there were 467

Roman Catholic separate schools in Ontario. Since English-French schools were not officially a distinct class of schools, their number was a sub-set of this group of 467 schools. If Whitney's approximations were correct, in 1910, out of a total of 467 separate schools, 195 or a staggering 41% were English-French. If the separate school system had an Achilles' heel, this was it. Any attempt on the part of the government to rein in English-French schools, for whatever motive or reason, legitimate or otherwise, would affect separate schools far more than public schools. As a result, the only road to survival was to let bilingual schools, which were more French than they would ever be English, die a quiet, government-inflicted administrative death.

****

Regulation 17 of June 1912 was divided into fifteen paragraphs. The most contentious of these were paragraphs 3, 4, 5 and 9 (2). They covered the use of French as a language of instruction and communication, French as a subject of study and the duties of Supervising Inspectors in English-French Schools:

3. Subject, in the case of each school, to the direction and approval of the Supervising Inspector, the following modifications shall also be made in the course of study of the Public and Separate Schools.

The Use of French for Instruction and Communication
(1) Where necessary in the case of French-speaking pupils, French may be used as the language of instruction and communication; but such use of French shall not be continued beyond Form 1 [Grades 1 and 2], excepting during the school year of 1912-13, when it may also be used as the language of instruction and communication in the case of pupils beyond Form I who, owing to previous defective training, are unable to speak and understand the English language.

Special Course in English for French-Speaking Pupils

(2) In the case of French-speaking pupils who are unable to speak and understand the English language well enough for the purposes of instruction and communication, the following provision is hereby made:

(a) As soon as the pupil enters the school he shall begin the study and the use of the English language.

(b) As soon as the pupil has acquired sufficient facility in the use of the English language he shall take up in that language the course of study as prescribed for the Public and Separate Schools.

French as a Subject of Study in Public and Separate Schools

4. For the school year of 1912-13, in schools where French has hitherto been a subject of study, the Public or the Separate Board, as the case may be, may provide, under the following conditions, for instruction in French Reading, Grammar, and Composition in Forms I to IV [Grades 1 to 8] . . . in addition to the subjects prescribed for the public and Separate Schools:

(1) Such instruction in French may be taken only by pupils whose parents or guardians direct that they shall do so.

(2) Such instruction in French shall not interfere with the adequacy of the instruction in English, and the provision for such instruction in French in the time-table of the school shall be subject to the approval and direction of the Supervising Inspector and shall not in any day exceed one hour in each classroom.

(3) Where, as permitted above for the school year of 1912-13 French is a subject of study in a Public or Separate School, the text books in use during the school year of 1911-12, in French Reading, Grammar, and Composition shall remain authorized for use during the School year of 1912-1913.

Inspection of English-French Schools

5. For the purpose of inspection, the English-French schools shall be organized into three divisions, each division being under the charge of a Supervising Inspector and an Inspector.

9. (2) The Supervising Inspector shall have the sole control of the organization of each school so far as is provided in 3 and 4 (2) above.[4]

The government made what it considered two conciliatory amendments to Regulation 17 in August 1913. In the original version of the Regulation, after the 1912-13 school year, no school would be allowed to ask for an exception to the rule that French could not be used as the language of instruction beyond Form I. The first amendment ended any time limit on a school's right to ask for this exception. The second amendment addressed the contentious issue of the Supervising Inspectors. The amendment abolished this category of inspector. In its place, two inspectorships were created, one for each of the two divisions established for English-French schools, and each inspector was required to report not to the trustees but to the minister of education.[5] Although these two compromise amendments did not alter the substance of Regulation 17, in the right hands they would have been sufficient to effectively circumvent the government's intentions and save bilingual schools from their intended demise.

However, any good that these two amendments might have achieved, at least in the realm of public relations, had been negated well in advance when the government published Instructions 18, on 12 October 1912. Draconian and punitive in its intent, this circular was initially a response to the refusal of the Ottawa Separate School Board, at the instigation of French-speaking trustees, to implement Regulation 17. The board's refusal was a direct challenge to the government's authority, and Whitney could ill afford to ignore it. Instructions 18 applied to all boards. Not only trustees but teachers as well were responsible for enforcing Regulation 17. Teachers were told that they were answerable not to the trustees who had hired them but to the minister of education and that they would face the loss of their teaching certificates if they failed to abide by the Regulation. Trustees were warned that if they did not follow *all* Department of Education regulations their board would forfeit the legislative grant and not be allowed to pay teachers' salaries from taxes levied on their supporters. No money meant no schools. The same punishment would apply if trustees hired non-qualified teachers as a means of operating their schools without benefit of the legislative grant and property taxes.[6]

****

Let us now examine the sequence of events that led up to Regulation 17. To do so, we must keep in mind that Regulation 17 was not an innovation. It had a quarter century of regulatory precedence and therefore was the logical result of prior administrative changes and of the findings and recommendations of several commissions and reports on English-French schools. These reports sought to address specific problems within the context of a growing anxiety about the "official" status of the English language.

Those changes began in 1885, when the government for the first time made the study of English compulsory in all public schools. Also, every candidate for a teacher's certificate who took his exams in either French or German was required to pass additional examinations in English grammar and translation. Authorized English-language readers were the means by which the Department of Education enforced what was known as Regulation 155. The mandated hours for the study of English were hardly onerous: two hours minimum per week for the first four years and four hours minimum per week for the final four years of elementary school.[7] But such minimum requirements produced the desired results: after four years, there was no school in which English was not taught.

In 1889, the government made its next move. It appointed a three-man commission to examine the quality of the teaching of English in those public schools in which the French language was taught. No mention was made of examining the quality of the teaching of the French language, and it is unclear if the commission's mandate included the examination of the then relatively small number of bilingual separate schools. The members of the commission were John J. Tilley, county model school inspector, Reverend Alfred H. Reynar, professor at Victoria College, and the Reverend D.D. McLeod of Barrie. They examined English-French schools in Essex, Kent, Simcoe, Prescott and Russell counties. Their report rested on a dangerously contradictory approach to the language question, one that would bedevil the whole debate on bilingual schools up to and well beyond Regulation 17 but seems to have escaped the notice of the commissioners themselves. It was a contradiction that took on a life of its own and was to reappear in future regulations.

The contradiction went like this. On the one hand, the commission asserted that English must be the primary language of instruction in English-French schools if children were to have a chance at finding their place in the world in which English was the dominant language. "Any departure from this rule," wrote the commissioners, "should be only partial and in accommodation to the peculiar circumstances of certain sections of the country, in order that the end sought may thereby be more fully attained."[8] English as the language of instruction was the norm; the use of French was a generous but only temporary exception restricted to certain areas of the province. On the other hand, the commission duly acknowledged a prevailing sentiment among French parents about the primacy of the French language in the lives of their children. "They have lived for a long period in the localities where they are found, enjoying the use of their native language. They are strongly attached to it. It is the language of their fathers, and the language used in their homes and spoken by their children. It is natural that they should cherish it with affection, and desire their children to acquire a knowledge of it."[9]

How, then, would the government accommodate a sentiment about the French language that was surely at odds with the assertion that English must be the language of instruction and communication in schools in historic French communities? It was a question conveniently left unanswered by the politicians and their underlings, the education bureaucrats. The government chose instead to play the role of the Roman god Janus: to look in opposite directions at the same time. This was accomplished in a circular of 18 October 1889.

Looking one way, the minister of education saw English as *the* language of instruction and communication, and he informed teachers in English-French schools that any teacher unfamiliar with the English language should immediately begin to study it. The reason for this was simple: "Not only shall the teacher conduct in the English language every exercise and recitation from the prescribed English text-books, but communication between teacher and pupil in matters of discipline, and in the management of the school shall be in English, *except so far as this is impracticable by reason of the pupil not understanding English*" [italics mine].[10] Looking the other way, as highlighted in the italicized words, the minister provided a convenient loophole by which trustees and teachers could easily ignore the government's policy on the primacy of English in Ontario's schools. Moreover, the government did not restrict instruction to the English language as a matter of policy. It did something quite the opposite. It provided a new series of English-French readers to be used in those schools "Where the French language prevails, and the trustees, with the approval of the Inspector require French to be taught in addition to English."[11]

These regulations were spelled out in greater detail in a circular of 10 February 1890.[12] According to Marilyn Barber, this circular assumed that any allowance for the use of French for instruction or communication was strictly temporary and never meant to delay or usurp the intended supremacy of the English language.[13] French as a subject of study was an entirely different matter and was treated like any other recognized subject. However, that 1889 loophole remained and what was intended by Toronto educationists to be a temporary measure of Anglo largesse had little trouble over time entrenching itself even more as a permanent feature in the bilingual schools of such far-away places as Essex and Kent counties in the southwest and Russell and Prescott counties in the northeast.

In 1893, the government appointed another commission, composed of the same three members, to investigate the teaching of English in the bilingual schools of Russell and Prescott. Tilley, Reynar and McLeod were satisfied that the teachers had progressed in their understanding of English and their ability to teach in it. They also reported that twenty-seven of the schools inspected in 1885 had become separate schools by 1889 (so that the children could learn the Catholic catechism) and that separate schools measured up to public schools in the matter of teaching in the English language.[14]

This reference to bilingual separate schools is curious. No such reference to these schools had been made in either 1885, 1889 or 1890, and no mention of the teaching of English in these schools can be found in separate school legislation during this period. The government's pre-eminent concern was the status of English in the bilingual schools of the public school system. By 1896, that concern found its way in "An Act Consolidating and Revising the Public Schools Act" (59 Victoria, Chapter 70). Section 76 (2) reads:

> To use the English language in the instruction of the school and in all communications with the pupils in regard to discipline and the management of the school, except where impracticable by reason of the pupil not understanding English. Recitations requiring the use of a text-book may be conducted in the language of the text-book.

That the government remained stubbornly Janus-like in its language policy is not the point. What deserves our attention is the preference of the education bureaucrats not to address directly the status of teaching in English in the bilingual separate schools. Applying departmental regulations to separate schools was left up to Catholics themselves as a matter of self-discipline.

The man most responsible for ensuring that separate schools obeyed the regulations was none other than inspector J.F. White. His chief desire that Catholic separate schools achieve parity in every major respect with their public school counterparts naturally extended to the English-French separate schools under his inspection. As a matter of public record, White heartily endorsed the notion of the absolute necessity of teaching in English. He made known his views as early as 1882, in his first report:

In several places in Essex [County], and in the counties adjacent to the Ottawa [River], French is the language of the people and of the schools. Though the attention paid to their own tongue is praiseworthy, and the progress made therein very fair, it is much to be regretted that English, the great language of the country, is so frequently neglected. In some of the places in Eastern Ontario, it is quite unknown to teachers and pupils. This necessitates the carrying on in French of the examinations of the classes, and of the whole work of inspection.[15]

At this stage, the neglect of English in the bilingual schools was more of an annoyance for White in carrying out his inspection duties than it was a problem for the separate schools. Four years later, however, the problem of the relative status of English and French had become more acute for all involved. White's 1886 report, in the wake of Regulation 155, details his inspection of what he called "French Schools" in Russell and Prescott counties. Although White was careful not to sound too alarmed by what he discovered, in effect the overall situation in these two counties was such a muddle as to border on the disastrous:

In some of the counties along the Ottawa River, but chiefly in the counties of Prescott and Russell, there are several Separate Schools in which French children form either the majority or the whole of those in attendance. In general, both the English and French languages are taught in all such schools; sometimes the principal part of the studies is in English, and the subjects taught in French are reading, grammar, composition, and religious instruction — this, even when the great bulk of the pupils speak French as their mother tongue. In other cases the two languages receive about equal attention, and sometimes the greater part of the teaching and instruction is given in French. However, of the whole number of teachers in these French schools — thirty — there were but two or three who were teaching exclusively in French; nor are these, I am told, schools in which English has never been taught, but the scarcity of teachers capable of giving instruction in both languages led to the engaging of those who knew only French, as that is the language of all the pupils in those particular schools.

As to these teachers' qualifications, many of them have diplomas obtained from Boards of Examiners in the Province of Quebec, several have certificates granted by the local Board in Prescott and Russell, and others have only temporary certificates. There are several difficulties to be overcome before there will be properly qualified teachers for such sections. The first is the lack of schools at which the French candidates can prepare for an examination to be conducted to a considerable extent in their own language . . . Then the amount of salary usually paid is too small to require teachers to make an expensive preparation for the profession or to tempt them to remain long in it; in Prescott and Russell the average salary for a female teacher in the Separate Schools was, in 1885, but $144 a year . . .[16]

White ended by hoping that the new French Model School, scheduled to open in September 1887, would improve "the art of teaching; for only when the teachers have a proper knowledge of English can we hope for it to be taught with satisfactory results."[17] White emphasized improving the ability of French teachers to teach in English. He never considered restrictions on the teaching in French as a way in which to improve English-French schools.

White agreed with the 1893 commission's conclusion that improvements had been made in the teaching of English, but he vehemently denied allegations from other quarters that so many public schools had become separate schools because French Catholics did not want to follow departmental regulations on the teaching of English. To the well-known fact that French Catholics wanted their children to be taught the catechism — legally impossible in the public schools — White asserted that all regulations concerning English-language instruction were strictly enforced in the separate schools.[18]

He should know. He was the one enforcing them.

****

There matters stood, quietly in most places, until 1908. On 30 October of that year, the Whitney government appointed Dr. F. W. Merchant, chief inspector of public and separate schools, to investigate a selection of bilingual schools in Ottawa and Sturgeon Falls and in smaller rural communities in the Ottawa Valley such as Plantagenet, Brook and Clarence Creek. Almost all of the schools which Merchant inspected were entirely French-speaking. His goal was to determine the level of English-language instruction and communication in these schools.

A well educated and seasoned civil servant, Francis Walter Merchant was to play a seminal role in the Regulation 17 controversy. Born in Oil Springs, Ontario, on 25 November 1855, Merchant earned a B.A. (1878) and an M.A. (1880) from Albert College and a Doctor of Paedogogy from the University of Toronto (1901). Beginning in 1908, he held a variety of posts in the education portfolio: chief inspector of public and separate schools; director of industrial and technical education; chief director of education; and chief adviser to the minister of education. His last posting came in 1930. He was also the author and co-author of three school texts.[19]

Merchant submitted his confidential report in January 1910. He painted a deeply disturbing picture of the state of bilingual education. Most damning was his judgment that neither French nor English was taught adequately. The whole system was a shambles. In nearly every school, French was the language of instruction and communication during Forms I and II (grades one to four). In many schools, that practice extended into Form III (grades five and six). Where there was a Form IV (grades seven and eight), the subjects for the high school entrance examination were taught in English, but in three schools he inspected they were taught in French. This made no sense. Although Merchant found no objection from trustees and teachers to English as a language of instruction, he also discovered that their strong attachment to French in the schools precluded any practical initiatives

216

about having their children taught in English. They were not hostile towards English; they were simply indifferent, a less emotional but more powerful sentiment.

Merchant concluded that any weaknesses in the bilingual schools could be corrected with better trained and professionally qualified teachers. To that end, he recommended special schools for English-French teachers and summer courses for those teachers who held temporary certificates. Regarding French as a language of instruction, he believed that as a matter of simple and practical justice, that it remain the language of instruction during the first four years.[20]

****

Shortly after Merchant had delivered his report to the government, the Catholic bishops, led by Archbishop Fergus McEvay of Toronto, finalized their position on changes to the Qualifications Act (in regards to Religious teachers), on sharing of corporate and utility taxes and on the need for publicly-funded Catholic high schools. Theirs was a radical agenda. Concurrent to the bishops' finalizing their demands, two members of the legislature sponsored individual private bills indirectly on behalf of the bishops. On 26 February 1909, Damase Racine, the Liberal member for Russell, introduced a bill on land assessment in favour of separate school boards. On 16 March, T.W. McGarry, Conservative member for Renfrew, sponsored legislation that would bring substantial relief to separate schools. McGarry's bill would have done the following: divide the taxes of public utilities and "bonus" industries between public and separate school boards according to the number of their respective supporters; amend the Qualifications Act so that Religious could continue to acquire second and third class teaching certificates on the basis of experience and attendance at Normal School summer sessions; amend the Assessment Act so that every Catholic ratepayer would automatically be listed as a separate school supporter and no longer would be required to submit a written notice of their support; and give separate school boards the right to establish Continuation

Classes. Both bills elicited howls of angry protest from the usual quarters.[21]

Whitney responded by informing the legislature on 2 April 1909 that the government had no intention of amending the Separate School Act during the present session. However, in return for Racine and McGarry withdrawing their bills, Whitney made the following promises: he would submit a stated case to the courts to determine the proper basis for the division of the legislative grant between the public and separate school boards — according to population, as was the current practice, or according to attendance, as demanded by separate school boards; he would provide relief to Religious teachers concerning their qualifications; and he would ensure that the cost of separate school textbooks would not exceed that of public school textbooks. Whitney also had R.A. Pyne, the minister of education, promise both Racine and McGarry that within a year the government would consider the whole separate school question.[22] Satisfied, both men promptly withdrew their bills.

Writing to Archbishop C.H. Gauthier of Kingston, on 24 March 1909, Whitney assured Gauthier (and by extension all the bishops) that "during the recess we will take hold of the several questions or points which have arisen in order that we may at the next Session be ready with legislation on them all."[23] There is no reason to doubt Whitney's sincerity. And there is every reason to believe that he repeated the same assurances he had given to Gauthier when he met Archbishop McEvay and Bishop R.A. O'Connor of Peterborough early in May. Also present at that meeting was J.J. Foy, the provincial attorney general and a leading Catholic member of Whitney's cabinet.

Archbishop McEvay was persistent if nothing else. He had taken a huge risk placing so much trust in Whitney. On 15 February 1910, McEvay wrote the premier, gently reminding him of his promise and of the bishops' willingness to believe that he would fulfill it: "when Sir James says a thing he means it and we have no reason to doubt the promise of the Hon. Premier."[24] The archbishop continued:

At present I merely wish to indicate in the name of the same Bishops some of the questions or points which have been brought to the attention of the Government from time to time and which require legislation and these may be classed under two heads — namely Educational and Financial.

In many places — for example Toronto — it is a great hardship to confine the Separate School system to the entrance class [grade eight]. When we are prepared to maintain efficient Schools and keep the regulations of the Education Department we should be allowed to have all the grades including the High School grades. As to Institutions of Higher Education, we are told there is a scarcity of teachers properly qualified throughout the Province. Then why shut out Convents and Colleges — Catholic or Protestant? Where a long experience has shown that this class of work can be done with success? Besides, parents who select such Schools have a right — it is admitted by the Government — to do so, and they have the further right to have the children prepared for Examinations in these Schools, and any legislation that tends to cripple such Schools in favor of Public Schools is unjust and unworthy of a great and strong provincial government. Inspect these Institutions as you wish, but do not kill them by a slow measure of petty technicalities.

As to the financial question — Catholics have no desire to get Protestant money for Separate Schools, but they do want all their own, and a fair share of taxes from Public Utilities. Surely the Protestants in this Province are able and for the most part willing to pay for the education of their own children. Why should Catholics pay their share of taxes to a bonused Industry and have all the School taxes of such industry go to the rich Public School? Such a thing is unjust on the face of it. Now, that such questions can be properly adjusted under our Constitution is clear from the Province of Quebec. Why should the minority there be more justly and generously treated than the minority in this Province?

This is the delicate and difficult question we expect you

to solve and if you get the answer into proper legislation we will be ever grateful, and the whole Province will have a splendid example that real difficulties can be solved justly by real Statesmen.[25]

Just how delicate and difficult that question had become for Whitney, in only a matter of weeks, was revealed in what must have been a bombshell of a letter from the premier to the archbishop. On 9 March 1910, Whitney informed McEvay of the government's decision not to proceed on its promise to address separate school grievances as outlined by the bishops. The government's about-face was triggered by the politically aggressive behaviour of the recent French Canadian Congress of Education.[26]

****

The first-ever French Canadian Congress of Education met in Ottawa from 18 to 20 January 1910. It attracted more than 1,200 delegates from every French-speaking corner of the province. In attendance at the public functions, at either the Russell Theatre or the Russell Hotel, were Monsignor Donato Sbaretti, the apostolic delegate, Sir Wilfrid Laurier, the prime minister, Robert Laird Borden, the leader of the opposition, Sir Etienne Taschereau, a former chief justice of the Supreme Court, Father William Murphy, the rector of the University of Ottawa, an impressive number of federal cabinet ministers and a cross-section of French-Canadian monsignors from Ontario, including J.O. Routhier, vicar general of the archdiocese of Ottawa.[27] Three members of the provincial cabinet represented Ontario, but unfortunately Whitney, Pyne and Foy each declined an invitation to attend. This was a political mistake. The delegates voted Senator Napoleon Belcourt as their president and established a permanent body, l'Association canadienne-française d'education d'Ontario (ACFEO), to carry its fight directly to the politicians and the courts. Belcourt had been counsel for the Christian Brothers during the teaching qualifications battle and was well versed in the language politics of the day.

What had offended Whitney were the fifteen resolutions adopted by the Congress and presented to him at a meeting with ACFEO representatives on 18 February, three days after McEvay's letter of 15 February. The ACFEO's timing could not have been worse for separate school supporters. The bishops had good reason to believe that they were on the cusp of convincing Whitney to transform the fortunes of separate schools. Whatever opportunity existed in 1909 to bring about that transformation vanished a year later because of the precipitous political behaviour of the ACFEO. Of course, the ACFEO did not intend to sideswipe the bishops in their diplomatic dance with the premier, but that is exactly what happened in February and March 1910. It was one lesson in the politics of self-destruction that the bishops were not to forget.

Central to the ACFEO's resolutions was a demand that the government of Ontario accept bilingualism and give a more official and prominent status to the French language in both elementary and secondary schools and in Ontario's teacher training schools. In practical terms, this meant that all schools in which the majority of students were French-speaking should be declared English-French. These schools should have French as the language of instruction and communication, with the appropriate readers and textbooks in French, and should have the right to continuation classes. In all schools where twenty-five percent of the students were French-speaking, there should be set aside for these students sufficient in-class time for instruction in French reading, spelling, grammar, composition and literature. All English-French schools and all those in which at least one quarter of the students were French-speaking should be placed under the supervision of bilingual instructors. The all important high school entrance examinations should have French subjects for students in bilingual schools and should also allow French students a lower passing grade on English subjects. The resolutions made no mention of the necessity or place of English language instruction in bilingual schools.[28] In 1910, when Ontario was still very much a Protestant province, and the Orange Lodge still a factor in provincial politics, all talk about official bilingualism and entrenching bilingual schools was pure fantasy bound to rouse the sleeping dog of anti-

French and anti-Catholic hostility.

The Conservative government and the ACFEO were far apart on the subject of bilingual education. No wonder Whitney rejected outright the ACFEO's resolutions and no wonder he promptly closed the door on the bishops' demand to expand the tax base for Catholic separate schools and to extend the separate school system to include high schools.

As soon as that door was closed, the bishops, with the exception of E.A. Latulippe, vicar apostolic of Témiscamingue, turned on bilingual schools. The shock of having been so easily rebuffed by Whitney on 9 March quickly turned into a fear, fed by the warnings of some parish priests — that the continuing existence of English-French schools, the majority of which were now under Catholic auspices, would sound the death knell for the entire separate school system. It may have been a leap of logic, but the logic of practical politics drew them to that conclusion. Archbishop Fergus McEvay made known his own frustration in a letter, dated 27 December 1910, to Archbishop Louis-Nazaire Begin of Quebec. It had been a long-standing custom, McEvay wrote Begin, for the bishops to present a united front when making proposals to the government on separate school legislation. McEvay continued:

> At the last Session of Parliament, many important requests, equally favoring French and English speaking subjects, were made by the Bishops of this Province, and the Government promised favorable legislation upon them. In the midst of all this, took place the Ottawa Congress, with the result that nothing was done to meet its long list of new demands, and worse than that the Government owing to the agitation aroused in the country, felt compelled to withhold the legislation which they had promised for the betterment of the Catholic System.[29]

This letter came at the close of the first round of the strictly Catholic battle over bilingual education. Much had happened to prompt McEvay to write it. The appearance of his protégé as the new bishop of London in the spring of 1910 had set the stage for that battle.

****

Michael Francis Fallon was consecrated bishop of London on 25 April 1910, to the applause of many who saw in him a brilliant champion of Catholic causes and to the utter dismay of many French Canadians who considered him the bête noir of the anti-French wing of Canadian society. It is not our purpose to discuss in detail the controversial career of this complicated man. That has been done elsewhere, although never in book length.[30] For our purposes, it is important to appreciate that before Bishop Fallon appeared on the scene, no Catholic bishop in Ontario had gone public with any kind of opinion for or against English-French schools. Fallon was the first to do so. Moreover, his episcopal colleagues almost to a man were quick to follow his lead when the crisis erupted and were relieved to have him deal directly with the government. Any fallout would be for Fallon to bear. We also note that Fallon had opposed the demands of the Congress and had congratulated Premier Whitney for standing firm in his opposition to any form of official bilingualism in the province's schools. Any views on bilingual education that Fallon held before he assumed official control of the diocese of London remained the same once he was raised to the episcopacy. He did not let his office temper his opinions or his willingness to give them. He was nothing if not consistent.

What exactly were Fallon's beliefs on bilingual education? According to C.B. Sissons, who wrote about Regulation 17 at the height of the controversy, Fallon did not object to the use of the French language. Rather, he denounced "the attempt to conduct the study of English and French simultaneously with the same pupils in the same elementary schools."[31] Fallon was fluent in both English and French and often preached in French. However, he was convinced that a bilingual approach to educating the young, as delivered in the province's English-French schools, was pedagogically unsound, producing an unfortunate class of student who was proficient in neither language and could not pass the high school entrance examination. What Bishop Fallon witnessed during his first confirmation tour — children who could not speak French or English very well as they tried to answer their catechism questions — convinced him that there was no practical hope of reforming such a system. It had to be abolished, and the sooner the better for the children who needlessly suffered under it and for the separate school system which had tolerated it for far too long.

Although Regulation 17 was strictly the government's doing, one might say that it had its genesis in a private conversation Bishop Fallon had with W. J. Hanna, provincial secretary and the member for Lambton West. Fallon asked to meet Hanna in Sarnia, where Fallon was scheduled for the next round of confirmations. Hanna happily obliged, and the two men met on 23 May 1910. Hanna wrote up the substance of their conversation in a memo dated the same day and addressed to Dr. Pyne, the minister of education. It appears that Fallon did most of the talking. He was thoroughly agitated.

> [Bishop Fallon] had resolved, so far as it is in his power, to cause to disappear every trace of bi-lingual teaching in the public schools of his diocese. The interests of the children, boys and girls, demand that bi-lingual teaching should be disapproved and prohibited . . . We belong to a Province of English-speaking people, part of an English-speaking continent, where all children leaving school to engage in the battles of life must be armed first of all with the English language, cost what it may.[32]

Fallon went on to complain about politicians and French-Canadian agitators who claimed that they (the French) controlled as many as fifteen or seventeen counties in the Ontario. He said that this was absolutely untrue, the result of "stuffed census lists," and that the sole purpose of such a false claim was "to control church and state, and that instead of being crushed or choked off they would dominate in both."[33]

Bishop Fallon despised French Canadian nationalism as much

as he did Protestant bigotry, at one time referring to them as two millstones, an upper and a lower, in between which was the Church.[34] Having fought against both forces all his life, Fallon believed that if they were allowed to battle each other over bilingual schools, the province's separate schools would be the only ones to suffer. At the annual retreat for diocesan priests at Assumption College in Sandwich, on 14 July 1910, Fallon spoke of the dangers of French Canadian nationalism in terms of a conspiracy. One of his priests, who was hostile to him, recorded his comments and forwarded them to the French press. At one point during his discourse, Fallon said:

> I am opposed to bilingual schools because they cannot provide an education suitable to our needs. The bilingual school has not succeeded in the Province of Quebec, and will not succeed in this Province.
>
> There is a conspiracy against the separate schools, and this conspiracy comes from a source I was loath to suspect; moreover, this conspiracy will lead us to the loss of our separate schools, because our enemies, once they see the division which exists among Catholics with reference to bilingual schools, will make use of this to weaken our position, and they will then deprive us of our schools.[35]

The Hanna/Pyne memorandum would explode on the front pages of the nation's newspapers if it ever found its way into the wrong hands. And that is precisely what happened. A full translation of the memorandum (along with other material such as the transcription of Fallon's remarks at the July retreat) appeared in a lengthy article by Michel Renouf for the 1 October 1910 issue of *Revue Franco-Américaine*. Renouf was one of Fallon's most strident and persistent critics in the French newspapers. Henri Bourassa printed Renouf's article in the 7 October issue of the more mainline *Le Devoir*. Bourassa was the most eloquent and influential French Canadian nationalist of his day. His paper was a thorn in the side of Bishop Fallon, who considered Bourassa's hostility a badge of honour. The memorandum had arrived on Renouf's desk courtesy of

H.C.A. Maisonville, the private secretary to Joseph O. Reaume, the member for Essex North and minister of public works in the Whitney government. Reaume was handy to Whitney because he was a French Catholic. Following an internal investigation, an unrepentant Maisonville was subsequently fired and Reaume was left severely embarrassed by the misbehaviour of his secretary. But the damage was done.

Fallon always relished a good fight. His reply came on 16 October, after Hanna's memorandum appeared in the *Globe*,[36] but before we examine it, we must mention two events that happened before that date. One, in his official capacity as spokesman for the Ontario bishops, Fallon had met Whitney on 16 August 1910. He told the premier that the Catholic bishops were opposed to bilingual schools. Whitney was confused. He believed that it was necessary to have French as a language of instruction for those children in the lower grades who spoke only French. Fallon agreed that that was the pedagogically sound thing to do. But he also made clear that instruction in French should not be extended beyond the lower grades. Rather, French-speaking children had to adapt to English-only instruction as quickly and smoothly as possible so that they could acquire enough proficiency in the English language to pass the high school entrance examination. On this crucial point the two men agreed.[37] Two, Fallon had already answered allegations, repeated in a half dozen French newspapers, that at the start of the 1910 school year he had forbidden the use of French in his diocese's separate schools. Fallon's emphatic and angry denial of 22 September 1910 was published in many Ontario newspapers.[38]

When it came time to respond to the publication of the Hanna/Pyne memorandum, Fallon was ready to blast his detractors. Writing from Goderich, another stop in his confirmation tour, Fallon confirmed the substance of the Hanna/Pyne memorandum and went on to amplify his opposition to bilingual education. Portions of it are reproduced below:

> The alleged bilingual system of education, as it prevails
> in certain parts of the Province of Ontario, is absolutely futile

as concerning the teaching of either English or French, and utterly hostile to the best interests of the children, both English and French. Let me cite a few facts, culled from a multitude, that I have collected on my tour through the Diocese of London.

The French-Canadian parishes of Belle River, Big Point, French Settlement, McGregor, Ruscomb, Staples, Stoney Point, Paincourt and Tilbury, with separate schools, and upwards of 2,000 children on the rolls, passed a total of ten pupils at the recent entrance examinations. It is from some of these parishes that the loudest noise comes regarding my insistence that these conditions are a disgrace. If the separate schools in these districts are bad, the public schools, also under the alleged bilingual system, are worse.

For the above-mentioned nine districts the public schools succeeded in getting only seven children through the entrance examination, of which Tilbury furnished four, McGregor, Big Point, and Paincourt one each, and the others none. And I could cite many other instances of equal inefficiency. All these facts have been supplied to me, over their own signature, by the pastors of the parishes I have named.

Is it any wonder that I should raise my voice on behalf of all the children who live in what might be called the bilingual belt of my diocese? And is it not monstrous that for so doing I should be charged with hostility to the French language and to the interests of the French-Canadian people? In the schools that are inflicted on these children neither English nor French is properly taught or decently spoken. The regulations of the Education Department are in many instances utterly disregarded. Because of the conditions that obtain, children are either not sent to school at all or are withdrawn in the face of the difficulties . . .

Now, the fault is not with the children or with the teachers — it is with the system, and it is against the system and the threatened extension of it that I protest. I base my protest on the rights of children to an education that will give them a standing in the community in which they are to live and that will open up to them the avenue of success. As things stand now, these children will either remain where they are, and then they will continue to be as they are, or they will move to Quebec to be classed as renegades because they do not know French, or they will go elsewhere to be hewers of wood or drawers of water because they do not know English. Essex stands lowest educationally amongst the nine counties that constitute the Diocese of London. Everything flourishes there except education. The land is heavy with rich harvests, choice fruits, and a generation of uneducated children. One would almost be inclined to believe in the existence of a well-contrived conspiracy among the enemies of the French-Canadian people to keep them in a position of self-perpetuating intellectual inferiority. To the contention that the language is the guardian of faith, I reply that it is a strange faith that would be preserved by the kind of English or French that is taught in the alleged bilingual schools of Essex, and I resent the inference that Catholicity and ignorance are convertible terms. . .

This whole question is not a contest between English-speaking and French-speaking Catholics; it is a matter of great public moment. On the one side of the discussion are a certain number of French-Canadians led by noisy agitators; on the other side are also French-Canadians in no small numbers with the rest of the population of the Province of Ontario, without distinction of creed or nationality. And let me hazard the prophecy that when this second division awakens to the gravity of the situation, it will make short work of an alleged bilingual school system, which teaches neither English nor French, encourages incompetency, gives a prize to hypocrisy and breeds ignorance.[39]

Fallon's statement was sensational. Wrapped in layers of brilliant rhetoric and damning facts, his words ignited intense newspaper coverage and editorial responses and aroused the slumbering Orangemen. In the topsy-turvy world of education politics, they became allies of Fallon but for reasons antithetical to the bishop's stated desire to preserve separate schools from extinction. Fallon's prophecy, given in the last sentence of his statement, did not quite come true. The fate of bilingual schools *did* divide French and English Catholics, and the "division" in society that attempted to "make short work of an alleged bilingual school system" was not the people, the grassroots opposition as envisioned by Fallon, but the government in the person of the premier.

****

Whitney's reaction to the ensuing uproar over Bishop Fallon's statement was to appoint F.W. Merchant to investigate Ontario's English-French schools, for a second time and far more thoroughly than he had in his previous report of January 1910. Beginning on 2 November 1910, Dr. Merchant examined 269 schools in which French was a language of instruction. These schools had 538 teachers and an aggregate enrolment of 20,645 pupils, of which 18,833 were French-speaking. They were located in the historic French settlements of Essex and Kent counties, in Russell, Prescott, Stormont and Glengarry counties in Eastern Ontario and in the city of Ottawa. Merchant also corresponded with another 79 schools with 104 teachers in what is now Northern Ontario.[40]

The Merchant commission was Whitney's way of buying time as he prepared his party for a 1911 election, which took place on 11 December, and also of deflecting the potentially damaging work of the *Toronto Star*. The *Star* had dispatched E.J. Archibald to report on bilingual schools in Essex and Kent counties, on the heels of Fallon's October statement. Archibald spoke fluent French and was sympathetic towards the children in these schools who spoke French at home but were expected to learn their lessons in English. Archibald concluded that any deficiencies in the bilingual schools were not the fault of the system. And the *Star* continued its reporting on bilingual schools the following year, when it sent Archibald and a second

229

reporter, H.M. Bolland, to Eastern and Northern Ontario. Bolland knew French and was a Catholic. Their stories appeared almost every day during November and December 1911.[41]

While Merchant was visiting bilingual schools, Whitney was active on the political front, ensuring that the general public (including Merchant) knew his government's stance on bilingual schools. On 22 March 1911, the legislative assembly passed the following resolution: "That the English language shall be the language of instruction and communication of the pupils of the Public and Separate schools of the Province of Ontario, except where, in the opinion of the Department of Education, it is found impracticable because the pupil does not understand English."[42] On many occasions during the election campaign, Whitney had recourse to this all-party resolution. It was an easy way to deflect questions on bilingual schools. He also had his lieutenants speak on the subject, but were they singing from the same hymnal? J.J. Foy told the press that "the English language should be thoroughly taught in our schools to every pupil by teachers competent to teach English; that no other language should be taught in these schools; that such is the law which should govern us; that there cannot lawfully be any Bi-lingual schools in the Province, and if any are found they must cease to exist and care should be taken to make all schools conform to the law."[43] This was no-nonsense talk from the attorney general: yes to English as the only language of instruction; no to bilingual schools. Period. Joseph O. Reaume, a fellow cabinet minister, put a different spin on the topic, taking care to be as ambiguous as possible and to attribute government policy on bilingual schools to the premier:

> Sir James Whitney's attitude is that while English should be made the language of the schools, as far as practicable, and while it is maintained that every child should receive an English education, we are not against the French-Canadians and Germans having their children started in their mother tongue, as a means to an end, and having their mother tongue taught in the schools as a subject when so desired by trustees representing the people of the school section.[44]

230

The "end," according to Reaume's way of thinking, did not mean an end to bilingual schools. What had to be determined was the length of time a child would be taught in his mother tongue and the teaching process by which he would learn English so that he could be taught in that language in the upper grades of elementary school. It would be Merchant's job to determine these things.

****

Premier Whitney won a landslide in the 1911 election, 83 seats for the Conservatives and 22 for the Liberals, with one Independent. J.O. Reaume was re-elected by only 53 votes. It appears that the French Canadians of Essex North were angered by his endorsement of a severely truncated form of bilingual education. Their displeasure was a harbinger of things to come. Dr. Merchant delivered his report on 24 February 1912, and the government tabled it in the legislature on 6 March, the last day of the session.[45]

In his *Report on the Condition of English-French Schools in the Province of Ontario*, Merchant concluded on the basis of pupil test results that bilingual schools were failing to provide their students with an adequate education so that they could meet the daily demands of life upon leaving school. In other words, they were inefficient. According to Bishop Fallon, this should have been enough to damn them into non-existence, but Merchant refused to pursue that direction. He said that the causes of their inefficiency were many, the chief one being that children who grew up exclusively in one language were required to learn another so that they could master their required school subjects. This would have been challenge enough for the brightest and most enthusiastic of students under the best of circumstances. But those circumstances were lacking in the bilingual schools. Student attendance was generally poor; far too many teachers were inexperienced, held the lowest teaching qualifications and were poorly paid; and there was confusion in the bilingual separate schools regarding their obligation to obey the regulations of the department of Education. It was a common belief among French-speaking Catholics that no Catholic separate school, bilingual or not, was obliged to follow departmental regulations. This was not true, of course, but local practice had a way of superseding regulations. Substantial reforms to the structure, management and teaching practices of bilingual schools were necessary if they were to be saved in some fashion and properly integrated into the provincial school system.

Merchant was under no illusion that the Whitney government expected every school in the province to have English as the language of instruction and communication, and that to achieve this some limit would have to be placed on the use of the French language. However, he was realistic enough to know that any attempt to abolish outright English-French schools would be a disaster and that to curtail too severely the use of French in the lower grades would only do more harm than good.

Merchant proposed better teaching training for current teachers and more effort to attract new French-speaking teachers. However, nothing could be done about the latter unless the department of education developed a closer working relationship between English-French schools and high schools and allowed some practical leeway to English-French students in the high school entrance examination. He also recommended more modern French textbooks.

Everything, though, hinged on the process whereby French-speaking students would learn English. To this all-important end, Merchant proposed a transition that would take place over five years. Form I would consist of grades one, two and three, and Form II would be grades four and five. During these years, English would gradually replace French as the medium of instruction. In those schools attended by both French and English students, a dual system of instruction would prevail until Form III, at which time all students would be taught in English.[46] A new group of Supervising Inspectors would enforce the will of the government.

Merchant's approach to the "problem" of English-French schools rested on a theory of transition, not a demand for abolition, on a gradual movement from French to English instruction, which assumed the continued existence of so-called bilingual schools as a legitimate part of the province's school system. The status quo could no longer be tolerated, but real change in conformity to political expectations had to be gradual with the best interests of the children always kept in the forefront of any administrative decisions concerning the future of bilingual schools.

For reasons best known to himself Premier Whitney chose to ignore Merchant's gradualist approach to language replacement and opted for what became Regulation 17. The political intent of this regulation was to abolish the existence of bilingual schools by limiting the use of French as an instructional language to Form I and by restricting the right to any exemptions to one year. John Seath, the superintendent of education, warned R.A. Pyne, the minister of education, that the prohibition of French beyond Form I would be injurious to the students and was illegal under the Public School Act. He argued to no avail. Even the 1913 amendment of Regulation 17 had as its intention the extinction of bilingual schools. This was how the ACFEO interpreted the government's actions, and Instructions 18, as we have already alluded to, only bolstered their opposition. Leaders of French Canadian opinion were spoiling for a fight, and the Ottawa separate school board provided a convenient battle ground.

****

Nowhere was the battle over Regulation 17 more bitter and disruptive than it was in Ottawa, where the French members of the separate school board took it upon themselves to defy the government. (In the previous chapter, we examined the politics of language combined with religion in the matter of the qualifications of Religious teachers.) Although the board was divided into two committees for administrative purposes — English trustees for English schools and French trustees for French schools — when meeting as a whole board, the French members formed a majority, which they used to great effect as the Regulation 17 crisis unfolded. At the urging of the ACFEO, trustee Samuel M. Genest convinced his French colleagues to pass two resolutions at a board meeting of 11 September 1912. These resolutions denounced the appointment of three English Protestant school inspectors, in place of the bilingual

233

Roman Catholic school inspectors, and a Protestant as head of the bilingual training school. As well, they warned that since the language requirements of Regulation 17 were pedagogically unsound, none of them would be enforced by the board in any of its English-French schools.[47]

To make clear its determination not to obey the law, Genest led a thirty-member delegation to Queen's Park, where, on 27 December 1912, they met Premier Whitney and four high profile cabinet members: R.A. Pyne, J.J. Foy, J.O. Reaume and James S. Duff. Nothing the delegation said could persuade Whitney to withdraw the Regulation. Indeed, the premier let it be known that "The reason why Separate schools exist is because of religious feeling, but the people of Ontario are not willing that a third kind of schools, known as racial schools, should exist."[48] (The phrase "racial schools" was political code for bilingual schools.) Whitney could not have been more forceful on this point, and he could well afford to be forceful because he had the vast majority of Ontario's electors behind him.

Undaunted, the French members of the school board continued to defy the government on Regulation 17. When they went on record as rejecting the August 1913 amendments to the Regulation and then refused to submit reports and to allow school inspectors into the schools, the government responded by suspending the legislative grants. This meant a loss of at least $4,000 a year, a considerable sum of money.

The English trustees were horrified at this turn of events. In November 1913, they launched what became a campaign to convince the government to establish two distinct language-based boards for separate school supporters. To this end, they sought and received the support of Ottawa's English-speaking priests and ratepayers. Meeting as a whole on 11 March 1914, the board refused to rescind the September 1912 resolutions. This prompted the English trustees to petition the government for their own English-language Catholic separate school board.

Since English-speaking Catholics provided the lion's share of tax money for separate schools, the French trustees interpreted this last move as a threat to the existence of bilingual schools. They

234

retaliated by intervening on behalf of two English candidates for the position of trustee who opposed Regulation 17, in the election of 24 April 1914. This action broke an old Ottawa tradition of non-interference based on language in trustee elections. Next, the school board asked the city of Ottawa for a by-law that would allow the board to raise $275,000 in debentures to cover the costs of paying teachers' salaries and building new classrooms and schools.

Six members of the English Committee of the school board protested this action. They were R. Mackell, J.F. Lanigan, Henry R. Sims, A.J. Brennan, James Finn and M.J. O'Neil. After writing to Archbishop Gauthier of Ottawa and to Premier W.H. Hearst (who had succeeded Whitney in September 1914) and R. A. Pyne, the minister of education, all to no avail, they sued the school board, winning an injunction in court on 29 April 1914.[49] The board appealed, on 28 November 1914 and 12 July 1915, losing both times, and took their case to the Judicial Committee of the Privy Council. In *Trustees of the Roman Catholic Separate Schools for the City of Ottawa vs. Mackell*, given on 2 November 1916, the Privy Council ruled that Regulation 17 and the Act of the provincial legislature that conferred authority upon it (5 Geo. V, c. 45) did not contravene any right conferred on Roman Catholics in the BNA Act of 1867. Trustees had a right, based on religion, to manage the schools under their stewardship, but they did not have a right to determine the language of instruction in those schools.[50]

As this case was winding its way through the courts, the Ottawa separate school board closed all its schools in June 1914, the day after the Conservatives won another provincial election, and the board kept them closed at the opening of the school year in September. More than 8,000 children were affected. The official reason for the closing was the government withdrawal of the legislative grant. But there was another motive at work: the board wanted the department of education to accept the board's hiring of twenty-three Christian Brothers, who were not qualified to teach in Ontario. Chaos in the school system was the result.

In April 1915, the Hearst government decided to restore order in Ottawa separate schools by abolishing the board of elected trustees and replacing them with an appointed commission of three to seven members. The Act was passed in April and the commission was appointed in July.[51] The members were Denis Murphy, Thomas D'Arcy McGee and Arthur Charbonneau.[52] Support for the commission, which was given all the powers of a school board, was split strictly along language lines. What followed in 1915 and 1916 were riots, marches and a children's crusade in Ottawa, Orange counter-rallies, protests from prominent Quebec nationalists, Quebec-based fund-raisers to re-open the separate schools as private schools, a House of Commons resolution and a flurry of charges and counter-charges of unpatriotic behaviour.

In the midst of all this, the French-speaking members of the disbanded Ottawa separate school board challenged the legality of the school commission, taking their case once again all the way to the Judicial Committee of the Privy Council. This time they won. In *Trustees of the Roman Catholic Separate Schools vs. Ottawa Corporation*, also presented on 2 November 1916, the Privy Council declared that the law giving the province the authority to disband a duly elected school board was unconstitutional.[53]

And there was a third Privy Council decision, reported in 1920. As soon as the Ottawa separate school board was back in operation, in 1916, it sued the commission members personally, as well as the banks from which they had borrowed funds, for the moneys that the commission had spent to operate the schools. Wanting to protect the commissioners from any personal liability, the government passed an Act in 1917 that declared that all moneys disbursed by the commission had been handled lawfully and that the Act itself could be used by the commissioners as a defense in any action brought against by the school board. The board challenged the constitutionality of this Act. However, in this matter they were unsuccessful. In *Trustees of the Roman Catholic Separate Schools for the City of Ottawa vs. Quebec Bank*, the Privy Council ruled that the Act was valid.[54]

****

In the face of the Ottawa turmoil and the loss of legislative grants to 190 bilingual schools in 1915, for failure to comply with Regulation 17, the Catholic bishops of Ontario decided to seek counsel from Rome. On 12 October 1915, seven of them, including Archbishop McNeil of Toronto and Archbishop Spratt of Kingston, met in Toronto and drafted a letter of explanation to the Holy See. Benedict XV responded in an Apostolic Letter of 8 September 1916. It was published in many Canadian newspapers near the end of October, and it was hailed by a broad cross section of Canadian society as "a masterpiece of wisdom and moderation."[55] Having reminded Catholics that "the one thing of supreme importance above all others is to have Catholic schools and not to imperil their existence," the pope laid out his arguments in two paragraphs:

> Nobody can deny that the civil Government of Ontario has the right to exact that children should learn English in the schools; and likewise that the Catholics of Ontario legitimately require that it should be perfectly taught, in order that their sons should be placed on the same level in this respect with non-Catholic children who frequent the neutral schools, and that they should not be eventually less fitted for the higher schools or be disqualified for civil employments. Nor on the other hand is there any reason to contest the right of French-Canadians, living in the Province, to claim, in a suitable way, however, that French should be taught in schools attended by a certain number of their children; nor are they indeed to be blamed for upholding what is so dear to them. . .
>
> How these two requirements are to be met, namely, a thorough knowledge of English and an equitable teaching of French for French-Canadian children, it is obvious that in the case of schools subject to the public administration, the matter cannot be dealt with independently of the Government. But this does not prevent the Bishops in their earnest care for the salvation of souls, from exerting their utmost activity to make counsels of moderation prevail, and

with a view to obtaining that what is fair and just should be granted.[56]

The bishops gathered in Ottawa on 24 January 1917 to issue a collective response to the pope's letter. The result was a pastoral letter that was read at all Sunday Masses throughout the province, without comment, on the first Sunday after its receipt.[57] In the letter, the bishops said that the faithful had to obey the Regulations of the government but at the same time show sympathy for French Canadian aspirations.

That should have put an end to public squabbling among Catholics and allowed the bishops to privately press the government for modifications to the Regulation, but the French Canadian side continued to lobby Rome for relief. This prompted the Apostolic Delegate to ask the bishops three questions, in a letter of 14 September 1917. Eight bishops gathered in Toronto on 11 October to formulate their responses:

Q. Was it possible to apply Regulation 17?
A. Yes. Since the Regulation had already been successfully applied to sixty schools, it could be applied to all the others.
Q. Should the Regulation be obeyed?
A. Yes. It is the law and the highest court of the land, the Privy Council, declared that it was within the jurisdiction of the province of Ontario.
Q. Should the Regulation be opposed?
A. No. "In Canada, all citizens have the right to oppose any civil law by argument, by influence, and by constitutional agitation, provided they obey the law in the meantime. The difficulty in connection with Regulation XVII, does not consist in the fact that it is opposed, but in the fact that, in a majority of the schools affected by it, the Regulation is not obeyed. In a Province so Protestant as Ontario, no civil government would dare make a change in the wording of this Regulation."[58]

The bishops finished their memorandum by reminding Rome that since the agitation over Regulation 17, no provincial government had had the political will or desire to improve the separate school system. Public opinion was against any improvements. Moreover, any overt opposition from the Catholic bishops to Regulation 17 would have prompted the abolition of the entire system. At the moment, the bishops were coping with a financially crippled system made all the more vulnerable because of the bilingual school crisis.

Benedict XV replied with a second Apostolic Letter, dated 7 June 1918. He declared that French Canadians had a right to appeal to the government for an explanation of the Regulation and to seek changes to it. They also had a right to have Catholic school inspectors, to speak and write French for certain subjects during the early years of school and to have teacher-training schools. However, in attempting to persuade the government for change, French Canadians must not rebel or invoke violent or illegitimate means to accomplish their goals.[59]

****

There the matter "rested" until 6 April 1925, when Premier G. Howard Ferguson, who was his own minister of education, announced in the Ontario legislature that he was not wedded to Regulation 17. In October of that year, he appointed a three-man committee to inquire into the conditions of the schools attended by French-speaking students. The composition of the committee was an act of political brilliance. The committee consisted of F.W. Merchant, chief director of education for Ontario and author of the 1910 and 1912 reports on English-French schools, Judge J.H. Scott, a prominent Orangeman from Perth, and Louis Coté, a French Canadian lawyer from Ottawa. The committee visited 843 classrooms in 330 schools and submitted its report, a hallmark of realism, conciliation and moderation, on 26 August 1927.[60] The government quickly accepted the report's recommendations.

Contrary to popular thinking, then and now, the Merchant-Scott-Coté report did not recommend the removal of Regulation 17.

Nor did it propose the abolition of bilingual schools, even though the commissioners found that the level of education and efficiency in most of the schools under investigation had actually declined since 1912. Instead, the authors of the report proposed a much different and fairer process whereby each school would be treated as an individual entity and judged on its own merits. Each school would be examined by inspectors, who would then consult with a departmental committee on the proper course of action to pursue. The committee would have three members — Director of English Instruction, a Director of French Instruction and the chief inspector — and they would report to the minister of education. Director of Instruction was a new position. Creating two to satisfy both sides of the language divide was a deft political move, because it instantly elevated the French side to a level of equality heretofore unknown in the department of education. The first two directors were W.J. Karr and A.J. Beneteau.

However, for anything good and lasting to come of this inspection and reporting, certain reforms had to be put in place and strictly maintained: the classification "English-French" would disappear, the traditional description of schools as either public or separate would be reinstated, "no rule which prescribes the medium of instruction for different forms or grades of a system [would] be applied impartially to all schools within that system,"[61] the course of study in French and English would be the same but curriculum reductions for those learning English would be allowed and finally teacher training would be significantly improved so that French-language students anywhere in Ontario would receive a standard of education at least equal to that received by their English-speaking counterparts. Concerning the quality of teacher training, the Ferguson government accepted the teacher-training program of the University of Ottawa, without challenging its pedagogical methods. The ACFEO took this as a sign of the government's good intentions and of its willingness to put to rest the bitterness of the recent past.[62]

****

However, the Merchant-Scott-Coté report failed to address the status of French in the high school curriculum and the perennial problem of separate school finances. Following the publication of Benedict XV's second Apostolic Letter in 1918, the bishops felt free to resume their lobbying for a share of corporate taxes and the right to claim publicly-funded high schools. These two issues were about to be addressed by the Whitney government in 1910, apparently to the satisfaction of the bishops, when the many-headed monster of English-French schools had overtaken their carefully orchestrated plans. Seventeen years later, another Conservative government found the right approach to Regulation 17. In the meantime, the bishops and lay leaders carried on their campaign to save and improve separate schools for future generations of Catholic children.

---

[1] As far as I know, John Moir was the first to use "double-minority" to describe the status of a particular group of Catholics in Canada. Credit, then, must go to him. He used the phrase to describe the position of English-speaking Catholics in the nineteenth century: "English-speaking Catholics shared the religious aspirations of French Canadian Catholics, but they often shared the political aspirations of English-speaking Protestants. The position of English Catholics may perhaps be described as a third solitude. They remained separated by language from their co-religionists and by religion from their co-linguists." See John Moir, "The Problem of a Double Minority: Some Reflections on the Development of the English-speaking Catholic Church in Canada in the Nineteenth Century," *Histoire Sociale/Social History* 7 (April 1971): 55. However, during the Regulation 17 debacle, the tables were turned, and French-speaking Catholics in Ontario found themselves the double minority.

[2] For an examination of how Regulation 17 affected the different federal and provincial political parties, see Margaret Prang, "Clerics, Politicians and the Bilingual Schools Issue in Ontario, 1910-1917," *Canadian Historical Review*, 41, no. 4 (December 1960): 281-307.

[3] Walker, *Catholic Education and Politics in Ontario*, 2: 246. A figure of 5,913 public schools and 467 separate schools, for a total of 6,380 elementary schools is given in J. Castell Hopkins, *The Canadian Annual Review of Public Affairs 1910* [hereafter cited as *Canadian Annual Review*] (Toronto: The Annual Review Publishing Company, 1911), 427. Whitney's figures were approximate for both the number of English-French schools and the number which were separate schools and public schools. One can only conclude that despite all the inspectors' reports, the government was unsure of the exact number of schools that were the cause of so much concern.

[4] *Report of the Royal Commission on Education in Ontario 1950* [hereafter cited as *Hope Commission*] (Toronto: King's Printer, 1950), Appendix A. Regulation 17 in its entirety can also be located in C.B. Sissons, *Bi-Lingual Schools in Ontario* (Toronto: J.M. Dent & Sons, 1917), Appendix II.

[5] Ibid., Appendix B.

[6] Walker, *Catholic Education and Politics in Ontario*, 2: 270-71.

[7] *Hope Commission*, 395, 398-99.

[8] Ibid., 399

[9] Ibid., 400.

[10] Ibid.

[11] Ibid., 396.

[12] Ibid., 401.

[13] Marilyn Barber, "The Ontario Bilingual Schools Issue: Sources of Conflict," *Canadian Historical Review*, 47, no. 3 (September 1966), 228.

[14] *Hope Commission*, 402.

[15] *Report of the Minister of Education (Ontario) for the Year 1882* (Toronto: C. Blackett Robinson, 1883), 131,

[16] *Report of the Minister of Education (Ontario) for the Year 1886* (Toronto: Warwick & Sons, 1887), 88-89.

[17] Ibid., 89.

[18] *Report of the Minister of Education (Ontario) for the Year 1893* (Toronto: Warwick & Sons, 1894), 183-84.

[19] "Merchant, Francis Walter," *The Macmillan Dictionary of Canadian Biography* (Toronto: Macmillan of Canada, 1978), 571; *The Canadian Who's Who*, 1936-1937 (Toronto: 1936-), 2: 776; Henry James Morgan, *Canadian Men and Women of the Time*, 2nd ed. (Toronto: William Briggs, 1912), 795.

[20] Walker, *Catholic Education and Politics in Ontario*, 2: 235-37; Barber, "The Ontario Bilingual Schools Issue," 237.

[21] Ibid., 224-25.

[22] *Globe*, 3 April 1909, 7.

[23] AO, F5 MU 3122, Sir James Pliny Whitney Papers, Whitney to Gauthier, 24 March 1909.

[24] ARCAT, ME AE0148, Archbishop Fergus McEvay to Sir James O. Whitney, 15 February 1910.

[25] Ibid.

[26] Walker, *Catholic Education and Politics in Ontario*, 2: 227, fn. 128. The Whitney government did live up to its promise to change the way in which the legislative grant was proportioned, with "An Act to amend the Department of Education Act" (10 Edw. VIII, c. 102); *Ontario Gazette*, 26 May 1910, 2. See also ARCAT, ME AE0151, George F. Shepley to Archbishop Fergus McEvay, 23 March 1910, plus a copy of Shepley's fees. In his letter, Shepley is obviously referring to the above Act, which was given Royal Assent on 19 March 1910. There is some confusion in the way in which this matter is reported in Choquette, *Language and Religion*, 89. Choquette's claim that "the Separate School amendments became law, but that the government refused to enforce them, because of the A.C.F.E.O. complication" is incorrect. Whitney fulfilled his promise to amend the law concerning legislative grants. This amendment became law on 19 March 1910. The bishops' proposals for amendments concerning corporate taxes and high schools, as outlined in McEvay's 15 February 1910 letter to the premier, went nowhere, due to the ACFEO's fifteen demands.

[27] Choquette, *Language and Religion,* 68-78.

[28] Barber, "The Ontario Bilingual Schools Issue," 240, *Canadian Annual Review 1910*, 420. A full text of the "A.C.F.E.O. Memorandum to the Government of Ontario, in February, 1910" can be found in Choquette, *Language and Religion*, Appendix.

[29] ARCAT, ME AE0158, Archbishop Fergus McEvay to Most Rev. L.N. Begin, D.D., 27 December 1910.

[30] John K.A. Farrell [O'Farrell], "Michael Francis Fallon, Bishop of London Ontario – Canada, The Man and His Controversies," CCHA, *Study Sessions* (1968): 73-90; Paul Baillergeon, "Bishop Michael Francis Fallon: Founder of St. Peter's Seminary," St. Peter's Seminary, London, Ontario, *Alumni Bulletin* (December 1966): 28-51; Michael Power, "The Mitred Warrior: A Critical Reassessment of Bishop Michael Francis Fallon, 1867-1931," *Catholic Insight*, 8, no. 3 (April 2000): 18-26. These three works contain references to many other works on Fallon. A very useful but highly critical look at Fallon is Robert Choquette's *Language and Religion: A History of English-French Conflict in Ontario.*

[31] Sissons, *Bi-Lingual Schools in Ontario*, 81.

[32] Ibid., 74-75.

[33] Ibid., 76.

[34] In a letter of 16 May 1916, Fallon wrote to Charles Murphy, a member of the House of Commons, "what is to become of us between the upper millstone of French-Canadian nationalism and the lower millstone of Protestant bigotry." As quoted in Prang, "Clerics, Politicians, and the Bilingual Schools Issue in Ontario, 1910-1917," 302.

[35] *Globe*, 13 October 1910, 2.

[36] Ibid., 1-2.

[37] ARCAT, ME AE01.55, Bishop M.F. Fallon to Archbishop C.H. Gauthier, 18 August 1910 (copy).

[38] *Globe*, 23 September 1910, 2.

[39] Ibid., 17 October 1910, 4.

[40] *Canadian Annual Review 1912* (Toronto: Annual Review Publishing Limited, 1913), 367-68.

[41] Sissons, *Bi-Lingual Schools in Ontario*, 81-89; *Canadian Annual Review 1911* (Toronto: Annual Review Publishing Company, 1912), 472.

[42] As quoted in Walker, *Catholic Education and Politics in Ontario*, 2: 258.

[43] *Canadian Annual Review 1911*, 473-74.

[44] Ibid., 474.

[45] F.W. Merchant, *Report on the Condition of English-French Schools in the Province of Ontario* (Toronto: King's Printer, 1912).

[46] *Hope Commission*, 405-8; *Canadian Annual Review 1912*, 367-70.

[47] Choquette, *Language and Religion*, 168; Walker, *Catholic Education and Politics in Ontario*, 2: 270

[48] *Canadian Annual Review, 1912*, 373.

[49] AO, Pamphlet 1915, No. 66, *The Ottawa Separate School Case*, (Ottawa: Printed Privately, 1915).

[50] *Hope Commission*, 409-10; for a copy of the decision, see Carter, *Judicial Decisions on Denominational Schools*, 49-58: Trustees of the Roman Catholic Separate Schools for the City of Ottawa vs. Mackell, Privy Council, 1917, A.C., 62.

[51] Province of Ontario, *Statutes 1915*, 5 Geo. V, c. 45.

[52] *Hope Commission*, 410.

[53] Ibid.; for a copy of the decision, see Carter, *Judicial Decisions on Denominational Schools*, 75-79: Trustees of the Roman Catholic Separate Schools for Ottawa vs. Ottawa Corporation, Privy Council, 1917, a.C., 76.

[54] *Hope Commission*, 410-11; for a copy of the decision, see Carter, *Judicial Decisions on Denominational Schools*, 80-85: Trustees of the Roman Catholic Separate Schools for the City of Ottawa vs. The Quebec Bank, Privy Council, 1920, A.C., 230.

[55] Walker, *Catholic Education and Polictics in Ontario*, 2: 298.

[56] Sissons, *Bi-Lingual Schools in Ontario*, 226, 227. Sissons reproduces the entire Apostolic Letter in Appendix III; *Globe*, 28 October 1916, 5.

[57] *Catholic Register*, 8 February 1917.

[58] As quoted in Walker, *Catholic Education and Politics in Ontario*, 2: 302-3.

[59] Ibid., 303-4; Choquette, *Language and Religion*, 213.

[60] *Report of the Committee Appointed to Enquire into the Condition of the Schools Attended by French-speaking Pupils* (Toronto: King's Printer, 1927).

[61] As quoted in Peter Oliver, *Public & Private Persons* (Toronto: Clarke, Irwin & Company, 1975), 115.

[62] Walker, *Catholic Education and Politics in Ontario*, 2: 314-21; *Canadian Annual Review 1927-28* (Toronto: Canadian Review Company, 1928), 380-82; *Hope Commission*, 411-14; *Globe*, 22 September 1927, 1-2.

CHAPTER FIVE

THE BISHOPS TAKE CONTROL
THE 1920S CAMPAIGN: CORPORATION TAXES,
HIGH SCHOOLS AND THE TINY TOWNSHIP CASE

*C*he 1920s form another tumultuous and colourful chapter in the long and complicated history of Catholic separate school politics in Ontario. The years 1921 and 1922, in particular, were the high-water mark in episcopal leadership on school matters, and the political duelling during these years will be the bulk of the narrative leading up to the Tiny Township Case, 1925 to 1928. Never before had the Catholic bishops of Ontario been so united and so determined in the advocacy and defence of the rights of separate school supporters. The bishops attracted thousands of the faithful to numerous school rallies, and for a brief interlude they even managed to disarm some of their severest critics, in a flinty war of words undertaken in the daily newspapers and in privately published pamphlets. For once, Catholics did not circle the wagons and proceed to shoot each other. This is what happened during the worst years of the Regulation 17 catastrophe. But irony is rarely in short supply. Never again after the 1920s would the Ontario bishops as a body exercise such a persuasive hold over Catholic opinion on this or any other constitutional issue directly affecting the rank and file of believers.[1] The 1920s ended a style of episcopal leadership rooted in the latter part of the nineteenth century, when the bishops were expected by their flocks to fight for them in the public square no less vigorously than they did in the corridors and back rooms of the political arena. And no single issue vexed and consumed the political energies of the Catholic hierarchy more than that of separate schools. In effect, the bishop-led agitation of the 1920s was the last hurrah for the unquestioned dominance of the episcopacy in the evolving sphere of separate school politics.

By the close of the 1920s, the bishops were worn down by indifference in the legislature and defeat in the courts. In the legislature, they encountered a generation of politicians who were only too happy to let the courts settle "the separate school problem."[2] A common refrain among politicians was that any attempt to give separate schools the right to have their own secondary schools would harm national unity. In the hands of the courts, the bishops placed nearly all their hopes for establishing, once and for all time, a future for the education of Catholic school children, from kindergarten to high school matriculation. The outcome, known in historical shorthand as Tiny Township, was a disaster. No wonder, then, that by the time of the Great Depression the bishops were ready to pass the political baton to lay hands.

However, before that momentous shift in leadership took place, close on the heels of Tiny Township, the bishops of Ontario mounted a separate school campaign that redeemed the noble failure of Bishop Armand de Charbonnel in his celebrated clashes with Egerton Ryerson during the 1850s. In Charbonnel versus Ryerson, the battle was a highly personal one, charged with raw emotion and religious antagonism. It took place when the small number of Catholic separate schools posed neither a present nor a future threat to the engineered predominance of the public schools [see Chapter One]. In the 1920s, the setting was very different. No bishop stood alone, and no bishop quarreled in public with an education bureaucrat. Instead, the bishops acted in concert, arming themselves with an encyclopedia of facts and at every opportunity arguing their case according to history, common sense, fair play and a shared Canadian citizenship lately won on the fields of France. Also, by 1922, there were more than 650 Catholic separate schools to defend.

Led by Archbishop Neil McNeil of Toronto, the scholar, and Bishop Michael Francis Fallon of London, the orator, the bishops took the offensive. Their principal aim was to persuade Ontario's Protestant majority to grant their Catholic neighbours the same rights concerning secondary education and broad tax support as those enjoyed since 1869 by the Protestant minority in Catholic Quebec.[3]

248

When it came to education and the BNA Act, this was the traditional Catholic interpretation of the Confederation agreement. It was an old song, to be sure, but one worth singing anew in a unified chorus with the bishops in the lead. Episcopal unity was all the more important in light of the many social and economic changes that Ontario society had been undergoing. A good number of these transformative changes were profound and unsettling, especially during and immediately after the First World War. Acutely aware of them, the bishops of Ontario feared that separate schools would never be able to provide the kind of education Catholic children needed to survive as *Catholics* in an increasingly urbanized and industrialized society.[4] The bishops to a man may have been born and educated in the latter half of the nineteenth century — for example, McNeil had been born in 1851 and Fallon in 1867 — but as pastors at the head of a growing and changing church membership, they knew that Ontario was no longer the rural society it had been up to 1900.

****

To understand the nature of the bishops' 1920s offensive, it would be helpful to highlight several points about the milieu in which the campaign was conducted; otherwise, we will not appreciate the rhetoric or logic of their arguments or the obvious passion of their beliefs. One, we must remember that Confederation, as an historical event, was still a living memory for many people in Ontario. After a mere fifty years, Confederation remained very much a part of the popular consciousness. The bishops, as leaders of Catholic opinion, took the business of interpreting the constitution very seriously and sometimes very personally. This goes a long way to explain why differences over the meaning and application of Section 93 of the British North America Act — the section that dealt with separate schools — were so hotly contested by them and their opponents, time and time again, and why separate school debates were always conducted as if a matter of fundamental justice were at stake. Two, the bishops believed that separate school rights were in effect minority rights, and that the protection of minority rights was a core concept of

Confederation. Three, the Dominion of Canada would not have come into existence without Section 93 as part of the BNA Act. Four, although the BNA Act was legislated in 1867, it was a living document, not a piece of historical parchment. Moreover, no country or any of its constituent parts stays frozen in time. The Ontario of the 1920s was hardly the Ontario of 1867. It was morally absurd, then, for anyone to believe that the framers of the BNA Act expected Catholic separate schools to function as if the social and economic conditions prevalent in 1867 would never change. As a result, it was incumbent upon the cabinet and legislature to treat Catholic educational rights *in ways consistent with changing times and practical realities* and to see Catholic separate schools as Catholic public schools or as a branch of the public school system. Five, the bishops were anxious about the long-term viability of separate schools. In this they were hardly alone. Catholic trustees, teachers and parents shared the same feeling. Unless the legislature allowed separate school trustees to operate their own high schools, and to receive their just portion of the legislative grants to do so, the separate school system would remain incomplete and second-rate and thus less attractive to the Catholic community. (This need for high schools became all the more urgent in 1921 when an amendment to the Adolescent Attendance Schools Act increased the school-leaving age from fourteen to sixteen years of age.[5]) And unless the legislature amended the Assessment Act to give separate school boards their rightful share of corporation taxes, Catholic schools would be always poor and flirting with insolvency.

****

This is where matters stood in June 1918, when Benedict XV issued his second Apostolic Letter on Regulation 17. Its immediate effect was to allow the bishops to confine organized opposition to Regulation 17 mainly to the Ottawa Separate School Board. If the French-speaking trustees in Ottawa insisted on carrying the torch for bilingual schools, they would have to do it on their own and suffer the consequences without a political lifeline to the episcopacy. That the bishops meant to insulate themselves from any further involvement with the Ottawa board was highlighted in February 1922, when not one bishop or bishop's representative was a member of an official delegation from Ottawa who met with Premier Ernest Charles Drury to discuss Regulation 17.[6]

As for the bishops, they understood their work in the immediate post-war period as saving a system of Catholic education that had been in place for more than seventy years and that deserved to have a future no less secure than that projected for the public schools. The separate school system was a victim of its own hardscrabble determination to survive. What was true for separate schools in the nineteenth century was also true for the first three decades of the twentieth: they grew greatly in number but their primary sources of public money stayed the same. They were the legislative grant and separate school property taxes.

As we have already seen in Chapter Two, between 1855 and 1899, there were increases in the number of separate schools, from 41 to 399; in teachers, from 57 to 764; and in students, from 4,885 to 41,796. Total revenues increased from £3,445 to $401,154. Figures for the years 1902, 1912, 1922 and 1929 (the year after all appeals in the Tiny Township case had been exhausted) show the same trend:

1902 — 391 schools, 870 teachers, 45,964 students; total revenue $485,503
1912 — 513 schools, 1,237 teachers, 61,297 students; total revenue $1,186,814
1922 — 656 schools, 1,958 teachers, 88,546 students; total revenue $4,049,044
1929 — 770 schools, 2,528 teachers, 105,518 students; total revenue $6,093,809[7]

Even more revealing than these figures is the incredible disparity that arose between the public elementary schools and the Catholic separate schools, in terms of the money each system was able to spend on a per student basis (the cost per student, enrolled attendance). For example, in 1911, the two systems spent nearly the same amount of money on a per student basis: the public system,

$20.50 and the separate system, $19.28, for a difference between the two of $1.22.[8] However, in 1915, the public elementary schools were able to spend $29.89 per student and the separate schools only $17.54 (an actual decrease from 1911 of $1.74) for a startling difference between the two of $12.35![9] All the second collections at Sunday Mass, all the increases in the mill rate for property taxes and all the efficiencies in spending could never make up such a huge gap in spending power. Indeed, the gap only widened. By 1925, the public elementary schools were able to spend $57.15 per student; meanwhile, the separate schools had only $38.15 per student at their disposal, making a difference between the two systems of $19.00.[10] Such practical inequality was a fundamental injustice, according to the bishops, all the more so as the separate school system continued to expand in nearly every part of the province.

****

In broad terms, as we have already noted, salvation for separate schools meant that Catholics had a constitutional right to have their own high schools and a right to a more comprehensive tax base that would support a full system of Catholic education. These sentiments need considerable parsing. Although intimately connected, as if they were a single issue — which was the way many bishops often treated them — high schools and taxes were actually two distinct issues: the resolution of one did not necessarily mean the resolution of the other.

The high school issue, beginning as early as 1915, can be divided into its constituent elements in this way. The main question was this:

> Did separate school trustees have the legal right to offer courses of study beyond the Fifth Form, or fifth classes, in effect grades nine and ten?

If the trustees had this right, three more questions follow:

1) Did separate school supporters have the right to exemption from paying a portion of their taxes to support public high schools?

2) Should the legislative grant be restructured to include separate secondary schools?

3) Should the distribution of corporation taxes be changed, from a system in which all corporation taxes were automatically directed to the public schools, except for that percentage determined by the number of Catholic shareholders who had gone to the trouble of declaring their holdings, to a system of distribution based on the number of enrolled pupils in both systems?

If separate school trustees had a right to offer courses beyond the Fifth Form, it only stands to reason that the answers to questions 1) and 2) must be in the affirmative. But it is less clear that the same holds true for question 3) on corporation taxes. It is possible to imagine the Ontario legislature recognizing a Catholic right to high schools and treating questions 1) and 2) as natural and practical consequences of having that right but, at the same time, not disturbing the status quo on corporation taxes. It is also possible to imagine the legislature insisting that separate school trustees had no constitutional right to offer to its students courses beyond the Fifth Form, but also that the same trustees had a *practical* right to a more equitable and modern distribution of corporation taxes because the separate school system had developed enormously since 1900, and it was obvious to everyone that corporation taxes were essential to the system's survival. But this second possibility was even more remote than the first one. The reason was purely political. It concerned huge sums of money, and the transfer of any sizable amount of that money, from the public system to the separate system, would bestow a benefit and a legitimacy on separate schools that a majority of politicians and voters in Ontario sincerely believed never existed. Political oblivion at the polls would be the fate of any government that tinkered with corporation taxes.

In the final analysis, the two possibilities, as outlined above, were just that — possibilities. Provincial governments, regardless of party, were loathe to address either possibility, preferring to send these issues to the courts for final adjudication. It was the old Pontius Pilate syndrome. When the bishops realized that the politicians had fallen into a pattern of washing their hands every time Catholics argued their case, they too saw the courts as the only avenue for a remedy. At the same time, though, the bishops restricted their petition to a constitutional right to secondary education. *Tiny Township had nothing to do with corporation taxes.*

****

At this juncture, then, we must ask ourselves: Why did the bishops in the 1920s think that they had a reasonable chance of achieving publicly-funded high schools? There were two main reasons. The first was situated in the history of provincial legislation on post-elementary education as well as in the widespread confusion about the meaning of the law on continuation classes, fifth classes and continuation schools. The bishops argued that over time a precedent for separate school education beyond the fifth classes had been established and that it could not be overturned by the government simply using its regulatory powers. The second reason was based on a 1915 Ontario Supreme Court ruling on the legal obligation of the Ottawa Separate School Board to adhere to the regulations of the department of education (see Chapter Four). As part of that judgment, Chief Justice William R. Meredith, a former Conservative politician and opponent of separate schools, wrote that separate schools were in reality public schools. His words constitute a significant departure from the usual manner in which Catholic separate schools had been described and treated:

> The right and privilege which the Separate Schools Act conferred when the Imperial enactment became law, and which the Separate Schools Acts have ever since conferred,

and still confers, was and is a right to separation, to separate public schools of the like character, and maintained in the like manner, as the general public schools. The machinery may be altered, the educational methods may be changed, from time to time, to keep pace with advanced educational systems. It was never meant that the separate schools, or any other schools, should be left forever in the educational wilderness of the enactments in force in 1867. . .

The modern fashion of applying the short name "public schools" to the general public schools, which were in earlier days called the "common" or "union school," and more appropriately so called, and of applying the short name "separate schools" to the particular public schools separated from the general ones under the Separate School Act, is no excuse for misunderstanding their true character of, all alike, public schools, maintained in the public interests and for the public welfare.[11]

Meredith's words convinced the bishops that when it came to Catholic separate schools in 1915, the nineteenth century mentality should give over to the modern world. The judiciary in the person of no less than the Chief Justice of Ontario seemed prepared to lead the way. This was proof enough for the bishops. Would the politicians follow? To answer that question, let us examine in some detail the history of provincial legislation on post-elementary education and the subsequent confusion that resulted.

In the days leading up to his Massey Hall appearance, in 1922, Bishop Fallon told the press that he wanted the department of education to restore to separate schools their right to teach higher work in the fifth form and also to exempt separate school supporters from paying taxes to public schools that provided this same work.[12] By "higher work," Fallon was referring to Middle School or grades eleven and twelve. When he spoke of the restoration of rights, he was calling for a return to 1899 legislation, the steady negation of which had culminated in the highly restrictive regulations of 1915.

The origin of those rights referred to by Bishop Fallon was a series of amendments to the legislation governing public schools, separate schools and high schools. In 1896, changes in the law provided for continuation classes for Form I of high school (grade nine), but only in those municipalities where no high school existed and as long as the students had passed the usual entrance examinations.[13] In 1899, an additional amendment allowed public and separate school boards to expand continuation classes to Form II (grade ten) and to offer courses beyond Forms I and II if the trustees requested it and if the inspector approved it. (Forms I and II were the Fifth Form or fifth classes, grades nine and ten, of the elementary schools.) The 1899 amendment also distributed grants to those school boards offering courses in Forms I and II.[14] In 1902, the Separate Schools Act was amended to incorporate these changes:

> The Separate School Board in any municipality or section in which there is no high school shall have power to establish in connection with the schools over which it has jurisdiction, such courses of study in addition to the courses already provided for the fifth form as may be approved by the regulations of the Education Department. The classes established under such courses shall be known as "Continuation Classes."[15]

From this amendment there can be no doubt that separate schools had a right to offer not only the courses in fifth classes (grades nine and ten) but also the courses for Middle School (eleven and twelve). The legislation did not mean that separate school boards had a right to set up publicly-funded high schools. However, in those municipalities and school sections in which there was no high school, continuation classes would constitute a legal and practical substitute for high schools as defined under the 1871 Act. Although the 1896 and 1899 amendments limited the exercise of this right to operate continuation classes to school boards in rural districts, a precedent, regardless of where in the province it takes place, is still a precedent. By 1904, there were fourteen separate schools, all of them in rural areas, with continuation classes.[16]

In 1908, the government took the first of what became four steps to deny the right of separate schools to offer courses beyond those in the fifth classes. Its aim was to take away what it had given in 1899, out of fear that if a tradition of separate school continuation classes were allowed to develop over time, this would provide a constitutional basis for Catholics to demand their own high schools.[17] The government's first step was to divide what had hitherto been called continuation classes into fifth classes and continuation schools. The practical effect of this distinction was twofold: to limit the work of fifth classes to courses for grades nine and ten and to treat continuation schools as rural high schools, with the goal of having one in each township of the province.[18] The government estimated that the province already had 300 fifth classes and 100 continuation schools. As of 1908, the separate school share of fifth classes and continuation schools was rather minuscule: fifth classes in Wallaceburg, Tilbury, Mattawa, Chesterville, Downeyville, St. Andrew's, Orleans and Mt. Carmel and continuation schools in Amherstburg, Eganville and Westport.[19] (The legality of the above three continuation schools produced considerable confusion for school inspectors, trustees and officials in the department of education.) The real danger for separate schools was not knowing the extent to which the government was planning to enforce the distinction between fifth classes and continuation schools. If the law were applied to its logical limits, one could hardly see how separate schools could continue to have the option of offering courses beyond the fifth classes, according to the 1899 legislation.

Bishop Fallon saw the potential harm to separate schools in the 1908 distinction, and his criticisms seemed justified in 1909, when the government legislated that no continuation school could be established or maintained in a high school district.[20] As if to make their intentions clear, the government then proceeded to create large high school districts, some of which covered up to twenty school sections.[21] In 1913, the government went one step further by changing the definition of "continuation school" from "public school" to "high school."[22] This move should have made it impossible for a separate school to operate a continuation school.

However, that did not put an end to the matter. Despite the intention of the legislation of 1908, 1909 and 1913, to short-circuit separate school ambitions in regards to publicly-funded secondary education, the law still allowed separate school fifth classes the right to offer their students Middle School courses in those municipalities and school districts where no high school existed. Thus, as late as 1924, there were seventeen Catholic separate schools offering course work beyond the fifth classes.[23] Nevertheless, this regulatory allowance (or loophole) assumed that the right to offer such courses did not imply a right to operate full-scale Middle Schools that could be passed off as continuation schools.

The nature of a loophole, if exploited properly, is to make way for the very thing it was designed to prevent. It did not take long for some separate boards to establish full Middle Schools and to tax their respective supporters accordingly. (There were several public boards guilty of the same thing, but their transgression was not a threat to the public school system.) By January 1915, the Conservative government was ready to respond. Dr. R.A. Pyne, minister of education, Dr. A.H.U. Colquhoun, deputy minister of education, and John Seath, superintendent of education, joined forces to demarcate the rights of separate schools. Catholic separate school education ended with the courses of the fifth class, grades nine and ten. No exceptions would be allowed. (The same ruling applied to public elementary schools.) The vast majority of separate boards were unable to provide fifth classes because of an inadequate tax base. But there were sufficient number that did make available fifth classes, and among these schools there were seven that offered Middle Classes. They were Youville and Water Street Convent schools in Ottawa and schools in Dublin, Douglas, School Section 10, Lancaster, Toronto and Hamilton.[24]

Seath, in particular, was highly suspicious of what he believed was an episcopal conspiracy to establish continuation schools as a bargaining tool in their quest for Catholic high schools:

As a matter of fact, however, it is so far as I know only Separate School Boards that desire to add Middle School Courses to Fifth Form Work in High or Continuation School districts and their object undoubtedly is to continue the Separate School system beyond the limits guaranteed to Separate Schools under the Confederation Act. Having formally obtained this concession, the next step of the Separate school supporters would be to ask for a further extension in the form of Separate High Schools.[25]

The result was a new regulation that emphatically put an end to offering high school work beyond the fifth classes and, as a result, implicitly reserved to the non-denominational public schools the work of continuation schools, high schools and collegiates. The department of education sent the regulation to all boards in January 1915 and published it as an educational order-in-council on 22 February.[26]

Nineteen fifteen, then, was a watershed year in the history of Catholic separate schools. It was the beginning of the long march to Tiny Township and, after that failure, the even longer march to full funding in 1984.

****

Patient, collaborative and courteous to a fault, Archbishop Neil McNeil preferred quiet diplomacy and amicable negotiation to public quarrelling and sabre rattling.[27] This is how he worked through and survived the morass of Regulation 17, reaching out to Quebec Catholics in French-language newspaper articles and working with a French delegation from Ottawa as late as March 1921.[28] However, Archbishop McNeil's personality was no match for that of Bishop Fallon's. In the end, it was Fallon who browbeat McNeil into agreeing to submit the question of Catholic high schools to the Privy Council, but it was McNeil who had to shoulder the fallout from the council's decision to deny all Catholic claims, because by 1928 ill health had forced Fallon out of the political picture.[29]

McNeil gave his initial reaction to the 1915 regulation in a public address on 23 April. He chose to emphasize the financial woes of the separate schools:

> Let us make our Elementary schools self-supporting. The Province is supposed to enable these schools to be self-supporting. They are not. The laws need to be amended. If we could turn the Church money that is going to the support of these Elementary schools towards higher education, we could be on a level with any other section of the community. What we need is financial justice in the support of our Separate schools.[30]

His next move was to establish a Bishops' Educational Committee, later known as the Catholic Educational Council, in July 1915.[31] The council's main objective was to act as a central clearing house for all separate school claims and representations to the government, in order to avoid internal conflict and to achieve strength in unity of purpose. The bishops would deal directly with the cabinet in regards to amendments to the school laws, and the council's full-time paid secretary would be an intermediary between separate school teachers and the department of education. Aside from McNeil, members of the council were Archbishop Michael J. Spratt of Kingston, Bishop Thomas J. Dowling of Hamilton, Bishop William A. MacDonell of Alexandria, Bishop Richard M. O'Brien of Peterborough and Bishop Michael J. Fallon of London. The council secretary was Michael O'Brien, a former separate school inspector in Ottawa.

The Catholic Educational Council spent the next five years frustrated at every turn.[32] After numerous interviews with the government, which produced many promises but no legislative remedies, the only forward action that the bishops achieved was a proposition from Premier Sir William Howard Hearst. On 9 August 1916, Hearst presented the council with two choices: one, the government would recognize the existence of the current separate continuation schools but would not tolerate any new ones; two, the government would take separate school claims concerning continuation schools and high schools to court in a friendly action, paying for all costs. It was a clever proposition, one that left the bishops on the one hand with practically no room to manoeuvre and on the other hand with the prospect of losing everything in court. Fearing endless stonewalling, yet confident in their cause, the bishops on the council did not hesitate to choose the second option, at a meeting with the premier on 21 May 1917. Hearst then formalized their choice in an order-in-council of June. It allowed the existing separate continuation schools to operate while the government and the bishops waited for the war to end, at which time by mutual agreement separate school claims would be submitted to the court. The same order-in-council also stated that the government did not in any way endorse those claims but only sought to have them resolved.[33]

The war ended but nothing happened. The council kept meeting with the government (Premier E.C. Drury and the United Farmers, beginning in 1919) but nothing happened. In protest, Bishop Fallon resigned from the council in February 1920 and took separate school grievances directly to the public.

****

Bishop Michael Francis Fallon was no stranger to controversy. We have already examined his pugnacious and at times divisive role in the Regulation 17 debacle. A majority of Ontario's English-speaking Catholics saw Fallon as the champion of all things Catholic and the defender of their interests in the public life of the province. However, in the eyes of French-speaking Catholics and the leadership of the Loyal Orange Lodge, Bishop Fallon was a contradiction in terms, a nemesis, a dangerous enemy for whom respect and recognition would be given only grudgingly. During the first half of the 1920s, Bishop Fallon was at his brilliant best on the podium and in print. He was the war-horse on the stumps who galvanized Catholic public opinion. No other bishop was his equal in front of an audience or on the editorial pages of the big city newspapers. According to *The Times*, "He had a forthright style of speech and a fearless pen, and he never shrank from using them freely when some cause dear to his heart was at stake."[34] One cause that was increasingly dear to his heart was separate schools. To their survival, he gave his all.

Bishop Fallon was a whirlwind of activity from February 1919 to April 1922. He delivered his opening salvo at Massey Hall, Toronto, on 13 February 1919, declaring that "Education and salvation cannot be separated" and that a Catholic atmosphere was necessary to educate the mind and soul of a Catholic child.[35] Next, he issued a pastoral letter, dated 9 August 1919, in which he said that in lieu of Catholic high schools and collegiates, Catholics should enroll their children in the public secondary schools. "Catholic money has helped to erect these schools," Fallon gently reminded his people, "and Catholic money contributes to their upkeep."[36] Moreover, Catholic students in the public high schools required the presence of Catholic priests to instruct them in the faith. Fallon was daring public school boards to accept the fact that since Catholics were being forced to pay a portion of their taxes towards the upkeep of their high schools, their children enjoyed the right to Catholic religious instruction, a proposition that was absolutely inimical to the department of education and to every public school board in the province.

In December 1920, Fallon gave a speech in London.[37] On 31 May 1921, he was a member of a delegation that met with the Ontario cabinet. The main topic was corporation taxes. Separate schools were on the brink of a financial crisis, according to an April 1922 province-wide episcopal letter. The solution was simple: a share of corporation taxes based on the average daily attendance in both the separate and public systems. Also on the agenda during the two-hour discussions were legislative grants and high schools.[38] Archbishop McNeil headed the delegation, as was his right, but one can hardly imagine Fallon not taking the lead as soon as everyone sat down behind closed doors. The meeting produced nothing for the Catholic camp. Fallon then returned to the road. He spoke in Kingston, in September 1921, in Peterborough, on 2 October 1921, and in London, on 25 October 1921.[39]

In the meantime, the Toronto School Board provided Bishop

Fallon, the peripatetic warrior, with an opportunity to take his campaign to a more provocative level of public engagement. At its regular meeting of 6 October 1921, the board unanimously adopted an eight-part resolution in response to a Catholic petition to the cabinet and legislature asking for relief as well as a firm legal definition of Catholic education rights. *The Catholic Register* described the Toronto board's resolution as uncharitable, bigoted and base.[40] This was the kind of hard-nosed rhetoric that appealed to Fallon and that probably prompted him to write his open letter of 21 January 1922. It was a lengthy point-by-point rebuttal addressed not only to the Toronto School Board but also for added measure to the London School Board, which had passed a similar resolution.

In his open letter, Fallon reproduced both the Catholic petition and the Toronto board's resolution. Since each in its own way is a classic statement of irreconcilable opinions on the constitutional status and practical future of separate schools, almost eighty years after the Scott Act, they deserve to be reproduced here. The Catholic petition of June 1921 reads:

Whereas, under the British North America Act, which is the constitution of Canada, the educational rights in the matter of denominational schools of the Protestant minority in Lower Canada and of the Roman Catholic minority in Upper Canada, were guaranteed by solemn compact, and

Whereas, amongst those rights are the full development of the common school system and the equitable division of the school taxes of minorities and the proportional distribution of all school grants, and

Whereas, the school system of the Roman Catholic minority of the Province of Ontario is deprived of its legal machinery for its complete functioning, and

Whereas, the Catholic school system of Ontario does not receive its just and proper share of certain school taxes and school grants, and

Whereas, the spirit of the constitution pertaining to denominational schools is fully carried out in the Province of

Quebec, where all schools receive their fair and just proportion of all rates and taxes and are given equal facilities for their full development,

Therefore, the undersigned respectfully request the Government and the Legislature of Ontario to enact such legal measures as will put the Roman Catholic minority of this province in the full enjoyment of its educational rights under the constitution.[41]

The Toronto School Board resolution, adopted on a motion by the Reverend H.A. Berlis and seconded by R.J. Miller, reads:

1. That, whereas an organized effort is being carried on at the present time in the Province of Ontario by certain Roman Catholic bishops, demanding an Amendment to the Assessment Act, whereby a portion of the school taxes on all corporations and public utilities, in proportion to the Roman Catholic population of Ontario, would be diverted to the support of Roman Catholic sectarian schools.

2. And, whereas, the Roman Catholic church authorities and organizations are conducting a province-wide propaganda, supporting these demands, with the evident intention of impressing the Government of Ontario with their numerical strength.

3. And, whereas, the demands now being made by the bishops are the same in principle as the demands made by the Roman Catholic church representatives before Confederation, viz., to receive public moneys for separate school support, not in proportion to the Roman Catholic taxable property, but in proportion to the population, though the ratio of that population may be many times that of the taxes they pay.

4. And, whereas, similar demands were denounced by Dr. Ryerson as 'a monstrous proposition,' and were rejected by the Government and Parliament of Canada in 1855, 1858, 1861 and 1862.

5. And, whereas, the Separate School Act of 1863 was

confirmed as 'a finality as to assumed rights' by the British North America Act of 1867, section 93, and adopted by the Parliament because of that belief.

6. And, whereas, to grant the present demands of the Roman Catholic bishops would not only violate the fundamental principle of the act of 1863, but would, in an arbitrary manner, define all Roman Catholics as separate school supporters, and result in the crippling of the splendid public school and nonsectarian school system of Ontario.

7. Therefore, be it resolved, that we, the Board of Education, of the City of Toronto, in the interest of public schools assembled, believing that it is the duty of all friends of the public school system of Ontario to express their opinion at this time, hereby accord an emphatic protest against the reopening of the school question by granting to the Roman Catholic bishops of Ontario any of the concessions demanded by them, or the adoption of any regulation or amendment by the Government or Legislature that would further extend sectarian schools in this province at the expense of the public schools, which are open to every class and creed.

8. Be it further resolved, that copies of this resolution be sent to the Hon. E.C. Drury, premier of Ontario; the Hon. R.H. Grant, minister of education, and to all public school boards in the Province of Ontario.[42]

If the Toronto and London boards were looking for a battle, Bishop Fallon would give them one.[43] Below is his response.

Paragraph No. 1: This was the most offensive part of the resolution, and Fallon divided his reaction into three sections: a) He took issue with the old Ryerson-era canard that it was only the Catholic bishops who were interested in separate school politics. "As a matter of undeniable fact that there has never been a time since Confederation when the Catholics of this province, bishops, priests and laity, have been so closely united, so practically unanimous in the matter of pressing for justice for separate schools. This they have demonstrated pretty conclusively already, and are prepared to give such further proof as will convince the most skeptical." b) The claim that Catholics demanded a share of corporation taxes based on population was completely false. Archbishop Neil McNeil denied it, and Fallon himself denied it, but the board went ahead and published their claim. [Several weeks later, the *Globe* supported Fallon in this instance, reprinting in its lead editorial his statement on the three options for dividing corporation taxes: in proportion to population, assessment or average daily attendance. Preferring the last option, Fallon said that it was the duty of the legislature to make the appropriate amendments to the Assessment Act.[44]] c) The term "Roman Catholic sectarian schools" may have found an audience among school board members, but it amounted to nothing more than a petty insult. "The legal description of our branch of the system of public education is 'Roman Catholic Separate Schools,' and name calling does not alter the fact that these schools of ours were at Confederation made part and parcel of the educational system of Ontario, and were guaranteed certain rights and privileges. That these rights and privileges be respected in the letter and in the spirit is the sum and substance of our demands."

Paragraph No. 2: There was no hidden intention, or secret agenda, on the part of Catholics when they petitioned the government on separate schools. Their intention was obvious for all to see. "Would it not be more sensible as well as more charitable," Fallon asked, "to believe that their activity is due entirely to a lively interest in the betterment of their schools? And that their 'evident intention' is to secure the enjoyment of their constitutional rights."

Paragraph No. 3: This was essentially a repeat of the baseless allegation already made in Paragraph No. 1 — that Catholics wanted a share of taxes according to population.

Paragraph No. 4: Fallon denied that Ryerson had denounced so-called similar demands concerning taxation and that the government rejected the same in 1855, 1858, 1861 or 1862. Moreover, "We have made no such demand as the Toronto Board of Education formulate for us." It was a fiction. All that the board accomplished with this allegation was to create a straw man and then proceed to knock it down.

Paragraph No. 5: Fallon called the Toronto board's interpretation of the "finality" of the 1863 Separate School Act both unhappy and misleading. Like Ryerson's ghost, the debilitating debate over "finality" had lively legs long into the twentieth century. The interpretation "is unhappy because, even allowing such rights to have been 'assumed,' they became definite, constitutional and sacred when confirmed by the unanimous agreement on which the British North America Act was based. Let it be very clearly understood that Catholics accept as a finality the act of 1863 and the constitutional guarantee of 1867. They are seeking no new rights or privileges; they are asking for no favors. But they are insisting on the full enjoyment of the things guaranteed to them by the act of 1863 and by the constitution of Canada; nothing more and nothing less." The interpretation was also misleading because the board did not give the full quote from which the words "a finality as to assumed rights" had been lifted. Fallon found the passage in question in a footnote on page 172 of J. George Hodgins's *The Legislation and History of Separate Schools in Upper Canada*. Hodgins wrote: "Finality as to assumed rights and as to such further demands, as would effect the integrity and stability of our public school system, but not, of course, finality in regard to administration, or as to which would be the better way to do things which the law allowed, or authorized or prescribed."[45] Catholics had no quarrel with Hodgins's opinion on "finality."

Paragraph No. 6: Fallon insisted that Catholic demands were not in violation of the 1863 Act. "A very cursory reading of the Act of 1863 would have clearly established that its main provision guarantees to Catholics that all the school taxes levied and collected on their property shall go to the support of separate schools, and expressly exempts separate school ratepayers from all taxation for common school purposes."

Paragraph No. 7: "The resolution adopted by the Board of Education of Toronto can scarcely fail to arouse prejudice, hostility and the most unfair opposition to Catholic educational claims." Catholics had no fear of the facts or arguments based on reason. But it was not a fact that separate schools would prosper at the expense of the public schools. Actually, the opposite was true: the existence of the separate schools was a stimulus to the efficiency of the public schools. "In education, as in other human activities, competition is the life of trade," wrote Fallon. If the separate schools were to receive their due portion of corporation taxes, they would only be receiving what was rightfully theirs. "Does the Toronto Board of Education think that its constituents are not able and willing to pay for the education of their own children without taking, by law or by force, what belongs to the children of the separate schools? If so, I am far from holding that opinion."

Paragraph 8: It was illegal for the Toronto board to have spent public funds distributing its resolution to all the public boards of Ontario. The school law did not allow for the expenditure of tax money on propaganda exercises. Moreover, a portion of those taxes came from Catholic ratepayers, the target of the board's resolution.

Bishop Fallon spent the remainder of his open letter hammering away on themes that would dominate the rest of his one-man road show: the utter impossibility of determining the number of Catholic shareholders in the era of the big corporation; the Protestant make-up of the public schools; the treachery of the 1915 regulation that ended Catholic continuation schools; the success of Quebec in implementing Section 93 in regards to secondary education, grants and taxes, and the abject failure of Ontario to match that success.

Bishop Fallon gave an electrifying and bravura performance, the greatest of his career, at a packed Massey Hall, on 10 February 1922, when he spoke for nearly three hours without notes on the history of separate schools and the rights of the province's Catholics to a full and properly funded school system.[46] The evening was a fund-raiser for the recently established Sisters of Service, and the proceedings were chaired by Mrs. P.G. Kiely of the Catholic Women's League of Canada. In a vigorous voice that held his audience spellbound, Fallon declared that Catholics in Ontario were entitled to "A common school system from the alphabet to the University; from the alphabet to the preparation of teachers; from the alphabet to the entrance into professional life; from the alphabet to the door of that other educational entity which follows on any school system; and the right and power of educating our children in that system from their fifth to their 21st year. That was given to us by the Constitution. It is the right we are standing upon to-day."[47] Hardly had Fallon finished speaking when the audience sprang to their feet as one and sang the national anthem.

Following Massey Hall, Bishop Fallon was busy as ever on all fronts. He gave a prepared speech to the Labour Forum in Toronto, on 12 March 1922, in which he quoted at length a 9 March 1916 letter from Richard Harcourt, then the minister of education, who supported the right of separate schools to offer continuation and high school work.[48] He wrote a letter to Premier Drury, dated 29 March 1922, asking him what he intended to do for separate schools during the present session of the legislature. Not receiving an answer, Fallon wrote an open letter to Drury the following month, reminding him (and everyone else) that the bishops were still waiting for some action from their meeting of 31 May 1921 and that the premier had yet to respond in any way to his letter of 29 March.[49] Since the premier chose to remain silent, Fallon wrote an open letter to the Ontario Legislature, dated 18 April 1922, reiterating in calm and careful language the entire range of Catholic school demands and the historical and practical reasons behind them.[50] Two days later, on 20 April, Fallon spoke to an overflow gathering in Cornwall, where the Fallon family was well known and respected. In the middle of his talk, he vented his anger against John Seath and the now notorious 1915 regulation: "In 1915, secretly, surreptitiously and shamefully, the late Superintendent of Education, an irresponsible official of a government department, issued a regulation forbidding the establishment of further continuation schools."[51] It had been Fallon's contention that Seath's 1915 regulation destroyed the natural and constitutional progress of separate schools, as they sought to deliver a full education to all Catholic children, and that it was also the primary cause of the enormous distress under which separate schools had been forced to plead their cause and to work for their continued existence.

For its part, the Drury government finally took action in the midst of Fallon's campaign, in a move one can only describe as brilliantly Machiavellian. In a meeting with the Catholic Educational

Council, on 15 March 1922, the premier announced that present-day separate school matters concerned points of law and should be decided by the courts.[52] This was very similar to what the Hearst government had promised to do in 1917, as soon as the war was over, but had never moved to fulfill its promise. The Drury government, however, seemed intent on handing over to the courts what was snowballing into a huge political headache, courtesy of Bishop Fallon.

Fallon had always been suspicious of political offers to go to the courts. He preferred the time-honoured route of petitioning the cabinet and legislature, which he always considered supreme in a democracy, and waiting for a definite refusal from the government before putting all their hopes into the hands of judges. Even after Drury announced his government's position to go to the courts, Fallon continued to act as if the Catholic cause would be heard by the elected representatives of the people. But when a person of the stature of William David McPherson publicly lectured Fallon from the pulpit of Cooke's Presbyterian Church, on the necessity of first having the courts decide the constitutionality of Catholic educational grievances before petitioning the government, Fallon knew in his heart that he and his fellow Catholics were cornered.[53] McPherson, a lawyer and king's counsel, had been the provincial secretary in the Hearst government and was currently Grand Master of the Loyal Orange Association. His hostility towards Catholic separate schools was well documented, and his legal opinions carried considerable weight with any government. When the bishops met in the King Edward Hotel, on the evening before the deadline for accepting the government's offer to take the case to court, Fallon put all his trust in British fair play and bullied McNeil (and any other indecisive episcopal colleague) into seeking relief from the Privy Council.

****

Let us return to Archbishop Neil McNeil of Toronto. The departure of Bishop Fallon from McNeil's Catholic Educational Council in February 1920 not only gave free rein to Fallon's instincts for public debate but also allowed McNeil some room to conduct his own style of campaign out of the shadow of the Mitred Warrior from London. McNeil preferred the written word and quiet consultation, although, as we shall shortly see, he too could give a solid speech.

The year 1921 was a busy one for McNeil. In March, he brought up the subject of publicly owned utilities and corporations, citing the example of the national railways. McNeil argued that since the national railways were owned by all Canadians, including Catholic Canadians, it was completely unfair that the railways' portion of education taxes in Ontario went exclusively to support the public school system. As a result, separate school supporters were deprived of their just share of these taxes and were forced to support the public schools in contravention of Section 93 of the BNA Act.[54]

During August and September, Archbishop McNeil (along with William G. Carroll) debated Benjamin Kirk of Toronto, in the *Globe*'s letters-to-the-editor column. The topic at hand was the proposal to amend the Assessment Act. Kirk objected to any amendments to the Act that would extend what he called the educational privileges of Ontario's Roman Catholic minority. Any school privileges that they enjoyed had been finalized in the BNA Act and had been denied to other denominations. Any attempt by Catholic authorities to have them extended would arouse hostilities. Separate schools were sectarian schools for Catholic children only; public schools were nondenominational and open to all children.[55] Benjamin Kirk's opinion was hardly unique. Since the days of Egerton Ryerson's administration, it was shared by most opponents of separate schools. Indeed, it reads as if it had been peeled right off the front pages of *The Orange Sentinel.*

McNeil's answer was in three parts: one, Catholic separate schools in Ontario are public schools and a constitutional right, not a privilege, granted in the first place to satisfy the Protestant minority in Quebec; two, the Fathers of Confederation realized that the inclusion of Section 93 on separate schools was a necessary condition

271

for Confederation itself; and three, amendments to the 1886 Assessment Act were justified because school taxes assessed against large incorporated companies should benefit all school children, and because trying to establish the religious persuasion of shareholders in large corporations was virtually impossible. On this last point, McNeil cited the case of Sturgeon Falls, which was brought to the Railway and Municipal Board in December 1915. He began by quoting Mr. Gibson, the secretary and a director of the Spanish River Pulp & Paper Mills:

> "In our own mills at Sturgeon Falls there are 87 per cent of Roman Catholic workmen and only 13 per cent of Protestant workmen. When this matter was brought to the attention of the board by Mr. Jones, although so far as I know, they were all Protestants, it struck the board that it was manifestly unfair that the taxes leviable against our property for school purposes should all be paid over to the public school supporters."

> It is not good for any country that the sense of justice should be thus in conflict with statute law. In the Sturgeon Falls case the directors of the company found that the law forbade them to direct one-third of the school taxes to the education of the children of 87 per cent of their workmen in a legalized school, unless they could also show that one-third of the company shares was owned by Catholics in the United States and other countries. This law was enacted in 1886, when companies were relatively few and small. It may have been possible then to know or ascertain to what churches shareholders went on Sundays. This knowledge is now impossible. Our law-makers have overlooked the vast economic changes which have taken place in the past thirty-five years, as far as Separate School support is concerned. The law seemingly enables such companies as the C.P.R. to divide its school taxes in Ontario. As a matter of fact, the law obliges the C.P.R. to support only the schools of the majority.

> What, then, has become of the provision in the

Constitution "to bind that compact of 1863 and make it a final settlement?" The answer is that it is not now fairly observed in Ontario. Part of the compact of 1863 is to the effect that Separate School supporters are to be exempted from all school taxes levied for the support of other schools. This is a very long way from being carried into effect. The National Railways are, in part, owned by Separate School supporters, though the law, as it now stands, directs all the school taxes assessed upon these properties to the support of the schools of the majority in Ontario. The same is true of the Hydro Commission as to its taxable property. The Catholic diocese of Toronto and other Catholic institutions, as well as many individual Catholics, are paying taxes to the Public schools through bank shares. Most of the banks are in much the same position as the Spanish River Pulp & Paper Mills. A list of the companies and public utilities in which the law, as it now stands, does not enable or allow observance of the compact of 1863, would take up too much space.

The Assessment Act needs to be amended in the interest of the pledges given and accepted at the time of Confederation, and in the interest of national unity, as well as of fair play.[56]

Kirk responded by reminding the archbishop that the majority of schools in Quebec were Roman Catholic and thus could not be compared to the nondenominational schools in Ontario and by quoting at length George Brown and Thomas D'Arcy McGee on the finality of the 1863 Scott Act. He ended by accusing the archbishop of reopening an old sectarian controversy and the Catholic hierarchy of never being satisfied. "A 'final settlement,'" Kirk wrote, "appears to be only a settlement so far as the hierarchy is concerned until plans are made for inaugurating a new campaign for fresh sectarian concessions."[57]

McNeil's rejoinder focused on the meaning and application of the word finality:

I did not revive the controversy of the sixties of the last century about the finality of the Separate School Act of 1863. On the contrary, I assumed that the settlement of 1863 was final, and went on to show that this finality placed upon the Legislature the duty of amending the Assessment Act from time to time in order to carry out the "final settlement" of 1863. It must be remembered that all school taxes which the Assessment Act does not expressly authorize a municipality to pay to a Separate School Board go automatically to the Public School Board. There is never any need of an amendment of the Assessment Act for the purpose of enabling a Public School Board to get its full share of the school taxes. It gets all the school taxes paid, unless part is diverted by way of exception, and this exception is determined by the Assessment Act. This act does make exceptions arbitrarily. It must be guided by the acts of 1863 and 1867.

It is absurd to contend that the assumed finality of the Act of 1863 means that the Assessment Act must remain as it stood in 1863. The former act expressed the principle involved. It did no more in no changeable a matter as assessment. The latter act applies, or should apply, that principle to the varying economic conditions.[58]

In early October, Archbishop McNeil found himself in another tug of war on the pages of the *Globe*. This one was mercifully much briefer than the Kirk episode. It began with a 28 September letter from R.F. Kenny, a Catholic from Holyrood, Ontario. Kenny complained about the public school practice of advertising only for Protestant teachers. W.L.L. Lawrence of Newmarket responded in a letter of 4 October, agreeing with Kenny but placing the blame at the doorstep of the Catholics, who had foisted upon the province a dual system of education. It was now McNeil's turn. He replied to Lawrence in a letter of 5 October. Blame was not the issue for the archbishop. A knowledge of history was. McNeil claimed that the legislature originally granted Catholics separate schools because

Protestants in the common school system insisted on teaching the Protestant Bible.[59]

This was a rehash of an old sore point. However, it seems that McNeil's letter was sufficient provocation for the Toronto Board of Education to issue its 6 October resolution against efforts by the Catholic bishops to have the Assessment Act amended. This was the same resolution that had so infuriated Fallon and to which he replied in an open letter of 21 January 1922, discussed above. In point of fact, McNeil had already given his own vigorous reply to the same resolution in October 1921, months before Fallon, in an article published first in the *Sunday World* and then in its entirety in the *Catholic Register*.[60] But Fallon was Fallon. His response in the London *Free Press* was like a red carpet leading the way to his February 1922 Massey Hall performance. McNeil's, on the other hand, was just enough to propel him to take the stage at the Canadian Club in Toronto, on 24 October.

Since Archbishop McNeil revisited territory familiar to anyone following the separate school debate, it is not necessary to repeat his main arguments or contentions, except one — that separate schools were public schools. McNeil was to trumpet this claim both before and after the Tiny Township case. It was a bedrock notion for him and every other Catholic bishop. It upheld any and all other claims concerning legislative grants, corporation taxes and Catholic high schools:

Perhaps I should emphasize the fact that [separate schools] are public schools. They are not private schools at all. They are a part of the machinery of public education in the Province of Ontario. Any laws that are made for the betterment of these schools are made by the Legislature of Ontario. Any regulations under which they operate are regulations passed by the Cabinet of Ontario. Their daily administration is under the Department of Education in Queen's Park. There may possibly be a doorkeeper or a caretaker in the Department of Education who is a Catholic. I have not enquired. There may even be a stenographer, for

275

aught I know, but of the men who have an administrative voice in the Department of Education of Ontario there is not one single Catholic. I am not complaining of that. They give us fair play. But I am pointing out to you that you have every possible safeguard as regards the general administration of the separate schools of Ontario in the fact that they are subject to the control and the daily administration of the Department of Education as it exists to-day. It is they who formulate the regulations. It is they who appoint the inspectors, who draw up courses of study, who prescribe text books, who lay down conditions under which teachers may be employed, who examine the accounts of all school boards, whether you call them public or separate. By the way, the [phrase] public school as used in Ontario is a localism. If the official reports had preserved the word 'public" in the Separate School nomenclature, there would not be the confusion in the minds of many people that exists to-day. They should have been called "Public Separate Schools," and not simply Roman Catholic Separate Schools as we find it in the reports. I mean that they are a part of the public school system of the Province of Ontario.[61]

Replying to Archbishop McNeil, on 1 November at the Canadian Club, was the Orange gadfly Horatio Clarence Hocken.[62] Among many other things, Hocken was a former mayor of Toronto, a past Grand Master of the Loyal Orange Association, a journalist and owner of *The Orange Sentinel* and a Conservative member of the House of Commons who was later appointed to the Senate.[63] He was a persistent and very able critic of separate school claims. Hocken never let an opportunity pass to denounce any attempt to extend the sphere of separate schools in either its curriculum or powers of taxation. To him, separate schools were not a public service but a special service available only to Catholics and limited in its application according to the Scott Act of 1863. Any burdens which Archbishop McNeil had to carry in order to keep separate schools open was his and not the public's responsibility.

Hocken went on to challenge Bishop Fallon's open letter of 21 January 1922[64] and to skirmish with Fallon after his speech in Massey Hall.[65] He also promised to lead a petition drive against any attempt to give separate schools a larger share of the taxes than they currently received.[66] Hocken made good on his promise. On 19 April 1922, on the day before Fallon spoke in Cornwall, Hocken delivered petitions with nearly 300,000 names, putting Premier Drury on notice that his government dare not accede to the demands of the Catholic bishops.[67] Hocken need not have worried. When Drury met with the Catholic Educational Council of Ontario on 15 March, he told the delegation: "All the schools of this Province have certain legal rights. There have, perhaps, been changes in conditions, but it is a question to be decided as a point of law."[68]

****

It took until 24 December 1925 for the case of *The Board of Trustees of the Roman Catholic Separate Schools for the School Section No. 2 in the Township of Tiny and Others v. The King* to reach court. The main reason for this lengthy delay was that Premier George Howard Ferguson decided to seek "friendly action" in the courts on legislative grants only in March 1924.[69] Friendly action meant that the government would pay the legal costs of both sides up to and including a hearing by the Privy Council in England. The distribution of legislative grants had become a point of contention as far back as 1907 when the government of the day introduced a process by which individual schools could earn a second level of grants based not on average attendance but on teachers' certificates, salaries and school equipment. Rural separate schools, however, had practically no chance to earn this extra grant money. In 1917, separate schools returned to the earlier practice of receiving their portion of the legislative grant based solely on average attendance, but any unearned moneys in the Separate School Fund were used for a second distribution of grants to the most deserving schools.[70] This created inequity as well as confusion.

In the meantime, Archbishop McNeil chose Thomas F. Battle,

secretary of the Catholic Educational Council and a Toronto lawyer, and Isidore F. Hellmuth, of the firm Hellmuth, Cattanach and Meredith, to represent separate school interests. McNeil also chose Tiny Township as the supplicant in the friendly action and limited its supplication to the courts to legislative grants to schools and the teaching of courses beyond grade ten. In consultation with the other members of the Catholic Educational Council, McNeil was quite prudent not to submit the matter of corporation taxes. He believed that such a move "would amount to submitting to the Courts the question whether Separate Schools have a right to exist at all or not, for their existence depends on the right of Separate School supporters to appropriate the school taxes paid by them for their schools."[71]

Tiny Township involved three areas of dispute in connection with the interpretation and application of Section 93 of the BNA Act. According to Franklin Walker, they were "the right of separate schools to teach high school subjects, the right of separate school supporters to exemption from taxes for the support of high schools not under jurisdiction of separate school trustees, and whether separate schools were entitled to all legislative grants for common schools, including all grants for the support of secondary schools."[72] Another way of describing the legal and constitutional issues under consideration can be put this way: "The question involved was how far the Legislature of Ontario could go in regulating and grading denominational schools. The contention of the Roman Catholic School Boards was that the British North America Act, combined with the whole body of law existing at Confederation relating alike to Separate and Common Schools, reserved forever to the boards of trustees of Separate Schools, the right to educate their pupils within certain limits, from kindergarten to university, and to share equally with Public Schools on a basis of average attendance in all legislative grants."[73]

On 13 May 1926, Mr. Justice Rose in a judgment from Osgoode Hall dismissed the petition of Tiny Township trustees. They had argued that the 1922 legislative grant for "common school purposes," as defined by the Act of 1863, would have been greater had it been apportioned according to the manner set out in the acts of 1859 and

1863.[74] The amount of money in question was $736. The trustees appealed, as planned. But the Appellate Division of the Ontario Supreme Court unanimously upheld the ruling of Mr. Justice Rose, in a decision of 23 December 1926.[75] From there, the case travelled to the Supreme Court of Canada, which divided evenly, three to three, in a judgment of 10 October 1927, thereby denying the appeal. Chief Justice Anglin, Justice Rinfret and Justice Mignault were in favour of allowing the appeal but with certain qualifications. Justice Duff, Justice Lamont and Justice Newcombe were opposed.[76]

The Judicial Committee of the Privy Council, sitting in London and composed of Lords Haldane, Buckmaster, Shaw, Wrenbury and Blancsberg, rendered its decision on 12 June 1928.[77] The Lords examined three questions:

Question No. 1:

Did the Trustees of the separate Catholic schools secure at Confederation the right to maintain, free from control or regulation by the Ontario Legislature, as respects the scope of instruction, denominational schools which could embrace the subjects formerly taught in the separate schools on their higher sides, and afterward taught in the undenominational high schools, etc., as developed after Confederation, or analogous subjects taught in the Catholic separate schools before Confederation, and the right to exemption from taxation for such undenominational educative organizations?

Question No. 2:

And did the Trustees secure a title to receive a share of every grant by the Legislature for common school purposes—construed as extending to the maintenance of education of the type given in post-Confederation secondary schools, as well as those that were merely elementary based on the number of pupils attending the separate schools, and independent of the subjects taught or the textbooks used, every separate school being entitled to its share calculated according to the statutory rate—however advanced, however rudimentary the education and textbooks might be?

Question No. 3:

The Provincial Legislature is supreme in matters of education excepting so far as Section 93 of the British North America Act restricts its authority. The question, therefore, is whether the Province could, then, as the law stood, so control the courses of study and the general range and quality of textbooks as to enable the educational authorities of the Province to prescribe the gradation of separate schools and the stages in which instruction could be given.

The answer to questions No. 1 and No. 2 were in the negative. The answer to question No. 3 was in the positive. Separate schools were only a special form of common schools, and although the province did not have a right to abolish separate schools, it had the power of regulation to determine the extent of education which they could offer. In other words, by regulation, the province could abridge the desire of separate school trustees to offer their students secondary education. "Such an abridgement," wrote the Lords, "may be in the usual course when a national system of education has attained a certain stage in its development and it would be difficult to forego this power if the grading which may be essential is also to be possible."[78] The last remaining remedy for the Tiny Township trustees was an appeal to the Governor-General-in-Council and through him to the Parliament of Canada for remedial legislation. Subsection 2 of Section 93 of the BNA Act gave the trustees this right, but unhappy memories of the Manitoba school crisis of 1895-96 pre-empted any talk of asking federal authorities to override the courts.

****

"It turns out," said Archbishop Neil McNeil to 25,000 men gathered for the 1928 Holy Name Society parade, " that the Privy Council has not proved to be the protector of minorities it was supposed to be."[79] To say that McNeil was bitter about the Privy Council decision of 12 June would be to understate the emotion of the moment as he stood in front of all those Holy Name men in Blantyre Park in Toronto to admit defeat in the most important court case in the

280

history of separate schools in Ontario. It was a cruel blow to him and his fellow bishops and to the thousands of Catholic parents who had sacrificed so much for so long to keep their schools solvent on what amounted to a widow's mite of public financing. But McNeil was not without hope. He told the men to have courage. It took years for Catholics to overthrow Regulation 17, but overthrow it they did. Knowing that the faith of the children was worth the fight, Catholics would carry on the battle to the finish.

In practical terms, McNeil regrouped the Catholic Educational Council in August 1928, hoping to restart negotiations with the Ferguson government on the vital issue of assessment. Conspicuous by his absence from the membership on the council was Bishop Fallon. He was to spend the final three years of his life out of the public view as he coped with the debilitating effects of diabetes. His death on 22 February 1931 symbolized the end to that style of episcopal leadership about which we spoke at the beginning of this chapter.

In December 1928, French-speaking and English-speaking Catholics met in Ottawa to devise a common plan of action. One direct result of that meeting was the replacement of the Catholic Educational Council with the more French-friendly Separate Schools Assessment Amendment Committee. Speaking to a convention of the Catholic Truth Society, in September 1929, McNeil said that the 1886 assessment act was the greatest stumbling block to freeing Catholic schools from poverty. Catholic school boards were asked to send petitions to the Assessment Amendment Committee. Parish priests in the archdiocese of Toronto were called upon to collect for funds for a general campaign fund and to interview their local member of provincial parliament. McNeil's goal was to present an impregnable front of Catholic opinion on separate schools as the surest means to influence public opinion as well as the government of Premier George S. Henry, who succeeded Ferguson in 1930.

But anything McNeil and the bishops did or said aroused the wrath of the traditional opponent of separate schools, especially the Orange Lodge and the Toronto *Telegram*. On 2 February 1931, more than a year into the Great Depression, Archbishop Neil McNeil invited prominent members of the laity to an informal dinner at the National Club on Bay Street, to discuss Separate School taxes.[80] Thus began the next chapter in the separate school struggle.

---

[1] Of course, one should not dismiss the work of individual bishops in later controversies. One thinks of Bishop Joseph Ryan's successful intervention with the Hope Commission, 1947 to 1950, to squash any attempt to scale back Catholic separate schools to grade six or seven.

[2] *Globe*, 16 March 1922, 15. In March 1922, Premier Ernest Charles Drury (United Farmers) informed a delegation from the Catholic Educational Council that "The Government has considered the matters which you have brought before us [secondary schools and legislative grants], and we have come to the conclusion that they are questions to be decided on points of law." Drury was not the first premier to propose going to the courts. Premier Sir William Howard Hearst proposed the same idea as early as 1917.

[3] *Catholic Register*, 22 February 1917, 1. This story reproduced a letter from J.C. Sutherland, the chief inspector of Protestant schools in Quebec, that showed that the Protestant minority in the province had complete control of their schools and did not have to pay any of their taxes to support of the Catholic schools. See also *Toronto Daily Star*, letter of S. Bond, 16 January 1917, and letter of Sir George Garneau, 12 February 1917.

[4] *Catholic Register*, 8 February 1917, 3. Between 1901 and 1911, the urban population of Ontario had grown by 41.93 per cent, and the rural population has decreased by 4.18 per cent.

[5] *Globe*, 10 October 1921, 4, "A School Revolution."

[6] Ibid., 3 February 1922, 10.

[7] *Report of the Minister of Education Province of Ontario for 1925* (Toronto: King's Printer, 1926), 66; *Report of the Minister of Education Province of Ontario for the Year 1930* (Toronto: King's Printer, 1931), 95.

[8] *Canadian Annual Review 1911*, (Toronto: The Annual Review Publishing Company, 1912), 440.

[9] *Canadian Annual Review 1916*, (Toronto: The Annual review Publishing Company, 1917), 487.

[10] *Report of the Minister of Education Province of Ontario 1925*, 58.

[11] For a full text of this decision, see Carter, *Judicial Decisions on Denominational Schools*, 58-63: Ottawa Separate School Trustees v. City of Ottawa, Ottawa Separate School Trustees v. Quebec Bank, Supreme Court of Ontario (1915), 34 Ontario Law Reports, 624.

[12] *Globe*, 3 February 1922, 11.

[13] *Statutes of Ontario*, "An Act Consolidating and Revising the Public School Acts," 1896, 59 Vic., c. 70.

[14] Ibid., "An Act to Improve the Laws Respecting Public Schools," 1899, 62 Vic. (2), c. 36.

[15] Ibid., "An Act to Amend the Separate School Act," 1902, 2 Edw. VII, c. 41.

[16] *Report of the Minister of Education (Ontario) for the Year 1904* (Toronto: King's Printer, 1905), 76.

[17] *Statutes of Ontario*, "An Act Respecting Separate Schools, Fifth Classes and Continuation Schools," 1908, 8 Edw. VII, c. 68.

[18] *Globe*, 26 March 1908, 5.

[19] *Report of the Minister of Education (Ontario) for the Year 1908* (Toronto: King's Printer, 1909), xi.

[20] *Statutes of Ontario*, "An Act Respecting Continuation Schools," 1909, 9 Edw. VII, c. 90.

[21] Robert T. Dixon, "The Ontario Separate School System and Section 93 of the British North America Act" (D.Ed. diss., University of Toronto, 1976), 57.

[22] *Statutes of Ontario*, "An Act Respecting Continuation Schools," 1913, 3-4 Geo. V, c. 72.

[23] Walker, *Catholic Education and Politics in Ontario*, 2: 337.

[24] As quoted in Walker, *Catholic Education and Politics in Ontario*, 2: 333.

[25] Ibid.

[26] Province of Ontario, *Sessional Papers* 1915, Report No. 56.

[27] McNeil was born in Hillsborough, Nova Scotia on 23 November 1851, educated at the Pontifical Urban College in Rome, from 1874 to 1879, and ordained there on 12 April 1879. After several parish appointments, he was professor and then rector of St.

Francis Xavier College in Antigonish, Nova Scotia. He was ordained a bishop on 20 October 1895 and served as vicar apostolic and then bishop of St. George's, Newfoundland, 1895 to 1910; archbishop of Vancouver, 1910 to 1912; and archbishop of Toronto, 1912 to 1934. He died on 25 May 1934. See ARCAT, "Clergy Biographical and Ministry Database, Biographical Information"; *The Ontario Catholic Year Book and Directory 1935* (Toronto: 1935), 35; George Boyle, *Pioneer in Purple: The Life and Work of Archbishop Neil McNeil* (Montreal: Palm Publishers, 1951).

[28] Peter Oliver, *Public & Private Persons* (Toronto: Clarke, Irwin & Company, 1975), 107.

[29] Dr. John M. Bennett, "Recollections of a separate school inspector," *Catholic Register*, 24-31 August 1991, ES14. The source for this article was a taped interview Dr. Bennett gave to Father Carl Matthews, S.J.

[30] *Canadian Annual Review 1915* (Toronto: The Annual Review Publishing Company, 1916), 497.

[31] ARCAT, ED SP05.06. "My Lord," 30 June 1915; OCCB, "Minutes of a meeting of the Bishops of Ontario held in St. Augustine's Seminary, Toronto on July 16, 1915."

[32] Walker, *Catholic Education and Politics in Ontario*, 2: 334-37, 342, 343, 346, 347; Dixon, "The Ontario Separate School System," 61-72.

[33] Dixon, "The Ontario Separate School System," 72.

[34] *The Times* (London, England), 24 February 1931.

[35] *Globe*, 14 February 1919, 6; 15 February 1919, 4; 19 February 1919, 8; *Canadian Annual Review 1919* (Toronto: Canadian Annual Review, Limited, 1920), 523.

[36] *Canadian Annual Review 1919*, 524.

[37] *Canadian Freeman*, 23 December 1920.

[38] Walker, *Catholic Education and Politics in Ontario*, 2: 342.

[39] *Canadian Freeman*, 5 September 1921; *Catholic Record*, 29 October 1921; *Toronto Daily Star*, 26 October 1921.

[40] *Catholic Register*, 13 October 1921, 4.

[41] *London Free Press*, 23 January 1922, 3.

[42] Ibid.

[43] Ibid. All quotes concerning Fallon's reactions to the eight-paragraph resolution of the Toronto Board of Education are taken from the same story in the London *Free Press*.

[44] *Globe*, 9 February 1922, 4.

[45] Fallon's transcription of the quote was not completely accurate. Hodgins actually wrote: "Finality as to assumed "rights," and as to such further demands for Separate Schools, as would affect the integrity and stability of Public School System; but not, of course, finality in regard to details of administration, or as to which would be the better way to do things which the law allowed, or authorized, or prescribed."

[46] *Globe*, 11 February 1922, 1, 2; *Catholic Register*, 16 February 1922, 1, 8; *Toronto Daily Star*, 11 February 1922, 10.

[47] *Canadian Annual Review 1922* (Toronto: The Canadian Review Company, 1923), 605.

[48] ARCAT, ED SPO1.73. "Some Aspects of the Separate School Question: Plain Facts for Fair Minds. An Address Delivered on March 12, 1922, in the Labor Forum Toronto, by Most Rev. M.F. Fallon, Bishop of London."

[49] *Toronto Daily Star*, 29 April 1922.

[50] *Canadian Freeman*, 4 May 1922.

[51] Ibid., 27 April 1922.

[52] *Globe*, 16 March 1922, 4.

[53] *Toronto Daily Star*, 17 February 1922, 2.

[54] Ibid., 18 March 1921.

[55] Kirk, *Globe*, 22 August 1921, 4; Carroll, *Globe*, 29 August 1921, 4; Kirk, 2 September 1921, 4.

[56] McNeil, *Globe*, 7 September 1921, 4.

[57] Kirk, *Globe*, 16 September 1921, 4. Carroll had intervened for a second time, Globe, 9 September 1921, 4.

[58] McNeil, *Globe*, 17 September 1921, 4.

[59] Kenny, *Globe*, 28 September 1921, 4; Lawrence, *Globe*, 4 October 1921, 4; McNeil, *Globe*, 5 October 1921, 4. The Lawrence and McNeil letters were reproduced in the Catholic Register, 13 October 1921, 3.

[60] *Catholic Register*, 20 October 1921, 1, 3.

[61] Neil McNeil, "The Separate School Question," 24 October 1921 in *Addresses Delivered before The Canadian Club of Toronto Season of 1921-22* (Toronto: Warwick Bros. & Rutter, 1923), 53-54. McNeil's speech was reproduced in *Catholic Register*, 3 November 1921, 1, 6.

[62] H.C. Hocken, "The Separate School Question," 1 November 1921 in *Addresses Delivered before The Canadian Club of Toronto Season of 1921-22*, 61-71.

[63] Hocken, Hon. Horatio Clarence," *The Canadian Who's Who: A Handbook of Canadian Biography of Living Canadians,* vol. 2, 1936-1937 (Toronto), 514; *The Canadian Parliamentary Guide 1936* (Ottawa: 1936), 97.

[64] *Toronto Star Weekly*, 28 January 1922.

[65] *Toronto Daily Star*, 14 February 1922, 13.

[66] *Globe*, 31 January 1922, 10.

[67] *Canadian Annual Review 1922*, 605.

[68] Ibid.

[69] *Globe*, 22 March 1924, 13.

[70] Ibid., 14 February 1922, 2; 16 March 1922, 1; 22 March 1924, 13; *Canadian Annual Review 1923* (Toronto: The Canadian Review Company, 1924), 552-53.

[71] *Catholic Register*, 4 October 1923, 4.

[72] Walker, *Catholic Education and Politics in Ontario*, 2: 337-38.

[73] *Canadian Annual Review 1925-26* (Toronto: Canadian Review Company, 1926), 359-60.

[74] *Globe*, 14 May 1926, 15

[75] Ibid., 24 December 1926, 12.

[76] Ibid., 11 October 1927, 21.

[77] Ibid., 13 June 1928, 12. For a full text of the Privy Council decision, see Carter, *Judicial Decisions on Denominational Schools*, 85-101: Roman Catholic Separate School Trustees for Tiny vs. Rex, Privy Council, 1928, A.C. 363.

[78] *Globe*. 13 June 1928, 12.

[79] Ibid., 25 June 1928, 13.

[80] ARCAT, MN PC19.03(a). N. McNeil to "Dear Sir," 2 February 1931.

THE GRAND EXPERIMENT
THE CAMPAIGN OF THE 1930S: MARTIN J. QUINN
AND THE CATHOLIC TAXPAYERS' ASSOCIATION

Introduction

$\mathcal{T}$he meteoric rise and fall of the Catholic Taxpayers' Association, during the 1930s, forms one of the strangest chapters in the history of separate school politics in the province of Ontario. The CTA's principal raison d'etre was to convince the provincial government, regardless of the party in power, to enact amendments to the Assessment Act that would guarantee a transparent and equitable distribution of corporation and utility taxes, according to the number of students enrolled in the two public school systems. It was as simple as that. The leading player from the CTA was Martin J. Quinn, a successful Toronto businessman turned pamphleteer and amateur politician. He was the first lay person to take centre stage in the separate school saga, an anomaly in Catholic political culture that initially thrived but then collapsed because there were no rules to govern such a novelty within the Catholic camp. Bishops were not used to handing over leadership on any issue affecting their flocks, and the laity were not used to the freedom of battling virtually on their own.

The organization of the CTA was very pyramidal. At the pinnacle stood Quinn, chairman and first among the five-member executive committee. Next were the remaining four members of the executive committee, and below them there was a general committee of influential Catholics, such as lawyers, doctors and educators, who were chosen from each of Ontario's nine dioceses and its one vicariate apostolic. Members of the general committee were in fact window dressing for the CTA and were not expected to have much, if any, say in the decision-making process. They lent their names to the official letterhead so that the CTA would have more credibility with both Catholics and Protestants. At the bottom of the pyramid was a province-wide network of parish priests and chairmen of parish committees, all of whom were directly linked to the CTA by a steady stream of missives from Quinn, the chairman, and to a lesser degree from W.T. Kernahan, the treasurer, and James E. Day, a Toronto lawyer.[1] The entire organization had the blessing of the bishops, who informally agreed to remain aloof from the public arena on what was considered a purely financial and political matter.

As the drama unfolded, beginning in late 1931, the CTA had to deal with the Conservative government of George Henry. Following the 1934 election, however, there was a new and more formidable opponent: Mitch Hepburn, the popular Liberal premier. Prior to the election, Hepburn promised to give the CTA exactly what they wanted, but during the election he was prone to speak in platitudes, comforting himself with speeches about Sir Wilfrid Laurier, and once he was premier, he treated Quinn with disdain. Off to the side yet always within earshot of Hepburn, who was a Protestant and a Mason, were the noisy and cantankerous rump of the Loyal Orange Lodge and the editorial opinions of Toronto's three largest newspapers, the *Evening Telegram*, the *Globe and Mail* and the *Toronto Daily Star*. Hepburn was able to contain the Orangemen, but he was ever mindful of the papers.

The denouement was yet another disaster for separate school supporters. Quinn went down to ignominious defeat, the CTA was dissolved, the bishops resumed control of school politics and, at the beginning of the Second World War, Catholic elementary schools were nearly as poor as ever. The only survivor was Mitch Hepburn. What happened?

This chapter will examine the historical origins and political strategy of the CTA under Martin Quinn's quixotic leadership and the Conservative and Liberal response to the CTA's campaign concerning corporate and utility taxes. Also important to our story are the reaction of the Ontario bishops to Quinn's shrill and confrontational style and his oft-repeated claim that Archbishop Neil McNeil had granted the CTA absolute independence, as well as the process by which the hierarchy ended this brief but explosive experiment in Canadian-style Catholic Action.[2]

Martin J. Quinn

Aside from his involvement in the Catholic Taxpayers' Association, from 1931 to 1939, and his many publications on separate schools during and after this period, we have precious few biographical details about Martin J. Quinn, the central character in this chapter. What he chose to reveal about himself, he did so not from a need to write his autobiography — he was egotistical but not in that way — but usually as part of an extended argument against someone in the Church or at Queen's Park. The oldest of nine children of Martin H. and Romona Quinn, Irish immigrants and longtime members of the Archdiocese of Toronto, Martin Joseph Quinn was born in August 1874 and received what formal education he had from the Christian Brothers in Toronto.[3] His time with the Brothers was an unhappy experience, one that he bitterly regretted in later life.[4] After he left school, he became a plumber.[5]

Regardless, Quinn remained a faithful and loyal Catholic all his life but one armed with a streak of anti-clericalism unusual for a church-going Catholic of his day. Subservience to the clergy had no place in his personality. He had no fear of them. On matters of faith or morals, the bishops and priests reigned supreme, but when it came to the practical realm, they were just as fallible as everyone else in the Church. For Quinn, this was undoubtedly true in the ill-defined universe of separate school politics. The bishops, as the unquestioned leaders of the Catholic ratepayers, had repeatedly failed in their efforts to convince a succession of provincial governments to render due justice to the children of Catholic parents. Although Quinn never referred in writing to the outcome of the 1928 Tiny Township case, he must have seen it as proof of the ineptitude of the hierarchy in the practical sphere of see-saw politics. The bishops, including Fallon, had been outwitted by politicians who had enough savvy to co-opt the judicial system on behalf of their own agenda, at the top of which was their own political survival.

Coupled to Quinn's wariness of clerical shortcomings was his outright contempt for those Catholics who had yet to shed their nineteenth-century inferiority complex. According to him, what began as self-pity among poor immigrants had become an entrenched mentality two generations later. Quinn insisted that any feelings of inferiority were linked directly to "the failure of parents to insist upon their **natural rights as defined by Church law**, to the end that our children will leave school imbued with a proper degree of self-reliance and courage, based upon a confidence-inspiring type of education, with some feeling of pride in our institutions (almost entirely lacking now), and of complete equality with those of any other religious belief."[6]

This is what Martin J. Quinn wanted for his own family. Quinn married Anna Josephine Sullivan, and they had nine children, all of whom attended the separate schools.[7] To support his family, Quinn parlayed his management skills into running the National Equipment Company and its subsidiary, National Peerless Water Systems. Quinn was the company's first manager, beginning in 1912. Located at 41-45 Wabash Avenue in Toronto, the company specialized in plumbing supplies, such as steel tanks, electric cellar drainers, "Q" foot valves and power pumps. It was highly successful supplying contractors for Toronto's booming housing market during the Roaring Twenties, and by extension it probably made Quinn a millionaire. He owned a home at 59 Oakmount Road and a summer cottage on Lake Simcoe and remained a prosperous man all his life. He belonged to the Empire Club and the Board of Trade, but, remaining true to his instincts about Church institutions, he adamantly refused to join the Knights of Columbus. Most importantly, Quinn made enough money to make substantial investments in the stock market. One of his investments, in the George Weston Company, was the first in a series of events that gave birth to the Catholic Taxpayers' Association. Moreover, Quinn was wealthy enough to work practically full time for the CTA and also to pay for secretarial staff out of his own pocket, without ever receiving a penny in compensation.[8] That Quinn was the sole member of the executive committee able to take advantage of such a luxury —

right in the middle of the Great Depression, no less! — went a long way to determine his own political fate and that of the CTA.

Shortly after Quinn resigned from the CTA executive, in January 1939, the *Canadian Freeman* crowed that the Cross would have to disappear from the Ontario landscape and the last Catholic school close its doors before Martin J. Quinn would be forgotten.[9] But just the opposite happened. Obscurity was his reward after more than eight years of unremitting toil on behalf of Catholic education. The moment his resignation was published, Quinn was yesterday's news, a cipher within Catholic society, an embarrassment. When he died ten years later, his passing went unnoticed in the *Catholic Register*. His obituaries in the *Globe and Mail* and the *Toronto Daily Star* gave no clue as to the high-profile role he had played in the Catholic Taxpayers' Association.[10] Only very recently has a clearly identified photograph of him been unearthed.[11] It may be difficult for us to imagine that someone who had publicly championed separate school rights from one end of the province to the other and fought two premiers of Ontario, with an unflagging passion for the cause, could suffer such a fate in so short a time. Sadly, that was Quinn's fate. To understand why, one must see that the political fortunes of Martin J. Quinn were so intimately tied to those of the CTA that the fall of one ushered in the dissolution of the other.

Origins of the Catholic Taxpayers' Association

The two people responsible for founding the CTA were Archbishop Neil McNeil and Martin J. Quinn. Although their respective backgrounds and temperaments made them unlikely allies, Quinn appeared as a Godsend to the archbishop, who had been at a loss since 1928 as to the direction in which he and his fellow bishops should take the separate school struggle. As for Quinn, he could not conceive of a more congenial prelate than McNeil. Unfortunately for Quinn, by the time the CTA came into existence, McNeil did not have many years left to live.

If nothing else, Catholic separate schools from their legal inception in 1841 had generated a mountain of words, both for and against their existence. McNeil and Quinn, as vigorous defenders of

293

separate schools, contributed to that tradition. As it happened, both men were writing about corporation taxes at about the same time in 1931. Despite their having worked in isolation from each other, it was inevitable that they would meet.

During the first half of 1931, Archbishop McNeil published a thirty-four-page pamphlet simply titled *The School Question of Ontario*. One should not be fooled by the generic-sounding title. The passage of time has not dulled its original lustre. It is still a minor masterpiece for its evenhanded presentation of the historical facts, its concise understanding of the evolving nature of taxation in an industrialized and urbanized society and its solid demonstration by way of concrete examples of the extent to which Catholic separate schools in Ontario were suffering because they had no legal access to their rightful portion of corporation and utility taxes.

McNeil's argument in favour of amending the Assessment Act can be broken down as follows:

1. The incorporation of the 1863 Scott Act into the 1867 British North America Act was a necessary condition of Confederation. No separate schools, no Confederation. Also — and this was the most original element in McNeil's paper — it was because of Confederation that corporation properties flourished and became so important to the economic well-being of the entire country.

2. Section 14 of the 1863 Scott Act reads in part that separate school supporters "shall be exempted from the payment of all rates imposed for the support of Common Schools." The operative phrase is "all rates," which was another way of saying "all taxes." The exemption meant that separate school supporters could not be forced to pay any part of their taxes for school purposes to support a school system other than their own.

3. In 1863, and by extension in 1867, "all rates" meant property taxes on homes, farms and small business. There were very few limited liability (incorporated) companies and public utilities did not exist.

4. However, during the next several decades, the growth in the number of limited liability companies forced the government to recognize their tax-paying potential for school purposes and, as a result, to amend the Assessment Act in 1886, so that separate school ratepayers who owned publicly-traded stock could direct the taxes on their portion of the stock towards separate schools. The amendment was a failure for two reasons: one, it was impossible to know the religion of stockholders in an age when stock was traded so widely, so often and so quickly; and two, even if a Catholic declared his ownership of his stock in a company, the law as written did not oblige that company to direct his portion of the company's taxes to the separate schools. It was purely voluntary, as denoted by the use of the word "may" and thus completely useless. The meaning of the phrase "all taxes" had evolved to include corporation taxes — and those taxes had become a central component of school revenue — but the exemption for separate school supporters had not kept pace. Consequently, separate school supporters, in the matter of corporation taxes, were paying by default some of their taxes for school purposes to support the common or public schools.
5. By 1930, the meaning of "all taxes" had come to include a massive corporation tax base, publicly-funded enterprises such as the CNR and the CPR, and a host of public utilities owned by all Canadians. But in the continuing absence of an exemption that covered the separate school portion of corporation and utility taxes, separate school supporters were denied their fair portion of these taxes.
6. This denial meant that the province was not living up to a common sense interpretation of the 1863 Scott Act.
7. As a result, Catholic separate schools were the poorer cousins of the public schools. Teachers' salaries were substantially lower. Property tax rates and debt loads were higher. Too many school buildings were unfit, equipment was outdated and textbooks were not free (as they were in the public schools).

8. The solution was simple: the two public school systems in Ontario would receive taxes paid by share-owned corporations and utilities in proportion to the number of students enrolled in each system. This was known as the Quebec Plan. In operation since 1869, it was a direct and equitable way by which the Catholic and Protestant school boards in that province each enjoyed their fair share of these kinds of taxes without the endless political squabbling and divisiveness over school taxes that still plagued Ontario.

9. It was the business and duty of the legislature of Ontario to make the necessary changes to the Assessment Act. The courts had no role in the matter.[12]

During the years to come, many of these same points were to be made, in one fashion or another, by a stable of separate school apologists. Among those who followed the archbishop, few improved on his basic argument or command of the facts. Catholic ratepayers knew the problem and knew the solution. Courtesy of Archbishop McNeil, they also knew that there was only one solution, the implementation of the Quebec plan.

****

The department of education's own statistics revealed the sorry financial state of Catholic separate schools.[13] For our purposes, we will examine statistics on average teacher salary, the revenue per pupil (net municipal expenditure plus legislative grant) and the legislative grant per pupil for both the Catholic separate schools and the public elementary schools, for the years 1917, 1927 and 1935.

1917	Average Teacher Salary	Revenue/Pupil	Legislative Grant/Pupil
R.C.	$426	$18.75	.90
Public	$688	$27.19	$1.84
1927	Average Teacher Salary	Revenue/Pupil	Legislative Grant/Pupil
R.C.	$816	$46.39	$3.64
Public	$1,293	$56.73	$6.19

296

1935	Average Teacher Salary	Revenue/Pupil	Legislative Grant/Pupil
R.C.	$734	$37.62	$5.38
Public	$1,137	$55.43	$5.35

Only in the area of the legislative grant did Catholic separate schools achieve a measure of equality and improve their financial situation. But the grant was far from enough, especially in light of the fact that just to stay afloat most Catholic boards were obliged to charge their supporters much higher tax rates. For instance, in 1935, separate school board supporters in Toronto paid a tax rate of 11.5 mills ($11.50 for every $1,000 of ratable property), but public school supporters in the same city paid only 6.9 mills ($6.90 for every $1,000 of ratable property).[14]

****

While Archbishop Neil McNeil was writing *The School Question of Ontario,* Martin J. Quinn was busy browbeating the George Weston Company for its decision not to comply with Quinn's request to have the taxes on his stock in Weston transferred to the Toronto separate school board. Relying on the 1886 amendment to the Assessment Act, Quinn made his initial request in a letter of 24 February 1931. He owned $92,000 in Weston stock that was worth about $900 in school taxes, a not inconsiderable sum of money sixteen months into the Great Depression. Weston stonewalled Quinn, but the longer the company procrastinated, the more truculent he became. Quinn loved to write letters — his preferred medium for conducting an argument — and he sent a steady flow of lengthy letters to the company directors. He was sure of his facts and figures, methodical (if somewhat plodding) in his presentation of them and unrelenting in pressing his case. Having acquired the hide of a rhinoceros, at some juncture in his public life, Quinn was not one to shy away from a good battle. Once he had convinced himself of the moral and practical rightness of his opinions, he was prepared to be David to anyone's Goliath.

Apparently, Weston's directors were so annoyed by Quinn, the gadfly shareholder, that company representatives paid a visit to Archbishop McNeil, assuring him that Weston would pay the $900 in taxes to the separate school board in exchange for Quinn promising not to publish their correspondence. McNeil told them that he could not accept the money, since that was a matter between Weston and the board, and that he had no right to tell Quinn what to do with his letters to the company.[15] In the end, Weston paid the taxes, if only reluctantly, and Quinn, using his own money, published their correspondence with the title *Injustice to Separate Schools, Assessment Act at Fault, Ontario and Quebec Compared.* He made sure that it was widely distributed.

In demolishing Weston's reasons for refusing to transfer the tax money to the separate school board, Quinn relied on many of the same arguments put forth by Archbishop McNeil in *The School Question of Ontario*, including the idea of the evolving character of property in Ontario. If there was one area in which Quinn's presentation improved on McNeil's, it was the attention Quinn paid to Ontario's Protestants. Quinn wrote that the vast majority of these people were thoughtful and fair-minded but that they were unaware of the burdens under which separate schools had to operate. Catholics would have to convince these people of the rightness of the separate school cause if Catholics were ever to receive justice at the hands of provincial politicians. (Odd is the fact that Quinn never referred to McNeil's *The School Question of Ontario*, not in 1931 nor in any subsequent publication of his.)

****

It was probably during the summer of 1931 that McNeil invited Quinn to meet him, on the strength of Quinn's (yet to be published) correspondence with Weston. A copy had arrived on McNeil's desk courtesy of one of Quinn's friends. This initial encounter brought three results. One, many more meetings took place during which a warm working relationship between the two men developed. Two, if we are to trust Quinn's memory of events, McNeil invited him to participate in drafting a letter from the hierarchy to the clergy. Three, almost immediately after the distribution of the bishops' letter, McNeil turned to Quinn and asked him to organize a gathering of influential Catholics in the archdiocese for the sole purpose of exploring with McNeil the question of corporation and utility taxes.

Dated 30 September 1931, and marked private and confidential, the episcopal letter was signed by all eleven bishops:

To the Right Reverend, Very Reverend and Reverend Clergy of the Province of Ontario:

1. This instruction to the priests of Ontario is not to be read in the churches or published.

2. You are hereby enjoined to study the duties of parents in the training of their children, and the question of our need and our right to a just share of the school taxes paid by Companies and Public Utilities for our Separate Schools.

3. The sources of information for you are, — the Holy Father's Encyclical on Education; Canon Law, especially Canons 1113, 1335, 1372 and 2319 Number 4 of the Codex Juris Canonici; the pamphlet of the Archbishop of Toronto on the School Question of Ontario; the Pastoral Letter of the Bishop of Hamilton on the subject; the open letter of Mr. M.J. Quinn. The last three mentioned documents will be forwarded to you.

4. Instruct your congregations at all Masses on the four Sundays following All Saints Day 1931, on parental duties and our Separate School rights, emphasizing the facts bearing on the question of taxes.

5. In addition to instructing the people in church, organize in this way: — Call in three intelligent men and discuss with them the unfair assessment under which we are suffering, appoint a day for a second meeting and ask the three men to invite, each, three other men, for further instruction and discussion. Then announce in church a general meeting of men for the purpose of forming an organization with President, Secretary and Treasurer, to carry

on the work of propaganda, and to discuss the matter in a friendly way with their Protestant neighbours. Then do the same for the women.

6. Take occasion in your instruction to state that if the Catholic Schools in cities and towns are crippled financially by the loss of taxes which are due them, the rural schools will soon find themselves more than equally crippled. Rural school supporters should be told that every Separate School Section, through which there is a railway, telegraph or telephone line or other public utility, has a right to a share in such taxes.

7. Make it clear to Separate School Trustees that they are in duty bound to become members of the Ontario Separate School Trustees Association, and to take an active interest in the work.

8. Please ask the prayers of your people, the Religious Communities and especially of the school children.

9. Each Pastor will send a written report to his Ordinary at the end of the year, setting forth what action he has taken and with what success and failure he has met.[16]

Even though the bishops welcomed the participation of both men and women in each parish to discuss the subject of corporation and utility taxes, it is very clear that the episcopacy, and by extension the parish priests, were still in control and that the flow of information went from priests to bishops, who alone would determine what use they would make of the year-end reports of their pastors. Moreover, nowhere in the letter is there mentioned the kind of concrete political action the bishops were prepared to take. It all looked like a recipe for busy work and unproductive anxiety.

Archbishop McNeil, however, did not let matters rest with the bishops' letter. Perhaps he suspected on his own that despite the letter's sincerity and unity of purpose, it would only lead to another dead-end. Perhaps, he allowed himself to be persuaded by Quinn to go directly to the rank and file of the local church. Regardless, on 7 October 1931, McNeil issued the following invitation: "I invite you to meet a number of citizens of Toronto here [at the archbishop's residence] next Monday evening [12 October] at eight o'clock and discuss ways and means of securing an amendment of the Assessment Act which will give to Separate Schools a fair share of school taxes paid by corporations."[17] To Quinn fell the task of finding enough prominent laymen in the archdiocese who would be willing to discuss the issue at hand. He came up with thirty-five names. Of these, only seven bothered to attend the first meeting, and only two showed up for the second.

Discouraged, McNeil asked to see Quinn. According to Quinn, this prophetic exchange took place:

McNeil: "Can you tell me, Mr. Quinn, why it is that intelligent and well informed Catholic laymen cannot be interested in such an important matter as our Separate School question?"

Quinn: "Yes, Your Grace, the reason, based upon many experiences, is that the thinking laity feel that it is quite useless to put great effort into any movement the result of which will be determined by a policy which can be developed and safely modified from time to time only by those whose practical experience is essential to a proper appraisal of the facts, because they fear that in the final analysis their work is quite likely to be destroyed by faulty judgment on the part of the Hierarchy, followed by ill-considered action on their part."

McNeil was so hurt by Quinn's words that Quinn tried to soften his remarks, but McNeil interrupted him with a wave of his hand: "Don't apologize, nobody ever spoke to me like that before, I wish to God they had. If you will go on with this work Mr. Quinn, and attempt to develop the movement along the lines we have discussed, I promise you that no clerical nose will be permitted to intrude itself."[18]

In Quinn's mind, McNeil's words were far more than a promise. They were a contract, and as such they were binding on McNeil and his successors as well as on all the bishops in Ontario.[19] It was a point Quinn was to press home in a letter of 7 January 1932. In that letter Quinn reminded McNeil not once but twice that the Separate School Tax Committee, the CTA's original name, "must speak with absolute authority." Quinn continued:

> That is to say, that we must be assured (as we think Your Grace intended to assure us) that there would be no public utterances, either in the press or otherwise, by the hierarchy or the clergy, and that they, in turn, would see to it that there would be no public action on the part of any organization, such as other existing committees, School Boards, etc., that might interfere with the plans of this committee . . .
>
> It appears to the committee tremendously important that we should be in a position to speak with absolute authority for everyone interested, and with the knowledge that any future action of the committee will be backed unhesitatingly, particularly by the hierarchy, whose moral support is, of course, so essential to such a movement.[20]

As envisioned by Quinn very early on, the committee would speak and act on behalf of all Catholic ratepayers on the subject of corporation and utility taxes, and would do so independently of the hierarchy. As for the bishops, they would remain quietly on the sidelines but entirely supportive of the committee's work, quietly guaranteeing the committee's position as the *sole* representative of Catholic ratepayers when dealing with the government and the department of education on this particular issue. Independence from the hierarchy, of course, implied a corresponding independence from the parish clergy. They too would be expected to work with the CTA executive but never attempt to control the agenda or to direct its strategy.

Quinn wanted the bishops and clergy to remain aloof from the public square to avoid any charges of clerical interference in the political process. In a letter of 17 January 1935, outlining the early history of the CTA for the benefit of W.T. Kernahan, Quinn wrote:

It was recognized by practical laymen that the subject is purely a political one, and that in no other sense would it be considered with either of the political parties, and thus it was necessary to organize for the purpose of, if necessary, making a demonstration of our strength in politics.

It was similarly recognized that public participation, in what might ultimately become a political dog fight, by either the hierarchy or the clergy, was to be avoided, and this chiefly for the reason that Bishops, particularly, are shining marks for the arrows of those whose weapon of warfare is the incitement of religious bitterness.[21]

There is no doubt that Quinn believed that the committee had authority free of episcopal control, that the bishops had agreed to this arrangement and that the bishops and priests were to stay out of the limelight for their own good and the good of the separate school cause. Quinn's modus operandi as general chairman of the CTA was defined and sustained by these beliefs. Otherwise, he would not have given himself so wholeheartedly to the CTA and sacrificed so much for its success. There is also no doubt that Archbishop McNeil came to accept Quinn's understanding of the committee's authority and independence of action. However, McNeil was not the hierarchy. As important as he was, he was still only one of eleven bishops. McNeil's imprimatur did not automatically include the imprimatur of any of his brother bishops. In 1932, the rest of the hierarchy did accept Quinn's leadership of the CTA and the political process he chose to employ in his dealings with the government. They did so at McNeil's behest and because they shared his enthusiasm for a fresh approach to separate school agitation. But as soon as Quinn began to fumble in his dealings with the political establishment, there were bishops who were quick to deny that they had abdicated their leadership on the separate school question in favour of that of the general chairman of the CTA.

****

As 1932 unfolded, the Catholic Taxpayers' Association of Ontario slowly took shape.[22] At first, there were two sections. There was an Eastern Ontario section "under" Archbishop Joseph Guillaume Forbes of Ottawa, and there was a Western Ontario section "under" Archbishop Neil McNeil of Toronto. The inaugural meeting of the Western Ontario section took place on 19 February 1932. Ten people, including McNeil, were present. They came from Toronto, Kingston, London, Peterborough, Sarnia and Hamilton. Senator George Lynch-Staunton was named chairman, and Martin Quinn was appointed treasurer. At a follow-up meeting, on 5 March, only four people were in attendance. Nonetheless, the names of many successful Catholics from around the province were added to the rolls and three working committees were struck: management and finance, legislation and publicity. Quinn belonged to the first committee. No clergy were present.

The Western Ontario section issued its first circular on 7 March 1932. It was addressed to all the priests of the archdioceses of Toronto and Kingston and of the dioceses of London, Hamilton, Peterborough, Sault Ste. Marie and Haileybury. In addition to reminding the clergy that it was the bishops who had put the political resolution of the taxation issue into the hands of the laity, the circular said that the instructions from the bishops (30 September 1931) were not enough by themselves: "But as motion alone is not progress unless directed to a definite and correct end, a complete organization was needed: hence this Central Organization."[23] McNeil expressed his support of the CTA in a letter to his own clergy, dated the next day, 8 March: "It would be foolish on the part of the Bishops to lead openly the campaign required. The Catholic electors must come forward and claim their rights."[24] The publicity committee, headed by James E. Day, addressed follow-up letters to those priests who had replied to the circular of 7 March and to those (the majority) who had not. Regarding this latter group, Day reinforced the idea that without the active co-operation of the parish priests, the CTA would not be able to organize the province for political action:

Either our people are behind the Movement or they are not. If they are, we will win. If our opponents can point to Parishes where the people are content that the Catholic people may be deprived of their just rights, neither Bishops, Priests nor Laymen can make Politicians believe that Catholic education is really the Church's doctrine.

It is not by our choice that we laymen are in this Movement, but Catholic Action by Laymen is an order to us. This is really the first movement of Catholic Action, and if it does not succeed in this one, having for its aim the relief of the pockets of our people and the salvation of our schools, the fault must lie with us. And as Catholic Laymen's Action can neither exist nor succeed without proper Ecclesiastical direction, we have to look to the Priests to find in the first instance some men who will act, on the call of the bishops.[25]

Whether Day realized it, he had summed up the essential paradox of the Catholic Taxpayers' Association, right from the start of its corporate existence. On the one hand, the CTA saw itself as acting independently of the bishops and their priests. On the other hand, it could not organize itself and do its appointed work without the support of the bishops and the active participation of parish priests.

Martin J. Quinn inherited this paradox when he was elected chairman of the Western Ontario section, on 23 April 1932. After Senator Lynch-Staunton had declined to continue in that role, Quinn was the unanimous choice of the executive to succeed the senator as chairman. His first move was to unite the western and eastern sections into one province-wide Catholic Taxpayers' Association, a process that was finalized in June 1932. Joining Quinn on the new executive were Dr. Edward Ryan, vice-chairman, Mrs. J.C. Keenan, second vice-chairman, W.T. Kernahan, treasurer, and R.L. Archambault, executive secretary.

At the same time this amalgamation was being carried out, Quinn was writing a second pamphlet that was to be titled *Some Pertinent Facts: The Separate Schools of Ontario*. It appeared under the imprint of the CTA and was available in both English and French. By July 1932 it was already in a second printing, and it appeared in the 16 August 1932 issue of the *Catholic Register*. Although *Some Pertinent Facts* was mainly another rendition of arguments already published by Archbishop McNeil and Quinn himself, it did arm Catholic ratepayers with a rather novel and quite compelling argument from the standpoint of *service to the state*. Having defined this phrase as the number of students in the Catholic separate schools, Quinn continued:

> It seems logical to argue that payment by the State in the matter of the education and development of Canadian citizens should be made on the basis of the actual service to the State, and in that connection it must be remembered that not only have Separate schools been declared by law to be a branch of the Public School System, but that both classes of schools are operated in precisely the same way under control of the Ontario Department of Education.[26]

If this were true, each branch of the public school system should enjoy a share of corporation and utility taxes according to the level of service it provided the state — the number of students it taught.

To prove his point, Quinn used the example of the separate schools in the city of Toronto. These schools taught one in six children, but their share of corporation taxes was one to ninety-one: for every dollar the separate schools received in corporation taxes, the public schools received ninety-one dollars. "This shockingly unfair inequality," wrote Quinn, "results from failure of the Legislature to perform its plain constitutional duty to amend the Assessment Act as changed conditions have the effect of shifting to the Public Schools a large part of the taxes paid by Separate School supporters. . ."[27]

Quinn wasted no time sending copies of *Some Pertinent Facts* to Premier Henry and every member of the Legislative Assembly. It was his opening shot and had the immediate effect of tranquilizing Queen's Park. No one on either the government or opposition benches knew how to respond. They kept quiet.

Premier Henry and the Conservatives

George Stewart Henry was to serve in the Ontario legislature for thirty years, from 1913 to 1943, and is regarded as the founder of Ontario's modern highway system, overseeing the extension of the province's paved highways from a mere 670 km to a truly impressive 3,888 km.[28] However, Henry had the political misfortune to have been premier during the Great Depression and to be seen by the public as dour and inept. Nothing could have saved him from defeat in the 1934 election. The arrival of *Some Pertinent Facts* only added to his woes. The thought of another round of the eternal separate school issue must have chilled his blood. Henry knew nothing of the pamphlet's author, Martin J. Quinn, or of its publisher, the Catholic Taxpayers' Association, and he could be excused if he thought that they could be treated as nothing more than a passing irritant. But that was not to be the case.

Quinn was nothing if not bullish in his political maneuverings. The CTA publication of *Some Pertinent Facts* and its widespread distribution marked the beginning, not the end, of his political lobbying. He was not going to wait for Premier Henry to respond. Instead, Quinn did the following four things: he consolidated the CTA's control over the parish-level committees already instituted by the bishops, in their letter of 30 September 1931;[29] he directed all such committees to draw up their own resolutions on the tax issue and forward them as soon as possible to their local member of provincial parliament;[30] he firmed up Archbishop Neil McNeil's support of the CTA (McNeil wrote three more letters to his priests, on 15 September and 2 November 1932 and again on 1 February 1933, in which he solicited their co-operation with the CTA's strategy);[31] and he personally directed a CTA public relations campaign as a lead-up to a formal presentation from the CTA to the government.

Quinn delivered speeches in London, Windsor, Ottawa and Kingston and in many other cities and towns across the province.[32] His energy never flagged, and his nerve never failed him. At each stop, he was greeted by large and enthusiastic crowds, as if he were a candidate on the hustings. Interestingly, his talks were always open to the general public. Quinn welcomed the presence of Protestants as a

307

demonstration of his bedrock belief that the proper division of corporation and utility taxes for the purpose of financing public education in a modern industrial society was a matter of fundamental justice that concerned every taxpayer.

In his London speech to the Catholic Women's League, Quinn declared that school taxes were not a political issue and that Catholics should no longer treat separate school grievances as if it were a battle between Catholics and Protestants. That was the old nineteenth-century way of thinking and had to be discarded for everyone's sake. The new way of thinking called for the education of both Catholics and Protestants in respect to the issue at hand — a realistic and equitable division of corporation and utility taxes.[33] Catholics had to accept that there was a "distinct tendency towards fairness and generosity on the part of the Protestant people." Quinn sincerely believed that if given all the facts and figures, free of political rhetoric, the majority of Protestant voters would side with the Catholics on this issue. Lastly, the debate about school taxes had absolutely nothing to do with religion. This was a veiled reference to the Loyal Orange Lodge, the traditional enemy of separate schools who would stop at nothing to invoke the spectre of religion.

On the dicey topic of the CTA's approach to governments and political parties, Quinn was reported as saying that Catholics were obliged to appeal to the government of the day and not to any particular party.

> If the Government refused to make the amendment, the Catholics, entirely without feeling, must elect some other party to obtain their ends, and if that party failed to grant their cause, elect yet another. Catholic people must for the time forget their political allegiance, and remember that they belong to one party, that of the Catholic School cause.[34]

Quinn repeated this message everywhere he spoke. It was a call for Catholics to dispense with party affiliation and to vote as a single bloc on the one cause that united them. It was a dangerous tactic, but as a threat, it could not be ignored by Premier Henry. His

Conservatives were the government of the day, and they would have to face an election within two years. As if to make his threat all the more real, Quinn later boasted that the CTA had 20,000 men and women in its ranks and 250,000 Catholic voters who supported the CTA's work.[35] It was a boast bound to boomerang if repeated once too often.

For the moment, though, Quinn had all the political momentum and was gaining allies along the way. Mayor David Croll of Windsor endorsed a fairer division of education taxes. The *Peterborough Examiner*, the *Kingston Whig-Standard* and the *London Morning Advertiser* came out in favour of the CTA.[36] It seems that the editorial writer for the *Examiner* had been swayed by the arguments in *Some Pertinent Facts* — much to the chagrin of the West Peterborough County Orange Lodge. Its legislative committee fired off a lengthy rebuttal. Alerted, Quinn replied with a lengthy letter of his own. Other support came from the Catholic Women's League. It sponsored a student essay contest that asked the question, "What Injustice Do Catholics in Ontario Suffer in Regard to Their Schools?" The winner was Gerrard Black of Campbellford.[37] For its part, the *Catholic Register* published a steady diet of editorials on the school question. One of the best was "Our Taxes." It argued that the Assessment Act did not reflect the reality of an industrialized society dominated by public share corporations and publicly-owned utilities. "The result is that we have lost millions of dollars of our school taxes. And the culprit in the case is the Legislature, or perhaps our men, for failing to insist on their civil rights."[38]

If there was an Achilles' heel to Quinn's strategy it had to be Bishop John T. McNally. Although McNally had signed the 30 September 1931 letter, in which his "Pastoral On Education" was recommended reading, and he had joined with all the bishops in giving Quinn freedom of action, his acceptance of the CTA was halfhearted at best. He did not encourage the formation of parish committees; he developed an active dislike of Quinn; and he used his diocesan newspaper — *The Catholic Voice* — to publish his own opinions on separate schools. Of course, McNally agreed with the CTA on corporation taxes. He parted company at the decision to hand over leadership to Quinn. As the CTA campaign heated up in the autumn of 1932, McNally was determined not to let Quinn's be the only voice on the public platform. To that end, *The Catholic Voice* published front-page articles such as "Separate Schools Are Not Receiving Fair Share of Taxes" and "Catholic Children Must Have Catholic Schools."[39] And McNally used the occasion of the commencement exercises at Hamilton's Catholic high schools to assail the government for its willingness to deny separate schools their just share of public funds. It was a story that made the front page of the *Catholic Register*.[40] This is not what Quinn bargained for when he accepted the general chairmanship of the CTA. He wanted complete independence from the bishops as well as their *public silence* as the CTA pursued the government.

While McNally was stirring up the dust in his own diocese, the CTA was busy preparing a brief for the government. On Friday, 13 January 1933, Martin Quinn led a deputation of fifty prominent Catholics, including the entire CTA executive, Senator Lynch-Staunton of Hamilton and William Louis [W.L.] Scott, the son of Sir Richard W. Scott, to Queen's Park. There was at least one delegate from each of the eleven dioceses in Ontario. They met Premier Henry, W.H. Price, the attorney general, and Charles McCrea, the minister of mines and the ostensible English-speaking Catholic representative in the cabinet. It was an impressive show of unity and purpose, every word and gesture being choreographed to full effect. Quinn spoke first. He was followed by Senator Lynch-Staunton. It was a one-two combination that impressed even the premier.

The sole purpose of the meeting was to lay before the government an "Application of Catholic Taxpayers' Association of Ontario for Amendment of the Assessment Act." Largely the work of W.T. Kernahan, the application was thoroughly researched, closely argued and well written. Its essential demand can be found in the opening paragraph:

> We are asking the Legislature to amend the Assessment
> Act so as to provide a fair and adequate means of assuring to
> separate public schools in the Province the share of school

taxes which we claim to be justly consistent with the true spirit and intention of existing school laws and regulations, which is that taxes for school purposes on every form of property of the supporters of each branch of the public schools should be available for the support of that branch of the public schools.[41]

Its solution to the financial woes of the separate schools can be found in the next to last paragraph:

The simplest and surest and most equitable remedy for the existing intolerable condition is to enact appropriate legislation which will ensure that corporation and public utility school taxes be divided between the branches of the public schools so that each branch will receive in part thereof proportionate to the number of children whose education is provided by that branch.[42]

The CTA's 1933 "Application" was the most important document it ever produced. Nothing that either Quinn or any other CTA representative said or wrote after that 13 January meeting with Premier Henry could have been more clear or more forthright. It contained the CTA's entire case on the matter of corporation and utility taxes and even offered a solution similar to the one in Quebec in operation since 1869. However, as Quinn, the novice politician, was soon to learn, ambiguity is the stuff of power and delay is the parliamentarian's craft.

Premier Henry took nearly fifteen months to formally respond to the "Application." During that time, he did little to welcome Catholics into the Conservative fold. From his position of strength in the legislature, he brushed off like so many annoying flies those newspapers that editorialized in favour of an amendment that would satisfy separate school supporters.[43] Among them could be counted the Cornwall *Standard-Freeholder*, the Windsor *Border Cities Star* and the *Toronto Daily Star*. Taken together, they formed a considerable body of public opinion, but politicians, especially from the safety of a majority, have a right to hold editorial writers in contempt. The people, though, should never be treated with contempt. Henry forgot this rudimentary rule of politics when he attended the 1933 version of the annual Twelfth of July parade in Toronto. His presence on stage was an insult to every Catholic in the province that was all the more offensive as a result of the behaviour of W.H. Dawson, the Grand Master of the Grand Orange Lodge of Ontario West. With the premier sitting close at hand, Dawson demanded a referendum on separate schools.[44] Horrified, many Catholics wondered aloud why the premier would join such an obviously anti-Catholic show of force.[45]

Something Martin Quinn said might have been partly responsible for the premier's presence and the Orange bravado. Speaking to the Toronto Council of the Knights of Columbus, on 13 March 1933, Quinn boasted that "The Catholic people of this Province control one-quarter of a million votes, and I believe that they are now fully awake to the fact that they must assert their rights if they are to enjoy them." He continued: "It is said that 'The meek shall inherit the earth,' but that is not true of Ontario politics. For many years a certain organization, which controls 50,000 votes, has worked steadily against us, but if the Government does not grant our requests, which we believe are fair and reasonable, we will go quietly to the polls and cast 250,000 votes and try to elect a Government which will give us justice."[46] These were bold words. It was easy to interpret them as a threat against Premier Henry and the ruling Conservative party and an attempt to goad the Orangemen into a public fight.

A reply from the latter was not long in forthcoming. A circular letter from the Grand Orange Lodge of Ontario West, dated 10 April 1933, roundly denounced Quinn and the Church of Rome and called on all its members to rally in defense of one school, one flag, one language.[47] The rally, a gigantic affair, took place at Massey Hall on 25 April.[48] Quinn defended his Knights of Columbus speech in a letter of 25 May 1933, to Charles McCrea, minister of mines.[49] Quinn was also in no mood to back down. In October, he responded directly to the political posturing of the Grand Orange Lodge of Ontario West with a series of three articles called "The True Position of the Orange Order in Ontario."[50]

312

Quinn's quarrel with the Orangemen, however dramatic and bellicose it might have been, was still a sideshow to the main event, which was Premier Henry's decision, on 29 March 1934, to refer the adjudication of the legal rights of the separate and public schools in regards to the division of school taxes to the Judicial Committee of the Privy Council. It would be a stated case, with the province paying all court costs. The referral to the Law Lords in London would be set in motion as soon as legal counsel had drawn up the questions. It was an adroit move, taken on advice from a former premier, Howard Ferguson, even though it appears that the government had previously intimated to Archbishop McNeil that it was considering reforms to the division of school taxes.[51] Yet nothing McNeil was told mattered. He was a supplicant who was used by the government. It was Ferguson who had Henry's ear. In a statement, the premier said:

> The government has given careful consideration to the argument of separate school supporters that, apart from the legal aspect, they are entitled to a larger share than falls to them under existing laws. But the government has had difficulty in finding a basis on which a larger share of school taxes may be paid which would take into account the question of legal rights.[52]

This was classic government dodging, in which delay was understood by its political practitioners as essential to survival. No wonder the *Catholic Register* exclaimed in a front-page headline, "Henry Seeks Cover in Downing Street" and in another, "Catholics be on Guard!"[53] And the *Register* was not alone in denouncing Henry for playing politics. It was joined by the *Canadian Freeman*, the *Catholic Record, Saturday Night*, the *Border Cities Star* and the *Toronto Daily Star*.[54] On 3 April, Henry prorogued the legislature, and on 16 May, he called a provincial election, to be held on 19 June 1934.

Quinn was apoplectic. He felt that the Henry government had treated the CTA's "Application" as little more than another opinion and the CTA itself as a nuisance factor in his political calculations. Anticipating the government's latest move, Quinn had already warned

W.H. Price, the attorney general, of the consequences of ignoring Ontario's Catholics. Quinn's letter to Price was dated 16 March 1934:

> I think I ought to say too that the claim of the Catholic people for their just share of taxation from two sources, viz.: — Joint Stock Companies and Public Utility Corporations, in both of which they, undoubtedly, have the same proportion of rights as non-Catholics, is so simple and so reasonable that any action on the part of the Government which would grant only a small measure of what is asked, would not only be entirely unsatisfactory but could not fail to cause offense to a large section of the community who, more than ever before are keenly conscious of the injustice to which, for so long a period, they have been subjected.[55]

In the face of Henry's 29 March announcement, which came at the end of the legislative session to spare the government any troubling questions, it was now time for Quinn to make good on his threat or be branded a bluffer.

First, though, Quinn had to convince the executive committee and the general committee that the time was right to end the CTA's political neutrality. The immediate effect of Henry's decision to go to the Privy Council was to divide Catholic opinion, both inside and outside the CTA, on the merits of that decision. As chairman, Quinn had to be cautious and patient so as not to upset the delicate balancing act he had achieved to keep the CTA from imploding.[56] It took him until the end of April to sway his colleagues of the political wisdom of breaking with the Henry government and urging Catholics to vote against it in the next election.

The shift in CTA policy is evident in Quinn's communications to parish priests and parish chairmen. In his 1 May 1934 circular to priests, Quinn had this to say of the Henry government:

> Though it is four weeks since the Legislature adjourned, and we had the statement of the Prime Minister [Premier] that questions to be submitted to the Courts were in

the course of preparation and would shortly be published, and some days afterwards a second reported statement of his that they would be published "in a few days", such publication has not yet been made.

On the contrary, we are in possession of indisputable evidence which indicates that the process of preparing these questions has not yet begun, nor does it appear possible that, even if started immediately, proper consideration would allow their publication under the next three or four weeks.

Obviously the conclusion that Mr. Henry continues to play the game that has gone on for the last sixteen months is inescapable, and this being so, only one policy on our part is possible. Complete information respecting this will be sent to you very soon.

The question that is going to be decided, by the Catholic voters at any rate, at the next election, is of far greater import than that applying to a fair distribution of school taxes. It is this: Shall the Catholic citizens, in any part of this province, be denied their ordinary rights of citizenship, because of the domination in provincial affairs of the Orange Order?

No greater service can be done the Province of Ontario than to declare, once and for all, that that kind of Government is repulsive to the moderate people of all classes, regardless of their religious beliefs.[57]

In a follow-up circular to priests, dated 16 May, the day the election was called, Quinn reiterated the CTA's opposition to the government's decision to submit the school tax question to the courts, and he promised that he would soon notify all parish priests of the CTA's policy in respect to the way that Catholics should cast their votes in the near future. In the meantime, at special meetings of the Catholic Taxpayers' Committee (and other societies too) of each parish, the priests should take the time to disseminate the policies and objectives of the CTA and to drum up the Catholic vote. Quinn reminded them that in the past the Catholic turnout on election day had been consistently low. That would have to change dramatically this time if Catholics were ever to triumph over their enemies in a matter that had become bigger than school taxes. It was now a question of the protection of minority rights.[58]

Premier Henry got wind of the CTA's exhortations to its members and wrote Quinn, on 28 May, asking him to refrain from concocting a political issue out of the fact that the government had yet to make public the questions to be submitted to the courts:

> When I stated in the legislature recently that the questions respecting separate school taxation would be proceeded with at an early date, I was not aware that the absence from the country of legal counsel for the Government would be extended longer than was then anticipated. In fact, my information was that the matter could be taken up at once. My promise to submit the conflicting claims of the parties in the case for final decision of the highest Courts still holds good. As far as it rests with me, this promise will be faithfully carried out. But, on reflection, I am opposed to introducing the subject as an issue during a political campaign. The issue is essentially one for judicial interpretation, and should not form part of the controversies that arise at such a time. I believe that you and your committee, as well as the advocates of public school rights, will recognize the wisdom and propriety of waiting for a few weeks before making the proposed questions public.[59]

Henry was being disingenuous. To take fifteen months to react to the CTA's "Application" was political; to take the question to court was also political; to vow to stay silent on the matter during the election campaign and to request that the CTA do the same were also political — and rather self-serving. The legislature did have the power to distribute school taxes more fairly between the two sets of taxpayers who supported the two types of schools as established by law and guaranteed by the BNA Act. Instead, Premier Henry chose to bypass the powers and responsibilities of the elected members — as

316

was his political right — and turn what was essentially an accommodation to modern reality into a full-blown question of competing rights.

In any event, nothing Henry had to say to Quinn at this moment in the history of the CTA would have made much of a difference in either the CTA's attitude or strategy. Henry's letter certainly did not deter Quinn from sending his next circular. Dated 29 May 1934, it was addressed to the parish chairmen and announced the Catholic voting strategy. It was an astonishing document:

> No doubt a great many of our Chairmen are wondering at what they may consider unnecessary delay on the part of the Executive in announcing <u>our final policy in respect to the coming election</u>, though a large majority of them have quite properly concluded what, of sheer necessity, it must be, if Catholics are to maintain their self respect.
>
> As our people are aware, no statement, oral or printed, has ever been made by us that the whole world might not know about, but having observed the willingness of some of the not too scrupulous opposition to quote part of our statements in an effort to create an impression entirely foreign to that which would be conveyed in its complete form, we hesitate at this time to go as far as we would like in stating our case as it now stands, but for your information, we would say that the proposal of the Government to submit stated questions to the Court is regarded as merely a <u>final attempt to side-step their very definite responsibility.</u>
>
> It may be quite unnecessary to remind you that our campaign from the beginning was based upon recognition of the fact that the <u>Government is the only source</u> from which relief can come, and thus <u>responsibility for fair treatment of 25% of Ontario's population rests entirely upon it</u>. We, however, also had a duty which was, by the publication of the facts in every possible way, to remove, as far as possible, the obstacle of opposition, based upon lack of information, from the Government's path — a duty which it is conceded on all

sides has been well performed.

We draw attention now to our oft repeated statement, both in our printed propaganda and at our public meetings all over the province, that if, under these circumstances, the Government failed to grant us the relief as freely provided under exactly the same Legislation for the Protestant minority of Quebec, we would avail ourselves of every proper means in an effort to elect another party to power at the first opportunity. Not only have the Government not taken any action whatever in respect to our request, but in their failure to do so have treated us with a degree of discourtesy amounting to absolute contempt.

The natural indignation that will have been aroused by the flagrantly insulting attitude of the Government toward Catholics will, in the interests of their own self respect, prevent them from voting for a Government candidate, and it is the special business of your Committee to see that every Catholic man and woman in your district casts their ballots in the coming election, thus making it clear, not only to politicians, but also to that great body of moderate fair minded Protestant citizens, who desire that justice be done, that the Catholic people are showing a reasonable degree of dignified interest in their own affairs.

A VOTE FOR AN INDEPENDENT CANDIDATE IS A VOTE LOST — WE CANNOT AFFORD TO LOSE ANY VOTES.[60]

Quinn never mentioned the Liberals by name, and he did not even hint that Mitch Hepburn, leader of the Liberal Opposition, had promised to give Catholics the concessions that the Henry government had refused them. However, since he had castigated the Conservatives and warned Catholics against voting for independent candidates, he left no choice for Catholics but to vote Liberal on 19 June.

For the first time in living memory, Catholics had been directed to vote for a particular party on the basis of a particular grievance —

school taxes. This direction was conducted quietly and privately among Catholics themselves so as not to invite political trouble. Quinn and the CTA would have escaped censure if a copy of his circular had not landed in the office of the *Evening Telegram* in Toronto, that scourge of separate school supporters. The newspaper decided to publish the entire letter as is, including the CTA masthead and the names of the members of its executive and general committees, on the front page of its issue of 13 June 1934.[61] The *Evening Telegram* even published an accompanying photograph of Martin J. Quinn. Publication of the letter was a journalistic coup of the first order.

Tension increased when the *Catholic Register* ran a front-page article in its 14 June 1934 issue, supporting the CTA in its call to unseat the government of Premier Henry:

> Next Tuesday [19 June] will be a fateful day in the Catholic history of Ontario. It gives the Catholics of this province a chance they have not had since Confederation of defeating the forces of bigotry that have so long been successful in obstructing the realization of those rights in which Catholic schools are entitled on grounds of natural justice, as well as by the spirit and intentions of the Separate School Act of 1863 and the Pact of Confederation.[62]

The remainder of the article was devoted to exposing the "deceit" of Premier Henry and calling upon Catholics to vote. It ended on an aggressive note: "Ontario Catholics are determined to have Catholic schools for their children at all costs."[63]

The *Telegram* published the entire *Register* article, presumably as a good example of organized Catholic perfidy in a democratic state, and it devoted its lead editorial of 14 June to a scathing denunciation of the Quinn letter of 29 May.[64] Premier Henry, meanwhile, purchased a front-page advertisement in the 15 June issue of the *Telegram*. He took Quinn and the CTA to task for trying to control Catholic votes:

The organized attempt to corral the Catholic vote must shock all decent-minded citizens, whether Catholic or Protestant, Liberal or Conservative. It is a startling invasion of the democratic system. It can only injure the cause it espouses by consolidating against it all citizens who value the privilege of using their own unfettered judgment in the exercise of the right to vote.[65]

Henry was not without his Conservative allies on the CTA's general committee. One such ally was a Charles P. McTague, a prominent Windsor lawyer. He resigned from the general committee — on election day, no less — because of Quinn's 29 May circular and also because of the *Register*'s 14 June call for Catholics to vote against the Conservative government. McTague condemned the letter and the newspaper for stirring up a "religious political campaign." He told one newspaper that he fully intended "to exercise my franchise as if the regrettable letters and editorials had never been written, and I believe my fellow Catholics are entitled to exactly the same privileges without fear of criticism from any properly constituted authority."[66]

At the end of the day, Premier Henry and the Conservatives suffered a massive defeat on 19 June. After languishing twenty-nine years in opposition, the Liberals, led by the charismatic and wildly popular Mitch Hepburn, won 65 seats to the Conservatives 17 (at the time of dissolution, the Conservatives held 84 seats to the Liberals' 15). Eight cabinet ministers, including Charles McCrea, went down to defeat. McCrea, the so-called Catholic representative in cabinet, had been excoriated by at least one newspaper for failing to defend separate school demands in the presence of his cabinet colleagues.[67]

As for Quinn and the CTA, they could take pride in helping to defeat a government that had not taken seriously the "Application" of 13 January 1933. Ontario's Catholic press, though, gave too much credit to Quinn for Henry's loss at the polls.[68] (So too did Henry himself, the Orangemen and the *Evening Telegram*.) And Quinn committed the unpardonable political blunder of believing his own press clippings. Although it is safe to say that a significantly greater number of Catholics voted in the 1934 election, and that many of them probably cast their ballots in favour of the Liberal party, no one then (or even now) could possibly determine the actual number of Catholics who voted, to which political party they had given their votes and why they voted the way they did. That Quinn (and many others) sincerely believed that he controlled over 250,000 Catholic votes was a fantastic illusion, one that would wreck havoc on the CTA when the time came for Quinn to deal with Mitch Hepburn.

Another portent of things to come was the death of Archbishop Neil McNeil, on 25 May 1934. His passing could not have happened at a worse time for Quinn. It deprived him of his one sure episcopal ally. McNeil's successor, Archbishop James Charles McGuigan, was not appointed to the Toronto See until December 1934 and was not installed until 20 March 1935. He knew little about the separate school issue, but he proved to be a quick study, especially in the art of how not to offend provincial politicians.

Premier Hepburn and the Liberals

Mitch Hepburn played all his political cards on the school tax question with the perfection of a seasoned politician. Timing was everything: when to stay silent and watch his political foes swing in the wind; when to tell Catholics what they wanted to hear (always in private, never in public); when to deny and when to blame others; and when to let an overzealous enemy such as Martin Quinn hoist himself by his own petard and disintegrate in midair. As Hepburn dealt with the school question, he was by turns evasive, vague and forgetful, as well as a master in delay tactics, all in the name of political survival. He was not above lying to a large election-eve crowd, as we shall see, and, he never believed for an instant that he owed his 1934 election victory to Martin Quinn and the CTA.

Quinn's initial contact with Hepburn was on 21 January 1933, the day Quinn sent the then leader of the opposition a copy of the CTA "Application." In his covering letter, Quinn remarked that he had discussed the tax issue with their mutual friend, Senator William H. McGuire, who had assured him of Liberal support if the Henry government introduced legislation in accordance with the CTA's expectations.[69] Hepburn did not answer until Quinn wrote him a second time at the beginning of February. In his reply, Hepburn stepped around the issue, telling Quinn that he was waiting for the Henry government to announce its policy, and, as soon as that happened, he would take the entire matter to the management committee of the Liberal Party. In other words, a response to the "Application" was Henry's headache, not Hepburn's. The Liberal opposition did not respond to the brief, in any concrete fashion, and it was carefully quiet when Henry announced his intention of taking the school tax question to the Privy Council.

The silent treatment continued during the 1934 election. Not even the *Evening Telegram*'s publication of Quinn's CTA circular of 29 May 1934 aroused much of a response from Hepburn. He dodged the issue wherever he spoke. Instead of answering the question he was often asked by reporters on the campaign trail — What did he consider fair treatment for separate school supporters? — Hepburn would invoke the memory of Sir Wilfrid Laurier and promise to treat Catholics in the same fashion as Laurier had treated Protestants. On at least one occasion, he simply lashed out at the *Telegram*.[70] Hepburn was so evasive the *Telegram* started a rumour that the Liberals had secretly pledged themselves to overhaul the Assessment Act in favour of Catholic demands. Before long, this rumour had assumed a life of its own. To counteract it, Hepburn chose a Massey Hall speech on the weekend before the election to flail the Tories and the *Telegram* for fomenting religious division in the province and to claim that his Catholic friends had never brought up the separate school question with him. He promised that as soon as they did, the Catholic minority would receive proper consideration of their claims.[71]

If Hepburn had ever uttered a lie in the course of a political speech, this was it. In March 1933, Senator McGuire had arranged a conference between Quinn and Hepburn at the Liberal Party headquarters on King Street in Toronto. At that meeting, Hepburn made two promises to Quinn: if the Henry government introduced an acceptable amendment to the Assessment Act, the Liberal opposition would support it; and if the Henry government failed to do so, and if the Liberals won the next election, Hepburn would introduce the appropriate legislation during the first session. Quinn wrote up his version of the Hepburn meeting in a letter to McGuire, dated 2 March 1934. He then met with the senator at the Ontario Club later in the month to confirm the contents of this letter. Not satisfied that McGuire understood the true importance of the Hepburn pledge, Quinn sent yet another letter to him, this one dated 30 March 1934, in which he reviewed their meeting at the club. Not once did McGuire contradict Quinn's version of events or object to his use of the words "arrangement" and "promise."[72]

During the 1933 Christmas holidays, Hepburn visited the Carty family in London and made promises very similar to the ones he had given Quinn. The Cartys were a high-profile Catholic family. Treating Mitch Hepburn as a friend, they advised him not to appear to be selling out to the Catholics, a mistake that the Tories would exploit. Hepburn assured them that Senator McGuire, Peter Heenan and Arthur Roebuck had convinced him to help separate schools but that he would put nothing in writing.[73] (Heenan and Roebuck would serve in Hepburn's first cabinet.)

No wonder, then, that Hepburn said nothing of substance on the school question during the 1934 election, and that Quinn not only refused to criticize him for staying silent but also went out of his way to reassure his colleagues in the CTA that Hepburn would deliver on his promises. Quinn was so confident that he had Hepburn in the bag, so to speak, that when directly challenged by the Windsor lawyer Charles P. McTague on the wisdom of the CTA organizing the Catholic vote for the Liberal Party, Quinn answered by declaring that Hepburn had committed himself to giving Catholics legislative relief during the first session and, furthermore, that he had made this promise in circumstances that would make denial impossible. McTague, a Conservative, did not believe Quinn, who was a Liberal in politics, and, as we have already seen, McTague had his name removed from the CTA's general committee. Quinn may have been a Liberal (so too were many others in the CTA), but as he also told McTague, he would not let his politics get in the way of exposing Hepburn if he ever tried to deny the March 1933 arrangement.[74]

Following the June 1934 election, Quinn's duty as CTA chairman was to find ways to cajole Hepburn into living up to his promise to give Catholics the tax legislation they needed to fund their schools. Quinn's failure to convince Hepburn to hold his nose, if necessary, and do what was morally right and not just politically expedient led to the self-destruction of the Catholic Taxpayers' Association and a tragic end for Quinn himself.

From Premier Hepburn's perspective, he was obliged to do something for Catholic separate schools, but exactly what conveniently eluded him once he was leader of the government. A concerted attempt to divide and conquer the Catholic bishops was the first order of the day. Hepburn sent Heenan and McGuire to speak to Bishop Félix Couturier of Alexandria, who was seemingly sympathetic to the government's desire to delay introducing legislation, and also to Bishop McNally of Hamilton, who was adamantly opposed. Their next interview was with Quinn. For three hours Heenan and McGuire tried to convince him to put party above Church and accept a delay, but he refused to budge an inch. Quinn described Heenan's behaviour as worse than that of Judas Iscariot, who at least had "the decency to be so thoroughly ashamed of his treachery that he went out and hanged himself with a halter."[75] Archbishop McGuigan's visit to Toronto, where he was met by all the Ontario bishops on 10 January 1935, put an end to Hepburn's ham-fisted attempt to influence the hierarchy.[76] The bishops were united. The premier would have to face the Catholic Taxpayers' Association, an unappetizing prospect.

On 22 January 1935, Martin Quinn and the CTA met Hepburn and his entire cabinet at Queen's Park and presented them with an "Application for Legislative Amendments of Existing Laws Relating to School Taxes."[77] Except for a few cosmetic changes, it was the same document presented to Premier Henry a little more than a year earlier. According to the *Evening Telegram*, the CTA was asking the government to amend the Assessment Act so that corporation taxes would be divided between the public and separate schools according to their respective school populations.[78] At some point during the presentation, Hepburn remarked that if what the CTA wanted was something along the lines of the Quebec legislation, he could see nothing wrong with that.[79] It was clear, though, that his comment was not for quoting. To the reporters waiting for an official comment on the meeting, Hepburn said that no decision could be made until he had heard the other side. As events were to play themselves out, this would be the first and last time Quinn met Hepburn in person.

The other side came in force on 14 February 1935. Led by C.M. Carrie, chairman of the Orange legislation committee and the Toronto public school board, the deputation consisted of two hundred representatives of Protestant churches, public school boards, municipal councils and Orange lodges from across the province. They also were given the privilege of addressing Hepburn and his cabinet. At least on that score no one could cry foul. They protested against the unconstitutional demands of separate schools, attacked the Quebec panel system of apportioning corporation taxes and insisted that no further concessions be made to Catholics.

The meeting went poorly for the deputation. Hepburn told them that he was not going to be cowed by their numbers or their propaganda, and that he was annoyed at having to remind them that he too was a Protestant and even a Mason and considered himself a good Canadian. Time was of the essence, he said, and soon he would make a decision. In the interim, he had ordered a detailed examination of the Minority School Act in Quebec.[80]

Unbeknownst to the Protestant side, Hepburn had asked the CTA to forward "as quickly as possible" its own version of school tax legislation, if it had one, to Attorney General Roebuck. The CTA did have a proposed bill on hand and wasted no time sending it to Roebuck. Following several rounds of negotiations with him, the CTA delivered a complete bill with a memorandum attached to it, explaining each detail of their proposed legislation.[81]

It was all for naught. The cabinet met on 15 February 1935. After three hours of intense debate the ministers agreed that some measure on school taxes should be introduced during the current session, but as to what that legislation might be they could find no consensus among themselves. Anxious to preserve ministerial unity and to avoid the appearance of political paralysis, so early in his first mandate, Hepburn sought to postpone any decision, and Martin Quinn inadvertently gave him the perfect excuse.

On 10 April 1935, Quinn wrote Hepburn to remind him of promises he had made in March 1933.[82] The next day Quinn wrote Senator McGuire to refresh *his* memory of Hepburn's promises and included a copy of Quinn's letter of the previous day to Hepburn. McGuire took two weeks to reply and ended his curt response with a denial: "You refer to an arrangement with Mr. Hepburn in your letter to him, also you refer to it again in your letter to me. I do not know what it is that you refer to."[83] Quinn was dumbfounded and fired off another letter to McGuire, trying but failing for a second time to have the senator jog his memory as to what they had agreed upon two years ago at Liberal Party headquarters and the Ontario Club.[84]

Quinn had done the unforgivable, according to Mitch Hepburn, who never liked to be reminded in writing of the promises he had made in private. He took his revenge soon enough. On 11 April 1935, Hepburn informed the legislative assembly that the government would not deal with school taxes until the fall session.[85] Then on 3 May, he established a Commission of Enquiry to investigate the cost of both primary and secondary education. The issue of corporation taxes would constitute only one aspect of the commission's work. The chairman was Dr. Duncan McArthur, deputy minister of education. Other members included inspectors Dr. George F. Rogers and V.K. Greer and two Catholics, Ernest C. Desormeaux of the Ottawa Separate School Board and W.T. Kernahan of the CTA.[86] It has been a dubious political tradition in Canada for governments to buy time by appointing commissions of one sort or another. Hepburn needed time to find his way through the school tax thicket, and a commission headed by Dr. McArthur, who was openly hostile to separate school claims, was the best way for him to buy that time.

The fall session came and went, but Hepburn did nothing. His excuse this time, notwithstanding all his denials, was Mackenzie King, the leader of the Liberal opposition in Ottawa. King asked Hepburn not to deal with the school tax question until after the Dominion election, which took place on 23 October 1935 and returned the Liberals to power.[87] Hepburn, who wanted to stay on King's good side, willingly obliged him.

As upsetting as this additional delay was to Quinn, he still believed that Hepburn would deliver the promised legislation. To Frank O'Connor, a fellow Catholic and Hepburn's political confidante, Quinn wrote on 28 October 1935 that "I have never had any doubt, and have not now, that Mr. Hepburn intends to take action along the lines adopted by Quebec, which is what every Catholic in the province desires."[88] (O'Connor himself believed this. He was so positive that Hepburn would adopt the Quebec plan he told Archbishop McGuigan it was a sure thing.[89])

The Catholic camp would have to adopt a stance of stoic silence. After Quinn convinced Archbishop McGuigan not to make independent inquiries to the government,[90] Quinn sent a circular, dated 5 December 1935, to parish priests:

> Obviously, the negotiations that have been going on with the present government for some time are of a very delicate nature politically, publicity of any kind would provide our enemies with the fuel necessary to fan into being a fire that might prove exceedingly dangerous.
>
> On the other hand, we have plenty of evidence from various parts of the province that Catholics are becoming suspicious that all is not well, that the government is attempting to dodge the issue, and that ultimate failure of our work is inevitable. Thus there is arising the danger of explosive utterances that may do us incalculable injury.
>
> I am, therefore, requesting that you will see to it that your Parish Committee affiliated with us, the School Board (if there is one), and any others whose names will be suggested by your best judgment, will be quietly informed that the situation at the present time seems perfectly satisfactory.[91]

Ironically, Quinn would be the one guilty of "explosive utterances." He was too candid in a letter to a person he thought he could trust, and remarks he made to what he assumed was a private meeting came to the attention of one of the premier's friends. In both instances, Quinn's words found their way to Hepburn's office in record time, and in either case, what he said amounted to political suicide.

In a letter of 7 February 1936, addressed to Robert Kerr of Rodney, Quinn repeated an old threat:

> If we are satisfied to accept less than we have asked, then, obviously, we either admit that we have asked more than we are entitled to, or that we are slaves, willing to accept less than our rights, and so far as I am personally able to influence the future of our Association, the desires of our people will be registered at the ballot box in the way of protest or of gratitude, and, as a liberal, I do hope that it will be in the latter direction.[92]

There was nothing wrong with Quinn's logic and nothing new in his threat to defeat any government that did not satisfy Catholic demands concerning school taxes. His only mistake — and it was an honest one — was to put any of these thoughts on paper and send them to Kerr, who immediately dispatched the letter to Hepburn.

Two days later, on 9 February, Quinn delivered a fire-and-brimstone speech to the Knights of Columbus in Oshawa. The correspondent for the *Toronto Daily Star* reported Quinn as saying: "If the Hepburn government does not give separate schools of Ontario a more even distribution of school taxes the Catholic Taxpayers' Association will defeat it in the next election."[93] Quinn wired Hepburn the next day to deny that he had uttered this threat. However, before Quinn had a chance to explain himself more fully in writing, Hepburn was in possession of an edited remarked Quinn had made about him: "If that bird doesn't come across now we'll kick him out." This was all the ammunition Hepburn needed to inform Quinn that the separate school tax issue would be settled on its own merits, regardless of what Quinn had to say on the subject.[94] As events would later prove, Quinn was no longer a part of the political dialogue, and his exclusion from the process effectively ended any meaningful participation by the CTA.

Quinn was finished, and Hepburn knew it. So too did the

Toronto Daily Star. In a lead editorial of 11 February 1936, the paper remarked: "As for the Hepburn government, it is pledged to grant the separate schools some measure of relief in the matter of dividing company taxes. No doubt it will grant as much as it believes public opinion warrants. No government is ever likely to grant more."[95] Hepburn referred Quinn to these words and took them as his cue to proceed as he saw fit.

Even more troubling were the emerging doubts within Catholic circles about Quinn's leadership. Brother Alfred Dooner of De La Salle Oaklands told Archbishop McGuigan that Quinn's Oshawa speech was "a great mistake."

> His speech was a deliberate challenge. He seemed to forget that we are a minority in this Province. The Editorial in last night's Star showed a strong reaction on the part of that newspaper which has been our friend for years on the Question. Nothing will be gained at this critical moment by stirring up dormant Protestant sentiment. We have to-day a perfect setting for the solution of our School difficulties. It is however, a question heavily charged with dynamite and a slightly false manipulation might blast everything.[96]

Murray Mulligan, a member of the CTA general committee, asked the lawyer James E. Day what had happened to their friend Quinn, who had always preached absolute discretion when dealing with the government. Day answered that there was no excuse for Quinn's "break." He should not have accepted the invitation from the Knights to speak in Oshawa.[97] Quinn had displayed poor judgment at a critical moment, and once more he had needlessly antagonized Hepburn.

But Hepburn had his own problems. In conscience, he could no longer delay implementing the government's school tax policy, but first he would have to establish that policy. That would require him to go not only to his cabinet but also to his caucus and among them find a modus vivendi on an issue that had the potential to destroy party unity in the legislature. When Hepburn finally decided to do something for the people who eat fish on Friday, as he wrote to his friend Chubby Power,[98] he discovered that he had scant moral authority over many of his fellow Liberals. Meetings with his cabinet on 27 February and 21 March and with the caucus committee on 24 March 1936 revealed a growing desire not to proceed with legislation of any kind.

Hepburn's solution was to march forward. He sincerely believed that he was capable of establishing, once and for all, a reasonable compromise between two competing and irreconcilable claims over the legal division of corporation taxes to fund the province's two school systems. Hepburn introduced Bill 138, "An Act to Amend the Assessment Act," on Friday, 3 April 1936. Drafted by Dr. McArthur and done in such haste that only typewritten copies were made available at the time of introduction, the bill was a complicated, even Byzantine, piece of legislation, with Sections 33(a) and 33(b) being the most important. There were now two types of corporations, for the purpose of apportioning school taxes based on assessment: those that could and those that could not determine the number of separate school supporters among their shareholders. Instead of quoting directly from the legislation, we will turn to the historian C.B. Sissons for a concise summary of each section.

> For Section 33(a): "Each corporation of the first type was required, not permitted as in previous legislation, to make a return to the clerk of the municipality showing the ratio in its assessment which the shares held by such separate school supporters as had filed a notice with the company to that effect might bear to the remainder of the shares." This was a definite improvement on the 1886 legislation. The word "shall" replaced the word "may," making compliance compulsory.
>
> For Section 33(b): "A corporation which was deemed to be of the second type, that is, one incapable of classifying its shareholders, was to have its assessment and taxes divided on an entirely new principle. The share assigned to the support of separate schools was to be in the same ratio as the

assessment roll of individuals supporting separate schools might bear to the assessment roll of individuals supporting public schools in the particular municipality where the corporation owned or occupied ratable property."[99]

Following a week of bitter and protracted debate, witnessed by throngs of public and separate school supporters sandwiched together in the galleries, the bill was passed into law by a vote of 65 to 20, in the early hours of 9 April 1936 (*Statutes of Ontario*, 1 Edward VIII, c. 4). The Liberals did not allow the bill to go to committee, where it would have faced the prospect of closer scrutiny and possibly amendment. As the close of the spring session was at hand, they were also anxious to avoid the glare of any further controversy. As soon as the voting ended, the Tories immediately promised to repeal it.[100]

Despite the fact that Bill 138 left all public utility taxes in the hands of the public school boards, Quinn accepted the legislation because, as he told the *Catholic Register*, "it finally establishes the principle of our right to share in taxes arising from any form of property in which Catholics have an interest, and for which we have contended almost ever since Confederation."[101] Right below this story, the *Register* ran another one, predicting that the Toronto Separate School Board would enjoy an additional $150,000 in tax revenue as a direct result of the legislation.

In May, Quinn initiated a massive campaign, via the parish priests, the parish committees and the separate school boards, to distribute copies of the all-important Forms attached to the legislation.[102] Form 14 (Section 33c) was a Notice from Shareholder or Member of a Corporation; Form 13 (Section 33a) was a Notice of Corporation; and Form 15 (Section 33b) was a Notice from Corporation. The priests and parish chairmen were in charge of the distribution of Form 14, and it was the duty of school board secretaries to see that every publicly-traded corporation in their respective municipalities returned Forms 13 and 15. It was an enormous and tedious task for everyone involved, taken up by Catholics across the province in good faith, but the Assessment Act, as revised, left no option for separate school supporters if they wanted their rightful share of corporation taxes.

To maintain morale among the CTA rank and file, as the months rolled by and the results of the campaign were disappointing, Quinn mailed to every Catholic parish in the province a copy of Attorney General Arthur Roebuck's speech of 6 April 1936 to the legislature. Quinn thought that it was a splendid document: "Not only is it a carefully prepared exposition of the main facts, but its chief importance lies in the fact that the Protestant Attorney-General in a Protestant Government is telling the people of Ontario that the claims made by the Hierarchy during the past fifty years, and more recently along different lines, by the Catholic Taxpayers' Assn., are entirely justified by the facts."[103] It is impossible to gauge what effect, if any, Roebuck's speech had on the CTA's ground-level troops. Roebuck's speech was just a speech. It had no bearing on the drafting of the legislation or on its practical application, as Quinn and others were soon to discover.

Roebuck's speech was attached to a circular of 23 July 1936. Two weeks later, Quinn's enthusiasm for the legislation had vanished. For all his efforts to have Catholic shareholders enrolled on the assessment lists and corporations comply with Hepburn's amended Assessment Act, he was forced to conclude that the Act was all smoke and mirrors. His loyalty to the Liberal Party, and his hope that the CTA had finally won something for Catholic ratepayers, blinded him to the obvious, which other Catholics, such as Senator Louis Coté, had seen from the moment the Bill had been tabled in the Legislature. The Act actually worked against the interests of separate schools. It ensured that only those Roman Catholics who had filed as separate school supporters, and whose name appeared on the rolls as such, could direct their corporation taxes to the separate schools. (In other words, it did not assume that all Roman Catholics were separate school supporters, the way in which school tax legislation in Alberta and Saskatchewan did.) The consequences of this restriction were drastic and immediate. Automatically excluded from the assessment rolls were "all non-property holders such as wives, sisters, children, roomers, estate executors, corporate shareholders, and all non-residents of Ontario."[104] (One example of the way in which the Act worked against Catholic interests was the J.E. Clements Inc. of Quebec City. For many years, Clements had its subsidiary in Ontario pay its corporation taxes to the separate schools. Under the revised legislation, since Clements was a corporation and not an individual tax-paying shareholder, and since corporations did not have a religion, it was required to pay its taxes to the public schools.) Then there was Section 33(b). It dealt with corporations unable to classify their stockholders and was worse than useless to separate school boards because there was nothing in the Act to compel these corporations to divide their taxes according to relative assessment. It was much simpler and far less costly for them to give Notice under Section 33(a) and declare that no Roman Catholics were shareholders. Dozens and dozens of corporations, including the Bank of Commerce, made an open mockery of the Act.

Quinn pointed out these and other flaws in the legislation in a four-page letter to Hepburn, dated 7 August 1936. He saved his most telling comment for the end:

> At the risk of prolixity, and with a view to finally arriving at some reasonable basis on which this vexed question may finally be settled, may I suggest, with a full appreciation of the political difficulties, that much could be done to produce a better understanding of the question if the public could be made conscious of the fact that the old tradition that taxes are paid by capital owned by stockholders of any faith, in any corporation, is a pure myth which cannot be supported by the slightest tittle of evidence.
>
> The fact is that every corporation, selling either service or goods, includes in their cost and passes on every dollar of every form of taxation, plus a profit, to the actual consumer.[105]

Quinn's analysis of the nature of taxation in a society of consumers was completely correct and in advance of its time. Although it was one of the most sensible things he had written during his tenure as CTA chairman, Hepburn had no intention of even listening to him, let alone replying in writing. Quinn repeated his argument in a letter of 22 February 1937.[106] Annoyed to the point of anger, the premier complained to Frank O'Connor, a Liberal senator since 1935: "I am now in receipt of another letter from Quinn, which I believe will cause considerable trouble if given publicity. As you know, I have absolutely no use for him. I believe he is so hot-headed and irresponsible that he makes little headway in any undertaking."[107] Hepburn's assessment of Quinn was only half right, but politicians with large majorities have the luxury of being half wrong. At times Quinn *was* a hothead and irresponsible, but there were times when he could speak the plain truth. He did precisely that on the tax question. Hepburn, however, wanted none of it.

Be that as it may, by the time Hepburn had written O'Connor, a variety of events had rendered Quinn and the CTA impotent and irrelevant within the ongoing political process concerning the future of the 1936 Assessment Act. First there was the 1936 Conservative Party convention. On 28 May, delegates adopted a resolution calling for repeal of the legislation.[108] This was no mere window dressing, designed to attract new recruits to the party in advance of a provincial election. The resolution served notice to separate school supporters that corporation taxes were off limits and it put the Liberals on the defensive for having raised Catholic expectations. It also highlighted the hopelessness of the Liberal legislation.

The implementation of the Act had brought nothing but chaos to the assessment process. School boards on both sides of the political divide had filed thousands of assessment appeals. By September 1936, it was evident to most separate school boards that they would be receiving fewer — not more — dollars in taxes from corporations, an appalling irony that forced them to petition the Toronto Separate School Board as well as the Catholic Taxpayers' Association to seek legal advice on amending the Act so that it would function according to their needs.[109] A case did end up in the Court of Appeal, but its ruling on 11 January 1937 confirmed the worst suspicions of separate school boards. The Court found that the Act did not automatically count all Roman Catholics as separate school supporters, that since corporations had no religion, all subsidiaries with head offices in

Ontario had to pay their taxes to the public schools and that corporations which fell under Section 33(b) were not obliged to carry out its provisions.[110]

The biggest blow to Quinn and the CTA was the East Hastings by-election on 9 December 1936. It was occasioned by the death in October of the sitting member, James F. Hill, a Conservative, who had won the riding in 1934 by a mere 418 votes. It was a singularly vicious campaign. The Conservatives used the occasion to attack the Hepburn amendment to the Assessment Act, repeating their pledge to annul it, and the Liberals treated the election as a vote of public confidence in their administration. Hepburn took it so seriously that he moved into the constituency and campaigned as if he were the one running for the seat. Each side accused the other of arousing religious passions and of introducing religion into politics. The whole atmosphere was poisoned by silly rumours, nasty denunciations and the disgraceful return of anti-Catholic and anti-French bigotry. (Perhaps it was a good thing that Quinn was in Australia at the time.) On election day, Harold E. Walsh, the Conservative candidate, easily defeated Harold A. Boyce, the Liberal standard-bearer. Hepburn interpreted the result as a repudiation of his attempt to find a middle way on the school tax issue. No one was happy with his legislation. Protestant electors wanted repeal, and among them were a good many who hoped for the abolition of separate schools. Catholic electors wanted a different and better amendment, one that would produce a more just division of corporation taxes.

Repeal it would be. Hepburn was relieved when the Conservatives gave him an opportunity to rescind his own legislation. Determined to live up to the Conservative party's resolution of 27 May 1936, and the promises the party had made during the East Hastings by-election, George Henry introduced Bill 96, "An Act to repeal Chapter 4 of the Statutes of Ontario, 1936." On 24 March 1937, Hepburn accepted his Bill, declaring to the Speaker: "I say that it is my responsibility now to forestall at whatever cost the possibility of a religious war in this Province. I am man enough to stand up in this Legislature and swallow what is a very bitter pill. I want in this respect to commend the Toronto Star for its fairness. At least it has been manifestly fair, and I think I should even go out of my way to commend The Globe and Mail for pointing out the dangers of religious warfare in Ontario."[111] In a front-page editorial of 24 March 1937, the proprietor of the recently amalgamated *Globe and Mail*, the thirty-three-year-old George McCullagh, gave Hepburn a gift-wrapped argument for accepting the opposition's Bill. In part, it said:

> The separate schools are with us, whether we agree with them or not, and there is nothing we can do to eliminate them. Repealing the Act should have no effect in weakening the support given them, for the sons and daughters of Roman Catholic citizens are entitled to an atmosphere as healthy as that of the public schools, and equal opportunities for education. With this all thoughtful Protestants will agree. Therefore the separate schools must be maintained. But the way this is done is incidental to the issue. Mr. Hepburn can assure his Catholic friends that adequate provision be made through grants, in accordance with past practice.[112]

This argument was exactly the kind of moral ammunition Hepburn needed to reject a piece of legislation of his own making. On the one hand, it gave him the political license to declare that "An even greater responsibility than bringing justice to a religious minority rests on the Government. It is the responsibility of maintaining peace and harmony."[113] On the other hand, it freed him "to give the definite assurance to the Catholic minority of Ontario that the Liberal Party will give justice and equity to all people regardless of race and religion."[114] It was a brilliant contradiction, one that would pay handsome dividends for many years to come. Justice and equity for Catholic separate school supporters would forever be at the mercy of the convenient fear of religious warfare.

After speaking for nearly an hour, and accepting congratulatory applause from both sides of the House of Assembly, Hepburn invoked closure to cut off any chance of debate. A rarely-used motion, it precipitated a wild scene in the legislature that lasted for almost twenty minutes and resulted in the ejection of Leopold Macaulay, a

Conservative. Following his return to the House, on a motion from Hepburn, a division was taken on second reading of the Bill. The vote was 80-0 in favour. How times had changed! The Act was given Royal Assent on 25 March 1937, the same day the legislature was prorogued (*Statutes of Ontario*, 1 George VI, c. 9).

The Catholic struggle for a fair share of corporation taxes had come to an ignominious end, at the hands of fear-mongering and weak-willed politicians for whom phantom phobias about religious strife and the editorial opinions of Toronto newspapers meant more than any call for justice based on reason and modern realities. Martin Quinn and the Catholic Taxpayers' Association had been badly outflanked by both Conservative and Liberal politicians, so much so that Catholics had lost their place in the democratic battle and were politically obliged to interpret repeal as a victory for Catholic ratepayers. In one sense, it was a victory: since the legislation was so absurdly flawed, it would never work in their favour. In another sense, though, repeal signaled the total defeat of the Catholic cause: the likelihood of any government attempting to introduce a new amendment to the Assessment Act, according to the CTA's 1933 and 1935 demands, was remote at best. A whole generation would have to pass before the political culture would grapple with the question. In the meantime, Catholic ratepayers would have to be satisfied with the 1886 legislation and an increase in legislative grants, which were subject to the advice of bureaucrats and the generosity of the government and which were always inadequate.

Epilogue

Days before the 1936 Hepburn amendment became law, Martin Quinn told a friend that his work for the CTA was nearly finished and that it would be best for someone else to carry on the work.[115] Tragically, that never happened. If Quinn had followed his own intuition, he would have avoided an immense amount of suffering and anger that plagued the rest of his life, starting in 1937. However, having been thoroughly bested in the political arena, Quinn's fate was to fall from grace and to be condemned to an undeserved obscurity. The Catholic community soon forgot him.

Since the story of Quinn's fall would take another chapter, we must limit our attention to the major events that contributed to his demise. In the weeks leading up to repeal in March 1937, Quinn lost the confidence of his fellow members on the CTA's executive committee, who decided to exclude him from the next delegation to interview the premier;[116] Quinn's circular (No. 141) to parish priests of August 1937 demonstrated that he had lost touch with political reality;[117] the bishops of Ontario re-asserted their authority on separate school matters, in a decision of 2 September 1937;[118] Quinn's publication of *The Case for Ontario Separate Schools* in 1937 was deemed untimely and unhelpful and angered Archbishop Michael Joseph O'Brien of Kingston to the point where he felt compelled to declare in a letter to Archbishop McGuigan that he had had no part in giving Quinn "'full and supreme authority in all matters pertaining to this question of the schools;'"[119] the bishops with the support of the executive committee convinced Quinn to keep silent during the provincial election of 6 October 1937 (it was another Liberal victory);[120] a newly-minted general committee of the CTA repudiated Quinn for publishing *Catholics are Counted but They Don't Count* (15 June 1938);[121] Quinn submitted his resignation as chairman of the CTA on 21 January 1939;[122] after completely re-organizing itself, the CTA in conjunction with L'association canadienne-française d'education de l'Ontario conducted one last public relations campaign on the school tax issue and completely failed to persuade Hepburn to introduce a new amendment;[123] the CTA general committee then gave itself a new name, the Ontario Catholic Education Council. It was an ad hoc committee of bishops and prominent laymen that met occasionally, especially during times of crisis, until the 1960s. In addition to the Ontario Catholic Education Council, the bishops, headed by Archbishop McGuigan, established the English Catholic Education Association of Ontario. On 8 September 1942, Father Vincent Priester of the diocese of Hamilton was appointed the association's executive director, his chief tasks being to represent the bishops and to act as a liaison between them, the separate school boards and the department of education.[124]

Martin J. Quinn, who had carried the Catholic Taxpayers'

Association on his own shoulders from 1931 until 1937, spent the rest of his life writing letters and pamphlets justifying himself and attacking the bishops, politicians and all those he called turncoat Catholics. His final publication, *The Frustration of Lay Catholic Effort in Ontario* (June 1945), is tedious, self-serving and defamatory in places. It all makes for sad reading. The Catholic Taxpayers' Association was a noble experiment, and Quinn ended up the sacrificial lamb on the high altar of provincial and local church politics. Brilliant, aggressive and decisive, he could not accept the fact that he had been beaten in the game of high stakes politics at Queen's Park and the Archbishop's Palace. Martin J. Quinn was meant for another time in Church history.

He died on 8 July 1949 and was buried in Mount Hope Cemetery, next to his wife and parents.

---

[1] Metropolitan Separate School Board [hereafter MSSB], Archives, CTA Papers, Series 46, File #5, M.J. Quinn to James E. Day, 27 July 1933.

[2] *The New Catholic Encyclopedia* defines two types of Catholic Action, the second one being "a tightly structured organization that serves as an arm of the hierarchy in lay life. The mandate is essential." The CTA fit this definition perfectly. *NCE*, 3: 262.

[3] Information supplied by Peter Meehan. Quinn's parents were originally buried in St. Michael's Cemetery. Angry at the dilapidated state of the cemetery, Quinn removed them to Mount Hope on 30 October 1925.

[4] M.J. Quinn, *The Frustration of Lay Catholic Effort in Ontario* (Toronto: The Catholic Primary School, 1945), 12.

[5] Quinn is listed as a plumber in the 1891 Census. Information supplied by Peter Meehan.

[6] Ibid., Foreword, [4]. The emphasis in boldface is Quinn's. This was part of his style of writing and rhetoric, but in future instances the boldface will be left out because Quinn resorted to it so often as to render it ineffectual.

[7] Anna Josephine Sullivan was born in February 1874 and died on 14 May 1946.

[8] Archbishop James C. McGuigan to Thomas Marshall of Dunnville, 22 October 1940. "He [Quinn] worked absolutely without fee." Reproduced in Quinn, *The Frustration of Lay Catholic Effort in Ontario*, 33.

[9] *Canadian Freeman*, 2 February 1939. Reprinted in Quinn, *The Frustration of Lay Catholic Effort in Ontario*, 34.

[10] *Globe and Mail*, 9 July 1949, 20; *Toronto Daily Star*, 9 July 1949, 26. Father Carl Matthews, S.J. noted the lack of a photo. See Carl Matthews, S.J., "The saga of Martin Quinn: tireless champion of Ontario separate school taxpayers," *Catholic Register* (29 February 1992), ES2-ES3.

[11] A photograph of Quinn with his name in the caption below it was published in the *Evening Telegram*, 13 June 1934, 1.

[12] Neil McNeil, *The School Question of Ontario* (1931).

[13] *Report of the Minister of Education Province of Ontario for the Year 1936* (Toronto: King's Printer, 1937), 103.

[14] Walker, *Catholic Education and Politics in Ontario*, 2: 416.

[15] Quinn, *The Frustration of Lay Catholic Effort in Ontario*, 15. A note of caution: one must be judicious in dealing with Quinn's version of events as presented in this 1945 publication. For instance, Quinn is fond of recounting conversations with Archbishop McNeil, sometimes word for word, but he never gives the dates on which those conversations supposedly took place. Also, his chronology of crucial events can be confusing, forcing one to decipher his version of the past in terms of probabilities.

[16] ARCAT, MG 5026.285 (a), Private and Confidential, 30 September 1931; reproduced in Walker, *Catholic Education and Politics in Ontario*, 2: 356-57. The encyclical was written by Pius XI and was dated 31 December 1929. The pastoral letter referred to was "Pastoral Letter on Education from the Bishop of Hamilton to the Clergy and Faithful of His Diocese," *The Catholic Voice* (1931?).

[17] Ibid., MN P917.16 (b), McNeil to "Dear Sir," 7 October 1931.

[18] Quinn, *The Frustration of Lay Catholic Effort in Ontario*, 15.

[19] Ibid.

[20] MSSB, Archives, CTA Papers, Series 46, File #6, Quinn to McNeil, 7 January 1931.

[21] ARCAT, MG SO20.01(a), Quinn to W.T. Kernahan, 17 January 1935.

[22] This was the full name of the association as it appeared in its letterhead, but I have chosen to drop the "of Ontario" because these words appeared in much smaller type under "Catholic Taxpayers' Association" and also for the sake of simplicity.

340

[23] Quoted in Walker, *Catholic Education and Politics in Ontario*, 2: 360.

[24] Ibid., 2: 361.

[25] Ibid., 2: 364. Walker makes much of the fact that the CTA's Western Ontario section had great difficulty in finding the names and addresses of all the priests in Ontario for their mass mailing campaign. See *Catholic Education and Politics in Ontario*, 2: 362. One wonders, though, if the publicity committee ever consulted a current issue of *The Ontario Catholic Year Book and Directory*, the most up-to-date source for such information.

[26] M.J. Quinn, *Some Pertinent Facts: The Separate Schools of Ontario*, 2nd ed. (Toronto: Catholic Taxpayers' Association of Ontario, July 1932), 13.

[27] Ibid., 14.

[28] "Henry, George Stewart," *The Canadian Encyclopedia* (Edmonton: Hurtig Publishers, 1985), 2: 806-7.

[29] Walker, *Catholic Education and Politics in Ontario*, 2: 366; Quinn to Chairmen of Parish Committees, 22 July 1932.

[30] Ibid., 2: 368-69; W.T. Kernahan to Chairman of Parish Committee, 9 November 1932.

[31] Ibid., 2: 367, 368 and 373.

[32] In fairness to James E. Day, we should note that he too was a public speaker. See the *Catholic Register*, 3 November 1932, 1, 4. He spoke in Mimico and Brantford.

[33] ARCAT, MG SO20.01 (a), Quinn to W.T. Kernahan, 17 January 1935.

[34] *Catholic Register*, 27 October 1932, 1; originally reported in the *London Free Press*, 18 October 1932.

[35] *Ottawa Citizen*, 28 November 1932.

[36] *The Ontario Separate School Question: What Some Orangemen Say, The Catholic Reply* (Catholic Taxpayers' Association of Ontario, [1933]); *Catholic Register*, 22 December 1932, 1; Ibid., 12 January 1933, 1.

[37] *Catholic Register*, 29 December 1932, 3.

[38] Ibid., 10 November 1932, 4.

[39] *The Catholic Voice* (Hamilton), February 1932, 1-2; July-August 1932, 1. This last one was written by Reverend P.L. O'Brien and was followed on the next two pages

with "Some Interesting Tax Facts."

[40] *Catholic Register*, 24 November 1932, 1; *The Catholic Voice*, December 1932, 1.

[41] Ibid., 19 January 1933, 1.

[42] Ibid., 3. The entire Application is reproduced in Walker, *Catholic Education and Politics in Ontario*, 2: Appendix.

[43] *Catholic Register*, 19 January 1933, 3; *Border Cities Star*, 18 March and 1 June 1933; *Toronto Daily Star*, 27 March and 28 April; *Toronto Weekly Star*, 6 May 1933.

[44] *London Morning Advertiser*, 14 July 1933.

[45] *Canadian Freeman*, 28 June 1933.

[46] *Globe*, 14 March 1933, 10; *Catholic Register*, 16 March 1933, 1.

[47] ARCAT, MG SO20.294(g), Circular Letter, 10 April 1933.

[48] *Catholic Register*, 4 May 1933, 1.

[49] ARCAT, MG SO20.294(c), "Meeting Orange Propaganda."

[50] Ibid., MG SO20.294(d), "The True Position of the Orange Order in Ontario."

[51] *Catholic Register*, 14 June 1934. McNeil spoke about this at Columbus Hall in Toronto, in February 1934.

[52] *Mail and Empire*, 30 March 1934.

[53] *Catholic Register*, 5 April 1933, 1.

[54] Ibid., 12 April 1934, 2.

[55] ARCAT, MG SO20.292(a), Quinn to W.H. Price, 16 March 1933.

[56] MSSB, Archives, CTA Papers, Series 46, File 4, Quinn to Chairman of Parish Committee, 2 April 1934 and 12 April 1934.

[57] ARCAT, MG SO20.298, Quinn to "Reverend and Dear Father," 1 May 1934.

[58] Ibid., MN AE11.25, Quinn to "Reverend and Dear Father," 16 May 1934.

[59] Quoted in Walker, *Catholic Education and Politics in Ontario*, 2: 395-96.

[60] ARCAT, MG SO20.300, Quinn to Parish Chairman, "Dear Sir," 29 May 1934.

[61] *Evening Telegram*, 13 June 1934, 1.

[62] *Catholic Register*, 14 June 1934, 1.

[63] Ibid.

[64] *Evening Telegram*, 14 June 1934, 1-2.

[65] Ibid., 15 June 1934, 1.

[66] *Globe*, 19 June 1934, 2.

[67] *Eganville Leader*, 8 June 1934.

[68] MSSB Archives, CTA Papers, Series 46, File 7. Editorial opinions of the *Canadian Freeman* (21 June 1934), the *Catholic Record* (30 June 1934) and the *Catholic Register* (28 June 1934) were reprinted as *The Ontario Separate School Question: Some Comments of the Catholic Press Upon the Result of the Ontario Election June 19, 1934* (Catholic Taxpayers' Association of Ontario, [1934]).

[69] Senator William Henry McGuire was a successful Toronto lawyer, a King's Counsel (1933) and a leading member of the Liberal Party in Ontario. See *Canadian Parliamentary Guide* 1936 (Hull, Quebec: Labour Exchange, 1936), 108-9; Walker, *Catholic Education and Politics in Ontario*, 2: 374-75, Quinn to Hepburn, 21 January 1933.

[70] *Evening Telegram*, 13 June 1934, 1; 15 June 1934, 1-2.

[71] John T. Saywell, *'Just call me Mitch': The Life of Mitchell F. Hepburn* (Toronto: University of Toronto Press, 1991), 161.

[72] ARCAT, MG SO20.12(c), Quinn to McGuire, 26 August 1935; MGS020.148(c), Martin J. Quinn, *"Catholics are Counted but Don't Count"* (15 June 1938), 5-6.

[73] Saywell, *'Just call me Mitch'*, 125.

[74] ARCAT, MG SO20.23(c), McTague to Quinn, circa 19 June 1934.

[75] Ibid., MG SO20.96(b), Quinn to E.C. Desormeaux, 18 February 1937.

[76] Saywell, *'Just call me Mitch'*, 209-10.

[77] ARCAT, MN AE11.26, "Application," 22 January 1935; *Catholic Register*, 24 January 1935, 1.

[78] *Evening Telegram*, 22 January 1935, 1.

[79] ARCAT, MG SO20.232(c), Quinn to Gordon Conant, 6 March 1943.

[80] *Evening Telegram*, 14 February 1935, 3.

[81] ARCAT, MG SO20.232(c), Quinn to Gordon Conant, 6 March 1943.

[82] Ibid., MG SO20.09(c), Quinn to Hepburn, 10 April 1935.

[83] Ibid., MG SO20.12(b), McGuire to Quinn, 23 April 1935.

[84] Ibid., MG SO20.12(c), Quinn to McGuire, 26 April 1935.

[85] *Globe*, 12 April 1935, 11.

[86] *Report of the Minister of Education Province of Ontario for the Year 1937* (Toronto: King's Printer, 1938), Part III, *Report of the Committee of Enquiry into the Cost of Education in the Province of Ontario*. The Committee submitted its report in March 1938. "In answer to a question raised by Mr. Desormeaux, the Chairman [Duncan McArthur] expressed the opinion that the Committee would not be expected to make any recommendation on the question of the division of corporation taxes between the public schools and separate schools of the Province, but that it would be in order to collect data relating to that question." See Appendix B, page 47.

[87] ARCAT, MG SO20.36(b), Quinn to Archbishop M.J. O'Brien, 4 December 1935.

[88] Ibid., MG SO20.32(c), Quinn to F.P. O'Connor, 28 October 1935.

[89] Saywell, *'Just call me Mitch'*, 258.

[90] ARCAT, MG SO20.31, McGuigan to Bishop John T. Kidd, 25 October 1935.

[91] Ibid., MG SO20.37(b), Quinn to "Reverend and Dear Father," 5 December 1935.

[92] Walker, *Catholic Education and Politics in Ontario*, 2: 424, Quinn to Kerr, 7 February 1936.

[93] *Toronto Daily Star*, 10 February 1936, 17.

[94] Walker, *Catholic Education and Politics in Ontario*, 2: 424-25.

[95] *Toronto Daily Star*, 11 February 1936, 4.

[96] ARCAT, MG SO20.44(a), Brother Alfred Dooner to McGuigan, 12 February 1936.

[97] Walker, *Catholic Politics and Education in Ontario*, 2: 426-27.

[98] Neil McKenty, *Mitch Hepburn* (Toronto: McClelland and Stewart, 1967), 79.

[99] Sissons, *Church and State in Canadian Education*, 105.

[100] All the Toronto newspapers devoted extensive coverage to the debate on Bill 138.

[101] *Catholic Register*, 9 April 1936, 1.

[102] ARCAT, MG SO20.51(a), Quinn to McGuigan, 11 April 1936; MG SO20.54(a), Circular letter to Parish Priests, 12 May 1936; MG SO20.54(b), Circular Letter to Parish Chairmen, 12 May 1936; MG SO20.56(a), Circular Letter to Secretaries of School Boards, 18 May 1936.

[103] Ibid., MG SO20.70(b), Circular to Parish Chairman, 23 July 1936.

[104] Saywell, *'Just call me Mitch'*, 296-97.

[105] ARCAT, MG SO20.72(b), Quinn to Hepburn, 7 August 1936.

[106] Ibid., MG SO20.97(a), Quinn to Hepburn, 22 February 1937.

[107] Walker, *Catholic Education and Politics in Ontario*, 2: 446, Hepburn to O'Connor, 26 February 1937.

[108] Ibid., 2: 439.

[109] ARCAT, MG SO20.76(a), J.G. Kelly to "Dear Sirs," 21 September 1936.

[110] Saywell, *'Just call me Mitch,'* 298.

[111] *Globe and Mail*, 25 March 1937, 1-2.

[112] Ibid., 24 March 1937, 1.

[113] Saywell, *'Just call me Mitch,'* 299.

[114] *Catholic Register*, 1 April 1937, 4.

[115] Walker, *Catholic Education and Politics in Ontario*, 2: 436-47, Quinn to Edward F. Murphy, 7 April 1936.

[116] MSSB, CTA Papers, Series 46, File 11, "Minutes of the Meeting of the Executive Committee, 6 March 1937."

[117] ARCAT, MG SO20.108, Quinn to Parish Priests, 7 August 1937.

[118] Quinn, *The Frustration of Lay Catholic Effort in Ontario*, 27-28.

[119] ARCAT, MG SO20. 313(C), O'Brien to McGuigan, 17 September 1937.

[120] Ibid., MG SO20.113, Father F.J. Brennan to McGuigan, 25 September 1937.

[121] Ibid., MG SO20.148(a), Edmond Cloutier, Arthur Murphy, E.C. Desormeaux and J.A. McNevin to McGuigan, 2 September 1938.
[122] *Catholic Register*, 23 February 1939, 1.

[123] *Catholic Register*, 2 February 1939, 1; Ibid., 2 May 1940, 1.

[124] Walker, *Catholic Education and Politics in Ontario*, 2: 481.

COMPLETING THE SEPARATE SCHOOL SYSTEM
THE TRUSTEES FIND THEIR VOICE:
THE ONTARIO SEPARATE SCHOOL TRUSTEES'
ASSOCIATION

Introduction

*T*his chapter deals with the history and contributions of the Ontario Separate School Trustees' Association, in relation to the politics of funding and completing the separate school system and to the maintenance of the system's Catholic nature and characteristics. The trustees formally established their association in 1930, keeping their name until 1997, when they changed it to the Ontario Catholic School Trustees' Association. In each of the previous six chapters, we have dealt with the issues of funding and completion in several different contexts. For decades, the issue was as basic as the rescue of separate schools from wholesale collapse. Extinction due to a lack of money was a very real threat that did not disappear until the 1960s. So far, we have written about the work (and the ensuing controversies) of a number of bishops, priests, religious teachers, individual trustees and lay people, such as John F. White and Martin J. Quinn. Each in his own way sought to have the constitutional rights of Catholic separate school supporters recognized by the government in terms of practical legislation. As we have already seen, they experienced failure far more frequently than success, and on several celebrated occasions they fought each other to the detriment of the Catholic children they professed to serve.

However, as separate schools evolved in the first half of the twentieth century from local examples of Catholic independence from public schools, into their own distinct provincial system, it was only natural for there to emerge a province-wide organization of trustees that could speak and act on behalf of all separate school boards vis-à-vis the government and education bureaucrats at Queen's Park. The need for such an organization was obvious to practically every defender of separate schools during the 1950s. The Hope Commission's hostile attitude towards separate schools had demonstrated the vulnerability of separate schools to narrow and punitive interpretations of the BNA Act and to a weakness in the defense of separate schools for their need to rely on the good graces of the premier to save them from the commission's recommendations. By the 1960s, the need for a professional trustees' association had became paramount. It was a time when equal opportunity for every child in every publicly-funded school had taken on the rhetoric of an unquestioned right, and when scores of politicians and policymakers believed that continuous and integrated education, from kindergarten to grade thirteen, was the only way to ensure that more students completed Grades 12 and 13 and entered post-secondary education.

For separate school ratepayers, equal educational opportunity for their children could not be achieved without some radical overhaul of the legislative grants. (After 1936, the fight for corporation and utility taxes was a dead issue.) By the mid-1950s, property taxes, parish subsidies, the lower salaries of religious teachers and the traditional legislative grants, which bore little relation to the ability of taxpayers to support their schools, could no longer sustain a system that was always expanding but barely able to cope with its own success. And the idea of continuous and integrated education, as expounded by premiers and ministers of education, would never be a reality for separate school students, if their publicly funded education stopped at Grade 10.

Who then would emerge as the chief manager of the political process by which Catholics would finally convince the government to treat their separate schools as an integral part of public education in the province of Ontario? That is an historical question, at least from our perspective, and the answer is simple: the Ontario Separate School Trustees' Association (OSSTA). But one should not be misled by the apparent simplicity of the answer. We must keep in mind two

348

points. One, although the Scott Act of 1863 mentions only two kinds of stakeholders in separate schools — Catholic ratepayers and their elected representatives, the trustees — it took more than sixty years for even a small minority of the trustees to organize themselves into an association. Two, it then took more than thirty years after OSSTA's formation for it to take its first meaningful step towards assuming its rightful stake in the often confusing world of lobbying on behalf of separate schools. The story of the association's assumption of leadership, after decades of standing on the sidelines as a second-string actor, is a complex one that needs some preliminary parsing prior to any detailed examination of its various parts.

In the wake of the collapse of the Catholic Taxpayers' Association, the bishops quickly reasserted their control over the separate school agenda. They created the Ontario Catholic Education Council, in 1938,[1] and next the English Catholic Education Association of Ontario, in 1943. Although the Ontario Catholic Education Council made a special effort to bring together French and English representatives and, as time went on, to invite other groups such as the trustees to its table, it met irregularly and had no permanent office. The council was most active (but not necessarily all that effective) during times of crisis, and it was still meeting as late as the 1960s.[2] Altogether, it was a conduit of discussion and decision-making controlled by the bishops. In terms of a political presence, though, the English Catholic Education Association of Ontario (ECEAO) was intended to be a far more valuable asset. It acted as the eyes and ears of the bishops on all matters involving separate schools and as the principal liaison between the hierarchy, on the one hand, and the premier and his minister of education, on the other. Its Catholic Education Office in Toronto acted as a clearing house for information, an idea initially suggested to the bishops by the larger Catholic boards.

Besides ECEAO, there were other players in the Catholic educational camp. Each had its own voice, and each was anxious to be heard as the crisis in finances approached the breaking point around 1960. These players included l'Association canadienne-française d'éducation d'Ontario (1910), the forerunner of ECEAO and an inspiration for the latter's establishment; l'Association des commissions des écoles bilingues d'Ontario (ACEBO, 1944), the French trustee counterpart to OSSTA; the Ontario English Catholic Teachers' Association (OECTA, 1944); the Federation of Catholic Parent-Teacher Associations of Ontario (FCPTA, 1949); and lastly the Association of Catholic High School Boards of Ontario (ACHSBO, 1967, Grades 11 to 13), which came on the scene as the political push for completion began.

In the midst of all these voices, OSSTA found its own.[3] It was then able to play a lead role in championing the Ontario Foundation Tax Plan, in 1964, in supporting the amalgamation of school boards, in 1969, and in writing and promoting the historic brief, "Equal Opportunity for Continuous Education in Separate Schools of Ontario," also in 1969. The trustees found a way to work as equals with the bishops, eventually superseding them as the "natural" leaders on the school question, to co-operate with the French-speaking trustees' association and to outflank ECEAO.

Of course, there is more to OSSTA's story than a new tax plan, board amalgamation and a single brief, momentous as each one was in the history of separate schools in Ontario. It is the intention of this chapter to introduce the reader to OSSTA's history as an organization and to detail its corporate involvement in the major issues that confronted Catholic education, up to and including completion of the separate school system. Our narrative will begin in 1925, when Catholic separate school trustees first gathered to discuss the formation of their own association, and it will end in 1984, when Premier Bill Davis bestowed his imprimatur on completion.

The chapter will be divided into ten sections: Early History, 1925-1950; The Hope Commission, 1945-1950; At Mid-Century, 1950-1960; The Three-Mile Limit, 1959-1963; The Ontario Foundation Tax Plan, 1964; The Hall-Dennis Committee, 1965-1968; Larger Units of Administration (Amalgamation of School Boards), 1969; The Campaign for Completion, 1966-1971; A Political Interlude, 1971-1984; Premier Davis Says "Yes" to Completion, 1984.

Early History, 1925-1950

It had been a tradition for some individual separate school trustees from the larger boards to attend the annual convention of the Ontario Educational Association (OEA), as representatives of their own boards. Founded in 1861, the OEA had evolved into a provincial association of teachers, trustees, school inspectors and parents.[4] By the 1920s, the association was large enough to be divided into four departments — elementary school, college and secondary school, supervising and training, and trustees and ratepayers — as well as at least twenty-three different sections. Most of these were devoted to specific subject areas, but they also included urban and rural trustees and high school principals. Notably absent was any section representing the interests of separate school trustees.

Although prudence dictated the practical wisdom of their attendance at OEA conventions, individual separate school trustees did not possess much of an identity to offer their public school counterparts, and they certainly had little influence in what was an overwhelmingly Protestant public school culture. This was not only unfortunate but also unacceptable. In 1925, there were at least 1,600 Catholic trustees in charge of more than 500 separate school boards in all parts of the province. This was impressive but only superficially. The absence of political unity under the guidance of a single body doomed separate school trustees to irrelevance in the bigger scheme of things.

It was precisely this fear of irrelevance that led a small group of separate school supporters to absent themselves from the OEA convention, on 15 April 1925, so that they could meet on their own for the first time. They were C.J. Driscoll from Sarnia, who was chosen as chairman, Mr. Bailey from Kingston, who acted as secretary, Mr. Butler and Mr. McNamara from St. Thomas, Mr. Laprairie from Timmins, Mr. Davis from Port Arthur, Mr. Sills from Seaforth and James Henderson from Ingersoll. Joining these laymen were two priests, Father G.R. O'Gorman from Cobalt and Father M.A. Brisson from London, and Brother Gregory from Windsor.[5] We should consider these eleven people the founders of OSSTA.

They talked about the need for separate school supporters to organize themselves, so that they could have better representation in their dealings with the OEA and also with the bishops, and to assume some of the work presently carried on by the bishops. Organizing the Catholic laity was uppermost in their minds. Sills of Seaforth thought that the phrase "separate schools" created a stigma against Catholics and suggested that "public separate schools" was a more accurate description. At the same time, they feared antagonizing public school supporters while the Tiny Township case was still in the hands of the courts.

As the meeting was about to end, the group drafted a letter to be sent to all separate schools boards, advising trustees that they had met and inviting them to attend the 1926 OEA convention. The letter went on to claim that only an association of trustees, teachers, inspectors and all those of good will could awaken in the Catholic laity an interest in educational matters. It also laid out the four objects that this hoped-for association would have as its raison d'etre:

1) To encourage, foster and promote greater and more active interest in school affairs on the part of Catholic people.
2) To encourage Catholics to assume the full share of their moral and legal responsibilities in school management and matters of interest to Catholic education.
3) To promote greater efficiency both within and without the school.
4) To promote more active co-operation between home and school.[6]

This was all fairly inoffensive and safe, but the fact that it was articulated at all, with a view of continuing their discussions the next year, was a distinct departure for the trustees. So too were the formation of a committee to recruit members for the 1926 convention and of a five-person provisional committee to consist of a president, vice-president, secretary-treasurer and two trustees. This committee looked very much like an executive, but if that was the intention, it was an executive without an association or even a name.

For the next three years, from 1926 to 1928, no progress was made in founding an association. Separate school delegates continued to meet at the annual conventions, and new people joined their group, but the members felt bound by the advice of Archbishop Neil McNeil of Toronto. He suggested that they wait for the courts to pass judgment on Tiny Township before they set up anything so potentially provocative as their own trustee association. Meanwhile, the members were scarcely idle. They promised at their 1926 gathering to work with the Ontario Catholic Educational Council (the bishops and their lawyers) on corporation taxes and to ask separate school inspectors to drum up more trustees for the 1927 convention. At that convention and the one in 1928, the delegates vigorously opposed public school resolutions on the division of taxes. These resolutions were intentionally hostile to the welfare of separate schools. It was a taste of battles to come.

Finally, on 2 April 1929, McNeil gave his blessing to an association, and the Ontario Catholic Educational Association was born. This was OSSTA's original name, but it was a poor choice and lasted only a year. It looked and sounded too much like the Ontario Educational Association and the Ontario Catholic Educational Council, the bishops' organization. Moreover, it made no mention of trustees. The initial goal of having a single organization for Catholic trustees, teachers and inspectors was simply unworkable due to competing interests. Since the association was a trustee initiative from its very inception, it would be an association for trustees. Monsignor J.L. Hand told the delegates that the time had come for the separate schools to have a recognized body that could freely discuss questions of interest to Catholics.[7]

Present were forty-one delegates from eighteen boards. The largest contingent naturally came from Toronto (James G. Culnan, Monsignor J.L. Hand, Herbert L. Conlin, F. Coates, Father F. Fitzpatrick, Father J.J. McGrand, Father T.J. Morrissey, Thomas F. Battle, a well-known lawyer, Brother Jarlath, E.F. Henderson, who twenty years later was one of four Catholic members of the Hope Commission, and Father J.E. Rowan). Other delegates came from:

East Windsor (Dr. Damien St. Pierre); Eganville (J.A.

Lambertus); Ford City, now a part of Windsor (Thomas Hebert, J.A.E. DeHetie, Dr. M.G. Brick); Hamilton (A.E. Ford, Father J.W. Englert); Kingston (Dr. V.A. Martin); Kitchener (Father M.S. Hinsperger, C.S.); London (Father M.A. Brisson); Ottawa (Aurélien Bélanger, MPP, E.C. Desormeaux, T.R. Donovan); Perth (T.J. Meagher); Sarnia (C.J. Driscoll); Stratford (P.H. Hishon, C.J. Stewart); Tecumseh (Norman B. Lassaline); Timmins (J.E. Newton, F.J. Kehoe); Waterloo (Reinhold Lang); Windsor (Charles A. Cada, J.A. Renaud, R.J. Desmarais, Damien Gourd, Dr. J.A. Clairoux, Brother Gregory, T. Schwart); Riverside, now a part of Windsor (Dr. F.J. Furlong); Woodstock (F.D. Burk).[8]

The first full executive was C.J. Driscoll, president; Father J.W. Englert, vice-president; E.C. Desormeaux; secretary-treasurer; and F.J. Kehoe, Dr. Damien St. Pierre, Dr. V.A. Martin and Thomas F. Battle, directors. It was a fairly representative executive, with no one school board or geographical area dominating. Desormeaux was an excellent choice for secretary-treasurer. He was perfectly bilingual and thus able to correspond in both English and French. He was also on the executive of l'Association canadienne-française d'éducation d'Ontario (ACFEO). Many English-speaking trustees admired the ACFEO for its spirited and successful defense of bilingual education during and after the Regulation 17 fiasco.

Aurélien Bélanger, MPP for Russell, and Thomas F. Battle spoke on the division of taxes, and Dr. J.A. Clairoux moved a motion that their association co-operate with the newly-minted Separate Schools Assessment Amendment Committee. It was seconded unanimously.[9] Interestingly, Battle was secretary-treasurer of this committee, which had replaced the bishops' Ontario Catholic Education Council.[10]

OSSTA spent its first decade, 1929 to 1939, slowly defining itself as a corporate body with its own distinct identity, on the one hand, and carefully jockeying for a meaningful role to play as a member of the Catholic education establishment, on the other. It succeeded in the first task but failed to make much progress in the second.

The process of defining itself forced the executive of OSSTA to seek the approval of the official Church, in the person of the archbishop of Toronto, to open lines of communication with all Catholic school trustees and to forge new relationships with non-Catholics in the OEA. Church approval came easy and came first. Archbishop McNeil had already given his permission. To reinforce his assent, E.C. Desormeaux wrote him a letter, dated 1 May 1929, claiming that the association would work on behalf of Catholic schools in Ontario in three areas. It "would offer an excellent channel of more rapid and effective propaganda in favour of a fairer apportionment of public taxes between Public and Separate schools; would assure the cohesion of Catholic forces in support and defense of Catholic schools; and would bring about closer co-operation between the English-speaking and French-speaking elements of the Catholic Church in Ontario."[11] This would have been music to McNeil's ears. The archbishop was on side. Two years later, all the bishops followed his lead by endorsing the OSSTA in the seventh instruction of their famous circular of 30 September 1931: "Make it clear to Separate School trustees that they are in duty bound to become members of the Ontario Separate School Trustees' Association, and to take an active interest in their work."[12]

In spite of episcopal exhortations, OSSTA had to spend considerable time advertising itself to Catholic trustees. Membership was only one dollar per board per year, which was hardly exorbitant. But it would take years for the association to sign up trustees from at least fifty per cent of separate school boards. Apathy confounded by poverty on the part of the numerous smaller boards, many of which were rural school sections of three trustees and one schoolhouse, would be the bane of OSSTA's existence until the 1960s. But OSSTA was not without fault in this matter. The fact that the executive took more than thirty years to hire a permanent secretary to work out of a central office militated against its ongoing recruitment drives.

Ironically, OSSTA initially seemed to have an easier time connecting with non-Catholic trustees. It applied for and received affiliation in the Ontario Educational Association, as a section of the

Ontario Trustees' and Ratepayers' Association. OSSTA's application was filed under its own name, which was necessary for it to maintain its Catholic identity. C. J. Driscoll was listed as the Separate School section representative of the OEA for the first time in 1931-32.[13] In addition to bestowing a measure of legitimacy to Catholic claims that separate schools were public schools, sectional affiliation in the OEA granted OSSTA, and by implication every separate school trustee, recognition and also validation. In practical terms, OEA affiliation made the president of OSSTA an ex-officio member of the executive of the Ontario Educational Association and the president, vice-president, secretary-treasurer and two directors of OSSTA members of the executive of the powerful Ontario Trustees' and Ratepayers' Association. (In subsequent years, OSSTA was also a member of the influential Ontario School Trustees' Council, which held its first meeting on 2 December 1949.)[14]

Internally, the association fashioned itself into a forum for opinions and problem solving and into a springboard to political action. In effect, the annual meetings became a necessary training ground for trustees. The vast majority of them had little contact with one another during the year. Also, when the rural school section was still the basic geographical unit for hundreds of separate school boards, many trustees remained tied to a nineteenth-century model of trusteeship. OSSTA was acting as a bridge to the modern world, linking urban and rural trustees in an atmosphere of unity and co-operation. Nowhere was this more apparent than in their open-floor discussions. Among a wide range of topics, the delegates discussed debentures, legislative grants, the perennial tax question, religious education, the duties and responsibilities of school boards and safety in the schools. In the 1950s, when school finance and constitutional questions had become so complex and worrisome, these discussions turned into lengthy question-and-answer periods hosted by experts.

A steady diet of special speakers was another prominent feature of the annual conventions and also an essential component of OSSTA's teaching mission. Among those who delivered lectures during OSSTA's opening decade were priests, politicians, school inspectors, teachers and education bureaucrats. Examples were Father

John Burke ("The Status of Separate Schools"); W.J. Lee, separate school inspector for Toronto (legislative grant distribution and "The Rotary System"); Father Lamoureux ("Our Separate Schools: Their Aim and Their Achievements"); Louis Coté, MLA for Ottawa ("The Distribution of School Taxes Paid by Companies and Corporations"); Miss A.C. Rowan, secretary-general of OECTA and the first woman to speak to an OSSTA convention ("What do Teachers Expect from School Boards?"); V.K. Greer, chief inspector of public and separate schools ("A Few Standards for Elementary Schools"); F.S. Rutherford, provincial supervisor of vocational training ("Vocational Training"); Charles Quenneville, business administrator of Windsor separate schools ("Separate School Statistics"); Father William G. Borho, CR ("The Church, Home and State in Education"); Senator Gustave Lacasse ("The Place of Health in Education"); and, not surprisingly, Martin J. Quinn of the Catholic Taxpayers' Association. Quinn spoke at three OSSTA conventions, one before and two after the 1936 amendments to the Assessment Act.

Political lobbying took the shape of annual resolutions on amendments to the Separate Schools Act that were packaged as petitions to the lieutenant-governor. The subject was invariably the division of taxes payable by publicly-owned utilities and incorporated companies. At one point during the 1933 annual general meeting, J.A. McNevin, president, reminded the delegates that "The public school boards pass 60 to 70 resolutions, all calling for amendments to the Public School Act. They are everlastingly hammering away at it. Working up amendments is the only way we can bring these matters to the attention of the department [of education]."[15] In 1937, OSSTA presented its first-ever brief. Written by A.H. Murphy and Father F. J. Brennan, it was a submission to the Royal Commission on Dominion-Provincial Relations.[16] Beginning in the late 1950s, the submission of briefs would become a staple of OSSTA's existence. For the moment, though, the clearest indication of OSSTA's policies and goals, as it solidified its identity as a provincial association of trustees, can be found in a fourteen-part resolution in support of a proposed policy platform of the Ontario School Trustees' and Ratepayers' Association. The resolution was published in the *Minutes* of the eighth annual general meeting, 30-31 March 1937:

1. That equal educational opportunities should be given to every child in Ontario.

2. That 50% of school expenditures should be borne by the State [province of Ontario].

3. That greater co-operation between school boards should be fostered in the interest of boys and girls.

4. That a Province-wide medical examination should be given at least once each year during the elementary and secondary school life of the child.

5. That a permanent record should be kept of every school child throughout his elementary and secondary school life.

6. That a more practical course should be provided for all primary and secondary schools leading to a standard diploma which would be recognized by business firms, agricultural colleges and other practical professions.

7. That our teaching profession be assured of a greater tenure of service and a minimum salary of $700.00 and greater freedom of citizenship.

8. War being the greatest menace to civilization and democracy, every effort should be made by teachers to encourage international peace and to teach the truth about war.

9. That every effort be made to encourage a better class of moving pictures and that all educational films should be stamped.

10. That assistance be given by the Federal Government to the Provincial governments for the vocational training and employment of youth.

11. That all real property taxes be based on a Provincial equalized assessment.

12. That we make a thorough study of the unit of administration [size of school boards] for the purpose of securing the greatest economy and efficiency in our educational system.

13. That every effort be made to increase interest in education in order that our citizens may be well prepared for life.

14. That there be the greatest possible co-operation between our Association [OSSTA] and the Department of Education.[17]

Of immediate concern to OSSTA were No. 1, on equal educational opportunity, which would become the rallying cry of the 1960s; No. 2, on the government's share of school expenditures; No. 11, on equalized assessment; and No. 12, on larger units of administration, which were achieved in 1969. However, when it came to leadership on these issues, or, for that matter on anything of significance affecting separate schools, OSSTA was more of a follower than a leader, at best a silent and submissive partner in the school politics of the 1930s.

At the first annual general meeting of the Ontario Separate School Trustees' Association, held on 24 April 1930, Archbishop McNeil told the one hundred delegates in attendance that the hierarchy had done everything in its power to obtain a fair division of corporation and utility taxes on behalf of separate schools. It was time for the Catholic laity to impress upon the government the justice of their claims.[18] When McNeil spoke to the annual general meeting the following year, on 8 April 1931, he invited the trustees to take a lead in solving the many difficulties faced by their schools. He could not have been more open and forthcoming. Yet it was the association itself, unsure of its status in the Catholic pecking order, who shied away from the challenge and assumed a subservient position.

Thomas F. Battle, for one, thought that it was the right of the bishops to negotiate with the government and the duty of the trustees to act as a vehicle of propaganda for the bishops.[19] Battle's view seems to have held sway and could account for OSSTA's willingness always to play second fiddle, first to the Separate Schools Assessment Amendment Committee and then to Quinn's Catholic Taxpayers' Association, which obviously had taken McNeil's cue on lay leadership of the school question. So anaesthetized was OSSTA that when it came time for the trustees to enter the debate about the myriad of problems generated by Premier Hepburn's 1936 amendment to the

Assessment Act, it was not the trustees as an association that intervened but individual school boards that took action, as if OSSTA did not exist. On 21 September 1936, trustees representing sixteen separate school boards gathered in Toronto and resolved to engage a Catholic solicitor to examine the amendment and suggest revisions to it. These revisions would then be forwarded to the government.[20]

Things did not improve much for OSSTA in the 1940s. If anything, its profile actually diminished. OSSTA had yet to assert its identity and press its claim to leadership because it had neither the members nor the money to do so. Caution bordering on timidity ruled OSSTA's ambitions. One example of this will suffice. At OSSTA's 1942 annual general meeting, the delegates were extremely anxious to express their loyalty to the hierarchy's current separate school agenda, above anything else they themselves might have had in mind for the schools. They did this by passing a multi-point resolution, later forwarded to the bishops, that supported a reconstituted Catholic Taxpayers' Association, good working relations with l'Association canadienne-française d'éducation d'Ontario and, most importantly, the bishops' plans to establish a central office and appoint a permanent secretary "to deal with educational problems and legislation."[21] This was the beginning of the English Catholic Education Association of Ontario.

****

ECEAO's inaugural meeting took place at Teefy Hall, St. Michael's College in Toronto, on 26 April 1943, attracting almost 100 delegates. The bishops wanted their new organization "to unify and co-ordinate all efforts for the promotion of elementary and secondary education among English-speaking Catholics and to provide a medium of official Catholic expression and action on questions affecting elementary and secondary education."[22] Later, a third aim found its way into the association's literature: "to bring together groups and individuals interested in the cause of Catholic Education."[23] Membership was open to Catholic school children and their families and to any group or organization that had an interest in

Catholic education. In due time, the three groups that formed the principal constituent parts of ECEAO were the school trustees (Ontario Separate School Trustees' Association), the teachers (Ontario English Catholic Teachers' Association) and the parents (Federation of Catholic Parent-Teacher Associations of Ontario.[24]

As if to make sure that everyone knew that the bishops were in charge, Archbishop McGuigan chaired both the fourteen-member General Council and the six-member executive committee. E.F. Henderson, one of the founders of OSSTA, was first president of the Governing Council. The remaining members of the council were the Archbishop of Kingston (hierarchy), Monsignor J.W. Englert, another OSSTA pioneer, and Father T.J. Sloan (clergy), Arthur Kelly, a future member of the Hope Commission and William Kelly (private schools), J.P. Allen and P.J. Dunlop (separate school trustees), E.V. McCarthy and Mr. McCarney (parents) and Father F.J. Brennan and Dr. D. Dolan (delegates at large). A teacher representative had yet to be chosen, but that he or she would come from the diocese of Hearst was agreed upon in advance by the delegates. The executive committee was composed of Archbishop McGuigan, Monsignor J.W. Englert, Father Vincent Priester, J.P. Allen, E.V. McCarthy and Arthur Kelly. Representing ECEAO on the Ontario Catholic Education Council were four laymen — J. A. McNevin, E.V. McCarthy, A.H. Murphy, Arthur Kelly — and one priest — Father Priester.[25] It was understood that ECEAO had replaced the Catholic Taxpayers' Association and that it would co-ordinate all school matters with l'Association canadienne-française d'éducation d'Ontario, under the sponsorship of the Ontario Catholic Education Council.

****

The one individual who best personified ECEAO was Father Vincent Priester, the association's executive director and secretary and the only day-to-day presence at the Catholic Education Office. Born on 5 June 1908, in Linwood, Ontario, he was the son of William Priester and Florence Ball and was educated in Drayton and Elmira prior to entering St. Augustine's Seminary. Following ordination to the priesthood, on 31 May 1936, Father Priester was assistant at St. Ann's and then St. Mary's in Hamilton while he taught at Cathedral High School, from 1936 to 1942. His ECEAO appointment was the longest of his clerical career, lasting from 1943 to 1965.[26]

Father Priester was given an office and just enough financial support to operate, and he enjoyed a close working relationship with Archbishop (later Cardinal) James C. McGuigan and with Premier Leslie Frost. Quiet diplomacy was Father Priester's modus operandi. Trustees, teachers, inspectors, school board officials and the always invisible separate school ratepayers were at best minor players in Father Priester's way of conducting business, which was usually with an iron hand. He "was definitely of the old school," remembered Father Joseph P. Finn, long-time chaplain to OSSTA and Father Priester's immediate successor at the helm of ECEAO. He "did not hesitate to keep youngsters like myself in line whenever we came up with thoughts or recommendations contrary to what he had in mind for the best interests of Catholic education in Ontario."[27] Such strength of character served him well for many years. Only once during his long tenure was his resignation from ECEAO ever seriously considered. That was in April 1950, four months after the publication of the Hope Commission's final report, which was a low point in the fortunes of Catholic separate schools. It was Cardinal McGuigan, Father Priester's principal patron, who persuaded Bishop Joseph F. Ryan of Hamilton to let him stay at the helm.[28]

Father Priester remained but was not allotted complete independence. His time was shared with his home diocese. In addition to his duties for ECEAO, he was administrator of St. Theresa's in Elmira, for the first half of 1954, and of St. Mary's in Mount Forest, from 1956 to 1957. His next pastoral assignment was St. Andrew's in Oakville, from 1957 to 1965, by itself a position that would have taxed the energies and devotion of the most committed priest.[29] It was also one that inevitably weakened Father Priester's ability to manage ECEAO's affairs in an effective and imaginative way as the staggering financial crisis of the late 1950s and early 1960s overtook the separate schools and threatened to destroy their very existence. As we shall see later in this chapter, the ECEAO's exclusion from the 1962 political run-up to what became the Ontario Foundation Tax Plan, the most important breakthrough in decades, signaled the beginning of the end of Father Priester's contributions to Catholic education.

The ECEAO papers reveal an executive director hard at work on every separate school issue that crossed his desk. Father Priester collected statistical information on the schools; he co-ordinated the transfer of Episcopal Corporation school property to local school boards; he was involved in the Hope Commission and published and distributed *Historical Sketch of the Separate Schools of Ontario and Minority Report*, the official Catholic response to the commission's recommendations; he oversaw the formation of new separate schools, salary schedules for religious teachers and revisions to the Separate Schools Act; he proposed names of candidates for the post of inspector, helped to establish parent-teacher groups and maintained a working relationship with the teachers and trustees; he corresponded with bishops and school boards and sponsored Franklin Walker's *Catholic Education and Politics in Upper Canada* and *Catholic Education and Politics in Ontario*, the first two volumes of what became a three-volume history of separate schools.[30] The above represent only a sampling of Father Priester's energy and devotion to the separate school cause. The bishops expected him to do nearly everything, and he almost succeeded.

We have already alluded to his political style, that of the quiet diplomat working the back corridors of Queen's Park to build positive relationships with those in power, and how that style neatly dovetailed with the Ontario bishops' understanding of ECEAO's primary role, which was to act as an unobtrusive listening post on developments in education policy and as the only intermediary between the hierarchy and the government. Personal pressure from Father Priester did yield some early results that tended to confirm the wisdom of his approach to school politics. He persuaded J.G. Althouse at the department of education to designate J.C. Walsh as Catholic assistant superintendent of elementary education, and A.L. Lake as a Catholic high school inspector.[31] We also know that the legislative grant was altered in December 1944 to a formula based on school population for urban areas and on the number of classrooms for rural areas. (After the first year, the new formula was not so favourable to separate schools.)[32] To what extent this initially promising change was the direct or indirect result of Father Priester's lobbying would be difficult, if not impossible, to determine, but even more difficult is it to imagine that he had *no* influence on those at Queen's Park responsible for bringing in the change.

But all this is beside the point. One must keep in mind that any long-range plans that Father Priester and Cardinal McGuigan may have had in store for ECEAO were completely derailed by the Hope Commission, for the five years that it took to complete its public hearings and deliver a report and for a long time afterwards, as public hostility towards separate schools continued to run high. As a direct result, the ECEAO was unable to accomplish much in the one area that mattered most to separate schools in the 1950s — the dire need for more public money.

Perhaps Father Priester's greatest accomplishment was the organization of the annual Easter-week Catholic Education Conference. These were huge gatherings, drawing hundreds to the ballroom of the Royal York Hotel to listen to cardinals, bishops, priests, politicians and education officials. Premier George Drew and Premier Leslie Frost also participated on occasion.[33] Given plenty of publicity in the Catholic press, these conferences served as an excellent venue for sharing information and ideas and as a public exercise in morale boosting. Apathy was always a problem when Catholic demands for justice in education started to sound like tired old complaints.

OSSTA was very much in evidence at these conferences. Their annual general meetings took place at the same time and under the umbrella of Father Priester's Catholic Education Conference. Their participation was valuable because it showed a unity in purpose among the different groups defending separate schools, but, at the same time, it helped to stunt OSSTA's growth as the collective representative of the only group of people empowered by law to act on behalf of separate schools — the trustees.

Father Priester himself had a low opinion of OSSTA. In a letter of 26 January 1948, to H.A. Ducharme of the Stratford Separate

School Board, he gave this rather dismissive assessment: "The trustees' Association is the link with the Ontario Education Association and as far as performing any particular duties or service for the boards, I do not know what they do except form that link."[34] Unflattering and probably all too true. As such, it did not bode well for the association as it prepared itself to deal with the state of separate schools at mid century and beyond. First, though, we must examine the political dynamics of the Hope Commission.

The Hope Commission, 1945-1950

On 21 March 1945, Premier George A. Drew, who was also minister of education, announced the formation of a Royal Commission on Education in Ontario, the first of its kind in living memory. Mr. Justice John Andrew Hope was chair of the Commission, and from that day to this, the Commission has been called the Hope Commission. He was assisted by twenty commissioners, four of whom were Catholic and were members of the commission precisely because they were Catholic. They were E.F. Henderson, Arthur Kelly, Henri Saint-Jacques and Joseph Pigott. Henderson was a familiar face in separate school circles. He was a co-founder of OSSTA, in 1930, and the first president of the governing council of ECEAO, in 1944, as well as the veteran business manager of the Toronto Separate School Board. Arthur Kelly, a Conservative, was the solicitor for both the archdiocese of Toronto and the school board and the favoured nominee of the bishops. Saint-Jacques, another Conservative, was also a former teacher and a practicing lawyer. He was appointed to represent French-Canadian interests. That he was nominated by J.G. Althouse, director of education for the province, and V.K. Greer, superintendent of elementary education, should not go unnoticed. Their nomination of Saint-Jacques shows that there was some effort, at least on the part of the education bureaucracy, to give separate school supporters a fighting chance on the commission. Pigott, meanwhile, was neither a lawyer nor an administrator but a highly successful contractor from Hamilton. He was chosen primarily for his knowledge of technical education and apprenticeship training.[35] After only several months had passed, the

Catholic commissioners realized, to their utter dismay and perhaps even to their horror, that they would have to conduct an all-out battle in defense of separate schools.

The terms of reference for the Hope Commission were extraordinary for being so all encompassing:

> to inquire into and report upon the provincial education system, and without derogating from the generality thereof, including courses of study, text books, examinations, financing, and the general system and scheme of elementary and secondary schools involving public schools, **separate schools** [emphasis mine], continuation schools, high schools, collegiate institutes, vocational schools, schools for the training of teachers and all other schools under the jurisdiction of the Department of Education, as well as the selection and training of teachers, inspectors, and other officials of such schools, and the system of provincial and local school administration.[36]

Little wonder that it took the Commission almost six years to fulfill its mandate. The Commission as a whole sat for 142 days, received 258 briefs and 44 memoranda and listened to 474 witnesses. Committees assigned specific tasks sat another 116 days, and the Editing Committee alone spent 93 days on the final report. The Commission conducted most of its hearings in Toronto, but it did visit Northern Ontario in an honest bid to see for itself the special problems in education faced by the people there. As well, individual members and certain committees travelled to other provinces, to certain states in the United States and to the British Isles, Sweden and Denmark.

The commissioners submitted their *Report* to Premier Leslie Frost on 15 December 1950. Divided into 30 chapters, it was an astonishing 1,179 pages in length (500,000 words) and consisted of a Majority Report (1,015 pages) signed by 15 commissioners, memoranda from four of the 15 signatories, a Minority Report written by two commissioners who were also signatories of the Majority

Report, an Historical Sketch of the Separate Schools of Ontario and a Minority Report submitted by the four Catholic commissioners, a memorandum from one of the Catholic commissioners on French as a language of instruction and a statement of dissent from one more commissioner (in addition to the four Catholics) who refused to sign the Majority Report.

The Hope Commission made 300 major recommendations on the re-organization of the education system, school administration, separate schools, the use of the French language for instruction, school programs, the training of teachers and financing the system. The Commission openly admitted that the subject of separate schools was the most nettlesome. The Majority Report devoted two chapters to Catholic separate schools. Chapter XVIII, "Origins and Development of Separate Schools in Ontario," dealt with the past as understood by commissioners for whom Catholicism itself was still something of a foreign element in the public life of the nation. Chapter XIX, "Roman Catholic Separate Schools in the Reorganized Educational System," promulgated the future of publicly-funded Catholic education as envisioned by fifteen members of the Commission, and that future was not very promising. In the end, the Catholic commissioners hived off themselves from the rest of their colleagues to write their "Minority Report" and "Historical Sketch."

One should not be too surprised that the Catholic commissioners had to circle their wagons. When Premier Drew unveiled the Royal Commission on Education in Ontario, separate school supporters sincerely but naively believed that the Commission would see the justice of their long-held claims concerning corporation and utility taxes and Catholic high schools and spell out in their final report the appropriate remedies. Many wondered aloud if the Commission would tell the government to put an end to the limits on separate school rights. On the other side of the Rubicon, as many Catholics saw it, was full equality of educational opportunity for their children. Would the commissioners dare to cross it and try to bring the government along with them?

Catholics could not have been more wrongheaded in their expectations. As it turned out, they were not only naive but also terribly ill-prepared to deal with what was in effect the final assault of old Protestant Ontario against the very existence of Catholic separate schools. Although the Drew government had not intended the Hope Commission to be a forum for separate school bashing, it was inevitable given the nature of the Commission itself, which was designed to be a platform for practically any and all opinions on every aspect of education. And it took only one brief to arouse the latent anti-separate school sentiments of a majority of the commissioners. That was Brief 113, submitted by the Inter-Church Committee on Protestant-Roman Catholic Relations, on 3 December 1945.

The Inter-Church Committee boasted representatives from the Canadian Baptist Federation, the Churches of Christ (Disciples), the Church of England in Canada, the Evangelical Church, the Presbyterian Church in Canada, the Salvation Army and the United Church of Canada. Among its members were prominent churchmen, lawyers, educators and professors. The Majority Report unequivocally stated that the Inter-Church Committee "expressed the views of a very considerable section of our population."[37] An observation is in order. Although the official title of the Inter-Church Committee included the words "Roman Catholic," there were certainly no Roman Catholics on the committee to talk about Protestant-Roman Catholic relations. All the criticism flowed in one direction, with no allowance for a Catholic countercurrent.

George A. Cornish, a retired professor from the University of Toronto, was the author of Brief 113. More than 180 pages in length, the Inter-Church Committee brief was anything but brief, but its lack of brevity was more than compensated by Cornish's encyclopedic knowledge of separate school legislation and educational regulations and by his ability to deliver one brilliant rhetorical punch after another. Professor Cornish knew the history of separate schools better than any defender of separate schools — better than any bishop, priest, administrator, trustee or teacher, and better than anyone associated with either the English Catholic Education Association of Ontario or the Ontario Separate School Trustees' Association. How ironic that it took a Protestant professor's Protestant brief to convince Catholics — in the persons of the four Catholic commissioners — to write and publish what became the first substantial history of separate schools and to incorporate that history into their Minority Report.

A dominant theme of the Cornish analysis was that Catholic separate schools were a threat to shared democratic values, and that bilingual separate schools, especially in northern Ontario, were the worse form of that threat. It was an allegation older than the BNA Act but one that had gained a whole new life following the Second World War. The entire tone of the brief was accusatory. Cornish was nasty but always brilliantly nasty. He leveled so many charges against separate schools, on this, that and every subject in between, as to leave bewildered even the most ardent separate school apologists and to make it virtually impossible for any Catholic author to reply, charge by charge.

One of the more succinct summations of Brief 113 has been given by the historian Franklin Walker:

> A reply to specific charges would have been pointless in any event for the inter-church argument was that separate schools from the beginning were the result of unjust privileges which the clergy had extorted from weak-minded politicians, that the financial problems of the schools were the fault of separate school supporters who, as the victims of "clerical authoritarianism" had been coerced into rejecting the public school system, that irresponsible government had allowed a steady growth of privileges and that while constitutional guarantees must be continued, nothing beyond a rigid interpretation of the 1867 settlement must be permitted.[38]

This was the ghost of Egerton Ryerson speaking. His was still a mighty voice in Ontario, carefully distilled by the current defenders of public schools. And it was in the presence of his ghost that separate school supporters presented their submissions to the Hope Commission.[39]

Of the eight briefs and one supplementary brief submitted to the Hope Commission in support of separate schools, we will examine the submission of the Ontario Catholic Education Council,

Brief 146, the lengthy supplementary to this brief and the Statement of the Catholic Bishops of Ontario, identified as Brief 196.[40] We will also examine transcripts from the proceedings of the Royal Commission that feature several testy exchanges between the Commission and separate school defenders.

Dated 28 December 1945 and presented to the Hope Commission on 10 January 1946, the brief of the Ontario Catholic Education Council was written by Father Frank Brennan and signed by Father Vincent Priester in his capacity as secretary of the Council. Its opening paragraph stated that the Council was composed of representatives from the English Catholic Education Association of Ontario and l'Association canadienne-française d'éducation d'Ontario and that it spoke on behalf of the Ontario Separate School Trustees' Association, l'Association des commissions des écoles bilingues d'Ontario, l'Association de l'enseignement français d'Ontario and the Ontario English Catholic Teachers' Association. The Council made it clear to the Commission that it represented all the separate school stakeholders, in particular the children.

The brief took as its unifying principle the theme of "equality of financial treatment for every child attending separate schools in relation to every other child attending public schools in the Province."[41] This theme was founded on a statement in the 1943 *Report of the Minister of Education*, which said that "Every child in the Province of Ontario has the moral right to the best education he can receive consistent with his ability, and it is the moral obligation of those charged with his care to see that this is provided."[42] The aim of the brief was to "show that the present legislation affecting taxation and assessment for school purposes and the existing regulations for Government grants are far from being in accord with the principle of equality, and the children of separate schools are grievously penalized."[43]

The brief went on to demonstrate six points: separate schools were granted as a minority right and not as a special privilege; the rights of conscience created the need for separate schools; the parent, not the state, is the natural teaching authority for the child; separate schools are public and democratic, they train their students for citizenship and they are regulated by the Department of Education; there is a financial inequality between public and separate schools; and separate schools are deprived of their rightful share of taxes.

In detailing its argument about the rights of conscience, the brief gave the classic Catholic reason for separate schools:

> Religion is more than a set of intellectual beliefs, it is a way of life, it is indeed the very life of the soul; it should inspire all conduct and determine our scale of moral values . . . For the Catholic education of Catholic children it is essential to have schools integrally Catholic, schools which are the allies and not neutrals or antagonists of Catholic homes and the Catholic Church. Religion must permeate all education.[44]

Concerning the claim of financial inequality, the brief pointed out to the Commission that in 1943 the average cost per pupil, estimated on average attendance, was $77.32 in the public schools and $47.94 in the separate schools. "The Separate Schools Boards have no magical power enabling them to get for $47 what the Public School Boards spend $77 to obtain," the brief declared.[45] It continued:

> The real costs are the same when the two kinds of Boards are doing the same kind of work. The difference in the costs of the Public School Boards and the Separate School Boards is paid for by the children and the teachers in the separate schools. The children suffer from inferior buildings, lack of equipment, understaffing of the schools, and restricted services. The teachers suffer from the same causes and they suffer also from the lower scale of salaries they receive as compared with their colleagues in the public schools. We believe that by dint of sacrifices made by teachers, parents and others on behalf of Catholic schools, the children receive some compensation for the disadvantages they suffer, but the fact of inequality and injustice remains. Sacrifices are imposed on children and teachers. These sacrifices persist in spite of the fact that in most localities the mill rate for

separate school support is substantially higher than that for public school support.[46]

There followed a Table showing figures for the differences in costs and grants per pupil and the mill rate, between the public and separate school boards in twelve of the province's largest municipalities.

On the subject of taxes, the brief addressed not only the matter of corporation and utility taxes but also Roman Catholic estates administered by trust funds, co-operatives and mutual corporations, jointly-owned businesses and those "cases where children are legally entitled to attend, and do attend, separate schools, there is no legislation to enable that the assessment of property occupied by the parents or guardians is marked for the support of separate schools."[47]

The new grant legislation of December 1944 also came under heavy criticism. The brief claimed that although the legislation lightened the burdens of both separate and public ratepayers by decreasing the mill rates for both sets of ratepayers, separate schools — pupils, ratepayers and boards — continued to function under a heavy and persistent burden of inequality.

The brief urged the Hope Commission to accept the principle of equal educational opportunity, as enunciated by the premier and the minister of education, and to recommend changes that would remove inequalities in tax revenues and grants.

The Ontario bishops were next. Their brief was dated 9 October 1946. The bishops stressed that the schools existed for the children of the laity, that the organizations represented by the Ontario Catholic Education Council were staffed by the laity and that it was no longer necessary for the bishops to be the most important champions of separate schools. If there was a weakness to this line of thinking it was this: since the episcopate was primarily a teaching office, the bishops could hardly disinterest themselves from Catholic education.

The thrust of their brief was simple: "Catholics have always held that there cannot be true religion without education, and moreover there cannot be true education without religion."[48] They reminded the commissioners of the situation in the public schools of the United States, where the teaching of religion was completely

372

absent from the curriculum. But the American way was not the British way. The bishops welcomed recent efforts in Ontario's public schools to provide better religious training for its students, in an atmosphere of religious (if not doctrinal) unity among Protestants, but they could never accept non-denominational Christianity for Catholic school children. There was too much at stake:

> It is needless for us to say that we believe that religion is necessary to morality, which is equally necessary to human society. The weakening of family ties, unbridled greed for material gain, and class antagonisms, will grow and become insoluble problems if the influence of religion is not strong in the community. It is the mission of religion to direct men to the true ends of life, to keep them in the ways of justice and foster in them the spirit of charity towards their fellows. In the absence of religion, teachers have become sadly conscious of the want of a regulating and unifying principle in the school curriculum. In the absence of Christian doctrine some other creed will be offered to the human mind. In the absence of God there will be some other object of worship. History, ancient as well as recent, enables us to discern what would be the alternative to the Christian Church. The State would take the place of the Church; the State would be the supreme teacher of the purposes of human life. The power over the formation of minds would be monopolized by the holders of political power. The State itself would be a compulsory Church; or it would create or enslave a puppet Church to promote its philosophy of life devoid of all spiritual ideals or principles. There would be no division of spiritual and temporal powers. Caesar would be deified.[49]

The bishops' brief was a thinly veiled warning against the inherent dangers of a godless educational system, the adoption of which could help to usher in the tyranny of the State over every aspect of life and then be used by the State to elevate itself to the status of a god. There was a wide audience for such rhetoric, both inside and outside the Catholic Church, but the Majority Report commissioners, although sympathetic to a large degree, brushed off the bishops, treating their warning as nothing more than a high-pitched interpolation of no real significance to the proceedings at hand.

The Ontario Catholic Education Council's supplementary to Brief 146 was dated 17 October 1946.[50] It was presented by T.N. Phelan and Gaston Vincent, representing English- and French-speaking Catholics in an obvious show of unity. They were assisted by John Connolly, J.O. Trepanier and Henry Somerville. Once again, Father Priester signed the document. The supplement, at nearly twenty-nine, single-spaced pages, dwarfed the original brief, which was fifteen and a half double-spaced pages. The supplement addressed many of the same issues, but it provided greater historical and statistical detail. It also made specific recommendations:

a) fair treatment of separate school concerns

b) teaching religion

c) salaries for teachers

d) retention of Section 21 of the Separate Schools Act (the right to establish separate schools in unorganized districts)

e) larger units of school administration

f) amendment of Section 56 of the Separate Schools Act ("to permit a Roman Catholic to remain a separate school supporter when the school, of which he was legally a supporter by the provisions of the above section 56, is closed, under a Union Separate School Board, the pupils being provided with transportation to another school or schools"[51]

g) the establishment of "a full elementary, secondary and high school education for all Catholic pupils under the charge of such Separate School Boards from the age of 5 up to 21 years, as originally granted in pre-Confederation Statutes"[52]

h) legislation that would make available the proper share of legislative grants for secondary and high school education

i) pending such remedial legislation, the retention of Grades IX and X and Continuation Classes, the Continuation Schools Act and the Regulations governing them, prior to

1946, and Section 73 of the Separate Schools Act

j) in the event that the government decides to erect intermediate schools up to the end of Grade X or composite high schools, that "legislation be enacted to protect the autonomy and authority of separate school boards over all classes in Separate Schools affected by this type of grading,"[53] and that the appropriate legislative grants be made to support such a system of grades and classes

The Hope Commission turned a deaf ear to all of this. This was clearly the case at the 28 November 1946 proceedings of the Commission. Instead of discussing the substance of the supplementary, Mr. Justice Hope, the chairman, and Major Angus Dunbar, legal counsel, interrogated T.N. Phelan and John Connolly about nuns: whether they received individual contracts or if separate school boards signed contracts with their religious communities; whether they paid income tax on a salary of more than $600 per year; and whether they received room and board as part of their salary. At one point, Mr. Justice Hope was so annoyed with Connolly, he asked a member of the audience, E.V. McCarthy, for his opinion on the income tax line of inquiry. McCarthy, a member of the Ottawa Separate School Board for many years, was surprised at the invitation but not shy about giving his opinion. He said that any questions about income tax were outside the scope of the Commission. Before he could continue, the chairman cut him off in mid sentence.

The Chairman: We are grateful to you, Mr. McCarthy, for your opinion on that, but, after all, we will follow up our own line of enquiry.

Mr. McCarthy: Yes, but my thought was that that was something that the federal authorities have dealt with, and I believe they have; and while I am not positive on it, I think they have ruled as to some of them that on account of the low salaries they do not pay income tax.

The Chairman: It is a very pertinent question, I may suggest to you, Mr. McCarthy. Grants are paid out of public funds;

you are asking for grants; public funds come from taxation mainly, and if certain people are exempt from taxation, then that might very well be taken in – I think that you will agree with me, in all fairness – when grants are being made. I think the two matters are very much akin and are directly within the scope of this Commission, with all respect to your opinion. These matters must be considered.[54]

The same kind of aggressive hostility manifested itself on the question of the constitutional right of separate school boards to build new schools outside the regulatory jurisdiction of the department of education that applied to public school boards. Mr. Justice Hope brought up the example of Mattawa. For forty years, he said, Catholics and Protestants attended the local public school, but then "some enthusiast, some young man, comes in there, he is an enthusiast for his own ideas, and he gets five members, heads of families, together, and there is no overriding authority which can, in the interests of community and of the public treasury, control, as I understand it."[55] Phelan replied: "It is going to be a very difficult problem, because you have two principles coming into conflict: You have the principle of the right to establish a school, and you have the principle of what is in the interest of the community from an economic point of view."[56] After a lengthy intervention from Father Priester, Mr. Justice Hope pressed on about ministerial approval for new separate schools, the same as that applied to new public schools. In the end, he forced Phelan to agree with him that if there was no finality to the 1863 Act, there was no finality to the right of separate school boards to establish new schools without ministerial approval.

The exchange that took place at the open session of 28 November 1946 was only a taste of things to come in the Majority Report of December 1950. The majority of commissioners opened Chapter XIX of the *Report* with these words: "No phase of our inquiry has consumed more time or proved more difficult than that of Roman Catholic separate schools. Here we encountered a conflict of principles which still makes the problem as impossible of solution by agreement as it has been for the past hundred years."[57] However, having declared the impossibility of finding a solution by agreement (as if Catholic separate schools should have been treated as a problem in the first place), the Majority Report did not hesitate to position itself squarely on one side of the conflict and propose its own solutions to the separate school problem. The side it chose to take was the side occupied by the Inter-Church Committee, among others.[58] Brief 113 was an inspiration, a guiding hand. The Majority Report rejected the Catholic version of separate school history and also any Catholic interpretations of the overall intention of the 1863 Act in regards to taxation and secondary education. Any recommendation submitted by the supporters of separate schools was measured against Brief 113 and, if found wanting, was dismissed.

The Majority Report made forty-five recommendations on Catholic separate schools. They dealt with their status within the broader framework of provincially funded education, curriculum and the teaching of religion, teachers and salaries, administration, formation of new school boards, union separate school boards, qualifications of trustees and electors, attendance of pupils, finances and, most importantly, the status of separate schools within the Commission's proposed grading system. This last-mentioned recommendation reads as follows: "that Roman Catholic separate schools be authorized by the Legislature to provide the educational programme only as proposed for elementary schools in the reorganized educational system, including nursery schools and kindergartens."[59]

What did this mean? One of the more curious recommendations of the Hope Commission, and the one that proved its undoing, was the proposal to restructure the system into six years of elementary school (Grades 1 to 6), four years of high school (Grades 7 to 10) and three years of junior college (Grades 11 to 13), which would include vocational training and university preparation. The Commission may have had its pedagogical reasons for recommending this 6-4-3 pattern, but it would have limited Catholic separate schools to the elementary panel, Grades 1 to 6. If ever implemented, this recommendation would most likely have killed Catholic separate schools and most assuredly have re-opened the whole separate school debate, which would have been a nightmare for any government. By proposing the 6-4-3 restructuring, the Hope Commission "flew directly in the face of the historical realities of Ontario," according to the historian Robert Stamp.[60] On the one hand, the Commission's proposal would have deprived Catholic ratepayers of "their constitutional and customary rights of from eight to ten years of denominational education."[61] Up from the Catholic ranks would come the cry of religious persecution. On the other hand, any attempt by the government to extend separate school rights to include the proposed second tier of education, thus guaranteeing ten years of education instead of the usual eight, would have earned the wrath of many public school supporters. From them would have come the charge of special privileges for a religious minority who had no right to privileges of any kind.

Cardinal McGuigan spoke for all Catholic ratepayers when he issued a press release immediately after the unveiling of the Commission's report. "I note that the Majority Report proposes that Separate School Boards should have jurisdiction over children only up to the age of 12 years. This proposal will cause astonishment and consternation among Catholics, especially as it is accompanied by a statement that the rights and privileges of Separate Schools under the British North America Act are to be continued."[62] By highlighting this obvious contradiction, McGuigan also wanted to stir up some astonishment and consternation among the politicians, and he succeeded admirably in his self-appointed task.

For Leslie Frost, who became premier in 1949, another protracted battle over separate schools was the last item on his political agenda. Frost had too many Catholic friends, including Cardinal McGuigan and Father Priester, to chance offending the substantial Catholic community on the always sensitive issue of separate schools. Indeed, he torpedoed the Hope Commission before it even issued its *Report*. On 3 November 1949, Dana Porter, the minister of education, told a stunned crowd in St. Thomas of the government's plan to revamp the grading system. There would be four curriculum divisions: primary (Grades 1 to 3), junior (Grades 4 to 6), intermediate (Grades 7 to 10) and senior (Grades 11 to 13).[63] Porter also announced the abolition of the high school entrance examinations. (The failure of so many Catholic children to pass these exams, earlier in the century, had been a sore point for Bishop Fallon and one of the reasons why he supported Regulation 17. They were now gone from the political landscape.) At a meeting on 21 December 1949, Porter promised the executive of l'Association canadienne-française d'éducation d'Ontario that the new grading system would not interfere with existing separate school rights or limit bilingual education.[64]

Astonishment and consternation were also found within the ranks of the opposition Liberals. Their leader, Farquhar Oliver, contemptuously referred to the final report as "The Thing" and announced that his party had no intention of ever implementing a report that did not commend itself to the people of the province and that it should be tossed into the wastepaper basket. That it took five years to compose and cost approximately $600,000 did not bother Oliver (or Frost for that matter) as much as the thought of a nasty political backlash from Catholic voters.[65]

The lessons to be learned from the Hope Commission were many for separate school supporters. Chief among them was that there was still enough of an organized opposition to Catholic separate schools to make Catholics feel distrustful of the political process, but that same opposition, no matter how sophisticated it was, was losing its influence over the Conservative party and public opinion. They could do nothing to stop Frost from shelving the *Report*. Another lesson was that Catholics needed to know the history of their own schools and be prepared to defend them on the basis of historical facts. That is why the Minority Report's *Historical Sketch* (ghost written by a young Franklin Walker) was such a psychological breakthrough for the Catholic community. Sensing its importance, the ECEAO published and distributed 4,500 copies of the *Historical Sketch*. The third lesson was all about financing. Separate school rights were nothing without the money to turn them into practical realities for Catholic children. The official apologists and defenders of separate schools, all well intentioned and hardworking, would have to forge a brand new strategy on legislative grants, if separate schools were to have a fighting chance at survival.

What lesson should OSSTA have learned? It should have learned that the trustees as an association had virtually no independent identity, and thus no discernible voice of their own, within Catholic ranks during the life of the Hope Commission. Despite the bishops' claim regarding lay leadership, it was the ECEAO, the creature of the bishops, that held sway in the Ontario Catholic Education Council. Father Priester, Father Brennan and everyone else who was involved in the drafting and presentation of Brief 146 and the major supplementary to it did excellent work and should be commended. Yet, one wonders, a half century later, if Catholic education might have been better served if OSSTA had been allowed to play a more active role in defending the rights of separate schools, especially at that unfortunate public session of 28 November 1946. We will never know. But surely there must have been any number of trustees who wondered aloud, if only to each other, why they were marooned on the sidelines for the past five to six years. It was time for OSSTA to begin to move towards the centre stage of school politics and become a lead actor in the unfolding drama of Ontario's Catholic separate schools.

At Mid-Century, 1950-1960

At the 1957 annual general meeting of OSSTA, Father Joseph Finn, the chaplain, remarked: "We know that our headaches are many and that they seem to be getting worse all the time." It was a candid comment, but what did he mean by "headaches" and why were they "getting worse all the time"?[66] At mid century, following the near debacle of the Hope Commission, Catholic separate schools were approaching that point in their collective history where they might fail because they had succeeded so well. It was another version of the same paradox that had governed separate schools since their legal inception in 1841. Having refused to wither away in the nineteenth century, despite all the legal and financial disabilities they were required to endure, separate schools quietly soldiered on and grew steadily in number in all parts of the province as the twentieth century unfolded. How can one explain this phenomenon? One of the best answers is found in the fact that there was a wholeness to Catholic life and culture in Ontario that was particularly vivid in Catholic parishes during the 1950s, the zenith of the pre-Vatican II Catholic experience, and included in that wholeness was a strong loyalty to separate schools. They were indisputably one of the public pillars of Catholic identity. However, so goes the paradox, there might come a time — probably in the near future — when the separate school system would implode because its sources of revenue, defined in the nineteenth century, had become woefully inadequate to sustain an expanding enrolment, from kindergarten to Grade 10.

The statistics for separate schools bear this out.[67]

Enrolment
1950-51: 127,253 Catholic separate school students
1960-61: 282,651 Catholic separate school students
(This was an increase of 2.22 times. The increase for public elementary enrolment for the same time period was 1.33 times.)

Percentage of Total Elementary School Enrolment
1950-51: 20.7% of all elementary enrolment was Catholic separate school
1960-61: 25.0% of all elementary enrolment was Catholic separate school

Number of Schools
1950-51: 947 Catholic separate schools
1960-61: 1,356 Catholic separate schools
(This was a net increase of 409 schools. During the same period, public elementary schools experienced a net decrease of 203 schools, but this was mainly because the public school boards consolidated more one-room schools.)

Percentage of Total Number of Elementary Schools
1950-51: 13.8% of elementary schools were Catholic separate schools
1960-61: 19% of elementary schools were Catholic separate schools

Legislative Grants (per pupil)
Catholic separate schools: 1950 ($36.50); 1960 ($103.50)
Public elementary schools: 1950 ($44.95); 1960 ($92.90)

From these figures it is obvious that by 1960 the separate schools were receiving more than the public elementary schools in legislative grants per pupil (and would continue to do so). But one should not be led astray. In terms of total revenue (taxes plus grants) the separate schools remained far behind their public school counterparts, which enjoyed all to themselves the relative riches of corporation and utility taxes.

Revenue (per pupil)
Catholic separate schools: 1950 ($88.21); 1960 ($186.54)
Public elementary schools: 1950 ($130.59); 1960 ($279.40)

Despite overtaking the public elementary schools in legislative grants, in 1960, the Catholic separate schools were able to spend $90.65 less than the public elementary schools, which was more than double the shortfall of $42.38 in 1950. Nowhere was this discrepancy in expenditure more painful than in the expenditure on instruction. In 1950, Catholic separate schools were able to spend a mere 5.3% of their total expenditures on instruction, including the low salaries they paid religious teachers, while the public elementary schools spent 36.3%. Ten years later, the percentages had hardly improved. Catholic separate schools were able to spend 6.4% of their total expenditures on instruction, an increase of 1.1 percentage points, while public elementary schools spent 32.2%, a decrease of 4.1 percentage points.

The headache mentioned by Father Finn was knowing that there was an imminent crisis of huge proportions but not knowing how to address it. How, then, did OSSTA help its trustee members cope with the prospect of being in charge of a school system that could fail because it was too successful? Answers to that question can be found in OSSTA's *Minutes of the Annual General Meeting*, for the years 1952 and from 1955 to 1960 (*Minutes* for the years prior to 1952 and for 1953 and 1954 are missing).

The *Minutes* for these years reveal an association diligently working on many different levels. For one thing, OSSTA had membership problems that it had to solve before it could claim to truly represent Catholic school trustees. In 1950, there were more than 700 Catholic separate school boards; in 1960, the total number had not changed significantly; in 1962 there were more than 750 Catholic separate school boards. One must keep in mind that in any given year during the 1950s and early 1960s, upwards of 300 of these separate school boards were French-speaking and therefore belonged to l'Association des commissions des écoles bilingues d'Ontario.[68] So, membership in OSTTA was drawn from the remaining 400 to 450 English-speaking separate school boards. One must also remember that the majority of these boards, whether English- or French-speaking, represented small schools in rural school sections. A school section was a nineteenth-century geographical division based on the single-school model, which did not change (at least for public school boards) until 1964, when the township became the basic administrative unit. As a result, the sheer number of these small school boards, found all over the province, made OSSTA's recruiting efforts a practical nightmare. In 1952, only 67 out of 300 or so separate school boards were members. M. Palezcny, president of OSSTA in 1952, was surprised that so few boards had bothered to join:

> I realize it is difficult to operate a business on a voluntary basis and it takes money to operate a central office, with a paid secretary, or a part time secretary. Nevertheless gentlemen, in my travels up and down the province many Boards have told me that they have arrived in Toronto to go to the Department [of Education] for help, financially of

course, and they did not know where to go for advice. They wanted to see someone to confide in regarding their problems and to get some direction. With the growth of our school system this idea should be considered.[69]

It was the old conundrum: trustees needed OSSTA, and OSSTA was established to represent them, but trustees had to join the association if they ever hoped to improve their ability to safeguard the interests of their schools. Negotiating on one's own with the department of education was so out-of-date as to be laughable. For any separate school board to be acting alone, as late as 1952, was not only appalling and intolerable but also an unmistakable signal to the government and the education bureaucracy that separate schools were not serious about being part of the modern world.

The only way for OSSTA to be taken seriously was to fill its ranks with new members, unite them in a common purpose under its leadership and hire a permanent secretary or director to co-ordinate their political lobbying. During the remainder of the 1950s, the association's executive spent countless hours conducting recruitment drives and was generally successful. In 1954, OSSTA had 74 members; in 1955, there were 86 members; in 1956, there were 158 boards which had paid their dues; in 1957, that number had increased to 210 boards; and by 1958, OSSTA had 235 members. The more members there were, the more work OSSTA could do on their behalf and the sooner it could turn itself into a professional organization. It was Bishop Ryan of Hamilton who initially suggested, at the annual general meeting in 1957, that OSSTA hire a full-time employee to co-ordinate the association's business on a daily basis without having to sacrifice time to another job. Unfortunately, because of a lack of funds, it took until 1961 for OSSTA to hire Robert Laidlaw as its first executive director and to set up its first permanent office, at 102 Eglinton Avenue East in Toronto. Andrew Sheedy, OSSTA president in 1958, put it best when he told his fellow trustees the hard truth: "We must unite and we must organize if we are to solve our problems. We must put our own house in order. We can only do that by uniting and organizing and, in an endeavour to assist the government in solving our problems, by attempting to form some solution ourselves."[70]

To its steadily increasing membership, OSSTA continued to act at its annual general meetings as an information clearing house and an educational forum for trustees. As the separate school situation became more complex and threatening, the need for information and education, prepared and given by an assortment of experts, was all the more necessary. Among the topics that were presented, and usually discussed in lengthy question-and-answer periods, were the need to aggressively search for every piece of assessable property, changes to legislative grants, the implications of a local improvement tax, the three-mile limit, debentures, teacher shortages, public relations, curriculum, building costs for new schools and additions, payment for textbooks, choosing school sites, insurance for older buildings, differential in costs per pupil between a separate school board and a public board within the same city, urban and rural schools, paying competitive teacher salaries and, of course, dramatic yearly increase in enrolment that threatened to swamp the separate school system. Everything seemed to be in flux. Premier Leslie Frost told OSSTA delegates in 1957 that they would need all their wits, all their understanding and all their energy to cope, if only in some way, with all the problems facing education.[71]

In addition to the annual information sessions, OSSTA encouraged the formation of regional and diocesan trustee associations, as a means to keep the lines of communication open among trustees year round; it fostered the growth of sub-groups within the association, such as school business officials, board secretaries and the legal committee, each one of which conducted their own sessions; it maintained fruitful working relations with the Ontario School Trustees' Council, the Ontario Educational Association and OECTA; it published two books, *Manual for Separate School Trustees* and Francis G. Carter's *Judicial Decisions on Denominational Schools*; and, most significantly for the long term, it began to hold regular joint executive meetings with l'Association des commissions des écoles bilingues d'Ontario, starting in 1959. This partnership with the French-language trustees would develop into a united front for separate schools in the lead up to the 1962 brief on the foundation tax plan.

This brings us to the subject of presenting formal briefs or position papers to the government. This was a time-honoured way of lobbying and was familiar to separate school lobbyists. The Ontario bishops, the Catholic Taxpayers' Association, individual separate school boards, the Ontario Catholic Education Council, on behalf of the English Catholic Education Association of Ontario and 'l'Association canadienne-française d'éducation d'Ontario, all submitted briefs to the government at one time or another. Of interest to us is that during the 1950s, OSSTA took a more serious interest in the presentation of briefs. The association concentrated on the inequalities in both revenue and expenditure between the two publicly-funded systems of education, and on the extent to which Catholic separate schools were being pushed to the brink of extinction because of those inequalities. The association's executive quickly learned the advantages of actively supporting the briefs of the larger separate school boards and submitting briefs of their own, in conjunction with the French-language trustees, as the only practical way to make their voice heard and to have the government treat them as serious participants in the politics of public education. The more investigations OSSTA conducted, the better they understood the situation of their schools and the more adept they became at presenting their case to the government.

Let us look at some of their work. On 7 January 1957, John Middleweek, secretary of OSSTA, led a trustee delegation to see William J. Dunlop, minister of education. At this meeting, Middleweek presented a statistical table detailing the difference between the percentage of pupils in separate schools and the percentage of assessment to support those schools, in seven selected cities:

City	Percentage of Pupils	Percentage of Assessment
Brantford	16.60	7.148
Sarnia	25.00	9.00
Sudbury	9.01	3.002

Cornwall	60.00	30.00
Windsor	40.06	17.40
Hamilton	23.20	9.09
Toronto	19.36	4.31[72]

In early April 1957, the London Separate School Board delivered its own brief to the government. Supporting the London board were members of the Toronto Separate School Board and the OSSTA executive. Monsignor J.A. Feeney, chairman of the board, said:

> We had a wonderful presentation that morning, a wonderful means of telling the Department [of Education] what our difficulties and problems were. I think for one of the first times the Prime Minister [Premier Leslie Frost] began to realize that we are in serious difficulties, we are in trouble and without their help we cannot get out of trouble. He said, Well, we are going to do something for you in 1958. I told him I had been listening to that for twenty-one years, listening to promises, and we can't live any more on promises. He insisted something would be done in 1958. My answer to that was, it is much better to keep an organization going than trying to redraft a wreck a year later, it can't be done. He is really conscious that the large urban Boards especially are in serious difficulty and in trouble.[73]

What Frost gave separate schools in 1958 was uniform assessment for the purposes of the legislative grant. The Ontario School Trustees' Council, of which OSSTA was a member, had submitted a brief on that very subject in 1955. Three years later, the Frost government finally agreed to implement the council's suggestion.[74]

The major project for 1957-58 was another statistical report and brief. It was compiled and written by Robert Wilson of the Toronto Separate School Board, with the co-operation of both the English- and French-speaking trustee associations. Andrew Sheedy said:

The two organizations working together, with a common objective, produced a scientific and mathematical proof of the disparity in financial conditions between the School Boards of the province. The logical conclusions which follow from the comparative figures and percentages clearly indicated that many of our Catholic Schools were slowly but surely dying of malnutrition or lack of financial nourishment. There is nothing wrong with the patient, all that is needed is substantial and continued financial stimulation.[75]

For 1958-59, the two trustee associations compiled a survey of twenty-eight cities, "showing the relationship between public and separate schools with regard to assessments, taxes, number of children educated"[76] and incorporated the results in that year's brief. It concluded that the new granting structure had indeed helped smaller rural boards but that it had done nothing to relieve the dire financial straits of large urban boards within the separate school system.

The next brief, delivered in December 1959, was once more signed by the presidents of both trustee associations but limited its statistical report to separate schools in five large cities: Toronto, Hamilton, Ottawa, London and Windsor. It is worth quoting at some length:

The grant regulation dealing with urban municipalities of 90,000 or more was designed to assist the five large School Boards but does not do so in a manner considered satisfactory.

The Report of the Minister for 1958 shows a total provincial enrolment for elementary schools of 1,027,598 pupils of which 784,167 attend Public Schools and 243,431 attend Separate Schools . . . 212,460 pupils or 20.7% of the total are registered in the schools of these five cities, and of this number 64,704 or 30.5% are attending Separate Schools.

The Government of Ontario has been noted for promoting legislation affording equality of treatment to all its people regardless of race, colour or creed. Financial considerations therefore should not be a factor in preventing the pupils enrolled in the Separate Schools of the five major cities from receiving educational opportunities equal to those enjoyed by public school pupils in the same five cities.

The enrolment in the Public Schools in these five cities has, over a period of four years, from 1955 to 1958, increased by 12,510 (an increase of 9%) and in the Separate Schools by 12,045 (an increase of 23%). The number of classrooms in the case of the Public Schools has grown from 3,864 in 1955, to 4,221 in 1958, or an increase of 358; and in the case of the Separate Schools, from 1,504 to 1,848 or an increase of 344 during the same period.

For the education of the 12,510 additional pupils referred to above, the Public Schools received from direct municipal taxation an amount of $9,197,387, and for the education of their additional 12,045 pupils the Separate Schools received from the same source only $1,173,017. It is therefore clear that additional relief should be given to the Separate School Boards in the five larger Ontario Municipalities . . .

The financial plight of Separate Schools is of course due to the fact that they benefit so little from Corporation taxes. In the case of the five larger Cities, 97% of the commercial-industrial assessment, or $1,593,692,918, is applied in favour of Public Schools and only 3%, or $50,243,697, in favour of Separate Schools . . .

By reason of corporation taxes available to them, the public School Boards in the large cities have been able to spend an additional $44.65 per pupil from 1955 to 1958 whereas Separate School Boards in the same period have been limited to an increase of only $5.58 . . . [77]

The two trustee associations were persistent. In a brief dated 31 July 1961, they pointed out that separate school boards had no money for supervisory staff and specialists in the classroom and barely enough money to maintain minimum-size administrative staffs. Also, they were forced to pay teacher salaries well below those paid to public school teachers. Nowhere was this more embarrassingly true than in the city schools, where the average salary in 1960 for separate school teachers was $3,552 and for public school teachers was $5,455, a difference of nearly $2,000. In the whole province, in 1960, there was only one separate school teacher who earned in excess of $6,250. In the public elementary system, many teachers earned this amount or even more and some earned as much as $12,650.[78]

However, for all their pleading and proofs, OSSTA and ACEBO failed to convince the Conservative government of the severity of the financial crisis then gripping separate schools. All discussion regarding corporation taxes, no matter how reasonable and factual, fell on deaf ears. Tinkering with the structure of the legislative grants was obviously no solution. Modest changes to it, although always applauded and gratefully accepted, produced only modest outcomes. It was the whole granting structure itself that had to be overhauled and based on the concept of need. As long as need was left out of the calculations, separate schools would be perennial beggars in a land of plenty. They were rich in students, having registered twice as many (proportionately) during the past ten years as the public school system, but paralyzed by poverty when it came to providing the calibre of schools their children deserved.

Underscoring the kind of frustration that Catholic lobbyists faced when dealing with the government on separate school issues was a 29 August 1961 meeting arranged by Father Priester at the Catholic Education Office. At that meeting were three members of the hierarchy, Archbishop Philip Pocock, Bishop Joseph F. Ryan and Bishop Thomas J. McCarthy, along with Robert Wilson, statistician of the MSSB, John Middleweek of the MSSB and OSSTA, Thomas Meyer of the Hamilton Separate School Board and, of course, Father Priester of ECEAO. On the government's side was Premier Leslie Frost and his aides. The meeting was called to discuss the effect of the application of the special per pupil grant known as the Residential and Farm Act Assistance Grant and to request that the government give secondary school grants to Grades 9 and 10 of separate schools.

During the discussion on the Residential and Farm Act Assistance Grant, it became clear to the Catholic contingent that Frost was unaware of the enormous difference between separate schools and public schools in the amount of assessment available to them. On the subject of secondary grants to Grades 9 and 10, the premier was armed with plenty of technical objections and did not hesitate to give them.[79]

Such was the state of affairs in Catholic separate schools, as understood by OSSTA, on the eve of the introduction of the Ontario Foundation Tax Plan. It was time for the association to assume the mantle of leadership and to become the chief negotiator for separate schools.

The Three-Mile Limit, 1959-1963

An interesting sidebar in the history of separate schools in the lead up to the introduction of the Ontario Tax Foundation Plan in 1964, was the search for a practical resolution to the problem of the three-mile limit, as it applied to union separate schools in rural areas. Section 19 of the 1863 Scott Act states: "No person shall be deemed a supporter of any Separate School unless he resides within three miles (in a direct line) of the site of the School House."[80] Although intended to protect separate school rights, by defining an administrative unit in terms of a three-mile radius with the school as its centre, and calling the area a school section, Section 19 effectively hobbled the operation of rural separate school boards in three significant ways.[81] One, the three trustees had to build a schoolhouse prior to applying the direct line from it that would determine the three-mile radius and thus the school district. Two, all those children enrolled in a separate school outside the three-mile radius became a financial burden to the separate school board, which educated them but could not tax their parents for doing so. This was often the fate of small town school boards. Their schools were often the only Catholic schools for many miles around and consequently attracted students from well beyond the three-mile limit. Father Joseph Finn remembered the story of Mr. and Mrs. Smith of St. Mary's parish in Simcoe. Although they lived outside the three-mile limit, they sent their two children to the separate school in Simcoe. Once a year, Mrs. Smith would give the parish priest ten dollars for the tuition of her children. The priest duly handed over the money to the trustees, who recorded it in the board's financial books as a voluntary subscription in lieu of taxation.[82] This type of payment had become a widespread practice among Catholics unable to direct their taxes to the separate schools, but in no way did it compensate for the loss of tax revenue. Three, union separate school sections were another headache. A union separate school section was defined as the union of two or more school sections as "one school for all Roman Catholic separate school purposes" under the management of three trustees. However, the schoolhouses in the sections under union had to remain in operation for the parents of the children attending them to be recognized as separate school supporters. For example, if one school in a two-school union (the usual combination) were to close for any reason, the local municipality would refuse to continue to assess the parents of the children of the now closed school as separate school supporters.

A legal challenge to this interpretation of the three-mile limit was begun in 1959. That year the trustees of the Roman Catholic Union Separate Schools, for the United Section Number 6 in the Township of Middleton and Number 22 in the Township of North Walsingham, decided to close the school in Middleton and bus its twenty-three pupils to the school in North Walsingham. The Middleton school was a one-room school with one teacher in charge of all eight grades. It was a relic from another era and hardly a desirable place to send one's children. The North Walsingham school had four classrooms with two grades to each classroom and was even enlarged in anticipation of the arrival of the Middleton students. It was a significant improvement over the Middleton school, a fact no one denied. But as soon as the Middleton school was closed, the Township of Middleton assessed the separate school supporters as public school supporters because they resided outside the three-mile limit of the North Walsingham school.

The school board — Robert Causyn, Joe DeVos and Cyrile DeWale — decided to challenge the township in court and took the case all the way to the Supreme Court of Canada, which handed down its ruling on 15 December 1961. The major plaintiffs were Andre and Yvonne Vandekerckhove, separate school ratepayers from Middleton whose children were directly affected by the township decision. They were represented in front of the Supreme Court by the Hon. Arthur M. LeBel and Francis G. Carter, of OSSTA.

The ruling was unanimous and in favour of the Vandekerckhoves. The justices based their decision on a practical interpretation of the relationship between sections 33 and 57 of "The Separate Schools Act" (*Revised Statues of Ontario*, 1950, c. 356). Here are the two sections:

33. (1) The majority of the supporters of each of the separate schools situate in two or more public school sections, whether in the same or in adjoining municipalities, at a public meeting duly called by the board of each separate school may form a union separate school of which union the trustees shall give notice within 15 days to the clerk or clerks of the municipality or municipalities and to the Minister, and every union separate school thus formed shall be deemed one school for all Roman Catholic separate school purposes, and shall every year thereafter be represented by three trustees to be elected by the supporters of the union separate school as provided by section 26.

(2) The trustees shall be a body corporate under the name of "The Board of Trustees of the Roman Catholic Union Separate School for the United Sections number .... in the ...."

57. Subject to the other provisions of this Part, no person shall be deemed a supporter of a separate school unless he resides within three miles in a direct line of the site of the schoolhouse.

Did section 57 trump section 33? That was the key question. The justices did not think so. Mr. Justice Cartwright delivered the judgment for the court. The appellants referred to are the Vandekerckhoves:

It is not questioned that the appellants have all the qualifications and have taken all the steps necessary to entitle them to be assessed as Roman Catholic Separate School supporters, unless they are prevented from being so dealt with by the terms of section 57. The prohibition in that section is expressly made subject to the other provisions of the Part in which it is found. If, therefore, as counsel for the appellants contends, the terms of section 33 are effective to give the appellants the right to be assessed as separate school supporters that right will not be destroyed by the terms of section 57.

Following the union which took place in 1944, the schools in Middleton and in North Walsingham became in the eyes of the law one school, not merely, as was suggested for argument, for purposes of administration, but in the words of sub-section (1) of section 33 "for all Roman Catholic separate school purposes." Once that happened, if the Board in the interests of efficiency decided to transport the pupils who were in attendance at one of the school-houses forming part of the one school resulting from the union to the other school-house they were in our opinion free to do so. It would be a startling result if on doing this they must suffer the loss of the revenue from the assessment of the parents of the children so transported. Such a construction would fail to give effect to the word "all" which is in bold face above. This result, can, and in our opinion, should be avoided by limiting the effect of section 57 to disabling from being a separate school supporter a person whose residence is not within three miles of the site of either of the two school-houses which on the union became component parts of one school, regardless of whether both or one only of the school-houses continues to be used.[83]

The Supreme Court handed down a common sense judgment. It did not abolish the three-mile limit. Rather, it ruled that a literal interpretation of the limit did not apply when a union separate school closes one of its schools for reasons of efficiency. In essence, the three-mile limit was an anachronism at a time when more and more rural students were being bused to centrally located schools.

The magazine *Municipal World* applauded the Supreme Court's decision and told its readers that the court had opened "the way for the formation of Roman Catholic separate schools which could operate in the same manner and over as large an area as the township area schools now do in the public school system."[84] In a bold move, it called upon the Ontario legislature to repeal the three-mile limit, which it described as a fictitious and outmoded barrier that hampered the growth of a legally-instituted, publicly-funded school system.

The legislature must have been listening because it passed a series of important amendments to the Separate Schools Act, including a lengthy one on the three-mile limit. Commonly known as Bill 97, the changes became law on 26 April 1963.[85] In an editorial, the *Catholic Trustee* described the amendment concerning the three-mile limit:

> The amendment is an important one. Section 57 — the three-mile limit section — has been repealed and in its place a lengthy section has been substituted. While the new section retains the measurement of three miles to determine the limits of a separate school zone, it need no longer be measured from a school house or site, but from a parcel of land approved by the supporters for the purpose of determining a centre. This means that a separate school board may now have a territory under its authority even though it owns neither a school nor a site. This amendment will permit the establishment of central schools for separate school supporters in rural areas without the necessity of building several satellite schools which were opened only to be closed. The retention of a three-mile diameter under this new circumstance will permit an orderly growth of the separate school system without harming the general public school system.[86]

The issue for separate schools in 1963 had been centralized

accommodation for students. Although the government did not abolish the three-mile limit, it did replace the phrase "rural school section" with "separate school zone," a change that pointed in the direction of the inevitability of even larger and more functional administrative units. Moreover, even if the 1964 amendment to the Public Schools Act, which mandated the township as the basic administrative unit (it had been voluntary since 1925), was not replicated in any amendment to the Separate Schools Act, it was only a matter of time and common sense that what was good and necessary for public school boards should be applied to separate school boards.[87] We will examine all this in greater depth in a later section of this chapter.

The point to be underlined here is the interconnectedness of change. The 1963 modification in the three-mile limit, and the 1964 introduction of the township as the basic school area (for public schools) were two of the building blocks on which the government made its decision to designate the county as the basic administrative unit for all school boards. This brought about a drastic reduction in the number of school boards, the disappearance of the one-room schoolhouse and the three-member board of trustees, a building boom in new centralized schools and an increase in the number of school buses to transport the students to them. Lastly, the evolution in the size of administrative units was a necessary condition for the proper and long-term application of the Ontario Tax Foundation Plan.

Then there is the interconnectedness of effort to bring about change. The successful challenge to the traditional interpretation of the three-mile limit, in regards to union separate schools, was the result of a concerted effort on the part of ratepayers, trustees and good lawyers, one of whom was a high profile member of OSSTA. Except for Father L. Langan, the local parish priest, who acted as moral support, there were no priests or bishops involved in the pursuit of the case up to the Supreme Court. In a way, the story of the challenge to the three-mile limit was a harbinger of things to come for OSSTA, which early on accepted and exploited the interconnectedness of change (larger administrative units, centralized schools and the Ontario Foundation Tax Plan) and eventually took this interconnectedness to its logical conclusion by advocating completion of the separate school system.

The Ontario Foundation Tax Plan, 1964

The Ontario Foundation Tax Plan saved separate schools from financial collapse. Assuming the principle of equality of opportunity in education for all Ontario children, the foundation tax plan gradually established financial equity at the elementary school level, between the public and separate school boards, regardless of geographical location or local tax base, in order to maintain a province-wide minimum standard of education. No financial equity, no equality of opportunity.

In its simplest terms, the foundation tax plan, as devised and fine-tuned by the government in the 1960s, achieved financial equity by a system of grants that were allocated to individual school boards on a pro-rata basis — in inverse ratio to local assessment. Poor school boards received larger grants than rich boards, the words "poor" and "rich" being terms relative to a board's ability to raise sufficient funds by means of local taxes on residences, farms, businesses and corporations. The political genius of the foundation tax plan was that it was never a question of separate schools "stealing" money from the public schools, as the charge went during the 1930s, and that it was also a significant benefit to small rural public boards. The foundation tax plan did not take local tax money away from the public schools and redistribute it to the separate schools but devised a non-political formula for the distribution of grants that would help all boards make equality of opportunity a concrete reality for every child in every Ontario classroom. That separate schools as a group were the major beneficiaries of the plan said a great deal about the shortcomings of the old system of legislative grants and nothing about special privileges for Catholic ratepayers.

The immediate and long-term effect on the financial welfare of Catholic separate schools and their ability to offer a much higher quality of education was nothing short of revolutionary. The Ontario Foundation Tax Plan, an idea more than six decades old and originally American, freed separate schools from the suffocating financial straitjacket of the nineteenth century and allowed them to cope with the staggering increase in enrolment as a result of the post-war baby boom and unprecedented immigration. Moreover, as time passed, the financial equity achieved by the separate elementary schools came full circle as a core argument in favour of enlarging the concept of equal opportunity in education to include the completion of the separate school system.

There were two major streams of political and bureaucratic activity that gave birth to the foundation tax plan. These streams were independent of one another but eventually merged to form a single current of political thought and action on a foundation tax plan that would apply to all boards but would not be a threat to the public school system. The Catholic educational establishment was responsible for one stream of activity, which took shape in two related but separate briefs to the government, one written by the bishops and the other by the two trustee associations. Premier John Robarts and Bill Davis, the newly-appointed minister of education, stood at the head of the second stream. To them we owe recognition for having the practical wisdom to accept the idea of a foundation tax plan and the political élan to implement it.

****

It took an editorial writer for the *Peterborough Examiner* to describe the plight of separate schools, in 1962, in a way so succinct and clear as to make it obvious to everyone. Separate school supporters were cornered: "they have an elementary system, partly paid for, a quasi-secondary system [Grades 9 and 10] which is supported at elementary rates and a high school system which is carried by church supporters entirely. If this system is not to atrophy, the Roman Catholic Church must press for a complete system largely supported by the general taxpayer."[88] There was the rub. Catholic schools in Ontario were of three kinds. The first kind, the elementary grades, were in the system but on life-support; the second kind, grades nine and ten, was half way in and on an even more tenuous life-support; the third kind, grades eleven to thirteen, was not in the system and did not even exist in the minds of education bureaucrats in Queen's Park. The whole Catholic education edifice might very well collapse if a radical renovation in financing did not occur, if not to the whole edifice, at least to its foundation, which was the elementary panel, kindergarten to Grade 10. From the Catholic point of view, the ideal was full-funding for a complete system of Catholic separate schools. The more realistic approach, in 1962, was to have the government guarantee separate school boards financial equity with their public school counterparts that left untouched public school money.

The above quote from the *Peterborough Examiner* was part of a lengthy and intelligent response to the bishops' brief of 27 October 1962. The brief, 4,000 words in length, was a collaborative effort.[89] Bishop Gerald Emmett Carter of London was the principal author, Francis G. Carter of OSSTA wrote the section on the legal history of the public nature of separate schools and Robert Wilson, statistician for the Metropolitan Separate School Board, provided the statistics on the significant gap in expenditure per pupil between the separate and public boards, for the years 1940 and 1960.

The main strength of the bishop's brief was twofold: its assertion that financial equity was a necessary condition of equal opportunity of education, a claim that gained political currency in the months following the brief, and its dire warning that the financial inequality long suffered by separate schools was pushing these schools to the brink of insolvency. "There can be no question of our desire to meet the highest conceivable standards. Our financial ability to do so may soon be called into question if we do not receive financial assistance in the same proportion as that given to the secular public schools."[90] The central weakness of the brief was its failure to provide a politically practical solution to the constant problem of financial inequality. Instead, the bishops asked the government to give separate school boards more influence over the curriculum and textbook selection; to explore the possibility of Catholic teachers' colleges; to apportion to separate schools their fair share of corporation taxes; and to enact fundamental changes in policy (and attitudes) towards Catholic secondary education. The bishops also complained about the unfair level of funding for Grades 9 and 10, which were treated as elementary grades in the separate schools but as secondary grades in the public schools, and the inability of separate schools to participate in the federal government's Technical and Vocational Training Assistance Act (1960).

Their brief was doomed regarding any of these specific items. They looked too much like demands (even if they were not) and sounded too much like old-style rhetoric. Curiously, though, the brief did not die. It had legs and plenty of running room in political and press circles. The bishops were bound to be taken seriously, because the public still listened to Catholic bishops in the public square, and they *were* taken seriously — by Premier Robarts, Davis, his education minister, and members of the legislative assembly, each of whom had received a copy of the brief, by religious leaders of all stripes and by every daily newspaper in the province.

The bishops' brief had its critics. Rt. Rev. Ross. K. Cameron, moderator of the Presbyterian Church in Canada, was one of them. He was anything but moderate in his criticism. He told the press that tax-supported separate schools were a vicious system and that the bishops' plans for them would make an already vicious system even more vicious. "I have always taken a stand that separate schools drive a wedge between children," he was quoted as saying. "Separate high schools would drive the wedge in further."[91] A United Church commission on church and state in education unequivocally stated that the changes proposed by the bishops could not be justified either in law or in the public interest and were a direct threat to Ontario's public school system.[92] Then there was this reaction from the Public School Trustees' Association of Ontario:

1. No tax-supported Roman Catholic separate high schools under any conditions or in any guise
2. No tax-supported Roman Catholic separate teachers' colleges under any conditions
3. No control by the Roman Catholic Church of the curriculum of any tax-supported schools, elementary or secondary

4. No selection by the Roman Catholic Church of textbooks used in any tax-supported schools, elementary or secondary

5. No federal or provincial funds for the building or operation of Roman Catholic separate technical schools and colleges.[93]

The public school trustees denounced every tenet of the bishops' brief but left untouched its principal selling point, that financial equity made possible equality of opportunity. Such an omission may seem rather odd, but the public school trustees were well aware of something else. They were entitled to bash away at the bishops' brief, but it would have been foolhardy of them to attack the sympathy that many high-profile people showed for the financial plight of separate schools as they struggled to cope with rising enrolments. Donald C. MacDonald, the NDP leader, confirmed his party's 1961 platform on separate schools when he stated that he was in "basic agreement" with the bishops' pleas.[94] (The Liberals under John Wintermeyer, a Catholic, would take a little more arm-twisting to fall into line.) Meanwhile, on the media front, the *Toronto Daily Star* told its readers that "there is a public responsibility to ensure that Catholic children in their elementary schools can get as good an education as public school children do in theirs"[95] and that "no child in this Province should be denied the opportunity to an equal education because of the religious beliefs of his parents."[96] John Bassett's *Toronto Telegram*, once a veritable bulwark of anti-Catholic hostility, editorialized that "as there are two sets of schools within our educational system, they should be treated as equals,"[97] and that "Above all other issues is the principle of equality of educational opportunity. The Separate Schools exist as of right. Separate school students should have access, as of right, to equitable instruction, school plant and equipment. And the only way to ensure this is to give them an equitable share of public funds."[98] How attitudes had changed at the *Telegram* since the days when it led the charge against the Catholic Taxpayers' Association.

If the bishops' brief accomplished anything, it revealed the existence of a broad-based sympathetic understanding of the concepts of equal opportunity and financial equity and the intimate relationship between the two, and of the very real crisis then affecting separate schools. The brief also prepared the way for the Ontario Separate School Trustees' Association and l'Association des commissions des écoles bilingues d'Ontario, to propose a foundation tax plan as the only way to undo the Gordian knot of financial inequality. This was a fortuitous if unintended turn of events.[99]

****

There is evidence that the trustees had some basic knowledge of the concept of the foundation tax plan — legislative grants based on an inverse ratio to local assessment — in the lead-up to their historic brief of December 1962. However, one is unsure if any of them, prior to the official adoption of the plan as trustee policy, appreciated its radical significance or how it might be applied in the real world of dollars and cents. For example, the minutes of a meeting of the OSSTA executive and directors in North Bay, 17-18 November 1961, show that P.J. Enright moved and Andrew Sheedy seconded that "Page 8 of the BRIEF be changed in direct inverse ratio in all the tables, doubled, tripled and quadrupled, whatever the case may be and that it be amended so that the per-pupil grant be increased proportionately to the assessment; this to be extended to all Boards, both Urban and Rural."[100] The all-important phrase "direct inverse ratio" certainly appears, and for the first time in OSSTA's records, but the reference to "doubled, tripled and quadrupled" is confusing since such multiples are totally arbitrary. The brief referred to might have been the one dated July 1961, some statistics of which Dr. R.W.B. Jackson of the department of education demanded be changed. And the revised brief might have been the one of 18 December 1961, which was mentioned in the *Catholic Trustee*.[101] It is possible that the trustees had been inspired by the November 1961 decision of the 1,000 delegates attending the Ontario Conference on Education to support a foundation tax plan for Ontario.[102] Or, having been informed of the success of a similar plan in Alberta, they may have (rightly) concluded that such a plan would also work in Ontario.[103] At a 27 September 1962 meeting of the Ontario Catholic Education Council,

Roland Bériault, the administrator of ACEBO, proposed that the Council study the foundation tax plan because it seemed acceptable to both Catholics and Protestants. To this proposal Archbishop Pocock replied that Premier Roberts felt that there was a constitutional barrier to the implementation of such plan in Ontario.[104] We do not know if the Council proceeded to investigate the plan — it is likely that nothing happened since the bishops would soon be off to another session of the Second Vatican Council — but we do know that Robarts changed his mind about the plan's constitutionality.

The pace of progress quickened when Robert Laidlaw, executive director of OSSTA, was approached by Carl Matthews, a Jesuit scholastic, to discuss the political and practical merits of adopting the foundation tax plan as the central plank in the trustees' next brief to the government, the one that was to complement the bishops' brief.[105] Laidlaw invited Matthews to make a presentation on the plan to a meeting of the English and French trustee associations scheduled for 20 November 1962, at the Lord Simcoe Hotel in Toronto.[106] Supported by John Wintermeyer, leader of the Liberal Opposition, and Donald C. MacDonald, leader of the NDP, Matthews showed a solid understanding of school finances and the history of foundation tax plans. He had little trouble convincing the trustees of the many merits of a foundation tax plan and of the fact that their public promotion of such a plan would be an astute political move on behalf of Catholic ratepayers. Circumstances were in their favour, a rare moment indeed. The government was actively considering the implementation of a foundation tax plan; the Liberals and the NDP were in favour of it; the Ontario Conference on Education (1961) and the Canadian Conference on Education (1962) had endorsed the concept;[107] therefore, it only made sense for Catholic separate school trustees to publicly retire their traditional claim to a just share of corporation taxes in favour of a plan that offered the best means to save their schools from certain collapse. Lastly, the request for a foundation tax plan should be the sole petition of the trustees' brief to the government.[108] Roland Bériault moved that the executives of both OSSTA and ACEBO accept Matthews' proposal. All were in agreement, and all were prepared to sell it to their board members.

Francis G. Carter, that veteran of separate school battles, wrote the lengthy introduction, and Matthews was responsible for the section on the foundation tax plan.

Dated 8 December 1962, the brief's essential argument was reduced to two propositions:

> 1. The Department of Education would determine in dollars and cents the total amount it costs to educate adequately a child in the schools of this Province;
> 2. This cost would be met in the following manner:
>   (a) by a uniform mill rate levied province-wide based on an equalized municipal assessment;
>   (b) by legislative grants.
> The plan presupposes equalized assessment throughout the Province.[109]

An article in the *Catholic Trustee* expanded on these two points:

> Every ratepayer, be he urban or rural, a corporation or an individual, a Public School supporter or a Separate School supporter, pays the same mill rate on his equalized assessment. Provincial grants then meet the difference between the amount thus raised locally and the amount required to meet the per pupil cost of education as presently provided by the better Public School Boards. [The intent would be to level up, not down.] If current trends continue, this foundation program level would regularly have to be revised upward. Because of the special needs of municipalities of varying sizes, perhaps there would be more than one recognized cost per pupil. In any event, trustees would have the same powers and responsibilities as at present. A poorer Board might have twice as much money to spend, and to spend wisely.
>
> The beauty of the plan is that general Public Schools and Separate Public Schools within a particular municipality would be considered on a par for all essential educational services and facilities from kindergarten to the end of grade ten.[110]

****

Premier John Robarts introduced the Ontario Foundation Tax Plan in the legislature, on 21 February 1963. He was unequivocal in his statement that the intention of the plan was to provide equality of opportunity in education for all the young people of Ontario.[111] No one could argue with him on that score without casting himself in the role of a political dinosaur. A full-scale debate on the plan took place on 26 March 1963.[112] When Bill Davis took the floor of the legislature, almost a year later, on 27 January 1964, to announce that regulations governing the grants would be ready for the fiscal year 1964-65, he began his speech by reiterating the objectives of the Ontario Foundation Tax Plan. They were "firstly—to provide equality of educational opportunity for every young person throughout the province, regardless of the wealth of the community in which he or she may live. Secondly—to ensure that the ever increasing costs of elementary and secondary school education do not bear too heavily upon the home owner and other municipal taxpayers of the province."[113]

The plan was divided into three types of grants: basic tax relief grants, special or stimulation grants and equalization grants. The equalization grants were then divided into three sections: corporation tax adjustment, which was amended in 1967; recognized extraordinary expenditures, such as debt charges, capital outlays and transportation; and the school tax equalization grant, which was the basic foundation grant and the one with the most immediate effect on the financial fortunes of separate schools:

> The principle of the basic equalization grant was that each board would be guaranteed sufficient revenue to meet a satisfactory level in terms of recognized operating costs. The equalizing grant would vary according to the wealth of the board. No board was to be forced to levy in accordance with the maximum number of mills specified, or to pay any amount into a provincial equalization fund. In fact, it could reduce taxes if it so desired, and was willing to bear the

405

consequences. From the point of view of the provincial taxpayer, the plan provided safeguards in that the total amount of aid the province wished to provide was fully controlled.[114]

The Ontario Foundation Tax Plan was an eighteen-month wonder for separate schools. In 1963, the per-pupil revenue of separate elementary schools was $206, of which $128 was in grants and $78 in taxes, leaving a deficiency of $83 when compared to the per-pupil revenue of public elementary schools In 1964, the per-pupil revenue was $265, of which $189 was in grants and $76 in taxes, leaving a deficiency of $70. And the wonder continued unabated. In 1967, the per-pupil revenue was $395, of which $299 was in grants and $96 in taxes, leaving a deficiency of $51. Financial equity had yet to be achieved, and it would only be achieved when the deficiency was zero, but the quick climb in revenue per pupil, largely generated by the staggering increase in grant money, was almost too good to be true for separate school supporters and their children.[115] Poverty was no longer their constant companion. And it happened without a tremor of public controversy.

Another immediate godsend of the plan, one that might not have been foreseen by OSSTA, was the tremendous increase in enrolment for Grades 9 and 10, as more and more boards opened up these grades in their schools. The new funding, even if it was still at elementary levels, made this possible and provided new hope that soon the separate school system would be extended upward and put on a par with public secondary education. Despite Premier Robarts's warning that the Ontario Foundation Tax Plan had nothing to do with extension, the successful application of the plan was a powerful practical reason for ending the unnatural truncation of the separate school system. A new era had begun. The nineteenth century had been laid to rest.

The executives and directors of OSSTA and ACEBO spent a great deal of their time during the remainder of the 1960s and early 1970s working hard to improve the grant regulations, so that actual financial equity between public and separate elementary school boards would finally be achieved. In October 1964, OSSTA appointed a Tax Foundation Plan Committee. It was comprised of Chris Asseff, H. Crowley, O. Cook and K. Lajambe. They were to investigate the effects of the Ontario Foundation Tax Plan on all separate school boards, no easy task when one considers that there were still hundreds of boards in 1964, and to incorporate the results of their findings in the next joint brief of OSSTA and ACEBO to the minister of education.[116] The board of directors also instructed this committee to conduct a province-wide survey "to determine future teacher requirements, teacher qualifications, the number of non-Catholic teachers in their employ, along with any further information they deemed desirable in maintaining an adequate supply of teachers."[117] Of special concern to the committee was the Corporation Tax Adjustment Grant, an element of the Ontario Foundation Tax Plan that dealt with assessment in urban areas. It was designed "to give the equivalent to what would come to each Board [public and separate in any given community] were the total corporate assessment in the community divided in the same proportion as the Separate School Board's residential and farm assessment for the community."[118] To monitor the effects of the Corporation Tax Adjustment Grant (and to study the entire financial system of the separate schools in the province), the OSSTA directors appointed a Special Advisory Committee on School Financing. Members of this committee included Dr. Joe Fyfe, Father Carl Matthews, Peter Meneguzzi, Don Lefebre and Chris Asseff.[119] At a meeting on 19 May 1965, the committee decided that it would be more beneficial to separate schools if the Corporation Tax Adjustment Grant were based on Average Daily Attendance instead of residential assessment, and that the two trustee associations should press the government for this change in the granting regulations.[120]

One of the trustees' best briefs on the Ontario Foundation Tax Plan was dated October 1966.[121] Many others in a similar vein were to follow.[122] Each of these briefs demonstrated a professional grasp of the many difficulties involved in refining what evolved into an ever more complex system of regulations and the mathematical formulae that accompanied them. Dr. Joseph W. Fyfe, a Sudbury physician, trustee, and president of OSSTA from 1964 to 1965, was the trustees' resident financial expert for more than twenty years and often dealt one-on-one with the minister of education. The government also recognized his expertise by appointing him to the Commission on the Reform of Property Taxation in Ontario (Report 1977) and to the Commission on the Financing of Elementary and Secondary Education in Ontario (Report 1985). Fyfe's diligent and untiring work, and the work of many others who assisted him, such as the Ontario Separate School Business Officials' Association, eventually produced the desired result. The December 1977 issue of the *Catholic Trustee* happily reported that "After generations of struggle, separate school supporters in Ontario now see their Catholic elementary schools on a near-equal financial footing with the public schools."[123]

****

In accepting the foundation tax plan, and spending years to fine-tune it, the two trustee associations showed that they were the true and rightful heirs to the leadership of separate school politics in Ontario. Their 8 December 1962 brief was a defining moment in the history of Catholic school trusteeship, and their follow-up briefs on the Ontario Foundation Tax Plan proved the wisdom of the Ontario bishops when they gave the trustees the task of finding practical solutions to the financial problems of separate schools.

One important development of this era was that no longer would the Ontario Separate School Trustees' Association have to work in the shadows of the English Catholic Educational Association of Ontario. The ECEAO would continue to function for some years, but its role as an effective lobbyist for Catholic separate schools was greatly diminished.

The Hall-Dennis Committee, 1965-1968

An order-in-council of 10 June 1965 set up the Provincial Committee on Aims and Objectives of Education in the Schools of Ontario, more commonly known as the Hall-Dennis Committee. Hall was Mr. Justice Emmett Hall of the Supreme Court of Canada. A prominent Catholic, he had been chairman of the St. Paul's Separate School District in Saskatoon and then chairman of the Royal Commission on Health Services. Hall was a highly respected and recognizable figure on the public stage whose presence alone imparted to the Committee's work and its findings an authority and respectability it could not have achieved otherwise. There is some suggestion that he accepted the chairmanship of the Committee, against the advice of many people, because he regarded it as "an historic opportunity to gain full tax support for Catholic secondary schools in Ontario."[124] If so, the Committee's recommendations on separate schools must have been a disappointment to him. Dennis was Lloyd A. Dennis. He was a Second World War paratrooper, a former school principal in Toronto and an education bureaucrat when he joined the Committee in 1966, on the suggestion of Mr. Justice Hall. Dennis became the Committee's co-chairman, secretary and research director. He worked well with Hall, assuming the lion's share of the daily workload as it became more onerous over time and because Hall was extraordinarily busy at the Supreme Court in Ottawa.[125] Dennis was the Committee's leading cheerleader during the course of its investigations as well as its most vocal defender on the publication of its report.

Of the Committee's twenty-four members, six were Catholic, including Justice Hall. They were Dr. J.F. Leddy, president of the University of Windsor and a friend of Justice Hall; E.J. Brisbois, a member of the board of directors of OSSTA, president of ECEAO and chairman of the management committee of the Metropolitan Separate School Board; Marcel P. Parent, a former trustee of the Ottawa Separate School Board and former chairman of the board of the Collegiate Institute of Ottawa; Sister Alice Marie, CSJ, supervising principal of the London Separate School Board and a member of the board of directors of OECTA and of the curriculum study committee of the Ontario Teachers' Federation; and Leopold Seguin, a teacher at St. Albert School in Cornwall and a member of l'Association des enseignments Franco-Ontariens. There had actually been one other Catholic member of the Committee. She was Sister Stanislaus, supervising principal for the Peterborough Separate School Board, who had died in 1965.

The Committee sat for three years, received 112 briefs and produced a coffee-table-type report called *Living and Learning* that prompted a chorus of praise from progressive politicians and the press and some literary, historical and pedagogical criticism.[126] The Committee's terms of reference, set forth in the order-in-council, were quite broad and thus open to many different avenues of exploration and emphasis:

–to identify the needs of the child as a person and as a member of society

–to set forth the aims of education for the educational system of the Province

–to outline objectives of the curriculum for children in the age groups presently designated as Kindergarten, Primary and Junior Divisions

–to propose means by which these aims and objectives may be achieved

–to submit a report for the consideration of the minister of Education[127]

A 14 April 1966 statement, issued by the department of education, made it clear that the Committee would be investigating the different ways of learning and mapping out an educational program for the future. That program would be flexible, diverse and continuous, and the aims and objectives agreed to by the Committee had to apply to the whole school system.[128] *Living and Learning* was "devoted to issues, ideals, values, and opinions about how learning should be promoted, along with many specific suggestions for the improvement of the school system."[129]

The Hall-Dennis Committee interests us not because of any pedagogical innovations it may have proposed for the classrooms of the province, but because of its treatment of separate schools, which was both positive and negative. The Hope Commission had regarded separate schools as a burden to be endured and tried to limit the education they offered. The result was *Historical Sketch of the*

Separate Schools of Ontario and Minority Report, considerable negative criticism and the instant death of the Commission's report after nearly six years' work. Keenly aware of the fate of the Hope Commission, the Hall-Dennis Committee decided to take a positive approach to separate schools, as they were presently constituted:

> The Province of Ontario is committed to a public tax-supported system of non-confessional and Roman Catholic separate schools. This two-fold system was in existence prior to Confederation and was written into *The British North America Act* as a condition of that union. Unless the constitution is changed, this is the pattern that will continue. That being so, it is imperative that the needs of the all children in Ontario be justly served in the spirit of co-operation, understanding, and good will that is increasingly noticeable in Ontario today.[130]

The Hall-Dennis Committee had stated the obvious, but at least it had stated it up front and without equivocation. It simply accepted the existence of separate schools, as a matter of history and the constitution, for the sake of the children who attended them and in the interests of public peace. Also, it was mindful that the Ontario Foundation Tax Plan, founded on equal opportunity and financial equity, was rapidly transforming the financial fortunes of separate schools.

However, for all the criticism the Committee would receive for being too progressive (or wishy-washy) on pedagogical issues, it was cautious to a fault when it came time to discussing the teaching of religion and completing the separate school system. Anxious to pre-empt any wrangling over religion, the Committee asked the Robarts government to establish a separate committee on religious education in the public schools of the province. This was done by an order-in-council of 27 January 1966. J. Keiller Mackay, a former justice of the Supreme Court of Ontario, was chairman.[131] When Hall broached the subject of completion with the Committee, in 1968, he faced such fierce opposition from Dr. Charles Phillips, a former director of

411

graduate studies at the Ontario College of Education, and Dr. Murray Ross, president of York University, that the matter died behind closed doors and was kept there out of sight of the general public.[132]

Regardless, the argument in support of separate school completion, so compelling to so many supporters, would not go away. Another version of it appeared in the main Catholic brief to the Committee. In an attempt to present a unified front of Catholic opinion, the Ontario Catholic Education Council reinvented itself and presented a submission, dated 11 January 1966. This latest reincarnation of the OCEC was made up of members of the hierarchy, the Ontario Separate School Trustees' Association, l'Association des commissions des écoles bilingues d'Ontario, the English Catholic Education Association of Ontario and l'Association canadienne-française d'education d'Ontario.[133] The OCEC hired Father Raymond Durocher, OMI, assistant editor of the *Catholic Register*, to write the brief.[134]

A French-speaking native of Minnesota, Father Durocher was analytical and articulate. In time, he would become editor of the *Register* and after that an important contributor to the composition of OSSTA briefs. He was responsible for writing the October 1966 brief on improvements to the Ontario Foundation Tax Plan, the May 1969 brief on "Equal Opportunity" and the November 1981 brief on "The Status of Secondary Education under Separate School Administration." OSSTA hired him as a consultant in June 1969 and then made him director of research and development and assistant editor of the *Catholic Trustee* in 1971.[135] Such was his reputation in the field of education that the government invited Father Durocher in 1973 to give advice on the amalgamation of the different education Acts into one Education Act (Bill 255). He was also an ardent supporter of an official entente with the French Catholic trustees on the issue of French-language secondary education.

Although OSSTA had presented its own brief to the Committee — it was dated 14 January 1966 and written by Francis G. Carter — it was clearly overshadowed by Durocher's work.[136] This being the case, and since OSSTA belonged to the Council and collaborated on the Council's brief, we will accept the Council's submission as the most notable voice of Catholic opinion heard at the hearings of the Hall-Dennis Committee.

Father Durocher composed the brief within the context of five areas of concern to all school systems. They were "home life, high school dropouts, national unity and bilingualism, the socialization of modern man and the religious renewal of modern times."[137] Within this context, the brief made many general and specific recommendations on a variety of topical issues. Of these, the following five are the most pertinent:

1. The need for Catholic teachers' colleges. If these were not feasible at the present time, [there was] the need for specialized credit courses for Catholic teachers in the teaching of religion as well as in the Catholic philosophy of education and the Catholic approach to all other subjects.
2. Department of Education subcommittees for both public and separate schools that would oversee teacher training, school inspection and the selection of appropriate text books.
3. Equalization of provincial grants to grades 9 and 10 in the separate system, and basic provincial grants to all schools providing secondary education.
4. Vocational-technical schools for the larger Catholic school boards, and joint management of these schools by public and separate boards (and even private schools) in smaller centres, religion always being part of the curriculum.
5. Legislation that would allow co-operation between school boards on common problems and common services.[138]

The Hall-Dennis Committee had listened to many arguments, both for and against, the proposal to extend the separate school system beyond Grade 10 and chose to ignore all but one of these recommendations. It would make something of No. 5, in terms of the larger units of administration, but of even greater significance was its recognition that any discussion about the extension of the separate school system "has an important and direct bearing on the aims and objectives of education in the K-12 continuous learning program which the Committee recommends for adoption in Ontario." In other words, if Ontario were to adopt the continuous learning program, it would have to adopt it for all school children, which logically implied publicly-funded separate schools from kindergarten to Grade 12. Separate school supporters would make much of the Committee's vigorous commitment to continuous learning. Taking their cue from the Committee, they would argue that extension was the only remedy for Catholic students if they too were to enjoy continuous learning. It made no sense for them to have to leave their schools after Grade 10 to complete their secondary education.[139]

Living and Learning made three recommendations concerning separate schools. The first had to do with legislating larger administrative units, and the second and third with co-operation between public and separate school boards:

> 252. Enact legislation which will form separate school boards into larger units of administration for separate school purposes, with boundaries coterminous with those of county and district boards of education.
>
> 253. In the implementation of the proposed plan for larger units of administration for education in Ontario, find some arrangement, acceptable to all, which will bring the two tax-supported systems into administrative co-operation, preserving what is considered by the separate school supporters as essential to their system, and at the same time making possible a great deal of co-operation and sharing of special services, avoiding duplication in many areas and services, and bringing to an end a controversy that has burdened the administration of education in Ontario since Confederation.
>
> 254. Develop patterns of co-operation between separate school boards and boards of education in the areas of transportation, school sites, health services, counselling services, computer services, in-service education and joint prospects where such co-operation will reduce costs and organizational impediments to equality of opportunity.[140]

414

It was the recommendation on larger administrative units that would find legislative expression. Premier Robarts first announced the government's intentions on this matter on 14 November 1967, and Bill Davis, minister of education, introduced the legislation in the Legislative Assembly on 28 June 1968. The history behind this legislation, in particular separate school support of it, and the legislation's usefulness as a building block in the separate school campaign for completion is the subject of the next section.

Larger Units of Administration
(Amalgamation of School Boards), 1969

Separate school trustees had been in the vanguard of the movement for larger administrative units. At the 1937 Committee of Enquiry into the Cost of Education, Arthur Kelly of Toronto was asked to give his opinion on the idea of a metropolitan-size school board. Kelly was able to report that as a result of special arrangements between the Toronto separate school board and a number of suburban separate school boards, a metropolitan unit of administration was already in existence and working well.[141] This arrangement was formalized as early as 1941 and considerably expanded in 1953, when the province created the Metropolitan Separate School Board, the largest separate school board in Ontario.[142]

In its second supplementary brief to the Hope Commission, the Ontario Catholic Education Council devoted a section to larger units of administration for rural separate schools. Although the Council recognized the fact that forty-two percent of rural public school sections had been absorbed into township school areas, on a volunteer basis, and that no such provision existed for the advantage of rural separate schools, it did not recommend to the Commission that separate schools be given the same privilege. Instead, the Council limited itself to asking for improvements to the machinery of establishing union separate schools, in reference to section 32 of the Separate Schools Act. It made three suggestions: one, that the number of trustees of a union separate school board be increased from three to five; two, that a referee (probably school inspector) be appointed to adjudicate sectional claims and disputes and that his decision be final;

and three, that the referee be given the right to recommend a special tax rate to be borne by one or more joining sections, in order to eliminate any differences in the respective contributions to the assets of the union. Along with these three suggestions, which were inspired by the legislation governing township school areas, the Council recommended:

> that the legislative facilities for establishing larger units of school administration for public schools be extended to the separate school portion of the Provincial school system; and that, due to the scattered nature of rural separate school distribution, the Separate Schools permitted to establish such unions be not restricted to location "in the same or in adjoining municipalities," as is the present Section 31, Separate Schools Act.[143]

Of course, nothing came of this modest recommendation. The Catholic commissioners did not hide their disappointment at being rebuffed by the Commission: "There is no evidence of any intention on the part of the majority of the Commissioners to accord to Roman Catholic separate schools the improvements in administration and supervision deemed essential for the other form of common schools."[144] They continued:

> we believe that a larger unit of administration determined with proper regard to the welfare of the children as well as to the economy and efficiency of internal operation is desirable, equally for both public and separate schools. But where larger units of administration are established for public schools only and corresponding units are not established for separate schools, a most confusing situation develops. This has happened under the present provisions for the formation of township school areas for public school purposes.[145]

It was not until the 1963 Supreme Court ruling on the three-mile limit that rural separate school boards were given some practical latitude to operate in the modern world. The trustees took advantage of the court's decision on union separate schools to eliminate hundreds of rural school sections, in a push for administrative efficiency and consolidated schools. In 1964, there were 723 separate school boards; in 1968, there were 455, for a decrease of 268.[146] If the township rule had applied to the separate schools, as it did to public schools, the decrease would have been even more dramatic and would have put separate schools in a more advantageous position when Premier Robarts outlined his government's plans to make the county (and the district in Northern Ontario) the basic administrative unit for school purposes.

Robarts made his announcement on 14 November 1967. The occasion was the dedication of a school addition in Galt. It was front-page news, but it mostly concerned the radical reduction in the number of public school boards. The *Globe and Mail* claimed that 1,500 boards would be replaced by 100 county-size units by 1 January 1969.[147] But the premier was also anxious to extend an invitation to the separate school boards. He told reporters that his government had considered merging separate school boards but held back any movement in that direction because separate schools presented special problems. By special problems, he must have meant that the explicit inclusion of separate schools in the constitution might entail a different way to consolidate their boards.

This was certainly not 1950. Conciliatory as always, Robarts left the door wide open for Catholic separate school trustees to come up with a solution to the amalgamation of their own boards. This is precisely what the trustees did. And they conducted their business with the government in an atmosphere of mutual trust and co-operation. Representatives from both the Ontario Separate School Trustees' Association and l'Association des commissions des écoles bilingues d'Ontario met several times with Bill Davis, the minister of education, and Dr. J.R. McCarthy, the deputy minister. The OSSTA delegation consisted of Dr. J.W. Fyfe of Sudbury, C.F. Gilhooly of Ottawa, Wm. J. Hillyer of Owen Sound and A.E. Klein of North Bay, who was president at the time.[148] Davis told the legislature that their advice and support had been helpful in developing what became Bill

417

168.[149]

OSSTA's brief on amalgamation, dated 29 March 1968, was written by Dr. Joe Fyfe, Father Durocher, Father Matthews, Ed Nelligan, Hank Lottridge of Welland and Chris Asseff. Once again, the trustees capitalized on Robarts's invocation of "equality of educational opportunity." They liked nothing better than to hear the premier repeat these words that had become a mantra for his government and called the proposed improvements in school board organization a means of achieving that equality. The benefits of amalgamation far outweighed any loss in local control over schools or in the more traditional relationship between trustee and ratepayer. The argument, largely irresistible, went like this. If the county were to become the basic administrative unit for separate schools, school boards would be in a position to offer a more extensive range of programs to all children; to meet the needs of special students; to recruit the proper personnel for audiovisual equipment, libraries, guidance and special education; and to finance additional classrooms in French-language schools "where English shall be the language of instruction, or as the case may be, where both French and English shall be the language of instruction in the various subjects of the course of study in accordance with Curriculum 46."[150] This was all heady stuff. And there was more. Teachers would have "greater economic security, less isolation and more chances for promotion."[151] For the first time in separate school history, there would be an "equitable distribution of the tax load over the entire area."[152] Concerning board administration, the trustees stated that "larger units foster greater efficiency in operation, less duplication of facilities, greater development of more fully-trained personnel, and provision for sound planning over a reasonable geographic area."[153]

If this was not enough to convince the most recalcitrant school board, the OSSTA brief saved its best argument for last. If the prime objective behind the government's intention to reorganize school jurisdictions was "to offer a total school program to meet the needs and interests of the student and to provide for the great variety represented by individual differences in ability, background and experience,"[154] it only made sense to extend this offer of a total school

418

program to every child in the province. The implication was abundantly clear: "within the limits of the common good, the jurisdiction of separate school boards be extended to include all grades from Kindergarten to Grade 13. If acceptance of the general proposals means that our schools can reap the benefits of the change to the fullest, we cannot help but support such a forward step."[155]

The brief made five recommendations:

1. That legislation be enacted to have all separate school boards in a County or union of Counties considered a combined board;

2. That legislation be enacted to allow a combined board which has centres in more than one County to pass a resolution to determine the County Combined Board to which it would prefer to be attached;

3. That legislation be enacted that, when in the counties five or more heads of families resident in a former school section pass a resolution to establish a new separate school zone and establish a centre therefore, such a new separate school zone shall become a part of the County Combined Board forthwith;

4. That legislation be passed establishing Metropolitan Toronto and the cities of Windsor and Ottawa as separate school zones independent of the Counties in which they are located;

5. That legislation be enacted that trustees be elected from the various areas on the basis of residential, farm and business assessment.[156]

It appears that "An Act to amend The Separate Schools Act," given Royal Assent on 2 July 1968, incorporated almost all the recommendations made by the trustees.[157] Amendments to the Act brought about many startling changes to the administration of separate schools. The most dramatic was the disappearance of hundreds of small separate school boards and their one- and two-room schools. As of September 1969, there were sixty-three boards left in existence.[158] The role of school inspector was abolished. For the first time since the mid-nineteenth century, the department of education had no direct contact with individual schools.[159] To replace the inspectors, the trustees employed their own supervisory officers — directors of education and superintendents — and then proceeded to build large central offices to house a growing education bureaucracy that was expected by Queen's Park to act fairly independently as it streamlined services, consolidated schools, hired principals and teachers and provided educational programs. Two negative aspects to the amalgamation of boards and the elimination of small schools were that the larger the school board the less contact there would be between parents and the trustees and the fewer the number of schools the greater the distance children would have to travel to school, especially in the rural districts. The age of the ubiquitous yellow school bus was about to begin.

And there was one more change, peculiar to separate schools. Right up to amalgamation, it was often customary for the local priest to be the secretary-treasurer of the local rural school board. This all came to an abrupt end on 1 January 1969. Those small boards disappeared, and along with them went the traditional presence and influence of the parish priest in the administration of countless separate schools. (But his role in the spiritual life of Catholic students remained intact.) Although priests continued to sit as trustees in the new larger boards or on the established urban boards in Windsor, Toronto and Ottawa, they were usually only one of a dozen or more trustees, and even that minimal level of clerical participation in school trusteeship came under scrutiny from some quarters during the 1970s and 1980s.

In drawing up its brief, OSSTA had been careful not to tie their support of school board amalgamation to completion of the separate school system. To have done so would have been political suicide.[160] If the Ontario Foundation Tax Plan had been the opening chapter in the renaissance of separate schools, the trustees' acceptance and promotion of larger units of administration was the second. The two legislated changes quietly complemented each other to the enormous benefit of Catholic school children, and in both chapters the chief negotiator on behalf of separate schools had been OSSTA. All that remained was to find the most propitious moment to initiate the political action that would form the third and most important chapter in the rebirth of separate schools — completing the system.

The Campaign for Completion, 1966-1971

The word completion, in its broadest sense, meant the extension of separate school board administration to include Grades 11 to 13, the practical application of which assumed the implementation of financial parity between the two-publicly funded school systems. Looked at another way, completion would give separate school boards the right to absorb already existing Catholic high schools as well as the right to establish new high schools where warranted by demand. Completion was never about special grants to private schools, despite the claims of those who vehemently opposed completion. Opponents often cited the unknown costs of implementation (a legitimate concern) and the wasteful duplication of services completion would bring (a charge based more on fear than on facts), or they revealed their antipathy by questioning, for the umpteenth time, the very idea of separate schools, charging that by design these schools were socially and religiously divisive in a society increasingly defined by pluralism and ecumenism.

The word completion also had a particular pedagogical element to it that is worthwhile repeating. Completion was about equal opportunity for all school children to receive their kindergarten-to-Grade 13 education in a continuous and integrated fashion, regardless of where they lived or in which school system they were enrolled. "Continuous" and "integrated" were two words that soon came to bear special significance for the thousands of Catholic high school students who were unable to enjoy continuity and integration in their studies towards a high school diploma. In 1961, Premier Robarts introduced the Reorganized Programme, or secondary school streaming, into high schools: five-year and four-year arts and sciences, business and commerce, engineering, technology and trades.[161] Streaming was just fine for public secondary schools. Indeed, the programme must have been fashioned with them in mind.

Well funded, and a constituent element of a continuous and integrated system of education, they could easily absorb the change and flourish as a result. But Catholic secondary schools functioned in a very different universe. It was not only impossible for the typical Catholic high school — underfunded for the first two years and privately funded for the last three — to compete with the public schools in offering the Reorganized Programme, but also quite a challenge for many of them to retain their Grades 9 and 10 students for the full five or four years of the programs they could offer.[162] Completion, it was later argued, would put an end to such bifurcation, two parts public and three parts private, and would increase the number of "streams" available to Catholic high school students. It would keep existing Catholic high schools from closing and enable separate school boards to operate more of them. With a properly funded and complete school system, students would complete their schooling within the Catholic separate school system.

The years 1966 to 1971 form a compact and complex period in the history of separate school agitation. Kick-starting this round of agitation was episcopal concern over the financial well-being of the private Catholic high schools.[163] The overriding question on the minds of the bishops was, "How long would they survive?" These schools, Grades 11 to 13, operated hand-to-mouth on the proceeds from tuition, bingoes, raffles and various fund drives, annual parish donations and diocesan emergency loans. It was all quite heroic, but heroism, like enthusiasm for any cause no matter how noble, has its limits. The rising costs of education, the professionalization of teachers, the steady decline in the number of religious teachers and the diminishing degree to which individual bishops and different religious communities could devote their own resources to subsidize the last three years of Catholic secondary education — all of these factors militated against long-term sustainability.

For the 1968-69 school year, there were 75 English-language Catholic high schools offering at least some secondary grades. (This was down from 89 in 1966 to 79 in 1967.) Of these 75 schools, six were junior high schools that ended at Grade 10 and the remaining 69 went up to Grade 12 and in many cases to Grade 13. There were 35 large schools (400 or more students), 15 medium schools (more than 200 but fewer than 400 students) and 25 small schools (fewer than 200 students). Of the 35 large schools, all of them offered the five-year arts and science program, but 13 of the 35 offered only this program. Eleven large schools offered the four-year arts and science program, 15 offered the business and commerce program but only six could offer all three programs. No school made available programs in engineering, technology or trades. Of the 32,611 students enrolled in Catholic high schools, ninety percent were in the five-year arts and science program. No wonder that these schools were open to the charge of elitism. Regardless, enrolment had increased by 1,643, from 1966 to 1968-69. The increase was hardly huge; nonetheless it was an increase and a bellwether of the popularity of Catholic secondary education. The average total revenue per pupil in the publicly-funded Grades 9 and 10 was $425, up from $376 in 1967. The average total income per pupil in the privately-funded Grades 11 to 13 was $309, up from $276 in 1967. There were a total of 1,729 full- and part-time teachers, of which 782 were Religious and priests and 947 were lay. Of the 947 lay teachers, only 97, or six percent, were non-Catholic. The percentage of teachers who were Religious and priests had declined from fifty-four percent in 1966 to fifty percent in 1967 to forty-five percent in 1968-69. That trend would continue into the 1970s and 1980s (see Chapter Three). Operating deficits were the obligation of Religious communities in sixty percent of the schools; the local parish or the diocese in fifteen percent of the schools; and lay boards in twenty-five percent of the schools.[164]

Complicating matters for the bishops, the religious communities and lay boards who had a direct interest in the welfare of Catholic high schools, and for the separate school trustees who ran Grades 9 and 10, was the decision by the Robarts government, on 30 May 1968, to introduce legislation that would allow on a permissive basis the establishment of French-language secondary schools. Bill 140, "An Act to amend the Schools Administration Act," provided three options based on the number of students: one, French as the language of instruction for certain subjects; two, a French-language department or section within an English-language school; three, composite French-language schools, in which instruction for all subjects would be delivered in French.[165] In an adroit move that showed Robarts to be at the top of his political game, the premier declared that any French secondary schools that were a result of the amended legislation would belong to the public school system. He calculated that separation in education based on language would be tolerated by the public and that any further separation based on religion would not be.

The results were predictable and a blow to the hopes of those Catholic ratepayers and apologists for whom completion had become the sine qua non of Catholic separate schools. The unity-in-action, so carefully fostered since 1959 by the Ontario Separate School Trustees' Association and l'Association des commissions des écoles bilingues d'Ontario, petered out, forcing OSSTA to work without their French trustee colleagues when it wrote its completion brief in 1969 and took control of the completion campaign.[166] In September 1968, the Welland Board of Education, the first public board in Ontario to have bilingual schools, became the first public board to operate a French-language high school. Called Confederation, it attracted about five hundred students. The vast majority of them were Catholic and had attended a school conducted by the Sisters of the Sacred Heart. When their school went bankrupt, the sisters doffed their habits and followed their students into Confederation. All of this produced quite a shock to supporters of Catholic education. How easy it was to lose a school. Much the same thing happened in Ottawa. There the Ottawa Collegiate Institute Board gladly welcomed the addition of seven high schools, a move that cost taxpayers only $2 million. This trend of opting to join the public school system continued until the number of Catholic French-language high schools had declined from twenty to four. By 1971, a mere three years after the introduction of the legislation, there were 28,000 students in French-language public secondary schools.[167]

Let us return to the bishops and their anxieties about Catholic high schools. They had good reason to worry, and they wisely did not wait for events, such as the above, to shape their policies or actions. In April 1966, they engineered the formation of the Association of

Catholic High School Boards of Ontario (ACHSBO). Timothy J. McKenna, a Hamilton lawyer, was president, and Bishop Ryan of Hamilton was honourary president. Having collaborated on school problems for many years, the two men worked well together in their new roles. Sadly, McKenna's premature death in June 1968 robbed separate schools of a selfless and tireless advocate.

Next, the bishops approved the nomination of Father Patrick Fogarty, CSC, as executive director of ECEAO, succeeding Father Joseph Finn in that post. Fogarty took up his duties on 2 August 1966 and did not relinquish them until his death nineteen years later. Patrick Harmon Fogarty was a native of Moncton, New Brunswick and was educated at St. Joseph's University, in Memramcook, New Brunswick, Holy Cross College in Washington, D.C. and the University of Toronto, where he received an M.A. in 1946 and then his Ontario Teachers' Certificate. He joined the Congregation of Holy Cross in 1940 and was ordained to the priesthood on 10 June 1945. Father Fogarty was a co-founder of Notre Dame College School in Welland as well as its second principal, from 1952 to 1958, and the founder of Denis Morris High School in St. Catharines and its first principal, from 1958 to 1966. He died at the age of sixty-six years, on 19 January 1985.[168]

Bishop Thomas J. McCarthy of St. Catharines was directly responsible for Fogarty's nomination and had no trouble convincing Bishop G. Emmett Carter to agree to it. To Father Fogarty goes the credit of lifting the ECEAO from the ashes of irrelevance, brilliantly if only briefly, from 1966 to 1969, at which time OSSTA assumed full command and control of the political agenda and agitation for completion. Father Fogarty forged a close connection to the Association of Catholic High School Boards of Ontario, carefully concentrating ECEAO's attention and efforts on the precarious state of Catholic high schools. And he was front and centre of ACHSBO's highly politicized public relations project, the Provincial Education Program or PEP, which was launched in November 1967.

The inspiration for the Provincial Education Program can be found in a speech given by Arthur Maloney, on 4 November 1967, at the second annual study congress of the Association of Catholic High

School Boards of Ontario. Maloney was a well-known and highly respected Catholic lawyer who would later become Ontario's Ombudsman. "A Reasonable Solution to the Problem of Catholic Public Schools" was a superb example of a new kind of separate school rhetoric, perfectly tailored to the 1960s, that was confident in its claims, patient in its delivery of the facts and figures and deliberately careful to avoid stirring up political rancor or fear among public school supporters. Absent was any suspicion of religious hubris.[169]

The Provincial Education Program was well underway at the beginning of 1968. PEP's principal goal was to reach, inform and convince three different audiences on the rightness and timeliness of completing the separate school system. Catholics were the first audience. Many of them were woefully ignorant of the history of separate school claims or just plain apathetic, a complaint that was often levelled (sometimes unfairly) against parish priests. PEP reached their fellow Catholics by means of leaflets and pamphlets, sermons at Sunday Mass and public rallies, where Father Fogarty was often the featured speaker. Crowds attract the attention of politicians, who either love them or hate them, and of journalists, who usually love them because they make for easy copy. Fogarty did a decent job of galvanizing Catholic opinion, but his presence on the stage also aroused trenchant criticism from a few Catholic university professors, who refused to believe that Catholics wanted or needed separate schools. The second audience was composed of those public school ratepayers who were always waiting in the wings for another round in Ontario's long history of school controversies. Some members of this audience suffered the existence of separate schools but hotly opposed completion. For others their antipathy was such as to loathe the entire separate school system. The third audience were the politicians, in particular the premier and his minister of education. The fate of any argument or agitation on behalf of completion was in their hands.

However, the Provincial Education Program nearly ended before it had a chance to begin. During the latter half of 1967, there was a serious move afoot in London to lease Catholic Central High School, Grades 9 to 13, to the public school board for the nominal sum of one dollar per year. The public board would administer the school; in return, it would guarantee the right of Catholic Central's board to approve of both students and teachers, the wearing of religious habits in the classroom and the traditional place of teaching the Catholic faith in the school's curriculum. This was the basic framework. The details had yet to be determined and formalized in a contract. Moreover, any agreement would require the government's approval.

The driving force behind the merger proposal was John F. Bennett, a separate school trustee and Conservative supporter who honestly believed that amalgalmation of this sort was the only hope for Catholic Central's survival. He had the endorsement of Bishop Carter of London and the diocesan senate of priests, once they had seen a draft agreement in November 1967. Carter was especially supportive. In a letter to Father Fogarty, dated 7 December 1967, he described the draft agreement as "the first real break in the Ontario high school picture"[170] and as a complement, not an impediment, to the current completion campaign under Fogarty's direction. Carter thought that if a merger could take place in London on the right terms, it could serve as a model for future mergers in other cities and towns and usher in "a universal solution."[171]

One cannot blame Bennett for his sincerity or Carter for his enthusiasm. Neither man had to show his curriculum vitae on Catholic education to anyone. But sincerity and enthusiasm are never enough in politics. If ever the wish was father to the thought, the London merger plan was it.

Father Fogarty was horrified. He was not alone. So too was Timothy J. McKenna, president of the Association of Catholic High School Boards of Ontario. (However, Albert E. Klein, president of the Ontario Separate School Trustees' Association, was initially in favour of the merger insofar as Grades 11, 12 and 13 were concerned. He subsequently changed his mind.) When the merger plan was floated before the bishops, few were convinced that it would provide the appropriate Catholic setting for Catholic students or that the Robarts government, busy pursuing its own multi-layered agenda on education, would ever give its approval. More than one critic pointed

427

out the constitutional problem of a separate school board handing over Grades 9 and 10 to a public school board.

Nothing came of the merger talks.[172] The two boards failed to arrive at an agreement, and Bennett's initiative died at the table. While the negotiations were stalled, Bishop Carter had a change of heart. He had been willing to listen to objections to the merger idea. One person who filed an objection within a week of Carter's letter to Fogarty was Klein of OSSTA. He delivered a brilliant thirteen-point position paper in which he stated that Catholic educators in the province were coming to see that there was only one worthwhile objective — to convince the provincial government of the need to complete the separate school system. Any deviation from this objective might jeopardize the entire system. Local solutions would never bring about the long-desired goal of completion.[173]

It was this position paper, in response to the London merger talks, that convinced OSSTA of the necessity of embracing completion as its policy for Catholic secondary education in the province. This happened at the executive meeting of 6 February 1968 and was confirmed by a motion passed without dissent at OSSTA's annual meeting in April.[174] Having embraced completion, OSSTA proceeded to remind its allies in separate school politics — the Ontario bishops, the English Catholic Education Association of Ontario and the Association of Catholic High School Boards of Ontario — that by rights OSSTA was now in charge of the plan of campaign. OSSTA would call for submissions, write and present the brief and control the political pressure.[175] Everyone agreed.

The trustees' association set up a Working Committee on the Extension of the Catholic Public School System in May 1968. Members of the committee were Albert E. Klein, chairman, Dr. Nicholas Mancini, William J. Hillyer, M. Earle McCabe, Dr. Bernard J. Nolan, Chris Asseff and Father Dennis J. Murphy, OSSTA chaplain and now moral advisor to the committee. Edward J. Brisbois joined the committee in early 1969. Assisting the Working Committee, which was composed exclusively of trustees, with the exception of Father Murphy, was a panel of Advisory Members. They were Francis Kovacs of Welland, a lawyer and president of ACHSBO, Father Frank

Kavanagh, OMI of OECTA and Mrs. M. Robida of St. Catharines, who represented the FCPTAO. To their number would be added Michael W. Carty of Kingston, Ed Nelligan of the Metro Separate School Board, Bishop Joseph F. Ryan of Hamilton, Father Patrick Fogarty, CSC, executive director of ECEAO and also secretary of ACHSBO, Father Raymond Durocher, author of the brief, and Jerry Collins (and later Joseph Redican) of the Ontario Catholic Student Federation.

The Working Committee divided itself into three sub-committees: Durocher, Klein, Nolan, Kovacs and Murphy on assessing the submissions, making formal presentations and drafting the brief; McCabe, Mancini and Kavanagh on public relations; and Hillyer, Robida and Asseff on format (i.e. ten point font size, 5,000 print run, press release letterhead). Two more sub-committees were to follow: a pedagogical sub-committee to work with the drafters of the brief and an implementation sub-committee, which wrote a five-page position paper on financing extension and post-May 1969. To financially support the Working Committee in 1968 and 1969, OSSTA took $25,000 from the Teacher Recruitment Fund.[176]

Each OSSTA member of the Working Committee was a war-horse in the history of separate school politics. They sacrificed a great deal of their time (and if they were self-employed professionals, a great deal of money) serving the cause during the late 1960s and into the 1970s. Albert Klein, president from 1966 to 1969, was a lawyer from North Bay. When he was shown in December 1968 that all secondary grades were seamless, as defined by government policy on continuous education, he stood in the forefront of OSSTA's support of separate school extension. Nicholas Mancini was a dentist from Hamilton and chairman of the Hamilton-Wentworth Separate School Board. He succeeded Klein as OSSTA's president, serving from 1969 to 1972, and he presented the 1969 brief to Premier John Robarts and led the ensuing campaign to convince the Conservative government of its merits. William J. Hillyer was chairman of the Owen Sound Separate School Board and the Bruce Grey Separate School. He became a member of the OSSTA board of directors in 1965, and he was president from 1976 to 1977. M. Earle McCabe was a long time director whose diligence and passion for separate schools was rarely surpassed by any of his contemporaries. Bernard Nolan, a dentist from Windsor, was a trustee of the Sandwich West Separate School Board and the Windsor Separate School Board and chairman of the latter for five years. He was president from 1972 to 1974. Chris Asseff was president from 1962 to October 1963 and executive director from 1964 to his retirement in 1985. He participated in every major separate school event during those years, beginning with the Ontario Foundation Tax Plan and ending with Premier Davis's 1984 announcement on separate school completion. Having run as a Conservative candidate in the 1962 provincial election, Asseff was always welcomed at Queen's Park. Father (later Monsignor) Dennis Murphy is a priest of the diocese of Sault Ste. Marie with a doctorate in religious education. Now retired, he was a pastor, a general secretary of the Canadian Conference of Catholic Bishops and the founding director of the Institute of Catholic Education. As chaplain to OSSTA, from 1966 to 1986, he served on numerous committees and was never far from the centre of decision-making. Ed Brisbois was a natural leader. He was a trustee and then chairman of the Metro Separate School Board and president of OSSTA from 1974 to 1976. A loyal Tory in politics, he enjoyed excellent access to Premier Robarts and always believed that one day in the not-too-distant future separate schools would offer all grades up to university entrance. However, he never lived to see the fulfillment of his hopes, dying of cancer in December 1977.

The Working Committee invited individuals and organizations to make formal submissions as part of the process of writing the now historic OSSTA brief, "Equal Opportunity for Continuous Education in Separate Schools of Ontario." The deadline was 31 October 1968. Twenty groups, mainly separate school boards, submitted briefs. The committee consulted the Ontario bishops, prominent Catholic educators, the English Catholic Education Association of Ontario, the Federation of Catholic Parent-Teacher Associations, the Ontario English Catholic Teachers' Association and the Association of Catholic High School Boards of Ontario. The last named association submitted a 102-page brief with five appendices. Titled "Completing

430

Their Schooling," it was the most thorough brief that the Working Committee had to digest.[177]

It was a bumpy road for OSSTA on the way to Queen's Park. Father Durocher, hired to write the brief, did not like the word "completion." He preferred "up-dating" and only reluctantly accepted "extension."[178] His first draft stressed three points:

(1) That re-organization and integration were reasons for up-dating;

(2) That continuity of religious instruction should go through the adolescent period;

(3) The requirement for obtaining teachers for the separate school system.[179]

Moreover, Father Durocher believed that the Hall-Dennis Committee's central recommendation of a continuous, integrated programme of non-graded studies from kindergarten to Grade 13 would not become government policy for at least five or ten years.[180] This accounts for the absence in the first draft of any pedagogical reasons for extension. This provoked strong rebuttals from Father Kavanagh, Francis Kovacs and Dr. Mancini. For his part, Father Kavanagh of OECTA brilliantly insisted that the basis of the brief had to be pedagogical and that it had to adopt as one of its major arguments that only a complete separate school system — not one that ended at Grade 10 — could provide a non-graded continuum of studies.[181]

In the end, the brief played up the pedagogical side of the argument. For extra measure, it did not mention the teaching of religion, which the committee felt was a matter between the school trustees and parents and not between Catholics and the legislature.[182] Its inclusion in the brief would have given the critics of separate schools another chance to kick Catholicism around as if it were nothing more than another political football, all at Catholic expense and embarrassment.

Then there was the sensitive topic of funding completion. Bishop Carter for one was adamant that the brief not concede "the legitimacy of the diversion of the tax base to the public schools at any level."[183] In this, he supported Ed Nelligan.[184] Nelligan did not want OSSTA to propose the Ontario Foundation Tax Plan as a means to fund Grades 11 to 13. He did not even want it to be used for any phase-in period. On the other side of the divide stood those who felt that it would be self-defeating to stir up that old and dangerous hornets' nest of accusations that separate schools were after public school money. There was no need to do that. One of the reasons why the Ontario Foundation Tax Plan had worked so well was its political neutrality. Its application was a matter of departmental regulations and arithmetical fine tuning. Since it did wonders for the elementary schools, with the minimum of negative political fallout for both separate school supporters and the Conservative government, there was no reason to suspect that the plan as applied to Grades 11 to 13 would not be just as politically benign. Only after completion had taken place should there be a change in local assessment. The executive of the Association of Catholic High School Boards of Ontario, Bishop Ryan and Father Fogarty accepted this argument, but to make peace, Father Fogarty changed his mind and joined Ed Nelligan.[185]

The brief came down in the middle, opting for a certain measure of ambiguity. On the one hand, it claimed that "every board, vested with its full powers and entire educational responsibilities, should enjoy equal control over its financial resources, with the province acting in its role as the great equalizer."[186] In practical terms, this meant that separate schools "would draw tax support for its services from K to 12 (13)," and any shortfall would be the responsibility of the government.[187] On the other hand, due to the fluid state of school finance, "the application of the above principle might take any one of many forms."[188] In other words, having agreed to completion, the government might choose to finance the phase-in part of completion by means other than a change in local assessment.[189]

The most pertinent parts of the "Equal Opportunity" brief are sections 4 to 8 inclusive:

4. The purpose of this brief is to obtain for separate public schools of Ontario that equality which is basic to the

educational policy of the province, which is demanded by official promotion of continuous, child-centred education, and which is implicit in the modern reorganization of the school system.

5. This request means the removal of the pedagogical and financial shackles which restrain the separate schools from offering a complete educational service from Kindergarten to Grade 12 (13) at the present time. Arbitrary barriers and obsolete obstacles must not be allowed to prevent separate school pupils from participating as freely and abundantly in this progress as pupils in the other sector of the educational system.

6. These barriers and obstacles are well known. They include:

a) an archaic elementary tax base;

b) financing of grades nine and ten as elementary grades;

c) unavoidable retention of grade distinctions in an ungraded system;

d) limitation of jurisdiction to a K to 10 programme;

e) lack of adequate voice at departmental levels.

7. Since our presentation is concerned only with equal opportunity in the two sectors of publicly-supported education in the province, we are not dealing here with the distinctive philosophy of either sector, nor with educational institutions outside the publicly-supported system.

8. Our premise is that the basic ideal of equality, becoming more and more explicit in modern times, expressing itself now in the policy of continuous education and recently in the reorganization of school districts, demands that separate school boards be vested with the same responsibility and powers over the normal span of schooling as the public school boards. Progress in the public school sector should go hand in hand with progress in the separate school sector. No segment of the publicly-supported educational system should be "more equal" than the other.[190]

The Working Committee completed the brief by 1 May 1969, and OSSTA presented it to Premier John Robarts and Bill Davis, minister of education, on 26 May. Later that same day they presented copies of the brief to Robert Nixon, leader of the Liberal Party and official opposition, and to Donald C. MacDonald, leader of the New Democratic Party. There had been some talk of distributing copies to every member of the legislature, also on 26 May.[191] The precedent for this had been the bishops' brief and OSSTA's brief on the Ontario Foundation Tax Plan, in 1962. However, the trustees limited their lobbying that day to Robarts, Davis, Nixon and MacDonald. There had been some last minute anxiety from Father Fogarty that at least one bishop should be a member of the delegation waiting upon the premier and the minister of education, so that Robarts and Davis, both of whom had a great respect for church authority, might not think that the hierarchy did not support OSSTA's brief.[192] No bishop was present on 26 May, but the absence of an episcopal presence had no adverse effect on the political shelf life of the brief. Robarts and Davis took it seriously but gave no indication of the way that the government might officially react to it.

Immediately after the trustees' meetings with the three political parties at Queen's Park, Dr. Mancini of OSSTA, John Kuchinak of OECTA and Ed Masterson of FCPTA, in a show of unity, held a press conference at which they explained and defended the brief in a credible and professional manner. The *Catholic Register* published the full text of the brief on 31 May. Father Durocher wrote an explanatory and clarifying article in the May 1969 issue of the *Catholic Trustee*.[193] At the request of Chris Asseff of OSSTA, Bishop Ryan wrote to the Ontario bishops, asking them to bring the brief of 26 May to the attention of their priests and to have them preach on it, on Sunday, 1 June. Enclosed in Bishop Ryan's letter was a sample homily, which gave a very succinct and accurate summary of the brief.[194]

OSSTA and its allies had done well in its opening salvo, but before the day was out, everyone knew that the brief had to be more than a one-day or one-week wonder. The inherent danger was that it would become yesterday's news, too stale for politicians to bother digesting. It had to be kept fresh and alive with the leaven of concerted political action. The challenge facing Catholic separate school supporters was formidable. That challenge was best described in a letter to Chris Asseff, executive secretary of OSSTA:

> If we can convince the Premier and his Cabinet and the editors that Catholics are concerned with the common good, that we have no intention of weakening the Public high school system, that we don't intend to build a secondary school in every town with a Separate elementary school, that most of the 69 private school buildings would be handed over free, that we realize that some technical programs will be too expensive to provide even in the cities — then I believe our case can be won.[195]

The bar for success was set very high. There were many people who had to be convinced of the rightness of the cause. They included apathetic Catholics, hostile Catholics who wrote vigorous letters of protest to Premier Robarts and Archbishop Pocock, the Conservative caucus, especially those members who represented rural ridings, the two opposition parties, the big Toronto newspapers and the leading education bureaucrats. And there were those, such as the Ontario Public School Trustees' Association and the Ethical Education Association, who would never be won over but whose opinions and political influence had to be blunted from the outset. But there was only one person who held the final yeah or nay. He was the premier. He stood at the top of the parliamentary pyramid, and his judgment would be final. Convincing him would be the ultimate goal of the completion campaign begun on 26 May 1969.

What followed was the most organized, comprehensive and sustained public agitation in the history of separate schools, most of which was carefully orchestrated by OSSTA from its central office in Toronto. OSSTA absorbed the Provincial Education Program — but not before its people under Father Fogarty had arranged for the distribution of 375,000 copies of the brief — and then replaced PEP's organization with its own. The Working Committee was in charge of all aspects of the campaign and directed the actions of the second tier of command, the County Committees, which purposely corresponded in size with the separate school boards. (Windsor, Toronto and Ottawa were the three exceptions. In Northern Ontario there were District Committees.) Each county had it own committee, and the chairman of each committee was a director of OSSTA or another trustee designated for the task by the Working Committee. Membership on the County Committees consisted of local representatives of the different individuals and organizations dedicated to completion. They were parish priests, elementary and high school teachers, parent-teacher associations, the Knights of Columbus, the Catholic Women's League and a new group that came into existence in the autumn of 1968, the Ontario Catholic Students Federation.[196] Since completion was all about students, the federation's arrival on the scene was a highly fortuitous development. The executive of the trustees' association kept in steady contact with the county and district Working Committees by means of two monthly publications: "Equality Guidelines" and "Equality Newsletter."[197] The bishops gave their official blessing to the campaign on 28 September 1969 and encouraged their priests to champion the many merits of completion with their parishioners on a regular basis and to co-operate with the proper distribution of campaign literature. OSSTA was never busier or more concentrated in its endeavours than it was during the period when the trustees and their numerous co-workers across the province anxiously awaited Robarts's formal political response to "Equal Opportunity."

Catholics had to wait more than two years. In the meantime, OSSTA and its auxiliaries kept their people busy on an assortment of fronts, all meant to keep the public spotlight shining brightly on completion. There were letter-writing campaigns to politicians and the press; CWL petition drives; meetings with local members of parliament; advertising campaigns; radio interviews; the ongoing production of leaflets and pamphlets, including an OECTA-produced "Completion Handbook" that outlined the basic facts and arguments and the best ways to discuss the issue. It encouraged supporters to

436

politely remind the public-at-large and the politicians that the separate school system, with 418,433 students, 16,214 teachers and 1,343 schools, was huge, growing and here to stay. It was time to finish the job. For its part, the *Catholic Trustee* published a steady stream of articles, mainly for the edification of the trustees, who were naturally on the front lines of debate. Examples were "Continuous Education for Separate Schools"; "Government Studying School Equality Brief"; "School Extension Reasonable"; "Hear This . . . Trustees' Brief Demands Equality for Separate Schools"; and "'Implementation,' The 'How' of Separate School Extension.'"[198]

The campaign had its political triumphs. On 4 November 1969, Robert Nixon and his twenty-seven-member Liberal caucus issued a statement that called for the extension of separate schools to the end of secondary education. These schools would be fully funded and administered by the present publicly-elected separate school boards.[199] The NDP issued a discussion paper, "The Financial Crisis in the Catholic High Schools," on 16 October 1969, and the party joined ranks with the Liberals on the separate school issue, on 3 March 1970, when leader Donald C. MacDonald stood up in the legislature and called on the government to implement equality.[200] A grateful OSSTA executive asked the Catholic people to write letters of thanks to both Nixon and MacDonald.

The open support of both opposition parties was a necessary but not a sufficient condition to win the day. There was still the public, the premier and the education minister to convince. This brings us to the campaign's two other trophy moments during the completion campaign. There was Equality Sunday, on 22 February 1970. Held in Catholic parishes throughout the province, the day was a rare, and fairly successful, opportunity for Catholics as a community to ponder the meaning and future of Catholic separate schools, an institution founded by the laity over a century ago. At stake was the long-term integrity of their schools.[201] Then there was the great rally in Toronto, on 25 October 1970. Organized and hosted by the Ontario Catholic Students Federation, it attracted 17,000 students, parents, teachers, trustees and clergy to Maple Leaf Gardens. Another 3,000 had to be diverted to St. Michael's Cathedral. It was an historic event.

Archbishop Philip Pocock was in all his glory; eighteen-year-old Jerome Collins of St. Catharines, president of the federation, gave a stirring speech; speaking for the NDP was Donald C. MacDonald and for the Liberals their education critic, Tim Reid; also in attendance was Bill Davis, who praised the students for the positive and constructive way in which they had organized their show of strength. Davis was suitably impressed by the sincerity and model behaviour of the students, but he was not about to change government policy in the hothouse atmosphere of the Gardens. He skated in and out of the rally politically undiminished, his stature among Conservatives rising to unassailable heights. The rally lasted long past the planned two hours and ended with a folk Mass concelebrated by Archbishop Pocock, Bishop Ryan and Bishop Francis Marrocco.[202]

The great Catholic roar was answered by more silence from Queen's Park. The ruling Conservatives had other more pressing matters on their mind. John Robarts resigned from politics in early 1971. Highly respected on both sides of the legislative assembly, a politician so inoffensive as to be everyone's favourite uncle, Robarts never warmed up for an instant to the trustees' "Equal Opportunity" brief and chose to leave the separate school file to his successor. Bill Davis, who had been Robarts' minister of education since 1962, became premier of Ontario in February 1971. During his run for the leadership, he told audience after audience not to expect separate school extension. This had the effect of soothing opponents of extension, many of whom voted Conservative, and keeping OSSTA and its allies off balance and in the dark, wondering if the Conservatives had no intention of completing the separate school system, why bother continuing the completion campaign.

The one thing never in short supply at OSSTA was hope. If completion were a Christian undertaking, there had to be hope that some day, someone at Queen's Park would hear their plea. It was with hope, if not great expectations, that OSSTA continued its work in 1971. It had a full discussion on extension at its annual convention, on 1 April 1971, and it distributed copies of a twenty-seven-page transcript of the proceedings to each separate school board.[203] The months quietly evaporated, turning spring into summer, with still no

438

word from either Premier Davis or Robert Welch, the minister of education. To the political mix was added the general expectation of a provincial election, which made an already tense situation even more so. No one, apart from the more radicalized, wanted separate schools to become an election issue. The Church would have to keep the election out of the pulpit, and OSSTA would have to be neutral. Backing the wrong political horse would ruin its reputation as a partner in education and rob it of any currency with the new government. With all these worries at hand, the Working Committee organized a special Extension Convention for Monday, 30 August 1971.[204] The timing could not have been more ironic.

On Tuesday morning, 31 August, Premier Bill Davis gave his answer to the May 1969 "Equal Opportunity" brief. The answer was "No." Davis met with his cabinet for ninety minutes and afterwards visited Archbishop Pocock at the chancery office before he delivered his verdict at a press conference at Queen's Park. Reading from a thirteen-page statement, Davis said:

> If the government were arbitrarily to decide to establish and maintain out of public funds a complete educational system determined by denominational and religious considerations, such a decision would fragment the present system beyond recognition and repair, and do so to the disadvantage of all those who have come to want for their children a public school system free of a denominational or sectarian character.
>
> The government has therefore concluded that it cannot support the proposals of the Ontario Separate School Trustees' Association.[205]

Davis reassured separate school supporters that their elementary schools were a matter of constitutional right and had contributed greatly to the building of the province and that no government could abolish them. But he also told them that even though government support of Grades 9 and 10 "offered a practical and sensible solution for many who have been otherwise disadvantaged . . . it was never intended as an encroachment upon the principle of a free, non-denominational and non-sectarian secondary school system, accessible to all and supported by all."[206]

Premier Davis did not arrive at his answer without considerable personal anguish. He counted among his friends many Catholic bishops and priests, and he had maintained a good professional relationship with OSSTA during his tenure as education minister. Davis admired Catholic commitment to separate schools, but he was also a politician who was readying his fellow Conservatives for an election. Davis did not want to lose his party's hold on power because he was seen as waffling on separate schools or caving into the Catholics, who were and still are a minority. Davis had the support of his caucus, the cabinet and the Conservative hinterland, where rumblings about the merger of school boards (and in particular separate school boards), eighteen months earlier, were a strong caution against any more "concessions" to separate schools.

OSSTA produced a preliminary comment on 7 September. It was bitter and denunciatory, calling Davis's reply to the 1969 brief as "backward looking, misleading, irrelevant and even confusing."[207] The trustees decried the premier's introduction of "credal criteria into the solution of an educational problem." For OSSTA, the demand for separate school extension had never been about religion; rather, it was all about the right of separate school students to a continuous education. Incensed, OSSTA refused to accept Davis's answer as final, vowing to continue "to provide opportunity for 400,000 students, comparable to that in the other sector of provincially-supported education, in the spirit of Confederation and in accordance with modern needs."[208] There was hope that common sense would prevail one day.

The election of 22 October 1971 vindicated Davis's political instincts. The Conservatives cakewalked to a landslide victory. They won 78 seats, while the Liberals dropped from 27 to 20 seats and the NDP from 21 to 19 seats.

The executive of OSSTA met with Premier Davis and Robert Welch on 19 November 1971. They made it clear that the government's announcement of 31 August 1971 had to be taken literally and would not be changed. Also, it was not the government's intention to provide secondary school grants to Grades 9 and 10 but adjustments could be made in the weighting factors that had begun to help them. However, any rapid rise in Grade 9 and 10 enrolment would be closely watched and controlled. According to Dr. Nick Mancini, the government showed no concern over the transfer of students from one system to the other and absolutely no interest in private schools.[209]

A long winter chill had descended.

A Political Interlude, 1971-1984

Premier's Davis's announcement of 31 August 1971 put an end to any hope for completion in the foreseeable future. The Ontario Separate School Trustee's Association, always realistic in its political gamesmanship, knew that since the battle had been lost — decisively — it would be pointless to carry on the completion campaign, in any guise no matter how discreet. The horse had keeled over, and no amount of kicking would bring it back to life.

But OSSTA did not so much abandon completion as it embraced the separate school system as it was and participated in the politics of education in Ontario according to changing circumstances. During the next dozen or so years, OSSTA kept completion off its agenda and off the public's mind and concentrated its best collective efforts on improving the overall well-being of separate schools, especially Grades 9 and 10, and encouraging separate school boards throughout the province to offer these two grades to Catholic teenagers.[210] In the process, OSSTA grew in administrative sophistication, influence and profile, so much so that Ed Brisbois could boast: "One thing is certain. No other trustee association has ever, or will ever have, the specific knowledge, the human resources or the unity of purpose which are so vital in the service to separate school boards. O.S.S.T.A. remains the one trustee body which shares the common faith dimension around which all of our decisions must be made. When I refer to one body, I mean also our Franco-Ontarian counterpart . . ."[211] That counterpart was the Catholic section of l'Association française des conseils scolaires de l'Ontario (AFCSO).

****

OSSTA applied its considerable energy and expanding expertise to a wide range of issues that confronted (and sometimes bewildered) separate school trustees in the 1970s and early 1980s. It was a time of fiscal restraint and cutbacks, cyclic economic prosperity and decline, fluctuating enrolment and all its attendant problems, legislation concerning teacher negotiations, the search for a workable model of trusteeship for minority language schools within the separate school system and plenty of soul-searching on the definition and role of "Catholic education" in an increasingly secularized and indifferent culture. It was also a time of self-definition for OSSTA, which was now the major player in separate school politics, a position that solidified with the passage of time. The English Catholic Education Association of Ontario changed its name in 1973 to the Federation of Catholic Education Associations of Ontario and was still considered the official umbrella of Catholic education groups, including the school trustees. However, the designation was more honorific than practical, and it faded into insignificance.[212] The same fate awaited the Ontario Catholic Student Federation. The Maple Leaf Gardens rally was the high point of its corporate existence. It was a brilliant, even glorious, moment but one that was unable to sustain itself beyond the storied walls of the Gardens. As for the bishops, they stayed in the background, but they did resurface during the 1975-76 debate on Catholicity and the 1978 drive to persuade the government to give academic credit for courses in religious education.

OSSTA addressed constitutional reform in 1971 and 1980, on both occasions advocating in the strongest terms the privileged entrenchment of Section 93 of the BNA Act and an improvement concerning bilingualism in a reformulated Section 133. In a 1980 article, Father Raymond Durocher stressed that there were three kinds of rights that needed to be entrenched in any new constitution: individual rights, group rights and historic rights. Into the third category he placed Section 93. "What was entrenched in 1867," he wrote, "was in intent a historical fact of Canadian life, quite distinct from, and more concrete than, the philosophical principles upon which current stresses on human and social rights are based."[213]

On 23 May 1972, OSSTA submitted a brief to the Committee on the Costs of Education, sometimes known as the McEwan Committee. In part one of its submission, OSSTA said that there was a continuing need for additional funds for both elementary and secondary education; that the goal of common education was "equal opportunity for twelve years of schooling to enable any youth to attain a reasonable development of his talents and a beginning of maturity in this complex world;"[214] and that the government should complete "the correction of anomalies and inequities . . . with regard to the separate school sector of the publicly-supported school system."[215] The second part of the brief dealt with very technical matters such as ceilings on expenditures and the use of weighting factors (adjustments) to provide some financial relief, the accumulated financial burden of many boards which were unable to spend up to the grantable ceilings because of extraordinary expenditures not covered by the legislative grants and rationalizing assessment, a perennial concern.

In 1976, OSSTA and AFCSO, with the support of the Ontario Catholic Supervisory Officers' Association, presented a brief to the Commission on the Reform of Property Taxation in Ontario, known as the Blair Commission. The trustees agreed to a decrease in residential taxation, but they pointed out that separate school boards would not benefit from any decrease unless they had access to other forms of assessment. They also agreed to a single mill rate for municipal purposes and payments in lieu of taxes on properties controlled by the federal and provincial governments, but they opposed the inclusion of municipal and school board property in the policy. The trustees described proposals to tax the property of private schools as "unnecessary, punitive, small-minded."[216] Lastly, they recommended the pooling and distribution of public property tax and corporation taxes, or payments in lieu, on the basis of relative enrolment. *The Report of the Commission on the Reform of Property Taxation in Ontario* was published on 10 March 1977, and the two trustee associations filed a formal response to it on 23 September 1977.[217]

Other endeavours included briefs, resolutions and position papers on shared accommodation of school buildings (in 1972, OSSTA opposed in principle the idea of shared accommodation but realized that there might be exceptions); the re-organization of regional offices of the department of education (1972); "The Consolidation of Education Acts" (Bill 255, 1974); "The Education Act" (Bill 72, 1974); Human Rights in Ontario (1976); the education of the trainable retarded (1976); a joint task force with the bishops on credit courses in religious education for Grades 9 and 10 (granted on 29 May 1978); declining enrolments and the delivery of quality education (1978); responses to the Reville Report (1973) and the Matthews Commission (1981) on the negotiation process between teachers and school boards; a submission to the Secondary Education Review Project (1981, known as SERP, its report made 98 recommendations of which four, numbers 88-91, concerned separate schools); and, of course, the annual meeting between representatives of OSSTA and officials from the ministry of education.[218]

****

In the words of one historian, Premier Davis's decision to say "No" to completion "was made easier because of the growing difficulty of defining what a Catholic high school was, and of proving its religious effectiveness."[219] That difficulty rested not with the premier or anyone else in government but with the whole range of Catholic separate school supporters — parents, teachers, trustees, administrators, parish priests and bishops. It was no use answering the question, "What makes a school a Catholic school?" with "I know one when I see one." And how could anyone ever measure the religious effectiveness of a Catholic school, if by "religious effectiveness" one meant the actual number of Catholics who remained practicing Catholics because of their attendance at a Catholic high school. One academic suggested that a Catholic high school's effect on a student's commitment to his faith was very limited.[220]

Archbishop Philip Pocock gave his own answer to the first question in a widely published article in 1972. Non-Catholics who

444

questioned the existence of separate schools were his intended audience, but, one might be inclined to say, Catholics were his real audience. A Catholic school is much more than just a school in which the students and teachers were Catholic and where religion was taught several hours a week. "Basically a Catholic School is one in which God, his truth, his life are integrated into the entire syllabus, curriculum and life of the school."[221] A Catholic school aims for academic excellence, of course, but it keeps God in every area of study. It is a Christian community that "stresses the sacred character of man, his divine origin and destiny, his responsibility to God, to God's people and to the entire creation."[222]

But there was another question that had to be answered. Just how were Catholic separate schools to live up to the archbishop's definition of a Catholic school? The answer was (and remains) fundamental to the integrity and survival of separate schools. Kenneth Westhues thought that "the success of Catholic schools is dependent upon the extent to which they receive public legitimation, that is recognition and support by established governmental authority and popular culture. To the degree that such legitimation is lacking, the success of such schools is explained by religious commitment and ease of mobilization of the Catholic population."[223] To put this in the historical context of Ontario, we will understand "success" to mean "survival" and will define "survival" as the unqualified retention of the Catholicity of Catholic schools. Prior to 1962-63, the year the government introduced the Ontario Foundation Tax Plan, the religious commitment of the Catholic people ensured the survival of Catholic separate schools. They were legitimate because Catholics made them legitimate, and they were obviously Catholic for all to see. However, after 1962-63, the legitimacy enjoyed by Catholic separate schools began (albeit very slowly and subtly) to depend less on the religious commitment of the Catholic people and more on government generosity and a concomitant shift in popular opinion towards separate schools. As time passed, the separate school system became relatively more prosperous and its dependency on the government and popular opinion for legitimacy grew and grew. Although Premier Davis's 1971 refusal to grant completion signaled that the government and popular opinion were not ready to grant full legitimacy to separate schools, there were Catholics who already saw the paradox of one day having a separate school system that was complete from kindergarten to Grade 13 but lacked the depth of Catholic commitment that would ensure its Catholicity. Among these were the trustees. They realized that "all the legal and financial safeguards for separate schools were of little value unless the freedom provided by them was filled with genuine Catholic education."[224] Which returns us to Archbishop's Pocock's definition of a Catholic school — therein resided the conundrum for Catholic educators and trustees.

The conundrum, though, was not news to OSSTA. Central to Catholic education was the teaching of the Catholic faith. However, those who had been traditionally entrusted with this task — the sisters from the different religious communities — were beginning to decline in proportion to the overall number of teachers in the system, as early as the 1960s, and would soon begin a precipitous descent in absolute numbers, with little hope of regaining their former predominance. The only credible response to this emerging crisis would be to train qualified lay teachers to teach the Catholic faith and to have their training be given in the teachers' colleges and be recognized as an accredited course by the Ontario department of education.

This was a radical but necessary turn of events in the history of separate schools, made all the more necessary by the introduction of a new Canadian catechism, *Come to the Father*. Directing the politics of accreditation, as equal partners, were OSSTA and OECTA. Input from the bishops' committee on education, chaired by Bishop Carter of London, came in the bishops' approval of the course content. On 4 September 1968, Chris Asseff, executive director of OSSTA, and Mary Babcock, his counterpart at OECTA, presented the brief "On the Training of Teachers in Religious Education for the Separate Schools of Ontario," to Premier John Robarts and Bill Davis, the minister of education. Written by Paul Forestell, a lawyer from Welland, the brief was divided into three parts: Outline of Courses for Teacher Training; A Suggested Course of Studies in Religious Education; and Recommendations, which included "That a regular course in Religious Education be provided in the Teachers' Colleges of the Province, to be given by qualified instructors according to a timetable equivalent to that allotted for major subjects."[225]

Although Robarts and Davis promised an answer by the end of 1968, none came, and the trustees and the teachers decided to jointly sponsor and fund their own religious education course and to quietly lobby separate school boards across the province to have their teachers take the course. Certificates would be issued by OSSTA and OECTA. The first offering was a five-week course in the summer of 1969, in Toronto and North Bay.[226] Enrolment was low — only forty-one teachers registered in Toronto — because news of the course came too close to the summer holidays. However, a province-wide tour of separate school boards promoting the Religious Education course produced much better results in 1970. That year there were four winter courses followed by another summer course, the last one being recognized by the department of education.[227]

It was only a matter of time before full recognition was granted. An ad hoc committee on religious education, consisting of Albert E. Klein and Chris Asseff of OSSTA, John Kuchinak and Mary Babcock of OECTA and Bishop Joseph R. Windle of Pembroke, met with the department of education in 1970. The committee was able to satisfy the department's concerns about a common curriculum, an evaluation process and other requirements. Davis was satisfied. On 26 January 1971, the department accepted three religious education courses sponsored by OSSTA and OECTA. In the words of one historian, "It would now be possible for a teacher to obtain three credits equal to a university credit or to another Departmental course for advancement to the next standard of a teacher's certificate and/or toward the next salary level."[228] The significance of this was not lost on Franklin Walker, who wrote: "In the end the religious training of teachers which the teachers' association and the trustees provided would be the main support for the religious orientation of separate schools."[229]

Complementing the accreditation of religious education courses for teachers was the success of OSSTA and its allies in convincing the government to recognize religion courses in Grades 9 and 10 as credits towards the Grade 12 diploma. On 1 March 1978, members of the Ontario bishops, OSSTA and the Ontario Catholic Supervisory Officers' Association submitted a seven-page statement on "Credit for Courses in Religious Education" to Thomas Wells, the minister of education.[230] Representing the episcopacy in this joint task force were Bishop James L. Doyle, Bishop Eugene P. LaRocque and Bishop John M. Sherlock; representing the trustees were C. Frank Giloohy, Dr. Nicholas Mancini, William J. Hillyer and Chris Asseff; and representing the supervisory officers were Patrick J. Brennan and Kenneth J. Regan. The task force did an excellent job of bringing Wells to their way of thinking. On 29 May 1978, the government announced its intention to give credit for Grades 9 and 19 religion courses, beginning in September.[231]

The two victories of 1971 and 1978 dealt with the teachers of religion and the students who studied it for credit. In between those two victories, the trustees as an association turned inward to examine themselves, so that they could consider how best to exercise their trusteeship of the separate schools in light of both the Gospel and a changing world that wanted little or nothing to do with the Gospel. The quest for Catholicity (a word that would gain ever more currency during the 1970s and 1980s) concerned everyone involved in Catholic separate schools. It was a matter of reinventing one's identity. To that end, OSSTA set up the Focus on Faith for the Future, or 3-F program, in late 1973, and hired Sister Elaine Dunn, CSJ, as the program's full-time resource co-ordinator.

The main thrust of the program was "to reaffirm and to strengthen today, the vision and courage shown by the Catholic community more than a century ago when separate schools were first established."[232] One might call this the historical component — to know one's past, especially as a people, was necessary to live in the present and to prepare for the future. This search for the past was then followed by a call to action:

> that the Catholic Community of priests, parents, trustees and teachers seek *together* to create an educational environment in continuity with the home. This environment must be one wherein youth will, of necessity, be drawn into an alive, adult,

448

faith-filled Catholic Community which, while adapting to the new set of circumstances created by today's world, does not negate the rich traditions and values which are our heritage.[233]

The project was divided into three phases. The first phase concentrated on the faith of the trustees. More than 800 trustees and superintendents participated during 1974 and 1975. To facilitate these day-long gatherings, or Faith Celebrations, the province was divided into ten regions, with delegates in each region meeting on a specified date. The day began with Mass celebrated by a bishop who also delivered the sermon (many of these sermons were later published in *Catholic Trustee*). This was followed by small group meetings that featured trustees from different boards sharing their experiences and ideas, and finally by a plenary session that filled in the remainder of the program. The second phase lasted four years and was divided into two sections, both of which were devoted to the faith of parents. The first section involved trustees, administrators, their spouses and parent couples. They met region by region during 1975. The second part had parents, priests, teachers, trustees and administrators meet at the local board level, from 1976 to 1978, with a parish priest responsible for the Mass and sermon. Approximately 1,700 people participated in the second phase. Each participant was expected to make a conscious effort "to combine maximum personal participation and in-depth discussion, with liturgical preparation and celebration . . . in which unity of purpose and sharing of efforts were germane to the working out of the programme."[234] The third phase, from 1979 to 1980, was called "Trustee Leadership and the Faith Dimension."[235] Its purpose was "to implement at the various local levels the wishes and hopes expressed in Phase Two by our Catholic Parents. Naturally, the children in our schools will be the centre and object of this Phase and must involve, if it is to achieve its goal, the entire Catholic Education Team in a common enterprise of Faith."[236]

At the Focus on Faith for the Future meeting held in Belleville, on 10 February 1974, Bishop Francis A. Marrocco suggested that the trustees would not enjoy true satisfaction in their roles until they embraced the following four statements:

1) It is absolutely essential that every individual involved in the Separate School system have genuine Catholic Faith.

2) If every individual involved in the Separate School System has genuine Catholic Faith, together they will think and act like a Catholic Community.

3) Catholic parents are getting a full return from their creation of the Separate School System because it is a real Catholic Community.

4) The great advantage that Catholic parents have in sending their children to a Catholic school is that every last school in the Separate System is staffed by people who have genuine Catholic Faith and form a real Catholic Community.[237]

These statements were essentially ideals. Towards these goals the trustees and their partners in Catholic education had to strive, always, and with diligence and perseverance. It is a never-ending task. That the trustees had the wisdom to see this in 1972, so soon after the collapse of the completion campaign, speaks volumes about their desire to continue the good fight. And it says a great deal about their knowing that the fight was about more than taxes and grants and even completion itself. It was about the joy and the challenge of working with the Catholic community to fulfill the promise bequeathed to them to establish and maintain a system of Catholic schools for Catholic children. OSSTA's Focus on Faith for the Future program forced the trustees into a prolonged period of self-examination, which helped to foster a durable identity for themselves as an association and by implication for the schools under their governance.

****

Another pressing matter that rose to the top of OSSTA's agenda was the place of French-language minority rights within the separate school system, and the role of trustees in administering those rights. Any discussion on the matter, no matter how diplomatic, would be complicated by the fact that beginning in 1968, French-speaking separate school supporters had effectively abandoned the completion campaign and willingly turned over their secondary schools to the public boards in exchange for a continuity in French-language instruction. This left the French elementary schools in the separate school system exposed to a type of thinking that subordinated religion to language and treated French-language separate schools as obstacles to the development of French cultural and educational opportunities for Franco-Ontarians.[238]

In opposition to this type of thinking, there was l'Association française des conseils scolaires de l'Ontario. By the late 1970s, its membership had begun to reinvigorate its commitment to a Catholic faith-based system of education and to seek ways to improve and solidify its trusteeship over French-language instruction within the separate schools. So-called umbrella boards that would incorporate separate elementary schools and public secondary schools were out of the question because they would be impractical and unconstitutional. As for stand-alone French-language separate school boards — the ideal solution — they would have to wait until the government implemented completion. Until then, a workable solution had to be found within the current legal structure that defined and governed separate schools, which was Part IV of the "Education Act" (*Revised Statutes of Ontario* 1980, c. 129).

Pressure to adopt this approach had come from outside and inside the French Catholic community. An example of outside pressure was the Royal Commission on Bilingualism and Biculturalism. It published its final report in six volumes. In the volume called Education (1968), the commissioners were hardly enthusiastic about the continuing existence of separate schools, but they did not hesitate to recommend that in Ontario French-language schools should be kept as part of the existing school board structure.[239] From within the ranks of Franco-Ontarians there was the voice of O. Tremblay, director of education for the Sudbury District Roman Catholic Separate School Board. Speaking in 1981, he said that "All Catholic trustees in Ontario should realize that their educational system has much in common with the country itself and should clearly understand that the unity and harmony within the Catholic school system in Ontario could be a living example of the unity and harmony that should exist across the land."[240] Unity and harmony — these were the predominant political watchwords of the early 1980s, when the federal government repatriated the constitution and passed the Constitution Act with a Charter of Rights and Freedoms.

In 1983, l'Association française des conseils scolaires de l'Ontario and the Ontario Separate School Trustees' Association responded to Tremblay's call for unity and harmony among separate school supporters by entering into a formal entente on the trusteeship of minority-language schools in the Ontario Catholic School System. Dated 19 December 1983, the "Entente" was actually a submission to a ministry of education document, "A Proposal in Response to the Report of the Joint Committee on the Governance of French-Language Elementary and Secondary Schools." The two trustee associations sought to confirm two rights for the resident pupils of Roman Catholic separate school boards: the right to receive education in either one of the official languages of instruction and the right to attend a class or school using either one of the official languages of instruction. Separate school rights were rooted in Section 93 of the BNA Act and were protected in Section 29 of the Charter; language rights were guaranteed in Section 23 of the Charter, which gave constitutional standing to the educational aspirations of Franco-Ontarians. Other sources of affirmation were Sections 32 and 258 of "The Education Act."

The model of governance they proposed for each separate school board was a unified board divided into two sections, one for each of the two official languages. The board as a whole would be responsible for "those matters which constitute the unique corporate entity of the Catholic separate school board and particularly to all matters which directly affect the denominational character of such schools or which are commonly accepted as the primary concerns of a board." The two sections, meanwhile, would be responsible for "management and control of personnel, resources and facilities required for the provision of adequate instructional, supervisory, consultative and support services in the class or classes, school or schools or section of either official languages of instruction."[241] There would be adequate mechanisms in place so that the two language sections could co-ordinate their efforts and co-operate with each other "for the efficient and harmonious operation of the board."[242] An appeals committee would resolve conflicts. The apportionment of minority language trustees for each board would be based on the number of full-time students being instructed in a minority official language, in French or English as the case may be, with a minimum of three and a maximum of seven trustees. To demonstrate their good faith in the "Entente," OSSTA took charge of the separate school portion of a 1984 appeal to the Ontario Court of Appeal, in a matter involving minority language education rights.[243]

Tucked in at the bottom of page four of the "Entente" was this caveat: "the right to an education within the Roman Catholic separate school system will not be fully and equitably achieved until the completion of that system to the end of the secondary school program has become a reality."[244] Little did the trustees know that the reality they so eagerly sought was just around the corner.

Premier Davis Says "Yes" to Completion, 1984

On Tuesday afternoon, 12 June 1984, Premier Bill Davis rose in the Legislative Assembly to deliver a government statement on Roman Catholic secondary schools. This would be no ordinary statement; it would be a first-rate political bombshell, a rare and historic volte-face on separate school policy for both the Conservative Party and the ever cautious premier from Brampton. A half century of campaigning and lobbying on behalf of Catholic high schools was about to end in favour of separate school supporters.[245]

Davis informed the Speaker and the Assembly that "the government has undertaken a careful and fresh review of the outstanding issues surrounding public support for the Roman Catholic school system, and this afternoon I wish to outline a new course we have decided to pursue."[246] Nearly half way through his statement, Davis finally spelled out the government's new policy:

to permit the Roman Catholic school boards to establish a full range of elementary and secondary education, and, as part of the public system, to be funded accordingly. This new program will be introduced at the rate of one year of secondary education for each school year beginning September 1, 1985. This process will be accomplished in much the same way we are implementing the new special education provisions and will parallel the revised secondary school structure.[247]

Ever the political pragmatist, Davis was careful to address both sides of the School Question. He promised public school supporters that there was nothing in the new policy that "would cripple or limit the viability of our non-denominational public secondary school system, which is accessible to all and universally supported, and which will always remain the cornerstone of our education system."[248] Public schools would always have pride of place. At the same time, the government could not be a hostage to old arrangements. "The letter of the old law cannot substitute for common sense," Davis said, "historic benefits must keep up with changing times."[249] Now was the time, the premier continued, to satisfy "the aspirations of a good third of our families who have demonstrated their competence and determination to provide contemporary education for their children."[250] The families referred to were Catholic families with children in separate schools. Although Catholics were still a minority in Ontario, they were a large minority and did not wish to be isolated from the rest of society. They were very much a part of the mainstream.

The premier then went on to announce the formation of a planning and implementation commission, a commission on the financing of elementary and secondary education and a commission on independent schools. The last two commissions were to report by May 1985. The planning and implementation commission, meanwhile, would "guide and advise all parties" involved in the implementation process, "receive and adjudicate the plans submitted by the Roman Catholic school boards," advise on changes to the "'Education Act' and conduct arbitrations that may well be required in some instances arising out of the sharing or transfer of schools and school locations."[251] The commission would have for its members representatives from the ministry of education, the education community at large and the Roman Catholic community.

When Davis had finished speaking, he received a standing ovation from all three parties. Bob Rae, the NDP leader crossed the floor of the legislature to shake the premier's hand. It was an unprecedented show of unity on an issue that had bedeviled Ontario politics for more than a century.

The decision to complete the separate school system revealed more about Bill Davis than it did about the Conservative party or any constituent part of the Catholic community, including OSSTA. It was really his decision and his alone. No more than a dozen or so people knew in advance. Davis informed the Conservative caucus about fifty minutes prior to entering the Legislative Assembly, a move that left no one much time to stage a revolt. Much has been made of Davis's friendship with Archbishop Pocock and then with Cardinal Carter. According to Claire Hoy, Carter had secured Davis's promise to extend full funding to separate schools after the 1981 provincial election and spent the next three years pressuring Davis, in public and in private, to make good on the promise.[252] Rosemary Speirs mentioned a 1984 Goldfarb poll in which "for the first time more than half the citizenry supported extension of full funding to Catholic schools."[253] And there was the fact of Grade 9 and 10 separate school enrolment. In 1971, there were 18,882 students enrolled in Grades 9 and 10; in 1983, there were 37,393 students, who were part of an all-time record separate school enrolment of 430,000 students.[254] To this number of students in Grades 9 and 10 could be added the more than 30,000 students in the senior secondary grades.[255] Instead of fading away after 1971, as some had predicted, Catholic high schools were actually prospering, at least in terms of enrolment.

At the end of the day, it was Davis's conscience that ushered in a new era for Catholic separate schools. He had never felt comfortable winning the 1971 election at the expense of separate school supporters. Thirteen years later, on the cusp of retirement, separate schools were still an unresolved issue. Davis had three choices before him: confirm the status quo, abolish government support of Grades 9 and 10 or complete the system. He chose to complete the system. "I think I had come to the conclusion that in terms of equity, in terms of fairness, whatever way you wish to describe it, that it was the right thing to do."[256] In a simple, straightforward sixteen-minute speech, Bill Davis ended 160 years of separate school agitation.

---

[1] Not to be confused with the Ontario Catholic Educational Council, an earlier bishop-sponsored organization. See the Early History section of this chapter.

[2] Franklin A. Walker, *Catholic Education and Politics in Ontario*, vol. 3 (Toronto: Catholic Education Foundation of Ontario, 1986), 3.

[3] Walker, *Catholic Education and Politics in Ontario*, 3:106.

[4] W.G. Fleming, *Educational contributions of associations*, vol. 7 of *Ontario's Educative Society* (Toronto: University of Toronto Press, 1972), 1-6. See also Edwin C. Guillet, *In the Cause of Education* (Toronto: University of Toronto Press, 1960).

[5] Ontario Separate School Trustees' Association [hereafter OSSTA], *Minutes, 1925-1939*, 15 April 1925, [1]-[2].

[6] Ibid., [3].

[7] Ibid., 2 April 1929 [11].

[8] Ibid., [10]-[11]; R. Durocher, "After Fifty Golden Years Pioneer Spirit Unchanged," *Catholic Trustee* (March 1980), 3-4.

[9] OSSTA, *Minutes*, 1925-1939, 2 April 1929, [13].

[10] Walker, *Catholic Education and Politics in Ontario*, 2: 351.

[11] ARCAT, ED SO02.01, E.C. Desormeaux to McNeil, 1 May 1929.

[12] Ibid., MG 5026.285 (a), Private and Confidential, 30 September 1931.

[13] Ontario Educational Association, *Proceedings of the Seventy-first Annual Convention* (Toronto: King's Printer, 1932), Board of Directors, 1931-32.

[14] "Report of the Retiring President Francis G. Carter," *Catholic Trustee* (May 1962), 6-7; J.W. Fyfe, "President's Address," *Catholic Trustee* (June 1966), 8-10; P.M. Muir, "The Ontario School Trustees' Council," *Catholic Trustee* (January 1967), 4-5.

[15] *Catholic Register*, 27 April 1933, 1.

[16] Canada, Royal Commission on Dominion-Provincial Relations, "Brief of the Roman Catholic Separate School Trustees' Association of Ontario," No. 400, 31 May 1938. This brief was ten mimeographed pages.

[17] OSSTA, *Minutes*, 1925-1939, 30-31 March 1937, [80]-[81].

[18] Ibid., 24 April 1930, [19].

[19] Ibid., Educational Committee, 1 September 1930, [24].

[20] ARCAT, MG 5020.76 (c), J.G. Kelly to "Dear Sirs," 21 September 1936.

[21] Ibid., ED SO13.233, "Extract of Minutes of Meeting of the Ontario Separate School Trustees' Association Held in Teefy Hall on Wednesday, April 8th, 1942."

[22] *Canadian Register*, 8 May 1943, 1.

[23] ARCAT, ED SO02.71, Priester to Archbishop Philip F. Pocock, 30 March 1961.

[24] Ibid.

[25] *Canadian Register*, 8 May 1943, 10.

[26] Diocese of Hamilton, Clergy Files, "Priester, Vincent;" *Catholic Register*, 15 June 1985, 14.

[27] OSSTA, Joseph P. Finn, ["Memories"], 25 March 1991, 3.

[28] ARCAT, ED SO02.39, McGuigan to Bishop Joseph F. Ryan, 14 April 1950; MG FA16.24, Bishop Raphael H. Dignan to McGuigan, 15 April 1950; MG FA16.27, Archbishop Joseph A. O'Sullivan to McGuigan, 24 April 1950; ED SO02.292-.293, Bishop Joseph F. Ryan, Bishop Joseph G. Berry and Cardinal McGuigan, 24 April 1950.

[29] In 1963, Father Priester became Monsignor Priester, a prelate of honour. However, since the title came at the end of his tenure at ECEAO, it would be more accurate to refer to him as Father. He died on 29 May 1985 and is buried at Holy Sepulchre Cemetery in Burlington.

[30] ARCAT, SO02, Papers of the English Catholic Education Association of Ontario.

[31] Walker, *Catholic Education and Politics in Ontario*, 3: 12-13.

[32] C.F. Gilhooly, "One Word, 'Overtime', Sums up Association's Golden History," *Catholic Trustee* (June 1980), 5. For an in-depth explanation of this new system of grants, and why it failed to bring much relief to separate schools, see Robert M.

Stamp, *The Schools of Ontario, 1876-1976* (Toronto: University of Toronto Press, 1987), 185.

[33] *Canadian Register*, 22 April 1944, 10, "Premier Drew Addresses Catholic Educators"; 19 April 1947, 1, 7, "Distinguished Leaders, Clerical and Lay, Address Education Conference"; 23 April 1955, 1, "Leaders Hear Cardinal, Premier Frost Praise Good Work of Separate Schools."

[34] Walker, *Catholic Education and Politics in Ontario*, 3: 14, fn. 8.

[35] Ibid., 3:20.

[36] OSSTA, Black Scrapbook, "Report of the Royal Commission on Education," 1.

[37] Ontario, *Report of the Royal Commission on Education in Ontario 1950* (Toronto: King's Printer, 1950), 498.

[38] Walker, *Catholic Education and Politics in Ontario*, 3: 23.

[39] The Inter-Church Committee was not alone in its hostility towards separate schools. A Committee of the Ottawa Local, District No. 1 of the Ontario Men Teachers' Federation, in a "Report: A Suggested Programme for Post-War Education in Canada," had this to say about separate and parochial schools: "Religious instruction should be for Christian living; dogma should be taught in the church. Therefore, your Committee recommend that there be no Separate or parochial schools in Canada and that religious instruction be given, if all, before or after school hours." Except for the reference to Christian living, this is an opinion shared by many people today. Assumption University Archives, Record Group I, Box 8, File 137.

[40] AO, RG 18-131, The Royal Commission on Education in Ontario. The other briefs were from the Toronto and Suburban Separate School Board (Brief 145); the North Bay Separate School Board (Brief 241); the Webbwood Separate School Trustees and Supporters (Brief 242); the Cache Bay Separate School Board (Brief 243); the Trustees and Supporters of St. Patrick's Separate School, Kearney (Brief 254); and the Massey Separate School Trustees and Supporters (Brief 257).

[41] Ibid., Box 16, Brief 146, 1.

[42] Ontario, Department of Education, *Report of the Minister of Education 1943* (Toronto: 1943), 61.

[43] AO, RG 18-131, Royal Commission on Education in Ontario, Box 16, Brief 146, 1-2.

[44] Ibid., Box 16, Brief 146, 5.

458

[45] Brief 146 originally used the following figures on page 7: $80.69 and $56.51 (line 8) and $56 and $80 (line 12). The correction was made in a letter from Father Vincent Priester to Dr. R.W.B. Jackson, Secretary, Royal Commission on Education, 4 January 1946.

[46] Ibid., Box 16, Brief 146, 7.

[47] Ibid., Box 16, Brief 146, 11.

[48] Ibid., Box 18, Brief 196, 2.

[49] Ibid., Box 18, Brief 196, 5-6.

[50] Actually, the Ontario Catholic Education Council submitted two supplementary briefs. The first was a list of answers to questions submitted to the Council by the commissioners. The second, and by far the more important of the two, was the one referred to here, dated 17 October 1946.

[51] AO, RG 18-131, Royal Commission on Education in Ontario, Box 16, Brief 146, Supplementary, 17.

[52] Ibid., Box 16, Brief 146, Supplementary, 21.

[53] Ibid., Box 16, Brief 146, Supplementary, 21.

[54] Ibid., Box 16, Brief 146, Extracts from the Report of Proceedings, 28 November 1946, 5.

[55] Ibid., 9.

[56] Ibid., 10.

[57] Ontario, *Report of the Royal Commission on Education in Ontario, 1950*, 492.

[58] Ibid., 499-500.

[59] Ibid., 506.

[60] Stamp, The *Schools of Ontario, 1876-1976*, 189.

[61] Ibid.

[62] OSSTA, Black Scrapbook, "Cardinal McGuigan Press Release." See also *Toronto Daily Star*, 22 December 1950, 1.

[63] Stamp, *The Schools of Ontario, 1876-1976*, 190.

[64] Walker, *Catholic Education and Politics in Ontario*, 3: 68.

[65] Roberston Davies, "Don't be Flippant Toward a Half a Million," *Peterborough Examiner*, 14 February 1951. A typed copy of this editorial can be found in OSSTA, Black Scrapbook. Davies was very annoyed at the politicians for their willingness to jettison the entire report "because a few suggestions in it would lose votes for whatever party put them into effect." This was an oblique reference to the commission's suggestions on separate schools.

[66] OSSTA, *Minutes of the Annual General Meeting, 23-24 April 1957*, 3.

[67] W.G. Fleming, *The expansion of the educational system*, vol. 1 of Ontario's Educative Society (Toronto: University of Toronto Press, 1971), 43, 56, 95, 144, 147, 323-25, 334-36, 342-43.

[68] Ontario, Department of Education, *Report of the Minister 1950* (Toronto: 1950), 48; ibid., *Report of the Minister 1960* (Toronto: 1960), S-3; *Report of the Minister 1963* (Toronto: 1963), 3.

[69] OSSTA, *Minutes of Meeting of the Ontario Separate School Trustees' Association, 15 April 1952*, [3].

[70] Ibid., *Minutes of the Annual General Meeting*, 8-9 April 1958, 7.

[71] Ibid., *Minutes of the Annual General Meeting*, 23-24 April 1957, 84.

[72] Quoted in Walker, *Catholic Education and Politics in Ontario*, 3: 91, fn. 107.

[73] OSSTA, *Minutes of the Annual General Meeting*, 23-24 April 1957, 142-43.

[74] Ibid., *Minutes of the Annual General Meeting*, 8-9 April 1958, 24-25.

[75] Ibid., 8.

[76] Ibid., *Minutes of the Annual General Meeting*, 31 March-1 April 1959, 5.

[77] ARCAT, ED SO13.196 (b), OSSTA and ACEBO, "Statistical Report on Separate Schools of Ontario," (December 1959), 1-3.

[78] "Brief on Roman Catholic Separate Schools," *Catholic Trustee* (August 1961), 1-2.

[79] ARCAT, ED SP01.160, "Report on Education to their Excellencies the Bishops of Ontario," prepared by Father Vincent Priester for a bishops' meeting, Thursday, 5 October 1961.

[80] *Statutes of the Province of Canada*, 26 Victoria, c. 5, "An Act to restore to Roman Catholics in Upper Canada certain rights in respect to Separate Schools."

[81] It should be made clear that this problem did not extend to separate schools in incorporated towns and cities. School sections in municipalities were abolished as early as 1847. Subsequent legislation gave the right of public school boards to determine separate school divisions, but it failed. So too did an amendment that allowed the establishment of separate schools in each ward or a combination thereof. In 1863, separate school boards were finally allowed to manage schools for an entire municipality. See W.G. Fleming, The administrative structure, vol. 2 of *Ontario's Educative Society* (Toronto: University of Toronto Press, 1971), 157.

[82] OSSTA, Joseph P. Finn, ["Memories"], 11-12.

[83] For a full text of this decision, see Carter, *Judicial Decisions on Denominational Schools*, 358-60, or *Catholic Trustee* (February 1962), 1-2.

[84] *Municipal World* (January 1962), as quoted in *Catholic Trustee* (May 1962), 9.

[85] *Statutes of Ontario*, 1962-63, 10-11 Elizabeth II, c. 132, "An Act to amend the Separate Schools Act."

[86] *Catholic Trustee* (June 1963), 3.

[87] *Statutes of Ontario*, 1964, 12-13 Elizabeth II, c. 95, "An Act to amend The Public Schools Act."

[88] *Peterborough Examiner*, 30 October 1962. Robertson Davies was publisher of the paper at the time and may have written this editorial.

[89] OSSTA, Correspondence Roman Catholic Separate Schools 1962 (yellow binder), letter of Vincent Priester to Frank Carter, 22 November 1962.

[90] "Roman Catholic Bishops' Brief on Education," 27 October 1962, as reprinted in J. Bascom St. John, *Separate Schools in Ontario* (Toronto: Globe and Mail, [n.d.]), 37.

[91] Cameron's comments were widely reported. *Toronto Daily Star*, 30 October 1962.

[92] "The United Church replies to the R.C. Bishops," *The United Church Observer*, 1 November 1962.

[93] Fleming, *Educational contributions of associations*, 184-85.

[94] *Toronto Daily Star*, 30 October 1962; Fleming, *The administrative structure*, 239-40.

[95] *Toronto Daily Star*, 30 October 1962.

[96] Ibid., 13 November 1962.

[97] *Toronto Telegram*, 14 November 1962.

[98] Ibid., 17 January 1963.

[99] It had always been the intention of the special committee of English and French bishops and OSSTA and ACEBO representatives that the brief by the bishops would be followed by a brief from the two trustee associations that would provide a plan of action. However, no one knew, not even as late as September 1962, that the trustees would propose a foundation tax plan. See ARCAT, ED SO13.237, "Minutes of the Special Meeting with the Hierarchy," 27 September 1962, 2.

[100] OSSTA, *Minutes* 1961, 17 and 18 November 1961, 2.

[101] *Catholic Trustee* (May 1962), 8.

[102] Walker, *Catholic Education and Politics in Ontario*, 3: 117.

[103] Carl J. Matthews, SJ, "Foundation Program of School Finance as Applied in Alberta," *Catholic Trustee* (November 1962), 14-15.

[104] ARCAT, ED SO13.237, "Minutes of the Special Meeting with the Hierarchy," 27 September 1962, 2.

[105] Carl Matthews was a doctoral candidate in school administration and finance at the University of Toronto. He was a student of E.B. Rideout, who was one of two influential academic consultants to the powerful cabinet committee and the department of education committee that were debating the merits of a foundation tax plan. Matthews was ordained a priest on 4 June 1966.

[106] Carl J. Matthews, SJ, interview by Michael Power, 30 October 2001 and (by telephone), 8 January 2002; OSSTA, Correspondence Roman Catholic Separate Schools 1962 (yellow binder), letter of 13 November 1962, from Robert G. Laidlaw to Francis G. Carter.

[107] Fleming, *The administrative structure*," 239. See also The Federation of Catholic Parent-Teacher Associations of Ontario, *Petition Presented to the Prime Minister, to the Minister of Education and to the Members of the Legislative Assembly of Ontario* (4 February 1963). The federation made a strong case for financial equity but left it up to the government to find the proper solution.

[108] Matthews Papers, letter of 15 January 1963, from Carl J. Matthews, SJ to Robert Laidlaw.

[109] ARCAT, ED SO13.242, The Ontario Separate School Trustees' Association and l'Association des commissions des écoles bilingues d'Ontario, *Brief Presented to the Prime Minister, to the Minister of Education and to the Members of the Legislative Assembly of Ontario* (December, 1962), 6-7.

[110] Carl J. Matthews, SJ, "Background Comments on the Catholic Trustees' Brief," *Catholic Trustee* (January 1963), 34-35; ARCAT, ED S)13.245, OSSTA, *Proceedings of the Twentieth Annual Meeting of the Ontario Separate School Trustees' Association, 15-16 April 1963*, 15-18.

[111] "The Ontario Foundation Tax Plan 1964. Statement by the Honourable John Roberts, Prime Minister of Ontario, Delivered in the Ontario Legislature Thursday, February 21, 1963."

[112] Ontario, Legislature of Ontario, *Debates*, 26 March 1963, Afternoon Session, 2197-2212, 2223.

[113] "Statement by the Honourable W.G. Davis, Minister of Education on The Ontario Foundation Tax Plan made in the Legislature of Ontario, Monday, January 27, 1964," reprinted in *Catholic Trustee* (March 1964), 5.

[114] Fleming, *The administrative structure*, 248.

[115] David M. Cameron, *Schools for Ontario: Policy-Making, Administration, and Finance in the 1960s* (Toronto: University of Toronto Press, 1972), 155.

[116] OSSTA, *Minutes 1964*, 3 October 1964, 4.

[117] Ibid.

[118] E. Brock Rideout, "The Application of the 1964 Grant Plan," *Catholic Trustee* (June 1964), 13.

[119] OSSTA, *Minutes 1965*, 20 April 1965, 4.

[120] Ibid., *Minutes of the Special Advisory Committee on School Financing*, 19 May 1965.

[121] OSSTA, The Ontario Separate School Trustees' Association and l'Association des commissions des écoles bilingues d'Ontario, *Brief Presented to the Prime Minister and the Minister of Education of the Province of Ontario* (October 1966).

[122] See *Catholic Trustee* (March 1964), 11-12; (January 1967), 13-18; (May 1967), 21; (December 1974), 13-16; (December 1976), 36-37; (December 1979), 5-8; and (June 1981), 15-21. For various instalments of Carl Matthews' "Trends in Ontario Separate School Finance," see *Catholic Trustee* (February 1962), 4; (January 1963), 31-33;

(September 1966), 26-27; (September 1967), 6-7; (May 1969), 15; (June 1970), 10-11.

[123] Carl J. Matthews, SJ, "Equal Money Status Nears in Ontario Schools," *Catholic Trustee* (December 1977), 33.

[124] Dennis Gruending, *Emmett Hall: Establishment Radical* (Toronto: Macmillan, 1985), 104.

[125] Ibid., 107.

[126] Walker, *Catholic Education and Politics in Ontario*, 3: 216-20. Walker himself was a critic of the Hall-Dennis Report.

[127] *Living and Learning: The Report of the Provincial Committee on Aims and Objectives of Education in the Schools of Ontario* (Toronto: 1968), 4.

[128] W.G. Fleming, Schools, pupils, and teachers, vol. 3 of *Ontario's Educative Society* (Toronto: University of Toronto, 1972), 500.

[129] Ibid., 499.

[130] *Living and Learning*, 12.

[131] *Religious Information and Moral Development: The Report of the Committee on Religious Education in the Public Schools of the Province of Ontario* (1969). The Committee made twelve recommendations, including the abolition of religious education in the public elementary schools and the repeal of Regulation 45, which allowed public school boards to sanction the teaching of religion in selected schools, *Revised Statues of Ontario 1960*, c. 361. It was the existence of Regulation 45 that convinced many French Catholics to support the establishment of French-language public high schools in 1968. They believed that although these schools were public, they could still teach the Catholic faith. Consultants to the Committee included Archbishop Philip Pocock of Toronto, Bishop G. Emmett Carter of London, Father Patrick Fogarty and Father Dennis J. Murphy. A memorandum from ECEAO to the Committee, with a covering letter of 9 November 1967, concentrated on religious education in Ontario teachers' colleges and religious education of Catholic students in the public high schools of the province. The memorandum also stated: "We wish to make it clear that it is our present hope and expectation to obtain from the Ontario Department of Education the extension of the Separate School System from Grade 1 to Grade 12 inclusive, or as far as the high school grades extend." See ARCAT, ED SO02.98 (a) and (b).

[132] Gruending, *Emmett Hall*, 110.

[133] "Items of Interest," *Catholic Trustee* (March 1966), 6.

[134] OSSTA, *Minutes* 1966, 21 and 22 January 1966, 3.

[135] ARCAT, ED SO13.36 (b), OSSTA, Press Release, 8 April 1971.

[136] Ontario Separate School Trustees' Association, *Brief Submitted to the Committee on Aims and Objectives of Education in the Schools of Ontario* (14 January 1966), reproduced in a special edition of *Catholic Trustee* (March 1966).

[137] This is taken from the first page of a synopsis of the brief, "Ontario Catholic Education Council Presents Brief to Hall Committee," *Catholic Trustee* (March 1966), 1-5.

[138] Ibid.

[139] Fleming, *The administrative structure*, 168.

[140] *Living and Learning*, 203.

[141] Ontario, Department of Education, *Report of the Minister of Education Province of Ontario for the Year 1937* (Toronto: King's Printer, 1938), Part III, *Report of the Committee of Enquiry into the Cost of Education in the Province of Ontario*, 72.

[142] *Statutes of Ontario* 1941, 5 George VI, c. 82, "An Act respecting the Board of Trustees of the Roman Catholic Separate Schools for the City of Toronto"; ibid., 1953, 2 Elizabeth II, c. 119, "An Act respecting Separate School Boards in the Metropolitan Area of Toronto." See also, James S. Brown, "The Formation of the Metropolitan Separate School Board (Toronto), 1953-1978," in *Catholics at the "Gathering Place"*, ed. by Mark McGowan and Brian P. Clarke (Toronto: Canadian Catholic Historical Association, 1993): 275-91.

[143] AO, RG 18-131, Royal Commission on Education in Ontario, Box 16, Brief 146, Supplementary, 14-15.

[144] *Report of the Royal Commission on Education in Ontario 1950*, 784.

[145] Ibid., 784-85.

[146] Ontario, Department of Education, *Report of the Minister 1966* [Toronto: 1966], 97; *Report of the Minister of Education 1968* [Toronto: 1968], 44.

[147] *Globe and Mail*, 15 November 1967, 1.

[148] *Catholic Trustee* (June 1968), 3; J.R. McCarthy, *Creation of Larger Units of Administration: Address to the Thirty-Eighth Annual Convention of the Ontario Separate School Trustees' Association* (Toronto: 26 April 1968), 12-13.

[149] Ontario, Legislature of Ontario, *Debates*, 28 June 1968, 4922.

[150] OSSTA, "A Statement on the Reorganization of School Zones as Applied to the Separate Schools of Ontario" [29 March 1968], 4.

[151] Ibid.

[152] Ibid.

[153] Ibid., 5.

[154] Ibid., quoted from Province of Ontario, White Paper, "The Reorganization of School Jurisdictions in the Province of Ontario (January 1968).

[155] Ibid., 6.

[156] Ibid., 10-11.

[157] *Statutes of Ontario* 1968, 17 Elizabeth II, c. 125, "An Act to amend the Separate Schools Act"; Fleming, *The administrative structure*, 177-78.

[158] Ontario, Department of Education, *Report of the Minister of Education, Ontario*, 1969 (Toronto: 1969), Table 1.1.

[159] Gidney, *From Hope to Harris*, 51.

[160] ARCAT, ED SO13.25 (c), OSSTA, letter of 13 March 1968, from Albert E. Klein to Timothy J. McKenna; Walker, *Catholic Education and Politics in Ontario*, 3: 157.

[161] Walker, *Catholic Education and Politics in Ontario*, 3: 283-84.

[162] ARCAT, ED SO13.06 (a), OSSTA, Draft of Proposed Letter to His Grace Archbishop Pocock and their Excellencies Bishop Ryan and Bishop McCarthy [1962].

[163] W. G. Fleming, *Education: Ontario's preoccupation*, (Toronto: University of Toronto Press, 1972), 259.

[164] Carl J. Matthews, SJ, "Some Facts and Figures on the English Catholic High Schools in Ontario 1968-1969," *Catholic Trustee* (March 1969), 11-14.

[165] Ibid., 265; Stamp, *The Schools of Ontario, 1876-1976*, 213; *Statutes of Ontario 1968*, 17 Elizabeth II, c. 121.

[166] ARCAT, ED SO13.25 (c), OSSTA, letter of 13 March 1968, from Albert E. Klein to Timothy J. McKenna.

[167] Stamp, *The Schools of Ontario, 1876-1976*, 213-14.

[168] *Catholic Register*, 2 February 1985, 3; *Globe and Mail*, 21 January 1985, 19; *Toronto Star*, 19 January 1985, A8; "Fogarty, Father Patrick Harmon CSC.," English Canadian Province of Holy Cross, Obituary; Walker, *Catholic Education and Politics in Ontario*, 3: 123.

[169] Arthur Maloney, "A Reasonable Solution to the Problem Facing Catholic Public Schools in Ontario. Address to the Second Annual Study Congress of the Association of Catholic High School Boards of Ontario," (Toronto: 4 November 1967).

[170] Matthews Papers, letter of 7 December 1967, from Bishop G. Emmett Carter to Reverend P.H. Fogarty, C.S.C. [copy].

[171] Ibid.

[172] Walker, *Catholic Education and Politics in Ontario*, 3: 319-323.

[173] Ibid., "Position Paper of A.E. Klein, Q.C., President of OSSTA," [13 December 1967]; See Walker, *Catholic Education and Politics in Ontario*, 3: 337, fn. 83. This position paper was written by Father Carl Matthews, S.J.

[174] ARCAT, ED SO13.216, Bishop Joseph F. Ryan to Ryan Paquette, 29 April 1968.

[175] OSSTA, *Minutes* 1968, 10 May 1968, 2-3.

[176] Ibid., *Minutes 1968*, 1 November 1968, 1; *Minutes 1969*, 17 January 1969, 6-7; 14 February 5; 23 April 1969, 1; 6 May 1969, 1.

[177] Matthews Papers, The Association of Catholic High School Boards of Ontario, "Completing Their Schooling: A Submission to the Ontario Separate School Trustees' Association's Special Working committee on 'Upward Extension,'" [25 October 1968].

[178] ARCAT, ED SO03.27 (d), 21 March 1969, Francis J. Kovacs to Reverend P.H. Fogarty, CSC, 2.

[179] Ibid., 3.

[180] Ibid., 8.

[181] Ibid., ED SO03.27 (g), [Kavanagh], "General Comments re "Updating," 1; Robert Thomas Dixon, *Be a teacher: A History of the Ontario English Catholic Teachers' Association 1944-1994* (Toronto: OECTA, 1994), 222-23.

[182] Matthews Papers, letter of 1 June 1971, from Carl J. Matthews, SJ to Albert E. Klein.

[183] ARCAT, ED SO13.27 (a), letter of 25 March 1969, from Bishop G. Emmett Carter to Albert E. Klein.

[184] Carter sided with Nelligan, but in September 1969, Carter had changed his mind, prompting Nelligan to change *his* mind. Matthews Papers, letter of 29 September 1969, from Carter to Klein; letter of 2 October 1969, Matthews to Carter; letter of 7 October 1969, Carter to Matthews.

[185] Carl J. Matthews, SJ, interview by Michael Power, 30 October 2001.

[186] OSSTA, "Brief on Equal Opportunity for Continuous Education in Separate Schools of Ontario," 1 May 1969, typescript copy, 9. A forty-eight-page brief was published in glossy, landscape format with illustrations, onion skin sheets at the beginning and end and a light brown cover. Another version was printed in the thousands and distributed by each diocese in the province.

[187] Ibid., 10.

[188] Ibid.

[189] This is exactly what happened. The Ontario Tax Foundation Plan was used to finance completion of the separate school system over a three-year period, one grade per year. Following completion, a change in local assessment took place.

[190] OSSTA, "Brief on Equal Opportunity for Continuous Education in Separate Schools of Ontario," 1-2.

[191] Matthews Papers, letter of 7 May 1969, from Carl J. Matthews, SJ to Dr. N.A. Mancini.

[192] ARCAT, ED SO02.101, letter of 22 April 1969, from Reverend P.H. Fogarty to Archbishop Philip F. Pocock.

[193] Raymond Durocher, "Continuous Education for Separate Schools," *Catholic Trustee* (May 1969), 11-14.

[194] ARCAT, ED SP03.11 (a), circular letter of 15 May 1969, from Bishop Joseph F. Ryan to the Archbishops and Bishops of Ontario.

[195] Matthews Papers, letter of 11 January 1970, Carl J. Matthews, SJ to Chris Asseff.

[196] ARCAT, ED SO13. 33 (a), OSSTA, memo of 30 June 1969, from the Executive Secretary to the Directors of OSSTA.

[197] Ibid., ED SO13.77 (a)-(n), OSSTA, "Equality Guidelines" and ED SO13.78 (a)-(j), OSSTA, "Equality Newsletter."

[198] *Catholic Trustee*, (May 1969), 11-14; (October 1969), 3-4, 8-10; 21-22; (March 1970), 1-3.

[199] Liberal Party Caucus of Ontario, "Statement: Separate School Policy," 4 November 1969; *Toronto Telegram*. Metro Night Edition, 4 November 1969, 1; *Toronto Daily Star*, 4 November 1969, 1, 11 and 5 November 1969, 65; *Globe and Mail* editorial, "The argument is flawed," 6 November 1969.

[200] Fleming, *The administrative structure*, 172-76.

[201] ARCAT, ED SO13.248, OSSTA, circular letter of 15 December 1969, from Dr. N.A. Mancini and Chris Asseff to pastors.

[202] *Globe and Mail*, 26 October 1970, 1; "Selections from Major Statements at Students' Rally, October 25, 1970," *Catholic Trustee* (December 1970), 3-15.

[203] ARCAT, ED SO13.46, OSSTA, memo to All Separate School Boards, 15 June 1971.

[204] Ibid., ED SO13.49 (a) and (b), OSSTA, "Position Paper, Extension Convention," 30 August 1971 and "Convention on Extension." See also OSSTA, Briefs 1968-1971, Dr. N.A. Mancini, "Opening Remarks," Extension Convention, 30 August 1971, and Documentation, Convention on Extension, "Implementing Extension Now," 30 August 1971.

[205] *Toronto Star*, 1 September 1971, 1, 4.

[206] Ibid., 4.

[207] ARCAT, ED SO13.47 (d), OSSTA, "Preliminary Comment by Ontario Separate School Trustees' Association on Government Statement re Separate School Extension," 7 September 1971, 1-2.

[208] Ibid., 5.

[209] Ibid., ED SO13.52 (b), OSSTA, memo of 19 November 1971, from Dr. N.A. Mancini to the Directors of OSSTA.

[210] *Catholic Trustee* (June 1973), 1.

[211] Ibid., (June 1976), 1.

[212] Walker, *Catholic Education and Politics in Ontario*, 3: 369.

[213] R. Durocher, OMI, "Separate Schools and Entrenchment," Catholic Trustee (November 1980), 11; see also "Brief on Constitutional Reform Presented to Committee on Constitution of Senate and Commons," *Catholic Trustee* (September 1971), 6-8.

[214] "Ontario Separate School Trustees' Association Submission to Committee on the Costs of Education," *Catholic Trustee* (September 1972), 19.

[215] Ibid., 20.

[216] "Presentation to the Commission on the Reform of Property Taxation in Ontario," *Catholic Trustee* (December 1976), 25.

[217] "The O.S.S.T.A. Response to the Report of the Commission on the Reform of Property Taxation in Ontario," Catholic Trustee (December 1977), 8-19.

[218] *Catholic Trustee* (January 1973), 4-6 and (September 1979), 12; (June 1973), 1; (June 1976), 22-26; (December 1976), 4-16; (September 1978), 1 and OSSTA, Briefs 1977-1981, Catholic Bishops of Ontario, Ontario Separate School Trustees' Association and Ontario Catholic Supervisory Officers' Association, Briefs 1972-1981, "Statement to the Honourable Thomas Wells, Minister of Education, by the Joint Task Force on Credit for Courses in Religious Education," 1 March 1978; OSSTA, Briefs 1977-1981, "Fluctuating Enrolment and Quality Education: A Brief by the Ontario Separate School Trustees' Association to the Commission on Declining School Enrolments in Ontario," 11 April 1978; *Catholic Trustee* (March 1981), 23-33; (June 1982); 1-2; (February 1983), 3-5.

[219] Stamp, *The Schools of Ontario*, 1876-1976, 236.

[220] Josef Denys, "Commitment Through Education: A Study of Religious Socializing in Separate Schooling," in Richard Carlton et al. eds. *Education, Change and Society: A Sociology of Canadian Education* (Toronto: Gage, 1977), 211-24.

[221] Archbishop Philip Pocock, "What is a Catholic School?" *Catholic Trustee* (March 1972), 16.

[222] Ibid., 18.

[223] Kenneth Westhues, "Public vs sectarian legitimation: the separate schools of the Catholic Church," in *Canadian Review of Sociology and Anthropology* 75, no. 2 (1976): 137.

[224] *Catholic Trustee* (June 1974), 3.

[225] ARCAT, ED SO13.228-.229, OSSTA and OECTA, "On the Training of Teachers in Religious Education for the Separate Schools of Ontario." For the date of

presentation, see OSSTA, *Minutes 1968*, 20 September 1968, 2. See also Dixon, *Be a Teacher*, 206-12.

[226] OSSTA, *Minutes 1969*, 13 and 14 June 1969, 3.

[227] Ibid., *Minutes 1970*, 2 and 3 October 1970, 9.

[228] Dixon, *Be a Teacher*, 211.

[229] Walker, *Catholic Education and Politics in Ontario*, 3: 174.

[230] ARCAT, ED SO13.70 (c), OSSTA, "Statement to the Honourable Thomas Wells, Minister of Education, by the Joint Task Force on Credit for Courses in Religious Education," 1 March 1978.

[231] "A Bit of Good News," *Catholic Trustee* (September 1978), 1.

[232] *Catholic Trustee* (November 1973), 3.

[233] Ibid.

[234] Ibid., (June 1975), 21.

[235] Ibid., (June 1981), 14.

[236] ARCAT, ED SO13.183, OSSTA, "Focus on the Faith."

[237] *Catholic Trustee* (March 1974), 16.

[238] Raymond Durocher, OMI, "Separate Schools and French Language Education," *Catholic Trustee* (December 1978), 14.

[239] Ibid., 15.

[240] O. Tremblay, "The French Dimension of the Separate School System," *Catholic Trustee* (June 1981), 29.

[241] OSSTA, Briefs 1982-1986, "Entente Between l'Association française des conseils scolaires de l'Ontario and the Ontario Separate School Trustees' Association on the Trusteeship of Minority-Language Schools within the Ontario Catholic Separate School System" (19 December 1983), 6.

[242] Ibid.

[243] The government passed its legislation on minority language education rights and trusteeship on 14 December 1984. See *Statutes of Ontario 1984*, 32-33 Elizabeth II,

c. 60, "An Act to amend the Education Act," sections 17-27.

[244] OSSTA, Briefs 1982-1986, "Entente," 4.

[245] *Toronto Star*, afternoon edition, 13 June 1984, A1, A21 and editorial on A18; *Globe and Mail*, 13 June 1984, 1, M2 and editorial on 6.

[246] Ontario, Legislature of Ontario, *Debates*, 12 June 1984, 2414.

[247] Ibid., 2416.

[248] Ibid., 2415.

[249] Ibid.

[250] Ibid., 2415-16.

[251] Ibid., 2416.

[252] Claire Hoy, *Bill Davis: A Biography* (Toronto: Methuen, 1985), 264.

[253] Rosemary Speirs, *Out of the Blue: The Fall of the Tory Dynasty in Ontario* (Toronto: Macmillan, 1986), 24.

[254] *Catholic Register*, 16 April 1983, 4.

[255] Ibid., 21 May 1983, 4.

[256] Steve Paikin, *The Life: The Seductive Call of Politics* (Toronto: Penguin, 2001), 49.

EPILOGUE
1984-1997

Our story does not end with Premier Davis's historic announcement of 12 June 1984. It actually lingers on for thirteen more years, the time it took the politicians and the judges to fulfill his promise regarding the completion of the separate school system. The purpose of this Epilogue is to give a broad outline of the political dynamics and the legal process whereby Bill 30 became provincial law and was declared constitutional, and to examine, albeit briefly, some of the efforts on the part of Catholics to define Catholicity in the years immediately following the 1987 Supreme Court decision on Bill 30.

The legislature and the courts are never far from each other whenever politicians from different parties sitting in the same assembly are determined to enact a radical break with the past. Bill 30 was no exception. Catholicity, on the other hand, was a different matter. It was (and still is) a delicate debate among Catholics that takes the form of a foundational question: What makes Catholic education (or a Catholic school) truly and distinctly Catholic? The question had already surfaced in the mid-1970s. But answering it fully and unambiguously, in the era of Bill 30, when completion was a legislated reality, had evolved into a dilemma for every member of the Catholic education establishment, including the Ontario Separate School Trustees' Association. That dilemma surfaced as soon as the battle for completion had been decisively won.

The Political Dynamics

On the same day that Premier Davis startled the province with his volte face on separate school completion, he set up three commissions. These were extra-parliamentary bodies that conducted their public inquiries without benefit of proposed legislation. They and the public were expected to work together in ignorance of the government's intended plan of action. No wonder, then, that alarmist reactions, confusion, fear, bitterness and plenty of diplomatic dancing, at least on the part of separate school defenders, coloured the proceedings of each of the commissions.

The Commission For Planning and Implementing Change in the Governance and Administration of Secondary Education was arguably the most important of the three. Its mandate was to advise the government on the mechanics of any transition period, during which time teachers and schools (and students if they so chose) would be transferred from the public to the separate system. Up to July 1985, it had approved thirty-eight implementation plans for the school year 1985-86. This commission survived as an integral part of Bill 30, and its work continued for many years often under complex, trying and emotional circumstances. The second commission was an eight-member body on school finance. It was headed by H. Ian Macdonald, a former deputy treasurer of Ontario who was teaching at York University. The Macdonald Commission was given the rather daunting task of looking into the whole business of school financing, not just full funding, but, since the prospect of full funding for separate schools was the primary reason for its existence, it focused its efforts on recommending ways to eliminate the critical disparity in local taxes between the two systems. The third commission was an inquiry into Ontario's private schools. Chairing it was Dr. Bernard Shapiro of the Ontario Institute for Studies in Education. All three commissions were strictly advisory — completion was government policy — and they were expected to table their final reports by May 1985.

The Planning and Implementation Commission heard 190 briefs. The Ontario Secondary School Teachers' Federation and the Ontario Public School Trustees' Association, two of the most hostile opponents of the very existence of separate schools, warned of catastrophic consequences to the public school system if completion were implemented. OSSTF predicted a loss of 8,500 jobs and 100 schools. OPSTA warned of a drop in enrolment of perhaps 15 percent and in some areas of 75 percent.[1] Many rural communities, never having more than one high school and feeling quite proprietorial towards it, feared what the appearance of a Catholic high school in their midst might do to "their school."[2] At times there was plenty of heat but little light at the public hearings. To all those attending the hearings, it was painfully obvious that Catholic separate schools, now on the cusp of completion, could still provoke unfettered feelings of hostility and the occasional caustic criticism that seemed to be reserved for Catholic education.

In its fifty-seven-page brief to the commission, written with force and clarity, OSSTA made many workable recommendations concerning programs, funding, facilities, student transfers, teacher and school staffing provisions, board organization, sharing in non-educational areas, changes in legislation and school boundaries. OSSTA eschewed emotion and hectoring (and any hint of arrogance) and instead concentrated on the facts, premising its presentation on the fundamental need to retain the Catholic character of all Catholic schools in the province, which were guaranteed by law and expected, by friend and foe alike, to be distinctly Catholic:

> Catholic schools are defined as those schools operated by a class of people, in whom rights and privileges have been vested by law outside the public sector, who have been empowered with respect to denominational schools. They do not enjoy the right to operate anything but a denominational school. They do not operate Alternative schools.

> A Catholic school is one in which the tenets of the Catholic faith are taught; the precepts of the Church are preached; and the values existing, inseparable within that faith, permeate the total curriculum and are practiced by the Catholic school community.[3]

The Macdonald Commission had its own problems. It had to find ways and means to protect the public school system from unacceptable harm due to an expanding separate school system and it had to protect the confessional nature of Catholic schools as they opened their doors for the first time to what many expected (and some feared) would be large numbers of non-Catholic teachers and students. Then there was the francophone community. It had fought hard in many different parts of the province to establish French-language secondary schools with the public system. By 1985, there were no fewer than 25,000 francophone children attending public schools. To many francophone parents, the promise of full funding for separate schools was a mixed blessing at best.

One reporter saw the emerging conflict over the distribution of tax money to the two school systems this way:

> Two entirely different portraits were drawn for the commission. Catholic politicians, educators and administrators say the new financing arrangement will only mean the addition of a few grades to a well-established school system and changes will be minimal.
>
> They emphasize the unique aspects of a religion-dominated school and argue for protection of the system's Catholic nature. They also press for rapid transfer of public school buildings.
>
> Public school supporters see massive upheavals in their system. They attack the announcement of controversial changes without consultation and implementation without legislation.
>
> They raise concerns about restrictions limiting non-Catholic access to the separate schools, the impact on public school programs and the potential disruption if local schools were transferred to the Catholic school system to accommodate the expansion.[4]

On the delicate topic of non-Catholics in Catholic schools, Catholics themselves were divided. For example, Cardinal Carter, archbishop of Toronto, stated that the Catholic bishops of Ontario had assured Premier Davis in advance of his June 1984 announcement that separate schools would co-operate in hiring non-Catholic teachers declared redundant due to completion. The Cardinal also publicly disagreed with the demand of the Bishops Commission on

Education that Catholic teachers make up a minimum of 90 percent of a school's staff. In February 1985, he was quoted as saying: "I think it is silly to postulate that, if there are 11 percent non-Catholic teachers in your school, it's going to be a failure; if 90 percent, then the school is fine. That's ridiculous . . . The Spirit of the school is what is going to matter and you could have a very wide range of Catholic and non-Catholic teachers in a school and still have a Catholic school."[5] In March, he went one step further, declaring that not only should non-Catholic students be allowed to attend separate schools but also that they could be exempted from religious instruction.[6] Opposing the Cardinal on the matter of non-Catholic students was Father Edward Boehler, chairman of the Metro Separate School Board. Father Boehler warned against universal access to Catholic schools, because the presence of substantial numbers of non-Catholics in a Catholic school would make it difficult for it to fulfill its mission, and he declared that religious education courses must be mandatory for all students.[7]

Dr. Shapiro's commission visited forty of Ontario's private schools, both elementary and secondary, and took in 514 briefs, almost half of which were submitted by individuals. In its brief of 4 March 1985, OSSTA agreed with the position of the Ontario Association of Alternative and Independent Schools — "That parents have a prior right to choose the kind of education that shall be given to their child, and its corollary, that it is the Government's duty to see that such right is afforded equitably to all, with discrimination towards none."[8] To this, OSSTA added the following caveat: "The manner of providing such funding must be as simple as possible so as not to require massive changes in tax or other legislation. It should not disturb the present property tax allocation but should provide appropriate relief for parents who wish to exercise their parental right to freely choose the education they wish for their child or children."[9] Parental rights had always been high on the Catholic educational agenda, making OSSTA's support of public funding of some kind for private schools a natural political move. In the end, though, Shapiro's commission was something of a smoke screen for the government. If it ever intended to follow through on any of the commission's sixty-one recommendations, the rancour and uproar generated by the other two commissions on completion convinced it to let Dr. Shapiro's final report die a quiet and hidden death.

While the three commissions went about their business, the political landscape of Ontario, long the preserve of the Conservative party, underwent a major alteration. Bill Davis resigned as premier in October 1985. This was not unexpected. He was succeeded by Frank Miller, who, in late March, called an election for 2 May. Since the Conservatives, Liberals and NDP were on record supporting completion, no party was foolish enough to turn separate schools into a political football. Their collective silence, however, goaded the *Globe and Mail* to do precisely that. A month into the campaign, it published a scathing editorial, "Not for discussion," in which it said that "The Miller government should have placed a moratorium on the Davis initiative until it had held a full public debate on the subject. The three leaders should have been prepared to field questions on the issue during a televised debate — a debate in which Mr. Miller refuses to participate. The question of extended funding should have been referred to the courts for a ruling on its constitutional validity."[10] These were sentiments shared by the Metropolitan Toronto School Board, which conducted a vigorous advertising campaign to smoke out the politicians, and by OSSTF, which had offered to fund the campaigns of independent candidates in twenty-seven marginal ridings (six were recruited) and had published a highly provocative pamphlet for wide distribution called "Preserve Public Education." Topics covered by the OSSTF pamphlet included Duplication of Services, Social Fragmentation and The Death of Democratic Government in Ontario.

The apparent death of democracy was taken up with great relish by the Anglican Archbishop Lewis Garnsworthy. On 25 April, a week before election day, Garnsworthy and Right Reverend Clarke MacDonald, a former moderator of the United Church, called a press conference to lift "the veil of silence" and to denounce the Conservative party's rule by decree. Garnsworthy did most of the talking. He hit a raw nerve when he compared Bill Davis's government to that of Adolf Hitler. Davis, Garnsworthy contended, had changed government policy on separate schools without consulting his party or the public. He did it by simply making a speech in the legislature without concern for the possible damage it might do to the educational and social fabric of the province. "This whole process was done by decree," said Garnsworthy. "It's the way Hitler made decrees in the Reichstag about education — without legislation, in a 12-minute speech."[11] Pressed by reporters to clarify his comments, Garnsworthy pressed on, saying that he was making a comparison between governments that ruled by decree. "What's the difference? This is how Hitler changed education in Germany, by exactly the same process, by decree. I won't take that back."[12] It was all bombast and balderdash, but if Archbishop Garnsworthy's aim was to get separate schools on the front pages, he succeeded admirably.

An uproar followed. Miller called Garnsworthy's remarks odious. Bob Rae, NDP leader, thought that they were inflammatory and demanded an immediate apology from the archbishop. David Peterson, Liberal Leader, also found Garnsworthy's comparison inflammatory, but he took the opportunity to accuse the Conservatives of failing to produce draft legislation and then to promise that a Liberal government would submit its plans on completion to a legislative committee.

The election results were a stunner. The Conservatives were reduced to the status of a minority government, winning only 52 seats. The Liberals came a close second with 48 seats, and the NDP managed to capture 25 seats. To what degree unhappiness among the electorate with the Conservative handling of the separate school portfolio brought about their fall from grace is difficult, if not impossible, to divine. On 18 June 1985, the Liberals and NDP formed a coalition of convenience and defeated the Miller government, bringing the Liberal party to power in Ontario for the first time since 1943. Central to the coalition's existence was the promise to introduce separate school legislation.

On 4 July 1985, Sean Conway, Liberal minister of education, presented Bill 30 to the Legislative Assembly. In his presentation, Conway told his fellow members that the legislation would embody the following six principles:

1. protection of the viability of the public secondary system
2. explicit clarification in the legislation of the spirit and the letter of the constitutional guarantees for Roman Catholic secondary education
3. in implementing the government's policy, the interests of all the students would come first (the attendance of non-Catholic students in Catholic schools would be limited only by the availability of space and non-Catholic students would be exempt from religious instruction)
4. no unemployment of teachers and other employees as a direct result of completing the separate school system
5. preservation of the distinctive (unique) mission of the Roman Catholic separate school system
6. adequate provision (money) for both school systems so that the transition would be orderly and cost-effective[13]

In addition to the six principles, Conway promised that the government would do three things: send the bill to committee immediately following second reading and not arbitrarily limit debate within the committee; refer the bill to the Ontario Court of Appeal, so that its constitutionality could be determined prior to third and final reading; and by way of an interim measure, amend the legislative grant regulations in order to provide full funding for Grades 9, 10 and 11, by September 1985, for those separate school boards whose plans for implementation had been accepted.[14]

Bill 30 received first reading on 4 July and second reading a week later, passing by a vote of 117 to one. Norm Sterling, a Conservative, was the single parliamentary holdout. The bill then went directly to the eleven-member Social Development Committee, chaired by Richard Johnston. Besides the chair, the committee was composed of four Liberals, four Conservatives and two NDP. It sat for sixty-five days, from mid July to mid November 1985, and heard 879 presentations. No one was turned away. Even Bill Davis made an appearance. He spoke for seventy-five minutes on 20 September.[15] Such was the overwhelming volume of work thrust upon the committee, as it travelled to every major region of the province, that on most days it held hearings morning, afternoon and evening and sometimes it even sat on Saturdays.[16] From the opponents of the Bill, the committee heard repeated concerns about non-Catholic access to separate schools, employment for public teachers displaced by full funding, transfer of public school buildings and compulsory religious instruction for non-Catholic students.[17]

In response, Johnston predicted thirty to fifty amendments to the bill. Ten of these amendments he classified as significant. For its part, OSSTA accepted Bill 30 as it appeared at second reading.[18] The trustees offered no amendments and were unwilling to accept any. The committee suspended its hearings in late November. It did not want to recommend any amendments until the Ontario Court of Appeal had ruled on the constitutionality of the proposed legislation.

Prior to discussing the Legal Process, we must jump more than a year and a half ahead in our narrative in order to clarify several things. Bill 30, "An Act to amend the Education Act" (35 Elizabeth II, c. 21), received assent on 24 June 1986, a little more than two years after Premier Davis's announcement on separate school completion. Important to remember is that before the Bill became an Act of the Legislative Assembly, it received four amendments. The first amendment provided options for financial assistance and retraining to any employee of the public school system designated for transfer to the separate school system who had conscientious objections to working in a Catholic school. The second abolished the clause that placed certain conditions on non-Catholic student access to Catholic schools; there were now to be no conditions. The third, linked to the second, did away with compulsory religious instruction for non-Catholic students in Catholic schools. And the fourth stated that after the Act had been in operation for ten years, Catholic boards would lose the right to hire Catholics over non-Catholics.[19]

The first amendment was non-controversial; the second and third amendments elicited cries of outrage from Catholic trustees and administrators; and the fourth, embodied as Section 136 of the Act, was a last-minute demand of the NDP. It was intended to mollify NDP backbenchers, many of whom had never been comfortable with Bill 30.[20] But the amendment was so potentially dangerous to the Catholic character of separate school that even the Liberals were prepared to go to court to challenge its own amendment. Also important to keep in mind is that the version of Bill 30 that was referred to the Ontario Court of Appeal and then to the Supreme Court of Canada was Bill 30 as it stood at second reading, the version accepted by OSSTA, and *not* the Act as amended and passed by the Legislative Assembly. This meant that any legal challenge to Section 136 would have to be a separate undertaking.

The Legal Process

There were actually two different issues that were appealed to the courts. The first issue concerned ministerial changes to the regulations governing the legislative grants. Sean Conway, the minister of education, initiated changes to the regulations on 4 July 1985, the same day he introduced Bill 30, in order to provide full funding for Grades 9, 10 and 11 in those separate school boards whose implementation plans had been accepted.[21] The money — $34 million, a considerable amount — was due to be paid by 15 December 1985. The Lieutenant Governor in Council approved of these changes on 10 September, and its order in council was published in the *Ontario Gazette* of 5 October 1985.

Contesting the government's decision were the Metropolitan Toronto School Board and the Ontario Secondary School Teachers' Federation. They won the first round, convincing Justice Potts that the minister of education had overstepped his power in apportioning money to Grades 9, 10 and 11 at the secondary level. The judge issued an interim order prohibiting the payment of the funds. His order was then appealed to a three-judge panel of the Ontario Supreme Court who sat as a Divisional Court. Justices Donald Steel, Richard Trainor and W. Gibson Gray lifted the interim order because it wanted to avoid the disruption of the educational system. Funds were ready to be distributed by 20 December. The judges also ruled, on 21 February 1986, that the minister did indeed have the power to extend funding to Catholic secondary schools under the "Education Act," Section 10(3), which read:

Subject to the approval of the Lieutenant Governor in Council, the Minister may make regulations, (a) providing for the apportionment and distribution of moneys appropriated or raised by the Legislature for educational purposes."[22]

The second issue, of course, was the Liberal government's reference to the Ontario Court of Appeal. The question it asked the court to decide was this:

Is Bill 30, an Act to Amend the Education Act inconsistent with the provisions of the Constitution of Canada including the *Canadian Charter of Rights and Freedoms* and, if so, in what particular or particulars and in what respect?

The court began hearing the arguments on 23 September 1985, sitting for two weeks. The two main combatants among the four dozen or so lawyers on hand were Ian Scott, the attorney general of Ontario, who took the unusual step for an attorney general and personally defended Bill 30 and would do so again in front of the Supreme Court, and J.J. Robinette, a leading expert on the constitution and a polemicist sporting a long track record of demolishing his opponents. A great-grandson of Sir Richard William Scott, architect of the 1863 Scott Act, Ian Scott had not only an historical interest in the fate of Bill 30 but also a genuine belief that the Liberal government had a constitutional right and duty to overturn the 1928 Tiny Township decision that had denied public funds for Catholic secondary education. For Scott, it had all come down to a matter of elementary fairness for a school system that had been in place for more than 120 years. Paradoxically, for all Scott's devotion to the constitutional status of Catholic separate schools, expressed in his brilliant performances in front of the Ontario Court of Appeal and the Supreme Court of Canada, in his own words he was "no longer a practicing Catholic, nor a believer, in any of the accepted senses, of the teachings of the Christian church."[23]

We have reproduced the question put to the Ontario Court of Appeal in 1985. It was the same question entertained by the Supreme

Court of Canada in 1987. Both courts tested Bill 30 in light of section 93 of the BNA Act of 1867 (Constitution Act, 1867) and Sections 2(a), 15 and 29 of the Constitution Act, 1982, Part I, Canadian Charter of Rights and Freedoms. Below, one will find the Preamble to Bill 30, which encapsulates the reasons for the legislation, as well as the relevant sections of the constitution:

Preamble to Bill 30

Whereas section 91 of the *Constitution Act, 1867* embodies one of the essential conditions which facilitated the creation of a united Canada in 1867 by guaranteeing to Roman Catholics in Ontario certain rights and privileges with respect to denominational schools; and whereas the Roman Catholic separate schools have become a significant part of the school system in Ontario; and whereas it has been public policy in Ontario since 1899 to provide for public funds to support education in the Roman Catholic separate schools to the end of Grade 10; and whereas it is recognized that today a basic education requires a secondary as well as an elementary education; and whereas it is just and proper and in accordance with the spirit of the guarantees given in 1867 to bring the provisions of the law respecting Roman Catholic separate schools into harmony with the provisions of the law respecting public elementary and secondary schools, by providing legislative recognition of and funding for secondary education by Roman Catholic separate schools; and whereas the foregoing facts were affirmed by the Premier of Ontario in his statement to the Legislative Assembly on the 12th day of June, 1984 . . .

Section 93 of the Constitution Act, 1867

93. In and for each Province the Legislature may exclusively make Laws in relation to Education, subject and according to the following provisions:

1. Nothing in any such Law shall prejudicially affect any Right or Privilege with respect to Denominational Schools which any Class of Persons have by Law in the Province at the Union:

2. All the Powers, Privileges, and Duties at the Union by Law conferred and imposed in Upper Canada on the Separate Schools and

School Trustees of the Queen's Roman Catholic Subjects shall be and the same are hereby extended to the Dissentient Schools of the Queen's Protestant and Roman Catholic subjects in Quebec:

3. Where in any Province a System of Separate or Dissentient Schools exist by Law at the Union or is thereafter established by the Legislature of the Province, an Appeal shall lie to the Governor General in Council from any Act or Decision of any Provincial Authority affecting any Right or Privilege of the Protestant or Roman Catholic Minority of the Queen's Subjects in relation to Education:

4. In case any such Provincial Law as from Time to Time seems to the Governor General in Council requisite for the due Execution of the Provisions of this Section is not made, or in any case any Decision of the Governor General in Council on any Appeal under this Section is not duly executed by the proper Provincial Authority in that Behalf, then and in every such Case, and as far only as the Circumstances of each Case require, the Parliament of Canada may make remedial Laws for the due Execution of the Provisions of this Section and of any Decision of the Governor General in Council under this Section. [Note: The opening sentence of Section 93 is referred as the plenary powers of the province in respect to education.]

Constitution Act, 1982, Part I,
Canadian Charter of Rights and Freedoms

Section 2: Everyone has the following fundamental freedoms: (a) freedom of conscience and religion

Section 15 (1): Every individual is equal before and under the law and has the right to the equal protection and equal benefit of the law without discrimination based on race, national or ethnic origin, colour, religion, sex, age or mental or physical ability.

Section 29: Nothing in this Charter abrogates or derogates from any rights or privileges guaranteed by or under the Constitution of Canada in respect of denominational, separate or dissentient schools.

On 18 February 1986, the Ontario Court of Appeal, by a margin of 3-2, answered the government's referral on Bill 30 in the negative. Justices Thomas Zuber, Peter Cory and Walter Tarnopolsky ruled in a twenty-nine page decision that the Bill was consistent with the Canadian Constitution and the Charter of Rights and Freedoms. They concluded that the government had the power to finance Catholic secondary schools, and, once established and publicly funded, these schools would be protected by the constitution in the same manner as Catholic elementary schools. Dissenting were Chief Justice William Howland and Justice Sydney Robbins. Their eighty-eight-page opinion stressed that if the right to equality without discrimination based on religion, as stated in the Charter, was to have any meaning it must mean at the very least that the followers of one religion should not receive benefits denied to the followers of other religions.[24] The Liberal-NDP coalition then decided to amend and then pass Bill 30.

Since the decision on such a divisive matter was hardly conclusive, the case went to the Supreme Court of Canada. Arguments were heard on 29 and 30 January and on 2-5 February 1987.[25] Sitting in judgment were Chief Justice Brian Dickson and Justices Bertha Wilson, Jean Beetz, William R. McIntyre, Antonio Lamer, Willard Z. Estey and Gerard V. La Forest. Madame Justice Wilson delivered the unanimous opinion of the court on 25 June 1987. It too was a negative to the question referred. In upholding the Ontario Court of Appeal, the Supreme Court established three facts:

1. that Bill 30 is a valid exercise of the provincial power to add to the rights and privileges of Roman Catholic separate school supporters under the combined effect of the opening words of s. 93 [plenary powers] and s. 93(3) of the *Constitution Act, 1867*

2. that Roman Catholic separate school supporters had at Confederation a right or privilege, by law, to have their children receive an appropriate education which could include instruction at the secondary school level and that such right or privilege is therefore constitutionally guaranteed under s. 93(1) of the *Constitution Act, 1867* [in effect

overturning the 1928 Tiny Township decision]

3. that the rights or privileges protected by s. 93(1) are immune from *Charter* review under s. 29 of the *Charter*[26]

The field had been won. Coincidentally, on the very same day that the Supreme Court handed down its judgment, the Liberal-NDP coalition came to an end.[27]

There remained one last legal skirmish to fight. In 1995, the Ontario Separate School Trustees' Association and the Metropolitan Separate School Board initiated a constitutional challenge to Section 136, which would have taken away the right of separate school boards to hire only Catholic employees. The ten-year grace period was coming to an end in 1996. The issues at stake were:

1) Does s. 136 apply (a) only to secondary teachers? (b) at the point of hiring?

2) Does s. 136 infringe the rights guaranteed by s. 93(1) of the *Constitution Act, 1867*?

3) If s. 136 does infringe the rights guaranteed by s. 93(1), what is the appropriate remedy?[28]

Justice Sharpe of the Ontario Court (General Division) heard the case in November 1997. Peter Lauwers, the OSSTA lawyer, argued on behalf of the applicants. Sharpe rendered his judgment on 17 December 1997, declaring that Section 136 was of "no force or effect" because it prejudicially affected rights guaranteed by Section 93(1) of the *Constitution Act, 1867*.[29]

Catholicity

Few public institutions legislated into existence in nineteenth-century Upper Canada have survived intact into twenty-first-century Ontario. One of those institutions is Catholic separate schools. They not only survived, but they also flourished to the point that the Supreme Court of Canada, prompted by provincial legislation, restored rights given to separate schools at Confederation to conduct secondary education. This was the great victory, long anticipated by generations of Catholic clergy, trustees, parents and teachers. The reasons why separate schools remained in existence and even thrived, despite enormous and constant adversity, are as many and various as the people who carried on the fight and whose battles on behalf of Catholic education are the substance of this book. What was so heartening and empowering for the generation of the 1980s and 1990s was the Liberal government's determination to preserve the distinctive mission of the Roman Catholic separate school system. This was the fifth of the six principles enunciated by Sean Conway when he introduced Bill 30 in 1984. For the government of the day, full funding was indispensable to preservation.

Emboldened, separate school supporters pressed on in the post-1987 period. Separate school commissioners demanded educational equity and taxpayer equity in their 1992 Minority Report to the Property Tax Working Group of the Ontario Fair Tax Commission. Educational equity for all students depended on taxpayer equity, but the huge disparity in school board assessment wealth hindered the ability of assessment-poor boards, both public and separate, to deliver in a timely fashion provincially mandated services to their students. Bill 64, in 1989, improved but did not achieve equity in school financing. The solution, in the words of the Minority Report, was threefold:

> The province set a common mill rate for commercial and industrial assessment for education purposes;
> Commercial and industrial tax revenue be pooled;
> The pooled funds, together with provincial grants to school boards, be distributed so as to make up the difference between residential tax revenues and a realistically established grant ceiling or recognized level of expenditure.[30]

Separate school supporters also made their voice heard during the public hearings of the 1993-94 Royal Commission on Learning. As it turned out, they were quite effective in their lobbying. Critical to their success in convincing the commission to incorporate four (among a total of 167) recommendations that were absolutely crucial

488

to Catholic interests were "The Hope That Lives Within Us" —
OSSTA's submission — and the work of Monsignor Dennis Murphy,
one of the commissioners. The four recommendations were:

> 115. That section 136, which restricts preferential hiring in
> the Roman Catholic school system, be removed from the
> Education Act [the courts did this in 1997];
> 116. That, with reference to the role of the Roman Catholic
> education system, the Ministry of Education and Training
> ensure appropriate and influential representation from the
> Roman Catholic education system at all levels of its
> professional and managerial staff, up to and including that of
> Assistant Deputy Minister; and that the Minister establish a
> Roman Catholic Education Policy and Programs Team or
> branch in the ministry;
> 117. That the Ministry of Education and Training and the
> faculties of education establish a pre-service credit course in
> the foundations of Roman Catholic education, and that this
> course be available at all faculties of education in Ontario;
> 118. That the religious education courses currently offered at
> faculties of education receive full credit status and be made
> part of the regular academic program[31]

Strong and confident was the separate school lobby. It was
apparent that Bill 30, and its subsequent validation by the Supreme
Court, had imparted to the corporate identity of separate schools the
kind of validation that Catholics had sought for their schools since
their inception. Separate schools were now legitimate "in law, in
government budgets, in administrative tradition, and popular
culture."[32] But was legitimacy by itself enough to preserve Catholic
separate schools? Was it enough to guarantee their long-term future?

Apparently not. Having won the prize of completion so
convincingly on every contested point, the Catholic education
establishment, including OSSTA, felt compelled to define the essence
of Catholic education within the context of public funding. Victory in
the political and legal arenas, earned at great cost to many people, was

followed by a period of self-examination and self-reflection that was (and continues to be) far more intense and soul-searching than anything previously experienced.

Central to this self-examination and self-reflection was OSSTA's support for the creation of the Institute for Catholic Education in 1985. Catholic trustees and their educational partners were acutely aware that they could no longer rely on priests and religious to assure the Catholicity of their schools. They also recognized the corrosive effects of the increasingly aggressive forces of secularization coupled with a declining level in religious practice and a loss of credibility in Church teaching among the Catholic population.

This was the context, then, in which the Ontario Conference of Catholic Bishops moved to insert itself more significantly into the Catholic educational scene by the establishment of an office whose primary focus would be the Catholic characteristics and features of the separate school system. On the initiative of Bishop John M. Sherlock of London, the OCCB invited Monsignor Dennis Murphy to become the first executive director of ICE and to set up an office. Murphy informed Bishop Sherlock that he believed that such an office would be effective only if the major educational partners shared in its direction and funding. Jim Sherlock, president of OSSTA, and Father Frank Kavanagh, general secretary of the Ontario English Catholic Teachers' Association, were able to enlist the active support and co-operation of both the trustees and teachers. As a result, a new type of collegial Catholic educational model was put in place. Bishops, trustees, teachers, supervisory officers and other partners in Catholic education began to work together at the same table to determine the policies and directions of the Institute in its mission to help preserve and enhance the Catholic nature of Catholic schools.

Then there was the Blishen Report of 1990. It is one of the more useful and revealing of the many Catholicity studies produced in the wake of the 1987 Supreme Court ruling. Catholic separate schools were at a crossroads:

Ironically, Bill 30 provided the occasion for the Catholic community to assess whether the now completed Catholic school system for which they had struggled for more than 100 years was effectively achieving its stated goals. There were many reasons for this. To some it appeared that since the days of sacrifice and extra effort on the part of teachers, parents, trustees, clergy and students was over, and since the goal had been achieved, then it was possible that the consensual commitment forged by adversity could be weakening. Others felt uneasy at the prospect of the Catholic private high schools which had been governed by religious communities of men and women now falling under the direction of large and supposedly impersonal administrative structures of publicly funded Catholic school boards.[33]

Prosperity has a way of evaporating the past and convincing people that the future will be much like the present. Nothing is more self-defeating than to forget one's collective history, and nothing is more dangerous than to be complacent about the future. On the other hand, no institution can wed itself so completely to the past that it is unable to envision for itself a viable future, one that is true to its mandate and yet able to adapt to changing circumstances.

Catholic supporters of separate schools must be brave enough to ask themselves if they still accept the following proposition:

> From a Catholic perspective, the purpose of education is not only the transmission of knowledge, but also the formation of the whole person of the students through bringing them to the personal integration of faith and life. Separate schools are responsible for imparting Christian doctrine in an organic and systematic way, in order to initiate students into the fullness of Christian life and to elicit in response a personal commitment to that way of life.[34]

An emphatic "Yes!" must be the answer. If not, there is no reason to have separate schools, no matter how legitimate they might appear in law and social tradition. And that "Yes!" means that Catholics must be ready to deal with a multitude of problems that threaten the integrity of separate schools in an increasingly anti-Christian society and for which there are no easy answers, no quick solutions. Among those problems are religious indifferentism, non-participation in the liturgical and charitable life of the Church, moral relativism, the worship of the individual and cultural conformity.

These are huge problems. They will not disappear overnight. However, Catholics are called to be a people of faith, hope and charity, who are willing to work together to build the Kingdom of God. Catholic separate schools are very much a part of that Kingdom. "Faith is the assurance of things hoped for, the conviction of things not seen" (Heb. 11:1).

---

[1] Gidney, *From Hope to Harris*, 131.

[2] Ibid., 132.

[3] OSSTA, Presentation to the Planning and Implementation Committee [1985], 7.

[4] *Globe and Mail*, 22 March, 17.

[5] Ibid., 21 February 1985, M1.

[6] Ibid., 22 March 1985, 17.

[7] Ibid., 23 July 1985, 16.

[8] OSSTA, "A Submission to the Commission of Enquiry on Private Schools in Ontario," 4 March 1985, 3.

[9] Ibid.

[10] *Globe and Mail*, 8 April 1985, 6.

[11] Ibid., 26 April 1985, 2.

[12] Ibid.

[13] Ontario, Legislative Assembly, *Hansard*, 4 July 1985, 451.

[14] Ibid., 452.

[15] *Globe and Mail*, 21 September 1985, 1, 2.

[16] Ibid., 22 November 1985, A14.

[17] Ibid., 21 November 1985, A24.

[18] OSSTA, "A Final Submission by the Ontario Separate School Trustees' Association to the Standing Committee on Social Development of the Legislative Assembly of Ontario on Bill 30 An Act to Amend the Education Act," 12 May 1986, 8.

[19] Gidney, *From Hope to Harris*, 137-38.

[20] *Globe and Mail*, 24 February 1986, A11.

[21] Edward Nelligan, vice chairman of the Planning and Implementation Commission, told separate school trustees that seven conditions were essential to securing funds. They were 1) "Separate School Boards must indicate they are prepared to offer a complete K to 13 program"; 2) "The implementation statement must contain a timetable for the phasing in of the completion"; 3) "The implementation statement must not be dependent upon new capital for buildings"; 4) "The R.C. implementation statements would have to indicate they were prepared to hire non-Roman Catholic teachers [or R.C. teachers] declared redundant as a result of student transfers from the public high school system"; 5) "R.C. schools must be prepared to accept non-Catholic students"; 6) "The R.C Plans must not impact negatively on the public school system"; 7) "R.C. School Boards should not expect that all the rights they had for a K to 10 operation will be automatically extended into the operation of R.C. high schools." See "Seven Conditions Outlined as Essential to Getting Funds," *Catholic Trustee* (Fall 1985), 6, 25.

[22] Gregory M. Dickinson and A. Wayne Mackay, *Rights, Freedoms and the Education System in Canada: Cases and Materials* (Toronto: Emond Montgomery Publications, 1999), 3-7; *Globe and Mail*, 22 February 1986, A17; Tom Reilly, "Bill 30 extends full funding to separate schools," *Catholic Register*, 24-31 August 1991, E17.

[23] Ian Scott (with Neil McCormick), *To Make a Difference*: A Memoir (Toronto: Stoddard, 1987), 151.

[24] *Globe and Mail*, 19 February 1986, A1, A8.

[25] Ibid., 29 January 1987, A4; 30 January 1987, A1-A2; 3 February 1987, A4; 5 February 1987, A4; 6 February 1987, A4.

[26] Dickinson and Mackay, *Rights, Freedoms and the Education System in Canada*, 66, 67, 68; *Globe and Mail*, 26 June 1987, A1, A9.

[27] There were provincial elections on 10 September 1987, which returned a Liberal majority, on 6 September 1990, which returned the first-ever NDP majority, making Bob Rae premier, and on 8 June 1996, when the Conservatives under Mike Harris were returned to power.

[28] *Daly v. Ontario (Attorney General), Dominion Law Reports*, 4th ser., vol. 154 (Aurora, Ontario: Canada Law Book Inc., 1998), 469.

[29] Ibid., 504.

[30] *Bringing Fairness to Payers of Education Taxes in Ontario: A Minority Report of the Property Tax Working Group of the Ontario Fair Tax Commission* (1992). The twelve signatories included Patrick V. Slack, executive director, and M. Earle McCabe, deputy director, of the Ontario Separate School Trustees' Association. See also *Fair Taxation in a Changing World: Report of the Ontario Fair Tax Commission* (Toronto: University of Toronto Press, 1992), 673-90.

[31] Ontario, Royal Commission on Learning, *For the Love of Learning: A Short Version* Toronto: (1994), 76.

[32] Kenneth Westhues, "Public vs Sectarian Legitimation: The Separate Schools of the Catholic Church," 149.

[33] Institute for Catholic Education, *Catholic Education in the Separate School System of Ontario* (1990), 15. This report is often referred to as the Blishen Report after Bernard Blishen, whose name appears first in the list of participating staff. Unlike many other reports of its kind, this one still commands one's attention and respect.

[34] Completion Office – Separate Schools, *Catholic Education and Separate School Boards in Ontario* (April, 1988), 1-3. This was quoted in *Catholic Education in the Separate School System of Ontario*, 19.

PRESIDENTS OF OSSTA/OCSTA
1961 to the Present

[Note: This list begins with the establishment of a permanent office.]

The Hon. Francis G. Carter, London
April 1961 to April 1962

Chris Asseff, Thunder Bay
April 1962 to April 1964

Dr. Joseph Fyfe, Sudbury
April 1964 to April 1966

Albert E. Klein, Q.C., North Bay
April 1966 to April 1969

Dr. Nicholas A. Mancini, Hamilton
April 1969 to April 1972

Dr. Bernard J. Nolan, Windsor
April 1972 to April 1974

Edward J. Brisbois, Toronto
April 1974 to April 1976

William J. Hillyer, Owen Sound
April 1976 to April 1978

C. Frank Gilhooly, Ottawa
April 1978 to April 1980

Mary C. O'Connor, Kirkland Lake
April 1980 to April 1982

Charles F. Yates, Cambridge
April 1982 to April 1984

Joseph H. Duffey, Kingston
April 1984 to April 1986

James V. Sherlock, Burlington
April 1986 to April 1988

Omer J. Gagne, Sarnia
April 1988 to April 1990

Betty Mosely-Williams, North Bay
April 1990 to April 1992

Mary Hendriks, Grimsby
April 1992 to April 1994

Patrick Meany, Mississauga
April 1994 to April 1996

Patrick Daly, Hamilton
April 1996 to April 1998

Regis O'Connor, Sault Ste. Marie
April 1998 to April 2000

Don Petrozzi, Lasalle
April 2000 to December 2000

Louise Ervin
January 2001 to the present

1977

Edward Brisbois	Metropolitan Separate School Board
James Copeland	London & Middlesex County RCSSB
Eileen Coombs	London & Middlesex County RCSSB
Sr. Bernadette Boivin	Kirkland Lake-Timiskaming District RCSSB
Joseph Donihee	Frontenac-Lennox & Addington County RCSSB
John Johnson	Windsor RCSSB
Morgan O'Connor	Durham Region RCSSB
Msgr. Delaney	Lincoln County RCSSB
Rev. Dr. Francis Grant	Peterborough Victoria Northumberland & Newcastle RCSSB
Rev. Bernard Cox	Hamilton Wentworth RCSSB

1978

Msgr. Charles Colgan	Hamilton RCSSB
Dr. John Andrachuck	Metropolitan Separate School Board
Jean Paul Parent	Cochrane-Iroquois Falls, Black River-Matheson RCSSB
Daniel Murawsky	Waterloo Region RCSSB
Sylvia Brown	Windsor RCSSB
Eugene Jacobs	York Region RCSSB
Dr. Bernard Nolan	Windsor RCSSB

1979

Rev. Blake Ryan	Wellington County RCSSB
Nicholas Marino	Lincoln County RCSSB
Rita Desjardins	Ottawa RCSSB
A.C. Thompson	Dufferin-Peel RCSSB
Rosario Paquet	Nipissing District RCSSB
Robert Butler	Huron-Perth County RCSSB

1980

Almon Doolan	Frontenac-Lennox & Addington County RCSSB

| John Pearson | Lincoln County RCSSB |
| Alexander Kuska | Welland County RCSSB |

1981

Aime Arvisais	Ottawa RCSSB
John Trepanier	Brant & Haldimand & Norfolk RCSSB
Janis Bunkis	North of Superior District RCSSB
Rev. L.P. Casartelli	Hastings-Prince Edward County RCSSB
Dr. J.W. Fye	Sudbury District RCSSB
Albert (Ab) Klein	Nipissing District RCSSB

1982

Sr. Emeline Forbes	Windsor RCSSB
Rev. Ken A. Burns	Welland County RCSSB
Mary Cowley	Lambton County RCSSB
Joseph Hugel	Dufferin-Peel RCSSB
Msgr. Percy Johnson	Metropolitan Separate School Board
Rev. Cornelius Siegfried	Waterloo Region RCSSB
Les Silaj	North Shore District RCSSB

1983

Lorne Charbonneau	Kirkland Lake-Timiskaming District RCSSB
A.F. Al Dunn	Elgin County RCSSB
C.F. Gilhooly	Ottawa RCSSB
Carl Q. Mundy	Lambton County RCSSB

1984

Gerald E. Dwyer	Windsor RCCSB
Frank E. Shine	Durham Region RCSSB
Archbishop J.L. Wilhelm	Frontenac-Lennox & Addington County RCSSB
Archbishop P.F. Pocock	Metropolitan Separate School Board

1985

Betty Biss	Dufferin-Peel RCSSB
Rev. Patrick Fogarty	Metropolitan Separate School Board
T.E. Ed Joyce	York Region RCSSB
Phil McAllister	Metropolitan Separate School Board
Chris Asseff	Thunder Bay RCSSB

1986

Rev. Raymond Durocher	Metropolitan Separate School Board
Frank Furlong	Waterloo Region RCSSB
John Hourigan	Wellington County RCSSB
James Jordan	Lanark Leeds and Grenville County RCSSB
Dr. N.A. Mancini	Hamilton-Wentworth RCSSB
B.E. Nelligan	Metropolitan Separate School Board
Pat Whelan	Lincoln County RCSSB

1987

Gerry Meehan	Dufferin-Peel RCSSB

1988

Kathleen Nolan	Hamilton-Wentworth RCSSB
Cecil Poirier	Kenora RCSSB
William Winters	Renfrew County RCSSB

1989

Martha Joyce	London & Middlesex County RCSSB
Angus MacLellan	Dryden District RCSSB

1990

Robert Hall	Dufferin-Peel RCSSB
Lillian O'Connor	Hastings-Prince Edward County RCSSB
Ferbie St. Cyr	Kirkland Lake Timiskaming District RCSSB

500

1991

Joseph Duffey	Frontenac-Lennox & Addington County RCSSB
Bertran Garrett	Hastings-Prince Edward County RCSSB
William J. Hillyer	Bruce-Grey County RCSSB

1992

Dr. Angelo Albanese	Welland County RCSSB
Robert O'Brien	Halton RCSSB
Chuck Yates	Waterloo Region RCSSB

1993

Jim Carpenter	London & Middlesex County RCSSB
Robert Flanagan	Welland County RCSSB
Paul Duggan	Metropolitan Separate School Board

1994

James Sherlock	Halton RCSSB
Mary O'Connor	Kirkland Lake-Timiskaming District RCSSB
Roberta Anderson	Ottawa RCSSB

1995

Fr. Carl Matthews	Metropolitan Separate School Board
John Shrader	London & Middlesex County RCSSB

1996

Msgr. Edward Boehler	Metropolitan Separate School Board
Michael Kelly	Ottawa RCSSB
Ray Voll	Waterloo Region RCSSB

1997

Mary Hendriks	Lincoln County RCSSB
Rev. Tom Day	Metropolitan Separate School Board

1998

Jacqueline
Legendre-McGuinty Ottawa RCSSB
Tina Rotondi-Molinari York Region RCSSB
Donald Schrenk Halton RCSSB

1999

Robert Hubbard St. Clair CDSB
Joseph Kraemer London & Middlesex County RCSSB

2000

A.J.M. (Art) Lamarche Ottawa Carleton CDSB

2001

Patrick Meany Dufferin Peel CDSB

2002

Donald Sunstrum Huron Superior CDSB

SELECT BIBLIOGRAPHY

Biggar, C.R.W. *Sir Oliver Mowat: A Biographical Sketch*. 2 vols. Toronto: Warwick Bro's & Rutter, 1905.

Cameron, David M. *Schools for Ontario: Policy-Making, Administration, and Finance in the 1960s*. Toronto: University of Toronto Press, 1972.

Carter, Francis G. *Judicial Decisions on Denominational Schools*. Toronto: Ontario Separate School Trustees' Association, 1962.

Choquette, Robert. *Language and Religion: A History of English-French Conflict in Ontario*. Ottawa; University of Ottawa Press, 1975.

Clarke, Brian P. *Piety and Nationalism: Lay Voluntary Associations and the Creation of an Irish-Catholic Community in Toronto, 1850-1895*. Montreal & Kingston: McGill-Queen's University Press, 1993.

Dictionary of Canadian Biography. 14 vols. Toronto: University of Toronto Press, 1966- .

Dixon, Robert Thomas. *Be a Teacher: A History of the Ontario English Catholic Teachers' Association 1944-1994*. Toronto: Ontario English Catholic Teachers' Association, 1994.

_____. "The Ontario Separate School System and Section 93 of the British North America Act." D.Ed. diss., University of Toronto, 1976.

Farrell, John K.A. "The History of the Roman Catholic Church in London, Ontario 1826-1931." Master's thesis, University of Western Ontario, 1949.

Fleming, W.G. *The administrative structure.* Vol. 2, *Ontario's Educative Society.* Toronto: University of Toronto Press, 1971.

_____. *Education: Ontario's preoccupation.* Toronto: University of Toronto Press, 1972.

_____. *Educational contributions of associations.* Vol. 7, *Ontario's Educative Society.* Toronto: University of Toronto Press, 1972.

_____. *The expansion of the educational system.* Vol. 1, *Ontario's Educative Society.* Toronto: University of Toronto Press, 1971.

_____. *Schools, pupils, and teachers.* Vol. 3, *Ontario's Educative Society.* Toronto: University of Toronto Press, 1972.

Gidney, R.D. *From Hope to Harris: The Reshaping of Ontario's Schools.* Toronto: University of Toronto Press, 1999.

Gruending, Dennis. *Emmett Hall: Establishment Radical.* Toronto: Macmillan, 1985.

Henderson, E.F. et. al. *Historical Sketch of the Separate Schools of Ontario and Minority Report.* Toronto: The English Catholic Education Association of Ontario, [1950].

Hodgins, J. George. *Documentary History of Education in Upper Canada.* 28 vols. Toronto: Warwick Bros. & Rutter, 1984-1910.

_____. *The Establishment of Schools and Colleges in Ontario 1792-1910.* 3 vols. Toronto: L.K. Cameron, 1910.

504

_____. *Historical and Other Papers and Documents Illustrative of the Educational System of Ontario, 1856-1872.* 6 vols. Toronto: L.K. Cameron, 1911.

_____. *The Legislation and History of Separate Schools in Upper Canada.* Toronto: William Briggs, 1897.

Hoy, Claire. *Bill Davis: A Biography.* Toronto: Methuen, 1985.

Kelly, Edward. *The Story of St. Paul's Parish Toronto.* Toronto: St. Paul's Parish, 1922.

Living and Learning: The Report of the Provincial Committee on Aims and Objectives of Education in the Schools of Ontario. Toronto: 1968.

McGovern, Kathleen. *Something More than Ordinary: The Early History of Mary Ward's Institute in North America.* Richmond Hill, Ontario: 1989.

McGowan, Mark G. *The Waning of the Green: the Irish and Identity in Toronto, 1887-1922.* Montreal & Kingston: McGill-Queen's University Press, 1999.

McKenty, Neil. *Mitch Hepburn.* Toronto: McClelland and Stewart, 1967.

McNeil, Neil. *The School Question of Ontario.* 1932.

Merchant, F.W. *Report on the Condition of English-French Schools in the Province of Ontario.* Toronto: King's Printer, 1912.

Moir, John S. *Church and State in Canada West.* Toronto: University of Toronto Press, 1959.

Murphy, Sister Mary Agnes. *The Congregation of the Sisters of St. Joseph: Le Puy, Lyons, St. Louis, Toronto*. Toronto: 1951.

Paikin, Steve. *The Life: The Seductive Call of Politics*. Toronto: Penguin 2001.

Quinn, Martin J. *The Frustration of Lay Catholic Effort in Ontario*. Toronto: The Catholic Primary School, 1945.

_____. *The Ontario Separate School Question: What Some Orangemen Say, the Catholic Reply*. Catholic Taxpayers' Association, [1933].

_____. *Some Pertinent Facts: The Separate Schools of Ontario*. 2nd ed. Toronto: Catholic Taxpayers' Association, July 1932.

Report of the Royal Commission on Education in Ontario 1950. Toronto: King's Printer, 1950.

Saywell, John T. *'Just call me Mitch': The Life of Mitchell F. Hepburn*. Toronto: University of Toronto Press, 1991.

Sissons, C.B. *Bi-Lingual Schools in Ontario*. Toronto; J.M. Dent & Sons, 1917.

_____. *Church & State in Canadian Education: An Historical Study*. Toronto: Ryerson Press, 1959.

Smythe, Elizabeth M. "The Lessons of Religion and Science: The Congregation of the Sisters of St. Joseph and St. Joseph's Academy, Toronto 1854-1911." Ph.D. diss., University of Toronto, 1989.

Somers, Hugh Joseph. *The Life and Times of the Hon. and Rt. Rev. Alexander Macdonell, D.D. First Bishop of Upper Canada 1762-1840*. Washington, D.C.: The Catholic University of America, 1931.

Speirs, Rosemary. *Out of the Blue: The Fall of the Tory Dynasty in Ontario*. Toronto: Macmillan, 1986.

Stamp, Robert M. *The Schools of Ontario, 1876-1976*. Toronto: University of Toronto, 1987.

Stortz, Gerald J. "John Joseph Lynch, Archbishop of Toronto: A Biographical Study of Religious, Political and Social Commitment." Ph.D. diss., University of Guelph, 1980.

Teefy, John R., ed. *Jubilee Volume of the Archdiocese of Toronto and Archbishop Walsh*. Toronto: Geo. Dixon, 1892.

Walker, Franklin A. *Catholic Education and Politics in Upper Canada*. Toronto: English Catholic Education Association of Ontario, 1955; reprint, Toronto: The Federation of Catholic Education Associations of Ontario, 1976; reprint, Toronto: Catholic Education Foundation, 1985.

_____. *Catholic Education and Politics in Ontario*. Vol. 2. Toronto: English Catholic Education Association of Ontario, 1964.

_____. *Catholic Education and Politics in Ontario*. Vol. 3. Toronto: Catholic Education Foundation of Ontario, 1986.

INDEX

accreditation of religion courses, 446-47

ACEBO. *See* l'Association des commissions des écoles bilingues d'Ontario (ACEBO)

ACFEO. *See* l'Association canadiene-française d'education d'Ontario (ACFEO)

ACHSBO. *See* Association of Catholic High School Boards of Ontario (ACHSBO)

"An Act Consolidating and Revising the Public Schools Act" (1896), 213

"An Act for amending the Common Schools Act" (1847), 36

"An Act for the better establishment and maintenance of Common Schools in Upper Canada" (1846), 36

"An Act for the better establishment and maintenance of Common Schools in Upper Canada" (1850), 37, 111, 112, 121, 129

"An Act for the better Establishment and Maintenance of Public Schools in Upper Canada, and for repealing the recent School Act" (1849), 36-37

"An Act for the establishment and maintenance of Common Schools in Upper Canada" (1843), 19, 84-85

Act of Union (1840-1841), viii

"An Act Respecting Public, Separate and High Schools" (1879), 60

"An Act respecting Separate Schools" (1866), 60-61

"An Act respecting the Qualifications of Certain Teachers" (1907), 194-95

"An Act supplementary to the Common School Act for Upper Canada" (1853), 43-44, 111, 121, 129

"An Act to amend the Assessment Act" (1936), 330-33

"An Act to amend the Education Act" (1986). See Bill 30

"An Act to amend the laws relating to Separate Schools in Upper Canada" (1855), 44-46, 129-30

"An Act to amend the Schools Administration Act" (1968), 423-24

"An Act to amend the Separate Schools Act" (1968), 419-20

"An Act to define and restore certain rights to parties therein mentioned" (1851), 39

"An Act to make further provision for the establishment and maintenance of Common Schools throughout the Province" (1841), 2, 16-17

"An Act to repeal Chapter 4 of the Statutes of Ontario, 1936" (1937), 335-36

"An Act to restore to Roman Catholics in Upper Canada certain rights in respect of Separate Schools" (1863), 54. *See* also Scott Act (1863)

"An Act to restore to Roman Catholics in Upper Canada certain rights in respect to separate schools, and to extend to the Roman Catholic minority in Upper Canada, similar and equal privileges with those granted by the legislature to the Protestant minority in Lower Canada," 58

Adolescent Attendance Schools Act: amendment (1921), 250

AFCSO. *See* L'Association française des conseils scolaires de l'Ontario (AFCSO)

509

Alice Marie, Sister, 409

Allen, J.P., 361

Althouse, J.G., 363, 365

amalgamation of school boards. *See* larger units of administration

Ambrose, Sister, 184

Anglican separate schools, 39

Anglin, Francis, 279

Anglin, Timothy Warren, 152

Appolonia, Sister, 178

Archdiocese of Ottawa: Grey Sisters of the Cross, 184-85; number of religious and lay teachers, 171

Archdiocese of Toronto, 16, 17, number of religious and lay teachers, 170-71; Sisters of St. Joseph, 175-78

Archambault, R.L., 305

Archibald, E.J., 229-30

Asseff, Chris, 407, 418, 428, 430, 434, 435, 446, 447, 448

Assessment Act, 217, 250, 271, 272; Catholic Taxpayers' Association, 289, 310-11, 330-33

l'Association canadiene-française d'education d'Ontario (ACFEO), 221, 237, 240, 338, 345-50, 354, 360; Dana Porter, 379; English Catholic Education Association of Ontario (ECEAO), 361; James P. Whitney, 221-22; Ottawa Separate School Board, 233-36

l'Association des commissions des écoles bilingues d'Ontario (ACEBO), 350, 383, 402; Ontario Separate School Trustees' Association, 385-86, 424

l'Association française des conseils scolaires de l'Ontario (AFCSO), 441, 451; entente with the Ontario Separate School Trustees' Association, 452-53

Association of Catholic High School Boards of Ontario (ACHSBO), 350, 425, 426; Working Committee on Extension, 431-32

Assumption College (Sandwich), 21

Assumption parish (Sandwich), 6, 10

Babcock, Mary, 446, 447

Baby, François, 1

Baby, James, 11

Bailey, Mr., 351

Ball, Florence, 361

Ball, Francis, 182

Banner, 85

Barber, G.A., 83-84, 97

Barber, Marilyn, 212

Barnett, Edward, 11

Basilian Fathers, 27

Bassett, John, 40

Bathurst, Lord, 4, 6, 7, 9

Battle, Thomas F., 277-78, 353, 354, 359

Bedingfield, Frances, 181

Beetz, Jean, 486

Begin, Louis-Nazaire, 222

Bélanger, Aurélien, 354

Belcourt, Napoleon A., 192, 220

Bell, Robert, 58, 102, 109

Belle River, 20

Belleville, 41-42

Benedict XV, 237-38, 239, 241, 250

Beneteau, A.J., 240

Bennett, John F., 427, 428

Bergin, William, 11

Bériault, Roland, 403

Berlis, H.A., 264

Bible, 18, 20, 31, 83

bilingual schools, 186, 195, 203, 206-12; separate schools, 213-16

Bill 30, 473, 474; amendments, 481-82, 486; Blishen Report, 491; Court of Appeal, 483, 486; legal challenges, 482-87; preamble, 484; principles, 479-80; Section 136, 481-82; Social Development Committee, 480-81; Supreme Court of Canada, 486-87

Bill 64 (1989), 488

Bishops' Committee on Education, 476-77

Bishops' brief (October 1962), 399-402

Black, Gerrard, 309

Blair Commission. *See* Commission on the Reform of Property Taxation in Ontario

Blake, Edward, 52

Blanc, Antoine, 26

Blishen Report (1990), 490-91

BNA Act (1867), viii, 249, 250. *See* also Section 93 of the BNA Act (1867)

Boehler, Edward, 477

Bolland, H.M., 230

Bond Head, Francis, 78

Borden, Robert Laird, 220

Border Cities Star, 311, 313

Boulton, H.J., 11

Bourassa, Henri, 225

Bourget, Ignace, 16, 185

Bowes Bill (1856), 46, 92, 97

Boyce, Harold A., 335

Boyle, Patrick, 109, 142-44, 150; John Joseph Lynch, 146, 147

Boys Industrial School, 81

Brantford, 113-14, 118-19

Brennan, A.J., 235

Brennan, F.J., 357, 361, 370, 380

Brennan, Patrick J. 448

Brennan, Teresa, 178

Brick, M.G., 354

Brisbois, Edward J., 409, 428, 430, 441-42

Brisson, M.A., 351, 354

British North America Act (1867). *See* BNA Act (1867)

Brothers: list of teaching communities, 166

Brown, George, 23, 28, 46, 47, 49, 85-86, 120, 273; Charles Donlevy, 96, 98-100

Brown, Samuel, 178

Bruyère, Élizabeth, 185

Bruyère, J.M., 46-47, 92, 100, 178

Bunning, Mary Martha [Marie], 174, 177

Burk, F.D., 354

Burke, Edmund, 15

Burke, John, 357

Butler, John, 6, 13

Butler, Mr., 351

Cado, Charles A., 354

Cahill, Daniel P., 152, 153

Cameron, Malcolm, 36

Campbell, Ignatia, 178, 179

Canada Temperance Act (1878), 52

Canadian Conference on Education, 403

Canadian Freeman, 80-81, 93, 94, 95, 199-20, 122, 313; Scott Act (1863), 103, 108; separate school issues, 102

Carrie, C.M., 325

Carroll, John, 6

Carroll, John (priest), 86

Carroll, Maurice, 100, 105

Carroll, William G., 271

Carter, Francis G., 385, 393, 399, 404, 412

Carter, Gerald Emmett, 399, 425, 427, 428, 432, 455, 476-77

Carty, Michael W., 429

Carty family (London), 323

Catholic Central High School (London), 427-28

Catholic Citizen, 101, 109

Catholic Educational Council, 260, 269-270, 277, 278, 281

Catholic Education Conference, 364

Catholic Institutes, 126-30; separate schools, 127-30; demise, 130

Catholicity, 444-50, 473, 476-77, 487-92

Catholic laity and separate schools, Chapter Two

Catholic Record, 313

Catholic Register, 110, 293, 306, 309, 310, 313, 319, 320, 434

Catholic separate schools. *See* separate schools

Catholic Trustee, 395, 404, 408, 434, 437, 449

Catholic separate school inspectors, 60, 61, 75; 130-37; abolition, 420

Catholic Taxpayers' Association, Chapter Six; "Application for Legislative Amendment of Existing Laws Relating to School Taxes," 324; "Application of Catholic Taxpayers' Association of Ontario for Amendment of the Assessment Act," 310-11; Assessment Act, 289; bishops, 302-3; election (June 1934), 317-18, 320; George S. Henry, 307-21; Judicial Committee of the Privy Council, 317; Mitch

511

Hepburn, 321-37; Neil McNeil, 291, 293, 298, 307; organization, 289-90, 304; origins, 293-306; re-organization, 338

Catholic Voice, 309

Catholic Weekly Review, 109

Catholic Women's League, 308, 309, 436

Causyn, Robert, 392

Cazeau, C.F., 54

Charbonneau, Arthur, 236

Charbonnel, Armand-François-Marie de, 15, 22-48, 76, 80, 86, 100, 248; bishop of Toronto, 27; early career, 25-26; Egerton Ryerson, 22-25, 35, 39-46; later career, 47-48; Lenten Pastoral (1856), 46; separate schools, 27, 38; Sisters of St. Joseph, 173

Charlebois, Marie-Ursule, 185

Charter of Rights and Freedoms: Section 29, 452, 484, 485

Chatham, 40

Chisholm, James, 6

Christian Brothers, 21, 27, 130, 132, 166, 178, 183; Martin J. Quinn, 291; teacher certification, 186, 187, 189, 190, 191, 192, 235

Clairoux, J.A., 354

Clarke, Brian, 138, 151

Clergy Reserves Fund, 44, 46, 101, 108-9, 121, 124

Clerk, George Edward, 110

Coates, F., 353

Colborne, John, 4, 77, 78

Collins, Francis, 11

Collins, Jerry, 429, 438

Colonist, 82, 91

Colquhoun, A.H.U., 258

Come to the Father, 446

Commission For Planning and Implementing Change in the Governance and Administration of Secondary Education, 454, 474-75

Commission of Enquiry, 326

Commission on independent (private) schools, 454, 474, 477-78

Commission on the Financing of Elementary and Secondary Education (Report 1985), 408

Commission on the Reform of Property Taxation in Ontario (Report 1977), 408, 443

Commission on the teaching of English in bilingual schools (1899), 210-12

Commission on the teaching of English in the bilingual schools of Russell and Prescott (1893), 212-13

Committee of Inquiry into the Cost of Education (1937), 415

Committee on the Costs of Education, 443

Common Schools Act (1841), 2, 16-17 completion of the separate school system,

411-12, 441; Albert Klein, 428; Bill Davis, 453-56; Bill 30, 479-80, 484, 486-87; campaign (1966-71), 421-41; meaning, 421-22. See also extension of the separate school system

Confederation, 48-49, 56, 249-50

Congrégation de l'Enfant-Jésus, 6

Congregation of the Notre Dame, 181

Congregation of the Sisters of St. Joseph. See Sisters of St. Joseph

Conlin, Herbert L., 353

Conmee, James, 153

Connolly, John, 374, 375

Conroy, George, 141

"The Consolidation of Education Acts" (1974), 444

Constitution Act (1982), 452; Sections 2(a), 15 and 29, 484

continuation classes, 256-57

continuation schools, 257, 260-61; Regulation of 1915, 259, 269

continuous and integrated education, 348, 414, 422; "Equal Opportunity for Continuous Education in Separate Schools in Ontario" (1968-69), 430-34

Conway, Patrick, 145

Conway, Sean, 479, 482, 488

Cook, O., 407

Corbiene, Louis, 12

Cornish, George A., 368-69

Corporation Tax Adjustment Plan, 407

corporation taxes, 253-54, 262, 266, 271, 278, 290, 390; Neil McNeil, 295

Corrigan, Teresa, 183

Cory, Peter, 486

Cosgrove, Bernard, 127

Costello, J.E., 150

Coté, Louis, 239, 332, 357

Couturier, Félix, 324

Crevier, Joseph, 10

Croll, David, 309

Crooks, Adam, 59, 146

Crowley, H., 407

CTA. See Catholic Taxpayers' Association

Culnan, James G., 353

Cummie, Essie, 180

Cusson, Catherine, 184

Dalhousie, Earl, 9

Daly, Charles, 90

Daly, Thomas, 113

Davis, Bill, 350, 398, 400, 440, 446, 447, 473, 476, 480; completion (1984), 453-56; "Equal Opportunity for Continuous Education in Separate Schools of Ontario," 439-40; larger units of administration, 417; Maple Leaf Gardens rally, 438; Ontario Foundation Tax Plan, 405; resignation, 478

Davis, Mr., 351

Dawson, W.H., 312

Day, James E., 290, 304-5, 329

Dease, Teresa, 182, 184

De Blacquière, Peter B., 17

DeHetie, J.A.E., 354

Demers, Catherine, 187

Denis Morris High School (St. Catharines), 425

Dennis, Lloyd, A., 409

Desmarais, R.J., 354

Desormeaux, Ernest C., 326, 354, 355

Devine, Thomas, 141

Devlin, Elizabeth, 185

DeVos, Joe, 392

DeWade, Cyrile, 392

Dickson, Brian, 486

Dinan, Mary Bernard, 174, 175

Diocese of Hamilton: number of religious and lay teachers, 171

Diocese of London: number of religious and lay teachers, 171; Sisters of St. Joseph, 177-78

Diocese of Peterborough: Sisters of St. Joseph, 180-81

Diocese of Sault Ste. Marie: number of religious and lay teachers, 171-72

Diocese of Toronto. See Archdiocese of Toronto

Dolan, D. 361

Dollard, Patrick, 6

Donlevy, Charles, 28, 78, 93, 94, 95-101, 102, 118, 126; common schools, 96-97; Egerton Ryerson, 96, 97-98; George Brown, 96, 98-100; school trustee, 95-96

Donovan, Cornelius, 61, 136-37, 177

Donovan, Gonzaga, 183

Donovan, T.J., 354

Dooner, Alfred, 329

Doran, Austin, 180

Dowling, Thomas J., 260

Doyle, James L., 448

Doyle, Patrick, 127

Drew, George, 364, 365, 367, 368

Driscoll, C.J., 351, 354, 356

Drury, Ernest Charles, 251, 261, 265, 269-70, 277

Dubois John 16

Ducharme, H.A., 364-65

Duff, James S., 234

Duffy, St. Charles, 180

Duhamel, Joseph Thomas, 189, 190, 191, 195

Dunbar, Angus, 375

Dunbar, Samuel, 152

Duncombe, Charles, 1

Dunlop, P.J., 361

Dunlop, William J., 386

Dunn, Elaine, 448

Durocher, Raymond, 412; brief on larger units of administration, 418; constitutional reform; 442-43; Hall-Dennis Committee, 413; Working Committee on Extension, 429, 431, 434

East Hastings by-election (1936), 335

ECEAO. *See* English Catholic Education Association of Ontario (ECEAO)

"The Education Act" (1974), 444; Part IV, 451; Section 10(3), 482-83; Sections 32 and 258, 452

Egan, P., 178

Elmsley, John, 21, 53, 76-93, 101, 112, 126, 174; conversion, 78-79; defense of the Catholic Church, 82-83; diocese of Toronto, 81-82; early life, 76-77; Egerton Ryerson, 86-91; Famine, 80-81; Michael Power, 91-92; politics, 77-78; St. Paul's Church (York, Toronto), 79-80; school trustee, 83, 86; Scott Act (1863), 83, 93

Elmsley, John (chief justice), 76

Elmsley, Remigius, 93, 110, 190; Toronto Separate School Board, 140-41, 148-50

Englert, J.W., 354, 361

English Catholic Education Association of Ontario (ECEAO), 338; bishops, 349; early history, 360-61; name change, 442; Ontario Separate School Trustees' Association, 350, 360-65; 408; Patrick Fogarty, 425; Working Committee on Extension, 430

English-French schools. *See* bilingual schools

Enright, P.J., 402

equal educational opportunity for every child, 348, 358, 372, 397, 405; completion of the separate school system, 421-22; "Equal Opportunity for Continuous Education in Separate Schools in Ontario" (1968-69), 430-34

Equality Sunday (22 February 1970), 437

"Equal Opportunity for Continuous Education in Separate Schools in Ontario" (1968-69), 430-33

Estey, Willard Z., 486

Ethical Education Association, 435

Evans, George, 141, 142, 144, 146

Evening Telegram, 290, 319-20, 322, 324. *See also Toronto Telegram*

expenditures per pupil (1911, 1915, 1925), 251-52

Extension Convention (30 August 1971), 439

extension of the separate school system, 413-14, 419, 421, 438. See also completion of the separate school system

Fallon, Michael Francis, 10, 223-29, 248, 249, 259, 260, 261, 379; bilingual education, 223-24, 225; Hanna/Pyne memorandum, 225-28;

James Whitney, 226; Massey Hall, 262, 268; Regulation 17, 224; restoration of rights, 255-56, 259; separate school politics (1920s), 261-70

Farley, Bonaventure, 178

Farling, James, 12

Farrell, John, 6

Farrell, John (bishop), 52, 174

FCPTAO. *See* Federation of Catholic Parent-Teacher Associations of Ontario (FCPTAO)

Federation of Catholic Parent-Teacher Associations of Ontario (FCPTAO), 350, 361, 429, 430, 434

Feehan, D.K., 127

Feeney, J.A., 387

Felton amendment, 46, 97

Ferguson, G. Howard, 239, 313

Fergusson, Adam Johnston, 129

Fifth form, 256, 257

finality of the Scott Act (1863), 54, 57-58, 265, 267, 273-74

Finn, James, 235

Finn, Joseph P., 362, 380, 382, 391-92, 425

Fitzgerald, Gerald, 109-110

Fitzpatrick, F., 353

Flannery, Frank C., 144-45

Fleming, Gertrude, 182, 183

Fletcher, John, 82

Focus on the Faith, 448-50

Fogarty, Patrick Harmon, 425, 426, 427, 429, 432, 434

Fontbonne, Delphine [Marie Antoinette], 173, 174

Fontbonne, Fébronie [Antoinette], 173

Fontbonne, Jacques, 173

Fontbonne, St. Jean, 173

Ford, A.E., 354

Forestell, Paul, 446

Foy, J.J., 218, 220, 230, 234

Fraser, Christopher Findlay, 143, 188

Fraser, William, 32

French as a language of instruction and communication, 186, 203, 207-8; Hope Commission, 367

French Canadian Congress of Education, 220

French-language minority rights, 451-53

French-language secondary schools, 423-24

Frost, Leslie, 362, 364, 366, 385, 387, 390; Hope Commission, 378

Furling, F.J., 354

Furniss, Albert J., 150

Fyfe, Joe, 407-8, 417, 418

Gallagher, Mr., 13

Garnsworthy, Lewis, 478-79

Gaulin, Rémi, 17

Gauthier, Charles Hugues, 191, 218

Genest, Samuel M., 233-34

George Weston Company, 292, 297-98

Gilhooly, C.F., 417, 448

Globe, 47, 103-4, 130-31, 146, 266

Globe and Mail, 290, 336, 478

Goderich, 115-16

Gordon, George, 12

Gordon, Edward John, 174

Gore, Francis, 1

Gormley, St. Edward, 180

Gourd, Damien, 354

Grant, Chas, 9

Grant, R., 265

Grantham, J.D., 192

Gray, W. Gibson, 482

Greer, V.K., 326, 357, 365

Gregory, Brother, 351, 354

Grey Sisters of the Cross, 118, 184-85

Grouchy, Philip de, 110

Guelph, 117

Haldane, Richard, 279

Hall, Emmett, 409

Hall-Dennis Committee (1965-68), 408-15; Catholic members, 409; Committee on Religious Education in the Public Schools, 411; completion, 411-12; continuous learning, 414; Living and Learning, 410, 414-15; separate schools, 410-11, 414-15; terms of reference, 410

Halley, William, 127

Hallinan, J., 127

Hallowell, Mary, 76

Hamilton, John, 17

Hammond, Richard, 5

Hand, John Laurence, 152, 353

Hanna, W.J., 224

Hanna/Pyne memorandum, 225-28

Harcourt, Richard, 269

Harrison, S.B., 40

Harvey, John, 12-13

Hay, John, 6

Hayes, M.P., 126

Hayes, Michael, 109

Hayes, Thomas, 109

Hearst, William Howard, 235, 260-61

Heenan, M., 176

Heenan, Peter, 323, 324

Heffernan, Denis, 13, 126

Hellmuth, Isidore F., 278

Henderson, E.F., 353, 361, 365

Henderson, James, 351

Hennigan, Stanislaus, 184

Henry, George S., 281, 290, 335; Catholic Taxpayers' Association, 307-21

Hepburn, Mitch, 290, 318, 320; Catholic Taxpayers' Association, 321-37

Herbert, Thomas, 354 high school entrance examination, 379 high school issue, 252-53, 257, 259

Hill, James F., 335

515

Hillyer, Wm. J., 417, 428, 429-30, 448

Hincks, Francis, 39, 44

Hinsperger, M.S., 357

Hishon, P.H., 354

Hocken, Horatio Clarence, 276-77

Hodgins, J. George, 22, 267

Holy Family (Toronto), 183

Holzer, John, 117

Hope, John Andrew, 365; E.V. McCarthy, 375-76

Hope Commission (1945-50), 348, 364, 365-80, 410-11, 415; Brief 113, 368-69; Brief 146, 370-72, 380; Brief 196, 370, 372-74; Majority Report, 376-77; Minority Report, 379; Ontario Separate School Trustees' Association, 380; recommendations, 367, 377; re-organization of the school system, 377-78; Report, 366-67, 376, 378; separate schools, 367-68, 376-77; supplement to Brief 146, 374-75; terms of reference, 366

Horan, Edward John, 52, 130

Horton, Wilmot, 9

House of Providence, 27, 81

Howard, Marie-Antoinette, 185

Howland, William, 486

Hoy, Claire, 455

Hudon, H., 17

Huron tribe (Belle River), 12

Hutchinson, Berchmans, 182

Hutchinson, Ignatia, 182

IBVM. See Institute of the Blessed Virgin Mary (IBVM)

Immaculate Conception (Peterborough), 181

Institute of Catholic Education, 490

Institute of the Blessed Virgin Mary (IBVM), 21, 168, 177, 180, 181-84

Instructions 17. See Regulation 17

Instructions 18, 209-10, 233

Inter-Church Committee on Protestant-Roman Catholic Relations, 368-69

Irish Canadian, 109, 110, 143-44

Isidore, Chief, 12

Jackson, R.W.B., 402

Jamot, Jean-François, 148, 149

Jarlath, Brother, 353

Jarvis, Samuel Peters, 13

Jesuits, 21

Johnston, Richard, 480, 481

Jones, Mary, 185

Judicial Committee of the Privy Council: corporation taxes (1934), 313, 316, 317; Ottawa Separate School Board (1916, 1920), 236; teacher certification (1906), 193; Tiny

Township (1928), 279-80; Regulation 17 (1916), 235

Kane, Clement, 127

Karr, W.J., 240

Kavanagh, Frank, 429, 431, 490

Kavanagh, P.F., 127

Keenan, J.C., 305

Kehoe, F.J., 354

Kelly, Arthur, 361, 365, 415

Kelly, D., 152

Kelly, William, 361

Kennedy, William, 6

Kenny, R.F., 274

Kenrick, Francis, 173

Kernahan, W.T., 290, 302, 305, 310, 326

Kerr, Robert, 328

Keven, C., 176

Kiely, P.G., 268

King, John, 80

King, Mackenzie, 326

Kingston, 122-24

Kingston Whig-Standard, 309

Kirk, Benjamin, 271, 273

Klein, Albert E., 417, 427, 428, 429, 447

Knights of Columbus, 436

Kovacs, Francis, 428, 431

Kuchinak, John, 434, 447

Lacasse, Gustave, 357

Lacourse, Anthony, 12

Ladies of Loretto. *See*
Institute of the Blessed
Virgin Mary (IBVM)

Ladies of the Sacred Heart,
179

La Forest, Gerald V., 486

Laidlaw, Robert, 384, 403

Lajambe, K., 407

Lalu, A. L., 363

Lambertus, J.A., 353-54

Lamer, Antonio, 486

Lamont, John, 279

Lamoureux, Father, 357

Land, Reinhold, 354

Langevin, Louis, 58

Lanigan, J.F., 235

Laprairie, Mr., 351

larger units of
administration, 396,
415-21; county, 417;
Hall-Dennis Committee,
414-15; Ontario Catholic
Education Council,
415-16; Ontario Separate
School Trustees'
Association, 418-19

LaRocque, Eugene, P., 448

Lassaline, Norman B., 354

Latulippe, E.A., 222

Laurent, Joseph M., 145

Laurent, P.D., 180

Laurier, Wilfrid, 220, 322

Lauwers, Peter, 487

Lawrence, W.L.L., 274

Leader, 104

LeBel, Arthur M., 393

Leddy, J.F., 409

Lee, W.J., 357

Lefebre, Don, 407

legislation. See "An Act ..."

legislative grants, 90, 101,
112, 121, 124-25, 218,
337, 348; changes (1944),
363-64, 372; Egerton
Ryerson, 115-16; Grades
9, 10 and 11, 480; high
school issue, 253;
Regulation 17, 210, 237;
Tiny Township case, 277-
80; uniform assessment,
387

London Morning Advertiser,
309

London School Board, 263

London Separate School
Board, 387

Loretto Sisters. See Institute
of the Blessed Virgin
Mary

Lottridge, Hank, 418

Loyal Orange Lodge, 74,
206, 261, 290, 308

Lynch, John Joseph, 15, 47,
48-62, 82, 175; Catholic
Institutes, 130; early
career, 50-51; Egerton
Ryerson, 49, 52-53, 62;
finality of the Scott Act
(1863), 57-58; James G.
Moylan, 102; Oliver
Mowat, 49-50; Patrick
Boyle, 142-50; Remigius
Elmsley, 140-41, 148-50;
Richard William Scott,
52, 54-55; Ross Bible,
61; school inspectors,
131; school textbooks,
61; secret ballot,
1151-53; Toronto
Separate School Board
(1876-79), 138-51

"Lynch-Mowat Concordat,"
50, 59

Lynch-Staunton, George,
304, 305, 310

Lynn, Ignatia, 183, 184

Lynn, Samuel Goodenough,
21, 81, 83, 86, 184

Macaulay, Leopold, 330

Macdonagh, John, 6

MacDonald, Clarke, 478

MacDonald, Donald C., 401,
403, 434, 437, 438

Macdonald, H. Ian, 474

Macdonald, John A., 45, 52,
102, 109

Macdonald, John Sandfield,
54

MacDonald, W.P., 79

Macdonald Commission,
454, 474, 475-76

Macdonell, Alex, 144

Macdonell, Alexander
(bishop), 1-14, 47, 76, 79,
80, 141; career in Upper
Canada, 4; Catholic
schools, 5-6; growth of
the Catholic Church in
Upper Canada, 5; views
on Catholic education,
1-2

Macdonell, Alexander
(priest), 11

Macdonell, Alexander
Ranaldson, 3

MacDonell, Allan, 6

Macdonell, Angus, 6

Macdonell, Angus (priest),
52, 54

Macdonell, Antoinette, 178

MacDonell, William A., 260

Mackay, J. Keiller, 411

Mackell, R., 235

Mackenzie, Alexander, 52

MacMahon, Mr. Justice, 192

MacNamara, Joseph, 183

Macnamara, Michael, 11

MacPherson, James, 5

Maisonville, H.C.A., 226

Maitland, Peregrine, 1, 7, 8, 9

Mallon, James J., 101

Maloney, Arthur, 426

Maloney, Ellen, 133

Maloney, Susan, 180

Mancini, Nicholas, 428, 429, 431, 434, 441, 448

Maple Leaf Gardens rally (October 1970), 437-38

Margerum, Alphonsus [Sarah], 174

Marrocco, Francis A., 438, 450

Martin, V.A., 354

Masterson, Ed, 434

Matthews, Carl, 403, 404, 407, 418

Matthews Commission (1981), 444

Marvyn, John, 142

Maupas, Henri de, 173

Mauseau, A., 17

McArthur, Duncan, 326

McCabe, M. Earle, 428, 429, 430

McCarney, Mr., 361

McCarthy, E.V., 361; John Andrew Hope, 375-76

McCarthy, J.R., 417

McCarthy, Thomas J., 390, 425

McCoy, M.S., 126

McCrea, Charles, 310, 312, 320

McCrossan, Michael, 109, 148

McCullagh, George, 336

McDonagh, William Patrick, 79, 80

McDonald, Angus, 5

McDonald, John, 10

McDonnell, Angus, 126

McDonnell, W.J., 127

McDougal, Joseph, 13

McDougal, Peter, 14

McDougall, P.A., 115

McEvoy, Fergus, 217, 218-20, 222

McEwan Committee. See Committee on the Costs of Education

McGarry, T.W., 217, 218

McGee, Thomas D'Arcy, 49, 57, 102, 178, 273

McGee, Thomas, D'Arcy, 236

McGrand, J.J., 353

McGuigan, James Charles, 321, 324, 327, 329, 338; English Catholic Education Association of Ontario (ECEAO), 361; Hope commission, 378; Vincent Priester, 362

McGuire, Ursula, 178

McGuire, William H., 321, 322-23, 324, 325, 326

McIntosh, John, 6

McIntyre, William R., 486

McKenna, Timothy J., 425, 427

McLeod, D.D., 211, 212

McLoughlin, P.B., 13

McManus, Mr., 13

McNally, John T., 309-10, 324

McNamara, Mr., 351

McNeil, Neil, 237, 246, 249, 262, 266, 270; Catholic Taxpayers' Association, 291, 293, 298, 307; death, 321; fifth classes and continuation schools (1915), 259-60; Martin J. Quinn, 293, 298-300, 301-2; Ontario Separate School Trustees' Association, 353, 355, 359; The School Question of Ontario, 293-96, 298; separate school politics (1920s), 271-77

McNevin, J.A., 357, 361

McPatrick, Don Pedro, 13

McPherson, William David, 270

McSweeney, John, 6

McTague, Charles P., 320, 323

McTavey, Patrick, 96

Meagher, T.J., 354

Médaille, Jean Pierre, 173

Meneguzzi, Peter, 407

Merchant, Francis Walter [F.W.], 216, 239

Merchant Report (1910), 216-17; (1912), 229, 231-32

Merchant-Scott-Coté report (1927), 239-41

Meredith, William R., 185, 254-55

Metropolitan Separate School Board, 415, 487

Metropolitan Toronto School Board, 478, 482

Meyer, Thomas, 390

Middle School courses, 258, 259

Middleton, 392

Middleweek, John, 386, 390

Mignault, Pierre, 279

Miller, Frank, 478, 479

Miller, R.J., 264

Mills, Michael R., 20, 22

minority rights, 249-50, 316

Minority School Act (Quebec), 325

Moffet, Flavien, 190

Moir, John, 58, 241, fn. 1

Morris, Denis, 152

Morris, William, 8-9, 18

Morrissey, T.J., 353

Mowat, Oliver, 49-50, 59, 143, 187

Moylan, James George, 75, 93, 94, 101-9, 118; early life, 1012; Egerton Ryerson, 104-8; Scott Act (1863), 103-4; separate schools, 103

Mulligan, Murray, 329

Murdock, John A., 5, 8, 9

Murnane, James, 13

Murphy, A.H., 357, 361

Murphy, Denis, 236

Murphy, Dennis J., 428, 429, 430, 488, 490

Murphy, Martin, 144

Murphy, William, 220

Murray, Daniel, 182

Murray, Joachim, 183

Murtagh, Peter, 119-21, 126

Nelligan, Ed., 418, 429, 432

Newcombe, E.L., 279

Newton, J.E., 354

Nicolson, Murray, 80, 83

Nixon, Robert, 434, 437

Nolan, Bernard J., 428, 429, 430

North Walsingham, 392

Notre Dame College School (Welland), 425

Oakville, 108-9

O'Brien, M.T., 85

O'Brien, Michael, 260

O'Brien, Michael Joseph, 338

O'Brien, Richard M., 260

O'Brien, Robert, 127

O'Connell, Francis, 126

O'Connor, Denis, 191

O'Connor, Dionysia, 180

O'Connor, Frank, 327, 334

O'Connor, Roderick A., 82, 180, 218

OCSTA. See Ontario Catholic School Trustees' Association (OCSTA)

O'Donohoe, John, 148

OEA. See Ontario Educational Association

OECTA. See Ontario English Catholic Teachers' Association (OECTA)

O'Gorman, G.R., 351

O'Grady, William, 11, 14, 79

O'Keefe, Eugene, 148

Oliver, Farquhar, 379

O'Malley, Frances, 178

O'Meara, Theodosia, 180

O'Neil, M.J., 235

O'Neil, Peter J., 126-27

O'Neill, Patrick A., 101

Ontario Association of Alternative and Independent Schools, 477

Ontario Catholic Educational Association, 353

Ontario Catholic Education Council (1938), 338, 349, 354, 361, 380; Brief 146, 370-72; Hall-Dennis Committee, 412-13; larger units of administration, 415-16; Ontario Foundation Tax Plan, supplementary to Brief 146, 374-75

Ontario Catholic League, 130

Ontario Catholic School Trustee's Association, 347

Ontario Catholic Student Federation, 429, 436, 437-38, 442

Ontario Catholic Supervisory Officers' Association, 443, 448

Ontario Conference on Education, 403

Ontario Educational Association (OEA), 351, 355-60

Ontario English Catholic Teachers' Association (OECTA), 169, 350, 361, 434; accreditation of religion courses, 446-47; Institute for Catholic Education, 490; Ontario Separate School Trustees' Association, 385

Ontario Fair Tax Commission, 488

Ontario Foundation Tax Plan, 170, 350, 363, 397-408, 411, 432; Bishops' brief (1962), 402; different types of grants, 404; improvements to the grant regulations, 406-8; inverse ratio to local assessment, 397; improvements to the grant regulations, 406-8; objectives, 405; origins, 402-3; results, 406. *See also* legislative grants; School Fund

Ontario Public School Trustees' Association (OPSTA), 425, 474

Ontario School Trustees' Council, 256, 385, 387

Ontario Secondary School Trustees' Federation (OSSTF), 474, 478, 482

Ontario Separate School Business Officials' Association, 408

Ontario Separate School Trustees' Association (OSSTA), Chapter Seven; annual general meetings, 385; l'Association des commissions des écoles bilingues d'Ontario, 385-86, 424; Bill 30, 481; bishops, 359-60; briefs (1937), 357, (1957), 386-87, (1959), 388-89, (1961), 389-90, (1962), 402-4, (1966), 407-8, 412, (1968), 418-19, 430-34, 446-47, (1972), 443, (1976), 443-44; Catholicity, 446-50, 473; Catholic Taxpayers' Association, 359; Commission for Planning and Implementing Change in the Governance and Administration of Secondary Education, 475; commission on independent (private) schools, 477-78; completion of the separate school system, 428, 441, 453-56; constitutional reform, 442-43; early history (1925-50), 351-65; English Catholic Education Association of Ontario, 360-65; entente with l'Association française des conseils scolaires de l'Ontario, 452-53; "Equal Opportunity for Continuous Education in Separate Schools of Ontario" (1968-69), 430-34; Extension Convention, 439; first annual general meeting, 359; founding members, 351-52; French-language minority rights, 451-53; Hall-Dennis Committee, 408-15; Hope Commission, 380; larger units of administration, 415-21; leadership, 348-50, 359-60; membership, 383-84; Mid-Century (1950-60), 380-91; Mitch Hepburn, 359-60; Ontario Educational Association, 355-56; Ontario Foundation Tax Plan Committee, 407; organization, 385; original name, 353; publications, 385; resolutions (1937), 358-59; Royal Commission on Learning (1993-94), 488-89; Section 136 of Bill 30, 487; Special Advisory Committee on School Financing, 407; Three-Mile Limit, 391-97. *See also* separate school trustees

Ontario Trustees' and Ratepayers' Association, 356

OPSTA. *See* Ontario Public School Trustees' Association (OPSTA)

O'Reilly, James, 56

Orton, Henry, 117

OSSTA. *See* Ontario Separate School Trustees' Association (OSSTA)

OSSTF. *See* Ontario Secondary School Trustees' Federation (OSSTF)

Ottawa Collegiate Institute Board, 424

Ottawa Separate School Board, 185, 189, 192, 209-10; Regulation 17, 233-36, 250-51

Our Lady of Lourdes (Toronto), 183

Palezcny, M., 383-84

Parent, Marcel P., 409

Parent, Mr., 6

Parry, Peter, 13

PEP. *See* Provincial Education Project, 425-26

Peterborough Examiner, 309, 398

Peterson, David, 479

petitions, 121-24, 151, 263-64, 277

Phelan, Bonaventure, 182

Phelan, Patrick, 185

Phelan, T.N., 374, 375, 376

Phillips, Charles, 412

Pigott, Joseph, 365

Pinsoneault, Pierre-Adolphe, 178

Pocock, Philip, 390, 403, 435, 438, 439, 455; Catholicity, 445-46

Porter, Dana, 378-79

Potts, Mr. Justice, 482

Powell, William Dummer, 8, 11

Power, Chubby, 330

Power, Joseph, 1141, 142, 144, 146

Power, Michael, 15-22, 26, 43, 47, 76, 80, 141, 168, 182; bishop of Toronto, 16; Council of Public Instruction, 21-22; early life, 15-16; Egerton Ryerson, 21-22; separate schools, 19-20, 91-92

Power, William, 15

Price, W.H., 310, 314

Priester, Vincent, 338, 361-62, 370, 374, 380; executive director of the English Catholic Education Association of Ontario, 363; Hope Commission, 376; James C. McGuigan, 362; Leslie Frost, 362, 378; meeting of 25 April 1961, 390-91; Ontario Separate School Trustees' Association, 364-65

Priester, William, 361

private Catholic high schools, 422-23

Privy Council. *See* Judicial Committee of the Privy Council

Protestant separate schools, 16, 34, 39, 105

Provincial Committee on Aims and Objectives of Education in the Schools of Ontario. *See* Hall-Dennis Committee (1965-68)

Provincial Education Program, 425-26, 435-36

Public School Trustees' Association of Ontario, 400, 401

Pyne, R.A., 218, 220, 224, 233, 234, 235, 258

Qualifications Act, 217

Quebec Plan, 296

Quebec teaching certificates, 133, 134-35, 192

Quenneville, Charles, 357

Quinlan, Joseph, 113

Quinn, Martin H., 291

Quinn, Martin J., 291-93, 347; *The Case for Ontario Separate Schools* (1937), 338; *Catholics are Counted but They Don't Count* (1938), 338; fall from grace, 337-39; founder of Catholic Taxpayers' Association, 293; *The Frustration of Lay Catholic Effort in Ontario* (1945), 339; George S. Henry, 314-16; *Injustice to Separate Schools, Assessment Act at Fault, Ontario and Quebec Compared*, 298; James C. McGuigan, 327; Mitch Hepburn, 321-27; Neil McNeil, 291, 293, 298-300, 301-2; *Some Pertinent Facts: The Separate Schools in Ontario*, 305-6, 307; speeches, 307-8, 312, 357

Quinn, Romana, 291

Racine, Damase, 217, 218

Rae, Bob, 454, 479

Raizenne, Marie-Clotilde, 6

Reaume, Joseph O., 226, 230-31, 234

Redican, Joseph, 429

Regan, Kenneth J., 448

Regiolpolis College, 14

Regulation 17, ix, Chapter Four; aims, 203; amendments (1913), 209, 233; Catholic bishops of Ontario, 237-39; Merchant Report (1910), 216-17 and (1912), 233; Merchant-Scott-Coté report (1927), 239-41;

Michael Francis Fallon, 224; Ottawa Separate School Board, 233-36; paragraphs 3, 4, 5 and 9(2), 207-9; two questions to resolve, 204-6

Regulation 155, 210, 214

Reid, Tim, 438

religion courses for credit, 448

religion teachers: training, 446-47

Renaud, J.A., 354

Renouf, Michel, 225-26

Residential and Farm Act Assistance Grant, 390-91

Reville Report (1973), 444

Reynar, Alfred H., 211, 212

Reynolds, John, 96

Reynolds, Michael, 96

Rinfret, Thibaudeau, 279

Roach, Mary, 15

Robarts, John, 398, 400, 435, 438, 447; "Equal Opportunity for Continuous Education in Separate Schools in Ontario" (1968-69), 434; French-language secondary schools, 423-24; larger units of administration, 419; Ontario Foundation Tax Plan, 403, 405, 406; Reorganized Programme, 421-22

Robbins, Sydney, 486

Roberts, Miss, 13

Robertson, Charles, 126

Robertson, James E., 142, 144, 145, 157

Robida, M., 429

Robinette, J.J., 483

Robinson, Charles, 21, 83, 93

Robinson, Peter, 11

Roebuck, Arthur, 323, 325, 332

Rogers, George F., 326

Rolph, John, 39

Rooney, Francis Patrick, 141, 145, 152

Rose, Mr. Justice, 278-79

Ross, George, 61, 188

Ross, Murray, 412

Ross Bible, 61

Routhier, J.O., 220

Rowan, A.C., 357

Rowan, J.E., 353

Rowan, William, 5

Royal Commission on Bilingualism and Biculturalism, 451

Royal Commission on Education in Ontario (1945-50). See Hope Commission

Rutherford, F.S., 357

Ryan, Edward, 305

Ryan, J., 108-9

Ryan, Joseph F., 362, 384, 390, 425, 429, 432, 434, 438

Ryerson, Egerton, ix, 15, 49, 73, 74-75, 119, 164, 248, 264, 369; Armand de Charbonnel, 22-25, 35, 39-46; Charles Donlevy, 86-91; common school system, 29; early career, 28-29; finality of the

Scott Act (1863), 58; interpreter of school legislation, 111-18; James G. Moylan, 104-8; John Elmsley, 86-91; John Joseph Lynch, 49, 52-53, 62; later career, 48; Michael Power, 21-22, 91-92; non-denominational Christianity, 29-31; Peter Murtagh, 119-21; school inspectors, 130-31; Scott Act (1863), 52-54, 57; separate schools, 31-35, 39

Ryerson, Joseph, 28

Sacred Heart Orphanage, 175

Sacred Heart (Peterborough), 180

Saenderl, Simon P., 19, 22

St. Cecilia's (Toronto), 183

St. Dominic's (Lindsay), 180

St. Francis Xavier (Toronto), 183

St. Helen's (Toronto), 183

Saint-Jacques, Henri, 365

St. John's (Toronto), 183

St. Mary's (Hamilton), 177

St. Mary's (Lindsay), 180

St. Mary's (Peterborough), 181

St. Mary's parish (Simcoe), 391

St. Mary's (Toronto), 183

St. Michael's (Toronto), 183

St. Patrick's (Hamilton), 177

St. Patrick's (Toronto), 174

St. Paul's parish (York, Toronto), 10-11, 21, 27, 79-80

St. Paul's (Toronto), 174

St. Peter's (London), 178-79

St. Peter's (Peterborough), 181

St. Pierre, Damien, 353, 354

St. Raphael's parish, 4

St. Raphael's Seminary, 5

St. Thomas, 119-21

St. Vincent de Paul Society, 27, 81, 152

St. Vincent's (Toronto), 183

salaries, 169-70, 177

Sales, Francis de, 184

Saturday Night, 313

Sawyers, Joseph, 6, 13

Sbaretti, Donato, 220

School Act (1871), 48, 62

School Fund, 21, 29, 33, 36, 40, 44, 45, 46, 84. See also legislative grants; Ontario Foundation Tax Plan

Schools and Teachers in the Province of Ontario, 169

School Sisters of Notre Dame, 168

Schwart, T., 354

Scott, Ian, 483

Scott, J.H., 239

Scott, Richard William, 51-52, 483

Scott, William Louis (W.L.), 310

Scot Act (1863), viii, 46, 52-56, 75, 119-20, 124, 138, 349; *Canadian Freeman*, 102, 102, 108;

finality, 54, 57-58, 102; John Elmsley, 83, 93; Section 14, 294;

Section 19, 391, 392

Seath, John, 194, 233, 258-59, 269

Seath Act, 194-95

Secondary Education Review Project, 444

secret ballot in separate school trustee elections (1888), ix, 50, 110, 151-53

Section 93 of the BNA Act (1867), 49, 51, 55-56, 186, 249, 250, 443; Bill 30, 484-85; full text, 484-85; Regulation 17, 235. See also BNA Act (1867)

Section 136 of Bill 30, 481-82, 487, 489

Seguin, Leopold, 409

separate school boards: number, 417, 420

separate schools: Catholic Institutes, 127-30; Catholic laity, Chapter Two; continuation classes, 256-57; continuation schools, 260-61; different meanings (1850s), 67, fn. 63; Egerton Ryerson, 31-35, 39; enrolment (1971, 1983), 455; finances (1917, 1927, 1935), 296-96, (1943), 371; Hall-Dennis Committee, 414-15; Hope Commission, 367; Michael Power, 19-20; number (1851), 39, (1860), 47, 62, (1890), 62, (1855-99), 125-26, 251, (1902-29), 251;

Ontario Foundation Tax Plan, 406; public schools, 254-55, 275-76; seven cities, 386-87; statistics (1950-51, 1960-61), 381-82; teachers (1960s), 423

Separate Schools Act (1894), 153; continuation classes (1902), 256; Section 32, 415-16; Three-Mile Limit (1963), 395

Separate Schools Assessment Amendment Committee, 281, 354, 359

separate school trustees, 74, 75, 110-26; accomplishments (1855-59), 124-26; Belleville, 41-42; Brantford, 113-14, 118-19; Chatham, 40; establishing separate schools, 112-14; Focus on the Faith, 449-50; Goderich, 115-16; Guelph, 117; incorporation, 44; Kingston, 122-24; Ottawa, 185, 189, 192, 209-10, 233-36, 250-51; petitions, 121-24; Regulation 17, 210; St. Thomas, 115-21; Toronto (1876-79), 137-51; *Toronto Mirror*, 100-101

SERP. *See* Secondary Education Review Project

Shapiro, Bernard, 474

Sharpe, Mr. Justice, 487

Shaver, Peter, 13

Shea, John, 127

Shea, Magdalen, 183

Sheedy, Andrew, 384-85. 387-88, 402

Sherlock, Jim, 490

Sherlock, John M., 448, 490

Sherwood, Charlotte, 77, 82

Sherwood, Levius Peters, 77

Signay, Joseph, 18

Sills, Mr., 351, 352

Sims, Henry R., 235

Sissons, C.B., 223, 330

Sisters: list of teaching communities, 167-68

Sisters of Charity of Ottawa. See Grey Sisters of the Cross

Sisters of Charity of Providence, 178

Sisters of St. Joseph, 27, 168; Archdiocese of Toronto, 175-78; Diocese of Hamilton, 174, 177-78; Diocese of London, 178-80; Diocese of Peterborough, 180-81; early teaching in Toronto, 174

Sisters of the Sacred Heart, 424

Sloan, T.J., 361

Smith, David William, 8

Smith, Frank, 147-48

Smith, W.J., 142, 146, 148, 151

Somerville, Henry, 374

Speirs, Rosemary, 455

Splitlog, Thomas, 12

Spratt, Michael J., 237, 260

Stamp, Robert, 378

Standard-Freeholder, 311

Stanislaus, Sister, 409-10

Steel, Donald, 482

Sterling, Norm, 480

Stewart, C.J., 354

Stickney, Mehetable, 28

Strachan, John, 8, 17, 22, 23, 28, 39, 78-79

Sturgeon Falls assessment case, 272-73

Sullivan, Anna Josephine, 292

Sullivan, Francis, 127

Sullivan, Miss, 180

Sweeney, Peter, 9-10

Taché, Étienne-Pascal, 44

Taché Act (1855). *See* "An Act to amend the laws relating to Separate Schools in Upper Canada" (1855)

Tarnopolsky, Walter, 486

Taschereau, Etienne, 220

Taylor, Francis J., 142

teacher certification, ix, 166, 186-95

teachers: number of religious and lay, 170-72

Technical and Vocational Training Assistance Act (1960), 400

Telmon, Adriene, 185

Thamour, Louise, 184

Thibodeau, Élénore, 185

Three-Mile Limit (1959-63), 391-97; legal challenge, 392-95

Tilley, John J., 211, 212

Timon, John, 51

Tiny Township case, 254, 259, 277-81, 352, 353; Bill 30, 483; Judicial

Committee of the Privy Council, 279-80; Martin J. Quinn, 291; Supreme Court of Canada, 279

Toronto Daily Star, 290, 293, 328-29, 401

Toronto Mirror, 28, 78, 93, 94, 95, 100-101; common schools, 96-97

Toronto Savings Bank, 27

Toronto School Board, 262-63, 264-65, 275

Toronto Separate School Board, 76, 92-93, 95-96, 110, 387; conflict (1876-79), 137-51; secret ballot, 151-53;

Toronto Star, 229

Toronto Telegram, 401. *See also Evening Telegram*

Trainor, Richard, 482

Tremblay, O., 451-52

Trepanier, J.O., 374

Tribune, 109, 110

True Witness and Catholic Chronicle, 110, 130, 148

trustees. See separate school trustees

Turgeon, Pierre-Flavien, 18

Twomey, Celestine, 180

utility taxes. See corporation taxes

Vandekerckhove, Andre and Yvonne, 393

Vincent, Charles, 150

Vincent, Gaston, 374

Walker, Franklin, 20-21, 83, 151, 278, 363; Brief 113, 369; Hope Commission, Minority Report, 379; religious training of teachers, 447

Walsh, Harold E., 335

Walsh, J.C., 363

Walsh, John, 75, 130, 151, 178, 179

Walsh, Joseph J., 142, 144, 146

Walsh, Michael, 150

Ward, Marmaduke, 181

Ward, Mary, 181

Waron, Chief, 12

Welch, Robert, 439, 440

Welland Board of Education, 424

Wells, Thomas, 448

Westhues, Kenneth, 445

Whalen, Margaret, 180

White, James, 133

White, James Francis, 61, 169, 347; bilingual separate schools, 213-16; Catholic separate school inspectors, 133-37; teacher certification, 189-90, 191, 193-94

Whitney, James Pliny, 186, 193, 204, 206, 218, 220; l'Association canadiene-française d'education d'Ontario, 221-22

Williams, J.B., 40

Wilson, Bertha, 486-87

Wilson, Robert, 387, 390, 399

Windle, Joseph R., 447

Wintermeyer, John, 401, 403

Wright, Ursula, 181

Young, George Paxton, 130

D'Youville, Marguerite, 184

Zuber, Thomas, 486